Klaus-Peter König/Martin Hugo

9 MM PARABELLUM

Klaus-Peter König/Martin Hugo

9 MM PARABELLUM

A History of the World's 9MM Pistols & Ammunition

SCHIFFER MILITARY HISTORY
Atglen, PA

Photos on Dust Jacket courtesy of Robert Ball

Top left:
1908 Luger Semi-Automatic Pistol

Top right:
Walther P 38 Semi-Automatic Double Action Pistol, 9mm

Bottom:
Browning Model 1935 High Power Semi-Automatic Pistol

Translated from the German by Edward Force.

Library of Congress Catalog Number: 91-66337.

Printed in the United States of America.
ISBN: 0-88740-342-5

This title was originally published under the title,
9mm Parabellum - Waffe und Patrone,
by Motorbuch Verlag, Stuttgart.

Published by Schiffer Publishing, Ltd.
77 Lower Valley Road
Atglen, PA 19310
Please write for a free catalog.
This book may be purchased from the publisher.
Please include $2.95 postage.
Try your bookstore first.

Contents

Foreword

The subject of this book has its particular charm, but it also has very definite drawbacks. For me as an author, the charm was primarily that of bringing together the great variety of development that these guns and bullets have undergone in the last few decades. The understanding reader will realize that no account of this can ever be absolutely complete, partly because the development continues constantly and a book can only offer a selection of a history that is still in progress.

No bullet has become so widespread throughout the world as the 9 mm Parabellum, though it is limited mainly to the Western World, where it has been introduced in almost all countries as the official bullet for military and police use. Suited as it is to almost universal use, it has necessarily led to a great number of weapon developments, incorporating any and all imaginable and practicable bolt systems; from the unbolted mass breech or the bolted type to the turning barrel, every possibility within the bounds of this caliber has found a practical and technically feasible application.

War has always been "the father of technology", an unfortunate term that has not been able to lose much of its justification to this day. In the realm of pistols, it has always been chiefly the task of the military or the police to institute a new development, followed thereupon by civilian utilization. In recent years this has led to a steady increase in the numbers of pistols on the market: the German police sought a new service pistol, the U.S. Army went looking for new side arms. Many manufacturers, hoping for large-scale contracts, offered their newest developments. What was not accepted either disappeared from view or was subsequently offered as a weapon for private use.

New tendencies also made themselves known in the realm of the revolver with a certain trend, not to be denied, away from the classic revolver bullets; in this realm, the 9 mm Parabellum was at least promising as an alternative and a complement.

The subject also has its drawbacks for the person engaged in research. The pleasure of being able to work on a subject that has not previously been treated in unified form is intoxicating at first. But that in itself becomes more and more of a burden. A book does not originate in a vacuum, but rather out of a number of discussions between author and publisher. Both try to settle on a scope that can satisfy both the subject and the economic demands without leaving out too much. In the process, the pressing problem of limiting the contents arises, and this has seldom seemed to be as difficult to me as in the work that now lies before you.

I tried to find a sensible solution by portraying only what has been accessible to and practical for the private owner, and this (unfortunately) eliminated all mention of machine pistols. Instead, other areas are taken up in somewhat greater detail, such as the reloading of cartridges, tests made by individual manufacturers, as well as by the military and the police, and the whole realm of sport weapons. Here it was necessary to deal with a prejudice that has been repeated again and again to date without being tested, namely that the 9 mm bullet does not attain sufficient accuracy. Numerous examples prove conclusively that the sporting use of the 9 mm cartridge, combined with a good pistol, will more than satisfy requirements. Weapons can be viewed from many points of view, and many a reader has doubtless made his own personal assessment already. Any type of standpoint is proper; it is just not possible to combine all aspects here. One reader will be more interested in the historical development, another will take a more technical-scientific attitude, and still another will care more about the targeting effect or put his emphasis strictly on the sporting application.

Primarily, this book attempts to provide as complete a portrayal as possible of what has been developed to date and what is available to the collector, the professional or the private user — and that is a great deal. Many guns have become legendary. The Parabellum pistol is one that has already been treated in numerous studies. Legends also belong in a book like this, but always within the limitations of a certain equality of treatment and rank with other pistols that have not yet attained such widespread popularity.

Through numerous photographs and technical drawings an attempt has been made to present a very complex subject in the realm of weapon development as clearly as possible, an attempt that we hope has succeeded in practical form.

Selm, 1987 Klaus-Peter König

Acknowledgements

In order to compile a thoroughgoing treatment of a subject, one must depend on the friendly assistance of numerous firms. At this point I would like to express my hearty thanks to the firms that kindly provided me with more and more information and lent weapons and photographs.

My thanks to these firms:
Dynamit Nobel AG, Troisdorf
Heckler & Koch, Oberndorf
Korth-Präzision, Ratzeburg
Sauer & Sohn, Eckernförde
C. Walther, Ulm
Glock GMBH, Deutsch Wagram, Austria
C.W. Engels, Frankfurt
Wischo KG, Erlangen
E. Kettner, Münster Branch Office
Peters-Stahl, Paderborn
Manurhin-Defense, Mulhouse, France
W. Behmke, Tarp

Special thanks are due to my friend and collaborator Martin Hugo, who carried out many of the tests cited here and always found a way to place one rarity or another before my camera.

Klaus-Peter König

BULLETS

Of all the pistol bullets developed to date, few have been able to gain so much success as the 9 mm Parabellum cartridge, which can be fired from pistols, revolvers and machine pistols. It has spread throughout the western world, and is produced by every noteworthy bullet manufacturer. In Germany it has come more and more into the foreground in recent years as the individual state police organizations have been equipped with weapons of this caliber or with these bullets themselves. In the realm of police use alone, there are now numerous special bullets which are only known to the public under certain limitations; their manufacturers would rather be silent as to their particulars, and their standpoint must be respected.

Even in the USA, the 9 mm Parabellum (also known here as the 9 mm Luger), has been reinstituted in the most recent times. It has often been chosen to replace the familiar .45 ACP in official use. After long tests, a pistol of precisely this caliber was chosen. Some time after the Model 39 by Smith and Wesson was selected, more or less unofficially, as the service weapon of the Air Force.

Brief History of the 9mm Parabellum

The beginning of this century was characterized by a wealth of technology in weapons design, and the array of new products offered in the realm of ammunition for those designs was just as rich. Many military forces gradually turned away from the revolvers that had beend previously used, and began to introduce self-loading pistols that could offer, above all else, the advantage of increased firepower.

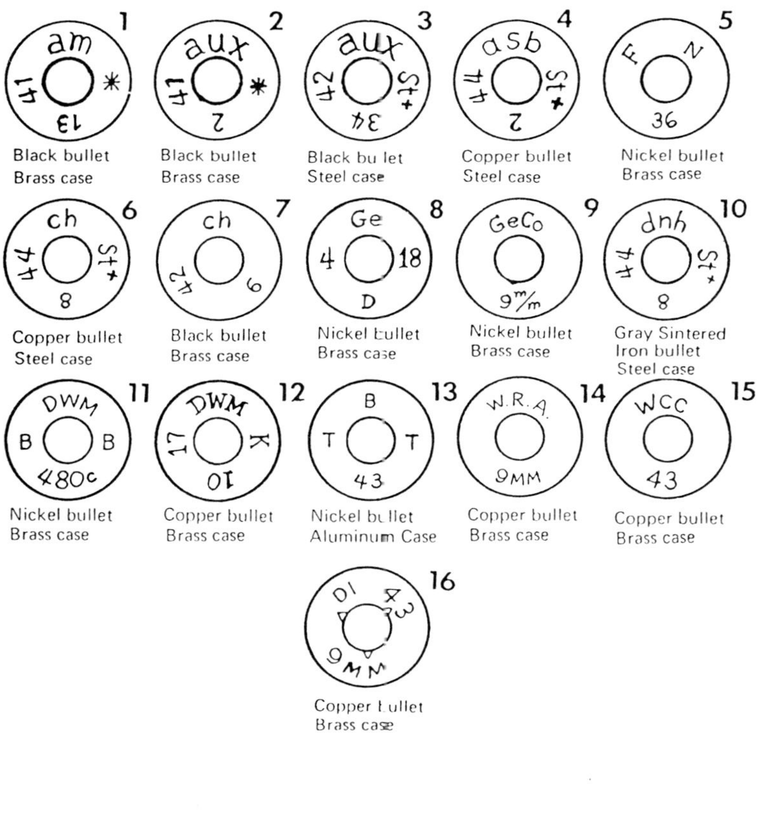

1. German: Otto Eberhardt Cartridge Factory, Hirtenberg
2. German: Polte, Magdeburg factory
3. German: Polte, Magdeburg factory
4. German: German Weapon and Ammunition Factory, Wuppertal
5. Belgian: Fabrique Nationale, Herstal (pre-war)
6. Belgian: Fabrique Nationale, Herstal (German occupation)
7. Belgian: Fabrique Nationale, Herstal (German occupation)
8. German: G. Dormheim, metal case factory (WW II)
9. German: Gustav Genschow (prewar)
10. German: Rhenish-Westphalian Explosive AG
11. German: German Weapon and Ammunition Factory, Borsigwalde
12. German: German Weapon and Ammunition Factory, Karlsruhe
13. Swiss: Federation Ammunition Factory, Thun
14. USA: Winchester Repeating Arms Co.
15. Canada: Defense Industries Ltd.
16. USA: Western Cartridge Co.

Pistolenpatronen

6,35 mm | 7,65 mm | 7,65 mm Parabellum | 9 mm Kurz | 9 x 18 Ultra (9 mm Police) | 9 mm Parabellum | 45 Automatik

Pistol cartridges made by GECO, comparing their sizes and ballistic performance. Not included are the different bullet shapes in 9 mm Parabellum caliber.

Kaliber	Geschoß-Art	Geschoß-gewicht (g)	Lauflänge mm	Fluggeschwindigkeit (m/s)				Auftreffenergie (J)			
				V_0	V_{10}	V_{25}	V_{50}	E_0	E_{10}	E_{25}	E_{50}
6,35 mm	Vollmantel	3,2	60	225	220	215	205	81	78	74	67
7,65 mm	Vollmantel	4,7	100	305	300	295	285	219	212	204	190
7,65 mm o. Abb.	Blei	4,7	100	305	300	295	285	219	212	204	190
7,65 Para	Vollmantel	6,0	125	360	355	345	330	392	383	353	324
9 mm kurz	Vollmantel	6,1	112	275	270	265	255	235	226	216	196
9 x 18 Ultra	Kegelstumpf	6,1	91	330	320	310	290	332	313	290	260
9 mm Para	Vollmantel	8,0	125	350	345	335	325	491	481	451	422
45 Automatik	Vollmantel	14,95	126	270	265	260	255	549	520	500	481

One renowned designer of this era was Hugo Borchardt, whose 1893 model pistol was, to be sure, a ground-breaking development. Though it was denied the success of being adopted officially by any military forces, his cartridge was none the less the first successful bullet for use in self-loading pistols. The bottle-shaped casing was loaded with nitro powder and had a nickel-plated steel-jacketed bullet. This cartridge was more or less the forerunner of such well-known cartridges as the 7.65 mm Parabellum, 9 mm Parabellum and 7.63 mm Mauser. Mauser was impressed by the cartridge that Borchardt had introduced and adopted it in an almost unchanged form for his Model C 96 self-loading pistol. The 7.65 mm Borchardt and 7.63 mm Mauser cartridges are almost identical, at least in terms of shape. But the Mauser cartridge had a stronger charge and thus a higher gas pressure, with a muzzle velocity of approximately 443 meters per second. The less powerful Borchardt cartridge fit into the Borchardt pistol but invariably caused considerable damage to the weapon. There are said to have been modified Borchardt pistols with a stronger recoil spring for experimental purposes, but this has never been proved conclusively by collectors' pieces; in any case, one should beware of modifications here. A similar potential for modification exists in comparison to the 7.65 mm Mannlicher cartridge, which also has a less powerful charge. A different situation is that of the 7.62 mm Tokarev cartridge. Its performance comes close to that of the Mauser cartridge, and can be exchanged for it without fear of pistol damage.

There were then noteworthy differences between Mauser, Borchardt and Luger, for in practice, Mauser had stolen the idea for "his" cartridge. In spite of that, an open battle could be prevented, for the business practices of the Loewe firm allowed the use of Mauser cartridges in exchange for licensing fees. When the proprietor of the firm of Loewe & Cie. sold his factory in Berlin-Charlottenburg and his shares of Mauser stock to the Mauser company at the end of 1896, the external peace was restored once again.

By Minor Changes to the 7.65 mm Parabellum

In 1898 Georg Luger changed the Borchardt bullet, giving it a somewhat shorter casing but keeping the jacket form. This step was presumably made to shorten the charge movement from that of the Borchardt pistol, but it is more likely that it was necessary to fit the diagonal magazine, for the new pistol made by Luger no longer had the nearly vertical grip angle. In addition, its recoil spring was located back in the receiver, which still had a curved leaf spring at that time. This concept

The 08 pistol made by the DWM for Finland. The pistol shown is of 7.65 mm Parabellum caliber.

simply demanded a shorter cartridge if the width of the frame was not to become impractical.

We know this cartridge today in almost unchanged form as the 7.65 mm Parabellum cartridge, and many pistols have been designed for this format. The 7.65 mm cartridge was thoroughly successful, and many self-loading pistols, such as those made in Switzerland since 1903, were designed specifically for this cartridge. The great interest in the 7.65 mm Parabellum encouraged numerous manufacturers to include it in their production programs and great numbers were built. It is still manufactured in many places today, though it no longer has anywhere near the importance it formerly had. A variation of the cartridge was developed especially for use with the Parabellum carbine, and can be recognized by its blackened case. The carbine cartridge develops a gas pressure approximately 20% higher than the normal version; the cartridges manufactured by DWM can be recognized by the "471 A" stamped on them.

Many pistols of the 9 mm Parabellum caliber can also be used with the 7.65 mm Parabellum cartridge. Both cartridges can be loaded into the same magazine, and have almost identical base dimensions, so that breech changes are not necessary. Generally it is sufficient to change the barrel and/or the recoil spring, which can easily be done, especially pistols with the Browning locking system. This has also been an advantage for the Parabellum pistols that so many Germans knew how to use so capably just before World War II. The conditions of the Treaty of Versailles forbade the production of pistols with a barrel length of over 100 mm and a caliber of over 7.65 mm by German manufacturers. Existing weapons in military or police stocks were not affected by these conditions, so that the 08 pistol could still remain in use. To be sure, 7.65 mm caliber pistols could be produced, and later were equipped with a different barrel, making sufficient numbers of 9 mm caliber Parabellum pistols available. In fact, there are times when legal limitations require ingenious developments in the realm of weapons production. For example, in Italy it is against the law for weapons and cartridges used by the military or the police to be privately owned. There too, there were and still are numerous 7.65 mm caliber pistols which have been offered alternatively for export in 9 mm caliber.

The 9 mm Parabellum in Military Use

The military need for greater durability and higher wounding capability could not be met by the 7.65 mm Parabellum cartridge. The 9 mm Parabellum offered by Georg Luger had better qualities, as it fired a heavier bullet at almost the same muzzle velocity.

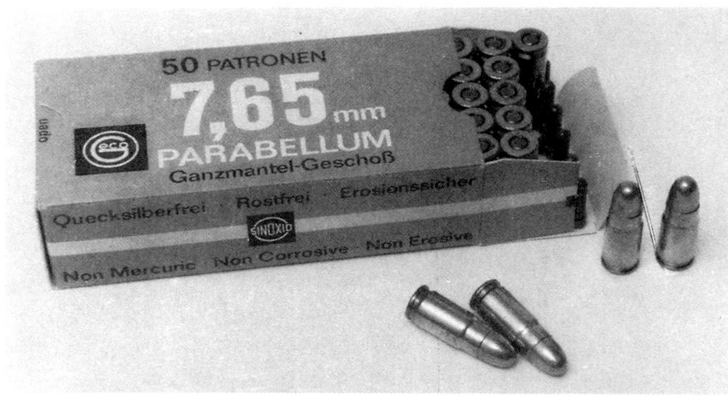

Cartridges in 7.65 mm Parabellum caliber from present-day production, packed in a plastic grid and fitted with fully jacketed bullets.

Over the years, the 9 mm Parabellum cartridge has been made with many different shapes and charges, only some of which could be shown here. In the bottom row are blank and training cartridges.

After initial testing, a cartridge with a slightly bottle-shaped case and a very flattened round-headed bullet was developed. It was offered to, among others, the British Small Arms Committee in 1902, but was not accepted, as it did not correspond to the values set forth in a special catalog of requirements as to bullet weight, bullet diameter and muzzle velocity. Soon afterward, Luger offered a cartridge with a different case, almost cylindrical and with a forward tapering at a slight cone. Here too, base dimensions were very close to those of the 7.65 mm cartridge, so that design advantages already noted could be retained.

The first to be used was a cartridge with a conical nose and flattened tip, however its further use on the front was banned by the Prussian War Ministry. Contradictory reasons have been given. Sometimes it is said that the further use of Dum-Dum bullets was not to be encouraged. These were bullets that caused more injury than was necessary, and thus were banned according to the stipulations of the Hague Convention for land warfare. Other sources state that the conical bullets caused difficulties in the drum magazines tested with the 08 pistol from 1916 on, and were therefore withdrawn. It was ordered that these bullets be used only within Germany and only for weapons training. The ogival bullet, with its apex in slightly modified form, which is the norm for the 9 mm cartridge to this day, was then introduced.

There was also a Parabellum carbine in 9 mm, for which different bullets had to be used. It's gas pressure was 15% greater and could not be fired from a pistol. To make it easy to recognize, it had a chemically blackened case (of brass), and should not to be confused with the blackened cartridges of later years; the color was meant to indicate that they were bullets with iron cores.

The basic concept of the 9 mm Parabellum cartridge was not changed during World War I. There were tests with armor-piercing bullets and even with multipurpose bullets, however, they were halted and were not of any importance until recently. Around 1916 the nickel plating of the bullet jacket was replaced by copper plating, however, it did not prove to be practical and was given up two years later. Such experiments were always based on wartime shortages of materials, and nickel was needed much more urgently in the production of steel alloys.

To make them impervious to oil, the bullets used in World War I had a covering of black paint between the

Cartridges made in Germany during World War II. At the far right in the picture is a cartridge with a sintered iron bullet. The blackened bullets have a steel core.

percussion cap and the cap chamber. During the period following World War I, the cartridge remained unchanged for a long time, and the extent of its production was strictly limited by the terms of the Treaty of Versailles. When the Third Reich began, rearmament of all kinds was initiated, at first secretly, then more and more openly. The need for bullets increased greatly for the many paramilitary units such as the SA and SS had armed themselves and needed bullets for use in training.

New testing was soon commenced, with the goal of using as little non-ferrous metal as possible, so as to reduce the consumption of copper and brass. In 1940 the first steel cases were introduced, replacing brass. At first these cases were coated with a corrosion-limiting layer of brass or copper; this coating was also necessary to guarantee the problem-free removal of the case from the bed. Later the metallic coating was replaced by a coat of paint which had the same purpose. As of about 1941 the painted steel cases with their light greenish color were seen regularly.

There were also tests to save non-ferrous metals, including lead, in the bullet. Experiments were made with bullets of soft iron or sintered steel. Sintered bullets

Cartridges made in Germany during World War II. Here too only a modest selection can be shown. The base stampings show the manufacturer, year of manufacture and production lot of each cartridge.

consist in practice of steel particles cemented together. For the bullet jacket, steel was eventually used, and its surface was also covered with paint.

During war production, percussion caps were also made of brass or copper, however towards the end of the war percussion caps of zinc-covered sheet steel were also produced.

During the war years, a number of different cartridge types were made, all more or less good for the purposes for which they were designed. The major identifying marks and their designations are listed briefly below:

9 mm Pistol Cartridge 08 (9 mm Pist Patr 08)

This is the usual standard version with a fully jacketed bullet in ogival form, the bullet weight varies from 7.45 to 7.97 grams. The case is made of brass (with a small star on its base for recognition), or of steel with a coating of brass, copper or paint; steel cases have the letters St on the base of the cartridge. The percussion caps are sealed with paint.

9 mm Pistol Cartridge 08 for the Tropics (9 mm Pist Patr 08 Trop)

Their creation was made necessary by wartime operations in Africa and other tropical regions. Primarily, they were sealed with paint between the bullet and the mouth of the case, so as to prevent the penetration of moisture. The percussion cap was sealed with black paint, or sometimes with red paint.

9 mm Pistol Cartridge 08 with Iron Core (9 mm Pist Patr 08 mE)

Introduced toward the end of 1940. The bullet had a steel jacket and an inner steel core, around which the so-called "lead shirt" was placed. On account of the lower specific gravity of steel (in comparison with lead), the bullet weight was only 6.29 to 6.55 grams; this resulted in a higher muzzle velocity with the same charge of powder. The bullet mantle was blackened and the percussion cap sealed with black paint. The case was made either of brass or steel with a greenish coat of paint.

9 mm Pistol Cartridge 08 with Iron Core for the Tropics (9 mm Pist Patr 08 mE Trop)

The bullet was made of sintered steel, baked from pulverized iron. The bullet weight was between 5.77 and 5.96 grams, which gave an even higher muzzle velocity than the bullet with lead shirt and iron core. It was introduced for use by the troops toward the end of 1943. This cartridge had a painted steel case and a brass or copper percussion cap sealed with black paint.

9 mm Pistol Cartridge 08 with Sintered Iron Bullet for the Tropics (9 mm Pist Patr 08 SE Trop)

The only difference from the previous version was the sealing of the case mouth.

9 mm Short-Range Cartridge 08

This was intended for weapons with attached silencers. The bullet weight was increased to 9.0 grams and the powder charged reduced to the extent that the muzzle velocity was just under the speed of sound. These cartridges are marked with an X on the base of the case.

9 mm Heavy Fire Cartridge 08

Just as today, cartridges with an overload of some 30% were made for heavy fire. The designation of such cartridges at that time was not always the same. Some were marked "Beschuss" on the base, while others had a percussion cap sealed in green and a green-painted cartridge base.

9 mm Poison Cartridge 08 (9 mm K Patr 08)

There is no clear agreement as to the actual existence of this cartridge to this day. According to statements that have been made about it (for example, by John Walter), it had a hollow-pointed bullet with a channel drilled into its interior. In it was a capsule of potassium cyanide, with a steel core behind it. On impact with a target, the steel core moved forward and made the capsule of poison burst, and the poison was sprayed out to the front. The poison cartridges are said to have been marked with a **K** on the base.

9 mm Explosive Cartridge 08 (9 mm Spr Patr 08)

Unconfirmed legends also envelop this cartridge. Whether it was actually introduced for use by the German Wehrmacht is not confirmed; it was at least a glaring violation of the rights of peoples at war and the Hague Convention, according to which bullets with unnecessary wounding effect were banned.

The explosive used in such small bullets may well have been lead acid, which does not ignite as long as it is under pressure from all sides. When the pressure is removed as the bullet fragments, the lead acid can act as an explosive.

Identifying Marks of the Bullet Boxes

The cartridges used in World War II are still available for collectors in relatively large numbers and at reasonable prices. For that reason it seems appropriate to describe, on the basis of several examples, the marking and packaging as well as the cartridges themselves. The statements given here are based on the data provided by John Walter, as well as the author's own research, and have been simplified only to the extent that designations previously published are included here.

The 9 mm cartridges were customarily packed in small cardboard boxes of sixteen, and separated within the box by a grid of cardboard or paper that curved around them. They were divided within a box into two rows of eight cartridges each, making two magazine loads, with every cartridge easily removable.

Fifty-two of these small packages were packed into a larger cardboard box, and five of these boxes were packed into a wooden crate; the last was the Cartridge Crate 88 or, for short, the PK 88.

Boxes for pistol cartridges essentially had a light blue label stuck onto them; this light blue color can sometimes turn to a light green, but in any case the bright blue label is an indication that normal cartridges were packed in the box. Packages with a dark blue vertical stripe on their light blue label contained cartridges with steel jackets. The dark blue stripe does not necessarily need to be very dark blue, for the color has sometimes faded and usually appears today as a medium blue. It is not clear whether a yellow label was used for tracer bullets, as tracer bullets were not always indicated in the same manner.

To acquaint ourselves with the number and letter code, let us look at two examples, one from a drawing, the other from a photo.

The first example is the drawing:

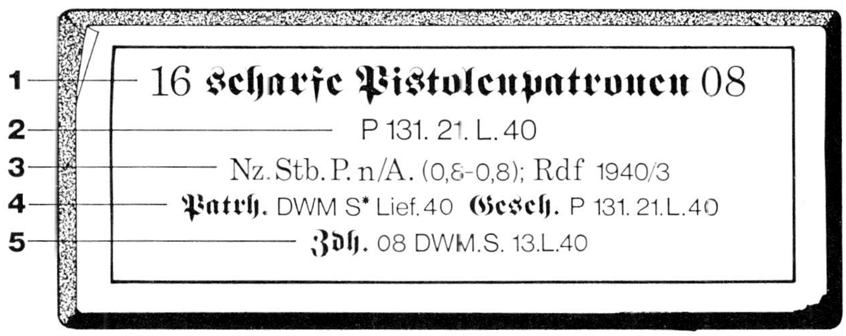

On the boxes and crates were a confusing variety of numbers, letters and abbreviations, but on close inspection, they amounted to a very logical system. On the basis of these markings, every shipment could be identified clearly as to its place of origin. This was not without importance in cases where bullet failures and problems had to be traced to their causes.

Line 1: "16 scharfe Pistolenpatronen 08"
This shows clearly that loaded cartridges are packed in the box, and not some other type such as training cartridges. The contents consist of 08 pistol bullets.

Line 2: "P 131. 21. L. 40"
The "P 131" is the code marking for the DWM branch factory in Berlin-Borsigwalde. It indicates that these cartridges were shipped as the 21st shipment of the year 1940 (Instead of only the letter L, sometimes the abbreviation "Lief." is used for "delivery").

Line 3: "Nz. Stb.P.n/A. (0,8-0,8); Rdf 1940/3"
This line indicates the type and production of the charge of powder. It is nitrocellulose particle powder of the new type as small-size powder with a diameter of 0.8 mm and a length of 0.8 mm. The powder was delivered by the Wasag Chemie firm from its factory in Reindorf, as the third lot of the year 1940.

Line 4: "Patrh. DWM S Lief. 40 Gesch. P 131.21.L.40"
Here are the indications of the cartridge case and the bullet. Cases were delivered by DWM in 1940 and are made of brass (the letter S with a star — only the star on the cartridge itself — is the symbol for brass). The bullets came from the manufacturer with the code designation P 131, thus from the Berlin-Borsigwalde factory, and were part of the 21st shipment in the year 1940.

Line 5: "Zdh. 08 DWM.S.13.L.40"
The last line concerns the percussion caps. They are brass caps which were delivered in 1940 as the 13th shipment from DWM.If we take as our second example the package shown in the photograph, whose label has suffered considerably but is still capable of being read correctly.

Line 1: "16 Pistolenpatronen 08 m.E."
In this box are sixteen 08 cartridges with iron cores. Accordingly, the cartridges in this box have had their cases painted black.

Line 2: "1944 emp 1"
The emp is the code designation for the Dynamit AG (formerly Alfred Nobel and Company), Empelde Works, Hamburg. The cartridges were assembled in 1944 and were part of the first shipment of the year.

Line 3: "Nz. Stb.P.n/A. (0,8-0,8) — 1943 mog 12"
Nitrocellulose powder of the new type is used, with its grains in bar form having a diameter of 0.8 mm and a length of 0.8 mm. The powder came from the Deutsche Sprengchemie AG, Moschwig Works. It was delivered in 1943 as the 12th lot or shipment.

Line 4: "Patrh. (Stahl) + lackiert 1943 emp 7"
The cases are made of steel and also painted. They were manufactured by the Dynamit AG as the 7th lot or shipment.

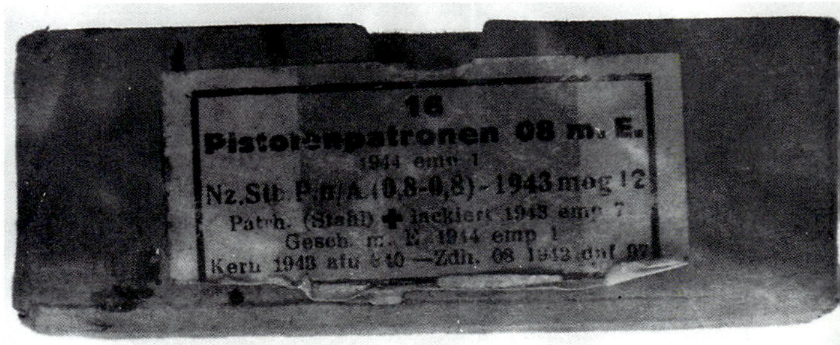

08 m.E. cartridges are those with iron cores in their bullets. The picture allows the label to be understood as explained in the accompanying text.

Line 5: "Gesch. m.E. 1944 emp 1"
The cartridges have bullets with steel cores and were assembled into complete cartridges in the year 1944 by the Dynamit AG, as the first lot or shipment.

Line 6: "Kern 1943 afu 340 — Zdh. 08 1942 dnf 97"
The afu is the code for the firm of August Winkhaus in Münster, Westphalia, where the cores were manufactured in 1943; they came from lot number 340. The percussion caps came from the Rheinisch Westfälische Sprengstoff

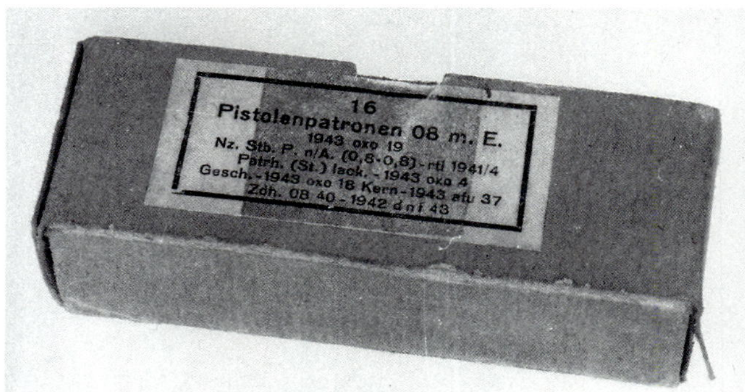

Cartridges with steel cases. A first indication is given by the dark stripe across the label.

AG (RWS), Stadeln Works, near Nürnberg (production of RWS and GECO cartridges is still going on there today). They came from the 97th lot of the year 1942. Although they are made of brass, the designation with the letter S is missing.

The type of inscription is not at all uniform, so we will find labels with different kinds of lettering, as well as varying types and sizes.

Markings on Cartridge Bases

A further means of identifying a cartridge is possible by reading the stampings on the cartridge base. This is true of older cartridges as well as those produced today.

Every cartridge base bears three or four bits of information, from which the year of production, the lot number, the manufacturer and the type of case can be determined. Let us first, once again, take several concrete examples from German 08 type cartridges.

Example 1: Marking dnh — 43 — star — 2
This cartridge has a brass case, as shown by the star; it was made by the Rheinisch-Westfälische Sprengstoff AG's Durlach Works near Karlsruhe (dnh is the code for this factory) and was made as part of the second lot for the year of 1943.

Cartridge base, example 1.

Cartridge base, example 2.

Cartridge base, example 3.

Example 2: Marking dnh — St+ — 3 — 43
Manufactured by the Rheinisch-Westfälische Sprengstoff AG Durlach Works near Karlsruhe. The case is made of steel with a coat of paint. The cartridge was made in 1943, as part of the third lot. The percussion cap is made of zinc-coated sheet steel and not coated with paint.

Example 3: Marking kam-St+ — 3-42
Hugo Schneider AG (Hasag), Eisen- und Metallwerke GmbH, Starzysko-Kamienna, Poland. Made in 1942, painted steel case, from the third lot or shipment of the year.

Code Markings for Bullets and Parts

The code is nothing more than a means of making it difficult for the enemy to identify individual factories of workshops and make them the targets of air raids. The so-called S codes, those for handguns and equipment, were set up as early as 1935. They were soon followed by the so-called P codes, which applied to the manufacturers and suppliers of cartridges, cases, bullets, gunpowder, etc. These codes consist of one capital letter with a following two- or three-digit number. They were replaced later by a different type of codifying: three, two or one small letter(s), and then the other indications, on the base of the cartridge and/or on the package.

P codes are seen again and again, however the list of them is not complete to date, since full information on them cannot be located. The following list includes only the codes definitely identified to date:

P 28 Deutsche Waffen- und Munitionsfabriken AG (DWM), Karlsruhe
P 69 Patronen-, Zündhütchen- und Metallwarenfabrik Schönebeck on the Elbe
P 94 Kabel- und Metallwerke Neumayer AG, Nürnberg
P 120 Dynamit AG (formerly Alfred Nobel & Company), Empelde Works, Hannover
P 131 Deutsche Waffen- und Munitionsfabriken AG (DWM), Berlin-Borsigwalde
P 151 Rheinsich-Westfälische Sprengstoff AG (RWS), Stadeln near Nürnberg
P 154 Polte Armaturen- und Maschinenfabrik AG, Grüneberg- Nordbahn, Silesia
P 181 Hugo Schneider AG (Hasag), Lampenfabrik,

Altenburg

P 198 Metallwarenfabrik Treuenbrietzen GmbH, Belzig, Mark

P 207 Metallwarenfabrik Odertal GmbH, Odertal

P 249 Finower Industriewerk AG, Finow, Mark Brandenburg

P 315 Märkisches Walzwerk GmbH, Strausberg, Potsdam District

P 316 Westfälische Metallindustrie AG, Lippstadt, Westphalia

P 334 Mansfeld Metallwarenfabrik AG, Rotheburg on the Saale

P 340 Metallwerke Silberhütte GmbH, St. Andreasberg in the Harz

P 346 Heinrich Huck Metallwarenfabrik, Nürnberg

P 370 Polte Armaturen- und Maschinenfabrik AG, Magdeburg

P 379 Metallwarenfabrik Scharfenberg und Teubert, Breitungen on the Werra

P 405 Dynamit AG (formerly Alfred Nobel & Co.), Durlach near Karlsruhe

P 490 Polte Armaturen- und Maschinenfabrik AG, Magdeburg

P 635 Munitionsfabrik Wolersdorf AG, Vienna

With the help of the letter coding, every cartridge can be assigned definitely to its manufacturer; according to what is known now, the list is almost complete. It is remarkable, though, how many small companies were involved in the production of cartridges.

ad Patronen-, Zündhütchen- und Metallwarenfabrik AG (formerly Sellier & Bellot), Schönebeck on the Elbe

afu August Winkhaus, Münster

aj Sörensen und Köster Aluminium- und Metallwerke, Neumünster in Holstein

ajn Union Sprengstoff und Zündmittelwerke, Alt-Berun

ak Patronen-, Zündhütchen- und Metallwarenfabrik AG (formerly Sellier & Bellot), Vlasim Works, Prague, Czechoslovakia

al Deutsches Leucht- und Signalmittelwerk Dr. Feistel KG, Schönhagen Works, Berlin-Charlottenburg

am Otto Eberhardt Patronenfabrik (owned by the Gustloff Works), Hirtenberg, Lower Austria

amh Büllmann-Werke Hans Büllmann, Gablonz-Schlag, Sudetenland

an C. Beuttenmüller und Compagnie GmbH, Bretten, Baden

ap Deutsches Leucht- und Signalmittelwerk Dr. Feistel K.G., Wuppertal-Ronsdorf Works

asb Deutsche Waffen- und Munitionsfabriken AG (DWM), Berlin- Borsigwalde

auu Patronenhülsen- und Metallwerke AG, Rokycany, Czechoslovakia

aux Polte Armaturen- und Maschinenfabrik AG ("Poltewerke"), Magdeburg

auy Polte Armaturen- und Maschinenfabrik AG, Grüneberg-Nordbahn, Silesia

auz Polte Armaturen- und Maschinenfabrik AG, Arnstadt

av VDM Halbzeugwerk GmbH, Werdohl branch, Westphalia

avt Silva Metallwerke GmbH, Magdeburg

avu Silva Metallwerke GmbH, Genthin

awt Württembergische Metallwarenfabrik AG, Geislingen

axq Erfurter Ladenindustrie, Erfurt-North, Thuringia

axs Berndorfer Metallwarenfabrik AG, Berndorf, Austria

ayg Julius Maurer, Oberstein an der Nahe

aym Carl Hoffmann Maschinenfabrik, Aue, Saxony

ba Sundwiger Messingwerke (formerly Gebrüder von der Becke) KG, Sundwig-Iserlohn, Westfalen

bb A. Laue und Compagnie, Berlin

bc Kupfer- und Messingwerke Becker und Compagnie KG, Langenberg, Rheinland

bch Augsburger Federnfabrik von Schwartzenberg und Oberplöderl, Augsburg

bd Metallwerk Lange AG, Bodenbach Works, Sudeten Region

be Berndorfer Metallwarenfabrik A. Krupp AG, Berndorf, Austria

bf Deutsches Eöhrenwerke AG, Mühlheim

bg Gebr. Böhler & Co. AG, Edelstahlwerke Branch, Berlin

bh Waffenwerk Brünn AG, Provázyska Bystrica Works, Czechoslovakia

bj Niebecker und Schumacher, Iserlohn, Westphalia

bk Metall-, Walz- und Plattierwerke Hindrichs Auffermann AG, Wuppertal-Oberbarmen

blu Sprengstoffwerke Blumau AG, Blumau near

	Felixdorf
blx	Michael Seidel Spiel- und Metallwarenfabrik, Zirndorf near Nürnberg
bmf	Mährische Stahl- und Eisenindustrie AG, Olmütz, Czechoslovakia
bnd	Maschinenfabrik Augsburg-Nürnberg AG (MAN), Nürnberg Works
bne	Metallwerke Odertal GmbH, Odertal
bqt	Eugen Müller Pyrotechnische Fabrik, Vienna, Austria
btn	Ernst Gösser Metallwaren- und Kunstharzpresswerk, Iserlohn, Westphalia
bvv	Rothmüller-Mewa Blechwarenfabrik, Vienna, Austria
bwq	Max H. Müller Brinker Eisenwerke, Hannover-Brink
bxn	Bayrisches Kabelwerk Riffelmacher und Engelhardt, Roth near Nürnberg
byc	August Klönne Brückenbau-Anstalt, Dortmund
byw	Johannes Schäfer Stettiner Schraubenwerk, Stettin
ca	Vereinigte Deutsche Nickelwerke AG (ex-Westfälische Nickelwalzwerke), Schwerte, Ruhr
cbl	Vereinigte Deutsche Metallwerke AG, Nürnberg-West
cdo	Theodor Bergmann Waffen- und Munitionsfabrik AG, Velten Works
cdp	Theodor Bergmann Waffen- und Munitionsfabrik AG, Velten Works, Berlin
cf	Westfälisch-Anhaltische Sprengstoff AG (Wasag), Oranienburg
cg	Finower Industrie GmbH, Finow, Mark
cgt	Josef Stefsky Posamentfabrik, Stockerau, Lower Danube
ch	Fabrique Nationale d'Armes de Guerre (FN), Herstal lez-Liege, Belgium
cma	Vereinigte Oberschlesische Hüttenwerke, Gleiwitz
cts	Märkisches Werk Wilmsmann GmbH, Halver
cwg	Westfälisch-Anhaltische Sprengstoff AG (Wasag), Coswig Works
cxm	Gustav Genschow AG, Berlin
czo	Heeres-Zeugamt Geschosswerkstatt, Königsberg in Prussia
dbg	Dynamit AG (ex-Alfred Nobel & Co.), Düneberg, Lauenburg
dbk	Richard Rinker GmbH, Neubrandenburg, Mecklenburg
dma	Heeres-Munitionanstalt, Geschosswerkstatt Zeithain
dms	Nürnberger Schraubenfabrik GmbH, Nürnberg-West
dnf	Rheinisch-Westfälische Sprengstoff AG (RWS), Stadeln Works, near Nürnberg
dnh	Rheinisch-Westfälische Sprengstoff AG (RWS), Durlach Works, near Karlsruhe
dnv	Fahr AG, Stockach
dom	Westfälische Metallindustrie AG, Lippstadt
dou	Waffenwerk Brünn AG, Povázska Bystrica Works, Czechoslovakia
dph	Interessen-Gemeinschaft Farbenindustrie AG (IG Farben), Autogen Works, Griesheim, Frankfurt-am-Main
drh	Gebrüder Thiel GmbH, Ruhla, Thuringia
drz	Eltron Dr. Theodor Stiebel, Berlin-Tempelhof
dsb	Alexander Beck Holzwarenfabrik, Schmalkalden, Thuringia
dut	Spindel- und Spinnflügelfabrik AG, Neudorf, Erzgebirge
dwo	B. Thies Spezialmaschinenfabrik, Coesfeld, Westphalia
dye	Erste Alpenländische Pyrotechnische Fabrik Eduard Pitschmann und Co., Innsbruck, Austria
dza	Bleiwerke Dr. C. Schülcke, Hamburg
eba	Metallwarenfabrik Scharfenberg und Teubert, Breitungen on the Werra
ebd	Fatra, AG Erzeugung technischer Gummiwaren, Napajedl, Czechoslovakia
ecc	Oskar Lünig Pyrotechnische Fabrik, Möhringen (Fildern)
ecd	Karl Lippold Pyrotechnische Fabrik, Wuppertal-Elberfeld
edg	J.A. Henckels Zwillingswerk, Solingen
edq	Deutsche Waffen- und Munitionsfabriken AG (DWM), Schlutup near Lübeck
edr	Sachsenwerk Licht- und Kraft AG, Radeberg, Saxony
edy	Gebrüder Müller Armaturenfabrik, Luckenwalde
edz	Pickhardt und Gerlach Metallwarenfabrik GmbH, Werdohl, Westphalia
eef	Heine und Sohn Schrauben- und Mutternfabrik, Vöhrenbach, Black Forest
eeg	Schürhoff & Co Metallwarenfabrik, Gevelsberg
eej	Märkisches Walzwerk GmbH, Strausberg District, Potsdam
eel	Metallwarenfabrik ex-H. Wiesner AG, Brotterode Works, Hessen-Nassau
eem	Selve-Kornbiegel Dornheim Munitionsfabrik

AG, Sömmerda, Saxony

een Josef Burger Söhne Metallwarenfabrik GmbH, Schonach

eeo Deutsche Waffen- und Munitionsfabriken AG (DWM), Posen Works, Poland

eeq Walter Helkenberg, Fassondreherei, Velbert, Rheinland

eev Friedrich Braun Metallwarenfabrik, Tembach-Dietharz, Thuringia

eey Metallwarenfabrik Treuenbrietzen GmbH, Röderhof

emh Georg Allgaier Stanz- und Presswerk, Uhingen, Württemberg

emp Dynamit AG (ex-Alfred Nobel & Co.), Empelde Works, Hannover

enc Georg Eckhardt Maschinenfabrik AG, Leipzig

eom Heinrich Huck, Metallwarenfabrik AG, Nürnberg

ern W.G. Dinkelmeyer Metallwarenfabrik, Nürnberg-West (This manufacturer seems to have used the "erm" code before 1942)

evz Bergbau Tiefbohrgeräte- und Einrichtungen, Salzgitter

exw Metallwerke GmbH, Holleischen, Mies District, Sudetenland

fa Mansfeld AG, Hettstedt, South Harz

faa Deutsche Waffen- und Munitionsfabriken AG (DWM), Karlsruhe Works

fb Mansfeld AG, Rothenburg on the Saale

fc Mansfeld Metallwarenfabrik AG, Copper and Brass Department, Allerstedt

fd Stolberger Metallwerk AG (ex-Asten, Lynen und Schleicher), Stolberg, Rheinland

fde Dynamit AG (ex-Alfred Nobel & Co.), Förde Works

fee Augsburger Wagenfabrik Ludwig Pfister, Augsburg

fer Metallwerk Wandhofen GmbH, Schwerte

fko Bernhard Bruns Maschinenfabrik, Bad Zwischenahn, Oldenburg

fva Draht- und Metallwarenfabrik GmbH, Salzwedel

ga Hirsch Kupfer und Messingwerke AG, Finow, Mark

ghf Fritz Kiess & Co. GmbH, Suhl, Thuringia

gtb J.F. Eisfeld Pulver- und Pyrotechnische Fabriken GmbH, Güntersberge Works

gxy Gebr. Klinge Lederwarenfabrik, Dresden-Löbtau

gyy Gladitz Glühlampenmaschinenfabrik GmbH, Schwäbisch-Gmünd

gyz Steatit-Magnesia AG, Dralowid Works, Teltow

ha Wielandwerke AG, Metallhalbfabrikate, Ulm on the Danube

ham Dynamit AG (ex-Alfred Nobel & Co.), Hamm Works

has Pulverfabrik Hasloch, Hasloch on the Main

hgs W.C. Gustav Burmeister, Pyrotechnische Fabrik und Signalmittelwerk GmbH, Trittau District, Hamburg

hhw Metallwerke Silberhütte GmbH, St. Andreasberg in the Harz

hla Metallwarenfabrik Treuenbrietzen GmbH, Sebaldushof Works

hlb Metallwarenfabrik Treuenbrietzen GmbH, Selterhof Works

hlc Zieh- und Stanzwerk GmbH, Schleusingen, Thuringia

hld C.F. Esser, Fabrik für Eisenkonstruktionen und Fensterbau, Cologne

hle Lilpop, Rau & Loewenstein- AG, Warsaw, Poland

hre C.W. Motz und Co. Metallwarenfabrik, Brandenburg, Havel

hrn Presswerk GmbH, Metgethen in East Prussia

htg Polte Armaturen und Maschinenfabrik AG, Duderstadt Works

jry Hermann Herhold, Olbernhau

jtb Société Anonyme Belge Tavaro et Companie, Ghent, Belgium

jua Danuvia Waffen- und Munitionsfabrik AG (Femaru Fégyvér es Löserdyár), Budapest, Hungary

k **Luck und Wagner AG, Suhl/Thüringen**

ka Gerhardi und Companie, Lüdenscheid, Westphalia

kam Hugo Schneider AG (Hasag), Eisen- und Metallwerke GmbH, Skarzusko-Kamienna, Poland

kfg Gesellschaft zur Verwertung chemischer Erzeugnisse mbH, Kaufering Works

klb J.F. Eisfeld Pulver- und Pyrotechnische Fabriken GmbH, Kieselbach

krl Dynamit AG (ex-Alfred Nobel & Co.), Krümmel near Hamburg

kry F.A. Sening Maschinenfabrik, Hamburg

ksb Manufacture d'Armes de Lavallois, Paris, France

kum Hartmann & Braun AG, Frankfurt-am-Main

kun J.F. Eisfeld Pulver- und Pyrotechnische Fabriken GmbH, Kunigunde Works

kus	Dörries-Füllner-Maschinenfabriken AG, Bad Warmbrunn
kye	Ernst Hilker & Co. Möbelfabrik, Detmold
kyn	Astra, Fabrica Romana de Vagoane, Motoane Armament si Munitiuni, Brasov, Rumania
kyp	Rumänisch-Deutsche Industrie- und Handels-AG, Bucharest, Rumania
kzu	Thonet und Mundus, Bistritz am Harz
ldb	Deutsche Pyrotechnische Fabriken GmbH, Berlin-Malchow Works
ldc	Deutsche Pyrotechnische Fabriken GmbH, Cleebronn Works
ldn	Deutsche Pyrotechnische Fabriken GmbH. Neumarkt Works, Oberpfalz
ldp	Krebs & Co. Möbelfabrik, Brand-Erbisdorf, Saxony
lge	Kugenfabriken Schulte & Co., Tente, Rheinland
lkm	Patronen-, Zündhütchen- und Metallwarenfabrik (ex-Sellier und Bellot), Veitsberg Factory, Prague, Czechoslovakia
lpk	Servotechna AG, Prague, Czechoslovakia
ma	Metallwerke Lange AG, Aue, Saxony
men	J.A. Kluge, Oberaltstadt, Werke Bleicherei und Färberei, Hermannseifen, Hohenelbe District
mog	Deutsche Sprengchemie AG, Moschwig Works
mpr	Société Anonyme Suisse Hispano-Suiza, Geneva, Switzerland
mrb	Aktiengesellschaft (ex-Skoda Works) Pilsen, Prague-Smichow Works, Czechoslovakia
myx	Rheinmetall-Borsig AG, Sömmerda, Saxony
na	Westfälische Kupfer- und Messingwerke AG (ex-C. Noell), Lüdenscheid, Westphalia
nbe	Hugo Schneider AG (Hasag), Czestochowa, Poland
ndn	Heinrich Blücher, Fabrik für technische Bürsten, Bürstein-Spremberg
nfx	Rheinisch-Westhälische Sprengstoff AG (RWS), Warsaw-Pragna, Poland
nrh	Johannsen & Ziegner Metallwerk, Oranienburg near Berlin
nyv	Rheinmetall Borsig AG, Unterlüss Works
nyw	Otto Eberhardt Patronenfabrik (owned by Gustloff-Werke), Meiningen Works
oa	Eduard Hueck Metall-, Walz- und Presswerke, Lüdenscheid, Westphalia
osn	Bünder Tonwerk Heinrich Hensiek, Bünde, Westphalia
oxo	Teuto Metallwerke GmbH, Osnabrück
oyj	Ateliers de Construction de Tarbes, Tarbes, France
pcd	Theodor Bergmann Waffen- und Munitionsfabrik AG, Bernauwerk, Berlin
pmt	Kabel- und Metallwerk Neumayer AG, Nürnberg (?)
pvf	Reichertwerk AG, Vienna, Austria
qa	Wilhelm Prym, Stolberg, Rheinland
qrb	Pirotechnico di Bologna, Bologna, Italy
qve	Carl Walther Waffenfabrik, Zella-Mehlis, Thuringia
r	Rheinisch-Westfälische Sprengstoff AG, Berlin-Niederschöneweide
rdf	Wasag-Chemie, Reinshert Works
s	Dynamit AG (ex-Alfred Nobel & Co.), St. Lambrecht Works
skd	Selve-Kornbiegel-Dornheim AG, Suhl, Thuringia
t	Dynamit AG, Werk Troisdorf
ta	Dürener Metallwerke GmbH, Berlin-Borsigwalde
ua	Osnabrücker Kupfer- und Drahtwerke AG, Osnabrück
va	Kabel- und Metallwerke Neumeyer AG, Nürnberg
vsk	Hirtenberger Patronenfabrik (ex-Keller und Co.), Hirtenberg, Lower Austria
vzg	Vereinigte Zünder- und Kabelwerke, Meissen
wa	Hugo Schneider AG (Hasag), Leipzig
wb	Hugo Schneider AG (Hasag), Berlin-Köpenick
wc	Hugo Schneider AG (Hasag), Meuselwitz, Thuringia
wd	Hugo Schneider AG (Hasag), Taucha-Leipzig
we	Hugh Schneider AG (Hasag), Langewiesen
wf	Hugo Schiender AG)Hasag), Eisen- und Metallwerke GmbH, Kielce, Poland
wg	Hugo Schneider AG (Hasag), Altenburg
wh	Hugh Schneider AG (Hasag), Eisenach
wj	Hugo Schneider AG (Hasag), Oberweissbach
wk	Hugo Schneider AG (Hasag), Schlieben
wm	Hugo Schneider AG (Hasag), Dermbach, Thuringia
xa	Busch-Jäger Lüdenscheider Metallwerke AG, Lüdenscheid, Westphalia
y	Jagdpatronen-, Zündhütchen und Metallwarenfabrik AG, Werk Nagytetený, Budapest, Hungary
ya	Sächsische Metallwarenfabrik August Wellner Söhne AG, Aue, Saxony
zb	Kupferwerk Ilsenburg AG, Ilsenburg in the Harz

Present-Day Bullet Production

The 9 mm Parabellum cartridge is produced in almost every country in the Western World and is available as a reliable cartridge. Only brass is used as the material for the case, with the only exception to date being the cartridges made by Blazer, which are available with aluminum cases, a material that is neither completely uncritical nor suitable for reloading.

Packages of cartridges made by GECO to date. Each package contains fifty cartridges.

The full-jacket cartridge is customary, but there are also other types of cartridges, such as those with partial jackets, with open hollow points, or made completely of lead. The cartridges made exclusively for police use are unique; they are action cartridges with a bullet that is open on the inside and has a plastic covering. Another type made for typical police use is the French developed T.H.V. cartridge (the abbreviation stands for Très Haute Vitesse: very high speed). On a test barrel of 110 mm this cartridge reaches speeds of about 700 meters per second, and fired from the longer barrel of a machine pistol, it even reaches 880 meters per second.

The THV cartridge is one of the most interesting developments in recent years, as it made it possible to combine several previously impossible demands in one ideal police cartridge. It must be capable of being fired from any weapon that can fire its caliber, thus even in the case of the 9 mm Parabellum from pistols, revolvers and machine pistols. It must show good precision even at 50 meters, and must be easy to fire with little recoil. A further demand is a high stopping effect, but with correspondingly little penetrating effect against soft targets and simultaneously a high penetrating power against hard targets. Thus the bullet of the THV cartridge, fired from a 9 mm pistol at a short range, will penetrate 4 mm of sheet steel when fired vertically, which

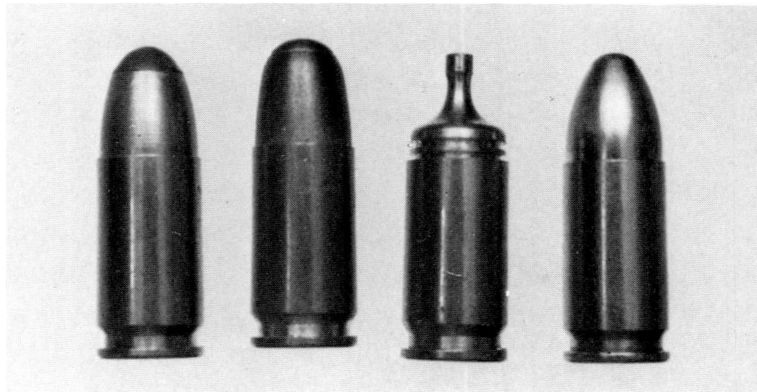

Present-day special cartridges. From left, the Action cartridge by GECO, the Quick Defense by MEN, the THV from France and a normal cartridge with FMJ (Full Metal Jacket) bullet, generally available to the private user.

is not attained by a cartridge with the usual bullet. The range should be considerably shorter than those of other cartridges, and no contradiction of the Hague and Geneva Conventions may be attained. To meet these last demands, the bullet may not reshape itself drastically in the body of the target, nor may it cause excessive wounds.

Schematic diagram of an early THV bullet.

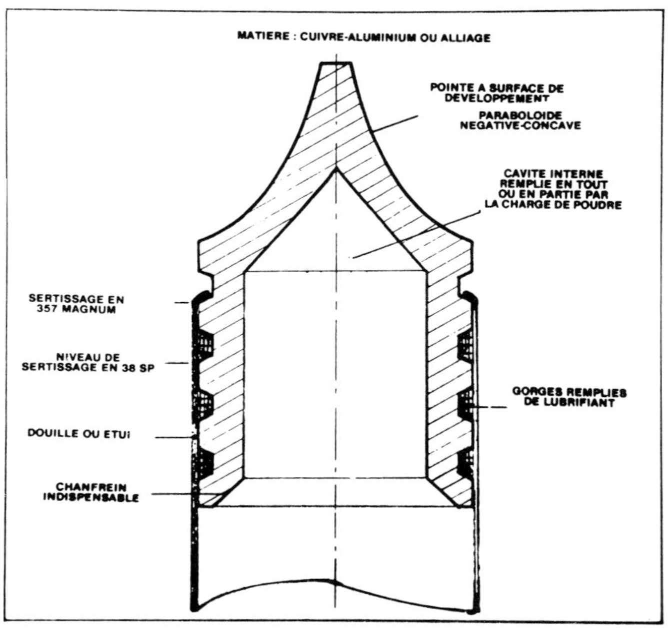

Cartridges with full jackets have the disadvantage of too great penetration against soft targets; numerous accidents have proved this again and again, and their range was and is too great, and this also leads to the endangerment of uninvolved persons in police use. A good, practical solution in its time was offered by the "Quick Defense" made by MEN and the "Action" made by Dynamit Nobel; good stopping effects and good penetration of hard targets such as automobiles, with correspondingly slight penetration of soft targets. Their main problem was that of changing form in the target.

The bullet of the THV cartridge was now able to fulfill all demands. The special feature is the composition of the bullet. It is made of a copper alloy, has several grease grooves, is relatively light, and attains its great speed from an increased charge of a specially developed powder. This makes it capable of cutting smoothly through hard targets such as metal; bulletproof vests scarcely offer any effective defense against it and are penetrated. When used against human targets, it has a greater stopping effect than is the case with hollow-pointed bullets, and transmits its complete energy to the target without penetrating deeply. This is achieved by its negatively parabolic shape, which results in a compression of the material in the target. The bullet alone cannot achieve the described effect; a certain minimum speed is necessary, and this was achieved through the quantity and type of the powder as well as the low mass of the bullet, which is cylindrically hollowed out inside.

The low bullet weight offers a very essential advantage, namely a much shorter range, which is reduced more than 70% at the same angle of elevation.

The whole spectrum of these very effective cartridges neither can nor will be portrayed here. They are not available to the private user, and at the present time they are given out to the national police in France only under the strictest security measures.

The manufacturing of cartridges is done to strict standards, which offer a high degree of safety to the user,

9 mm Luger is the other name of the Parabellum cartridge. Only the name of Luger is necessary, but it looks very colorful as a whole. This is a package of 50 NORMA cartridges.

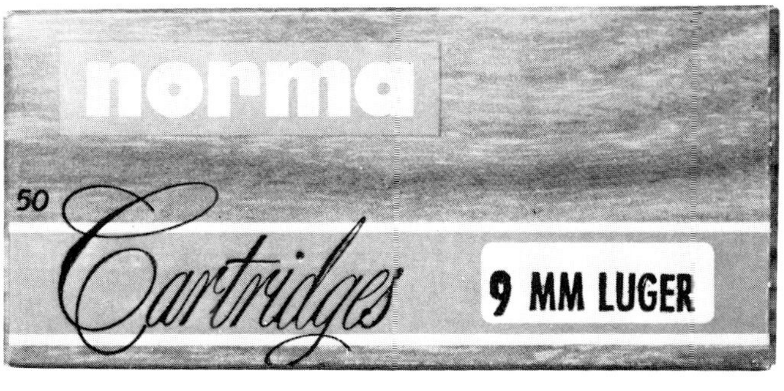

Breaking-in cartridges made in Germany and used for official breaking-in. They are loaded for excess pressure and have a rimmed base for identification.

whether in service or private. Many of the requirements are set forth in the STANAG 4090 (STANdard AGgreement). Specifications are recorded there in concrete details, as to terms of form, measurements, manufacturing techniques, achievement in use, maximal gas pressure, median gas pressure, or minimum and maximum values of muzzle energy as shown on a test range of 200 meters. In addition, very specific weapons are listed in which trouble-free functioning must have been shown without exception. Such weapons include the GP 35 (FN High Power), Walther P 38, the Italian Beretta Model 4 machine pistol, the Canadian Model C 1, and the French 1949 model. The type and sensitivity of the percussion cap is regulated.

Cartridges that correspond to the NATO norm bear a small cross in a circle on their base and thus differ from cartridges made for civilian use, without being significantly different. Production according to this norm has been carried on to date only in Germany, Belgium, The Netherlands and Canada. Production in the USA, using the XM 882 case, has only been experimental to date.

As for the reliability of the commercially available cartridges in the weapons used in Germany, malfunctions occur only rarely. The most frequent problems are malfunctions of the gun itself or in the feed from the magazine. The situation is different in terms of visible precision, as not every cartridge functions similarly in every gun, even as regards defensive weapons at short ranges. There are however striking differences, which can only be shown for the weapon in question through testing. Incompatibility of weapon and cartridge or bullet shape may show up clearly when the firing is done under constant conditions, such as from a shooting machine with a weapon built for low tolerance.

9 mm Luger (Parabellum)

Geschoßgewicht [g]	8,0	Hülsenlänge [mm]	19,1
Geschoßlänge [mm]	15,7	Lauflänge [mm]	125
a)  b)  Geschoßtyp: a) Vollmantel b) Bleirundkopf		Höchstzulässiger Gebrauchsgasdruck [bar]	2.600

Ballistic Data

Entfernung [m]	0	10	25	50
Geschwindigkeit [m/s]	350	345	335	325
Energie [J]	491	481	451	422
Flugzeit [ms]	0	29	73	149

7,65 mm Para

Geschoßgewicht [g]	6,0	Hülsenlänge [mm]	21,3
Geschoßlänge [mm]	14,5	Lauflänge [mm]	125
 Geschoßtyp: Vollmantel		Höchstzulässiger Gebrauchsgasdruck [bar]	2.600

Ballistic Data

Entfernung [m]	0	10	25	50
Geschwindigkeit [m/s]	360	355	345	330
Energie [J]	392	383	353	324
Flugzeit [ms]	0	28	71	145

Short Weapons with Rifled Barrels - Pistols

Lfd. Nr.	Handelsübliche Bezeichnung	Mindestwerte in mm							
		Patronenlagermaße				Übergang		Lauf	
		Länge vom Stoßboden bis Übergang L 3	Durchmesser Stoßboden- bzw. Randausfräsung R 1	Pulverraum-Ø hinten P 1	Hülsen-Ø vorne H 2	Länge des Übergangskegels G	Durchmesser des Übergangskegels hinten G 1	Feld-Ø F	Zug-Ø Z
1	6,35 mm	16,20	7,85	7,22	7,10	3,20	6,51	6,17	6,35
2	7,65 mm	17,60	9,20	8,74	8,61	1,66	8,61	7,72	7,90
3	9 mm kurz	17,30	–	9,72	9,58	2,21	9,15	8,84	9,02
4	9 mm Parabellum	19,15	–	10,03	9,68	3,64	9,09	8,84	9,09
5	30 M 1 Carbine	32,97	9,27	9,12	8,60	3,91	7,96	7,62	7,82

Maximum Cartridge

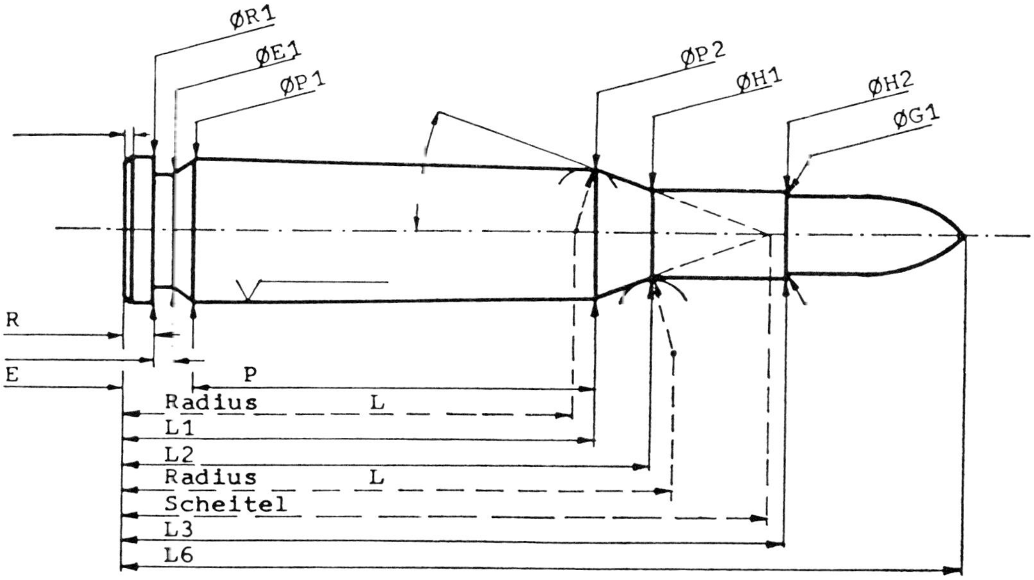

Values for Cartridges, Barrel 3.DVO WaffG 76

Patronenlagermaße für Pistolenmunition																
Kaliber	Länge			Boden			Pulverraum		Schulter		Übergang			Lauf		Verschluß-abstand
	L_1	L_2	L_3	R	ØR_1	E	ØP_1	ØP_2	ØH-	ØH_2	ØG_1	G	i oder 2 tg i	Ø F	Ø Z	
1	2	3	4	5	6	7	8	9	10	11	12	13	14	15	16	17
6,35 o. .25 Brown.	–	–	16,00	1,10	7,70	3,14	7,20	–	–	7,10	6,51	3,20	3°	6,17	6,35	–
7,62 Tokarev	19,26	21,07	25,45	1,10	10,01	3,20	9,91	9,62	8,58	8,50	7,86	3,10	1:12,92	7,62	7,84	0,15
7,63 Mauser	19,21	21,03	25,50	1,27	10,03	3,80	9,93	9,64	8,63	8,55	7,90	3,07	2°36′30″	7,62	7,85	0,15
7,65 Browning	–	–	17,20	1,25	9,20	3,17	8,64	–	–	8,55	7,94	2,41	1:7,52	7,63	7,83	–
7,65 lang	–	–	19,70	1,10	8,60	3,30	8,56	–	–	8,53	7,90	4,60	1:17	7,63	7,83	–
7,65 Parabellum	15,52	17,50	21,80	1,22	10,03	3,20	9,96	9,64	8,55	8,48	7,92	5,46	1°33′	7,62	7,83	0,15
8 mm Steyr	–	–	18,65	1,10	9,00	3,30	8,88	–	–	8,83	8,20	4,50	1:15	7,90	8,15	–
9 mm Berg. Bayard	–	–	23,00	1,30	10,05	4,00	9,91	–	–	9,61	9,09	3,75	1:15	8,84	9,09	–
9 mm Brown. kurz	–	–	17,30	1,15	9,65	2,95	9,65	–	–	9,55	9,09	2,58	3°	8,84	9,02	–
9 mm Brown. lang	–	–	20,20	1,25	10,25	3,20	9,78	–	–	9,75	9,15	2,21	1:7,13	8,84	9,09	–
9 mm Makarov	–	–	18,00	1,25	10,00	3,50	9,93	–	–	9,88	9,30	2,50	1:10	9,05	9,24	–
9 mm Mauser	–	–	25,00	1,20	10,00	3,20	9,88	–	–	9,63	9,09	3,75	1:15	8,84	9,09	–
9 mm Parabellum	–	–	19,15	1,27	10,05	2,46	10,00	–	–	9,68	9,05	3,35	1:14,56	8,82	9,02	0,15
9 mm Steyr	–	–	23,20	1,25	9,80	3,50	9,73	–	–	9,65	9,09	4,35	1:15	8,80	9,02	–
9 × 18	–	–	17,95	1,25	9,60	2,93	9,93	–	–	9,70	9,09	2,58	3°	8,82	9,02	–
221 Rem. Fireball	27,08	30,28	36,37	1,20	9,66	3,00	9,66	9,19	6,48	6,45	5,69	2,16	3°10′36″	5,56	5,69	0,10
357 Aut. Mag. Pist.	24,09	26,76	33,50	1,37	12,04	3,80	11,99	11,74	9,80	9,78	9,15	5,73	1:19,09	8,84	9,09	–
38 Wadcutter*)	–	–	29,64	1,57	11,28	–	9,65	–	–	9,65	–	–	–	8,79	9,04	–
38 Spec. A.M.U.	–	–	29,34	1,27	10,41	3,20	9,71	–	–	9,65	9,40	16,48	1°30′	8,79	8,97	–
38 Super Auto.	–	–	23,32**)	1,27	10,36	3,77	9,88	–	–	9,83	–	2,91	9°40′	8,84	9,02	–
44 Auto. Mag. Pist.	–	–	33,00	1,37	12,04	3,80	11,99	–	–	11,69	10,95	4,20	1:19,09	10,73	10,88	–
45 Auto (ACP)	–	–	22,81	1,24	12,22	3,75	12,22	–	–	12,04	11,48	2,81	1:11,24	11,23	11,43	–

*) Die Maße F und Z können bei starr verriegelten Wettkampfwaffen unterschritten werden, wenn die Sicherheit gewährle stet ist.

**) Dieses Maß kann bis auf 22,86 verkürzt werden, soweit dies die Funktion der Waffe erfordert.

BELGIUM

Only the Fabrique Nationale in Herstal (FN for short) can be named as a manufacturer of pistols in Belgium. The High Power, produced since the mid-1930s, has not been succeeded to this day by a more modern successor. For one thing, the design has certainly proved itself, and for another, the manufacturers were rather unlucky in trying to modernize their concept, which had been successful until then, and other firms came to rank far above FN in this respect. A similar situation in principle was experienced by the Colt firm, which had formerly produced several variations of the famous Government model, yet could not develop a successful new pistol despite the great need for one.

The Fabrique Nationale was created in 1889 through the financial assistance of several Belgian banks and the technical direction of Ludwig Loewe. The firm began by building Mauser guns under license for the Belgian armed forces. Shortly after 1890 John Moses Browning joined the new firm. Moses came from the USA, where he had just had a falling out with Winchester, and had not been able to have his automatic rifle manufactured in the USA. It went into production in Belgium. Afterwards, he applied himself to the developing of self-loading pistols and other guns. All in all, with the exception of Fritz Walther, there had never been such a moving spirit among weapon inventors. The slide mounted lock over the tilting barrel, which he designed, can still be found in most self-loading pistols today. This turn of the century technology has not been superseded even as the twentieth century nears its end. The name "Browning" is practically synonymous with the self-loading pistol itself, just as Colt stands for revolvers.

Moses' later development culminated in the Model 1935 pistol, which was also designated HP (for High Power) or GP (for Grande Puissance, which means the same in French). It was developed and technically completed between 1925 and 1935. In 1935 it was accepted for military use, hence the model designation of 35. After its adoption in Belgium, numerous other European countries put it into service, where many of them still use it today.

Only a few Colt M 1911 technical features can be found on the Model 35 — Browning had improved much and

One of the patent drawings for the Browning pistol, which led eventually to the successful High Power (GP 35) pistol.

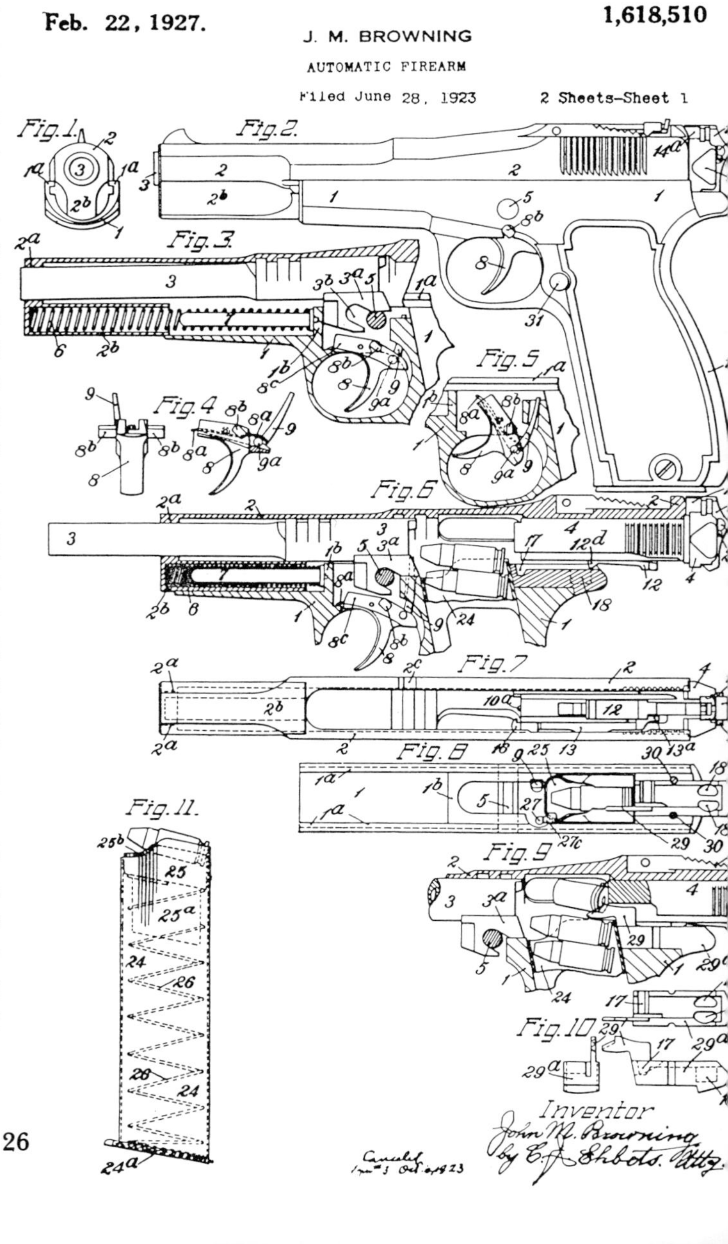

eliminated weaknesses.

Aside from the variations that resulted from the use of sights and external changes by various manufacturers in other countries, its technical basis has been retained essentially unchanged to this day.

The HP or High Power Pistol

Because of their high-quality workmanship as all-steel pistols and their reliable functioning, as well as their good shooting performance, HP's are still popular weapons today, even though they can no longer meet all demands on account of their simple single-action triggers. If they existed today with double-action triggers . . . their admirers have been lamenting this lack for years, and without success. The magazine holds thirteen cartridges stored in two rows. Because of this, the grip is somewhat wider, though not excessively wide if one compares its dimensions with those of other pistols with similar magazines. A certain external similarity to the Colt M 1911 may be present or hinted at, but noteworthy differences exist in the gun's details.

The movement of the barrel is not controlled by the chain link, not inconceivable in view of the pistol's performance, but rather by a control curve attached to the barrel. Here it benefits the testable precision to a great degree in that the barrel is forced to make the first part of recoil in a straight line, and is only then swung backward or downward by a bolt. Otherwise the trigger

Cutaway drawings of the most important pistols of our century. From the top: Colt M 1911, Tokarev 1930, MAS 1935 A, SIG SP 47/8, and FN Browning Model 1935.

The GP 35 pistol made by the Fabrique Nationale in Herstal, Belgium, set new standards and was one of the best self-loading pistols of its time. Typical features are the rounded hammer spur and the fixed sights, plus the wooden grip panels with herringbone pattern. The trigger can be pulled only when the hammer is cocked; to use the present-day expression, this is a single-action pistol.

is no different than those of similarly constructed weapons. The barrel and slide are firmly linked by two tabs on the barrel and slide, and after firing they move backward a short distance together, separating as soon as the barrel is moved downward in the area of the cartridge chamber.

The HP has no grip safety, but rather a magazine safety. It is not possible for a bullet to be fired without having the magazine in place. This arrangement is not wholly regarded in positive terms, for if the magazine is lost the pistol becomes nothing more than a projectile, though it may have a large supply of cartridges. The magazine safety is built into the magazine shaft. It works on the trigger bar and is released from the catch on the

Almost the same pistol in terms of design, made after the way. The spur was changed but the fixed sights were retained here.

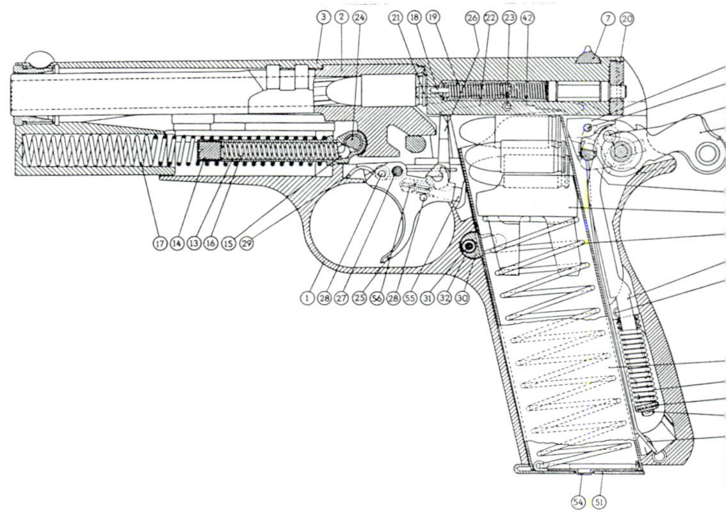

Cutaway drawing of the GP 35, a factory drawing of the FN firm.

sear.

Pistols made after World War II have different sights. The normal version is the "Vigilante", which has a rigid sight and lacks sight adjustment. The surface is highly burnished, with the grips being made of black plastic with a pressed-in pattern. The "Vigilante Renaissance" model of the pistol also has a fixed sight, but it is finely engraved and silver-plated. Choice of grip panels consists of either walnut or imitation mother-of-pearl.

The "Sport" model differs from the standard version in the addition of an adjustable sight. The Sport version known as "GP Special" or "Competition" offers a longer barrel, added front weight and adjustable sight. The slightly cut-back bar foresight is a part of the 74-gram front weight, which is held firmly in position by two Inbus screws. The barrel of the Sport pistol is 150 mm long, with the weapon's total length about 230 mm, and its unloaded weight about 980 grams.

After production commenced in Belgium just before World War II, two basic versions were built, one of which had the fixed sight. The second version had a sight with adjustable height, with the range of adjustment (devoutly to be wished) moving up to 500 meters — the sight was not much different in terms of operation from that of a rifle. The pistol with the 500-meter sight had an aperture machined into the rear of the grip to hold the wooden shaft.

In addition, there were already extensive factory experiments made at that time: A pistol with a sight adjustment of up to 1000 meters and the aperture for the shaft, a 7.65 mm Parabellum version with only an eight-shot magazine, and a version for the 7.65 mm long cartridge, this last being an attempt to attract orders from Switzerland or France. None of these experiments resulted in a production weapon, nor did a further version with an alternative switch to serial fire in connection with the wooden shaft proceed.

When German troops had overrun Belgium in 1940, the factory was immediately placed under German control. The production of pistols was allowed to proceed, and the weapons were put into German Wehrmacht service with the designation "Pistole Modell 640 (b)." Some 320,000 640 (b) pistols were produced. Some employees of the Fabrique Nationale fled to Britain before the German occupation, taking any available designs and drawings with them. Whether a small

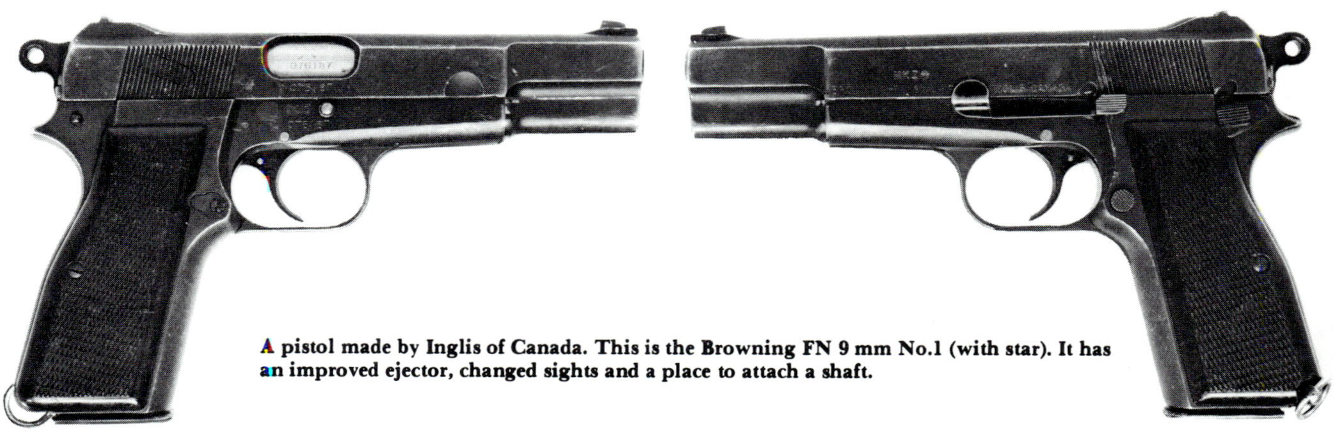

A pistol made by Inglis of Canada. This is the Browning FN 9 mm No.1 (with star). It has an improved ejector, changed sights and a place to attach a shaft.

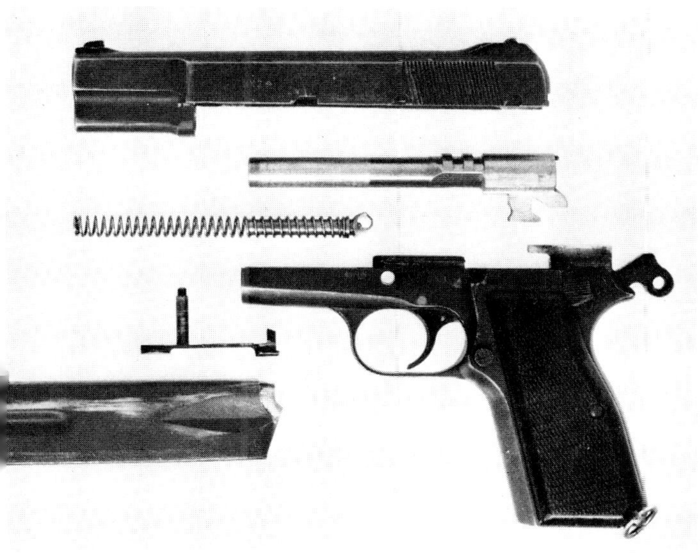

The same pistol dismantled for cleaning. The bolt using the two cam curves up on the barrel and the chainless downward guiding of the barrel are easy to see.

A version with sights adjustable to 500 meters, called the Browning FN 9 mm No.1 Mk. 1 pistol.

A pistol made after the war, with sights adjustable vertically as well as laterally.

number of HP pistols were built in Britain is not definitely known to this day, even to British authors. There was a "Browning 9 mm (FN) Automatic Mk 1 (UK) Pistol", but no evidence of its use by the British forces has been found to date.

Shortly thereafter, in 1942, the drawings reached Canada, and from then on the pistol was manufactured at the John Inglis factory in Toronto. Inglis continued to build the two hitherto successful versions for use by various fighting forces, including large numbers for Nationalist China. The pistol was accepted by the Canadian and British forces, as well as by numerous special units and commando troops. From this era, four versions in all are known to have been made:

Browning FN 9 mm No 1 Mk 1 Pistol with adjustable sight to 500 meters and attachable shaft.

Browning FN 9 mm No 1 Mk 1 Pistol,* like the Mk 1 but with an improved ejector, modified sight and attachable shaft.

Browning FN 9 mm No 2 Mk 1 Pistol with fixed sight and no provision for a shaft.

Browning FN 9 mm No 2 Mk 2 Pistol, like No 2 Mk 1 but with an improved ejector.

The end of World War II also saw the end of production by Inglis, and from then on production was resumed in Belgium. Pistols made for military use were known as Model 1946, the versions for the civilian market were called High Power. Actually, the 1946 model designation does not seem to have been accepted anywhere, for it continued to be sold everywhere as the Pistol 35, with the already denoted type names such as Vigilante or Capitain (the Capitain was a version with a sight adjustable only in terms of height).

Testing and Modification

The manufacturer could not ignore the demand for a modernized pistol with a cocking trigger, but private sales were not sufficient to assure financial success; there had to be government orders to justify the financial expenditure of putting a pistol into production.

The successor to the HP, as illustrated and described in numerous publications, was the so-called Geisterschiff (Ghost Ship), a weapon that ultimately did not go into production and exists only in a few handmade prototypes.

This pistol retained many of the GP's best features, including the steel grip. The trigger guard took on a modern shape, including the typically popular projection to the front, and the trigger was now finally a cocking trigger. The sight was improved, the hammer finally lost its very long and often unhandy spur, and the safety catch was located on both sides. At the same time, the cocked hammer could now be decocked safely over the lateral safety — all characteristics which other manufacturers already had on the market before that time. Without being lengthened downward, the two-row magazine now held 14 rather than the former 13 cartridges; grip panels of resistant plastic were applied, with a thumb position lightly marked on each side. An unusual, and not very practical, feature is (or was) the planned operation of the safety catch, which had to be pushed up from bottom to top to decock the hammer. Not much more can be told of this pistol, as the manufacturer has kept its details secret. The new pistol was designated BDA-9 S. To meet the needs of police and security forces, the BDA-9 S was used as a basis from which the BDA-9 M version was developed — it likewise

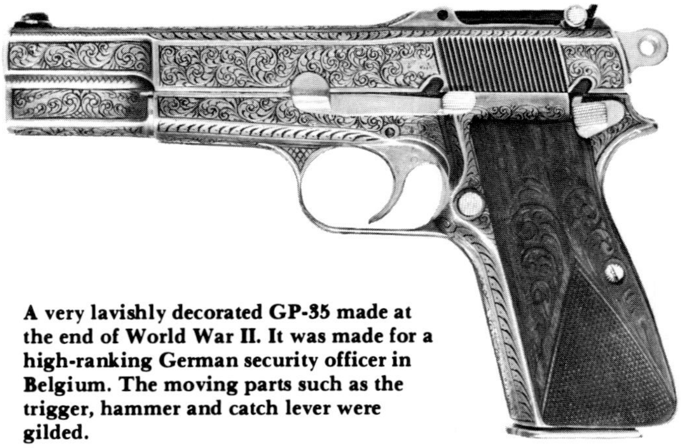

A very lavishly decorated GP-35 made at the end of World War II. It was made for a high-ranking German security officer in Belgium. The moving parts such as the trigger, hammer and catch lever were gilded.

held 14 cartridges in its magazine and used the same grips as the 9 S type. The barrel of this rather compact pistol was only 96 mm long, instead of 118 mm, as was the BDA-9 S. The difference in overall length was 178 mm, as opposed to 200 mm, and the weight saving amounted to 50 grams.

Here FN had taken up a very timely trend as other manufacturer's had. Namely a pistol with the same design and for the same cartridge, but easier to handle than the pistol intended for military use.

Another planned but not built version was the BDA-9 C type. A weapon that was trimmed down to extreme compactness, with a shortened grip and a magazine holding only seven cartridges. The grip was nothing more than a short stump — how one was to hold such a short grip was questionable. The heights of the pistols compare as follows: BDA-9 M, 130 mm; BDA-9 C, only 93 mm, with an overall length of 173 mm as compared to the 178 mm of the M type.

A somewhat modified version of the HP, in the 9 mm Parabellum caliber, was put on the market at the beginning of 1986 under the "Single Action" model name. At that time, however, it was intended only for export and not yet available for the domestic market. The exterior had been prepared economically. All surfaces had been sandblasted and parkerized, with only the magazine, which held 13 cartridges, still burnished. The sight was different, with a light rail between the backsight and the foresight. The long hammer spur, that often caught in one's clothing and did damage, was retained.

The manual safety catch was set on both sides, a long-awaited agreement to the demands of the world's shooters. Only the grips with the thumb marked position were reminiscent of the BDA model series, and were

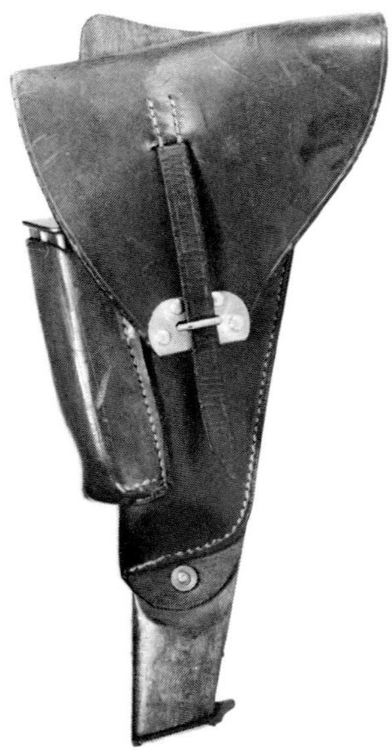

A leather holster with attached shaft, which could be attached according to the model. The holster also holds a second magazine.

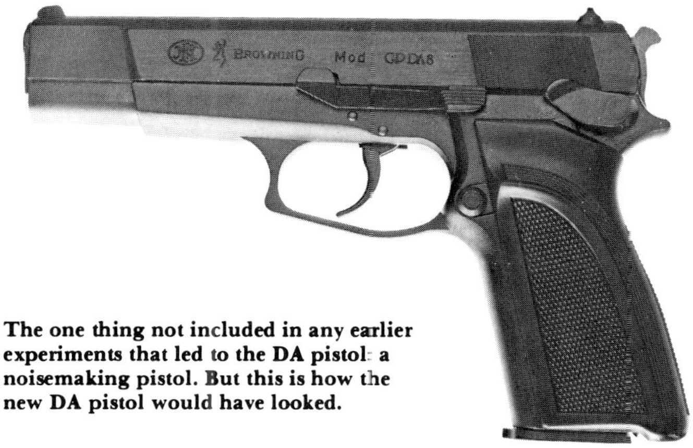

The one thing not included in any earlier experiments that led to the DA pistol: a noisemaking pistol. But this is how the new DA pistol would have looked.

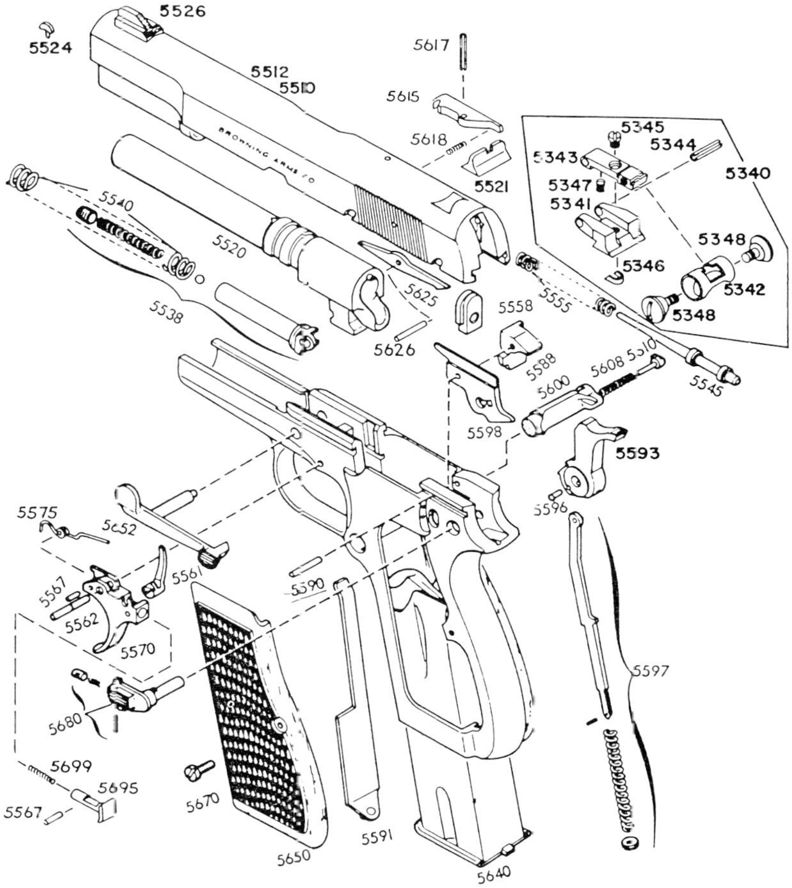

The individual parts of the FN Model GP 35 pistol. In the small box are the alternative parts for the adjustable sight.

Technical Data: FN HP Model 35

Manufacturer	Fabrique Nationale d'Armes de Guerre*
Year built	circa 1927-28
Caliber	9 mm Parabellum
Magazine	13 cartridges
Overall length	218 mm
Height/width	129 (136) mm 35 mm (depending on sights)
Barrel length	120 mm
Sights	fixed/adjustable/sport sights
Safeties	safety lever/safety magazine/safety rest
Material	Steel
Finish	burnished/painted.parkerized*

* by John Inglis, Canada

made of plastic. Whoever did not feel at home with them could exchange them for the earlier type of grips, as the screw holes were identical.

BRAZIL

Pistols by Taurus

The Brazilian firm of Forjas Taurus S.A., in Porte Alegre, began producing its own handguns in the mid-1970s. Since safety conditions have sometimes been chaotic in Brazil, the available market has been anything but small. The firm began by producing revolvers typically characterized by lengthwise cylinder flutings. In many ways, the lock resembled that of the Smith & Wesson revolver, but was made somewhat simpler.

Meanwhile, the firm's offerings could be enriched with its own line of revolvers, and their workmanship was such that they do not necessarily need to avoid comparison. A Model 85 S revolver in the author's possession shows such good workmanship in its excellent locking system that one can rank it among the best products of its kind without reservation. The Taurus firm's production program has become more and more extensive in recent

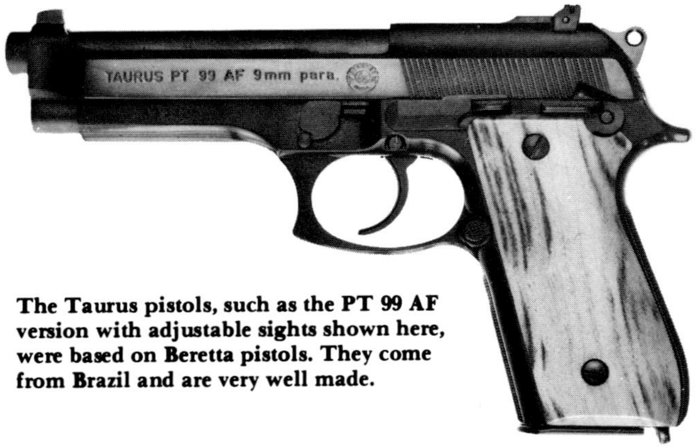

The Taurus pistols, such as the PT 99 AF version with adjustable sights shown here, were based on Beretta pistols. They come from Brazil and are very well made.

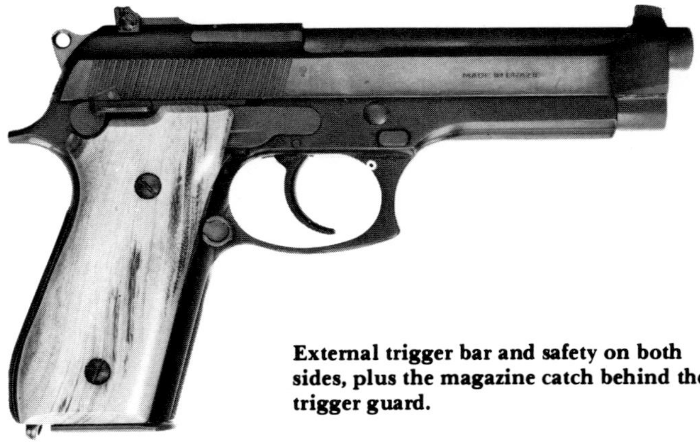

External trigger bar and safety on both sides, plus the magazine catch behind the trigger guard.

years, including not only revolvers, pistols and machine pistols, but also police equipment, air-pressure weapons, holsters, fishing tackle and crash helmets. The firm's self-loading pistols are made under license to the design of the Beretta 92 series, with the same being true of the Model MT-12-A machine pistol made by Taurus.

In the 9 mm Parabellum caliber, the firm first made the PT-92 model. This was nothing more than a Brazilian version of the Beretta Model 92 with a fixed sight and magazine catch in the grip. Technical information is identical, likewise the operation and technology, so that a further description need not be given here.

When the PT-92 model went out of production, the PT-99 AF and PT-92 AF models took its place. The PT-92 AF version still generally resembles the Beretta pistol externally — the sight is fixed, the surface is matte as far as the flanks of the slide, and the shape of the grip has been modernized. The trigger guard is curved to the front, profiled and grooved. The magazine catch has been moved upward, directly behind the attachment of the trigger guard. The safety catch was retained in the style of the Beretta 92, and consists of four safety devices working independently of each other: a lateral safety to lock the trigger and the slide, safety stops on the hammer, the firing pin as a flying ignition pin and loading indicator. The extractor projects out far enough when a cartridge is inserted to be seen or felt easily. The PT-99 AF version also has a vertically and laterally adjustable sight, which is set deep in the top of the slide.

To suit these presently produced pistols in terms of their safety, the PT-99 has been fitted with an additional lock for the firing pin. This safety is linked to the trigger and, by way of a lever, releases the lock on the firing pin only immediately before the hammer is released. Thus the Taurus pistol is an extremely safe design.

In actual testing, the pistols proved to be safe and

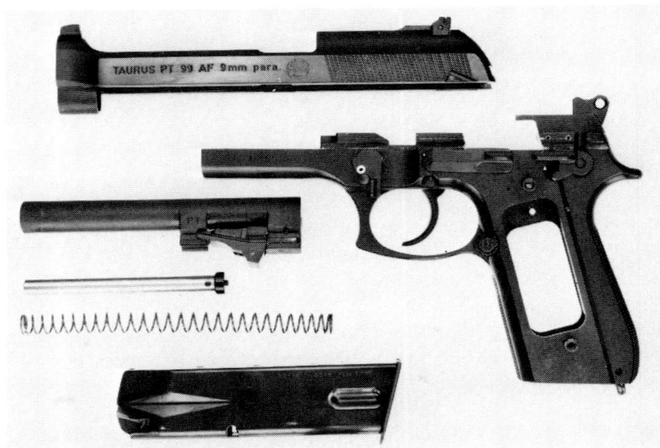

Dismantling is simple. These pistols have a swinging bolt, such as is commonly used by Beretta, under the barrel. The magazine holds 15 cartridges.

efficient. The trigger could move more easily, but that is often a question of personal opinion and preference. The shooting performance is notably good and scored, in groups of ten, in dispersion circles of 50 to 70 mm, depending on the cartridges used, with an inclined weapon at a range of 25 meters.

In this respect it may be of interest that there are almost

Cutaway view of the Taurus pistol. This drawing is not completely representative of the pistols shown here, which have their magazine catch immediately behind the trigger guard.

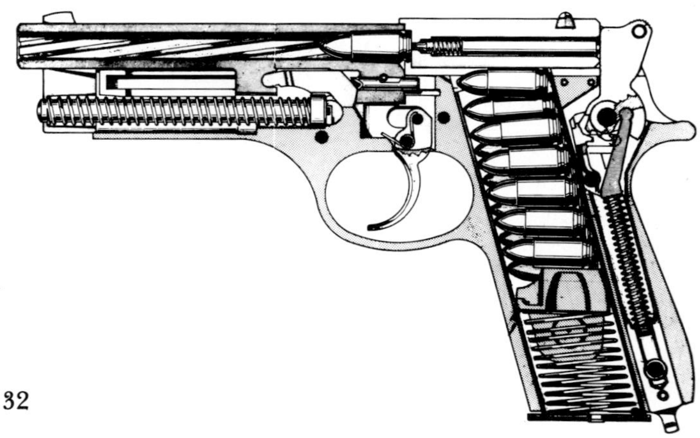

A version for the lover of shiny weapons. The surface is silk-matte nickel-plated. Here too is the deeply inset adjustable sight.

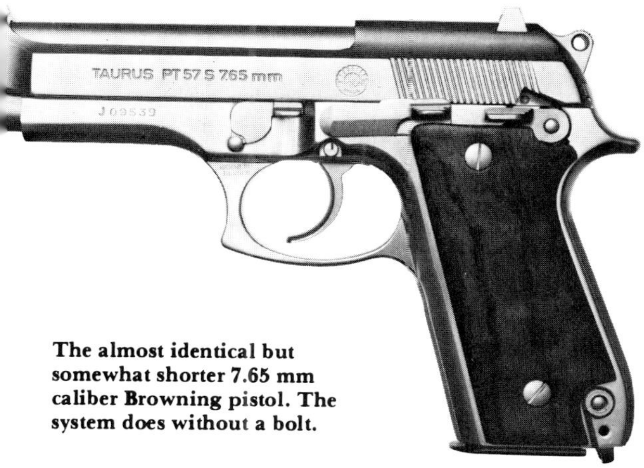

The almost identical but somewhat shorter 7.65 mm caliber Browning pistol. The system does without a bolt.

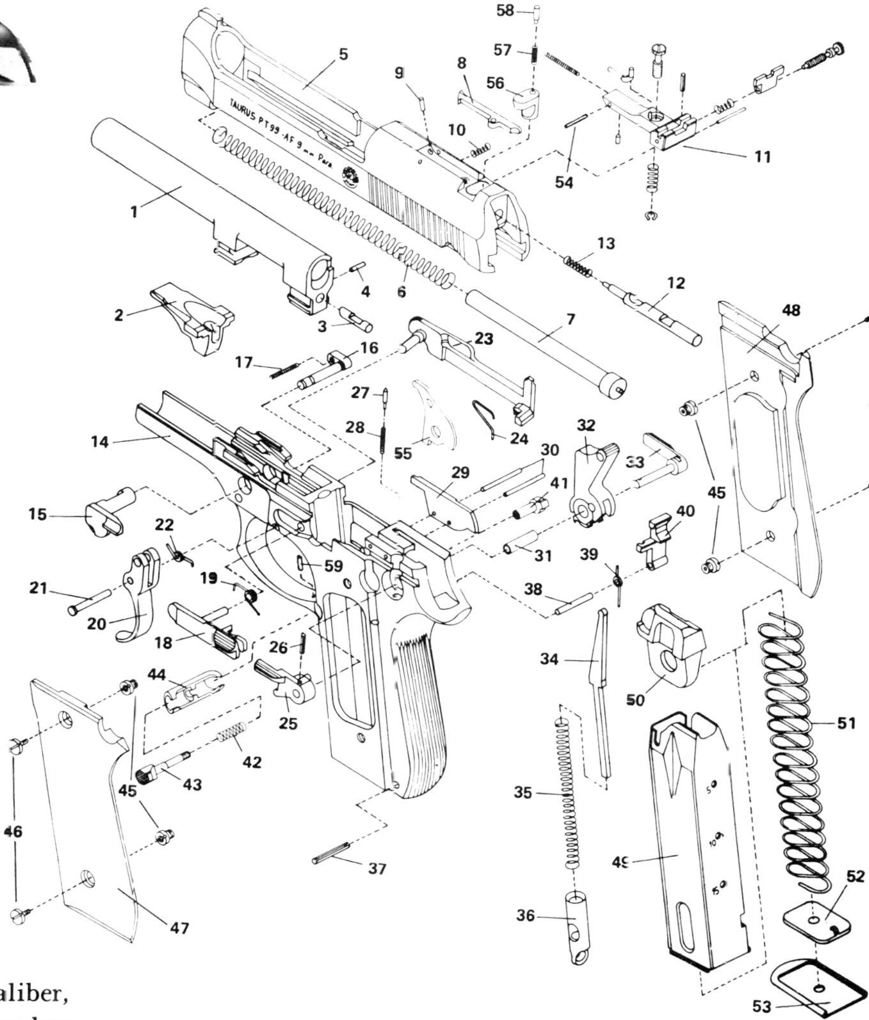

The individual parts of the PT 99 AF with adjustable sights and new safety.

identical pistols in the 7.65 mm Browning caliber, without locking by means of a swinging bolt, but rather a massive lock with a very powerful closing spring. The operation, dismantling and constructive design are so similar that a further description is unnecessary.

The barrel of the smaller pistols is some 8 mm shorter and the overall length somewhat less, however, the magazine holds fifteen cartridges in a two-row system,

Comparison of slides and barrels. Above is the locked system, below that of the unlocked pistol.

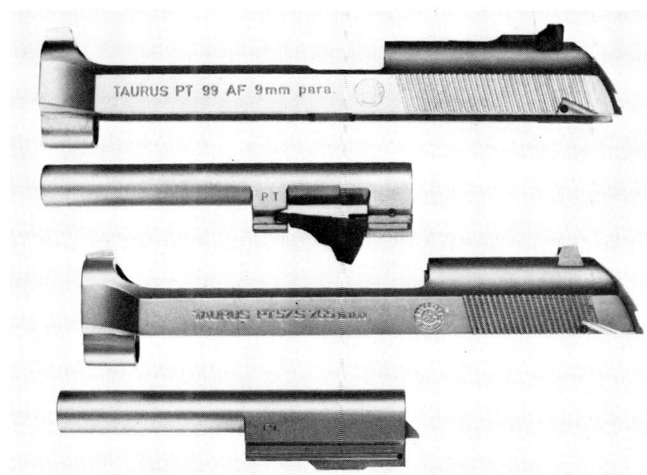

and an extra cartridge can be carried in the chamber without sacrificing any safety as well.

If one puts the hammer of a Taurus pistol in the safety stops and engages the safety catch, everything is blocked, the slide as well as the hammer.

Technical Data: Taurus PT-99 AMF

Caliber	9 mm Parabellum
Magazine	15 cartridges
System	Swinging bolt
Overall length	217 mm
Height	137 mm
Width	37 mm
Barrel length	125 mm
Barrel	6 riflings/right/250 mm long
Sight line	155 mm
Weight empty	980 grams
Sights	height & side adjustable
Finish	burnished or satin
Material	Steel, aluminum frame
Safeties	Safety rest/firing pin block/manual safety/ closing safety

GERMANY

Germany can be regarded as the birthplace of the 9 mm Parabellum cartridge as well as that of the most noteworthy self-loading pistols. So it may not be an exaggeration to describe this country as the classic land of pistols.

Many interesting and pioneering designs were made by German or German-speaking inventors. Naturally, constructive ideas also came from outside the country, such as the tipping-barrel lock based on Browning's ideas and hardly to be improved on. But as for variations to the system and their use for even the most powerful cartridges, these advances were first made in Germany.

Preference for the pistol, or more specifically for the self-loading pistol, developed early and led to the acceptance of Georg Luger's pistol, in its improved form, as the first self-loading pistol in military use — this was the version made for the Imperial German Navy and introduced there in 1904. The army followed with the 08 pistol in 1908. In both world wars, German troops used 9 mm caliber Parabellum pistols as their official side arms, aside from the fact that in times of crisis they used any pistol they could get their hands on.

After World War II as well, Germany has been inclined more to the pistol than the revolver. This was clearly shown in the 1970s, when new weapons were introduced for the police, which had been equipped until then almost exclusively with guns in 7.65 mm caliber, which could no longer meet the requirements. Manufacturers represented in Germany were encouraged to take part in the development of the new pistol, and with their developments they once again set new standards. For the private user, such developments always have the advantage that, after the official contracts have been fulfilled, a high-performance product is available very soon. All pistols introduced for service use are always available privately, as long as the legal requirements for their ownership have been met. The revolver per se, and more specifically the revolver for the 9 mm cartridge, remained a borderline item for sporting use, and is usually offered with the option of using a changeable cylinder to fire the 9 mm cartridge.

The Dreyse 9 mm

The name of Dreyse-Sömmerda was originally linked with the technology of the needle system that was used in rifles and carbines as well as pistols. When the Dreyse pistols appeared, Nikolaus von Dreyse was already long dead, and his name was used chiefly as a memorial to him.

The 9 mm caliber Parabellum pistol was this third development, and it was certainly an interesting weapon, though not a successful one. Its distribution was correspondingly small, and never officially introduced for military use. To be sure, officers liked to carry it as their sidearm, as it did fire the standard military cartridge. As of about 1912 it was placed on the civilian market, and remained in production until 1915. After that, production was halted as the available production facilities were needed for other weapons. Thus the Dreyse 9 mm Parabellum ranks today among the very rare items, and are seen only in really good collections.

Here as in his two other pistols, in 6.35 mm and 7.65 mm calibers, the designer used the principle of the unbolted spring-mass lock, which is not easyily adapted to the 9 mm cartridge. One needs either a very large locking mass or an extremely strong spring. In the case of the strong recoil spring, a disadvantage must be accepted, namely that such a weapon can barely be operated with normal strength. To minimize this typical disadvantage, Hugo Schmeisser developed the possibility of separating the top part of the slide from the strong closing spring, and inserting a cartridge into the chamber and cocking the lock without compressing the recoil spring. Thus the pistol can be cocked without using the

The 9 mm Parabellum caliber Dreyse was made only in small numbers and never officially introduced. Officers were happy to buy it privately. The pistol has no locking system.

With a little trick it is possible to introduce a cartridge from the magazine and cock the internal firing pin lock without cocking the strong recoil spring. One pushes the rod up, pulls it back and pushes it forward again, after which it rests at the back.

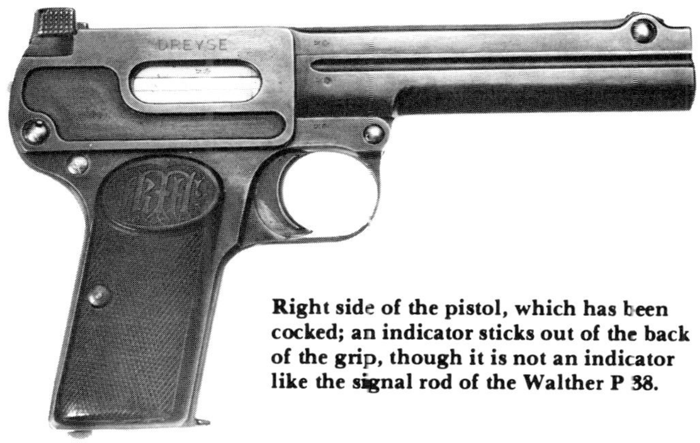

Right side of the pistol, which has been cocked; an indicator sticks out of the back of the grip, though it is not an indicator like the signal rod of the Walther P 38.

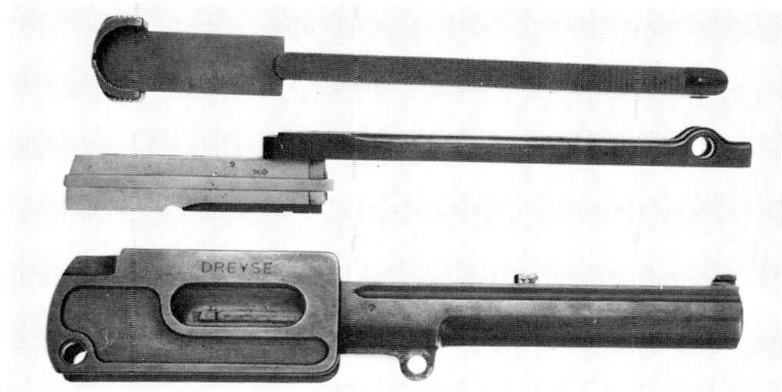

The recoil spring is wound around the barrel and thus not visible here. The pistol has a mass breech in the typical shape for the Dreyse pistol developed by Schmeisser.

recoil spring, a solution that was protected by patent 13800/1911.

The basic concept of the pistol resembles the 7.65 mm version in many ways. The closing spring is wound around the barrel and held by a box. The part of the slide extending out over the barrel is equipped with a cocking piece, a long steel rail with a tab on its underside. At the rear is a small handhold and the cutout for sighting. This rail can be folded up and is stopped again after firing. At the front end, it is movably attached by a stable bolt and held firmly by a small arresting spring. When folded down, it rests and is held in a cutout of the box in front of the recoil spring.

This requires some rethinking in terms of the loading procedure. The magazine is inserted as usual. The rail is now held by its rear handhold and moved up. Next, one moves the rail, along with the slide, which hangs onto it, backward and then pushed it forward, whereby a cartridge from the magazine is pushed into the chamber. This does not require any great strength, as only the pressure of the recoil spring has to be overcome, as the pistol has no hammer, but operates with customary firing pin ignition, which is well known in small-caliber self-loading pistols. One needs only to push the rail into its resting position by moderate pressure on its rear end for the pistol to be ready to fire. When fired, the locking mass moves backward along with the locked-in rail, after which one has no problem with the strong recoil spring. Not much can be said for the durability of this technically interesting solution. The rail with its tab was probably not made of hard enough material, and thus it soon becomes worn and no longer functions as intended. Ease of dismantling has been provided for. The complete upper part is attached to the receiver by two thick bolts. The weapon has a small arresting spring, similar to those of the G 3 rifle or the MP 5 by Heckler & Koch, to hold them.

A special feature of the Dreyse pistol is the cocking indicator at the back of the grip. As soon as the firing pin lock is cocked, this signal bar rises out of the back of the grip, where it is easy to see and feel. This also reappeared in more modern self-loading pistols.

Technical Data: 9 mm Dreyse

Designation	Dreyse 9 mm
Caliber	9 mm Parabellum
Functioning principle	Unlocked mass breech with firing pin lock
Magazine capacity	8 cartridges
Overall length	206 mm
Barrel length	126 mm
Barrel	6 riflings, to right
Empty weight	1050 grams
Sights	Fixed
Material	Steel, burnished
Lettering	Rheinische Metallwaren & Maschinenfabrik Sömmerda Dept. Dreyse

Pistols by Heckler & Koch

The firm of Mauser was a leading manufacturer of weapons before and during World War II. Mauser weapons such as the 98 and 98k rifle and carbine, or the 08 pistol rank among the world-renowned designs that. Because of their to their trouble-free robustness, these wepaons still have a high value today.

After World War II, the Mauser factory at Oberndorf on the Neckar was dismantled and the production facilities turned over to the French government as reparations. In the early 1950s, the production of weapons was gradually allowed in Germany. At this time a new and hitherto unknown firm took over the Mauser premises, the firm of Heckler & Koch, which is presently one of Germany's greatest producers of civilian, police and military handguns. Probably Heckler & Koch's best-known weapon was the G 3 rifle with its movably supported rolling breech, which was officially introduced into the Bundeswehr around 1965, replacing the G 1 rifle made by FN, which was in use at the time.

Using the design of the movably supported rolling breech as a basis, there appeared during the following years in the popular calibers of the time, an extensive family of weapons with further variations of the G 3, and included machine guns and machine pistols. These last were built for and accepted by the German police, and are also in service in numerous other western countries.

In the realm of self-loading pistols, Heckler & Koch specialized particularly in introducing new types of manufacturing technology. A typical example of this is the still-available P 9 S pistol, the handle of which is not machined out of solid material but welded together out of two stamped halves. Plastics are also being used increasingly for less stressed parts. In the P 9 S, for example, the magazine catch, grip panels and trigger guard are made of a resistant plastic, and has the advantage of weight saving's, in addition to cost saving's when put into large-series production.

When a new and, in particular, higher-performance self-loading pistol was wanted by the German police, Heckler & Koch was able to offer an interesting conception in the form of the PSP model, which was introduced with slight modifications as the P 7 pistol.

The P 9 and P 9 S Models

Development began with the P 9 pistol in 9 mm Parabellum caliber, and was produced until 1978. Its design differed from that of the subsequently produced P 9 S chiefly in the type of trigger, which was designed here as only an SA type. To fire, the internal hammer was cocked by either the lateral cocking lever or the movement of the slide.

The P 9 S version was equipped with a DA trigger and hardly differed externally from the earlier model. Over the years there were several changes, but only superficial: The shape of the trigger guard was changed and designed at its front making it possible to place a finger there when shooting with two hands. The grip panels of the earliest versions were smooth around the herringbone areas; now they are slightly roughened. The side panels of the slide were smoothed and polished in the earlier models, while later models have the sides matte-finished similar to the slide the top.

The identifying marks of the P 9 S pistol are the movably supported rolling breech, which results in the weapon's somewhat more favorable recoil action, and the polygonal barrel. As major parts of the basic conception, both deserve to be described more thoroughly. Another characteristic of the P 9 S is the already mentioned production out of stamped parts in practical combination with parts made of very tough plastic.

The P 9 S has a concealed hammer, which is an exception for self-loading pistols of this caliber. If not already engaged because of the movement of the slide, the hammer is cocked by a strong push on the lateral cocking lever. At the same time, the signal pin (part 9 in

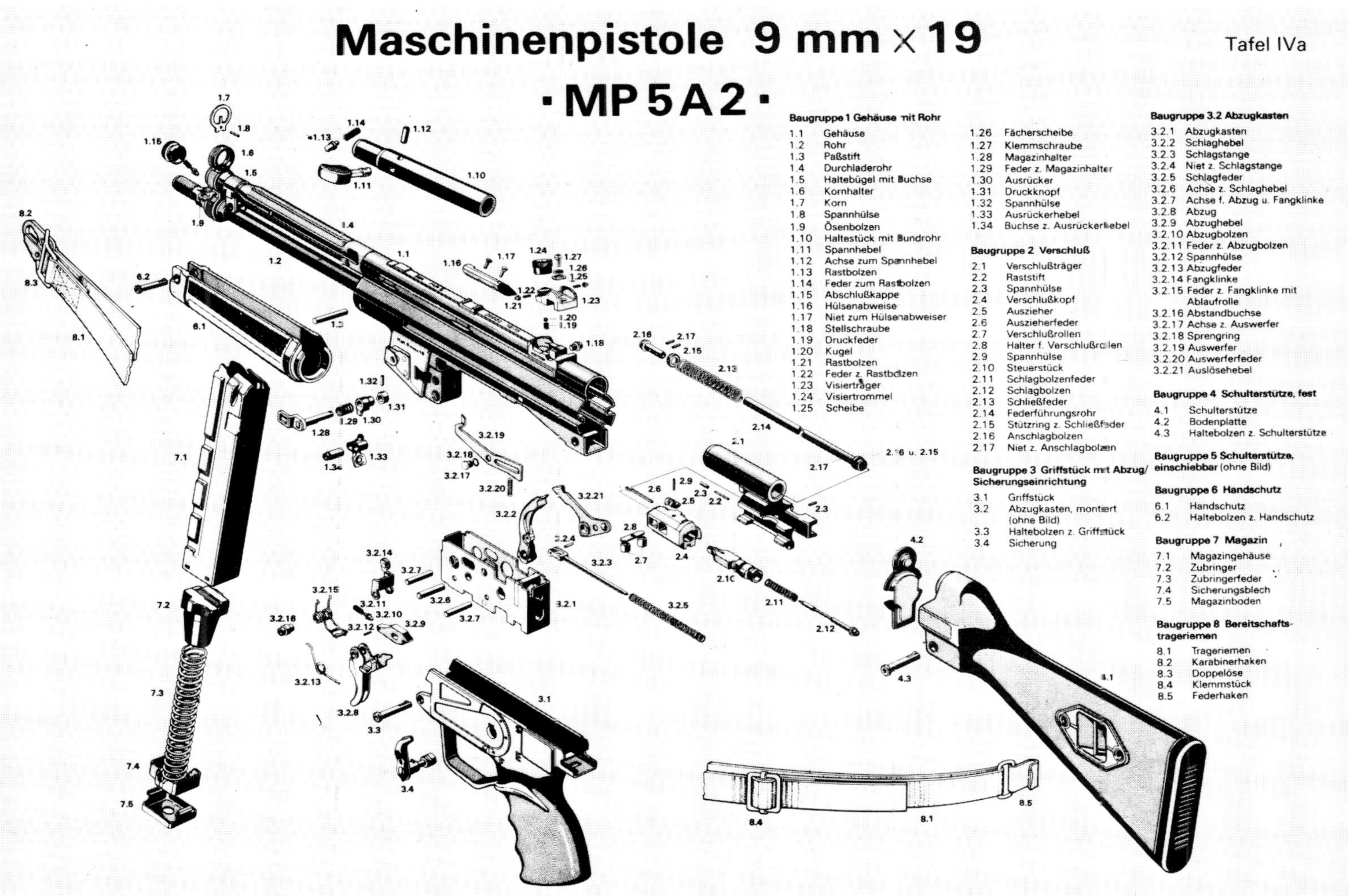

Heckler & Koch is an important producer of police and military handguns. A certain kit principle was used successfully by the firm.

the drawing on page 39) moves back slightly and projects a few millimeters out of the grip, becoming tangible and visible. In this way it is always possible to tell for sure whether or not the gun is cocked.

The lateral cocking lever also fulfills several other functions: if the slide is moved back when a full or empty magazine is in place, it is held there by the catch (part 62 in the drawing). By pressing downward on the cocking lever, it now functions as a "slide catch lever", pushes the catch down and frees the slide, which is under the pressure of the recoil spring, so that when the magazine is filled, and introduces a new cartridge into the chamber.

In addition, the hammer can be safely decocked by using the cocking (or decocking) lever. To perform this, the manual safety on the slide can be set at "safe",

With the self-loading P 9 pistol, Heckler & Koch made a successful start in the field of service and defense pistols. The P 9 model did not yet have a double action trigger. The internal hammer is cocked by pressing on the side lever.

The most modern production techniques could be utilized here. The frame is made of pressed parts but is very stable and thick-walled. The shape of the trigger guard was changed many times over the years.

Cutaway of the P 9 S pistol in 9 mm Parabellum caliber. It was also made in .45 ACP caliber.

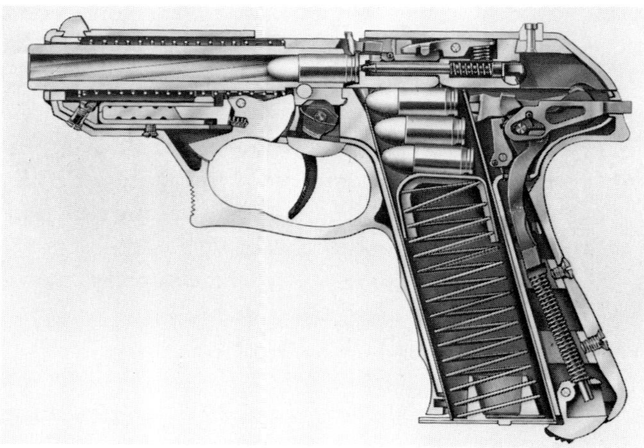

whereupon the white dot becomes visible. Now one pushes the cocking lever (part 61 in the drawing) down, pulls the trigger through (when the cocking lever is held down), and allows the trigger and cocking lever to move forward or upward again. This type of decocking may not please all users, especially if they have to do it under pressure of time.

All in all, though, the P 9 S has a safety system that works clearly and in several ways, and will be described briefly here. In addition to the cocking rest, the hammer has an additional safety stop by which it is caught to prevent its operating wrongly. The recoil safety (part 44 in the drawing) is very sensitive. Whereas many pistols still allow release of the hammer with an opening gap of 5 mm, in the P 9 S the hammer is released only when the gun is really locked. The lock is released after the slide has moved back about 7 mm, and the recoil safety works with a gap of about 3 mm. Two visible and/or tangible safety provisions inform the user as to the loading or cocking condition. One of these is the already mentioned cocking indicator on the rear of the grip. The other is the indicator over the extractor on the breechblock head. If a cartridge or case is in the chamber, then the upper part of the extractor sticks up more than one millimeter and can be seen or felt easily.

The safety located on the side of the slide covers the firing pin with its pivot and simultaneously blocks it. With all these independently working safety devices, the P 9 S should satisfy all requirements.

In terms of dismantling, there isn't a modern pistol that can be dismantled for cleaning as quickly as the P 9 S. After checking the safety devices, the barrel catch (part 34 in the drawing) is pressed forward in the trigger guard with the thumb lever, the upper part pushed forward

The grip after removal of the grip panels, a single piece held by two screws. The trigger guard shown here in modern form was installed by the author.

some 10 mm and then lifted off the receiver. Installing the upper part proceeds just as simply, by reversing the procedures: it is set into the grooves of the grip section, pushed down and slid backward.

Now the barrel is grasped by its attachment, pushed forward against the pressure of the return spring, lifted somewhat at the rear, and taken out of the slide (the breech housing in the drawing) rearward or upward. If the breechblock head is also to be removed, such as to clean the strike plate better, then a shank end of the locking piece on the barrel end is used to push on the catch between the breechblock head and the block itself.

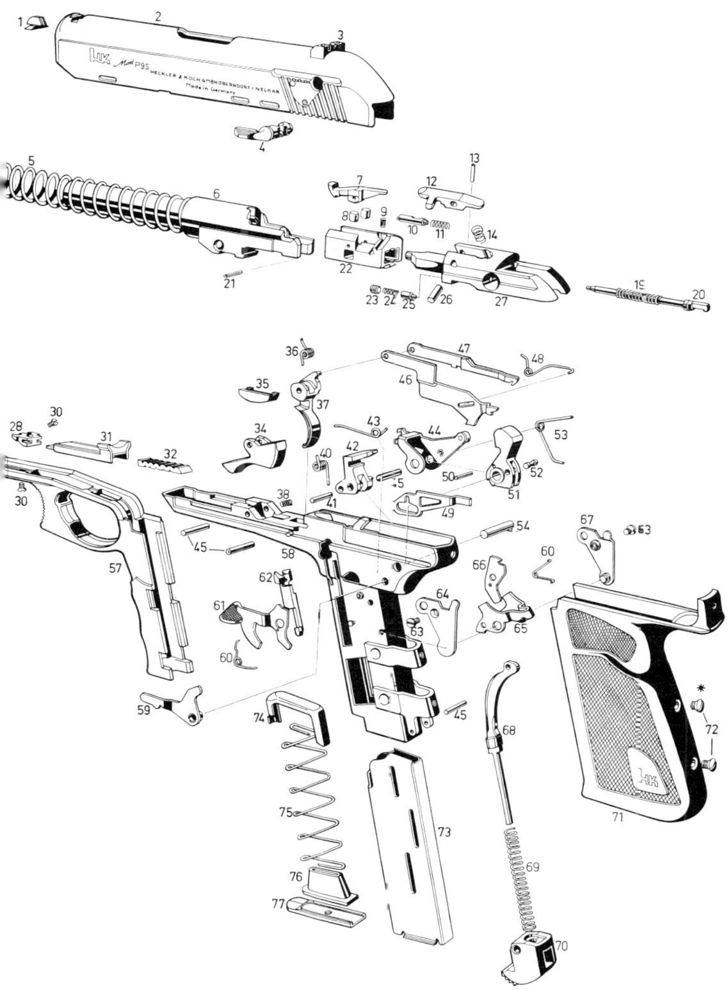

The breechblock head then moves slightly forward and can be removed. To install, it is pushed back onto the breechblock carrier, pressure is again put on the catch (with the help of the barrel), and the breechblock head is pushed back into its resting position.

The P 9 S sits in the hand comfortably and can be easily fired. This results first from the characteristics of the rolling breech, which divides the impulses, and also from the buffer fitted into the forward part of the grip section, which mitigates the slide's hard contact with its block during forward movement.

Numerous hits can be fired with various types of cartridges, and at 15 meters, used in a sitting position, the bull's-eye can almost always be hit. It is a down-to-earth high-performance pistol, and later inspired the manufacturer to produce a sport pistol on the basis of the P 9 S. High-performance firing is not necessarily provided by the presumed good qualities of the polygonal barrel. For some years there has been heated discussion of its advantages and disadvantages. Even the manufacturer may at best ascribe a slight increase in the attainable firing performance to the barrel's profile. The cause of it is rather the precise preparation and the typical nature of the P 9 S of having a barrel that remains firmly in place during the process of firing. It is held in place by its attachment so play-free that one can really call it a fixed barrel, even though its quick dismantling would not make it appear so at a glance.

The Polygonal Profile

With the exception of the HK 4, VP 70 and VP 70 Z models, the pistols made by Heckler & Koch have an unusual barrel profile, which deviates clearly from the earlier type of rifled barrels. In this Heckler & Koch is not alone, for the firm of Steyr also uses a similar principle in its Model GB pistol.

The word "polygon" comes from Greek and means "many-sided." In this sense, the designation applies to this type of barrel cross-section, which does not have the usual sharply defined rifling, but looks more like a square with rounded corners. A look through such a barrel shows only a shiny surface on which a the rifling can be seen only faintly.

Despite the new cross-section, the principle of rifling stabilization has been maintained. The cartridge derives its spin and thus its stability along its own long axis. The polygonal barrel offers a number of advantages, some of which are, of course, noticed only when the weapon is in constant use.

Sealing

The polygonal profile allows an almost complete sealing of the bullet from the wall of the barrel, whereas with an earlier barrel, comma-shaped gouges remained on the sharp angles of the profile. This concerns jacketed bullets and does not occur so noticeably with bullets made of lead. This can be clearly seen in the two combined photos (top page 41), for which a bullet was driven into each barrel. The barrel was cut through in the area of the bullet and photographed against a source of light.

The almost complete sealing results in several advantages, such as somewhat greater muzzle velocity and muzzle energy, and also less erosion. The powder gases rushing past the sharp angles contribute significantly to gun barrel damage. The sealing was tested experimentally with the help of compressed air. The schematic drawing shows the setup, in which **B** is the container of

P 9 Pistol Series

Model Designation	P 9	P 9 S	P 9 S-Sport
Caliber	9 mm/7.65 mm Para.	9 mm/7.65 mm Para.	9 mm Para.
Breech System	Roller	Roller	Roller
Trigger	Single-Action	Double Action	Double Action
Magazine Capacity	8-9 cartridges	8-9 cartridges	8-9 cartridges
Vo/Eo/9 Para.	350 m/s-500 J.	350 m/s-500 J.	390 m/s-620 J.
Vo/Eo/7.65 Para.	370 m/s-425 J	370 m/s-425 J.	–
Overall Length	192 mm	192 mm	230 mm
Overall Height/Width	137/34 mm	137/34 mm	149/49 mm
Barrel Length	102 mm	102 mm	140 mm
Sight Line	147 mm	147 mm	190 mm
Weight empty, minus magazine	850 g	850 g	910 g
Weight with magazine/full	1030-1000 g	1030-1000 g	1090 g
Barrel Weight	–	–	190 g
Sights	Fixed	Fixed	Adjustable

compressed air and L is the barrel with a driven-in bullet of the type to be tested. The container is filled with compressed air at 5.5 atmospheres. Then the time that elapses to let the pressure in the container decrease from 5.5 to 4.0 at over the contact point on the bullet is measured. A soft-core bullet with a tombak-plated steel jacket reaches this in a time of 0.5 to 1 minute in the rifling profile, but in the polygonal barrel, on the other hand, in 5 to 10 minutes. Bullets with lead cores and full tombak jackets (the usual jacketed bullets made by various manufacturers) reached 5 to 10 minutes in the usual profile and 10 to 15 minutes in the polygonal profile. Clear statistics as to the effect of the sealing can be derived and applied from this.

Longer Barrel Life

The values for these statistics were attained from steady firing from machine-gun barrels, whereby a barrel was regarded as shot out when the first ricochets resulted under cold barrel conditions. Earlier barrels achieved some 15,000 shots, but the polygonal barrel reached its end only after some 30,000 shots. This is dependent on the inner workmanship of the barrel and the type of ammunition used. First of all, such statistics are far more important for the durability of a military weapon than for the private use of a pistol, for who would fire 15,000 or 30,000 shots from his 9 mm pistol? But this advantage is not so completely unimportant, for the weapon or its barrel still remains "like new" longer. Negative effects of its overuse are shown only late, and most private owners will hardly see them.

This shows the difference between a polygonal barrel and an older rifled barrel. At right the so-called comma cuts, through which the powder gases pass the bullet, are clearly seen.

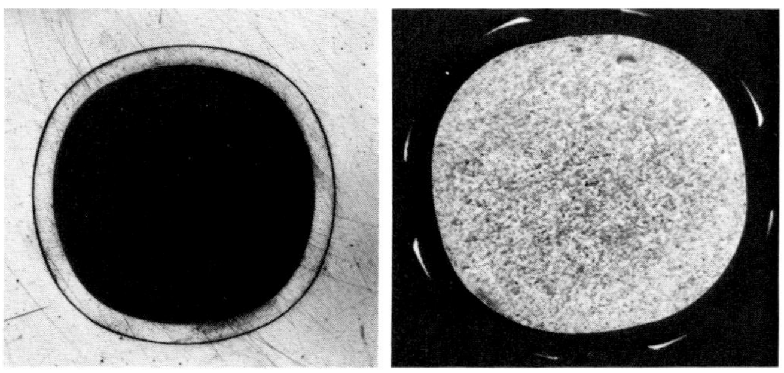

Higher Gas Pressure

The bullet is pressed into a polygonal barrel more firmly, with almost its whole surface touching. Thereby a slightly greater intensity of powder burning takes place, which results in a higher muzzle velocity. Depending on the material and construction of the bullet, an increase of 3% to 10% is shown in comparison to the earlier barrel type, and one may note, not without criticism, that such comparisons must always be somewhat vague and can be affected by numerous factors. The author's own measurements with a VM-25 measuring device made by the Weinlich firm, attest to the slight differences in velocity for jacketed bullets, but not for lead bullets.

Less Heating

In the earlier barrel, the aforementioned comma-shaped gouges occurred all around the barrel. In these spots, hot powder gases passed the bullet and rushed some distance ahead of it, as can be shown clearly by photographs with an opposed flash. The gases streaming past caused more heat to be given off to the barrel. Thus the polygonal barrel absorbs some 4% to 6% less heat. This is also

The bullet exits from the old-type barrel at left, where the bullet has already been passed by the powder gases. At right, from the polygonal barrel with its almost complete sealing to the bullet. Before the muzzie is a contact wire to trigger the flash in the opposing light.

relatively insignificant for a self-loading pistol, but may have a more obvious effect from the sustained fire of automatic weapons.

Less Bullet Nicking

From the sharp angles of the rifling, a jacketed bullet receives very visible nicks, and is inclined to fragment when it strikes a hard target. Bullets from a polygonal barrel do not get nicked, and thus their form remains more stable.

Better Precision

Opinions are divided as to a possible increase in precision; even the manufacturer does not ascribe any noteworthy increase in accuracy to his polygonal barrels. Extensive tests at the factory showed a slight increase in firing performance, however it was slight and depended on firing several series from the same weapon with the same cartridge type under constant conditions.

It would be more correct to say that the limitations on precision and hindering phenomena appear only later in a polygonal barrel, and that the existing precision is maintained somewhat longer. With the 9 mm Parabellum cartridge, very different accuracy patterns can be achieved with the same weapon, and in any sporting use it greatly depends on arriving at a charge exactly suited to the weapon. Even with small differences in the quantity of powder, the tested groups of ten extend from 25 to 100 mm.

Easier Cleaning

It is a real advantage of the polygonal barrel that it can be thoroughly cleaned more simply and effectively. Jacketed bullets leave more and more deposits behind on the sharp rifling angles, and can only be removed effectively with suitable equipment. Such material that rubs off jackets is rarely found in the polygonal barrel. Lead bullets, particularly when they are fired at higher speeds, make a an earlier-type barrel truly "thick" after 20 to 30 shots. The rubbed-off material is so heavy that tests for documented precision in sporting use can hardly be carried out meaningfully. The deposited lead is most effectively removed mechanically with a bronze pad, which should be done quickly after a long series of shots, with the barrel removed. Here the polygonal barrel is simply more agreeable, though it looks quite gray and dirty after firing lead bullets.

The Supported Rolling Breech

The P 9 and P 9 S pistols, as well as the automatic rifles, machine guns and machine pistols made by Heckler & Koch, have the so-called moveable supported rolling breech. The result is tangible to the shooter: the decreased recoil speed of the slide plus, all in all, a somewhat weaker recoil.

The recoil pressure of the cartridge case is initially transferred via the breechblock head to the two rollers. These transmit the received impulse — it is divided in the barrel because of the angles on the breechblock carrier and the curves in the barrel — backward in decreased strength. The barrel is firmly attached to the grip section, and on each side of its end has a forklike extension in which the semicircular depressions for the rolls have been machined. In a locked mode, the two rolls are set into them. When the gun is fired, the cartridge chamber presses on the breechblock head, and this in turn presses on the rollers in their lateral mountings. The rollers can now simultaneously put pressure on the extension of the barrel, as well as on the grip section and the angled surfaces of the breechblock carrier, which is mechanically linked to the breechblock housing (slide).

The advantage of this system is that it temporally divides the entire recoil, which, as in other weapons, is dependent on the weight of the bullet and its speed.

Models VP 70 and VP 70 Z

The production of Models VP 70 and VP 70 Z (the Z stands for Zivil: civilian) began in 1973 and has since come to an end. The VP stands for "Volkspistole" and may awaken some readers' memories of such terms as "Volkssturm" or "Volkssturm-Karabiner", which were crudely and cheaply built weapons used in the last phases of World War II.

The VP 70 is a simple design that lacks a lock, thus it ranks among the few self-loading pistols of 9 mm Parabellum caliber that get by with a simple spring-weight breechblock. The slide of this pistol is correspondingly massive and heavy.

The two models differ in the way that they are fired. The VP 70 version was planned as a simple pistol for police use and can, with an attached shaft, fire limited bursts of fire consisting of three shots each. This shaft is made of green-colored plastic and has a selector lever at the front, with positions 1 and 3; at the 1 setting, single shots are fired. The shaft simultaneously serves as a holster, and at the time the two were not available to the private customer for legal reasons, as the pistol is an automatic weapon. The VP 70 Z (this is also inscribed on the left side of the heavy slide) is the civilian version. Common to the two is the otherwise simple technology and the high magazine capacity of 18 cartridges, plus an additional round that can safely stay in the cartridge chamber.

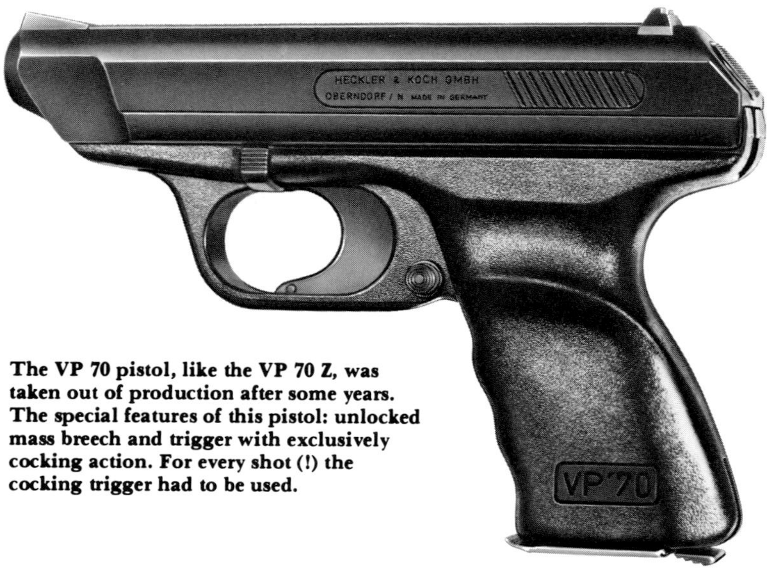

The VP 70 pistol, like the VP 70 Z, was taken out of production after some years. The special features of this pistol: unlocked mass breech and trigger with exclusively cocking action. For every shot (!) the cocking trigger had to be used.

Along with the attached holster shaft, the VP 70 can optionally fire single shots or limited bursts of three shots.

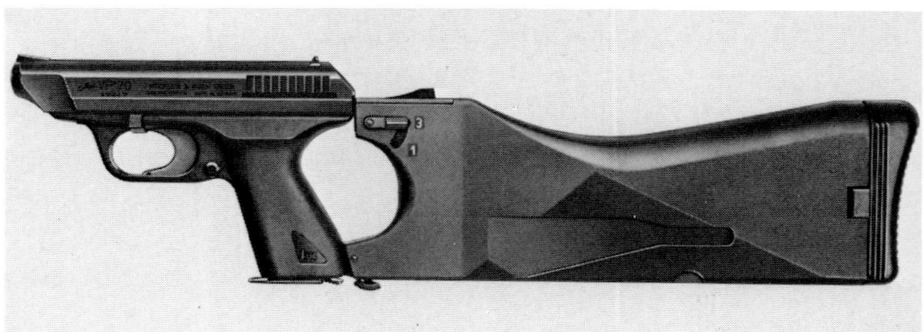

The civilian version is the VP 70 Z, set up only for single action. The moving parts are bedded in the cast plastic grip.

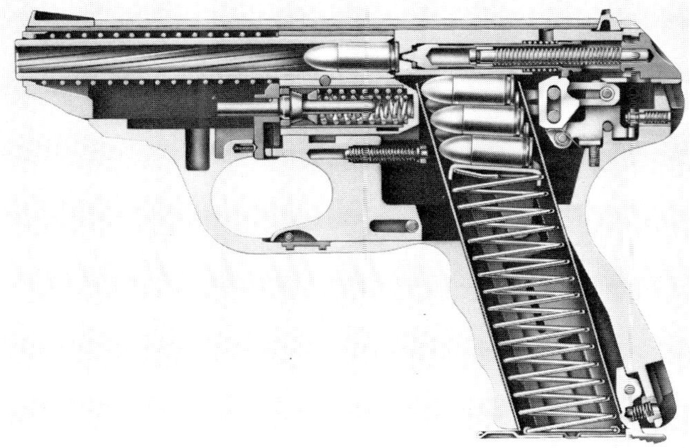

Cutaway of the VP 70 Z.

The strong recoil spring requires a pressure of 10 kilograms, which is considerably more than usual. The ignition takes place without a hammer via the cocked firing pin bolt. On account of its simple design, the VP 70 Z is probably the pistol with the fewest moving parts — there are just four moving components. The grip is made of plastic with cast-in steel parts. The barrel, slide and moving parts are naturally made of steel, the trigger itself of aluminum.

The trigger is unusual, as it functions solely as a cocking trigger. For every new shot it is released and then pulled all the way. Thus the pistol can be carried ready for use at any time without having any of its parts under spring tension.

The functioning of the trigger is as follows: during withdrawal, the firing pin is caught by the sear on the trigger bar and moved some 10 mm to the rear. The sear sinks down at the end of this motion and releases the firing pin, which then strikes the percussion cap of the cartridge. After the shot is fired, the slide moved backward, extracting and ejecting the empty case. The firing pin also makes this movement, as well as the immediately following move forward. However it cannot ignite the

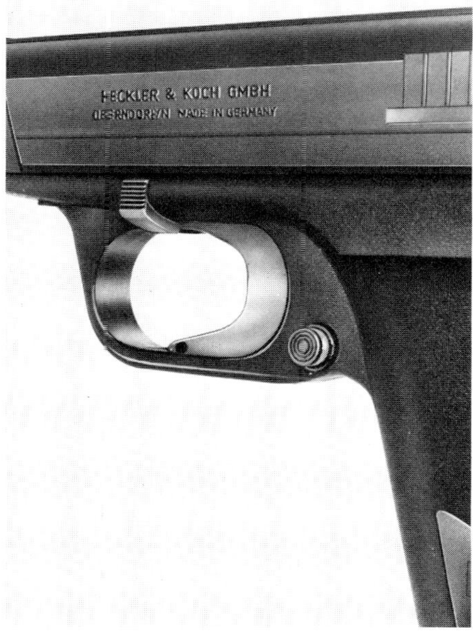

The magazine catch below in the grip, safety push-button right behind the trigger, and dismantling lever forward in the trigger guard.

One pushes the dismantling lever down, then draws the slide back and lifts it off.

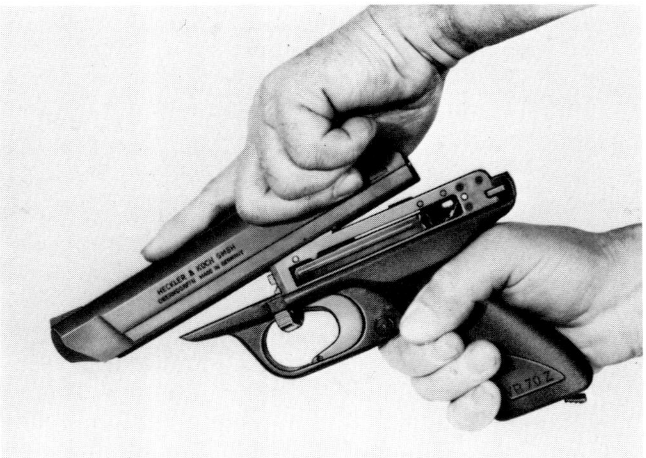

Lift the back of the slide and push it forward over the firmly attached barrel.

next cartridge in so doing, for a catching spring pushes it against the mainspring so that its movement energy is not sufficient for an ignition. With this trigger mechanism, the VP 70 Z can be regarded as a truly foolproof pistol, and if the shooter is not satisfied, he can block the trigger by using the safety button under the base of the trigger guard. When the red mark is visible, the weapon is released and the cocking trigger can be pulled all the way.

The sight operates on the light-shadow principle and provides quick sighting of a target even in poor light — the backsight, mounted to the side, can be adjusted.

Dismantling the VP 70 is quite simple: after checking the safety catch, the dismantling lever above the trigger is pushed down. The slide is drawn all the way back, lifted out at the rear and pushed forward over the barrel from the receiver. To remove the firing pin, the end cap at the rear, on the back of the slide, is given a quarter turn to the right, until first it and then the firing pin, complete with spring, can be removed.

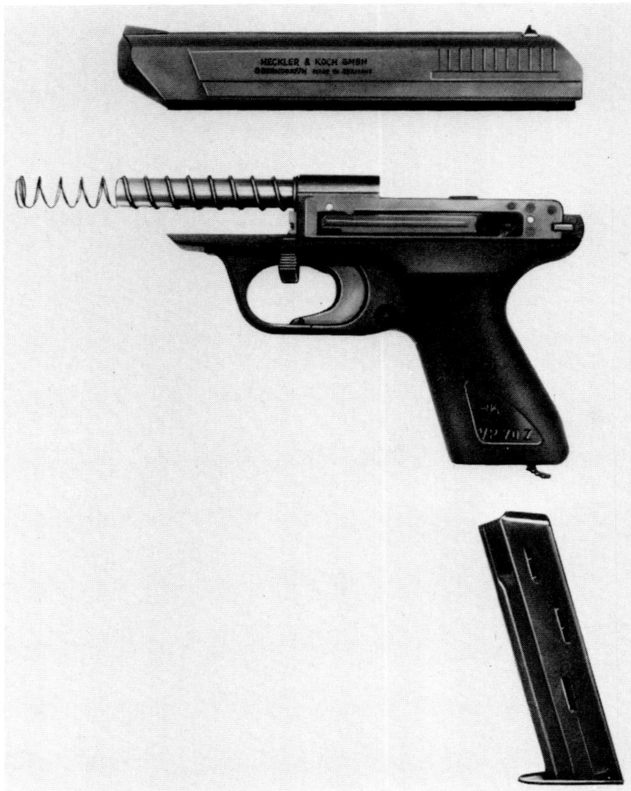

The VP 70 Z dismantled for cleaning.

The firing pin (see text) can be removed from the slide easily.

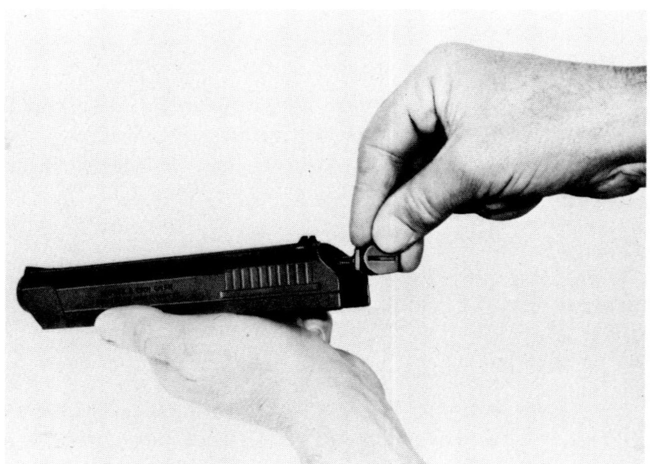

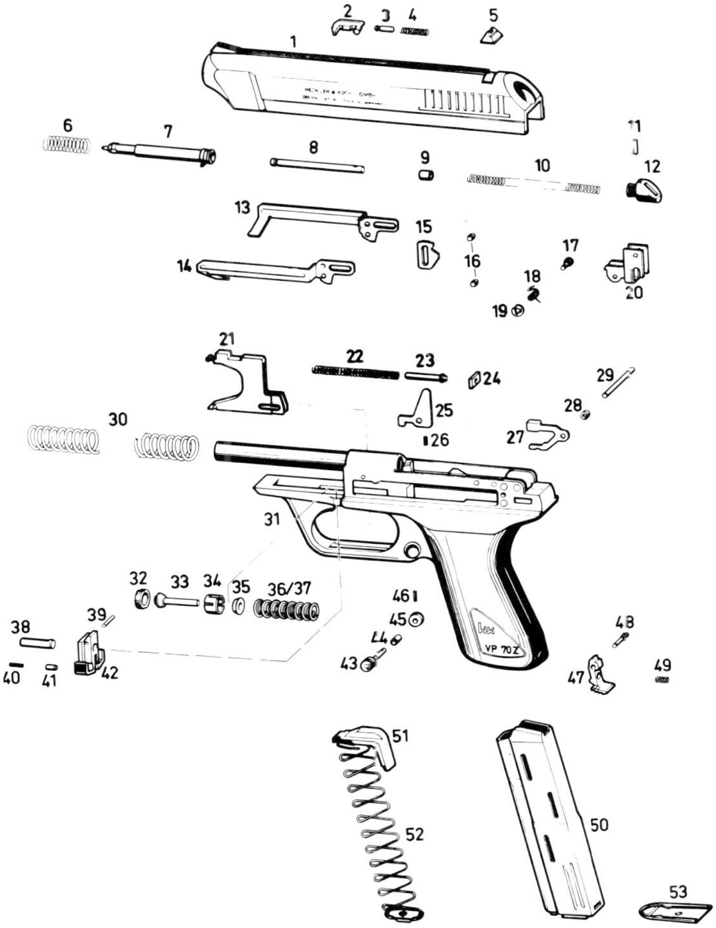

Components of the VP70Z Automatic Pistol
Calibre 9 mm x 19 (Parabellum)

1 Slide
2 Extractor
3 Pressure bolt
4 Extractor spring
5 Rear sight
6 Firing pin recoil spring
7 Firing pin
8 Recoil spring guide rod
9 Bush
10 Firing pin spring
11 Cylindrical pin
12 Rear cap
13 Trigger lever, right
14 Trigger lever, left
15 Drag lever
16 Trigger lever guiding bolt
17 Axle for elbow spring
18 Elbow spring
19 Circlip
20 Control lever
21 Trigger, compl.
22 Trigger spring
23 Trigger spring guide bolt
24 Support plate
25 Drop safety
26 Compression spring
27 Catch fork
28 Guide roller
29 Cylindrical pin
30 Recoil spring
31 Receiver with barrel
32 Threaded ring
33 Buffer spring guide bolt
34 Brake ring
35 Contact piece
36 Buffer spring
37 Buffer spring
38 Buffer bolt
39 Clamping sleeve
40 Compression spring
41 Retaining bush
42 Retaining catch
43 Safety button, compl.
44 Guide bush
45 Locking bush
46 Clamping sleeve
47 Magazine catch
48 Screw for magazine catch
49 Spring for magazine catch
50 Magazine housing
51 Follower
52 Follower spring with spring floor plate, compl.
53 Magazine floor plate

Technical Data: VP 70 Series

Model designation	VP 70 Z	VP 70
Functioning principle	Recoil loader	Recoil loader
Breech system	Mass Breech	Mass Breech
Magazine capacity	18 cartridges	18 cartridges
Types of fire	Single shots	Single shots – bursts of 3 shots
V_o/E_o	ca. 360 m/s-520 J.	ca. 360 m/s-520 J.
Weight without magazine	820 g	820 g
Weight, magazine filled	1140 g	1140 g
Shaft weight	–	420 g
Overall length	204 mm	204 mm
Length with shaft	–	545 mm
Barrel length	116 mm	116 mm
Sight line	175 mm	175 mm
Width/height	32/142 mm	46/144 mm (with shaft)

The PSP and P 7 Series

At the beginning of the 1970s, when the German police were looking for a new self-loading pistol in the high-performance 9 mm PARA caliber, officialdom took a different approach than before. Though they had always looked only at existing weapons in current production, this time they issued very specific requirements to the manufacturers. It was the so-called "Pflichtenheft" or requirement book, according to the terms stated in which the firms taking part in the competition were to provide a testable design. The type and extent of the tests were not easy, however their strictness was quite justified. All this led to a new weapon for police units, differing, to be sure, in the individual federal states, which had the right to place individual orders.

Heckler & Koch arrived on the market with a truly new

The PSP model was the forerunner of the present-day P 7 series, which includes numerous variations.

design, the Model PSP, from which the Model P 7 and its further developments were later derived.

Striking features of the PSP are compact construction and the completely new way of getting the weapon ready to fire. Instead of a double action trigger, the PSP, and this also applies to the variations derived from it, has a cocking handle that projects from the front of the grip. When this cocking handle is pressed, the firing pin is cocked. During firing, the firing pin is automatically cocked after every shot.

When the cocking handle is released, either intentionally or by accident, as for example the weapon is dropped, the firing pin is decocked and the weapon is automatically immobilized. In addition, the locking catch can be released by the cocking handle.

Before the other design features are described here, let us first describe the functioning of the breech system. The PSP/P 7 has a gas-delayed or gas-braked mass

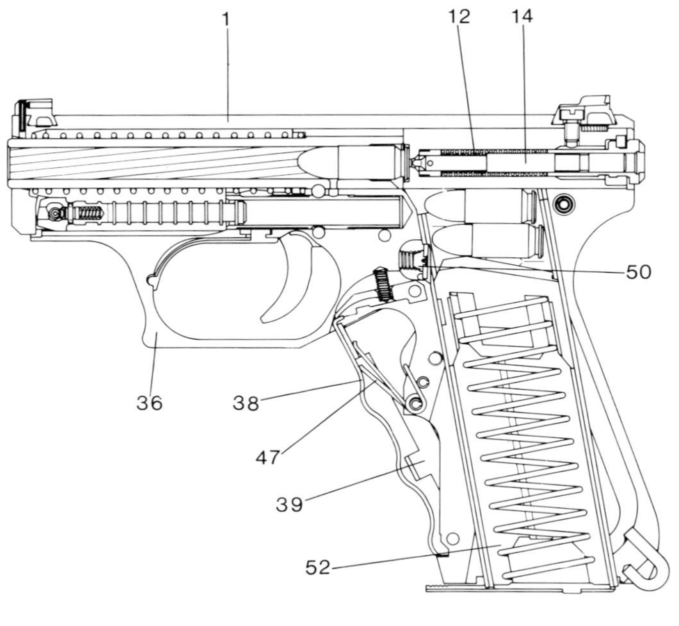

Cutaway of the P 7. The pistol is loaded and thus uncocked, and a cartridge can be inserted in the chamber safely.

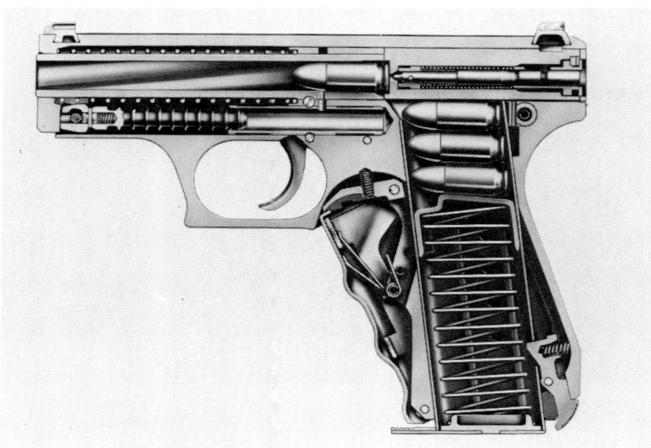

Cutaway of the PSP/P 7 pistol. The cocking handle is not pushed in; the weapon is loaded and the safety is set.

breech, which means that this breech holds itself closed by the gas pressure of the fired cartridges. Directly in front of the cartridge chamber, the polygonal barrel is bored out 1 mm. As soon as the bullet has passed this bore, a portion of the freed powder gases escapes through the bore into a cylinder situated below the barrel. At the front of the slide a moveable grooved piston is attached, projecting into the cylinder. As the powder gases push against the piston, the recoil of the slide is delayed and braked to the extent that no further locking of the system is necessary. Only after the gas pressure decreases in the cylinder can the piston, and with it the slide, move further backward, whereby the usual functions are carried out: extraction and ejection of the empty cartridge case, cocking of the firing pin, compression of the recoil spring, and then insertion of the new cartridge from the magazine.

This design has the advantage that, in the PSP/P 7, there are no external operating levers. Thus the weapon is made smooth and absolutely holster-friendly. The grip is machined from steel and the polygonal barrel is attached firmly to the receiver.

The cocking handle requires some rethinking when one is learning to operate the weapon quickly and safely: after pressing the cocking handle, no additional energy

The P 7 in open position after firing the last shot. The feed mechanism of the magazine (53) lifts the catch lever (26). If the slide is moved forward from this position, one pushes the cocking handle (38) in. The catch lever will release parts 41 and 39.

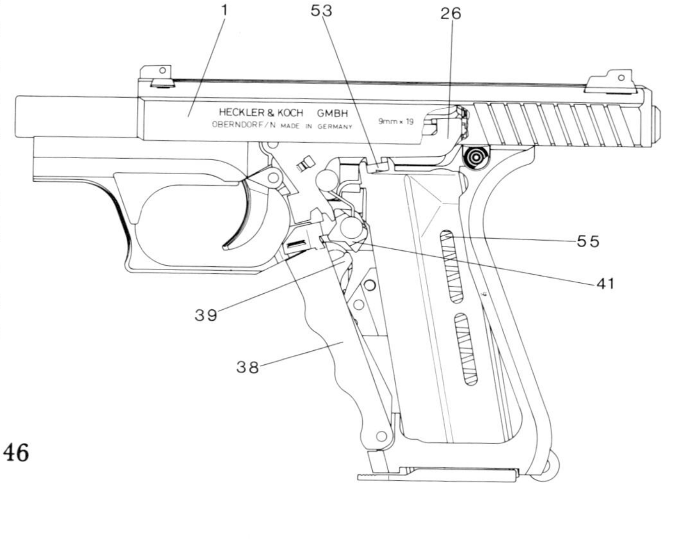

A P 7 with attached wooden grip panels, alternatively available to the private owner.

has to be expended for the first shot than for all subsequent shots, thus the shooter always has single-action shooting and cannot force the first shot over the (uncontrolled) cocking handle.

If a cartridge fails to fire, the cocking handle need only be released and pressed again, after which the trigger functions normally again.

During firing, no additional energy is needed to press the cocking handle than is needed to hold any other pistol.

After the last shot, the slide remains in its rearmost position. When a new magazine is inserted, the cocking handle is simply pressed and the slide moves quickly forward again, after which the pistol is immediately ready to fire again.

Lefthanded and righthanded shooters have no particular problems, because the weapon is built symmetrically. The PSP/P 7 has been criticized at times because it cannot be uncocked soundlessly in certain situations. It occurs soundlessly when one pulls the slide back about 10 mm with the other hand, releases the cocking handle, and then slowly moves the slide forward again.

Unlike other pistols, the magazine catch here can be operated more handily or ergonomically than before. The magazine catch is situated at the bottom of the grip and is not pushed backward, but rather forward. One pushes it in while simultaneously holding the magazine firmly onto the magazine base.

The weapon can be dismantled without a tool: Remove the magazine and check the cartridge chamber, let the slide move forward again Press the assembly button on the back of the grip, pull the slide backward until it is stopped, and lift it out upwardly, then push it forward over the barrel away from the receiver. During assembly, be sure to insert the piston into the gas cylinder in the correct manner.

After the PSP/P 7 came on the market, the manufacturer made several modifications to the pistol for the purpose of reacting quickly to the varying requirements of customers.

Model PSP

This was the first version, which is no longer in production in its original form. The side of the slide is still inscribed Mod. PSP.

Model P 7

It was introduced in this version as a police pistol. The magazine takes eight cartridges. The grip panels are inscribed HK P 7.

A P 7 in the "service" version. This variation is also identified at the bottom of the grip panels.

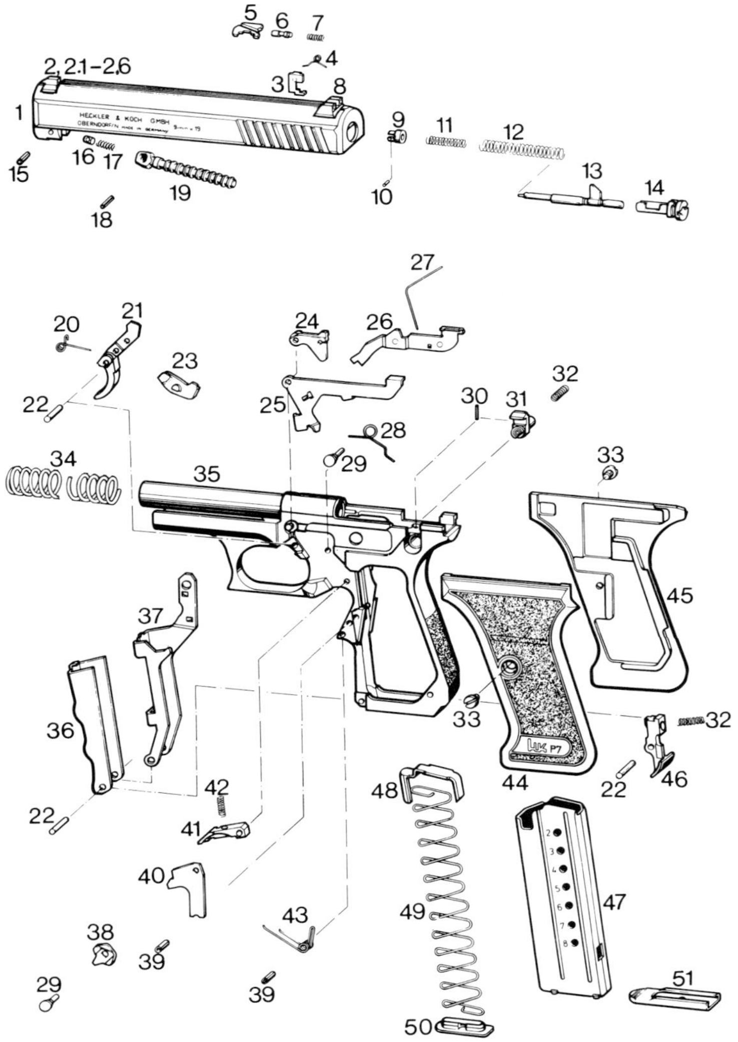

1 Slide
2 Front Sight
3 Drop Safety Catch
4 Drop Safety Catch Spring
5 Extractor
6 Extractor Spring Guide
7 Extractor Spring
8 Rear Sight
9 Firing Pin Collar
10 Firing Pin Collar Pin
11 Inertia Spring
12 Firing Pin Spring
13 Firing Pin
14 Firing Pin Bushing
15 Piston Pin
16 Piston Detent
17 Piston Detent Spring
18 Piston Retaining Pin
19 Piston
20 Trigger Spring
21 Trigger
22 Trigger Pin
23 Transmission Lever
24 Disconnector
25 Slide Catch Lever
26 Sear Bar Complete
27 Sear Spring
28 Rocker Spring
29 Rocker Spring Axle
30 Retainer Pin
31 Slide Retainer
32 Slide Retainer Spring
33 Grip Screw
34 Recoil Spring
35 Receiver with Barrel
36 Squeeze Cocker
37 Drag Lever
38 Rocker
39 Stop Pin
40 Stop
41 Cocking Latch
42 Cocking Latch Spring
43 Squeeze Cocker Spring
44 Grip Panel, Left
45 Grip Panel, Right
46 Magazine Catch
47 Magazine Housing
48 Follower
49 Magazine Spring
50 Locking Plate
51 Magazine Floor Plate

The individual parts of the P 7, with all parts named.

Model P 7 M 8

The P 7 M 8 pistol is substantially like the Model P 7 and has a magazine capacity of eight cartridges. Its differences from the Model P 7 are:
The magazine catch is attached on both sides under the catch lever, and operable equally from either side. This allows an even faster change of magazines. The plastic covering at the top of the trigger guard provides the shooter with protection there from the transmission of coldness or heat.

The backsight is linked to the slide and the foresight and is screwed firmly in place. This means that even under the hardest use, no unwanted displacement can take place. Unlike the P 7 and PSP, the firing pin can be removed without a special tool.

The P 7 M 8 version, which holds 8 cartridges. The sights, the magazine catch just above the cocking handle, the different shape of the trigger tongue and the inset at the top of the trigger guard are different here.

The P 7 M 13 version has a magzzine that holds 13 cartridges, and the grip is thus wider. The type marking is also seen on the side of the slide.

Model P 7 M 13

The technical differences from the Model P 7 M 8 apply only to the magazine capacity. The magazine holds thirteen cartridges, which increases the thickness of the grip from 29 mm to 33 mm. The grip panels are inscribed HK P 7 M 13.

Models P 7 M 8 S and P 7 M 13 S

The S stands for Sicherung (safety) — here the manufacturer actually came up with an anachronism, for the special feature of this design was that no manual safety measures were necessary. Since various users would accept only a pistol with a manual safety, the M 8 and M 13 models, otherwise constructed the same way, were additionally fitted with a safety catch.

The safety lever is located high on the right side of the weapon above the trigger guard, and works directly on the trigger. In safety position, the safety slide is pushed back and the two numbers 0 (white) and 1 (red) can both be seen. For shooting, this slide is pushed forward until it is stopped, so that only the red number 1 is visible. Thus the trigger is released and the pistol is ready to fire.

The P 7 M 8 and M 13 were equipped with a manual safety at a customer's request — actually a technical retrogression. The attached safety pusher works directly on the trigger. This version is not intended for private owners.

The P 7 M 8 dismantled for cleaning. Under the slide is the moveable piston.

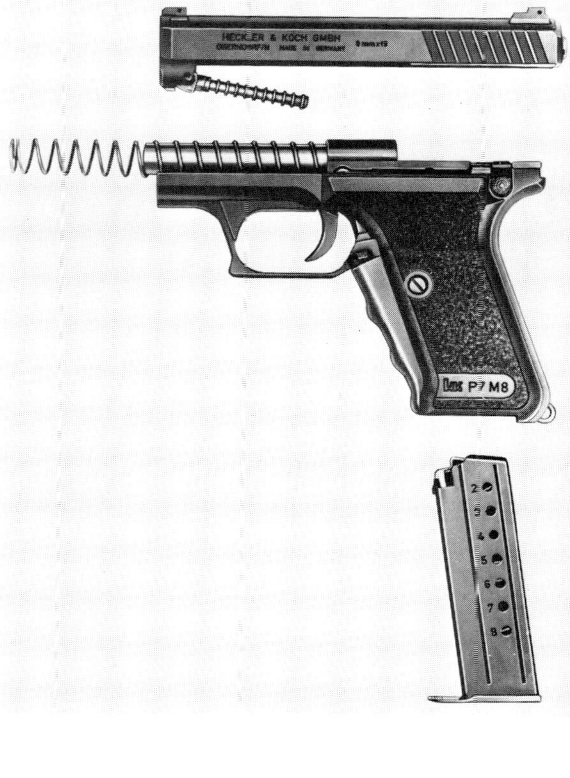

It should be noted that (as of 1984) this is exclusively a version made for a particular user, and the manufacturer absolutely does not wish to offer a version for the private buyer.

The technical features of the S versions do not differ from those already described.

Model P 7 PT 8

This is a version made to fire PT bullets at short ranges. PT is an abbreviation for "Plastic Training"; the cartridges are made by Dynamit Nobel and have sprayed-on bullets.

The PT 8 version allows the semi-automatic firing of these cartridges; all handling and operational functions are identical to those of the P 7 pistol.

It differs from the P 7 in having a magazine catch that can be operated from either side, plus a plastic inlay above the trigger guard. In addition, the backsight is screwed in place, and at the back of the grip there is an eyelet to hold a cord for carrying. To avoid confusion, the slide of the PT 8 has a large blue spot on each side.

The slide of the PT 8 had an attached gas piston and is some 50 grams lighter than the slide of the normal version. The recoil spring is copper-plated for easier recognition. The cartridge chamber is different, resembling the KK system of the Colt Government pistol; it is inserted so as to be longitudinally moveable and serves to increase the recoil in the familiar way.

The maximum shot range of the PT cartridge is 125 meters, and a safe distance of 170 meters is required. After a flight of just 25 meters, the energy of the PT bullet is so decreased that it falls below 10 Joule.

At a distance of eight meters, dispersion circles of some 10 cm can be attained with the PT 8, which is sufficient for practice-like training under limited space conditions. If necessary, the bullets can also be fired as live ammunition when damage to important surroundings is to be avoided. One realm in which they can be used is in the constant protection of aircraft whose pressurized cabins cannot be pierced.

For trouble-free functioning of the pistol, it must be kept in mind that the moveable cartridge chamber must always be well-cleaned and oiled before insertion.

Model P 7 K 3

The weapons in this new series do not belong within the scope of this book, it is true, but they will be noted here for the sake of completeness, and because they can also be used as practice weapons.

The K 3 is essentially identical in construction to the earlier P 7 and thus has the same cocking-handle system with all its advantages. The system is different in terms of locking; the gas piston and the cylinder for it are absent, since all versions get by with an unlocked mass breech. The K 3 is offered for use with 7.65 mm Browning, 9 mm short and .22 LR cartridges.

The barrel, 97 mm long (the P 7 barrel is 105 mm long), can be unscrewed with the help of a special wrench, so that a quick change of calibers from 7.65 mm to 9 mm is possible. The conversion kit for the .22 LR caliber has a lighter slide.

The P 7 PT 8 is made for the PT cartridge, which can be fired with the friction-ignition bullet at short ranges with the repeating function retained. It is also marked by the blue spot on both sides, just under the foresight.

The P 7 K 3 pistol can be equipped to fire any of three different cartridges. It has no braking over the gas piston but closely resembles the P 7 M 8 otherwise.

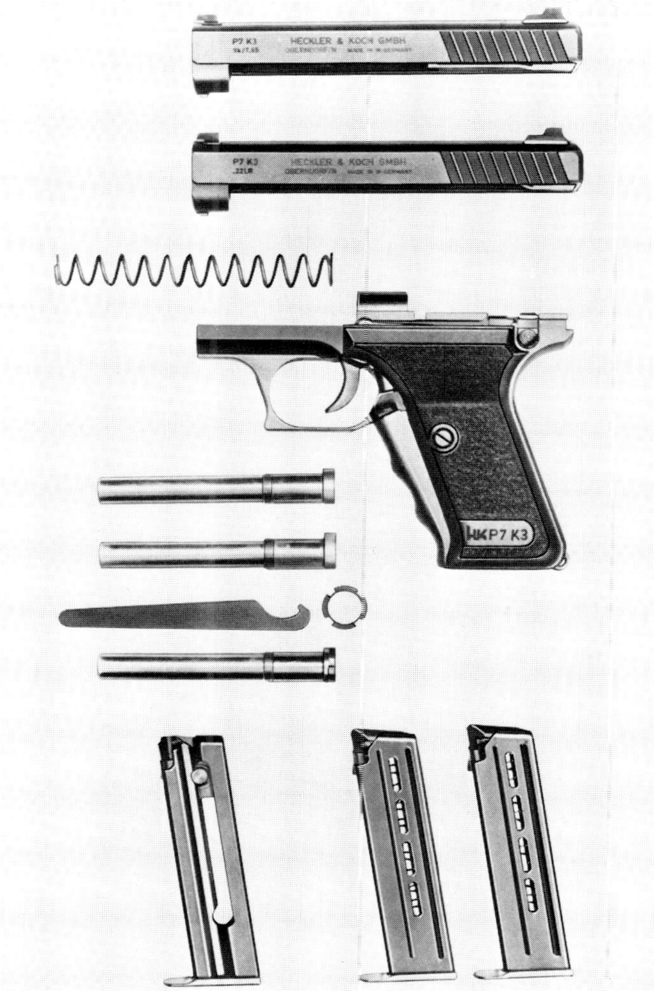

This is the equipment for use in three calibers. One slide is enough for 9 mm short and 7.65 mm cartridges, while a lighter slide is used for the .22 cartridge.

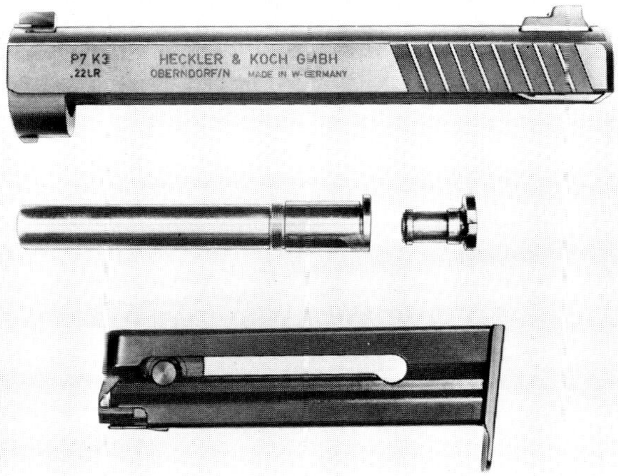

The switching system for .22 LR caliber use. Like other manufacturers, Heckler & Koch uses the principle of the flying chamber, the chamber being moveable and thus strengthening the recoil impulse.

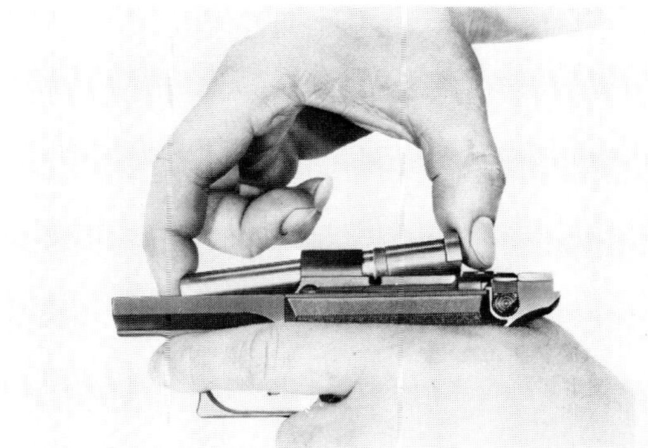

Changing the barrel of the P 7 K 3: the unscrewed barrel can be pushed out of its mounting to the rear, or inserted in the same manner.

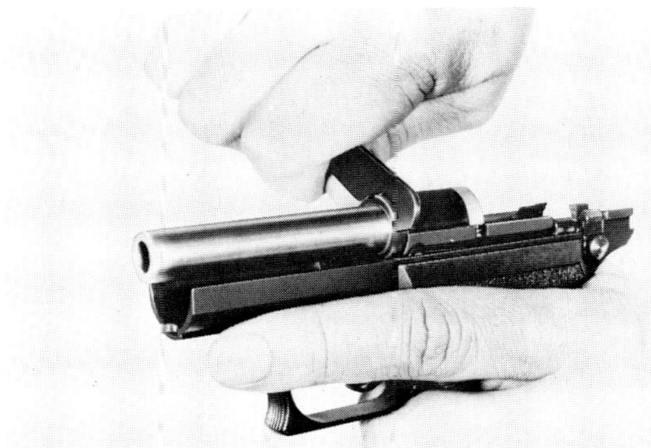

. . . and tightened with a special wrench that comes with it. After that the slide is installed.

Data Comparison: P 7 Pistol

	P 7 M 8	P 7 M 13	P 7 M 8 S	P 7 M 13 S	P 7 PT 8
Caliber	9 Para.	9 Para.	9 Para.	9 P ra.	9 Para./PT
Magazine capacity	8	13	8	13	8
Initial velocity m/s	ca. 351	ca. 351	cq. 351	ca. 35	ca. 400
Muzzle energy Joule	ca. 500	ca. 500	ca. 500	ca. 500	ca. 210
Overall length mm	171	175	171	175	170
Overall height	128	135	128	135	128
Grip width	29	33	29	33	29
Barrel length mm	105	105	105	105	105
Sight line mm	148	148	148	148	148
Weight empty grams	780	850	780	850	790
Weight loaded	950	1135	950	1135	–

The Pistol by Korth

The firm of Korth, located in Ratzeburg, has been known for years as a producer of high-quality revolvers in .22 LR and .357 Magnum calibers. These revolvers are valued for their excellent workmanship, which cannot find its equal easily. The basic technology of the Korth revolvers is shown in another way, for some of the models are available with alternate cylinder for the 9 mm cartridge.

As for a pistol made by Korth, for years there were only rumors, and then a prototype was exhibited several times at the Nürnberg Weapons Exhibition. Nothing more was to be heard for awhile, and in the trade press it was alternatingly stated that it would or would not be marketed.

The pistol makes a compact and yet elegant impression and is noteworthy for its grip, which extends downward. The magazine holds ten cartridges in a single row, thus the corresponding grip length, and fits comfortably into the hand with its milled grip panels. When first taken in hand — the prototype was not officially fired, and firing tests therefore had to be omitted — the trigger proves to move very smoothly for both types of use. When the hammer is cocked, the trigger is released as quickly and smoothly as a good revolver trigger.

Different from those of well-known pistols is the type of locking by a swinging bolt fitting between the barrel and the grip. The barrel is guided by a longitudinal extension inside the grip section, and makes no tipping movement during unlocking. This could be one of the causes of an outstanding locking performance, and yet,

Long announced: the Korth pistol from Ratzeburg. Korth had already celebrated its 30th anniversary as a manufacturer of high-quality revolvers. In this heavy all-steel pistol, many features are atypical in addition to workmanship and price.

The right side of the weapon with the slide back. The pistol's lines are striking at first glance.

When these lines were written (in mid-1986), the actual start of Korth pistol production had not been stated precisely, however the first delivery was suggested for the end of 1986. Thus these lines and photos could refer only to one of the available prototypes with the pre-series number of 005. It is not yet discernible to what extent the series production model may one day differ from it. The basic technology, though, will be retained and should at least be described to some extent.

for reasons already cited, cannot be done practically.

When the slide is drawn back, it comes to rest in its rearmost position when the empty magazine is still in the grip. An unusual feature is the visible catch on the left front side, which is moved by spring pressure into an extension on the grip when the barrel recoils and stops the barrel after a distance of 10 mm. When the slide moves forward in the course of repeating, the curved point of this catch moves onto a bar of the step between the flanks of the slide, is caught and releases the barrel for its further forward movement.

The dismantling lever has been swung downward. The side hook holds the barrel to the frame while the slide moves farther back.

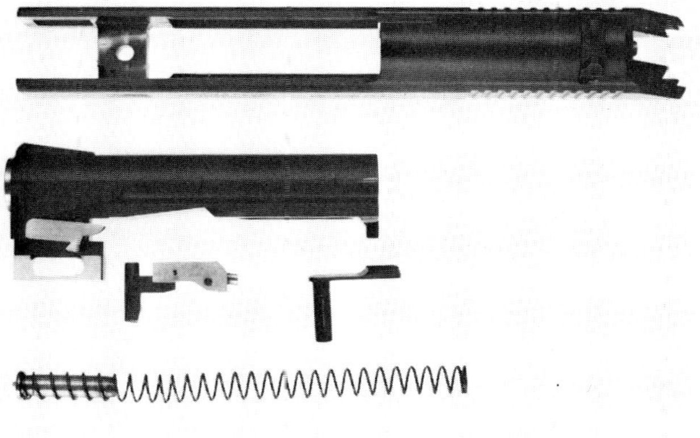

Barrel, slide and recoil spring of the Korth pistol. A similar principle to that of a weapon locked by a swinging bolt is used here.

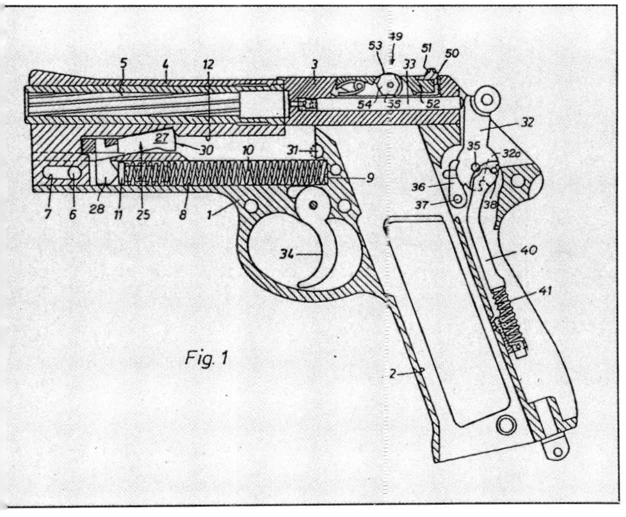

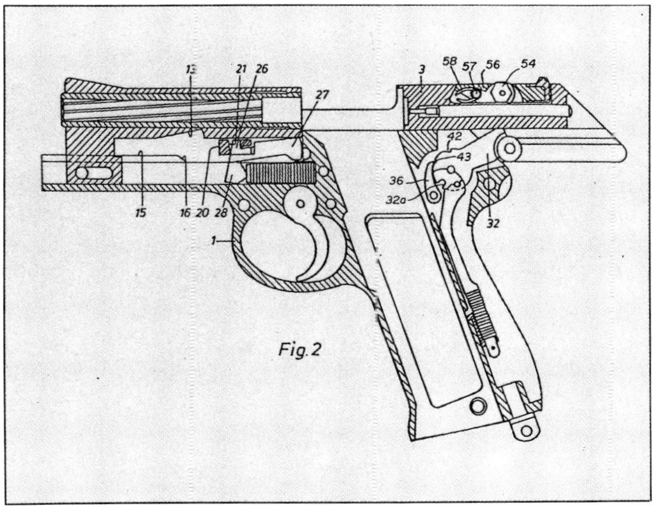

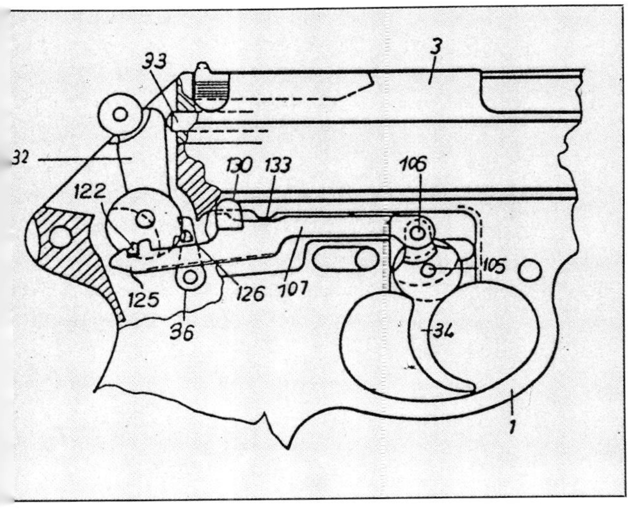

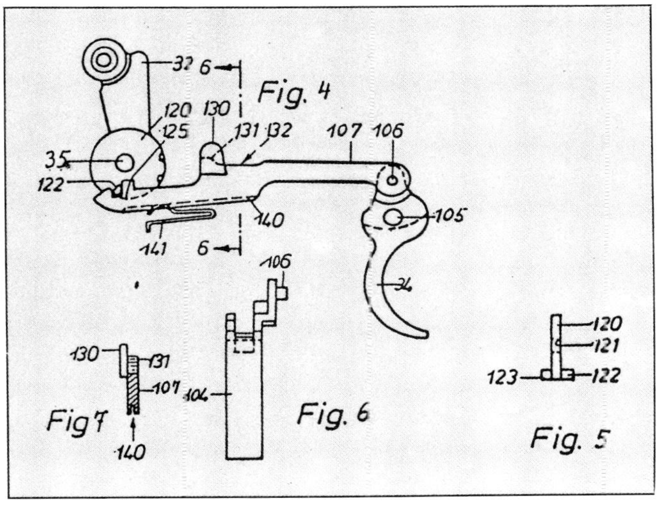

Cutaway drawings of the Korth pistol, also showing the trigger and safety functioning.

When the weapon is dismantled, the dismantling lever at the front of the grip is turned 90 degrees, which is not an easy operation, and removed from the side — the need to remove a part may not be a very modern method any more. The complete upper part can now be pushed out of the grip and dismantled further. On the frame, the neatly made rails on the upper section are noteworthy and have a step worked into them over which the swinging bolt, which extends downward, can slide out, so as to slide backward afterwards on the deep rails along with the slide. The recoil spring is set in the receiver and has a short guide housing, the point of which is to be fitted back into a guiding bore on the lower arm of the swinging bolt when being reassembled. The joint backward movement of barrel and slide measures 10 mm, and the contact surface for the lock is 54 square mm. The manufacturer describes this interesting type of locking as a, "rigidly bolted barrel with swinging bolt breech."

The hammered barrel, measuring 102 mm in length, has six riflings turning to the right. So far it has been made for the 9 mm Parabellum caliber, and additional calibers are being planned by the Korth firm.

A noteworthy feature of the Korth pistol, or at least of the available prototype, is that the hammer has no specific safety rest into which it can be drawn. Neither is there a manual safety nor the possibility of decocking the cocked hammer. Yet the Korth pistol is not therefore an unsafe weapon, for it has an effective safety which is engaged when the hammer would slide off while being cocked, or when the pistol falls on its hammer. The catch-rest safety and its functioning can be seen best when the pistol is dismantled. When the hammer is released by the trigger, it moves far forward, where at first the catch rest has no function. Only when the trigger is released again does the hammer fit into its catch rest. The Korth pistol is a very expensive weapon to produce, which naturally determines its price, which is said to be well over 4000 German Marks. All parts are machined out of solid material, and no stamped or cast parts are used. Thus the collector or user of high-quality weapons will not hold an everyday pistol in his hand.

Technical Data: Korth Pistol

Manufacturer	Korth, Ratzeburg
Model designation	unknown to date
Caliber	9 mm Parabellum
System	Rigid locked barrel with swinging bolt
Trigger	Double and single-action
Trigger weight	SA 1500 grams/DA ca. 5000 grams
Barrel	Hammered/six riflings to right
Safety	Closing/short firing pin/automatic catch rest safety
Sights	Ramp foresight/Fully adjustable
Magazine capacity	10 cartridges
Overall length	210 mm
Overall height	148 mm
Grip width	30 mm
Weight empty	1240 grams
Material	Steel
Finish	silky matte burnished

Pistols by Mauser

The Mauser works in Oberndorf on the Neckar were founded in 1869 by the brothers Peter Paul and Wilhelm Mauser for the production of rifles. Excellent weapons soon went into production and won a fine worldwide reputation. Probably the most famous weapon developed by Mauser was the 98 system which was used in the 98 rifle and 98 k carbine. No other system would be as successful, and to this day many hunting repeaters are based on this immortal system.

The company began pistol production in 1877, at which time a single-shot pistol (the Model 1877) was developed — however widespread success did not come to this pistol. The Mauser "Zick-Zack" revolver, so called because of the diagonal grooves on its cylinder, became well known. Officially it was the Model 1878 revolver, which could be opened for loading. Another little-known model was Mauser's first repeating pistol, the Model C 86, with a tubular magazine under the barrel. The C 96 pistol was one of Mauser's outstanding designs and appeared in many forms. It was followed by the development of the legendary Parabellum pistol and of numerous cartridges, the production of pocket pistols and much more. After World War II the Mauser works lost much of their reputation in the field of handguns, and even in the realm of pistols the magic seems to have been lost. Hunting guns and precision rifles are produced today, along with larger-scale weapons for purely military use.

The C 96 9 mm Caliber Parabellum Pistol

The C 96 pistol had a rather unusual fate, for it was, to be sure, planned as a military weapon. However, large-scale orders did not result, and the pistol later achieved worldwide distribution mainly in the private sector. This naturally did not exclude its use in various armies

When more and more pistols were needed in World War I, a version of the C 96 for the 9 mm Parabellum cartridge was built. They were not rebuilt weapons, but pistols made for this cartridge from the start.

Detail of a cutaway model made by the factory, showing the type of bolt and trigger function.

— for example, the German army officers in World War I liked to arm themselves with it, though it was never introduced officially.

Development began in 1894 and was basically a private pastime of the three Federle brothers, factory engineers, one of whom was the factory manager for a time. The first prototype was finished in 1885 and would be fired on March 15 of that year. On December 11, 1895 a German patent, number 90,430, was awarded — the British patent followed on January 14, 1896, and that was only part of the patent protection obtained. Mauser had this design patented in almost all the weapon-producing countries of the world.

The cartridges for the pistol were made by Borchardt and adapted by Mauser. From then on it was the 7.63 mm Mauser, almost identical to the Borchardt cartridge, but somewhat more powerful. The C 96 became one of the first self-loading pistols for a high-powered cartridge that was built in series and whose technical problems could be overcome. It was a locked pistol with its magazine in front of the trigger guard, and was loaded either individually or with the help of a charger. The charger was inserted into the grooves on top of the breech housing and the cartridges were pushed into the magazine box, then the empty charger was withdrawn and disposed of.

The barrel formed a rigid unit with the breech housing, and in the breech housing the chamber (or breechblock piece) moved — earlier in its development it had one, and later two, cutouts to hold the tabs of the bolt block. The complete upper section moved in the guiding grooves of the receiver, which had very few functions here: space for the integral magazine with 10 or 6 cartridges, the mount of the sprung trigger tongue, and the attachment points of the two grip panels with the typical Mauser diagonal grooves. The functioning parts of the lock could be removed as a complete unit, but first the follower of the magazine had to be removed.

Let us have a look at the functioning of the weapon when firing: the chamber is forward and is bolted, a cartridge is in the chamber, the hammer is cocked. The hammer, released by the trigger, strikes on the firing pin which runs longitudinally through the chamber, and then ignites the cartridge. The recoil moves the unit of barrel, breech housing and chamber back some 2.5 mm. This backward movement lets the bolt block slide over its lower angled surface; it moves back a small distance and then downward; in this movement its tabs (knobs) move out of the grooves of the chamber and release this to move the rest of the way back. In the process, the recoil spring is compacted; it lies inside the chamber against the holding wedge pushed in at the back. In the usual

For clear recognition, a big number 9 was cast and painted red on each side. Versions without it, or with black paint, are also known.

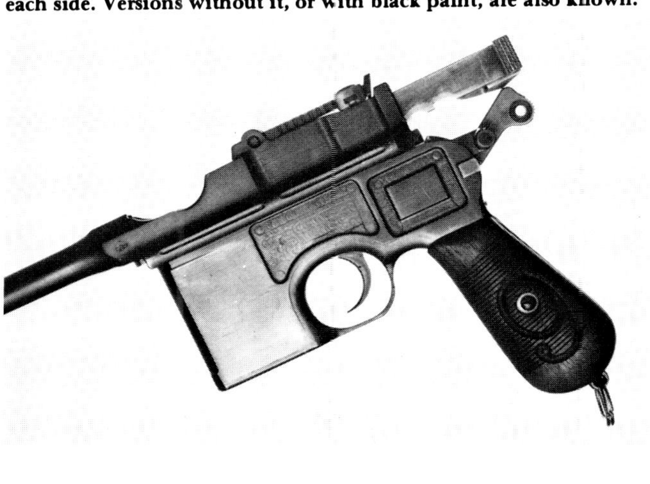

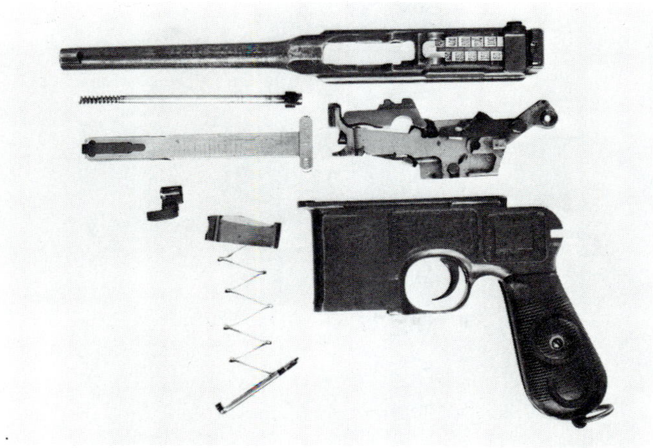

The dismantled C 96 in 9 mm Parabellum caliber. The sights of this version are adjustable to 500 meters.

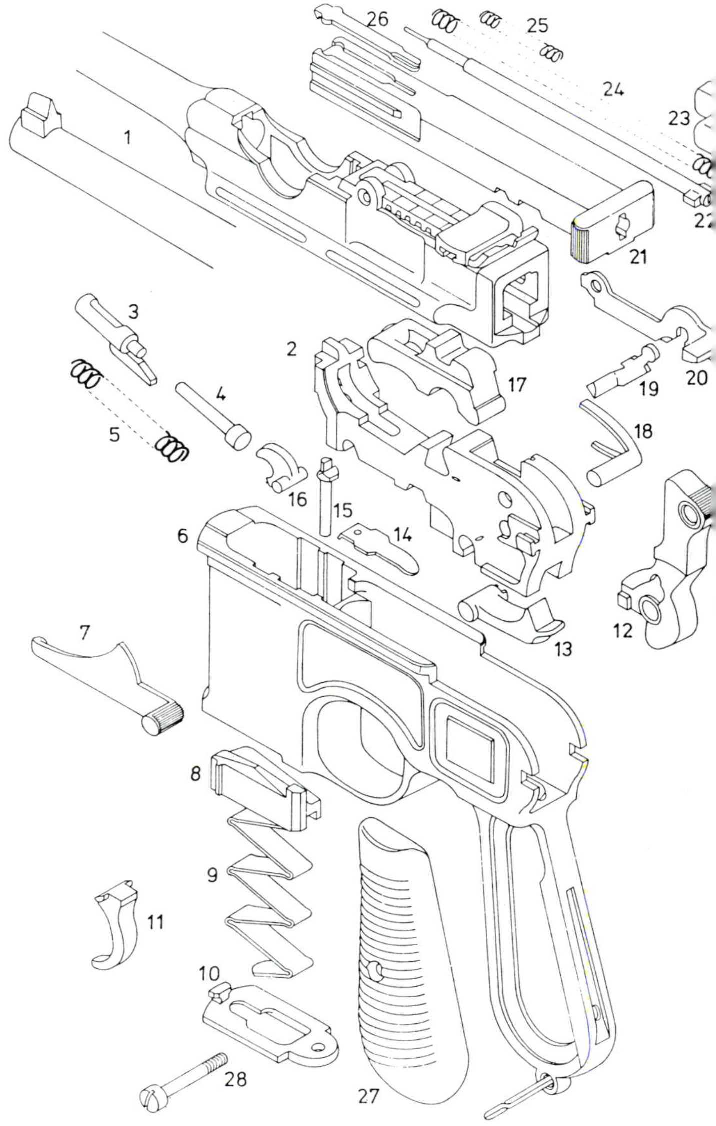

The parts of the C 96 pistol in the version with serial numbers from 35,000 up, with improved firing pin. The magazine of the C 96 is a permanent part of the frame.

manner the empty case is extracted, ejected and the hammer cocked again, as well as being caught in its rests. The chamber moves forward again under pressure of the recoil spring, and the barrel with the breech housing also move forward. The bolt block swings up again and locks the chamber in its forward position.

The lateral safety blocks the hammer, which cannot be cocked when the safety catch is applied. Over the years, many changes have been made to the C 96, including to the safety, which exists in three quite different versions. The 9 mm caliber Parabellum pistol has the so-called "C 12 new safety", recognized by the letters NS stamped into the back of the hammer.

During World War I the demand for pistols of any and all calibers by the German Army increased tremendously. To at least come close to filling the most serious deficits, the Mauser firm was contracted to prepare a large production series of its pistols for the 9 mm Parabellum cartridge. This course was faster and easier to follow than switching production to the new Parabellum pistol that was already in use by the army. This revision caused no difficulties worth mentioning, and much could be retained unchanged. To differentiate clearly, all 9 mm caliber pistols had a large number 9 cut into both sides of the grip panels; the 9 was originally painted red; later versions were painted black or had no numbers on the grip panels at all. The latter were specimens that were assembled from spare parts after the war. In all, some 150,000 pistols were prepared for the 9 mm Parabellum cartridge.

Among the main features of the C 96 is the sight that, depending on the model, was adjustable to 1000 meters — wishful thinking, for even with a normal rifle it is very difficult to hit anything at 1000 meters using an open sight, let alone with a pistol. This does not change another of this model's points of interest, the shaft that could be attached to it and likewise used as a holster. Production of the C 96 was ended about 1938, since no further need for such a big handgun could be foreseen.

Another version of the C 96 was built for sustained fire (rapid fire). With it, Mauser met the different requirements of markets in foreign countries, where very good Spanish copies of this pistol were being sold. The 1932 model had a switching system for sustained fire, a development by Mauser's engineer Nickl, and the later

Technical Data: Mauser C 96

Manufacturer	Mauser Weapon Factory, Oberndorf a. N.
Caliber	9 mm Parabellum
Magazine capacity	10 cartridges
Overall length	296 mm
Height/width	158 mm/35 mm
Barrel length	140 mm
Weight empty	1120 grams
System	Locked
Sight	Adjustable 50-500 meters
Safety	Lever
Material/finish	Steel, burnished
Grip panels	Wood, with carved 9

An 08 pistol made by Mauser in 1937. It was replaced by the P 38 pistol.

pistols had a system based on a development by Mauser colleague Karl Westinger.

Almost all pistols of this type were made in 7.63 mm caliber, while about 100 were produced in 9 mm Parabellum caliber and shipped to Yugoslavia.

Wartime Pistol Production

Mauser did not originally take part in the production of the service weapon introduced as the 08 pistol. This changed only in 1930.

On May 1, 1930 August Weiss began working for Mauser; his assignment was to build up the expanded pistol production. He brought with him 800 finishing machines from the Wittenauer factory of the Berlin-Karlsruhe Industrial Works, where part of the Parabellum production had gone on until then. Weiss successfully built up pistol production at the Mauser works. With a team of three engineers, ten masters, nine employees and some 1000 workers, he produced approximately one million Parabellum pistols during the next fifteen years, plus 10,000 7.65 mm caliber pistols (old model), another 400,000 7.65 mm (new model) pistols, and some 400,000 Model P 38 pistols, plus a total of some fifty million spare parts.

The sales of Parabellum pistols were extremely modest at first: 302 pistols to the Netherlands Navy, then smaller series to the Netherlands forces in East Asia, then more and more deliveries to the German Army, later the entire German Wehrmacht, which at this time was being equipped steadily.

Before and during World War II, Mauser was the only German pistol manufacturer allowed to export to other countries. Shipments were made to the following countries: Turkey, Portugal, Latvia, Iran, Sweden and Finland.

The high production costs led to a search for a pistol that was less expensive to produce, a search that led to the adoption of the P 38 made by Walther/Zella-Mehlis. The P 38 was at the time the first self-loading pistol in the 9 mm Parabellum caliber that had a double action trigger. In 1942, Wehrmacht High Command had production of the Parabellum pistol stopped and gave Mauser and other firms contracts to produce the P 38 pistol. Mauser used the code letters byf on these pistols. If one looks at the Mauser production figures (source: Wolfgang Seel, *Mauser — von der Waffenschmiede zum Weltunternehmen*), one can see that many were produced:

1939/40: 141,514 08 pistols	no P 38 pistols
1940/41: 157,109 08 pistols	no P 38 pistols
1941/42: 139,425 08 pistols	no P 38 pistols
1942/43: 11,583 08 pistols	99,680 P 38 pistols
1943/44: 507 08 pistols	162,454 P 38 pistols
1944/45: presumably none	ca. 65,470 P 38 pistols

Postwar Production

It was judged a small sensation when, in 1967, the Mauser firm announced in the press that the production of the HSc and Parabellum pistols would be resumed. At this time there was once again a worldwide demand, which existed despite the no longer up-to-date tech-

During recommenced production after the war, Mauser produced a series of nicely made anniversary pistols. This is the "70 years of Parabellum pistols, Russian Empire" version in 9 mm Parabellum caliber. Production was always limited to 250.

The "75 years of Parabellum pistols, Kingdom of Bulgaria" version in 7.65 mm Parabellum caliber, and with a longer barrel. The cocking buttons are different in this type.

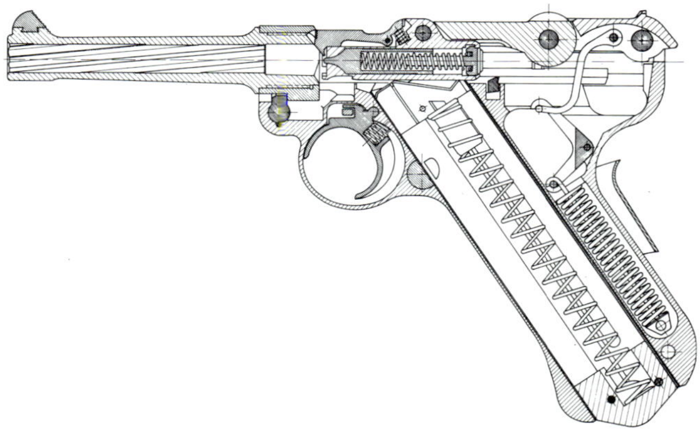

Cutaway of the Parabellum pistol made by Mauser after the war, shown in 9 mm Parabellum caliber.

The popular knee-joint breech demanded a high degree of precise production; no wonder the pistol was so expensive. Cyrillic lettering is on the safety and the extractor.

nology of this nostalgic pistol. In the USA the demand was particularly great; there these pistols have such a high value that the distinction is always made between "Lugers" and mere "pistols."

The first thoughts of resuming production came up at the end of the 1950s, but at that time there was a good deal of skepticism involved, for how should a pistol that was so expensive to produce be competitive against all the more reasonably priced designs made of stamped parts, cast parts and the like? When American authors visited Oberndorf and brought up this subject, there was still no resumption of production in sight. The expensive production — that of the receiver alone cost almost 1000 Marks — is still a problem for this pistol, which is therefore bought mostly by collectors and fans. The Parabellum has nothing remarkable to offer in terms of either price or technology. In the mid-1980s, newly made Parabellum pistols were offered at prices over 3000 Marks — a price beyond the "sound barrier", for weapons with the most modern technology cost scarcely half as much. It is no wonder that Mauser deliberately turned to the potent customers who wanted more of a piece of jewelry than a useful utensil: the expensive jubilee pistols on the one hand, and expensively engraved and decorated pistols on the other, are visible proof of this.

But back to post-World War II production. At the beginning of the 1960s, Samuel Cummings of an American firm, the International Armament Company (INTERARMCO), went to the Mauser firm in Oberndorf and the Eidgenössische Waffenfabrik in Switzerland to

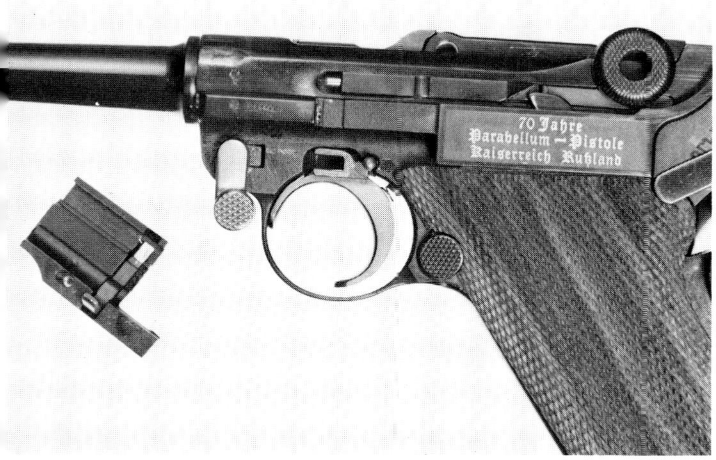

After removal of the side covering plate, the upper part can be pushed forward off the receiver.

The dismantled 9 mm Parabellum caliber pistol.

Producing the frame out of solid material requires many separate work processes by machine and hand.

make an initial study of expenses involved in a possible new production. Both firms began to make their initial project studies. August Weiss had been able to rescue considerable production records amid the chaos of the war's end, but no further progress was made. In Bern, on the other hand, there were designs, machines and statistics from the early Swiss production of ordnance pistols of the 06/29 W+F type. From this basis there arose a simplified 06/29 pistol, which was originally designated the 29/65 Pistol. The grip safety lever had been eliminated, the whole chamber was simplified technically, the transition from barrel to fork housing has a strongly built-up cone. This version was, in the end, not developed further, as in the meantime Mauser and Interarmco had been able to reach a financial understanding.

Around 1968, and based on the new contracts, Mauser produced new models, which looked like a new edition of the 06/29 W+F type. This Mauser pistol differed from its immediate predecessor in having a smooth rim on the wooden grip panels and a shortened grip safety lever. Additional prototypes, which resembled the Swiss Parabellum less and less, were built in 1969 and 1970 before

The version with a straight grip, as produced for Interarms in 9 mm Parabellum caliber.

Another Interarms pistol.

series production began. The hand-held surfaces of the magazine catch, locking piece and safety were again given a herringbone finish, as were the hinge pins of the joint. The transition from the fork housing to the barrel took on its familiar form with its outer angles. When series production at the Mauser works began again in 1970, the new pistol looked more like the Swiss 06/29 than the original 08 pistol.

Production began in the 7.65 Parabellum and 9 mm Parabellum calibers — serial numbers of the 7.65 caliber began with 10, those of the 9 mm caliber with 11. In November 1971, the grip was made in a somewhat different shape. It now no longer formed a straight line down the front but had a bulge in front. The sights were also changed, with the foresight no longer cut in the back, but having the shape of the 08 foresight instead. This pistol was known unofficially as the 06/73 version — this is the weapon shown in several photographss here. Along with series production, factory experiments went on, including in the .45 ACP caliber for the inviting American market. For the first time since 1907 there was again a Parabellum in this caliber. Smaller pistols, popularly known as "pocket pistols", were also tested, as well as sporting versions in both calibers. The 7.65 mm caliber Parabellum pistol has its barrel slightly flattened on the sides, while the barrel of the 9 mm caliber Parabellum sport pistol remained round. The adjustable sight was set into the rear joint.

More attention will be given to the 06/73 version, which became most widespread. It was produced as of 1971, and for a long time both types were available simultaneously. The grip had the familiar bulge to the front, and the foresight was like that of the 08 pistol. The tangible surface of the safety was no longer made round, but rather as a rounded rectangle with longitudinal grooves. On the forward joint was the Mauser banner emblem with the added word "Original", or the inscription "Mauser Parabellum" plus the caliber on the grip above the left grip panel.

The 06/73 version was available with barrel lengths of 100, 120 and 150 mm, as well as with varying and very striking surface decor.

This series was expanded by the so-called anniversary models or jubilee pistols, which were models of fine workmanship, but not without criticism as to their prices. The first of this series was made in 1974 under contract from the Italian manufacturer Renato Gamba (a well-known producer of hunting and sporting rifles); it was designed for the 7.65 mm Parabellum cartridge and had a barrel 100 mm long. The lettering on the right step of the grip was: "MAUSER P. 08 4" SERIE SPEZIALE RENATO GAMBA." An independent numbering system was used, with the letters RG before the number. There followed a series of 250 pieces for the anniversary of the introduction of the Parabellum as an army pistol. The inscription read: "75 Jahre/Parabellum-Pistole/1900-75." The further series' were likewise limited to 250 pieces, whereby the pistols in a series were numbered accordingly as, for example, 0234 of 250. Shown here are the "75 Years Parabellum Pistol, Kingdom of Bulgaria", the "70 Years Parabellum Pistol Russian Empire", "75 Years Parabellum Pistol Imperial Navy", "75 Years Parabellum Pistol Carbine Model" and "Model 1902 Cartridge Counter." The pistols were supplied in a tastefully designed case, lined with velvet, or in a hand-sewn leather case with partitioning.

Surely the pistols from Oberndorf are far better than many other pistols if one considers only the careful workmanship. Still in all, this new yet old pistol is no longer capable of lasting, for its technology is that of the turn of the century.

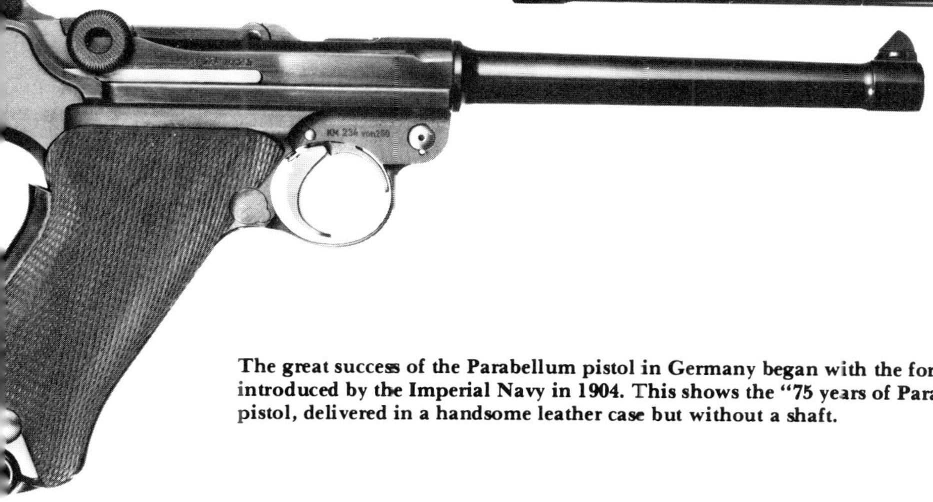

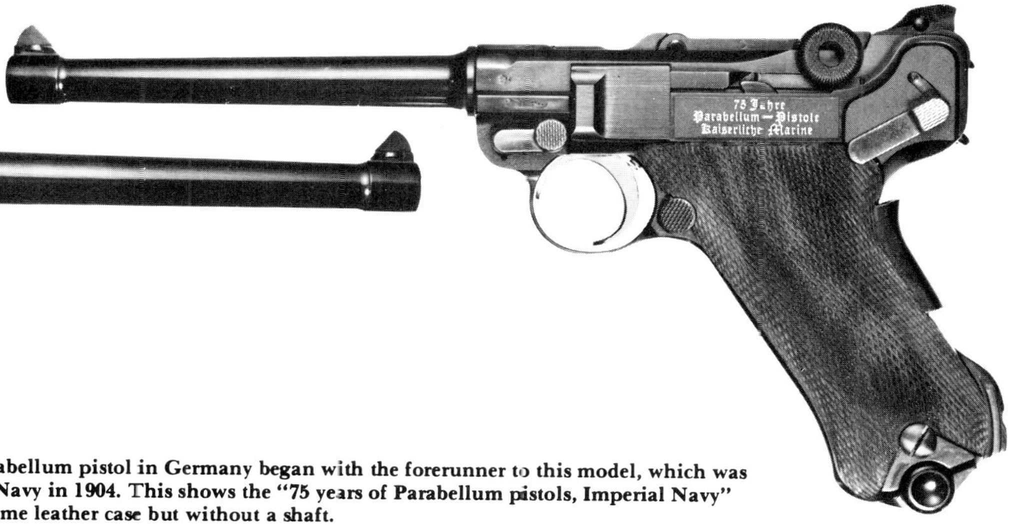

The great success of the Parabellum pistol in Germany began with the forerunner to this model, which was introduced by the Imperial Navy in 1904. This shows the "75 years of Parabellum pistols, Imperial Navy" pistol, delivered in a handsome leather case but without a shaft.

"75 years of Parabellum pistols, Model 08", introduced by the Imperial German Army in 1908.

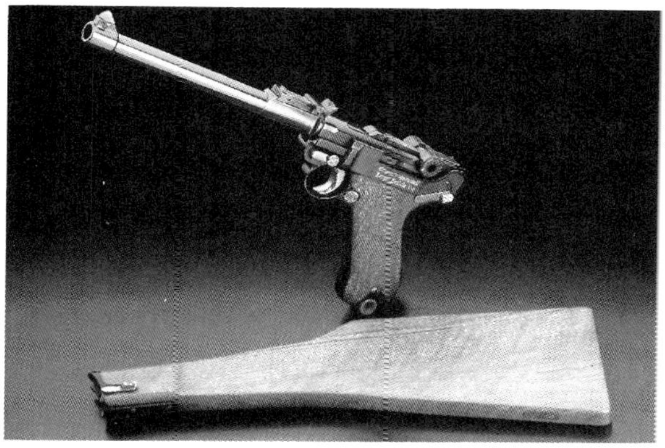

"Commemorative Model, Long Pistol 1908" with plinth.

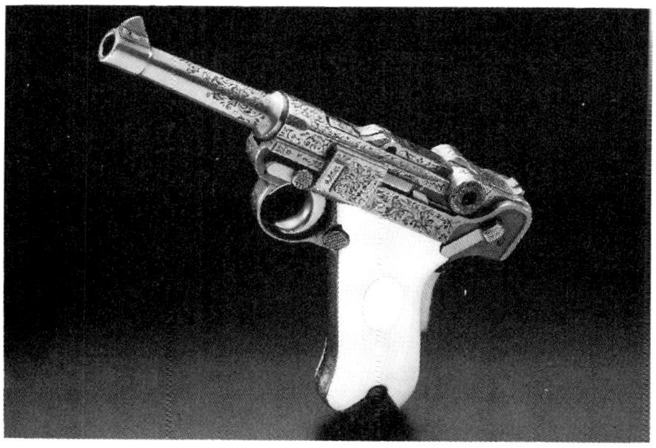

In terms of utility, the Parabellum pistols are long since outmoded and replaced by better designs. Mauser makes small quantities of very valuable pistols to order.

Navy Parabellum (reproduction) seen from above. The sight is adjustable in two steps to 100 and 200 meters.

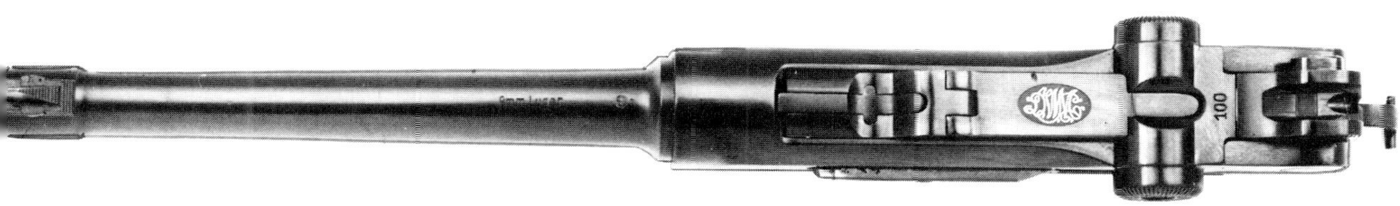

The Parabellum Pistol

As for the famous parabellum pistol, it is not merely a weapon, but a legend, especially as portrayed by American writers. There is still a differentiation there between handguns and Lugers, and the term "Luger" has made itself very much at home there. The term "Parabellum", on the other hand, has been limited to the continent of Europe. The designation "Pistol 08" would be less precise, for that is only one of a large family of weapons.

No pistol has achieved such worldwide distribution and popularity as the Luger or Parabellum, which numerous countries have put into service. After World War II, production was revived again for several years in Oberndorf. The Parabellum is much sought after, and it is no wonder, what with its good appearance, good workmanship and inexpensive price. Its entire history is too vast to recount here. Only a few essential details can be taken up, and not all variations made to date can be depicted here.

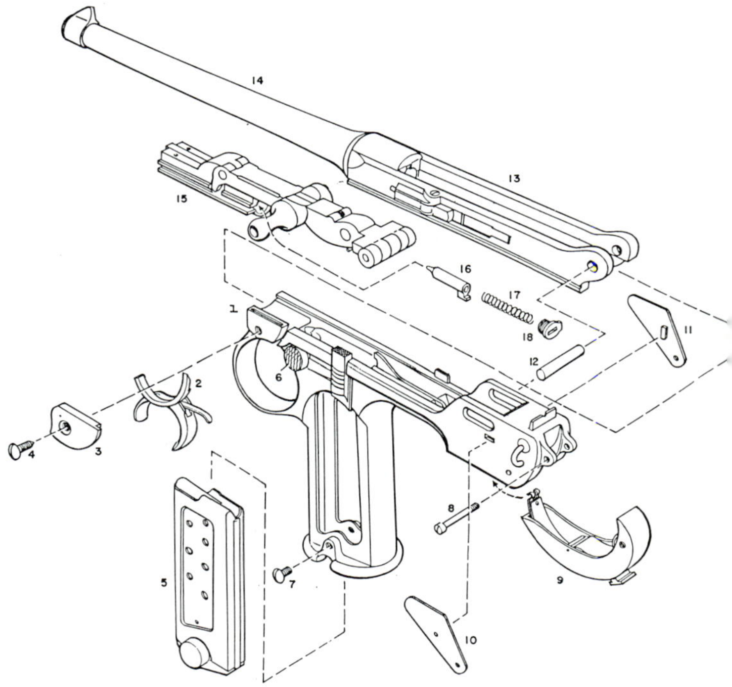

The Borchardt pistol can be regarded as the origin of the whol series of Parabellum pistols. It had a knee-joint breech, but it w installed in an insufficiently handy design.

The Borchardt pistol blazed the trail to later Parabellum pistols, but proved to be too unhandy.

There were four noteworthy personalities who created the Parabellum's history: Ludwig Loewe (1837-1886), his brother Isidor Loewe (1848-1910), Hugo Borchardt (1845-1921) and Georg Luger (1849-1923). The man who led the way was Ludwig Loewe, who created the mechanical requirements for the manufacture of the Borchardt and Luger pistols. There was not much said in Germany about Ludwig Loewe and his brother — he was Jewish, and that was not at all appropriate for a weapon that was used as a side arm in two German wars.

The end of the 19th century was an active time for inventors, but for many years they were stumped by the unavailability of usable cartridges. Only the development of dependably good cartridges made the self-loading weapon possible, whether machine gun or automatic pistol. The first repeating pistols (like those of Bittner and Schlegelmilch) formed a milestone on this path. In them, the next cartridge was introduced by moving a lever.

A further milestone was the machine gun developed by Hiram Maxim, which also took place in the days of Borchardt and Luger. After its successful development, the wish was often expressed to miniaturize this principle and apply it to pistols. A problem of this time was the invention of an interrupter, that is, a device that, after the first shot was fired, first put the trigger out of action until it was released and activated again. The interrupter was what turned the automatic weapon into a self-loading weapon with a semi-automatic function — there were and are pistols without interrupters, but they remained the not too practical exceptions.

Schönberger was one of the first who found a way to utilize the impulse of the cartridge to cause repetition. He designed a cartridge with a special percussion cap that could release pressure to the rear after the shot, thereby practically activating a lever system which in turn caused the opening of the breech. The Schönberger pistol was not a commercial success. Orders from armies did not materialize. One year later, in 1893, a pistol came on the market that was to become the father of the legend of which we speak here: the Borchardt pistol, which is generally regarded as the first practicable self-loading pistol.

Like many others before him, Borchardt too had gone to America to seek his fortune, but returned disappointed. He took a position with the Royal Hungarian Weapons Factory in Budapest, and there he had his first contact with Hiram Maxim's machine gun, a weapon with a descending knee-joint breech. Borchardt utilized the principle of the knee-joint but made it open upward rather than downward in Maxim's gun. In addition, for the first time in a pistol he used a bar magazine that could be removed from the grip at the bottom and filled outside the weapon. An essential prerequisite for his successful work was naturally the suitable cartridge, and shortly before this time he had developed a 7.65 mm caliber cartridge. To his pistol he added a removable shaft, and this too became a characteristic of numerous handguns in military use. Whether with or without a shaft, his pistol was very unhandy, and was one reason why it was not accepted anywhere. During the first three years it was in production, some 3000 specimens were built, yet unfavorable criticism remained.

On the basis of its design there arose a pistol developed chiefly by Georg Luger which must be regarded as the forerunner of the Parabellum pistol. Where the name Parabellum came from cannot be determined for sure. In any case, it originated from the Roman proverb "Si vis pacem, para bellum": If you want peace, prepare for war (Even in ancient Rome fear was aroused by heavy armament).

Luger had retained the knee-joint breech in principle, but he located the recoil spring (at that time still a bent leaf spring) in the receiver directly behind the magazine shaft. This resulted in a very noticeable shortening of the pistol, and thus it was gradually made competitive and could be offered to various countries for testing as the Borchardt-Luger pistol. The first country that introduced the Luger pistol was Switzerland. To be sure, the Swiss had requested several changes and improvements (see under Switzerland). In Switzerland the improved pistol was introduced in 1900 as the Ordnance Pistol 1900, System Borchardt-Luger. After the first shipments were delivered from Germany, the Swiss took up production themselves, and manufacturing began at the Eidgenössische Waffenfabrik in Bern. At that time the German manufacturers were more than fully occupied with supplying their troops in the war.

The Borchardt-Luger in the USA

This venture in the USA was not very successful at first, in fact, it was full of disappointments. Colt and Browning in particular opposed the pistol from Germany on the basis of an ostensibly violated patent. Their 1897 patent had basically prevented any kind of recoil loader.

After its introduction in Switzerland the interest on the other side of the Atlantic rose high. Though this new pistol was said to be very good, the Americans did not want to give up the revolver. It was also suggested that changing from the revolver to the self-loading pistol was too much for the common soldier, which would lead to numerous accidents. Accidents actually happened very soon and in ominous numbers, as many gunsmiths had adapted the new pistol according to what they thought would work. In military circles, therefore, all use of these pistols was strictly forbidden by order.

In the period from 1901 to 1907, the Borchardt-Luger in various versions and calibers was subjected to its first

Cutaway of the early Swiss Parabellum pistol, the Model 1900 in 7.65 mm Parabellum caliber. The leaf spring in the back of the grip is its most unusual feature.

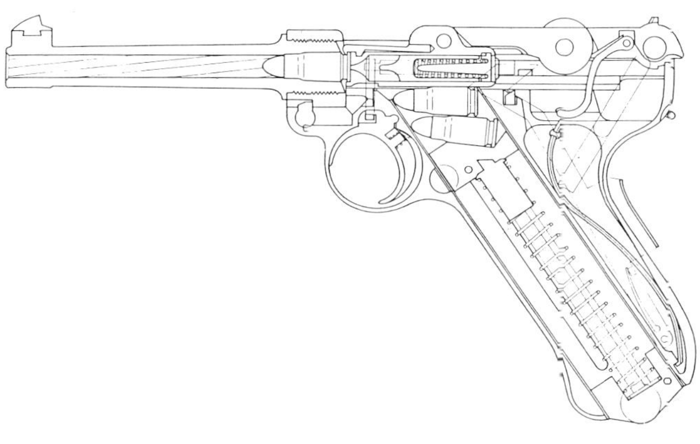

THE LUGER AUTOMATIC PISTOL.

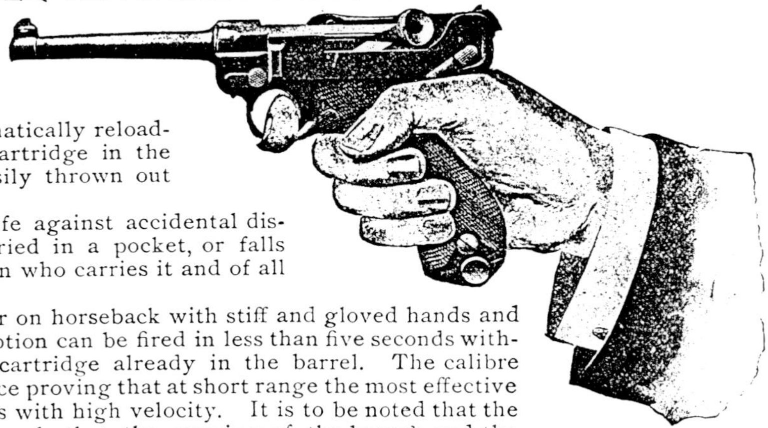

Modeled after the world-famed Maxim gun—using smokeless powder—capable of firing over 100 shots per minute—this wonderful weapon is a veritable triumph of the armorer's art. The Luger Pistol is a "repeater," automatically reloading and cocking itself, so long as there is a cartridge in the magazine. Magazines are interchangeable, easily thrown out and inserted, and contain eight cartridges.

Its construction makes it absolutely safe against accidental discharge, whether it dangles from a belt, is carried in a pocket, or falls upon the ground, insuring the safety of the man who carries it and of all around him.

This pistol can be loaded while on foot or on horseback with stiff and gloved hands and in every position. Nine shots without interruption can be fired in less than five seconds without changing the magazine, when there is a cartridge already in the barrel. The calibre chosen is .30 (765 mm.)—both theory and practice proving that at short range the most effective "stopping" shots are produced by small bullets with high velocity. It is to be noted that the construction of the Luger Automatic Pistol is such that the opening of the breech and the reloading occur after the projectile has left the barrel. This gives the greatest ballastic efficiency, because there is no escape of gases, which compels them to exert full and uniform pressure on the projectile. It also prevents fouling and burning of the mechanism. As a target pistol the Luger is pronounced the best. After 34,000 rounds of continuous firing the mechanism of one of these pistols acted as well as at the commencement of test. It can be used as a single loader, thus adapting it for target practice.

DIMENSIONS, CALIBRE, ETC.—Length on centre line, 9¼ inches; height, 5¼ inches; weight, 1 pound 15 ounces; calibre .30 (765 mm.); weight of bullet, 1/5 ounce; muzzle velocity of bullet, 1,150 feet; maximum range, 2,000 yards (elevation 27 30) Walsrode Smokeless Powder cartridges used with soft nose or steel-jacketed bullets.

Price of Pistol..........................$25 00, net   Cartridges..............................$2 50 per hundred

GOVERNMENT TEST AT THE SPRINGFIELD ARMORY.

The following details are extracted from the report dated April 3d, 1901, of a board composed of officers of the Ordnance Department, U. S. A., before whom the Luger Automatic Pistol was tested.

1st. DISMOUNTING AND REASSEMBLING.

Time required to dismount, 3¾ seconds; to reassemble, 12½ seconds.

2d. VELOCITY.

Velocity at 53 feet, 1153.35 foot seconds (mean of 10 rounds).

3d. ACCURACY AND PENETRATION AT 75 FEET.

Mean horizontal deviation 0.30 inches (mean of 5 rounds).
Mean vertical deviation 0.50 inches (mean of 5 rounds).
Mean absolute deviation 0.64 inches (mean of 5 rounds).

4th. RAPIDITY WITH ACCURACY.

30 rounds were fired at a distance of 25 yards at a target 2 x 6 feet. Trial by Recorder of Board. Time for 30 rounds, 52⅝ seconds. Number of hits, 24.

5th. ENDURANCE TEST.

500 rounds fired without cleaning; pistol cooled at every 50 rounds. The pistol was not oiled before beginning this test. These 500 shots were fired satisfactorily, except a few misfires owing to pistol not being well oiled. After the pistol had been thoroughly cleaned, the Endurance test was repeated. These 500 shots were fired with great satisfaction.

The report of the Board says: "The 50 rounds were fired without difficulty, the first 24 rounds being fired in 21½ seconds, or at the rate of 67 rounds per minute; the second 24 was fired in 17⅞ seconds, or at the rate of 80 rounds per minute." 534 in all were fired without difficulty of any kind.

6th. DUST TEST.

The pistol was exposed to a blast of fine sand dust for 15 seconds. The sand was then removed by rubbing with the hand and by blowing. 10 rounds were then fired in 11⅛ seconds, the action of the pistol being satisfactory.

7th. RUST TEST.

All oil was removed from the parts by boiling in a solution of sal soda. The pistol was immersed in a saturated solution of sal ammoniac for 5 minutes and then hung up in the open air to dry. At the end of 24 hours the pistol was taken for firing. As it had been hanging in a dry, steam-heated room, it was found to have rusted very badly. Time required to fire the 10 rounds, 3 minutes and 23 seconds. The pistol was then oiled on the outside. 10 rounds was then fired in 10½ seconds, the pistol working smoothly. Firing was then continued for 68 rounds more.

The Board is of the opinion that this pistol has successfully passed the test to which it was subjected.

Excerpt from an American advertisement for Luger pistols, with reference to the successful tests at the Springfield Armory.

tests. The impetus was provided by Captain William H. Beehler who, as military attache in Berlin, had attended a showing of the pistol at the Loewe factory and regarded it as a superior weapon, "far superior to any other handgun I have seen . . ."

In March 1901, further tests of two 7.65 mm caliber Borchardt-Luger pistols took place at the Springfield Armory. Two thousand shots were fired, and troubles occurred such as insufficient ignition because of a too weak firing pin impact, feed problems caused by bent magazine lips, or faulty cartridges. Damage was done to the breech lock, so that it no longer remained open after the last shot. The judging officers evaluated the pistol thus — the parts of the pistol were somewhat complicated in their composition and difficult to produce, as well as very expensive, but the pistol as a whole was not too complicated and could be dismantled quickly and easily for cleaning or lubrication with oil.

On April 16, 1901 Colonel Frank H. Phipps was authorized to order 1000 pistols of the Borchardt-Luger type as well as a great number of cartridges. The weapons were divided among the various arsenals and training centers, and reports of their use arrived steadily over the next few years.

Typical of this era is the assessment of a captain of the 13th Cavalry from Fort Robinson, Nebraska; he said sensibly, "The pistol shoots very well, it shoots fast and is well-balanced. The magazine, though, is too hard to load, especially for a mounted man, and with cold, clammy fingers it is fully impossible to load the cartridges because of the too-strong spring."

A year later, Georg Luger himself arrived in America and brought along a 9 mm caliber version of his pistol. Shortly before, he had developed a 9 x 19 mm caliber cartridge which was later to become known as the 9 mm Parabellum cartridge. On May 21, 1903 several pistols in 7.65 and 9 mm calibers were demonstrated to officers at the Springfield armory. In particularly, the effect of different barrel lengths was tested: 100, 120 and 175 mm for the 7.65 mm caliber and 100, 120 and 148 mm for the 9 mm caliber. In all, the 120 mm barrel was able to give the best results.

Firing tests on soft targets followedin order to give an impression of bullet effects — the smaller-caliber bullets had better penetration and caused bigger holes in blocks of soft material. Later these tests were rejected and shots were fired at "living flesh", the targets being drugged sheep under a veterinarian's care. The tests led to the awareness that the 9 mm cartridge was better suited to military use. Again there were tests in individual troop units, and again the same criticism was voiced as to the weapon's complexity, which the common soldier would neither understand nor learn to master. Naturally, this was always viewed in comparison to the simple revolver.

An interesting viewpoint from this era came from a Captain P. Francis Crosby, stationed in the Philippines, "Even officers and non-commissioned officers must take considerable care to understand this pistol. Without this understanding, the simple soldier will not be able to have as much confidence in the pistol as in his revolver."

In order to emphasize his impression even more, he told of an experience that had happened to him and was presumably typical: "After firing it, I left the pistol lying untouched for several months. When I wanted to fire it again, I did not notice that the holding lever in front was turned downward instead of backward (he meant the lever that held the covering plate). When I tried to cock the pistol, the plate fell out and it took me a good ten minutes before I understood how it had to be put back in . . ." In 1906 the Ordnance Department recalled all Luger pistols then being tested, and sold 700 of them at a public auction for ten dollars apiece. Additional pistols, including their holsters, were cleaned or polished up slightly and likewise sold privately.

In 1907 there was another Luger test, this time of long .45 ACP caliber pistols, however, they too did not find any general acceptance, and no large-scale order resulted. Thus no business was generated in the USA, with success limited only to Europe at first. Only after World War II could the Luger begin its successful reign in the USA, as a collector's piece.

The Luger in Europe

The first attempts to do business with the German Army were hardly successful. The Gun Testing Commission had already subjected several self-loading pistols to an examination, but the members were united in thinking that these pistols all had too small a caliber, were too delicate and too difficult to use. At that time the "first-born" self-loading pistols were being tested: a 9 mm version of the Luger pistol, various pistols by Mannlicher, the 9 mm Bergmann-Mars, the Schwarzlose 1893 Standard, models by Browning and the Mauser C 96. While the Army was still testing several variations of the

This version of the Parabellum pistol was officially adopted by the Imperial German Navy.

Luger pistol, the German Imperial Navy had already made their decision. As of December 12, 1904 the Reich Naval Office accepted the 9 x 19 mm Naval Model, Borchardt-Luger Pistol. The naval pistol had a 150-millimeter barrel, an extractor with simultaneous functioning as the loading indicator, and a sight with two adjustment steps (100 and 200 meters), protected by prominent side panels. In the 81,250 pistols delivered to the Navy there were, in the period from 1904 to 1918, a total of five different variations. An important change took place in the "new type" pistol in 1906. The leaf spring in the receiver was replaced by a coil spring, the

The 9 mm caliber Navy Parabellum, introduced in 1904, had a 150 mm barrel and two-step adjustable sight. Excerpt from a 1906 service manual.

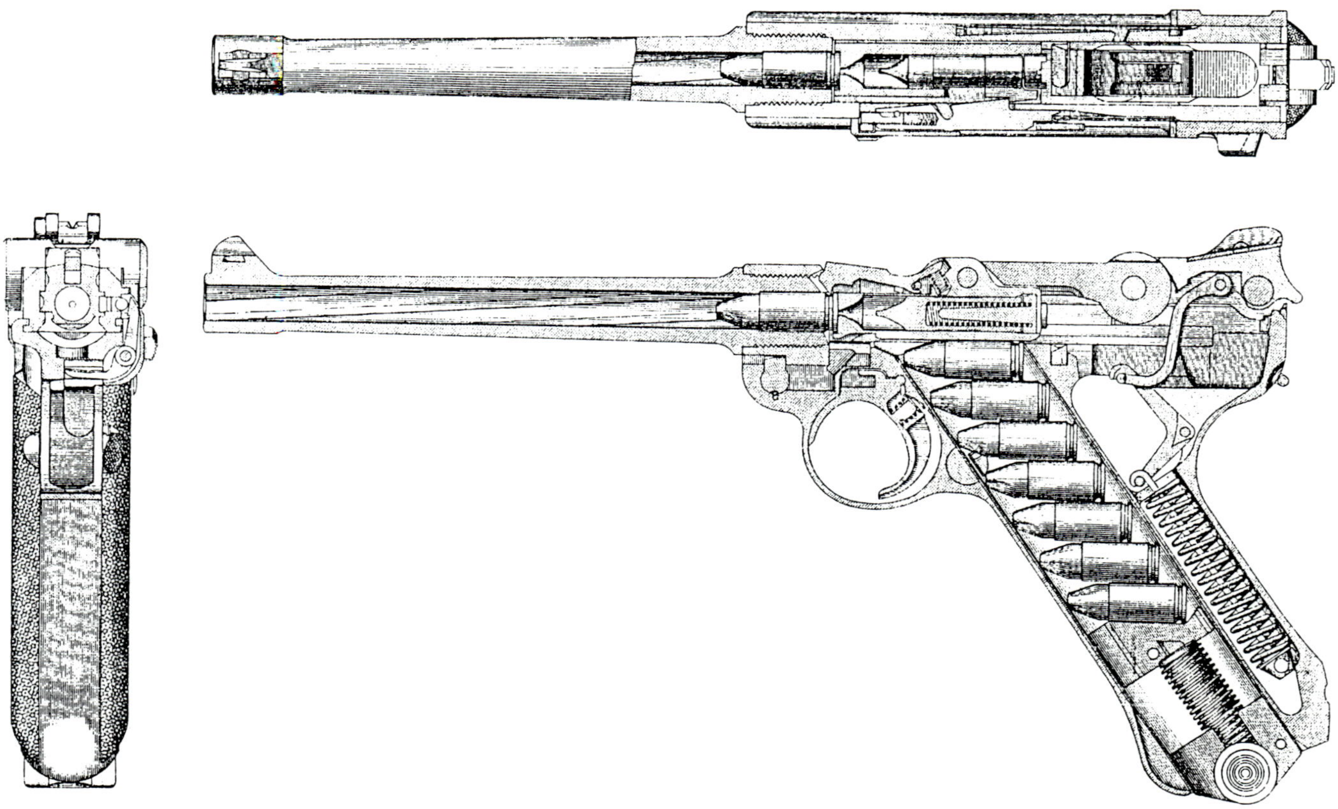

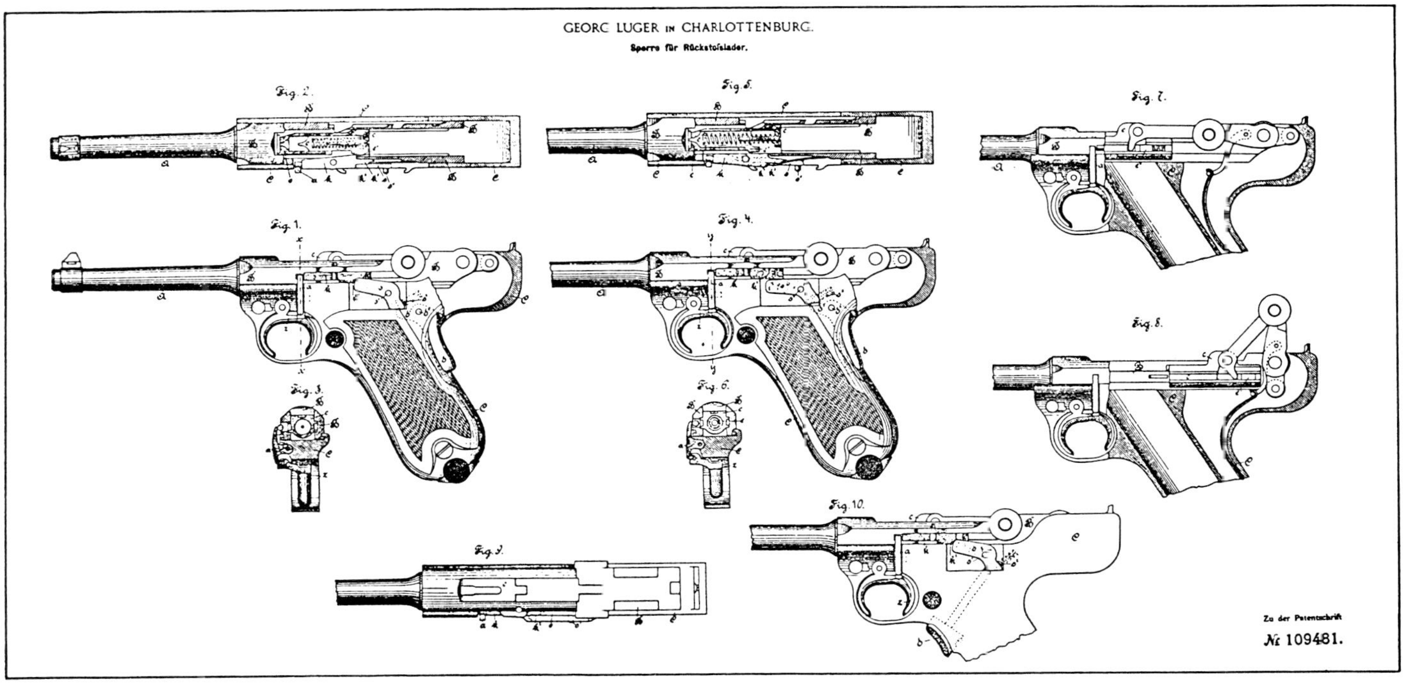

Eigenthum des Kaiserlichen Patentamts.

AUSGEGEBEN DEN 12. FEBRUAR 1900.

KAISERLICHES PATENTAMT.

PATENTSCHRIFT

— № 109481 —

KLASSE 72: Schusswaffen, Geschosse, Verschanzung.

GEORG LUGER in CHARLOTTENBURG.

Sperre für Rückstofslader.

Patentirt im Deutschen Reiche vom 30. September 1898 ab.

Durch vorliegende Erfindung soll eine gesicherte und vereinfachte Handhabung der Rückstofslader mit beweglichem Lauf erreicht werden. Die Erfindung besteht in einer Sperre, welche gleichzeitig den Lauf und Abzug selbstthätig feststellt und ohne besondere Handgriffe beim Umfassen des Kolbengriffes bezw. Kolbenhalses oder Vorderschaftes oder schliefslich beim Inanschlagbringen der Waffe ausgelöst wird.

Die Sperre kann für Geschütze, Gewehre, Pistolen u. s. w. Verwendung finden und der Art der Waffe entsprechend ausgeführt werden.

Die Fig. 1 bis 9 veranschaulichen eine Ausführungsform der Erfindung in Verbindung mit einer nach Art der bekannten Borchardtschen Rückstofslader angefertigten Pistole, und zwar zeigt

Fig. 1 die linke Seitenansicht der Pistole, theilweise im Schnitt und mit unverdeckten, in Wirkung stehenden Sperrtheilen,

Fig. 2 den achsialen Horizontalschnitt der gespannten Waffe nach Fig. 2,

Fig. 3 den Schnitt nach Linie x-x der Fig. 1 von hinten gesehen,

Fig. 4 eine der Fig. 1 entsprechende Ansicht, jedoch mit ausgelösten Sperrtheilen während der Schufsabgabe,

Fig. 5 den achsialen Horizontalschnitt von Fig. 4,

Fig. 6 den Schnitt nach Linie y-y der Fig. 4 von hinten gesehen; die

Fig. 7 und 8 zeigen als Ergänzung zu Fig. 4 die schematische Darstellung des Verschlusses beim Oeffnen des Verschlusses;

Fig. 9 ist der Grundrifs des Verschlusses in geschlossenem Zustande;

Fig. 10 zeigt eine zweite Ausführung der Auslösevorrichtung für die Sperre.

Wie bei Rückstofsladern im Allgemeinen üblich, besteht das hierzu gewählte System aus drei Haupttheilen, nämlich dem Laufe A mit der mit ihm aus einem Stück hergestellten oder fest verbundenen, hier gabelförmig gestalteten Hülse B, dem Verschlufsstück c und dem Gehäuse C, in welchem sich der Lauf mit der gabelförmigen Hülse führt und welches bei Faustfeuerwaffen zweckmäfsig in seiner unteren Fortsetzung als Griff ausgebildet wird. In diesen drei Haupttheilen sind dann alle zur Waffe gehörigen Einzelbestandtheile entsprechend angebracht. Der Gegenstand der Erfindung selbst ist hierbei folgendermafsen angeordnet:

An der Seite des Gehäuses C befindet sich ein daumenartiges Organ s, welches um den Stift s^1 drehbar ist und unter der Wirkung einer Feder s^2 immer nach oben in die Bahn der mit dem Laufe beweglichen Hülse B und gegen die an der letzteren angebrachte Abzugsstange bezw. deren Stütze k^2 gedrückt wird, wodurch ein Bewegen des Laufes und der Abzugsstange stets selbstthätig verhindert bezw. Lauf und Abzugsstange in ihrer Normalstellung mit dem Gehäuse C starr verbunden sind (Fig. 1). Aufser Eingriff wird die Sperre gebracht je nach Anordnung der Theile, und zwar bei den in Fig. 1 bis 6 veranschaulichten Einrichtungen durch festes Umfassen des Griffes C, wobei der nach hinten vorstehende, um den Stift d^2 drehbare Hebel d mit seiner Nase d^1 auf das Sperrstück s wirkt und dieses entgegen der Spannung der Feder s^2 vom Ansatz k^2 und der Abzugsstangenanlage k^3 herunterdrückt (Fig. 4), so dafs die mit dem Laufe bewegliche Hülse B freie Bahn zum Zurückgleiten bei der Schufsabgabe erhält. In ähnlicher Weise wird die Sperre bei der Ausführung nach Fig. 10 aufser Eingriff gebracht, wo jedoch der Drücker d vorn liegt und beim Umfassen des Griffes C von den Fingern verschoben wird.

Wie ersichtlich, ist in den hier gezeichneten Beispielen die Abzugsvorrichtung mit der selbstthätigen Sperre derart in Verbindung gebracht, dafs dem Abfeuern des Schusses stets eine Freistellung der Bahn für die Laufbewegung vorangeht, da beim Schiefsen mit festgestelltem Laufe das Sperrstück allein den Rückstofs aufnehmen müfste. Die selbstthätige Laufsperre dient gleichzeitig als selbstthätige Sicherung des Abzuges, da der die Laufbewegung sperrende Daumen s auch über die den Schlagbolzen e an der Nase e^1 gespannt haltende Abzugsstange k tritt, so dafs bei alleinigem Zurückziehen des Abzuges z, welcher den Druck vermittelst des Doppelhebels a auf die seitlich gelagerte, in waagrechter Ebene schwingende Abzugsstange k überträgt, die Schufsabgabe nicht erfolgen kann, vielmehr ist hierzu vorerst ein festes Umgreifen des Griffes C erforderlich, wodurch z. B. vermittelst des Hebels d die vorher selbstthätig gesperrten Theile freigegeben werden, welcher Vorgang durch die Fig. 1 bis 3 einerseits und Fig. 4 bis 6 andererseits dargestellt ist.

Die bisher nur als Beispiele gezeigten Ausführungen der Erfindung können der Gestalt und dem Verschlufs (z. B. Cylinder- und Blockverschlufs) der Waffe entsprechend abgeändert werden, auch können die Theile in anderer Stellung angeordnet und mittel- oder unmittelbar wirkend, sowie für einfach achsiale, für drehende oder für combinirte Laufbewegung eingerichtet werden. So kann z. B. der das Auslösen der Sperre bewirkende Drücker bei Gewehren an der Kolbenkappe oder im Vorderschaft angebracht werden, nur mufs der angestrebte Zweck, die gleichzeitige, selbstthätige und stete Sperrung des Laufes und des Abzuges, wenn nicht geschossen werden soll, erreicht werden, und dürfen weder die Abzugsvorrichtung noch der Lauf je für sich allein oder zusammen durch Zufälligkeiten aufser Eingriff mit der Sperre gebracht werden können.

Patent-Anspruch:

Sperre für Rückstofslader mit beweglichem Lauf, welche gleichzeitig den Lauf und Abzug selbstthätig und zwangschlüssig feststellt und ohne besondere Handgriffe beim Umfassen des Kolbengriffes bezw. Kolbenhalses oder Vorderschaftes oder beim Einsetzen der Waffe in die Schulter ausgelöst wird.

Hierzu 1 Blatt Zeichnungen.

BERLIN. GEDRUCKT IN DER REICHSDRUCKEREI.

Excerpts from patent documents by Georg Luger concerning the installation of a "block for recoil loaders."

Zu der Patentschrift 312919

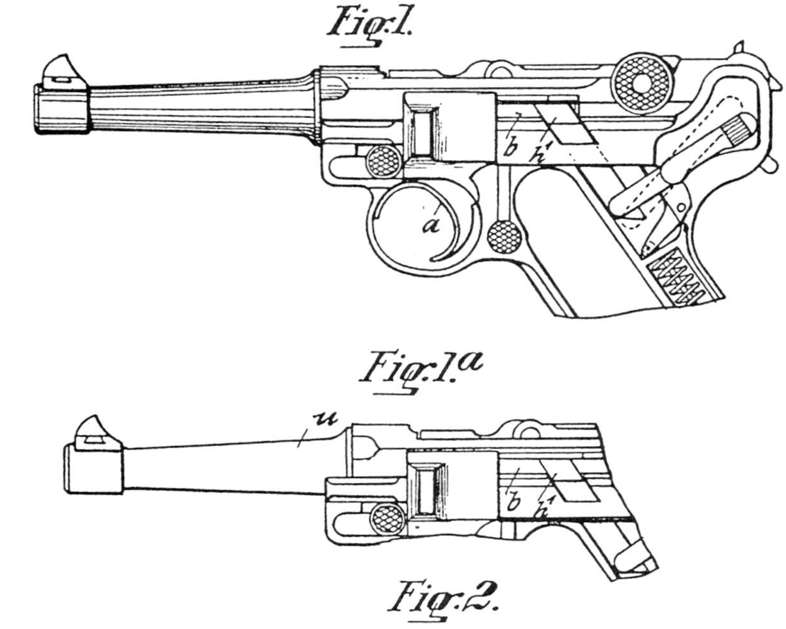

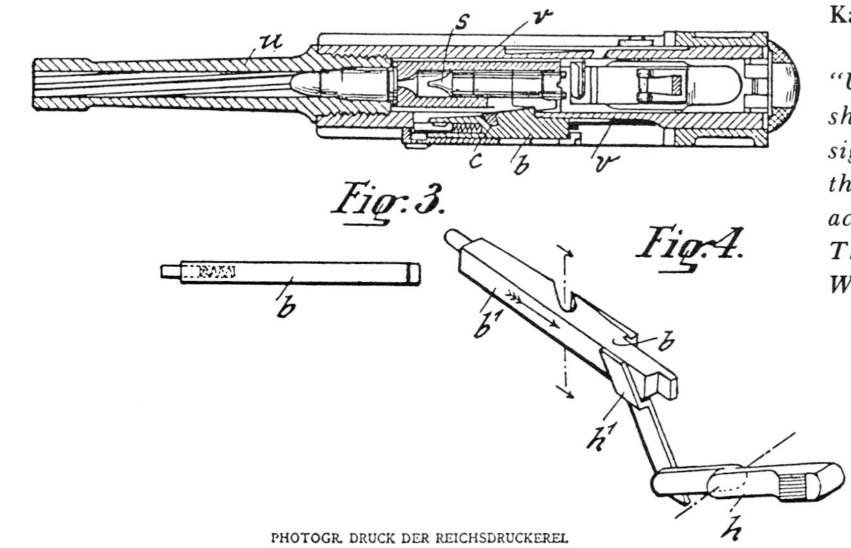

PHOTOGR. DRUCK DER REICHSDRUCKEREI

Drawings of an improved safety for the Parabellum pistol.

knee-joint lock was done away with entirely, and the safety catch, which in the first lots was still set by moving the lever upward, was changed. It was replaced by the other safety mechanism with its downward movement, and all other pistols, except those that had been mustered out on account of damage or the like, were sent to have their safeties reworked, either in workshops or at the factory in Berlin-Charlottenburg.

It was probably because of an Army requirement that Luger had to rework the safety again. The safety lever now affected the trigger bar directly via a bolt, and no longer by the grip safety, which thus became superfluous. This type of safety mechanism was used in the 08 pistol, as well as in the post-1909 08 pistol, which still retained the "long fork housing." All naval pistols were made for the attachment of a wooden shaft, of which two versions are known. The type introduced in 1910 had a stamped plate like that of the 98 rifle. As of 1916 the naval pistols had the "short fork housing", a 150-millimeter barrel, and an adjustable sight.

The 08 Pistol

After the success of the 1904 Naval pistol and the new type of 1906, the German Imperial Army adopted the slightly modified new-type pistol as of August 22, 1908. It was designated the Parabellum Pistol, Model 1908, and known simply as the Pistol 08 or P. 08. This took place, as usual, according to an All-Highest Order of the Kaiser:

"Upon the address given to me, I accept the model shown to me of a self-loading pistol under the designation — Pistole 08 — . The pistol takes the place of the Revolver 79 and 83. Its production takes place according to the standards of the available means.
The War Ministry is to conduct the matter further.
Wilhelmshöhe, August 22, 1908 Wilhelm v. Einem"

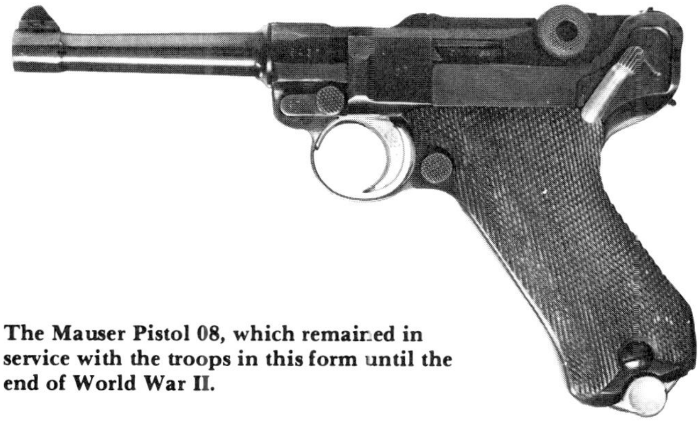

The Mauser Pistol 08, which remained in service with the troops in this form until the end of World War II.

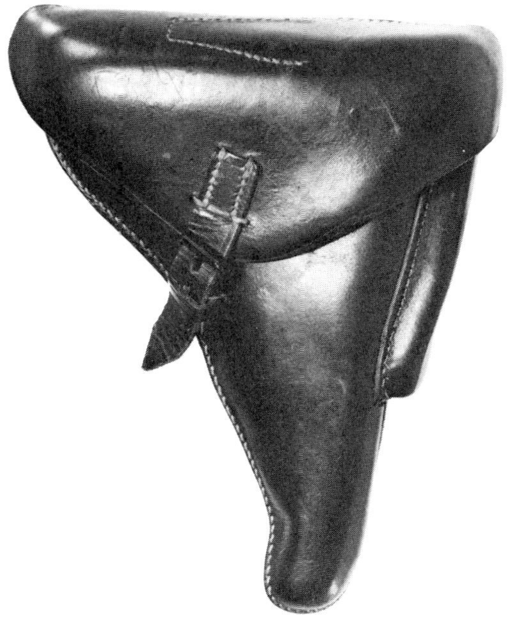

Holster for the Pistol 08, as used by the German Wehrmacht.

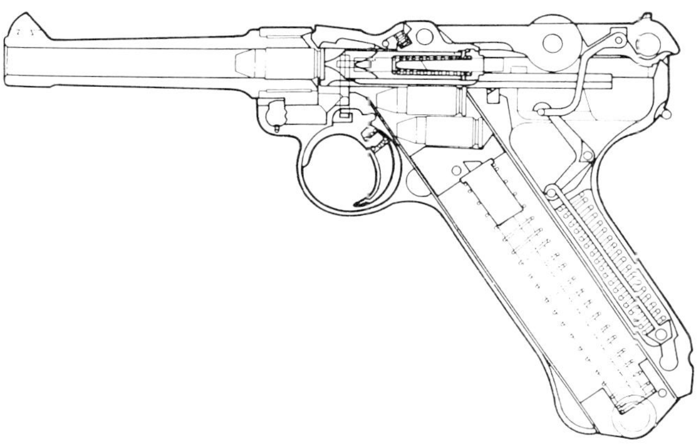

Cutaway of the Pistol 08 as it was introduced by the German Army.

At the same time, the DWM was given a contract to supply 50,000 pistols, which reached the troops in large quantities only in 1909, with the introduction of the Pistol Holster 08. With every pistol there came a holster, a second magazine and a screwdriver. A cleaning rod was issued for every six pistols. At that time the pistol 08 cost the government 46 Reichsmark — in comparison a Rifle 98 still cost 60 Reichsmark.

Like the 1906 model of the Luger pistol, the P 08 had a coil spring as its recoil spring, the extractor served simultaneously as the loading indicator, the grip safety was eliminated and the new safety (to activate, a lever was pushed at the side of the trigger bar) prevented the latter from moving sideways. Pistols made before 1913 as yet had no device to attach the shaft. Many of the pre-1914 pistols had no chamber catch, so in them the breech did not remain back and open after the previous shot —this was later changed.

The Army soon determined that DWM alone would not be capable of meeting their entire need for the Pistol

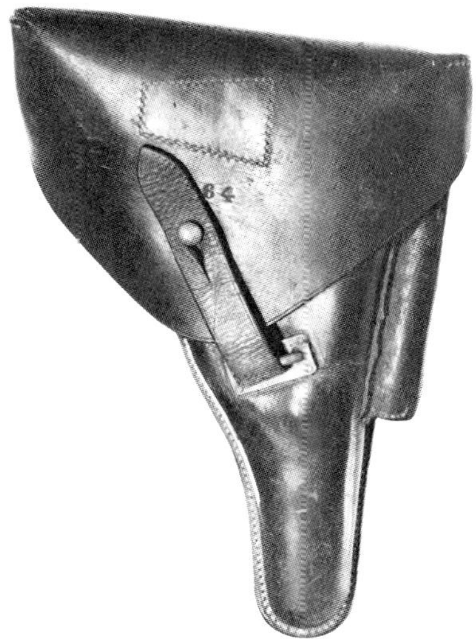

Holster for the Pistol 08, as delivered to Portugal.

Privately sold cartridges from shortly before World War II.

Long Pistol 08, the so-called Model 1917, made in Erfurt.

08 alone, as it had planned to issue them to officers and non-commissioned officers, as well as to various other units such as the telegraph troops, the trains and the medical service, to name only a few.

In order to assure speedy manufacturing, it was arranged to create a second production facility in Erfurt. This facility could not be limited to a small number of machines and cost 26 million Reichsmark at the time. The first pistols from the Erfurt Gun Factory were delivered in 1911. The state had to pay a license fee to the DWM and to Luger for every pistol made there.

By the start of World War I in 1914, the DWM had already delivered 250,000 pistols to the German Imperial Army. John Walter takes this to mean that in the time between 1909 and 1918 approximately 1.6 million of the Pistol 08 were built. In that case, production statistics for the P 08 would be as follows:

DWM for trade before 1914		15,000
DWM for the military	1908-1918	908,275
Erfurt for the military	1910-1918	660,000???

An additional 150 pistols were probably assembled at Spandau and stamped there.

As already noted, production of the Pistol 08 required very expensive facilities. In all of Europe there were only three such facilities: the DWM, Erfurt, and the Bern Weapons Factory. The DWM facilities were moved from Berlin-Charlottenburg to Berlin-Wittenau in 1916, and to the Mauser works at Oberndorf in 1930. The Erfurt factory was taken over by Simson/Suhl in 1919 and by the firm of Krieghoff in 1935. The Bern facilities remained there for many years and were moved, for the

The Long Pistol 08 with added drum magazine to hold 32 cartridges. The magazine did not stand up to long use by the troops.

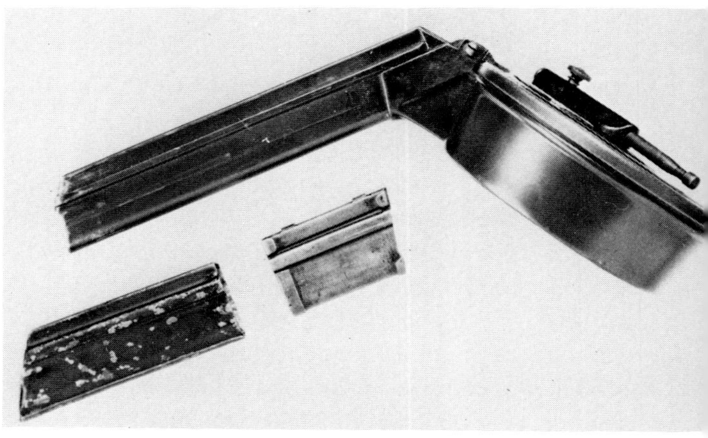

The magazine of the Long Pistol 08 with loading assistance.

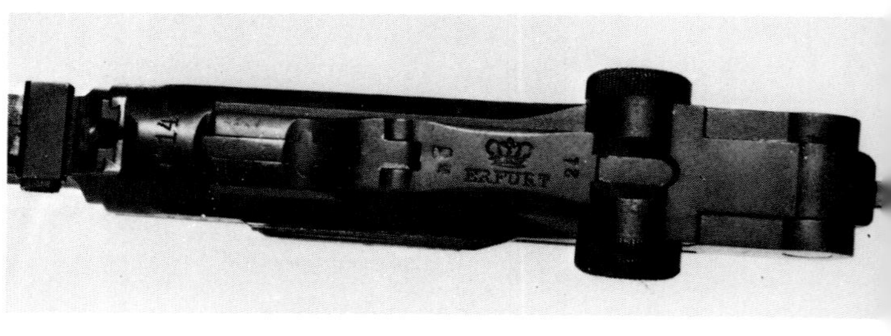

The breech of a Long Pistol 08 made in Erfurt. By order of June 3, 1913, the long pistol was introduced.

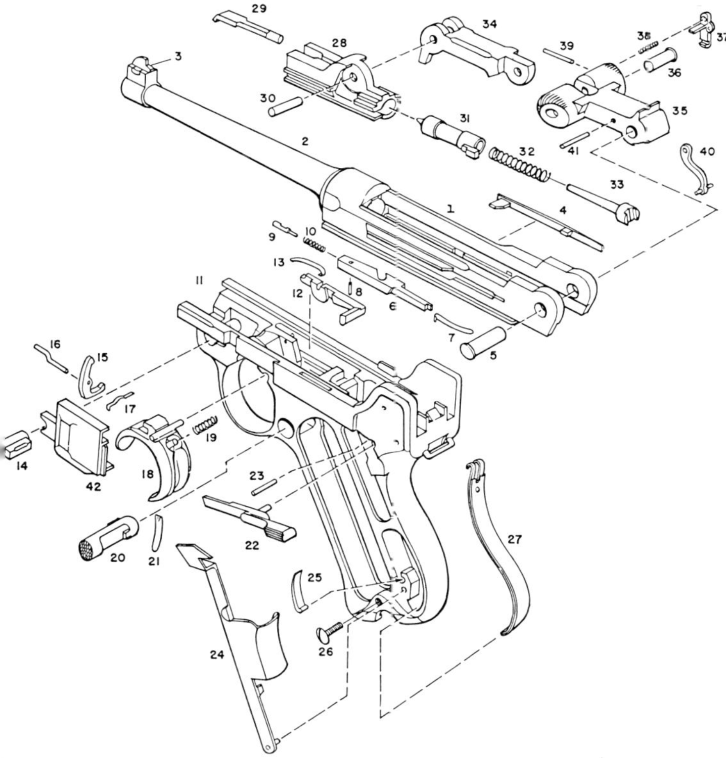

The parts of the early Parabellum pistol, here still with the leaf spring at the back of the grip.

most part, to the Mauser works at Oberndorf in 1967 for postwar production there. At its peak, production was done at full capacity: the DWM produced 700 pistols every day. In comparison are statistics from other manufacturers: Colt built 1325 of the M. 1911 pistol and 375 1917 model revolvers every day; Smith & Wesson could produce 725 1917 model revolvers every day, and Webley & Scott made 360 of their revolvers every day.

This quantity did not arrive anywhere near meeting the actual needs for the troops, and thus numerous other pistols were "called into service", including the Langenhahn 7.65 mm caliber, the Dreyse 7.65 mm and 9 mm Parabellum, the Beholla 7.65 mm caliber, the Walther Model 6 Parabellum in 9 mm caliber, and also a goodly number of Mauser C 96 pistols in 9 mm Parabellum caliber.

While the war was still raging, changes were being made to the recently introduced P 08. A chamber catch and a new trigger bar were installed, which finally allowed loading and unloading with a cocked breech and the gun on safety. Luger received a fee of one Reichsmark per gun for this work.

At this time the 08 formed a link to the development of the machine pistol. The trigger was rebuilt so that its interrupter function was eliminated and allowed sustained fire. These pistols used the cylinder magazine for 32 cartridges. It was later found to be difficult to load, and tests were therefore given up in favor of the MPi 18 machine pistol made by Bergmann.

A specialized form of the 08 Pistol was the "Long Pistol 08", which was introduced by decree in the states of Prussia, Saxony and Württemberg on June 3, 1913. This issue was intended for the field artillery, air forces, crews of watchtowers and observation posts, as well as fort and garrison personnel. This may be the origin of the incorrect designation "Artillery Model" (Ari-08 for short), but officially there was no designation.

As in the normal 08, because of different triggers, there was a "Long Pistol 08 with new-type trigger" and a "Long Pistol 08 with old-type trigger." The long pistol resulted from the need for a handy carbine that would be easy to use, but would have a longer-range effect than the pistol itself. Tests with a Parabellum carbine had been made previously and were successful. According to the

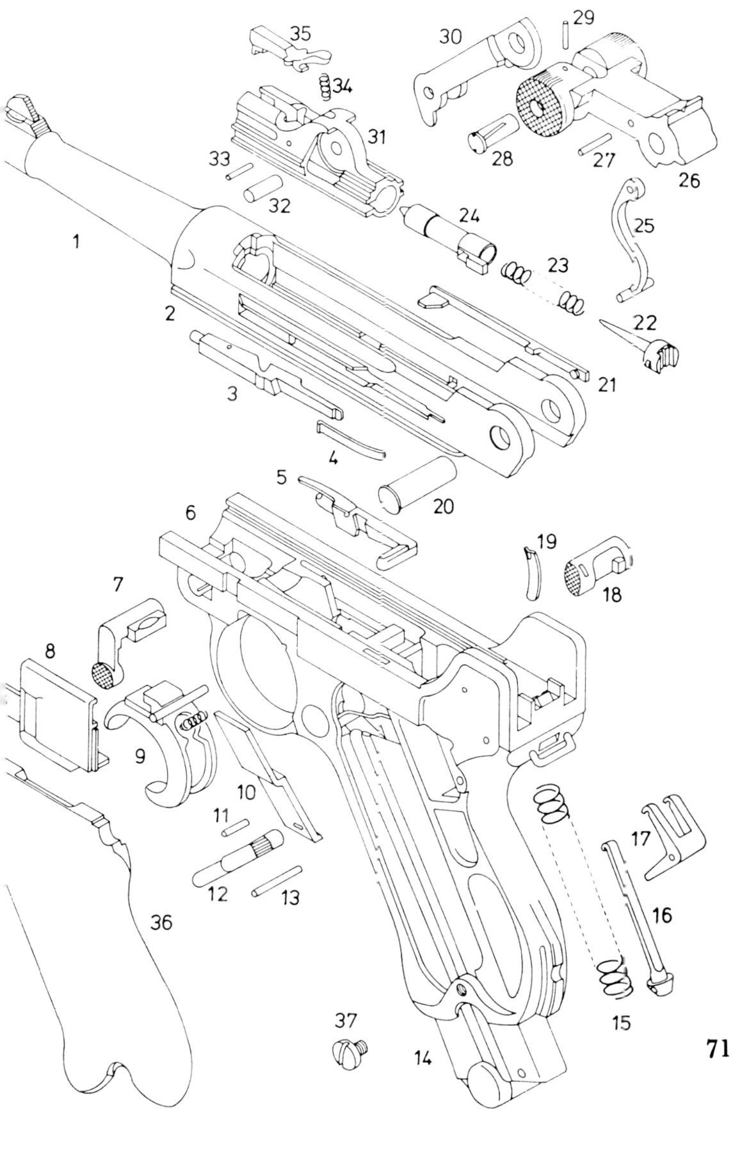

In comparison, the parts of the later Pistol 08.

instructions for handling and training, the performance of the long pistol against head targets was satisfactory up to 600 meters, and from 600 to 800 meters success could still be expected with the correct setting of the sight. Horse skulls and French steel helmets could still be pierced smoothly at 800 meters.

In its design, the long pistol corresponded to the standard Pistol 08. The barrel was 200 mm long and had an adjustable sliding sight with divisions in 100-meter steps, running from 0 to 800 meters. With increasing height, the sight flap swung synchronically to the left, in order to equalize the bullet's increasingly strong pull to the side. Many of the long pistols also had a separate adjustment to the back- and foresights by means of set screws.

Long pistols were used with the cylinder magazine that was built according to a patent by Friedrich Blum (Budapest 1915-16). It held 32 cartridges in all, 12 of them in the transition piece and 20 in the cylinder itself. It was hard to handle, for the cartridges had to be inserted against a strong pressure. An additional loading device was developed for it.

Approximately 198,000 long 08 pistols were built by the DWM and in Erfurt, but here too the quantities were not sufficient. Toward the end of World War I, more pistols were withdrawn from the artillery and turned over to the crews of gunboats and minesweepers. These pistols were stamped by the Navy on the front of the receiver.

After the defeat of World War I, the need for pistols came to an end. By the terms of the Versailles Treaty, the German Army was strictly limited to 100,000 men, 4000 of them officers. The needs of the Reichswehr and the police could be easily met from the remaining supplies, so there was no need to make many new guns. These pistols were built and finished at Erfurt, and can be recognized by the stamped "1920" on their casing, with the new year either stamped into the material in addition, or the original stamping ground away. The private demand was met in similar manner: old weapons were polished up and reworked, new barrels were installed, and tremendous quantities of leftover parts could be assembled as well. This in turn resulted in a colorful and, from today's standpoint, bewildering array of unofficial variations. The "civilian" Naval Pistol 04 and a modified version of the 08 long pistol were offered for sale. In the 7.65 mm Parabellum caliber in particular, all imaginable barrel lengths were on the market. The reason for this can be seen in the regulations of the times: the caliber of pistols could not be greater than 8 mm, the length of the barrel could not exceed 100 mm, and the production of ammunition was also regulated, no more than 60,000 pistol cartridges per day could be made.

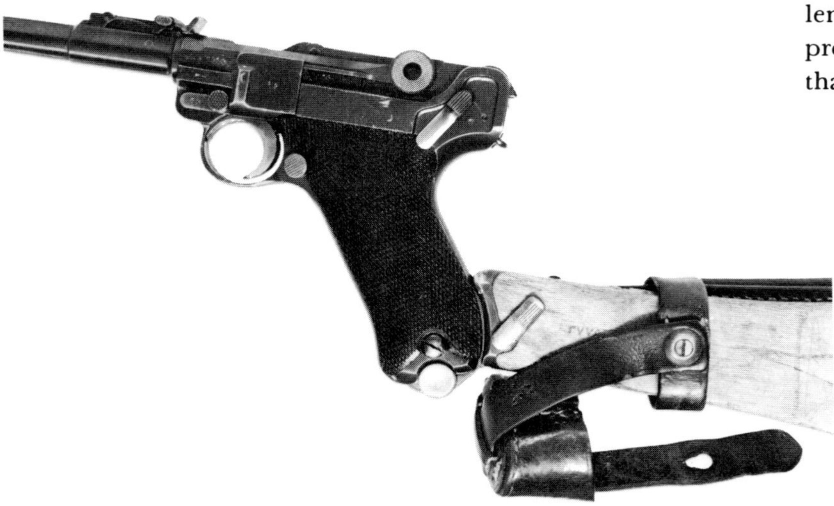

This shows how the pistol was attached to the shaft.

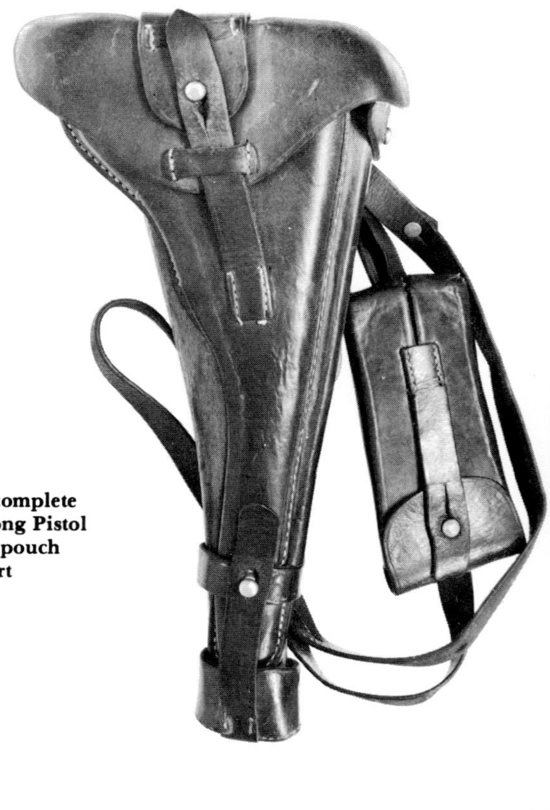

Holster with complete belt for the Long Pistol 08. The small pouch holds two short magazines.

A Pistol 08 made for Portugal.

A valuable beauty: the Parabellum carbine, which was reissued in small numbers by Mauser after the war as an anniversary model.

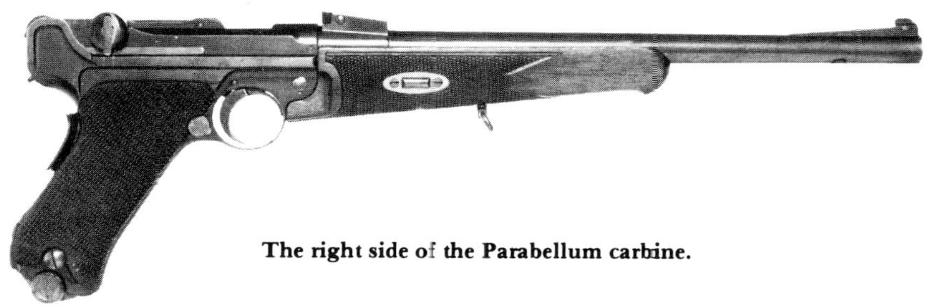

The right side of the Parabellum carbine.

At this time the firm of Simson & Co. in Suhl received permission to manufacture pistols for the Reichswehr and the police. The entire facility had been taken over from Erfurt at the right time. Only as of 1925 did Simson's own production really get into operation, where until then the firm had kept itself afloat by reworking old supplies. The pistols newly made by Simson bore the firm's trade mark on the front joint, plus the year. As of 1928 the year was omitted until 1933, one reason why such pistols are often assumed to be reworked weapons.

The firm was gradually able to attract a few foreign commissions, and so the Parabellum pistol once again made its way all over the world. The firm was able to sell a large portion of its products in America, where the firm of A.F. Stoeger Incorporated took over the profitable distribution and had the "Luger" trade name registered. Pistols were shipped to Finland (some 5000 of them) and to The Netherlands (3820 for the army air forces in the Netherlands Indies and 1484 for the navy).

The pistols needed no technical changes, so the Reichswehr accepted the pistol as it was, and as it was carried. The police caused a surprise, when at the beginning of the 1930s they suddenly required a magazine safety and a safety on the trigger bar. The first safety was supposed to make it impossible, in the manner still used today, to fire a shot as soon as the

The shaft of the carbine, also finished in a finely cut herringbone pattern.

Cartridges for the Parabellum carbine; they had stronger charges than the normal cartridges of the same calibers and could not be interchanged.

magazine was not inserted all the way. The second safety had more to do with the typical danger area of the 08. If a cartridge was in the chamber and the firing pin was decocked, after removing the upper part, the overlooked cartridge could be ignited by nothing more than lateral pressure on the trigger bar, which may well have caused many accidents in its day.

After Luger received one Reichsmark per weapon for the simple modification to the trigger bar (and in view of the large number of guns produced, that was a lot of money), many inventors also tried to earn something and submitted their designs. Carl Walther was one of them, however his magazine safety was not put into production. The actual competition was provided by Ludwig Schiwy of Berlin, whose invention was protected by German patent No. 501,267 of July 19, 1929. Schiwy's modification consisted of a leaf spring above the covering plate and the trigger bar, and riveted to the fork housing. On the front was a pin extending downward that, when the covering plate was removed, would fit into a ground-out aperture in the trigger bar, thus limiting its movement to the side. When the covering plate was put in place, this pin was pushed up out of the trigger bar.

Early in 1930 one of the most important changes in Parabellum production took place. In 1922 the DWM and the firm of Mauser had been merged into the "Berlin-Karlsruher Industrie-Werke AG", owned by the Quandt family. For the sake of practicality, pistol production was moved to Oberndorf, for which purpose some 800 machines and a part of the work force were moved to Oberndorf in the spring of 1930. Mauser continued, though, to use the registered trade mark of the DWM until 1935 — it is not definitely known why, but perhaps it was to be able to trade on the strength of such a well-known name for several more years.

The continuing Mauser production took place at a time when Germany began to orient itself to new politics. Rearmament had begun, even though it was

1934	ca. 10.000
1935	ca. 80.000
1936	ca. 80.000
1937	ca. 120.000
1938	ca. 143.000
1939	ca. 118.000
1940	129.420
1941	151.420
1942	102.760

A particularly impressive Pistol 08. It is said to have been a gift for Reich Marshal Hermann Göring, but this cannot be proved now.

Technical Data: Parabellum Pistol 08 etc.

Model designation	Model 1904	Long Pistol 08	Pistol 08
Manufacturer	DWM	Deutsche Werke AG, Erfurt	Waffenfabrik Mauser
Year made	circa 1900	circa 1900	circa 1900
Caliber	9 mm Parabellum	9 mm Parabellum	9 mm Parabellum
Overall length	269 mm	325 mm	220 mm
Height/Width	144 mm/39 mm	254 mm/112 mm	140 mm/39 mm
Barrel length	152 mm	192 mm	100 mm
Magazine contents	8 cartridges	8/32 cartridges	8 cartridges
Weight empty	970 grams	1585 grams	890 grams
Sights	100/200 m	100-800 m	fixed
System	knee-joint	knee-joint	knee-joint
Material/Finish	Steel/burnished	Steel/burnished	Steel/burnished
Grip panels	Wood	Wood	Wood
Safeties	Grip, lever	Lever	Lever
Lettering	DWM	Erfurt 1914	byf 42

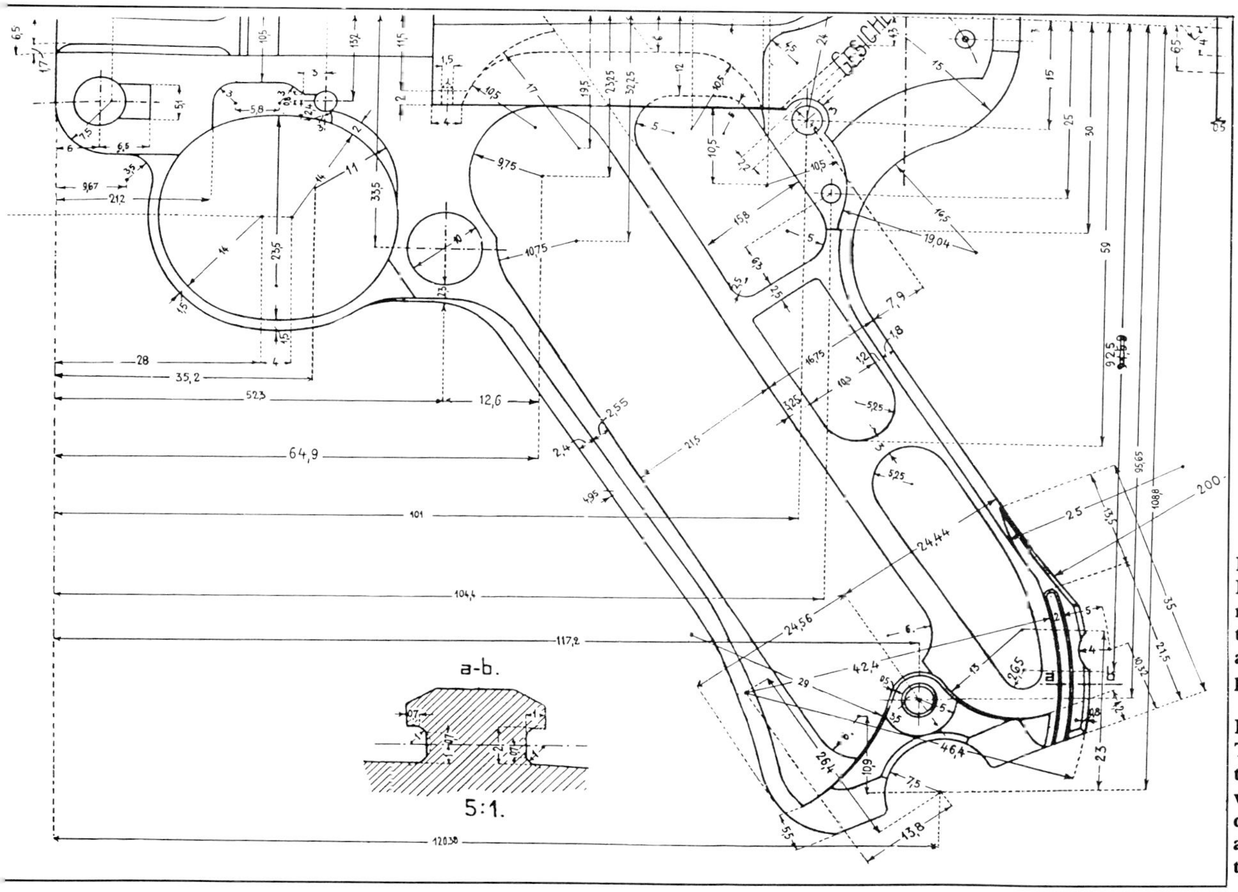

Left: Plans for frame production, with radius indications. Manufacturing such a part is not so easy.

Lower left: Plans for manufacturing the cover plate and trigger lever pin.

Lower right: The barrel of the Pistol 08 with its exact dimensions and allowed tolerances.

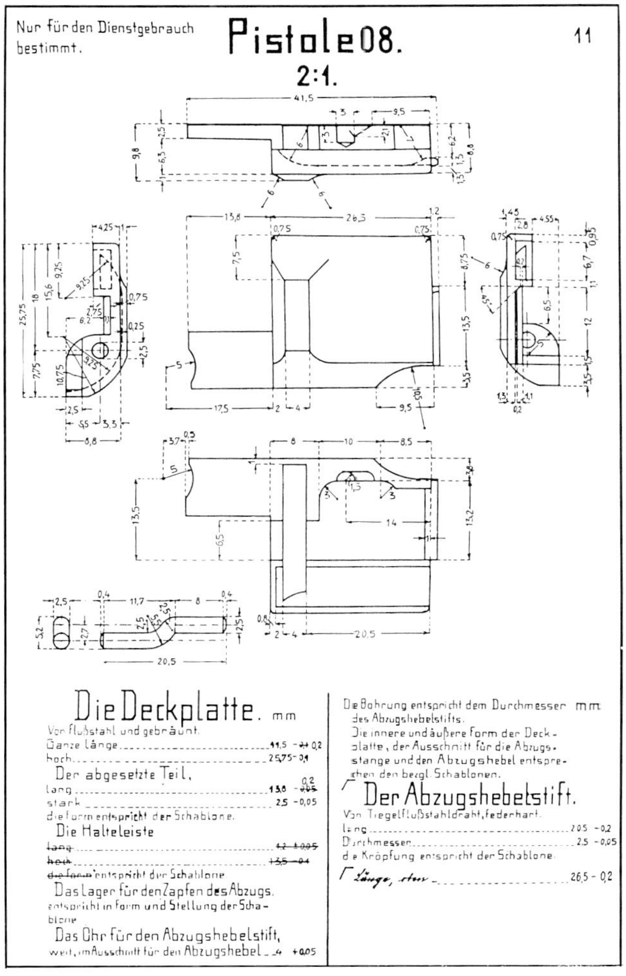

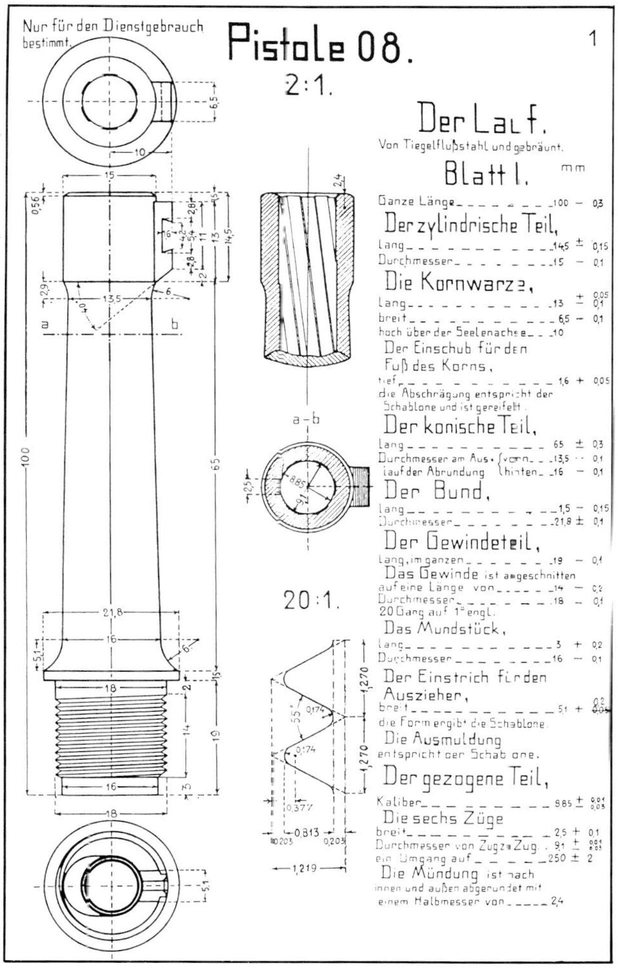

more or less secret, and the military and paramilitary organizations like the SA and SS urgently needed pistols.

In the period from 1934-1942, some 930,600 pistols were manufactured by Mauser for the German Wehrmacht, plus only about 9200 by Krieghoff and a few hundred by Simson & Co. If one adds up all the pistols built before, during and after World War I plus those built during World War II, then the result (according to J. Walter and F. Datig) is a total number of 2,818,000 pistols. The production figures, as far as is known, can be divided approximately as below for the period from 1934 to 1942:

At the end of the 1930s the German Wehrmacht began a search for a better, less costly pistol. One single 08 pistol required 12.5 hours of work time and a total of 778 individual work processes from beginning to end, 642 of them by machine and 136 by hand. In 1939 every 08 cost 11.50 RM to produce, and every machined magazine cost an additional 3.15 RM. A pistol equipped with two magazines cost 17.80 RM to produce and was sold to the government for 40.00 RM. The Walther P 38 cost only 5.60 RM to produce. From the aspect of cost alone, a change appeared to be beneficial. When Mauser also began production of the P 38 in 1943, the pistol cost the government 32.00 RM. Surely that was only one of the standpoints involved, but production could be done less expensively, and the new pistol conformed to the changed conditions in both its design and its use.

Top and center: the early version of the P 220 pistol. There were visible changes at the front of the slide and the rear handhold.

Pistols by SIG-Sauer

It is not completely correct to list the SIG-Sauer pistols under Germany, but it would not be right to list them under Switzerland either, for they were developed in Switzerland and manufactured for the most part in Germany by the firm of Sauer & Sohn in Eckernförde, while their sale was handled in part by the firm of Hämmerli (though some of those produced in Germany were assembled elsewhere). These pistols were likewise introduced in both countries: in Switzerland as the "9 mm Pistole 75" and in certain German states as Model P 225, with the abbreviation P 6. In addition, this family of pistols, meanwhile grown to three technically similar models, has enjoyed great popularity in many lands because of their precise and rugged workmanship. A version with a 15-shot magazine also took part in an

The present-day version of the P 220. Its hammer has a safety rest into which it can be placed by hand.

American competition for a new service pistol to be introduced there, though the decision went in another direction. Among the pistols made by SIG-Sauer today are three 9 mm caliber Parabellum models which differ only slightly: The P 220 pistol, the P 225, and the P 226 with its expanded magazine capacity.

The Development of the SIG-Sauer P 220

Development began in 1966, and its goal was the replacement of the SIG 210 pistol, which was too expensive to produce. It was clear that a pistol without a double action trigger would no longer meet the present-day demands, no matter how well it performed. Until it was ready for production in 1975, the development of the new pistol took place exclusively at SIG in Neuhausen, so that this weapon can be described without exaggeration as a purely Swiss development.

At first, attempts had been made to develop the SIG 210 further. These versions had a different slide, which was no longer machined expensively out of solid metal but welded together out of stamped pieces. This experimental model did not yet have a cocking trigger, as its main purpose was to provide the firm with experience with a lightly made slide. This was soon given up, and an essentially new design was taken up. Development leading up to the P 220 took place in six steps, which deserve to be looked at here in some detail because of the essential importance of this pistol.

P 220 Prototype, Basis 9

The first version was originally made exclusively for the 9 mm caliber Parabellum. At the same time, experiments with an alternative system for the .22 LR cartridge were already underway; this system had the so-called floating chamber, which was a moveable cartridge chamber, which slid backward while shooting was taking place and increased the weak impulse to the point where it was sufficient to move the slide. The alternating system of the Colt Government has a similar arrangement, as does the PT barrel of the Walther P 5, or the PT version of the Heckler & Koch pistol.

The prototype of the time allowed a quick change to the 7.65 mm Parabellum cartridge or the .38 SPL Wadcutter cartridge. Its shape strongly resembled that of the pistols built today, while the type of sight, the shape of the trigger and that of the hammer were completely different.

P 220 Prototype, Basis 45

The .45 ACP caliber tests were undertaken to achieve good chances of sales in the USA some day. In all, 45 of these pistols were made, based on the larger dimensions of the .45 cartridge. Two weapons from this series were used for sustained pressure tests in conjunction with the Schweizerische Gruppe für Rüstungsdienste (GRD), in the course of which 5000 or 10,000 shots were fired. The design proved to be durable, and only one minor defect, that of a spring in the trigger system, occurred. The goal of attaining the same degree of precision with this pistol as with the SIG 210 could not be achieved at that point in time.

The Automatic Firing Pin Safety

Until this point, the prototypes did not yet have the automatic safety on the firing pin. A third series of 30 pistols in all was built with the new safety. In August 1975, 25 of this version were turned over to the GRD and subjected to intensive testing. Tests were so positive that the P 220 was introduced as a service weapon that very same year — its official designation from then on was "9 mm Pistol 75." Thus its development reached a successful conclusion.

The Additional Safety

After testing, the GRD requested an additional safety for the 9 mm Pistol 75. It was to be built into the trigger tongue as a push-button safety. On the basis of the design, this was a superfluous addition that went against the very sense of the concept. The reasons for this safety were actually legal ones, for it was meant to make it possible for one to tell whether the shooter, in the event of a shooting accident, had his pistol's safety on or off. After several tests, the idea of an additional safety that only caused trouble was given up.

The Zero Series

Before the final acceptance of the pistol, the GRD had a so-called zero series provided, which already bore all the numbers, symbols and stamps that the weapons delivered to the army would have. Some of the zero-series weapons were used for additional durability testing, as well as the usual troop tests in mud, sand and extreme cold.

Improvements to the Material

Before the official deliveries of the pistol, now produced in series by the firm of Sauer & Sohn, were made, there was another brief delay. The material of the existing weapon was improved in two places. One change was a reinforcement of the slide in the area of the large ejection opening, the other was a change in a part of the receiver, where damage had appeared behind the trigger guard under extremely hard use. From then on, an improved aluminum alloy was used, and thus abrasion from the pistol's own movements could be eliminated.

In the beginning, the pistols for Swiss army use were made or at least assembled by SIG at Neuhausen, with parts coming from the firm of Sauer & Sohn in Eckernförde. Assembly was also done by Hämmerli in Lenzburg, where the assembled weapons were also tested and fired in. Today the SIG in Neuhausen is no longer involved with the direct production of the P 220 for military use or the P 225 for the police, but production of the P 220 for the civilian market still takes place there. Production of the P 6 pistol for the German police takes place exclusively at Eckernförde.

Handling and Function

All three models, the P 220, P 225 and P 226, as well as the P 6 version with the hammer spur that was slightly changed after a time, are technically identical to the extent that the same instructions can apply in terms of their handling, functioning and dismantling. The minor differences can be found in the tables, which include data on all the versions.

By its nature, the SIG-Sauer pistol is a mechanically locked recoil loader with automatic firing pin safety, double action trigger, decocking lever and external breech catch lever. With every shot, the next is loaded automatically until the magazine has been emptied. After that the breech remains in an opened position. This much can be learned from the introduction to the accompanying instruction book. In fact, instruction books are so detailed today that they really cover all aspects of the weapon they describe. This includes the instructions for finding and eliminating malfunctions in the SIG-Sauer pistol.

To show how specific such instructions are, the portions most important for understanding the weapon will be given here word-for-word and shown along with their illustrations. The German text shows a slight orthographic difference in the directions written for Swiss use.

The Main Characteristics

The automatic firing pin safety guarantees optimal safety whether the hammer is cocked or not. The shot can only be fired by activating the trigger.

Quick readiness to fire with the double action trigger is always guaranteed, which is not true of any manually activated safety.

The decocking lever allows the hammer to be decocked safely to its position in the safety rest without activating the trigger. In the process, the firing pin remains on safety.

The external breech catch lever is arranged so that it can be operated easily with the shooting hand.

The practical sight, also suited to critical light conditions, provides quick targeting.

All individual parts are replaceable.

The anatomically properly shaped grip panels, the ideal grip angle and the comfortable grip dimensions considerably simplify the process of quick, precise shooting.

The enclosed design does much to protect the weapon from getting dirty from outside influences.

Dismantling the Weapon

To begin, follow this sequence:

‡ Remove magazine.
‡ Pull slide backward until it makes contact and hold it in its opened position by pushing up the slide catch.
‡ Check chamber.
‡ Push dismantling lever downward.

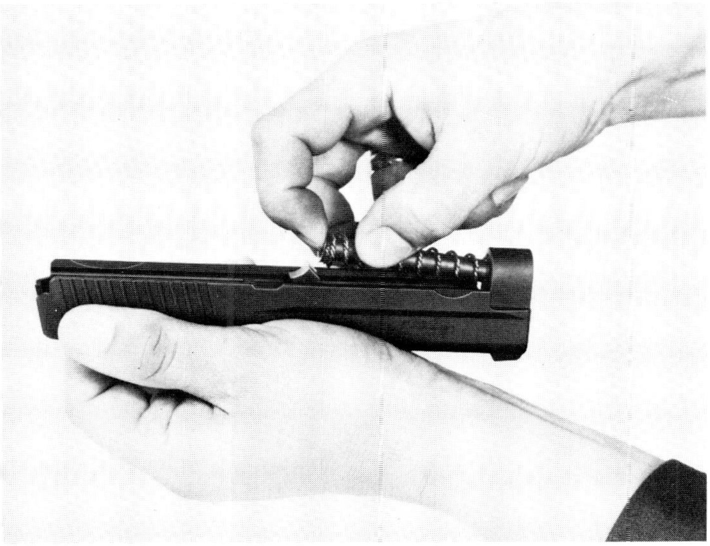

‡ Pull breech back lightly, so that the slide catch can come to rest, then move it forward by hand. Separate entire breech-tube-recoil spring system from receiver.
‡ Remove recoil spring.
‡ Remove barrel.

This dismantling suffices for a thorough cleaning after shooting.

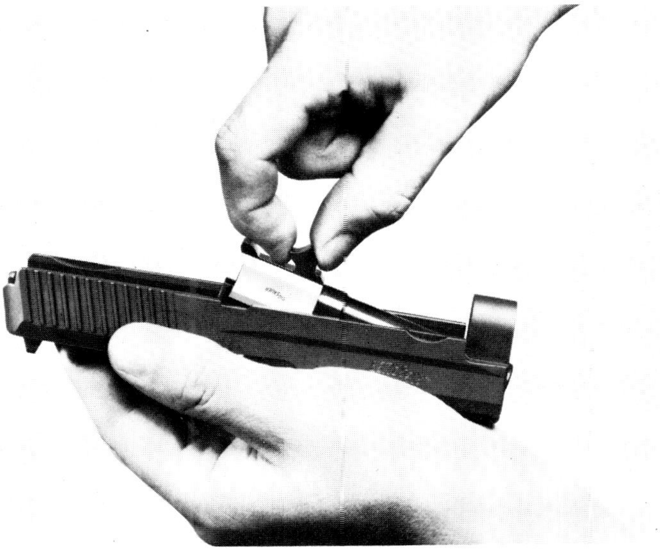

Further dismantling should be done only by trained specialists.

How the Weapon Functions

When the hammer is cocked, the shot is fired by pulling the trigger. The transition of movement takes place via the trigger bar, the safety lever of which moves the sear out of the firing pin-lever rest. At the same time, the safety lever raises the safety lock upward, whereby the safety lock lever is released just before the hammer is freed. The recoil impulse resulting from the shot activates the system, consisting of the slide and barrel, to move backward against the power of the recoil spring. After a distance of about 3 mm, the lock between the barrel and the slide is released, the barrel is swung downward and held in place. The slide continues its backward motion until it contacts the receiver; during this rearward motion the hammer is cocked. At the same time, the cartridge case is extracted and ejected by making contact with the ejector.

During the first phase recoil, the separation between the safety lever and the safety lock is achieved. Thus the automatic firing pin-safety takes effect again. In its further backward motion, the slide guides the trigger bar downward, whereby the break with the safety takes place. Under the effect of the sear spring, the sear and safety lever are moved back to their starting positions. After reaching the rear turning point, the compressed recoil spring pushes the slide forward. A cartridge is pushed out of the magazine and into the chamber. Shortly before the final forward position, the barrel is bolted to the slide again. Under the pressure of the recoil spring, the whole system takes up its final forward position. The forward release of the trigger couples the trigger bar with the safety lever.

The weapon is again ready to fire.

After the last cartridge is fired, the slide is held in its rearmost position by the slide catch, which is activated by the feed under pressure from the magazine spring.

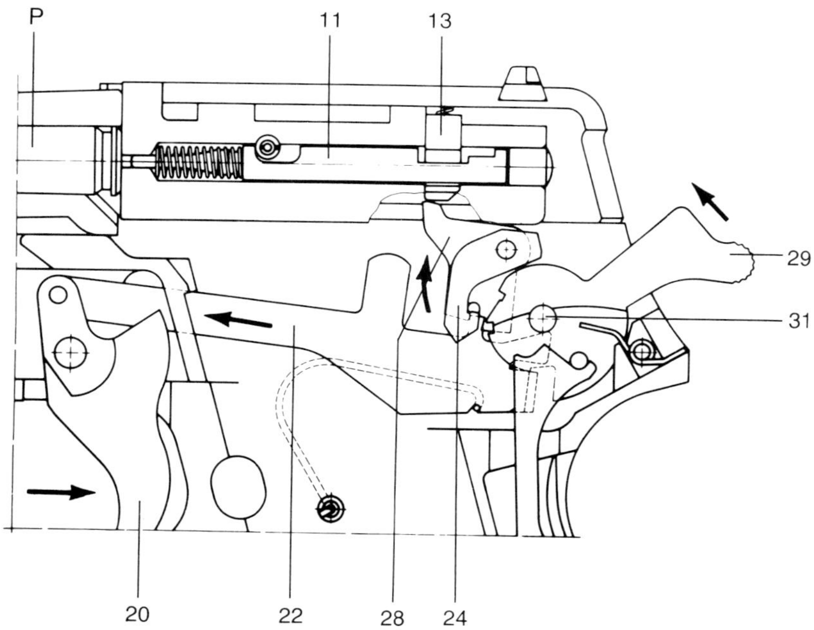

1. Double-action trigger
If the loaded weapon is not already cocked, the shot can be fired by way of the double-action trigger mechanism.

As the trigger (20) is pulled, the trigger bar (22), engaging the double-action notch, cocks the hammer (29). In the final phase of movement, the trigger bar (22) pivots both the safety lever (28) and the sear (24). Hereby, the safety lever (28) raises the safety lock (13) to liberate the firing pin (11). As trigger movement continues, the trigger bar (22) cam acts against the hammer pivot (31) to disengage the trigger bar (22) from the double-action notch. This trips the hammer (29) which strikes the firing pin (11) to discharge the shot (P).

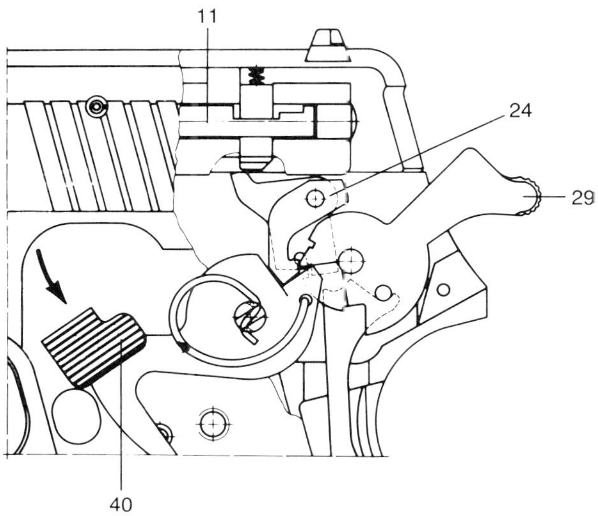

2. Decocking lever and hammer safety notch
Thumbing down the decocking lever (40) takes the sear (24) out of register with the full-cock hammer (29) notch. As the decocking lever (40) is released, main spring pressure drops the hammer (29) which is then caught by the sear (24) engaging in the safety intercept notch.

During and after decocking, the firing pin (11) remains constantly locked. The safety intercept notch also becomes effective in case of inadvertant hammer (29) tripping when thumbcocking the weapon. The safety intercept notch is the rest position of the hammer (29) when the main spring is not compressed.

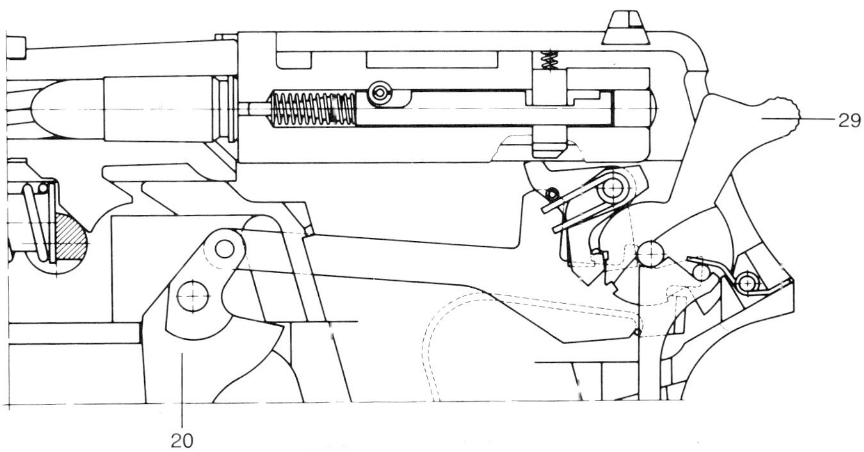

Safety features

1. Firing pin lock and hammer rebound into the safety notch
The automatic firing pin lock described in preceding sections, and which can only be deactivated by intentionally pulling the trigger (20), provides an optimal degree of inherent safety. In conjunction with the double-action trigger, it also greatly enhances immediate first-shot potential. This combination of locked firing pin and positive hammer (29) rebound into the safety intercept notch, effectively prevents accidental discharge of a chambered round, even if the loaded wepaon is dropped in either the cocked or decocked condition.

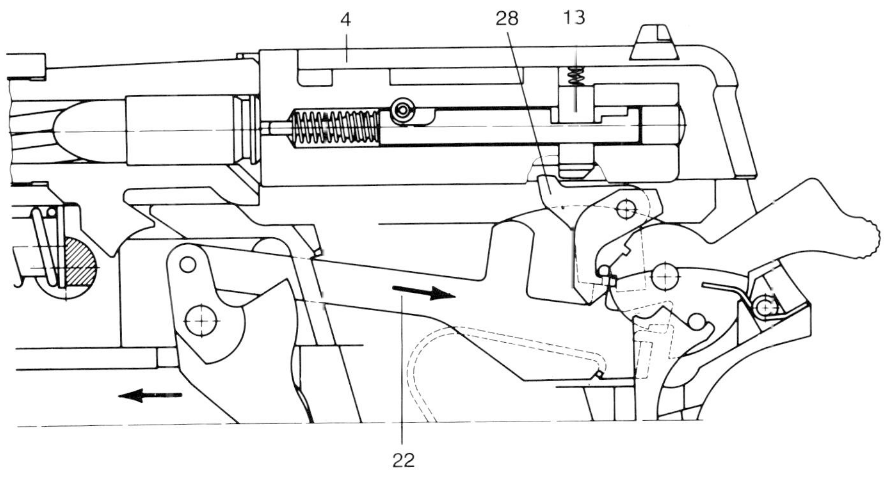

2. Disconnector safety
If the slide (4) does not return to the full forward position due to a weapon, magazine or ammunition malfunction, connection between the firing pin lock and safety lever (28) is not made. Therefore, deactivation of the safety lock (13) is automatically prevented.

In this disconnected state, the slide (4) also cams down the trigger bar (22) and effectively interrupts subsequent trigger functions.

Troubleshooting

If the weapon is maintained properly, malfunctions are not to be expected. If there is a malfunction during firing, proceed as follow:

1. Keep the pistol in firing direction.
2. Pull the trigger again.
3. If the malfunction still persists, check that the magazine is inserted correctly and cycle the slide.
4. If the weapon still does not function, unload it and look for the cause of the defect.

Malfunction	Cause	Elimination
Feed: No round fed into the chamber	Magazine not properly inserted or magazine is deformed or dirty	Insert magazine properl or change magazine
Slide does not close properly	Weapon or cartridge are fouled (dirty) or too heavily greased	Clean weapon and cartridge
	Weapon defective	Repair by armourer
Extraction: After firing the case stays in the chamber or is jammed in the ejection port	Insufficient recoil due to dirt or Weapon defective	Clean the weapon Repair by armourer
Ignition: Hammer drops but shot does not fire	Firing pin jammed in firing pin hole	Pull trigger again or clea the weapon
	Faulty ammunition	Pull trigger again or loa a new round
	Weapon defective	Repair by armourer

Pos.	Designation
1	Barrel
2	Guide, recoil spring
3	Recoil spring
4	Slide frame
5	Front sight 5/6/7/8/9/10
6	Rear sight 5/6/7/8/9/10
7	Inner pin H.D.
8	Outer pin H.D.
9	Breechblock
10	Extractor
11	Firing pin
12	Spring, firing pin
13	Safety lock
14	Spring, safety lock
15	Frame
16	Take down lever
17	Locking insert
18	Lever, slide catch
19	Spring, slide catch
20	Trigger
21	Pivot, trigger
22	Trigger bar
23	Spring, trigger bar
24	Sear
25	Spring, sear
26	Shaft, sear
27	Spring, pin H.D.
28	Lever, safety
29	Hammer
30	Hammer strut pin
31	Hammer pivot pin
32	Ejector
33	Strut, hammer
34	Main spring
35	Spring, pin
36	Seat, main spring
37	Stop, hammer
38	Spring, reset
39	Pin
40	Decocking lever
41	Bearing, decocking leve
42	Spring, decocking lever
43	Magazine catch
44	Support plate
45	Spring, magazine catch
46	Stop, magazine catch
47	Spring, magazine stop
48	Right grip plate
49	Left grip plate
50	Screw
51	Magazine tube
52	Spring, magazine
53	Feeder
54	Floorplate, magazine
55	Insert, magazine

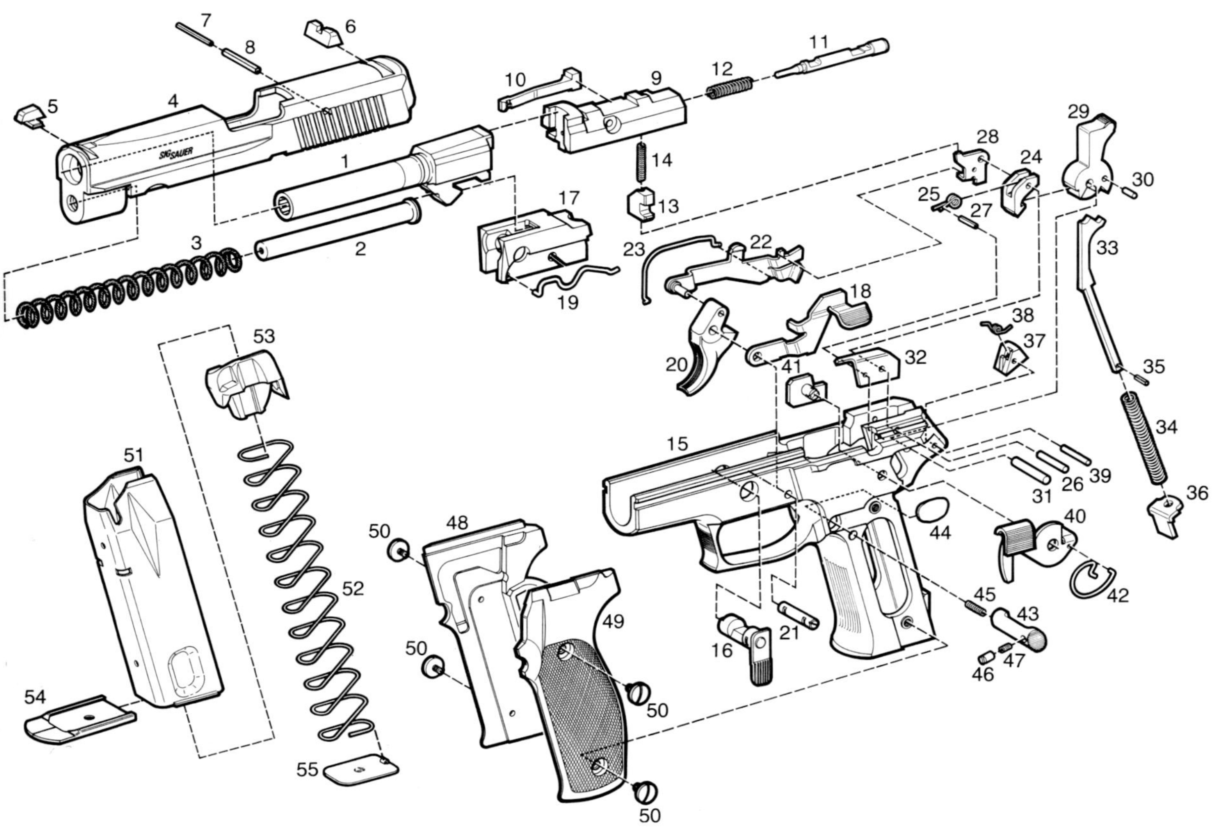

Differences Within the Production Run

The P 220, P 225 and P 226 models have the same basic design, but there are a few noteworthy differences that will be described briefly here.

The P 220 is the only one of the series that is equipped for other calibers. It is available for use with the 9 mm Parabellum, 7.65 mm Parabellum, .45 ACP and .38 Auto Super cartridges with small differences in weight. The comparative technical and ballistic data can be found in the following table. Another difference is the hammer which has a clearly defined safety rest, which can be engaged manually. When decocking it by using the lateral decocking lever, it is decocked in the safety rest. The spur has a different shape.

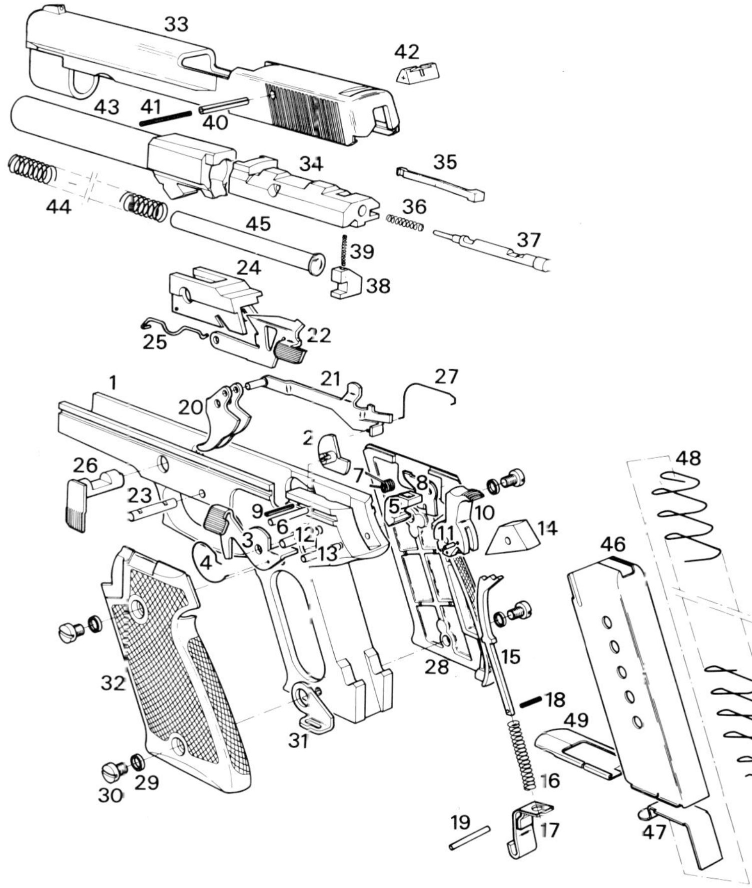

The individual parts of the P 220, with listing.

The individual parts of the P 226 (see page 82).

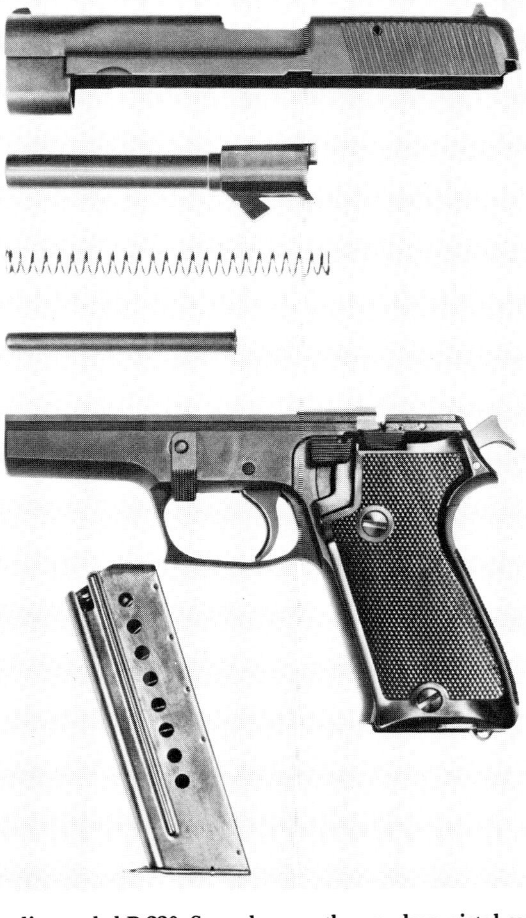

The dismantled P 220. Scarcely any other modern pistol can be dismantled so simply and quickly.

Pos.	Designation
1	Frame
2	Bearing, decocking lever
3	Decocking lever
4	Spring, decocking lever
5	Sear
6	Shaft, sear
7	Spring, sear
8	Lever, safety
9	Spring, pin H.D.
10	Hammer
11	Hammer strut pin
12	Hammer pivot pin
13	Pin
14	Stop, hammer
15	Strut, hammer
16	Main spring
17	Magazine catch
18	Spring, pin
19	Magazine catch pin
20	Trigger
21	Trigger bar
22	Lever, slide catch
23	Pivot, trigger
24	Locking insert
25	Spring, slide catch

Pos.	Designation
26	Takedown lever
27	Spring, trigger bar
28	Right grip plate
29	Washer
30	Screw
31	Strapring
32	Left grip plate
33	Slide frame
34	Breechblock
35	Extractor
36	Spring, firing pin
37	Firing pin
38	Safety lock
39	Spring, safety lock
40	Outer pin H.D.
41	Inner pin H.D.
42	Rear sight
43	Barrel
44	Recoil spring
45	Guide, recoil spring
46	Magazine tube
47	Feeder
48	Spring, magazine
49	Floorplate, magazine

The single-row magazine with an opening on the side holds nine of the 9 mm caliber Parabellum cartridges, as well as those of similar calibers. It holds only seven of the .45 ACP caliber cartridges.

The grip panels are made of black plastic with a clear herringbone pattern, and a strap loop is mounted detachably on the left side. The attachment of the holding screws for the grip panels does not use a separate threaded bushing — instead the screws go directly into the surface of the receiver.

The P 225 version (called P 6 by the police) was developed directly from the P 220. The description and instructions in the service manual at that time followed that of the P 220 in terms of its design, but not as to its dimensions. What was required was a weapon with a maximum overall length of 180 mm and height of 130 mm, whereas the P 220 measured 198 mm and 132 mm. Only the maximum weight of the loaded pistol, limited to 1000 grams, was not exceeded by the P 220.

On the basis of the P 220, a shorter version with the same technology was simply developed. The shape of the hammer is different, as is the receiver, the grip of which is designed with more rounded lines, but not so expansive to the rear and below. The hammer has a bigger spur with a rounded rear and is caught differently. It cannot be put into the safety rest position manually, but has to be pushed into the safety rest by means of a spring mounted in the rear of the receiver. After a shot is fired, it only goes to the safety rest position when the trigger is released, and then the spring goes into action.

The P 6 pistol was fitted with a different hammer spur after several years, a change that suggests a retrogression and is more or less a police "invention." The text of the service manual says: "If the weapon has fallen, it must be turned in to the workshop for examination.

"If it falls several times, especially on the hammer, components may become fatigued and be destroyed under further stress. The hammer therefore has a deformable spur which deforms or breaks off after a fall on the hammer."

This is therefore the reason why the spur of the hammer is pierced and opened to the bottom, as in a fall, it would bend or break, and there is no excuse for malfunctioning. All the same, this so-called improvement is somewhat questionable, for the safety system of the SIG-Sauer pistols is clearly and truly safe. If a user were to let his weapon fall once on its hammer, that would not result in the destruction of the safety function.

Thus the P 225, as the P 6, was introduced by many police units. Meanwhile it had acquired the deformable spur described elsewhere.

The P 225 in open position, with the slide to the back.

The dismantled P 225. Note the spiral recoil spring, which differed from that of the P 220.

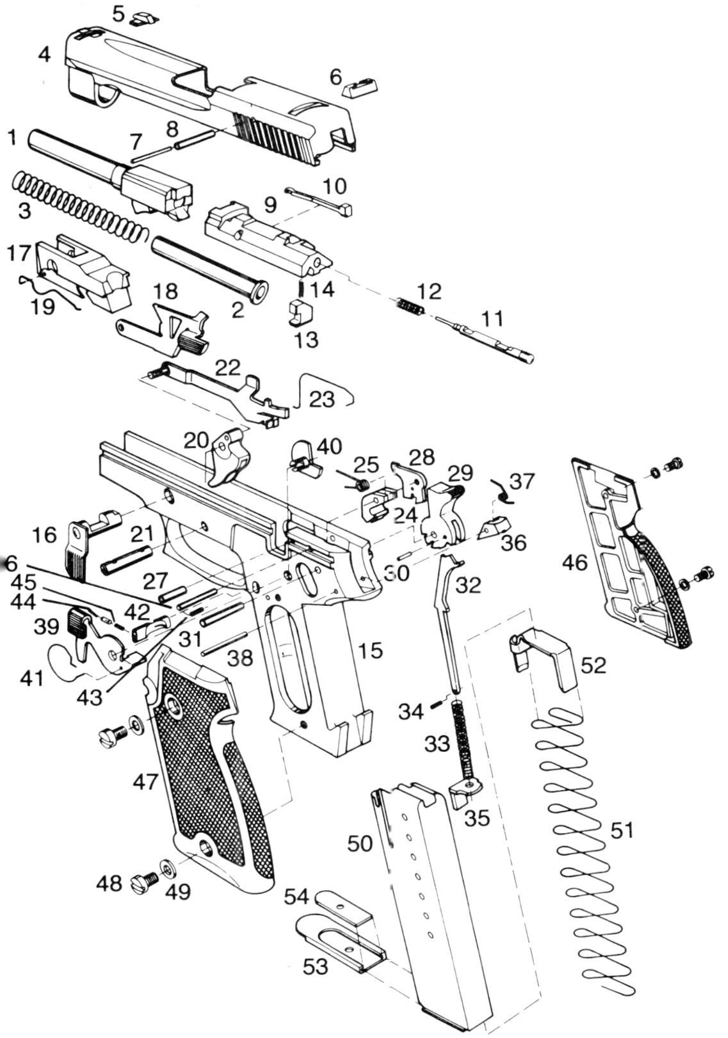

The individual parts of the P 225, here still without the so-called deformable spur.

Right side of the frame of the P 225/P 6. Note the extension of the trigger bar, which extends into the slide's track as a closing safety.

Cutaway model of the P 6, here with the newly "invented" deformable spur.

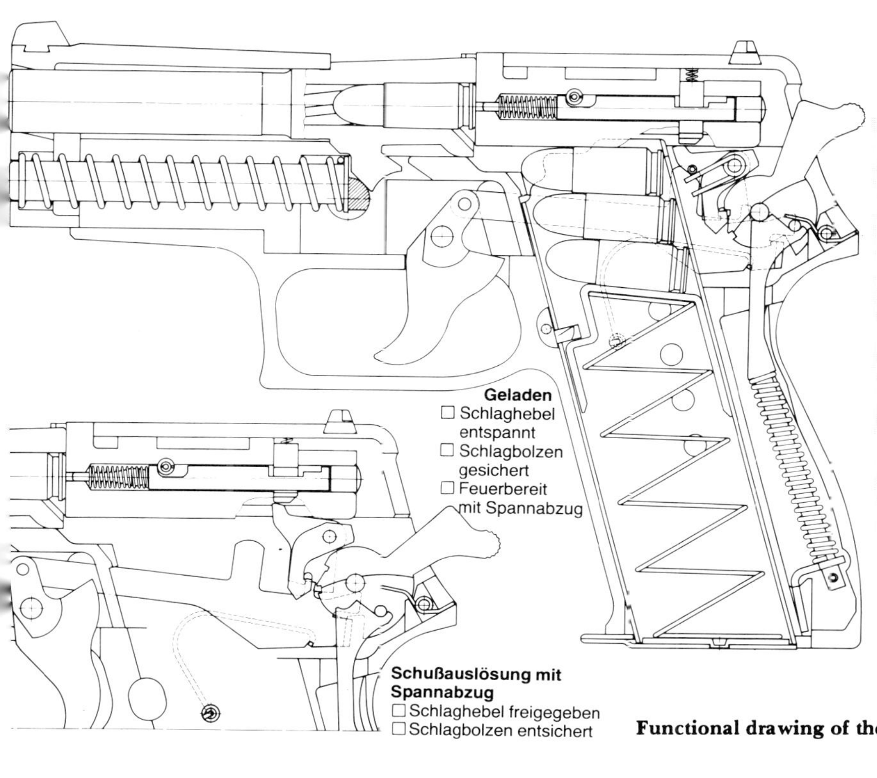

Cutaway model in detail. Note the lower mounting of the barrel and the position of its control surfaces.

Functional drawing of the P 225 (P 6).

But if it falls again and again one should perhaps be banned from the use of such an object as a firearm. Experiments have shown that all pistols have excellent firing performance and react well to varying manufacture or workmanship of the cartridges. The short-barrel P 225 also shoots very well, and in such tests, a somewhat longer barrel did not result in any great increase in precision.

Of particular interest in this respect was the comparison shooting of a P 6 from one of the first pilot lots. The weapon had already fired barely 10,000 shots and did not look it. Only the burnishing (blue finish) had suffered somewhat in spots. The measurable firing performance of the older pistols differed insignificantly from that of the new pistol, and the measured muzzle velocities were also the same, thus the barrel was far from being worn out, as barrels of this caliber are sometimes said to be.

A P 225 of the very early series as a pilotless weapon, with more than 10,000 shots already fired (according to the manufacturer's information). No performance deficiency could be noted.

The P 226 pistol is, as one might say, the P 225's big sister. It follows the new trend toward higher magazine capacity, this being 15 cartridges. Like the P 225, it has a small reversing spring behind the hammer lever, and a deformable spur is fortunately not required for the civilian market. The width of the grip in the area of the slide guide is identical to that of the P 225 to the extent that the two slides can be exchanged, though the functioning is not provided.

Center and bottom: The P 226 is made to hold 15 cartridges and took part with much success in the famous (or infamous) U.S. Army competition. It is a well-developed design with no reservations.

The grip panels are kept as flat as possible, otherwise the grip would be hard to handle because of the wider magazine shaft. It becomes so for some users when walnut grip panels are mounted, for they are somewhat thicker for reasons of stability. That is only a sensible alternative for shooters with big hands. The magazine catch, mounted behind the top of the trigger guard, is well situated. The trigger is grooved on its forward surface, as is the front of the grip. Some details of the sight: The foresight, like the backsight, has a deep white-painted marking for easy targeting in poor light. This groove is simply painted white, and no luminous materials are included as, for example, in the Beretta 92 F and 92 F-Compact. The foresight has a width of 3.6 mm, the backsight notch is 3.8 mm wide. For lateral adjustment, the fore- and backsights (only the backsight of the P 220) can be moved. The height adjustment can be made by catching the foresight and/or the backsight. Six backsight sizes are available, with differences of 0.28 mm, which gives a change of 4.8 cm at a range of 25 meters. Five foresight sizes are available, with differences

It is also available in electroless satin finish, plus with walnut grip panels. A disadvantage is that the grooves of the handhold are not easy to grip on account of the surface treatment.

The grip of the "bright" P 226. The course of the slide, with its channels, is different here.

A look at the self-acting firing pin safety.

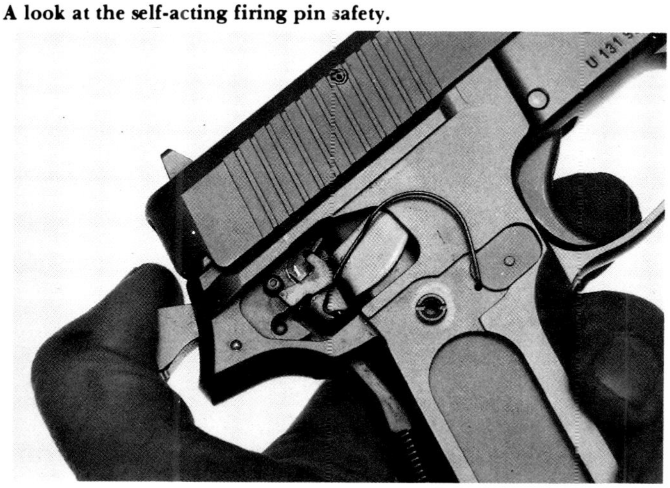

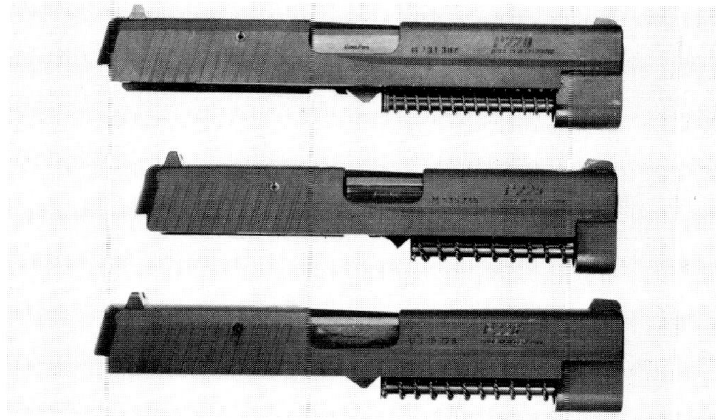

The slides of the three SIG-Sauer pistols for comparison.

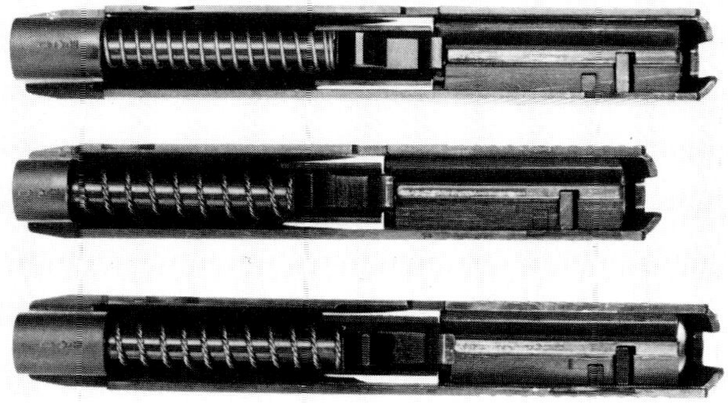

The same slides seen from below. They are not interchangeable.

of 0.14 mm, with an effect of 2.4 cm at a range of 25 meters. In this manner, a difference of 2.4 cm is always possible; this is very fine and already exceeds the requirements of actual use.

All three pistols have excellent triggers, which work as effectively as a sport trigger when the hammer is already cocked. It would be nice to have an adjustable stopping screw in the back of the grip or, even better, directly in the thick trigger tongue (advertising photos from the end of 1986 occasionally turn up that show a stopping screw in the back of the grip of the P 226).

Alternatively, the manufacturer offers as a matte nickel-plated version, a weapon for people who like shiny guns. Its sights are also nickel-plated, with the markings done in red. A sport pistol with a somewhat longer barrel and additional weight would be welcomed some day, and the pistol's shooting performance and reliability would justify such a step in any case.

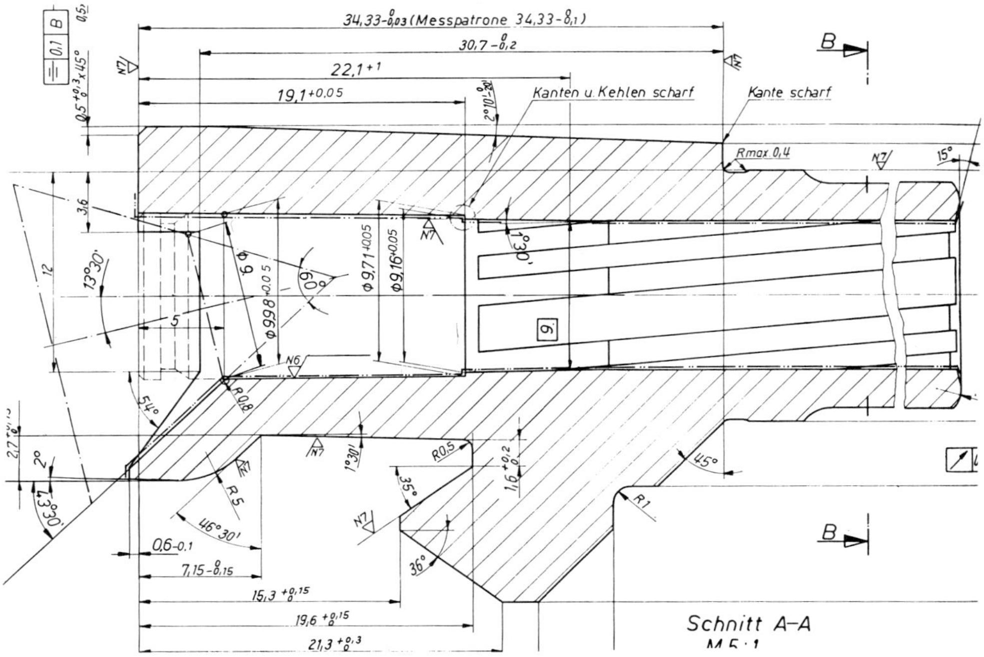

Excerpt from a blueprint of the P 225 pistol, with precise data on the chamber and locking piece.

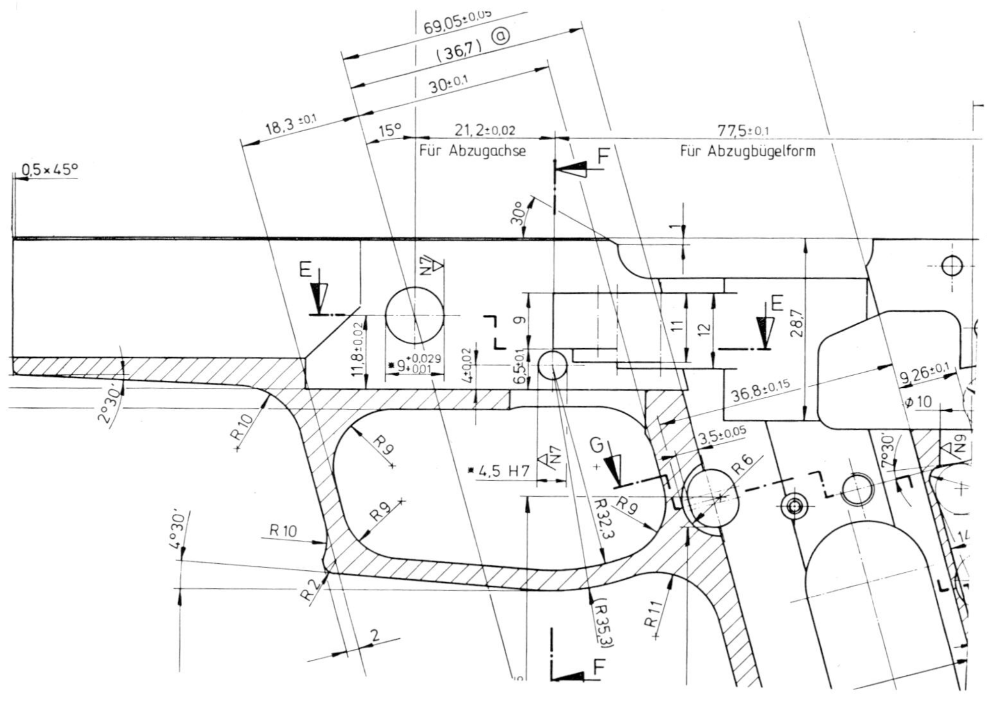

Plans for the frame of the P 225, with a cutout for the trigger guard.

SIG-Sauer 9 mm Parabellum Pistols

Model	P 220	P 225	P 226
Caliber	9 x 19 Para.	9 x 19 Para.	9 x 19 Para.
Overall length	198 mm	180 mm	196 mm
Overall height	143 mm	131 mm	139 mm
Overall width	35 mm	34 mm	37 mm
Barrel length	112 mm	97.6 mm	112 mm
Rifling length	250 mm/6	250 mm/6	250 mm/6
Sight line	160 mm	145 mm	160 mm
Weight - magazine	750 grams	–	750 grams
Weight + full magazine	–	920 grams	–
Magazine capacity	9	9	15
Muzzle velocity	–	ca. 325 m/s	–
Muzzle energy	ca. 500 J.	ca. 500 J.	ca. 500 J.

Pistols by Walther

The sport and hunting weapons factory of Carl Walther, presently located in Ulm on the Danube, originated in Thuringia, where in 1592 the cities of Zella and Mehlis founded a guild and began to manufacture weapons. The actual founding of the firm was done by Carl Walther in 1886, when he, then 26 years old, opened a small workshop. At first he concentrated on repairing rifles, then on building and copying matchlock and target rifles. Around the turn of the century, the development of small pocket pistols began in Zella-Mehlis, and the ever-growing firm was able to gain an excellent worldwide reputation. Further success was won in the realm of sport pistols, and worldwide acclaim was gained through victories in the 1936 Olympic Games in Berlin. Probably the best-known Walther pistol was the P 38, which was introduced in the German Wehrmacht as the successor to the 08 pistol, which was too expensive and laborious to produce. After World War II it was also produced in Ulm, and was built under license by the French firm of Manurhin, which still produces it today.

Walther brought an old tradition back with the all-steel construction of the P 38. The entire weapon is burnished to a high gloss and superbly made.

Unlike the wartime version, the postwar P 38 has an aluminum receiver but otherwise the same technology. In this firm it became the official side arm of numerous police forces and the German Bundeswehr. On the occasion of the IWA of 1986, in the same year as the firm's hundredth anniversary, another variation of the P 38 was offered for the aficionado; it has a grip made of steel and is highly polished on all external surfaces.

The Model 6

Before and during World War I, the Walther firm was able to put a considerable series of very handy and successful 6.35 mm caliber pocket pistols on the market. Today they are sought-after, and highly desirable collectors' items. Their principle, except for external differences, was always the same: an unbolted spring-weight breech and an inside firing pin ignition, plus the advantage of safe handling and easy dismantling. To keep up with increasing demands, numerous pistols in 7.65 mm caliber, their sizes suited to these cartridges, were offered.

Wartime demands called for greater numbers of higher-performance pistols, a demand that all the pistols in 7.65 mm caliber could hardly meet. Thus the Walther firm simply made the attempt to increase the size of an existing model so it would be usable with the 9 mm Parabellum cartridge. The basic type was the Model 4, and the enlarged version became the Model 6, a very large pistol, not easy to handle, which was ultimately built only in small numbers. According to Ezell in *Handguns of the World*, only about 1000 of them are said to have been delivered.

Production of the Model 6 began in 1915 and ended in 1917. The pistol has an unbolted spring-weight breech, and with the cartridge in question, this required both a high breech weight and a powerful recoil spring, which made using the pistol all the more difficult. The Model 6 is 215 mm long and has an empty weight of 964 grams. The safety is located on the side of the grip, and ignition is carried out via the interior firing pin lock.

The sights are fixed, though the backsight, inserted in the slide, can in fact be moved sideways with a tool. Both sides of the strikingly slim slide are inscribed; the left side is lettered "Selbstlade-Pistole Cal. 9 mm Walther's Patent" and also bears the Walther emblem. The right side, on which side the empty cartridge cases are ejected,

The Model 6 of World War I days was the first Walther pistol in 9 mm Parabellum caliber. It had no locking system and was not officially introduced for the troops.

reads "Carl Walther Waffenfabrik Zella St. Bl", the last being an abbreviation for the part of town, Sankt Blasii. Somewhat later, the location was changed to read "Zella-Mehlis."

The Path to the P 38 Pistol

During the 1930s, additional 9 mm caliber Parabellum pistols were manufactured by Walther, however they were only prototypes and model studies. They were made in very small numbers, only a few of them reaching production figures of 50 to 100 pieces. One of the well-known types was the Model MP-PP, which was, at that time, the new PP police pistol and was already a success on the market —Walther wanted to capitalize on this success in a larger caliber.

The development of the Model MP took place at the beginning of the 1930s. In principle, the MP was an enlarged PP pistol, a weapon with a modern cocked trigger, a modern safety system and an unbolted breech similar to that of the earlier Model 6.

It is often assumed today that the Walther firm contravened the restrictions of the Treaty of Versailles, which strictly forbade the production of 9 mm caliber Parabellum pistols by German manufacturers. Of course the entire development was kept secret, but the same thing is done to this day, and the Model MP was merely a prototype that led to the later P 38 pistol. Definite information as to actual production figures has not been found to date, and one reason for this may be that all manufacturer's records up to the end of World War II were lost. Not many of these pistols are known to exist to this day, and those known to exist are all in the USA — they are numbers 5004, 5007, 5008 and 5009, which leads one to conclude that their numbering began with 5000.

Another variant of the Model MP has a different hammer spur, which is rounded in the back. This version is part of the second series. The differences in the MP with the rounded spur include, for example, the catch lever attached to the left side, which required a corresponding machined-out area on the bottom of the slide. The magazine catch has been moved down into the receiver, and the pistol is somewhat smaller overall than the first Model MP (also called MP-PP; James L. Rankin, *Walther Pistols 1908-1983*). The system is different, for the MP version with the rounded spur has a delaying mechanism and thus a separate bolting piece — thus it is the only known PP pistol with an additional bolt.

Further tests followed, using a version with a concealed hammer. These MP versions with concealed hammers were exclusively handmade and can likewise be classified only as test models or prototypes. In the first versions of the MP with a concealed hammer, the barrel is free — this type is popularly known as the "bridgeless" Model MP. The pistol has two recoil springs running on rails in the receiver, a feature that was retained successfully in the later P 38. The sliding of the barrel on the rails in the grip proved to be insufficiently stable, despite the lateral reinforcements; the barrel could spring out of its grooves, and the performance of the bullets fired from this pistol was correspondingly outside the norm. However, it is important that many design features could be included in this version for further development.

From 1935-1937 the Model AP was developed with the letters AP standing for Army Pistol. Most of the AP pistols are of 9 mm Parabellum caliber, but a few were built for the .45 ACP cartridge. The Model AP can be regarded as a further development of the Model MP with a concealed hammer; both the Model MP and the Model AP were the forerunners of the Model HP and the P 38.

The Model AP has just one reinforcing rib on each side of the grip, where the MP had two ribs. The method of dismantling it was improved, with two separate levers being attached to the left side. The dismantling lever is to the front, and the slide catch is above the trigger — thus it was retained. What was eliminated was the serious fault of the barrel jumping out of its attachments. The slide had a bridge in front that became the typical feature of this whole series from then on.

The lock of the AP was a pioneering feature. It consists of the well-known swinging bolt under the barrel, with two upper extensions which fit into grooves inside the slide. After a short joint recoil of the barrel and slide, the locking bolt strikes its contact point in the frame and

Here is the patented swinging bolt as it was first portrayed in a patent drawing. Excerpt from a patent document for Fritz Walther and Fritz Barthelmes in 1938.

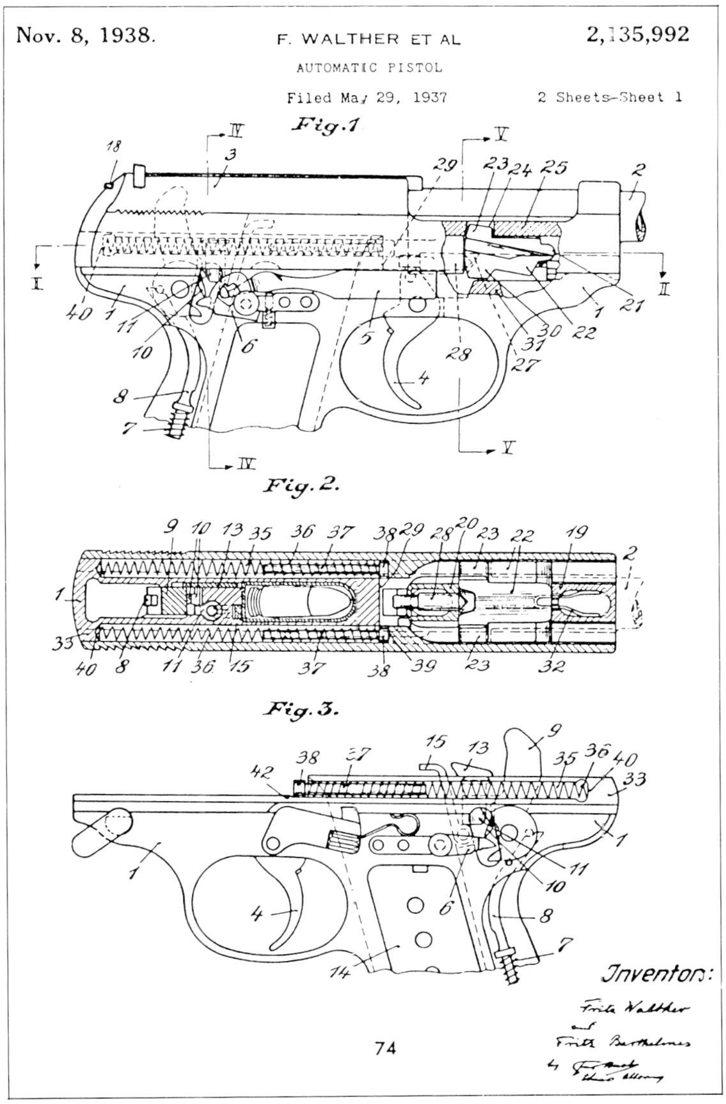

This shows the signal rod and the accompanying cover plate, from a 1939 patent document for Fritz Walther.

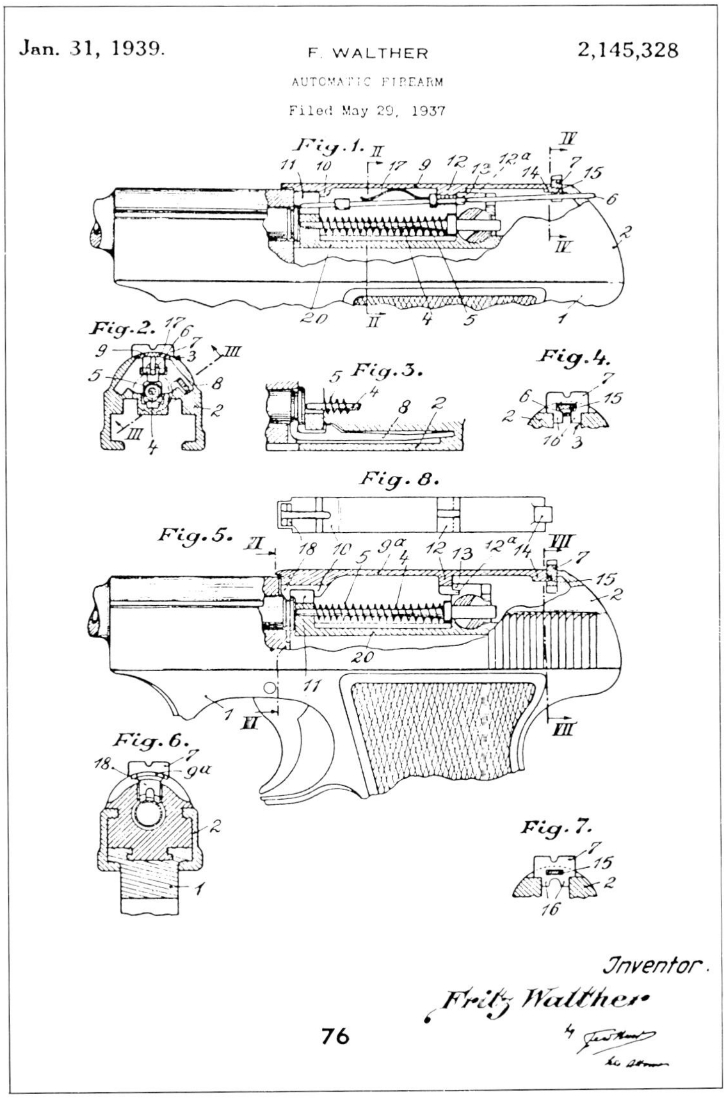

forces the swinging bolt downward. Its extensions move into the grooves in the slide, and the slide can move backward alone against the pressure of the two lateral recoil springs.

Within the AP series, Walther made numerous experiments, and versions are known to exist with varying barrel lengths, as well as a version with an overly long barrel and an attachable shaft, which can serve as a holster similarly to that of the Mauser C 96, along with a matching belt. No definite information on the production figures of the Model AP are available, but some 200 of them are said to have been built.

There was also a so-called second model of the AP type, this time with an external hammer, as the successor to a similar version that still had an internal hammer. This weapon is very similar to the HP pistol and the 38 Pistol. Even at that time, the mid-1930s, first attempts were being made to manufacture pistols out of stamped pieces of sheet metal, a production technique that led to further experiments at the Walther works toward the end of the war. A single Model MP made of sheet steel exists in the USA, and is said to be the only one in existence.

During the mid-1930s the Wehrmacht High Command called for a new pistol intended primarily to replace the 08 pistol, which was too expensive to produce. Simplicity in all components as well as individual parts was called for, plus as low a number of parts as possible, interchangeable parts despite their being made in different factories, and ease of dismantling; only the 9 mm Parabellum caliber was considered. Shortly thereafter, in 1937, four German firms offered their suggestions: the firms were Mauser, Walther, Sauer & Sohn, and the Berlin-Suhler Waffen und Fahrzeugwerke. The Walther firm had an advantage, for it had been able to gain much experience from its own pre-series weapons.

The responsible authorities required several minor changes to the Model HP pistol and then introduced it in 1938 — thus it was designated P 38 by the Wehrmacht. The Model HP continued to be produced for the civilian market. It was available in 9 mm Parabellum, .38 Super, /45 ACP and 7.65 mm Parabellum calibers. The firing pin was originally still angular. Only as of April 1940 was it made round, another simplification in manufacturing. Technically the Model HP was almost completely like the official P 38 pistol, which reached troops only in 1940 even though it had been adopted in 1938. The Swedish Army introduced the HP pistol in 1939 under the designation of m/39 and ordered about 1500.

The Model MP, one of the early stages on the way to the famous P 38.

A later Model MP that looks more like the P 38.

The frame is almost like the P 38, and the slide encloses the barrel as far as the muzzle. This was a first attempt at using price-decreasing stamped parts.

At least that many were delivered before production for foreign markets, as well as the domestic civilian market, but were entirely halted because of military requirements. The weapons sent to Sweden can be recognized by the letter H before the serial number on the right side of the grip at the front.

The early P 38's were almost identical to the Model HP, and many pistols were assembled using parts from HP production. The main features were the somewhat different inscription, the external extractor, the rectangular firing pin, the signal rod and the two operating levers on the left side of the weapon. In terms of attached grip panels, there were versions with black panels bearing a pressed herringbone pattern, panels made of bakelite with longitudinal grooves, and later pressed panels made of sheet metal.

Pistol slides made for the Wehrmacht had the familiar maker's name on the left side, the P 38 designation and the serial number. This remained unchanged until 1940, by which time some 13,000 pistols had been completed. The government then changed the inscription and, for the first time, introduced a code system that was intended to make it difficult for the enemy to identify the place of origin of military equipment. The Walther works in Zella-Mehlis were given the number 480, which was stamped on the left side of the slide instead of the Walther firm's name and emblem.

At the end of 1940 this code was changed and the better-known letter code was introduced. Walther was given the code letters ac. At the end of 1941 the Walther works in Oberndorf received a contract to manufacture P 38 pistols, and the code letters byf were used for these Mauser weapons. In 1943 the Spreewerke GmbH in Berlin also began manufacturing, using the code letters cyq. At the end of the war the code for the Mauser works was changed again, this time to SVW. Despite the codes, numerous P 38 pistols cannot be identified clearly from their markings, because in 1943 approximately 3000 pistols were delivered without any code lettering.

The prices of the two most important service pistols of those times are of interest. A document dated January 1943 gives a contractual price of 32 Reichsmark for the P 38, while the 08 pistol cost 35 Reichsmark at the same time. The difference in price may seem small, but when one thinks of the great quantities manufactured, one can see that even the smallest differences in prices add up. With a good million P 38's manufactured, the difference is enough to pay for about a dozen Tiger tanks. Seen from another angle, the Messerschmitt Bf 109 cost some 44,000 Reichsmark in 1944.

The Model HP can scarcely be told from the P 38 and shows no noteworthy design differences.

The lettering of another HP in detail, though scarcely visible in a photograph.

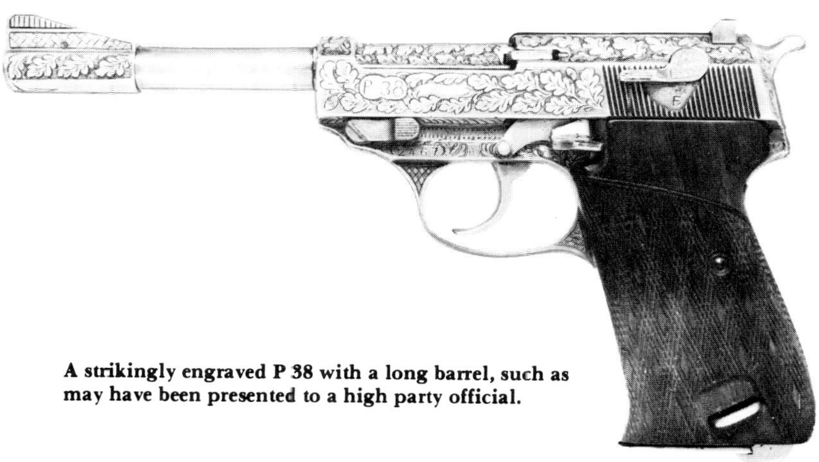

A strikingly engraved P 38 with a long barrel, such as may have been presented to a high party official.

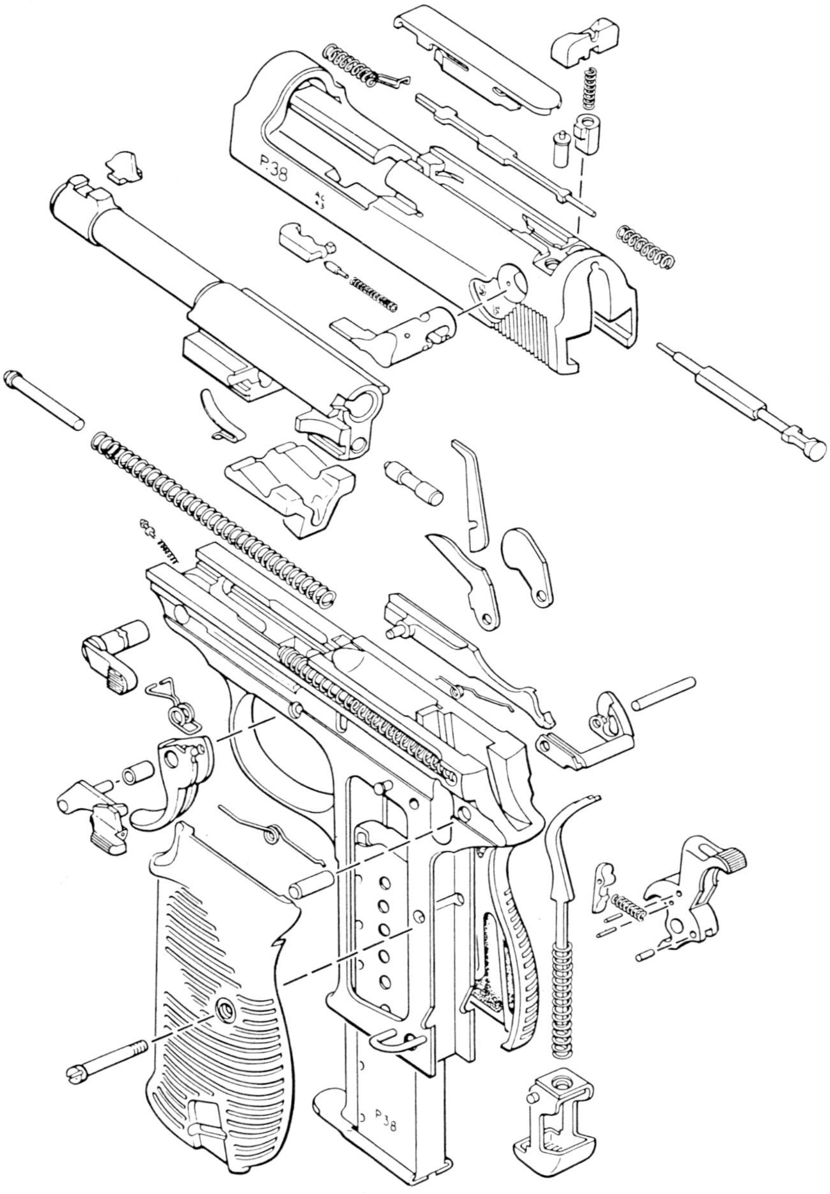

The parts of the P 38 as made in Germany during the war.

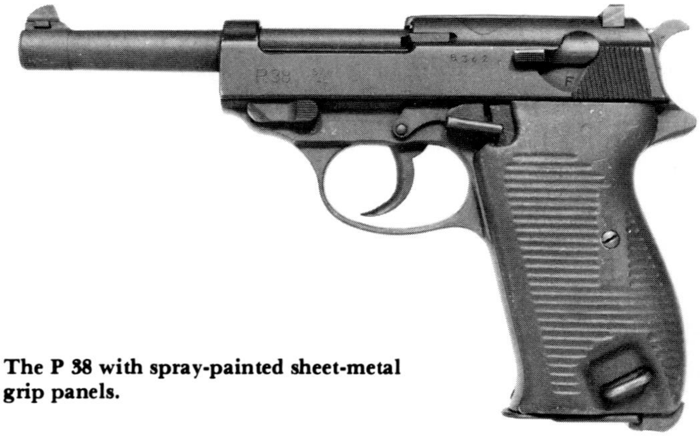

The P 38 with spray-painted sheet-metal grip panels.

The P 38 dismantled for cleaning. The swinging bolt under the barrel and the cutouts in the window of the slide are easy to see.

A P 38 with byf 43 code marking. This was the typical service pistol after series production began.

The war required economies of all kind. This P 38 has a gray phosphate surface.

The Walther "Tin Pistol"

To compensate for the high losses of weapons by the fighting forces, the Wehrmacht High Command promoted simplified designs and thus set up the following requirements: very simple production of all individual parts, easy weapon assembly, and trouble-free functioning with whatever cartridges were used.

During this time, several very unusual pistols were developed, including the famous Volkspistole (People's Pistol), whose origin is still disputed. The Walther firm probably developed at least three different prototypes or small series, though their production numbers are no longer known. One of them was a sheet-metal version of the P 38 with a similar locking technique, but assembled from stamped sheet-metal parts; only the actual receiver was still reminiscent of the P 38.

Another sheet-metal pistol shows similar technology to this version, which is depicted here. The essential difference is that it has a cocking trigger and a differently shaped slide.

The pistol shown here is owned by the Walther firm in Ulm and was reworked slightly as a showpiece. The barrel seems to have been made new. The weapon has the number 105 on the slide and the bottom, but it is not known whether this was meant to be a customary serial number. American sources at least assume that it was not. Toward the front of the slide, on both its inner and outer surfaces, the faint number 12 can be seen — the origin of this number cannot be determined either.

The "Tin Pistol" is striking from the outside, since it is obviously made of sheet-metal parts. The parts are relatively thin, an indication of how great the shortage of materials must have been at the time. Only four screws are used in the weapon, and hold the grip panels onto the receiver. The grip panels are made of hardwood, not of beech, with the herringbone pattern pressed into them, a cost-saving measure, for it would hardly have made sense to fit such a low-cost design with hand-cut grip panels.

The weapon fits into the hand well and has much of its weight to the front. This is caused by the heavy slide, for this pistol has no bolt, but works on the principle of the unbolted spring-weight breech, and has been used only infrequently in weapons of 9 mm Parabellum caliber. In any case, a heavy breech weight is required, and an extremely heavy spring less so. After pressure is applied to the magazine catch, which is made of a strip of sheet metal at the bottom of the grip, the magazine can be

The so-called Tin Pistol was an attempt at even cheaper production with as little use of material as possible. Even so, this pistol shows some very interesting design features.

The magazine is from a P 38. The recoil spring has a guiding rod of rolled sheet metal. Note the muzzle bulge to center the barrel in the slide.

The Tin Pistol dismantled. A simple design with many ideas.

removed. It is similar to the magazine of the P 38 and holds eight cartridges. The slide is held back after the last shot has been fired, and it remains there after the magazine has been removed.

The remaining technology is seen when the weapon is dismantled. Immediately in front of the trigger a bolt can be seen that is pushed down a little bit by pressure on the lateral dismantling lever just above it. When the massive slide is to the rear and the lever is pushed down, the barrel is released — it can be removed from the slide only to the front. Its central section is cylindrical, and it is thickened as far back as the cartridge chamber, with a hole in the bottom into which the bolt operated by the dismantling lever can be pushed. On the top of the rear end of the barrel a guide rail has been cut. A bar set into the slide from the top extends into it and thus provides for the halfway centric positioning during assembly.

In the muzzle area the diameter of the barrel increases slightly. It fits into the slide and centers itself by means of its conical shape.

The slide is assembled from several pressed half-shells, of which the outer shell somewhat overlaps or wraps around the inner shell. One of the pieces that links these two shells is the handhold at the back of the slide. Here the inner shell is pierced in several places, and the stamped-in points of the outer shell fit into these holes. This not only provides for firm attachment, but also offers a halfway usable handhold. The sights have been made in similarly simple form. The foresight is bored out, the backsight is a piece of stamped sheet metal, part of the outer shell, that is bent up at a right angle with a notch cut into it.

The only solid piece inside the slide is the insert which contains the firing pin. This insert is machined out of solid metal and has two wide tabs on its rounded upper side which fit into the corresponding notches in the slide's inner shell. The extractor, in the form of a curved spring, is fitted at the end with a bar that acts as a safety on the rounded firing pin. At the same time, a bowed-out section of this spring fits into a cut in the slide so that the insert is absolutely firmly in its place.

To dismantle the pistol as described above, one needs only a screwdriver or an ordinary nail to press the spring (extractor).

The recoil spring is removable from the slide along with its bar. The bar itself is a tube made of rolled sheet metal, and the recoil spring is held onto this tube by flanges on both sides. The front flanges are shaped so

The frame as seen from the right side. The thin sheets of metal are cleverly riveted. The mainspring works when pulled.

they will fit into two small grooves in the slide. Thus the spring, along with its guides, is easy to remove but at the same time hard to lose.

The receiver is a real masterpiece of technical improvisation, and in terms of the strength of its material it is not at all comparable with the stamped grips of present-day pistols of the P 9 S type. An interesting feature is the guiding of the slide, for which the thin sheet metal of the grip has five cutouts on each side, into which the slide fits without too much play. The parts of the receiver are riveted around the spot-welded inner magazine shaft — the rivets themselves are made cleanly. In order to provide the screws of the grip panels with a seat, two threaded inserts are pressed into each side of the sheet metal and held by a star-shaped clamp.

In terms of handling and safety, the sheet-metal pistol has several very modern features. The very wide external hammer has a safety rest and a striking rest. The lateral safety can be set as S or F, and the hammer can be cocked only in the F position. When the slide is pulled back with the lever in S position, it moves forward again into its safety rest. The cocked hammer can be decocked by means of the safety system; it is released and remains held in the safety rest. The handling safety depends primarily on the reliability of the safety rest. In addition, and simultaneously with the forward motion of the decocked hammer, a block attached to the decocking lever (also the safety lever) moves up far enough so that the hammer, while moving forward, cannot reach the firing pin. The procedure is thus that first of all, the rising block is pushed high enough, and only immediately before its final position is the cocked hammer released.

The weapon can be assembled in a few steps: the slide is pushed into its guides and fixed in its rearmost position by pushing the catch lever (which has no actual handle for it) up until it can engage. This can be done differently when the magazine is inserted and then the slide is simply moved backward. Then the barrel, with its guiding slots, is pushed up from the front and moved somewhat, so that the holding bolt can fit into its lower hole. Whether it has been inserted properly can be determined by the rising of the holding bolt, which is easy to see from below. When the slide is pulled back with the magazine drawn part of the way out, the slide moves forward quickly and the weapon is ready to fire again. This is a very effective solution in some ways, and was attained out of necessity.

The P 38 After the War

The Walther firm's facilities were completely destroyed at the end of World War II, and the machinery was disassembled by Russian forces. The Walther family moved to the west and was able to make a modest new start in Ulm on the Danube in the early 1950s. In 1954 the firm's owner, Fritz Walther, was able to sign a contract with the newly reestablished Bundeswehr for the P 1 pistol, and well over 100,000 pistols were produced in the terms of this contract. The postwar product, with an aluminum receiver, was designated P 1. As of 1957, production for the civilian market also commenced, contracts were received from various official agencies inside and outside Germany, and production under license was begun by Manurhin in France.

Technical Data: Walther Sheet-Metal Pistol

Model designation	none
Year made	ca. 1943-44
Manufacturer	C. Walther, Zella-Mehlis, Thuringia
Caliber	9 mm Parabellum
Magazine capacity	8 cartridges
Overall length	218 mm
Overall height	142 mm
Width of grip	30 mm
Barrel length	129 mm
Bolt	none
Trigger	only single action
Safeties	closing, safety rest, decocking lever
Material	sheet steel (1 mm), steel
Finish	phosphated/burnished
Weight empty	1100 grams
Weight of slide	480 grams

The basic design of the P 38 has been retained, with slight changes made to some moving parts, as well as grip panels of black plastic with a small thumb position on the left side.

Many other nations have adopted the postwar version of the P 38 as side arms for military or police use. For example, Pakistan's air force, Ghana's army, the armed forces of Venezuela, Columbia, Argentina and Uruguay. Of course sales of the P 38 have declined somewhat since the introduction of the P 5 pistol, but the well-known pistol still has as good a reputation as ever, especially in South America and Asia. The Walther firm's 100th anniversary in 1986 was celebrated jointly with another: the 50th anniversary of the P 38 pistol.

A few more comments might be added about the present-day P 38, which is currently available in 9 mm Parabellum, 7.65 mm Parabellum and .22 LR caliber. Even though pistols with better and more modern technology have meanwhile become available, the P 38 is still up to date. The magazine holds a single row of 8 cartridges, and the sights have white twilight markings with which targeting is much improved in unfavorable light conditions.

The hammer can be decocked by means of the safety lever, which is turned to the S position and then back to the F position to decock the trigger spring again. The safety, when the lever is turned to S, moves in front of the thickened area of the firing pin and prevents it from making any forward motion. In addition, the firing pin is still secured by the automatic firing pin lock when the hammer is decocked. Immediately before firing it is raised, releasing the firing pin. The signal rod arrangement is retained, though not in the .22 LR caliber version. It then pushes on the bottom of the inserted cartridge and then projects, easily seen and felt, from the back of the slide.

A P 38 made in Ulm in the 1970s. It was accepted by the Bundeswehr as the P 1 pistol. The frame is no longer made of steel, but of aluminum.

Cutaway of the P 38 as made in Ulm.

Factory cutaway model of the P 38, with many functions easy to see, especially the type of bolting and safety.

Slide back, recoil spring compressed, swinging bolt down.

P 38: Comparison in 3 Calibers

Caliber	.22 l.r.	7.65 mm Para.	9 mm Para.
Overall length mm	216	216	216
Height mm	137	137	137
Width mm	37	37	37
Barrel length mm	129	125	125
Weight empty grams	ca. 800	ca. 800	ca. 800
Magazine capacity	8	8	8
Muzzle velocity m/s	297	384	373*
Muzzle energy Joule	113	442	556*
Shooting-in range m	25	25	25
Maximum range m	1200	1600	1600
Penetration in			
fir at 25 m cm	12	21.5	23
at 50 m cm	11	20.5	22.5
Signal rod	no	yes	yes
Grip	aluminum	aluminum	aluminum

Finish - matte burnished, or polished burnished at extra charge

* Depending on cartridge or charge

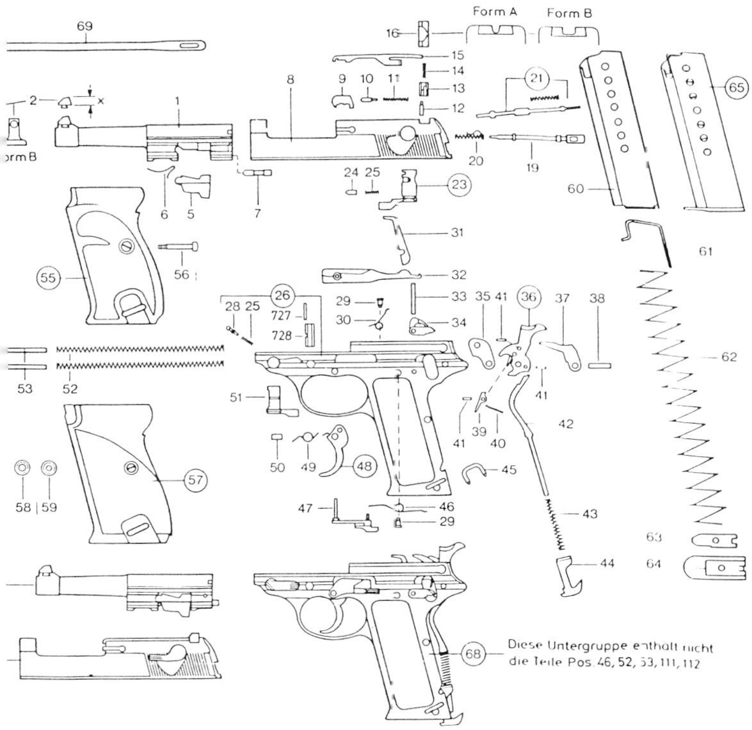

The parts of the P 38 as made in Ulm; excerpt from the Walther firm's archives.

Variations of the P 38

The existence of a shortened version of the P 38 during World War II still cannot be verified with absolute certainty. The statements of various authors contradict each other, sometimes quite drastically. A short version, which its owner says is authentic, is shown on page 100.

A shortened version, with the designation of P 38 k, was made after the war but is no longer part of the production program today. Its most noticeable characteristic is the shortened barrel. In the P 38 it still had a length of 125 mm, but the barrel of the P 38 k is only 70 mm long, and the foresight is therefore mounted on the bridge of the slide.

The P 38 and P 38 k models differ considerably in their security systems, while the P 4 and P 38 k are identical in this respect. The P 38 k does without any shooter-regulated safety, instead of which it has an decocking roller. This difference cannot be seen at all from outside, except that here the safety lever, or more properly the decocking lever, always points in the shooting direction. By turning the decocking roller inside, the raised firing pin is blocked. In the last third of its turning motion, the cocking piece (part 34 in the drawing on page 100) is

The P 4 pistol is not simply a shortened P 38. It is completely different in its safety system.

The upper parts of the P 4 and P 38. The P 4 has no signal rod and thus no removable cover on top.

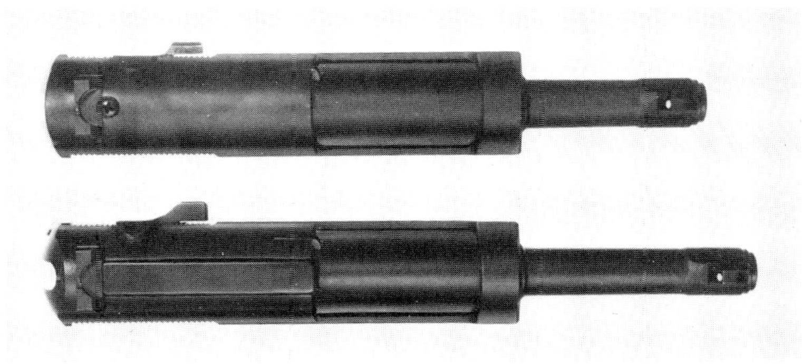

Cutaway of the P 4 with its different safety.

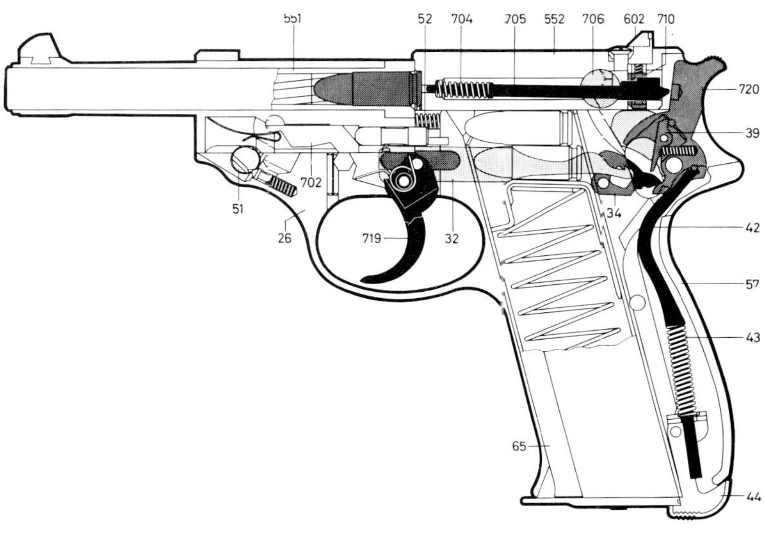

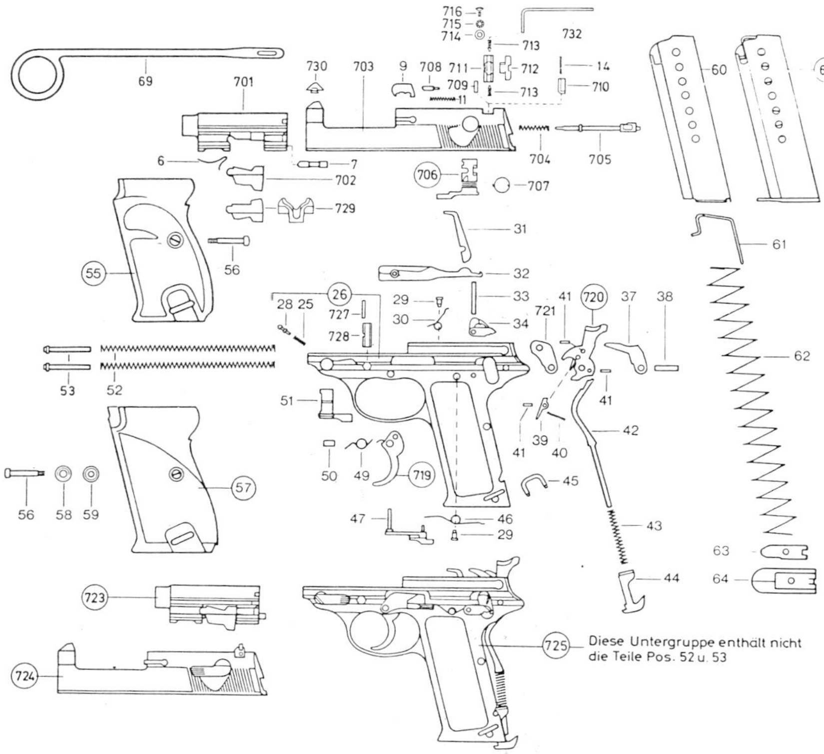

In comparison, the pieces of the P 38 K, which is almost identical to the P 4. The P 38 K and P 4 have a different safety system than the P 38.

The P 38 K is not a shorter P 38, but rather a shortened P 4. The P 4 and P 38 K have been out of production for some time.

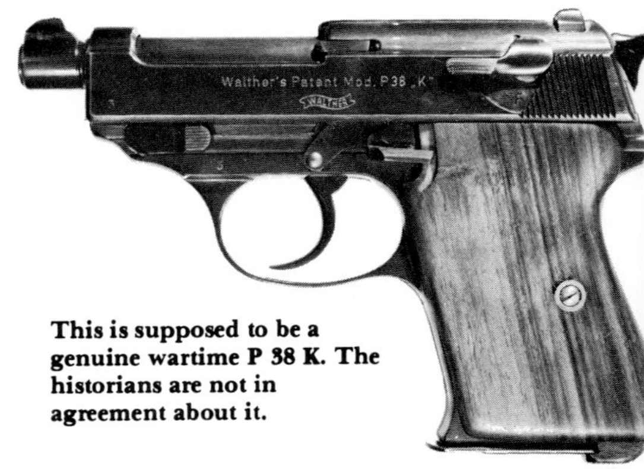

This is supposed to be a genuine wartime P 38 K. The historians are not in agreement about it.

Data on 9 mm Parabellum Pistols made by Walther in Ulm

Model	P 38	P 4	P 38 K	P 5
Caliber	9 mm P./7.65 mm	P. 9 mm Para.	9 mm Para.	9 mm Para.
BoltType	Bolt	Bolt	Bolt	Bolt
Overall length	216 mm	200 mm	160 mm	180 mm
Height\width	137/37 mm	139/35 mm	139/37 mm	129/32 mm
Barrel length	125 mm	110 mm	70 mm	90 mm
Magazine capacity	8	8	8	8
Weight empty	800 grams	800 grams	771 grams	800 grams
Signal rod	yes	no	no	no
Decocking lever	no	yes	yes	yes
Manual safety	yes	no	no	no
Sights	fixed	fixed	fixed	laterally adjustable
Material	Steel/aluminum	Steel/aluminum	Steel/aluminum	Steel/aluminum
Finish	burnished/nickel-plated/engraved	burnished	burnished	burnished/engraved

raised through the decocking piece (part 37 in the drawing), the hammer is thus released and moves forward. The decocking roller is under constant tension from a torsion spring and, after being activated, returns immediately to its original position, whereby the trigger is released and can move forward.

An additional safety feature provides constant safety along with constant readiness to fire. The hammer, like that of the P 4, P 5 and P 88 models, has a cutout and cannot strike against the firing pin as long as this is in its lower position. Only when the trigger is pulled backward and the firing pin is raised under the pressure of a spring-operated pusher (that is, the firing pin lock), can the hammer strike on its end with its full surface. Thus in every case the weapon is safe from faulty operation, or from falling or being hit.

The Model P 4 pistol is actually a transition piece between the P 38 and the P 38 k, of which it has its entire safety system. The barrel of the P 4 has a length of 110 mm, instead of the P 38's 125 mm. As with the P 38 k, the P 4 also has a backsight that can be adjusted laterally between two screws. Both pistols lack the signal rod to indicate that a cartridge is in place.

The first prototype of the P 5 pistol. The slide still resembles the P 38, the barrel has an oval cross-section, and a second lever is added as an decocking lever.

The barrel is still completely on the rails of the frame; this was not retained in that form.

The New Police Pistol - P 5

In the mid-1970s the German police were looking for a new service pistol, with the intention of having a so-called typical police weapon. Questions of handling safety were of minor importance, as the 7.65 mm caliber PP and PPK pistols had proved themselves well for more than forty years. A weapon with a more powerful cartridge was wanted, namely the 9 mm caliber Parabellum. There had already been one such search, which led to the development of the PP Super pistol, with several innovations, by Walther — it was designed for the 9 mm Ultra or 9 mm Police cartridge. As good as the weapon and cartridge basically were, this development did not become a commercial success. Several thousand of them were delivered to various police departments, and then new developments in this caliber were undertaken.

The frame of the first prototype. The position of the operating lever is easy to see.

The requirements for the new service pistol were published in a "Specification Manual for Hand Firearms" by the Technical Commission (TK) of Arbeitskreis II of the Innenministerkonferenz in 1974-75. The German manufacturers were requested to either

modify an existing weapon to equal the specifications in this manual and offer it as a new weapon, or to develop a weapon that equaled the specifications. The most important specifications in the manual were:
Caliber 9 mm (Parabellum)
Muzzle energy 500 Joules
Overall length approximately 180 mm
Overall height approximately 130 mm
Overall width approximately 34 mm
Weight when loaded not to exceed 1000 grams.

The same weapon with the slide open.

It had to be possible to carry and draw the weapon safely while ready to fire. Immediate fire by pulling the trigger had to be possible without additional activation of operating controls such as the safety, etc.

In addition, the weapon was not to fire when it was dropped or struck. A high degree of durability was also required. The main components, the barrel, breech, grip, recoil spring and firing pin spring, had to show no cracks or tears after firing 10,000 shots. Other parts, such as the firing pin or firing pin spring, had to show no damage after 5000 shots. The type and extent of the individual tests were also specified precisely in the manual. Four weapons manufacturers in Germany entered the competition: the firms of Heckler & Koch with the Model PSP, the Mauser firm with the Model HSP, the firm of Sauer & Sohn with the current Model P 6, and the Walther firm with the present Model P 5.

The P 5 pistol is a successful blend of time-tested elements with several new features. It provides easy and sure handling as well as constant safety and readiness to fire. The breech with the swinging bolt, which had been used in the P 38, P 38 k and P 4 models, was retained. The advantageous 9 mm Parabellum caliber, which the other models used, was also retained. So was the safety-less "safety system" with an decocking roller in the familiar manner. The grip and sights resembled the corresponding components of the PP-Super or P 38 k pistol in many respects. The backsight is laterally adjustable, an adjustment for height can be made by exchanging sight leaves, seven of which are available in all.

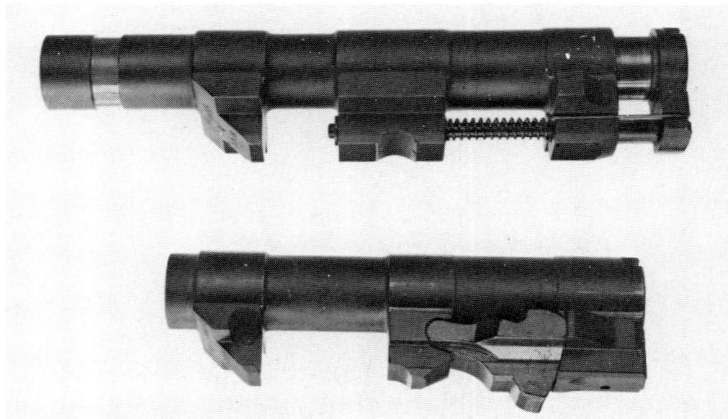
For use in practice, the Walther firm developed a PT barrel with a backward-moving chamber. It is fired with great accuracy, retaining the repeating function, at ranges up to 8 meters.

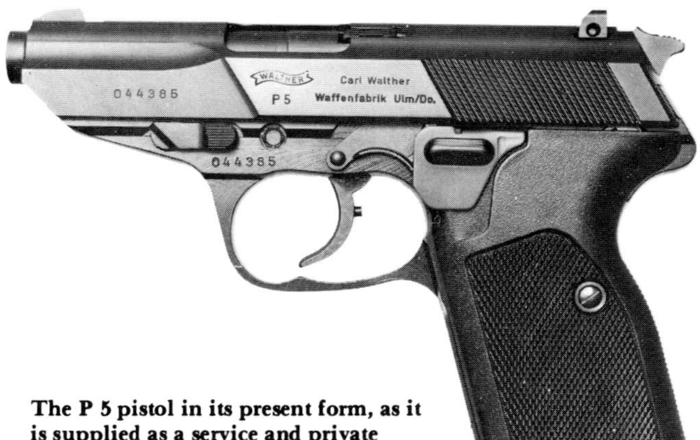

The P 5 pistol in its present form, as it is supplied as a service and private pistol.

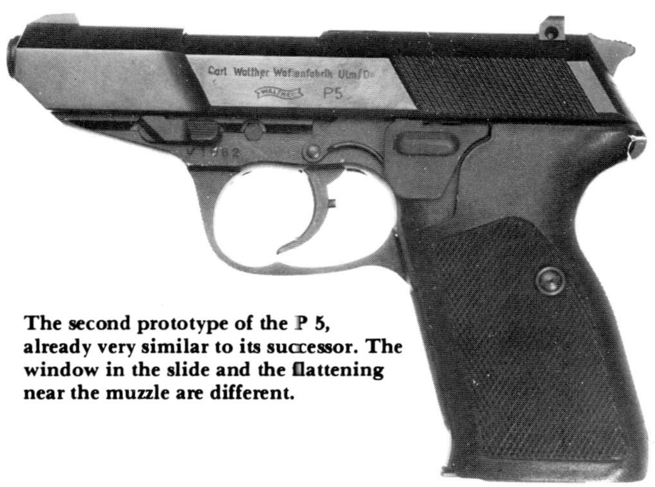
The second prototype of the P 5, already very similar to its successor. The window in the slide and the flattening near the muzzle are different.

utaway
the P 5
istol,
aded
nd
ncocked.
istol
aded
nd
ncocked

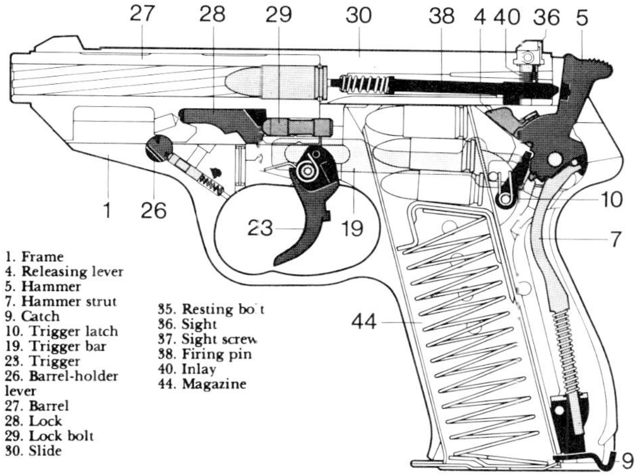

The cutaway model in detail, with a look at the safety and the hammer cutout.

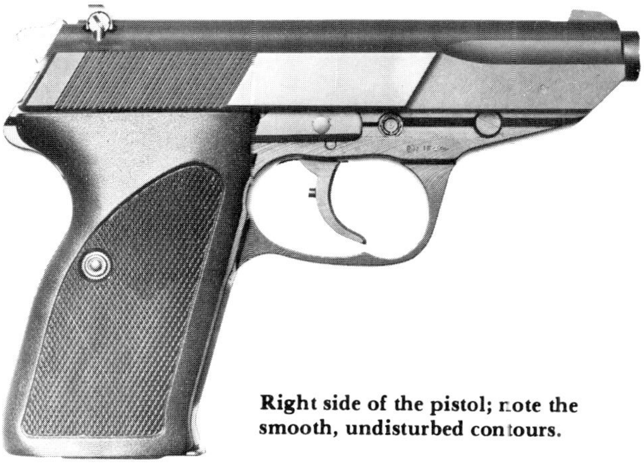

Right side of the pistol; note the smooth, undisturbed contours.

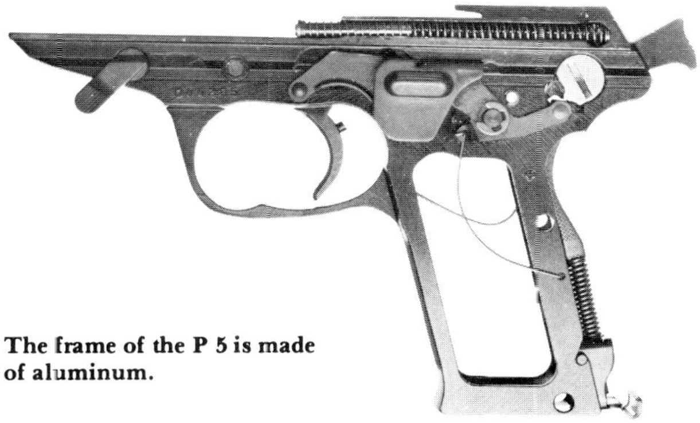

The frame of the P 5 is made of aluminum.

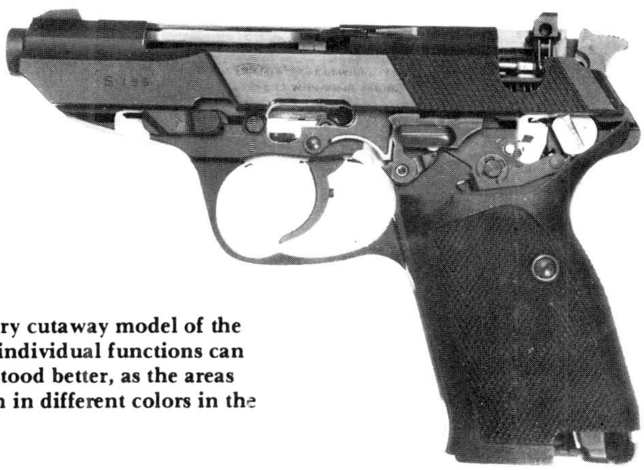

The factory cutaway model of the P 5. The individual functions can be understood better, as the areas are shown in different colors in the model.

Two half-finished P 5 frames are set up for further work.

The slides are immersed in the hardening bath.

This work only looks simple; shaping magazines.

The P 5 pistol dismantled for cleaning. One pushes the barrel back a bit after removing the magazine and swings the dismantling lever downward. The complete upper part can then be pushed off the grip.

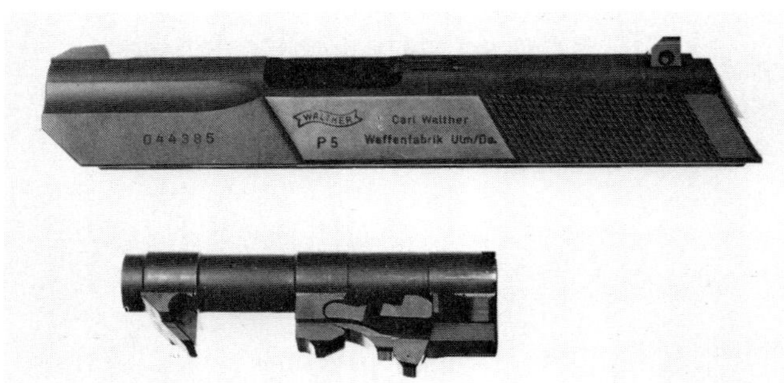

The P 5 also has the well-known swinging bolt.

In 1986 the manufacturers celebrated their 100th anniversary. For this occasion, small numbers of these pistols were made: burnished to a high polish, with gold trigger, hammer and writing. The pistols came in tasteful cases.

The weapon in its open position. Grip panels of walnut were attached; they were available from the manufacturer as accessories.

All the moving parts at a glance. The slide is made to move forward by pressure on the decocking lever.

Walther always knew how to make refined weapons. This one has a dark frame, dark grip panels with carving, and a less dark etched slide.

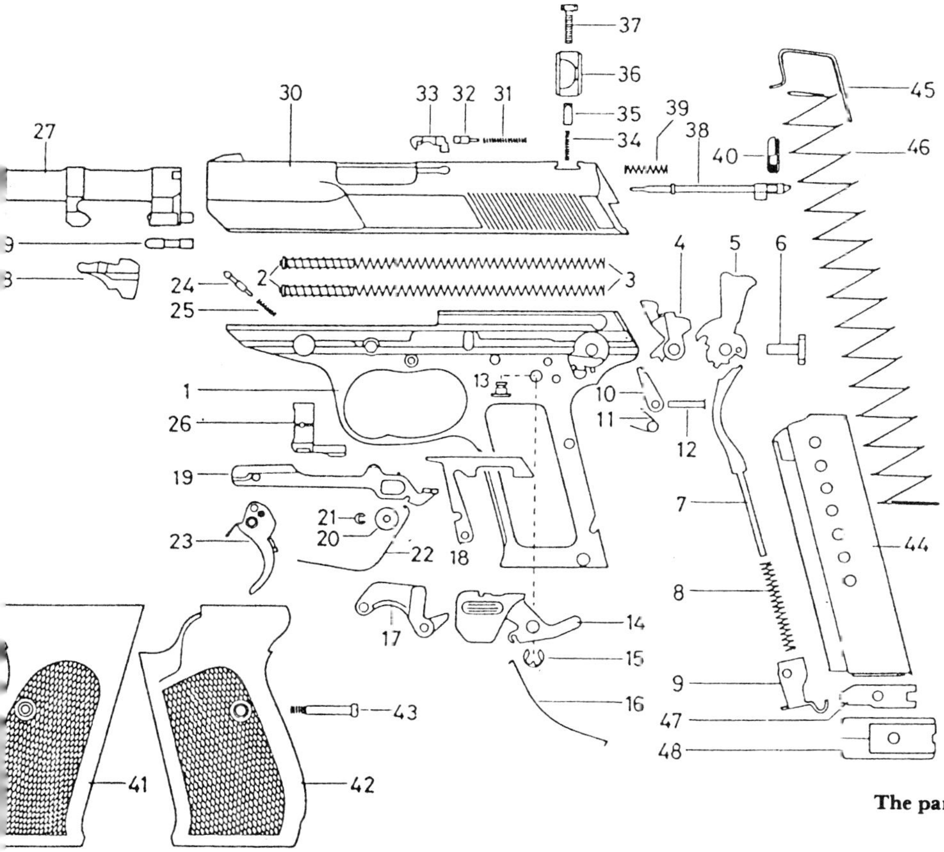

1 Griffstück	25 Druckfeder
2 Bolzen	26 Rohrhaltehebel
3 Druckfedern	27 Rohr
4 Auslösehebel	28 Riegel
5 Schlaghebel	29 Riegelbolzen
6 Schlaghebelbolzen	30 Verschlußstück
7 Schlagstange	31 Druckfeder
8 Schlagfeder	32 Auszieherbolzen
9 Magazinhalter	33 Auszieher
10 Abzugklinke	34 Druckfeder
11 Drehfeder	35 Rastbolzen
12 Zylinderstift	36 Visier
13 Bolzen	37 Visierschraube
14 Entspannhebel	38 Schlagbolzen
15 Sicherungsscheibe	39 Schlagbolzenfeder
16 Drehfeder	40 Einlage
17 Fanghebel	41 Griffschale rechts
18 Auswerfer	42 Griffschale links
19 Abzugstange	43 Linsenschraube
20 Bolzen	44 Magazingehäuse
21 Sicherungsscheibe	45 Zubringer
22 Abzugfeder	46 Magazinfeder
23 Abzug	47 Bodenhalter
24 Rastbolzen	48 Boden

The parts of the P 5 pistol as introduced for police use.

The operating lever attached to the left side fulfills two tasks. When the slide is back, it can be moved forward by pressing on the lever; at the same time, the slide can be held back with it by pushing the lever up. When the hammer is cocked, this lever serves as a decocking lever. When decocking, the firing pin remains in its lower position under the pressure of a spring, and in this position, on account of the cutout on the inside of the hammer (firing pin lever), it cannot be driven forward in any case. It is also held in its longitudinal direction. The hammer, moved forward over the "decocking lever", is held in its safety rest, and the trigger thus returns to its forward position. The process of cocking and decocking need not be described further here, as it is described in detail in the accompanying graphics (taken from the Walther firm's original service manual).

To sum up, the individual safety features of the P 5 are:

1. Longitudinal stopping of the firing pin
2. Cutout in the striking surface of the hammer
3. Safety rest on the hammer
4. Recoil safety (interrupter)

Only when the barrel and slide are in a bolted position and the trigger is pulled all the way can the hammer strike the firing pin and fire a shot; it would scarcely be possible to improve on the safety and simplicity of

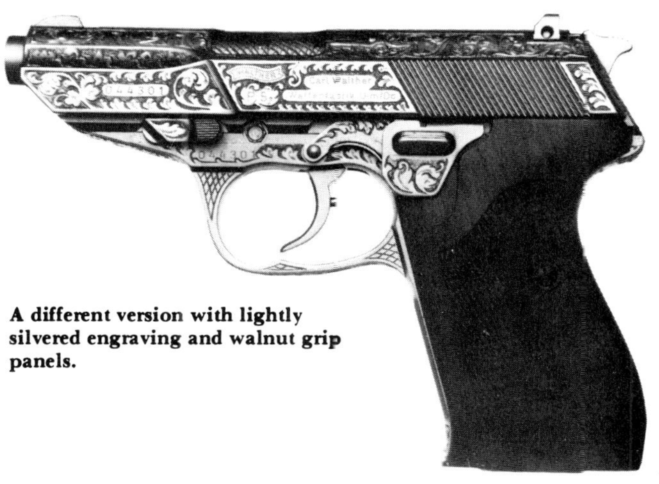

A different version with lightly silvered engraving and walnut grip panels.

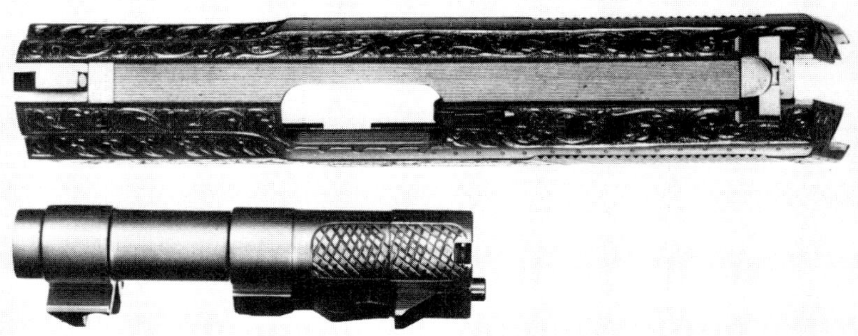

Careful workmanship in detail.

Decocked position
Firing pin (38) is held down by spring pressure with its rear and aligned opposite the recess (o) in the striking face of the hammer (5). At the same time, its forward motion is also blocked (see fig. 20 n). The hammer is decocked and its safety notch (g) is engaged. The trigger bar (19) is located in the double-action spur (p) of the hammer base.

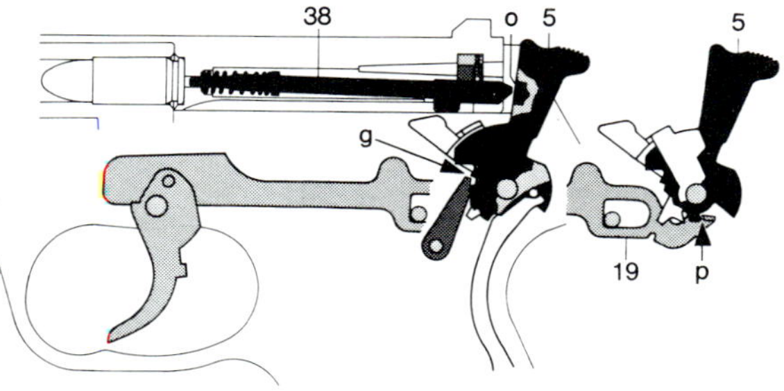

Hammer cocked
The hammer (5) is held in the full-cock position (a) by the sear (10). Trip lever (4) and the firing pin (38) are in the rest (safe) position. Forward motion of the firing pin is blocked (n). The trigger bar (19) is in contact with the hammer (b) and the trigger moves to the rear position on cocking.

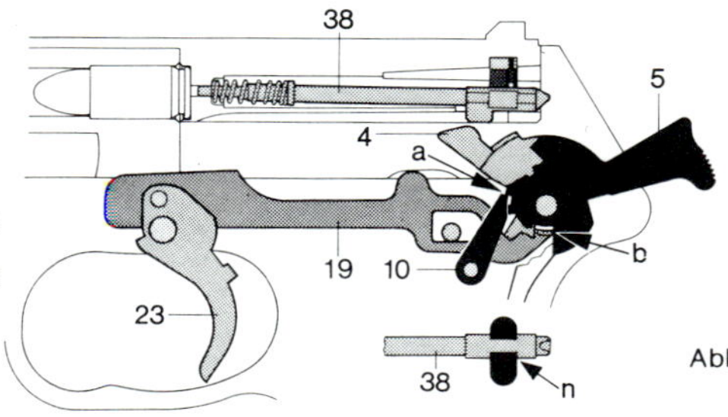

Abb. 20

Even smaller, handier and more compact, the P 5 COMPACT in prototype form. It was shown to the public in mid-1986.

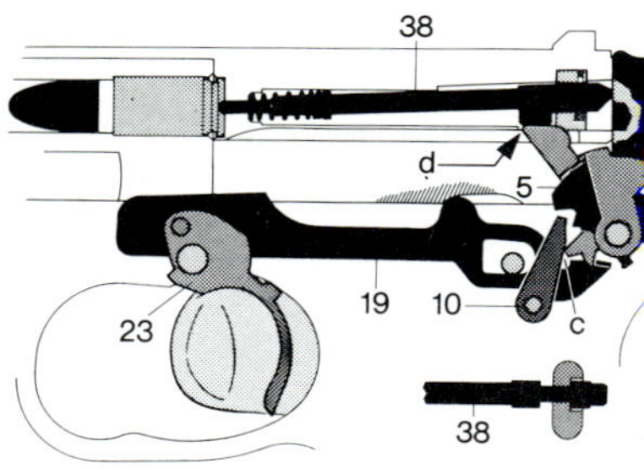

Abb. 21

Firing position
Pulling the trigger (23) causes the trigger bar (19) to pivot trip lever (4). The lower spur (c) of the trip lever disengages sear (10) from the hammer (5), while the upper segment (d) raises firing pin (38). Only in this position can the hammer strike the firing pin.

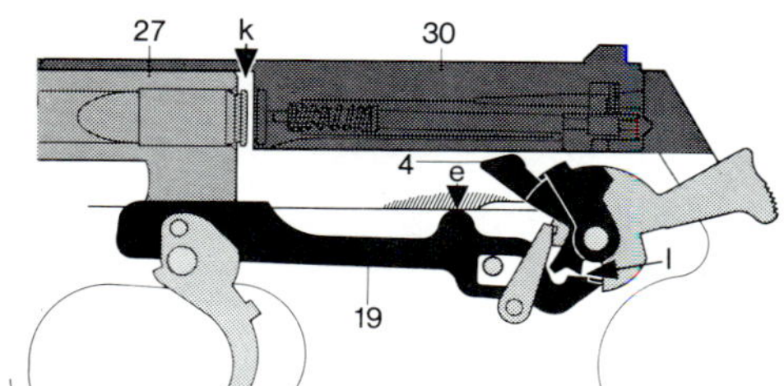

Abb. 22

Disconnected position
If the slide (30) is not fully closed (k), trigger bar (19) is pushed down (e) by the slide. This disconnects (l) the trigger bar and the trip lever. Firing a shot by pulling the trigger is not possible until the slide is fully closed.

Arrested position
When the last shot has been fired, the magazine follower (45) raises the catch (17) which arrests (h) the slide (30) in its rearmost position. Also, the pawl of the slide catch enters the action radius (i) of the decocking lever (14). When the recocking lever is thumbed down, it acts on the pawl and depresses (m) the slide catch, thus releasing the slide. The hammer is held cocked by the sear (10). Thumbing down the decocking lever a second time will decock the hammer.

The magazine holder above, behind the trigger guard, the hammer without the typical spur.

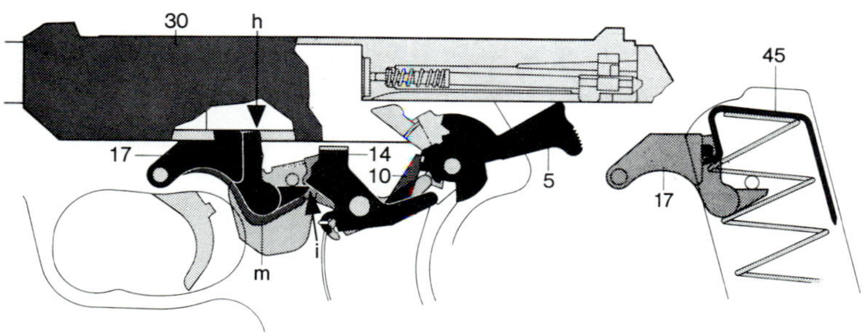

The individual functions of the P 5 explained, from the manufacturer's instruction manual.

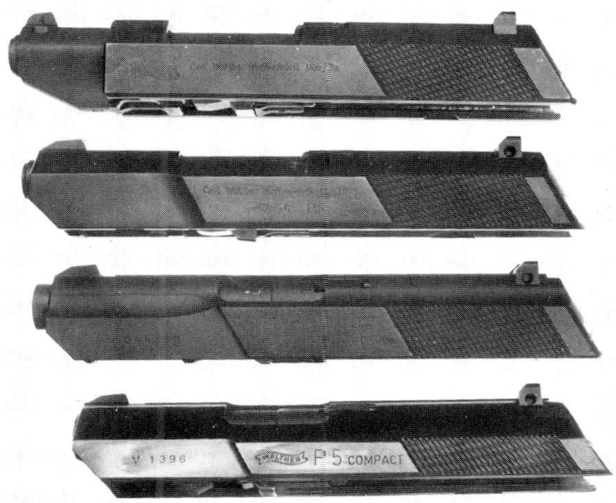

The slides of the four versions, for comparison. From above: first prototype, second prototype, P 5 production version and P 5 COMPACT prototype.

handling.

In the individual German states, three different pistols were introduced, which is less a testimony to the quality of one pistol than a political and economical decision, for if one huge contract were given to one manufacturer, this would result in a loss of possible work for the other manufacturers. The P 5 pistol was chosen by the states of Baden-Württemberg and Rheinland-Pfalz, and the first deliveries to the agencies involved were made in 1978. A year later the national police of The Netherlands also chose the P 5 pistol and bought more than 35,000 of them. They were followed by the stand-by police of the states of Baden-Württemberg and Rheinland-Pfalz.

In the manufacturing process, progress had been made so successfully that the lower limit of 10,000 shots has always been exceeded as a matter of principle, and 20,000 shots can be fired from a presently produced P 5 without any significant damage. This can be proved in practice, as after many years of regular use, there have been practically no complaints from the police about the functional capability of these pistols.

In mid-1986 the Walther firm first began to display a prototype of a shortened P 5 pistol to a limited audience. The new pistol is designated P 5 COMPACT, and as these lines were being written (1989), it had not yet been determined whether, how and when this shorter version would be put into series production.

Also, the barrel was shortened by 15 mm, the slide's front end is practically even with that of the barrel, and it was shortened 8 mm from that of the usual P 5.

In addition, the prototype includes several other changes. The magazine catch was moved to the base of the trigger guard and can be inserted there from either the left or right side. This corresponds to the requirements, more and more in demand today, for a quick change of magazines. The length of the grip and the

The barrels of these four pistols in the same order.

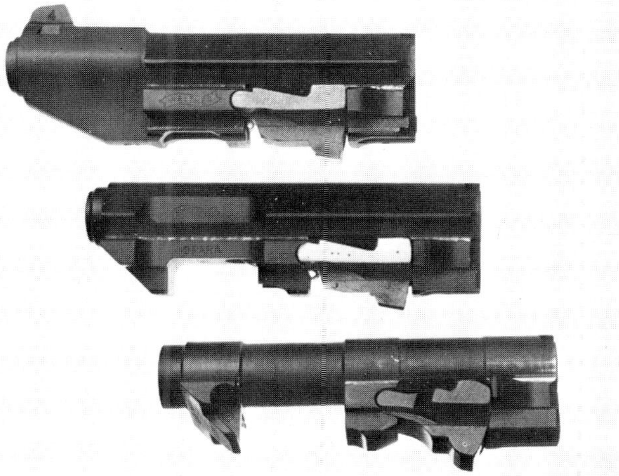

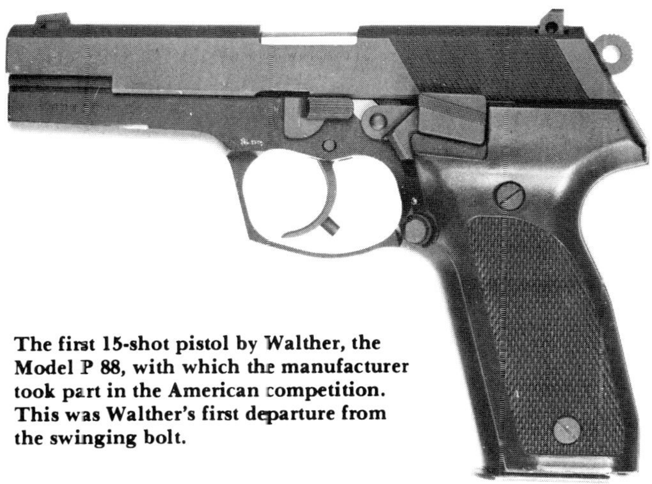

The first 15-shot pistol by Walther, the Model P 88, with which the manufacturer took part in the American competition. This was Walther's first departure from the swinging bolt.

magazine have not been changed, but in the back of the grip (provisionally at first) an insert of aluminum has been added.

The hammer no longer has an extended spur, but is very easy to cock, and at the same time impossible to snag on clothing. The shape of the sled was also changed, with its flat sides being shortened. Its top has the shape of a rounded triangle, so that this slide now bears more resemblance in shape to that of the second prototype, which is also depicted here.

All the rest of the technology, such as the ease of dismantling and the complete safety plus constant readiness to fire, has been retained and typifies the P 5, which has been able to prove itself well as a modern concept and make the P 5, now as before, the safest and best-functioning of pistols.

Moving parts as seen from both sides. Here too is the modern decocking lever with its double function.

Model P 88

The Walther firm, with its P 88, competed in the American competition when a search was made for an optimal pistol in 9 mm PARA caliber as a service weapon for the armed forces.

While many of the participating manufacturers simply expanded an already proven basic design to the required magazine capacity of 15 cartridges, Walther presented a fully new conception, which departed for the first time from the principle of the tipping swinging bolt which had been used exclusively up to that time. The P 88 has a bolt in the manner of the Browning bolt; the barrel is tipped downward in the rear and thus the connection between it and the slide is broken. Particular importance was placed on problem-free functioning safety, which has succeeded superbly in the P 88 along with the built-in safety system. Thus we have a combination here of time-tested safety devices and a bolt system that has proved itself in other weapons.

The hammer has a cutout and can only strike the firing pin when the latter is lifted by the action of the trigger and enters the striking zone of the hammer. It is not possible for a shot to be fired as a result of a fall or blow, or without the trigger being pulled. Likewise, no shot can be fired from a weapon that is not completely locked, because the trigger bar and sear are then separated. For all new pistols it was required that the hammer be decockable without pulling the trigger. This system is also used in the P 88, but with the advantage that the wide decocking lever can be used from either side. Thus it has the advantage of simultaneously pushing the catch lever for the slide back down after being pressed. This was already used successfully in the P 5 police pistol, where it was described as a one-lever operation.

In order to hold the slide fast, the lever on the left side below the decocking lever is pushed upward and pressed into the cutout on the underside of the slide. The slide is made to move forward by using the decocking lever, with both sides equal.

The magazine catch of the P 88 is of interest. It can be operated from either side, a technical innovation that seems to have existed only rarely before that time, but which is especially practical for left-handed shooters. Within the receiver is a sprung catch which is swung out by the angularly shaped push-button of the magazine catch.

The sights can be adjusted laterally, and the fore- and

The dismantled P 88 after the grip panels were removed. The frame is closed on both sides, the magazine catch is operable equally from either side.

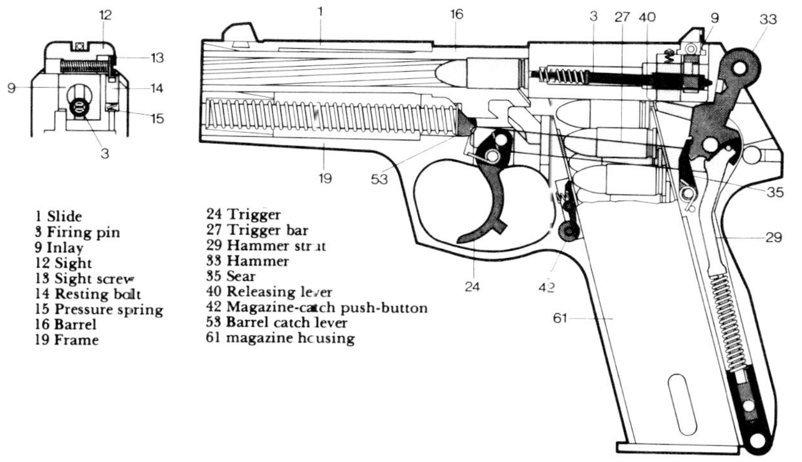

Cutaway of the P 88 pistol with which Walther took part in the American competition. The weapon has a breech with tipping barrel and a 15-cartridge magazine.

backsights bear the usual Walther markings in white.

The frame is made of aluminum-alloy and protected from corrosion with a black coating. No grooves have been included on the front or rear of the grip. The shape of the frame and slide has perhaps not yet been finalized. The grip extends to the level of the opening, while the slide is cut back in steps there to a length of some 30 mm. Optically, it would have been better if the slide did not have these steps, and there would also be less possibility of dirt getting into the guiding grooves. A good deal of experimentation appears to have been done to the trigger. The cocking trigger moves over its entire distance without any clearly tangible increase in weight, the SA trigger releases as quickly and cleanly as the trigger of a good revolver, and is supported by a trigger-stop which is added as a knob on the tongue of the trigger.

When the author first saw this weapon, it was not yet known what the results of Walther's competition in the USA had been. It was also not yet known whether a private version would be put on the market in Germany. The weapon at hand has the inscription on the right side of its slide, "INTERARMS ALEXANDRIA/VIRGINIA", as well as "Made in W. Germany."

Meanwhile it has become known that the P 88 will not be introduced in the USA. A slightly modified version will be available for civilian purchase.

Technical Data: Walther P-88

Manufacturer	C. Walther, Ulm
Caliber	9 mm Parabellum
System	recoil loader with tipping barrel
Trigger	Double Action trigger with trigger stop
Overall length	187 mm
Height/width	141 mm/38 mm
Barrel length	102 mm
Sights	laterally adjustable
Uncocking lever	both sides
Weight empty	ca. 900 grams
Weight loaded	ca. 1080 grams
Magazine capacity	15 cartridges
Material	steel/aluminum
Finish	matte burnished
Grip panels	plastic

FINLAND

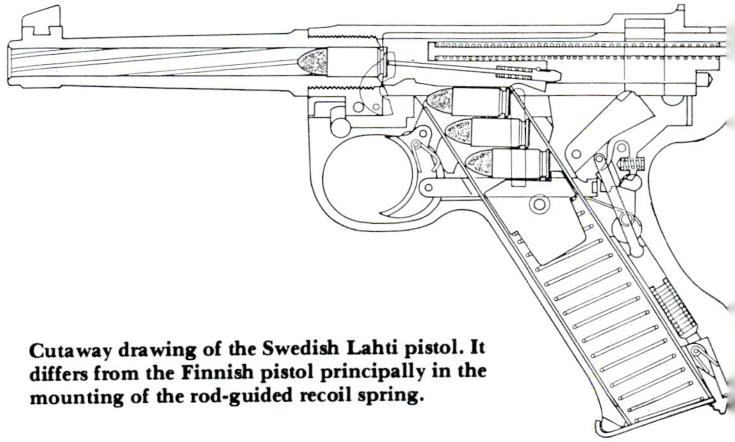

Cutaway drawing of the Swedish Lahti pistol. It differs from the Finnish pistol principally in the mounting of the rod-guided recoil spring.

After handguns from other countries had been put into service for many years, Finnish experiments were made with a modified version of the Parabellum pistol developed by A.E. Soloranta. They finally resulted in the L-35 pistol made by the Finn Aimo Lahti, a robust service pistol that remained in use for several decades and proved itself well, especially under the rough climatic conditions of that country.

Lahti rightfully enjoys a reputation in Finland similar to that of F. Walther or Mauser in Germany, and has successfully developed numerous independent designs in the realm of rifles, machine guns and pistols. The L-35 pistol was built by Valtion, the state weapons factory; series production began in 1935, the development having begun in 1929. The first prototype was built for the 7.65 mm cartridge, and the original intention was to offer the new pistol in both 7.65 mm and 9 mm Parabellum calibers. Few were built for the smaller caliber, and there was no series production. After the first experiments and troop tests were concluded satisfactorily, the Finnish Army introduced this pistol officially under the designation of "Pistoolit L-35", and series production commenced.

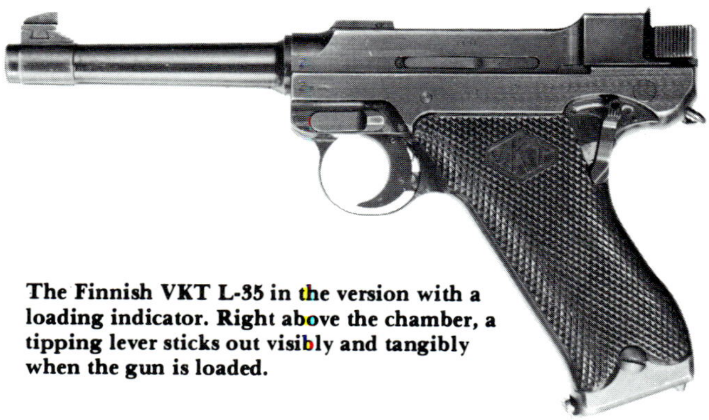

The Finnish VKT L-35 in the version with a loading indicator. Right above the chamber, a tipping lever sticks out visibly and tangibly when the gun is loaded.

The Finnish Lahti Pistol

Even though the entire outward appearance may be somewhat reminiscent of the Parabellum, it is really only external. There are no technical similarities between the two pistols. The L-35 has a bolt system that is as simple as it is original. The barrel and upper section (breech housing) form a screwed-together unit and slide in long and strong rails on the equally sturdy receiver. Within the breech housing, which is rectangular in section, slides the actual breechblock, in which the extractor and the firing pin are mounted. On its upper side, the breechblock has a cutout into which an angular U-shaped yoke can fit. In the breech housing there is a cutout that fits this yoke piece, and in which it lies in a locked state, thus creating a fixed link between the breech housing and the breechblock.

During the firing process, the whole upper section slides back some 8 mm. During this movement, the yoke is forcibly lifted upward over the guiding curves built into both sides of the receiver. This releases the breechblock which can then slide backward against the pressure of the recoil spring. When it moves forward, the yoke is pushed downward again and creates the rigid link again. This principle is well designed, simple in its overall conception and nearly as trouble-free as it is robust. In fact, one can install the yoke piece the wrong way around, and there are problems involved in dismantling the weapon, which is not at all possible without special

The later version of the Finnish pistol, this time without the loading indicator.

tools. In order to limit this error, the yoke has a stamped-in arrow that shows that it must be installed correctly in the direction of the shot and in no other way.

A special feature of the L-35 is the accelerator. In the left front of the breech housing there is a rugged turning lever that has the task of giving the breechblock an additional impulse and thus speeding up its rearward motion. In this manner, the breechblock has a greater recoil speed than the rest of the upper section. As for the justification for this accelerator, there are two different opinions, the truth of which is probably a mixture of the two. Some authors assume that this measure was necessary because of the long working distance of the system. Others assume that it became necessary to keep the pistol functioning properly even under arctic conditions. Owners of the L-35, on the other hand, are of the opinion that under the temperature conditions existing in Germany, the accelerator can simply be removed, so that the weapon is under less mechanical stress. Even at Valtion, the verdict on the accelerator was not always definite. One small series was built without it, and the reactions of the troops were awaited. All the pistols, though, were gradually returned, as they had not functioned without difficulties.

The production of the L-35 began only gradually, and only as of 1939 was it built in larger quantities. The early versions still had grip panels made of wood and a foresight welded fast to the barrel. After that came grip panels of plastic with the diamond-shaped VKT emblem, and the adjustable foresight was set in a welded-on

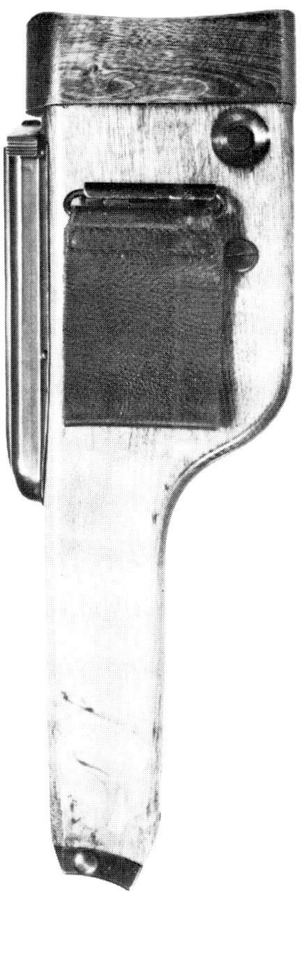

Holster box with extra magazine and fastener for mounting on the grip.

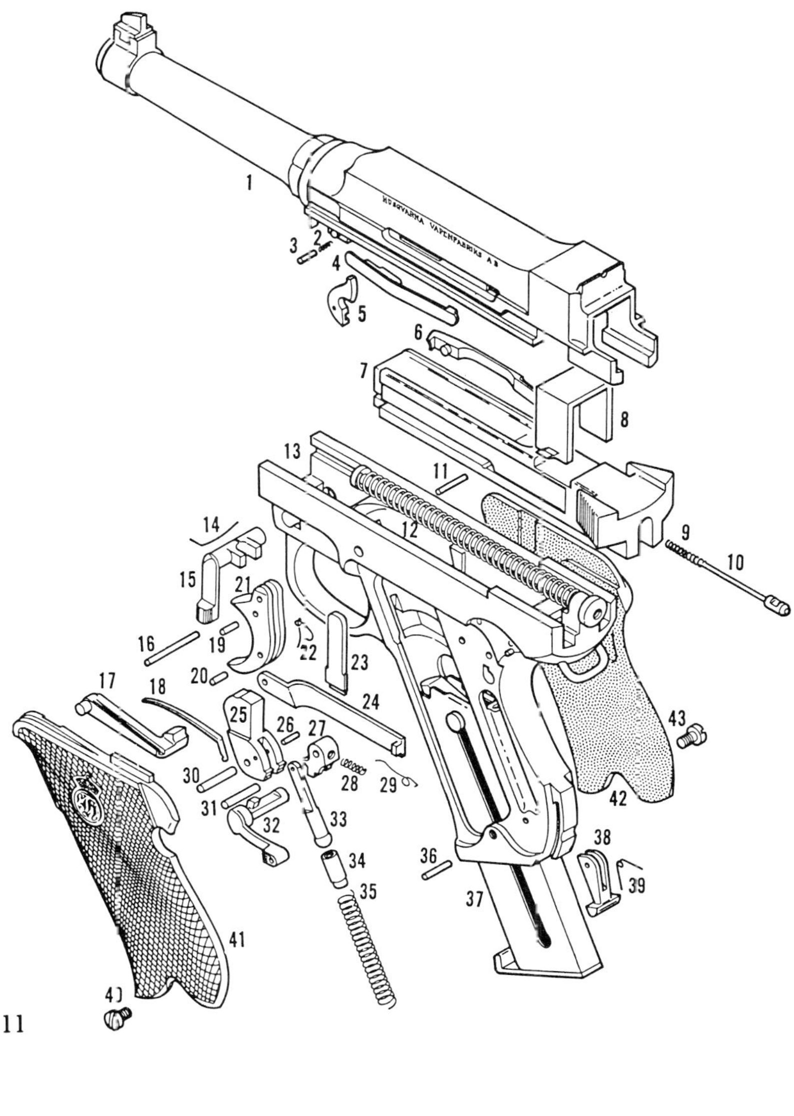

The parts of the Swedish Lahti pistol. Part 5 is the accelerator, part 8 the horseshow-shaped block that is guided upward for unlocking.

mount. These versions also had, low on the back of the receiver, a somewhat protruding attachment for a wooden box in the manner of the Mauser C-96. Only 200 pistols with this box are said to have been built, and they are thus rarely found in collections today. There are differences in the loading indicator, which is mounted high in the breech housing and shows whether there is a cartridge or its case in the chamber. Later versions lacked this, as well as the machined-out space to hold the box, and the Swedish version also lacked the loading indicator.

During the course of production there were several interruptions, usually caused by the Russo-Finnish War. The first interruption occurred in 1939-40, and production did not resume until 1941, though with small numbers produced. The next interruption came in 1944, after which pistols were produced again only as of 1946, continuing until 1954; in this period, some 9000 pistols were produced.
In 1958 another small series of 1250 pistols was produced under a military contract. This version has the somewhat smaller trigger guard of the Finnish version but the angular barrel attachment of the Swedish type.

All in all, the Finnish version was better made than the Swedish type, about which a few words will be said below. The material was chosen more carefully, more handwork was done in assembly and fitting, and the surface was finished better. Some people have gone so far as to compare the Finnish L-35 with the almost legendary SIG 210; as far as firing performance is concerned, the L-35 can bear comparison, an advantage of the non-tipping barrel. Few markings and inscriptions have been used on the L-35. The grip panels bear the initials VKT, the serial number is stamped into the side of the grip, and

The Swedish version of the Lahti pistol, without a loading indicator, with an attachment for the shaft and the other opposed mount for the recoil spring.

the top of the housing bears only the initials VKT and L-35.

Technical Data: VKT L-35 / 9.00 pist/.44

Model	VKT L-35	9.00 pist/.44
Manufacturer	Valtion Metalitehtaat	Valtion Kiväări Thedas
Kaliber	9 mm Parabellum	9 mm Parabellum
Overall length	235 mm	214 mm
Height/width	146 mm/35 mm	142 mm/36 mm
Barrel length	117.5 mm	110 mm
Weight empty	1240 grams	1085 grams
Magazine capacity	8 cartridges	8 cartridges
Safety	lever	none
System	vertical block	mass breech
Sights	fixed	fixed
Material/finish	steel/burnished	steel/burnished

Production in Sweden

Another "Lahti" came from Sweden and was produced by the Husqvarna Vapenfabrik AB in Husqvarna.

This manufacturer had already been active in weapon production for some time but had not developed any of its own designs. According to opportunity and contract conditions, other weapons were manufactured under license. An independent pistol design, a gas-pressure loader, was once tried but did not go beyond early the prototype stage. The Swedish "Lahti" was a rather pointless venture, as the Swedish government had

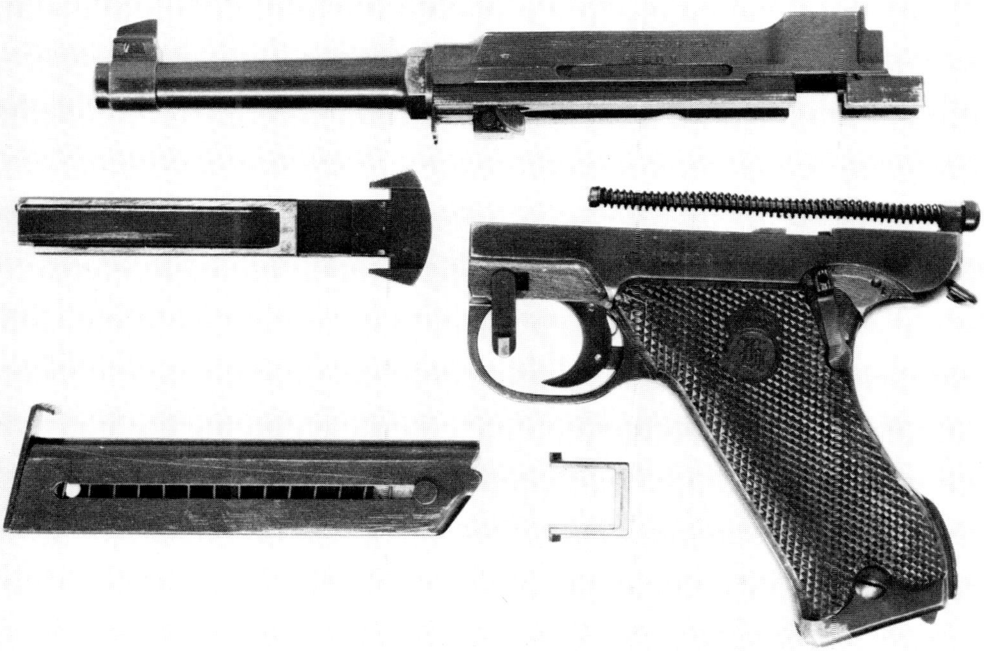

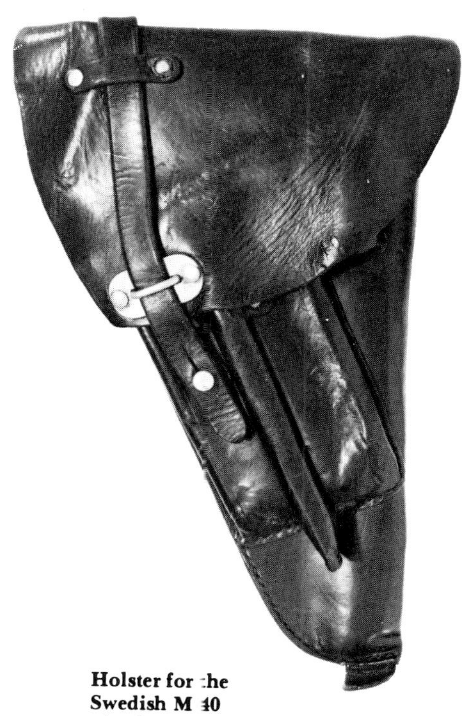

Holster for the Swedish M 40 pistol.

The dismantled Swedish pistol, which is largely identical to the Finnish version.

decided to introduce the Walther P 38 pistol. The contracts had already been signed, but the shipments were not sufficient, as after World War II began in 1939, Walther had to devote all its production to meeting its own country's needs. To take the place of the L-35, the Finnish L-35 was chosen, as it had proved itself very well in the Russo-Finnish War at that time. But since the Finns could not meet the Swedish needs as well as their own, they gave the Swedes a license to produce their "own" Lahti pistols.

There are several differences between the Finnish L-35 and the Swedish m/40. The m/40 has a slightly longer barrel, plus a hexagonal attachment that is screwed into the breech housing. The trigger guard is larger and sturdier, and the loading indicator was eliminated. The grip panels bear a wreathed H with a crown above, and as in the original, each is held by two screws.

The Swedish versions are said to have been made out of poorer material with generally inferior workmanship. Much has been recorded as to difficulties with the m/40, for it is said to have been tested insufficiently before being put into production. In Sweden 83,950 m/40 pistols were built, 950 of them intended for private sales where they remained in service for a long time.

Like the L-35, the m/40 could be fired easily and accurately, and both functioned trouble-free with present-day cartridges. Handling and dismantling either pistol is simple. After removing the magazine, the breechblock remains to the rear after the last shot and cannot be moved forward by an attached release lever, and the upper section is moved backward some 8 mm. The barrel catch is swung downward 90 degrees, and the upper section is pushed forward off the receiver. By holding the upper section with its underside upward, the yoke piece slides into its aperture and the breechblock can be pulled out. Very few pistols can be dismantled as quickly and easily.

The m/44 . . . A Non-Production Venture

In 1940, Finnish air force pilots were supplied with the Model 1935 High Power made by FN. During the war years of 1941-1943, the Finnish armed forces, who fought along with the German troops, were supplied with pistols from Italy, Spain and Czechoslovakia — captured weapons such as the Germans themselves used in great numbers.

Since there was a real need for 9 mm pistols then as before, the leadership of VKT considered a new concept,

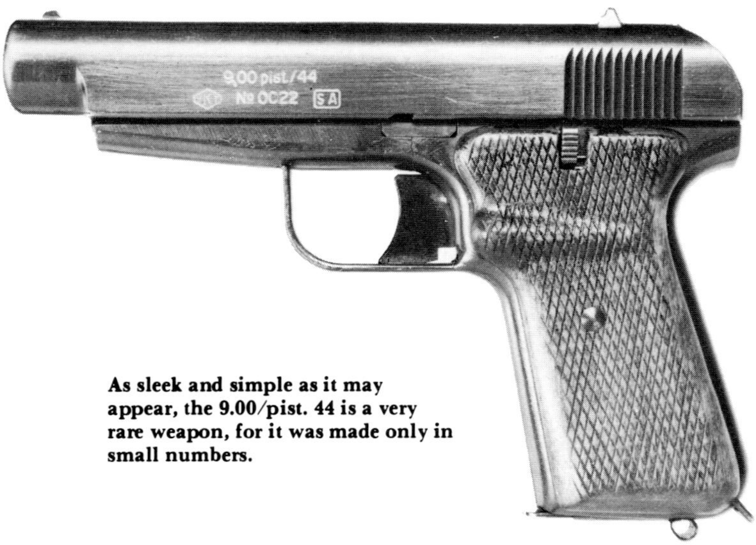

As sleek and simple as it may appear, the 9.00/pist. 44 is a very rare weapon, for it was made only in small numbers.

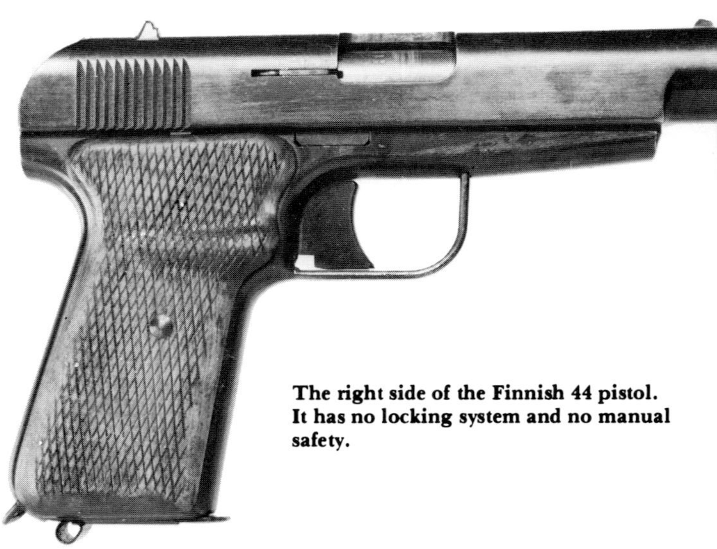

The right side of the Finnish 44 pistol. It has no locking system and no manual safety.

which was intended above all to allow simple and economical production. Thus the Model M/44, in 9 mm Parabellum caliber, was developed, and featured a frame and slide made of sheet steel. A bolt was not included as one of the measures taken to keep production costs low. The barrel was firmly attached, though not rigidly linked with the receiver. In similar manner as in the successful FN pocket pistols, the barrel had a sort of half-open thread comb on its rear section, with which it could be held firmly in place after being turned briefly into a corresponding attachment. The opposite piece was not rigidly linked to the receiver either, but was a removable unit. A spring bolt stuck out the front of this attachment piece, intended to contribute something to damping when the slide moved forward under the pressure of its recoil spring. As in the Tokarev pistol, the m/44 was made with its lock as a removable unit, a design feature that is seen relatively rarely.

In 1944 the Finns ended their involvement in World War II, and production of the m/44 was not taken further and was given up. Only 26 of these interesting pistols were built in all, so that the m/44, despite its simple appearance, ranks among the most sought-after rarities in the ranks of self-loading pistols. During the Russian occupation, members of the Allied Control Commission became aware of the m/44 — the design drawings, tools and one prototype were taken to Russia, but no further development was done.

In view of the fact that pistols were never built in great numbers in Finland, both the L-35 and the m/44 can be regarded as very good and very independent developments. Under the severe climatic conditions in particular, they have proved to be dependable where other weapons have failed.

FRANCE

The French armed forces were acquainted with the 9 mm Parabellum cartridge very late, and during World War I in particular had a remarkable collection of handguns in service. In World War I the French Army was equipped with the Model 1892 revolver in 8 mm caliber, plus the Model 1873 revolver in 11 mm caliber. During the war a large number of Spanish Ruby pistols were bought, mainly in the 7.65 mm Browning caliber (.32 ACP) — some of these not overly well-made pistols were still in service at the end of World War II. Between the two wars, two pistols were developed in France, both of them built for the 7.65 mm long cartridge. They were the M 1935 A and M 1935 S models. The French cartridge was very similar to the American .30 cartridge of 1918, for which John Browning had developed a self-loading pistol. It is said that after it was displayed, the French did not want Browning's gun, but they did want his cartridge . . . and brought it to France. In any case, it remained officially in service for pistols and machine pistols until 1949.

The pistols of the M 1935 series were based on patents by C. Petter and the SACM, and were basically modified Browning types which had undergone some changed, in comparison to the Colt 1911 A 1 pistol. The armed forces

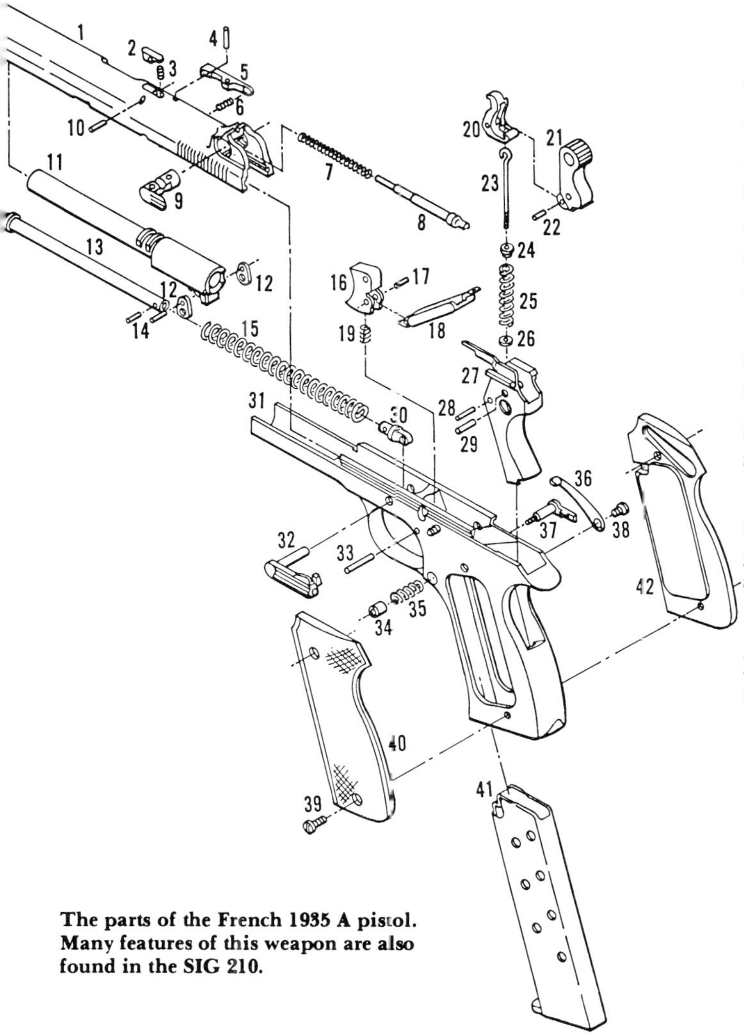

The parts of the French 1935 A pistol. Many features of this weapon are also found in the SIG 210.

stuck with these pistols until World War II and beyond, until their war in Indochina. In addition, handguns made in Britain and the Colt 1911 A 1 were used.

The 1950 Model

In many ways, a great similarity to the Colt 1911 A 1 can be discerned here. The barrel, with two cams on its top, fits into the inside of the slide and has a chain below, through a hole in which the axle of the catch lever fits. As in the Colt pistol, the trigger is designed only for single action — for the first shot, the hammer must be cocked by hand.

An advantage for rough military usage is the encapsulated, rod-controlled recoil spring, which can be removed completely after knocking out a holding pin.

Various safety features are built in, including a magazine safety. The magazine has a bulge on its left side which, when pushed in, reaches under a spring arm which then ceases to press on the trigger bar. When the magazine is removed, the trigger bar is immediately swung out of the area of the sear. The recoil safety works similarly here: its extension reaches into the course of the slide and presses the trigger bar down when the weapon is not locked.

The wing safety at the left rear of the slide locks the firing pin or covers it with a forward-moving pivot side to prevent the hammer from striking it. In the safety position, the lever reaches into the area of the hammer and indicates that firing cannot yet take place.

Similar to the SIG pistols, Petter, or now Star as well, the firing pin housing can be taken out of the receiver as a complete unit (without tools) from the rear and above. Thus the M 1950 is very easy to maintain.

The surface is parkerized in a medium gray, the grip panels are made of black bakelite and held in place by two small screws each.

The French M 1950 pistol in 9 mm Parabellum caliber is based on Petter's work and much resembles the 1935 A pistol.

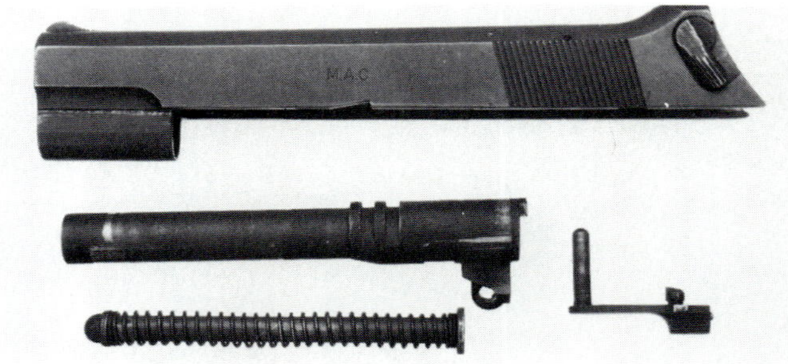

Tipping barrel with joint and two tabs, plus recoil spring with rod.

The weapon with safety on.

The surface is matte parkerized. The recoil spring is rod-guided for its whole length, and locking is done as in the Colt pistol.

The functioning lever in detail, with a view of the magazine safety. When the magazine is removed, the trigger bar is pushed away from the sear.

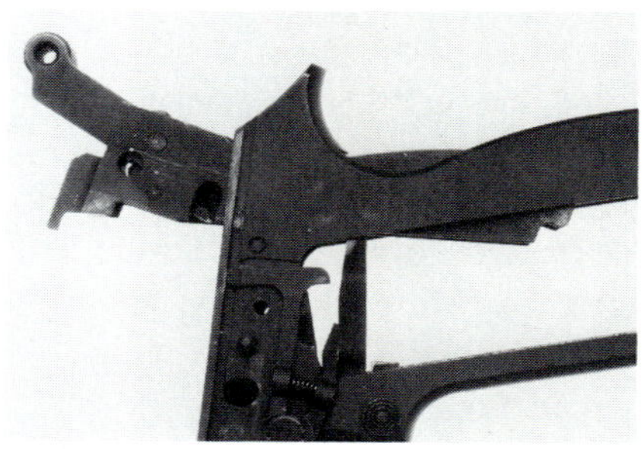

This design feature originated with Petter and is basically very practical. One can pull the whole firing pin unit up out of the frame.

Simple dismantling, as with most pistols of this type. The workmanship is solid and sturdy.

Technical Data: M. 1950 and PA-15

Model designation	Model 1950	PA-15
Manufacturer	M.A.C.	M.A.B.
System	Browning	Turning barrel
Caliber	9 mm Parabellum	9 mm Parabellum
Magazine capacity	9 cartridges	15 cartridges
Overall length	195 mm	200 mm
Overall height	143 mm	136 mm
Barrel length	111 mm	115 mm
Barrel	4 riflings, left	6 riflings, left
Width of grip	30 mm	40 mm
Weight empty	960 grams	1160 grams
Material	Steel	Steel
Finish	Phosphated	Burnished
Trigger	Single action	Single action
Sights	Fixed	Fixed
Safeties	Magazine, closing, lever	Magazine, closing, lever, safety rest

The PA-15 has an interesting locking system over the barrel, which turns on its own longitudinal axis. A high-performance SA pistol with good workmanship and 15 cartridges in the magazine.

Model PA-15

For sporting and possible service use, a new pistol in 9 mm Parabellum caliber was developed — it was introduced later and had a very interesting type of bolt. The "P-15 Competition" version has a barrel six inches long, an adjustable sight, and walnut grip panels. The forward mounting of the barrel, using a removable bushing housing, is a different feature of the sporting version. The official designation of the pistol is "9 mm PAP Mle F 1", the F 1 being the sport model of the MAB P-15. There is also another version with a magazine holding only eight rounds, while the pistol shown here has a magazine for 15 cartridges, and its trigger is set up as a simple single-action type.

The very neat workmanship and highly polished burnishing of the external surfaces are striking features of the P-15, setting it apart pleasantly from the matte-parkerized or black-painted French pistols.

The hammer has a massive safety rest, the firing pin is, as usual, a short flying ignition pin, a magazine safety, a firing safety (directly above the upward-arching trigger bar) and a manual safety on the back of the grip; like all the other parts, it is made of solid steel and makes a very robust impression.

The manual safety holds the slide fast in its cutout after insertion and blocks the sear by holding an extension under the flank of the sear.

The sights are fixed, andin fact, the foresight is a fixed part of the slide. The backsight block is pushed in place and can be adjusted laterally by striking it.

All versions of this pistol have the same bolt over the turning barrel, resembling the system of the Mexican Obregon pistol.

The barrel has a wide tab at the lower rear, and somewhat aside from it on the upper surface is a diagonally cut guiding tab which fits into its course within the slide, thereby guiding the slide forcibly in its forward and backward motion, which results in a turning of the barrel. The advantage is that the barrel does turn but cannot make any vertical movement in the muzzle area, as is the case with the tipping-barrel bolt. The lower cam fits into a massive intermediate piece that extends into the receiver and is held there by the pivot of the catch lever. At the same time, this intermediate piece is the carrier of the recoil-spring bar, and it also functions as a ramp for the cartridge. The recoil of the slide brings about a turning of the barrel, in the process of which the grooves of the intermediate piece serve as a turning joint; the upper tab comes out of its curve in the slide and moves into the straight part of its course, and the slide can then move backward against the pressure of the recoil spring, whereby the case is extracted and ejected. As it moves forward, a new cartridge is introduced. The turning of the barrel occurs only in the last seven to eight millimeters of its path, and the weapon is now locked again.

The PA-15 fits into the hand very well and can be used well and quickly thanks to the good location of the safety. Its only disadvantage is that it is not well known.

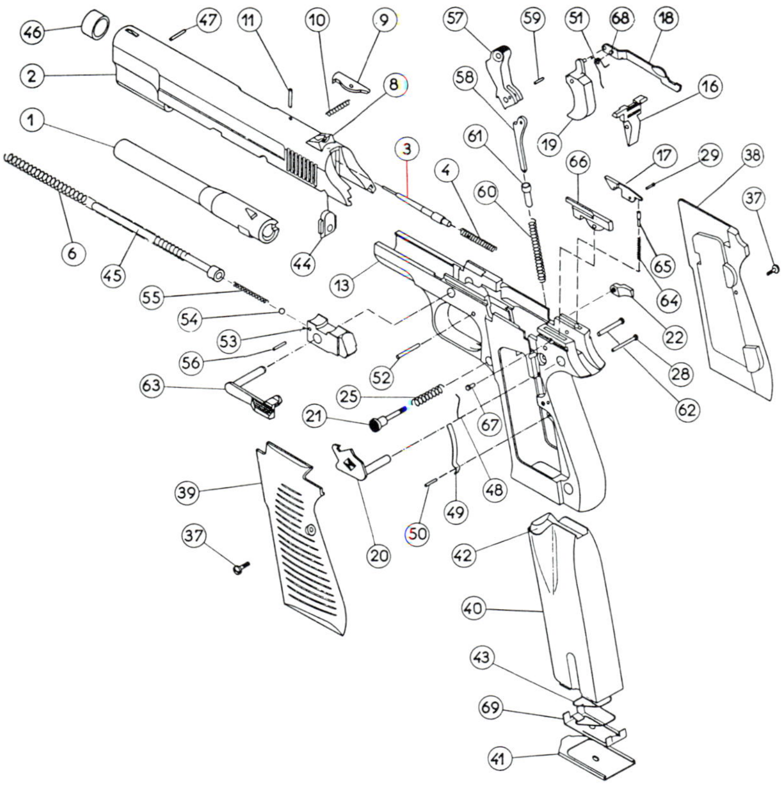

MAB Model P 15 Pistol

1 Barrel
2 Slide
3 Firing Pin
4 Firign Pin Spring
6 Recoil Spring
8 Rear Sight
9 Extractor
10 Extractor Spring
11 Extractor Pin
13 Frame
16 Sear
17 Magazine Safety
18 Connector
19 Trigger
20 Safety Lock
21 Magazine Catch Retainer
22 Magazine Catch
25 Magazine Catch Spring
28 Trigger Pin
29 Magazine Safety Pin
37 Grip Screws
38 Grip, Right
39 Grip, Left
40 Magazine
41 Magazine Floorplate
42 Magazine Follower
43 Magazine Spring
44 Firing Pin Retainer
45 Recoil Spring Guide
46 Slide Ring
47 Slide Ring Retainer
48 Safety Catch Spring
49 Sear Spring
51 Trigger Spring
52 Trigger Pin
53 Barrel Block
54 Ball
55 Slide Latch Spring
56 Recoil Spring Guide Pin
57 Hammer
58 Hammer Strut
59 Hammer Pin
60 Hammer Spring
61 Hammer Plunger
63 Slide Lock Lever
64 Magazine Safety Spring
65 Magazine Safety Plunger
66 Ejector
67 Ejector Pin
68 Spring Stud
69 Magazine Floorplate Retainer

The parts of the MAB Model P 15. For locking and unlocking, the barrel is forced to turn on its longitudinal axis and then releases the slide for its recoil.

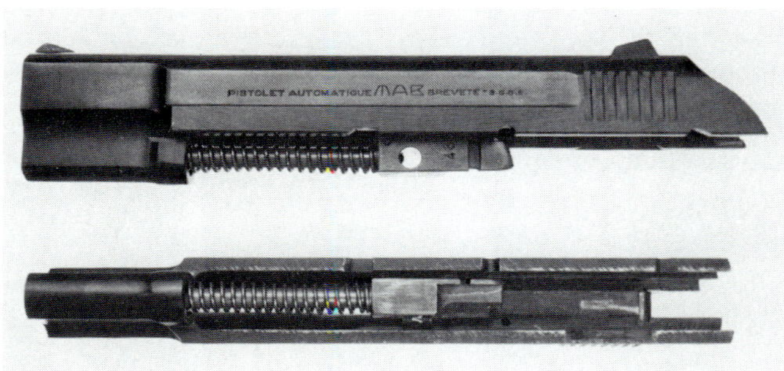

Slide with barrel and recoil spring in detail. The intermediate piece carries the recoil-spring rod and is also the feed ramp for the cartridge.

View of the ejection window. The guide for the turning barrel is easy to see.

Locking system in detail, strongly magnified. The tab forces the barrel to turn inside a rail of the slide.

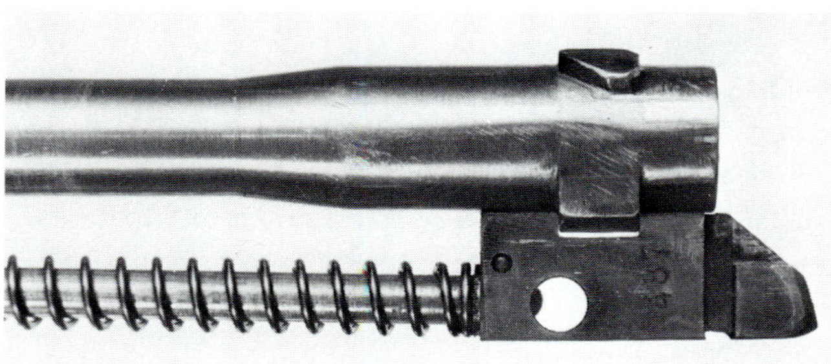

The dismantled PA-15 without magazine and grip panels.

ITALY

Italy has always had a flourishing weapons industry. Even today, hunting rifles compose the greatest part of the weapons manufactured there. The number of manufacturers is great, and one can always learn from the IWA in Nürnberg that Italy is strongly represented, with some seventy firms. At the present time, many superior and inferior replicas are coming from Italy. Most are copies of historical weapons, for the part muzzle-loaders. In the days of pocket pistols, the Italian firms were very active and did a lot to flood the market.

The best-known firms include that of Pietro Beretta, which have a long history of successful and varied products behind them.

Until World War II, the Italian Army used a wide variety of handguns, pistols and revolvers. One of the best-known pistols was the Glisenti, made for the 9 mm Glisenti caliber, a cartridge very similar to the 9 mm Parabellum, though weaker in terms of ballistic performance. At the beginning of the 1950s, the 9 mm Parabellum was accepted for military use and was also adopted by the police for their pistols and machine pistols. In Italy, good and well-made pistols were manufactured for use with the 9 mm Parabellum cartridge, these being made for the armed forces of Italy and other countries as well as for the police. The private owner is not allowed to possess such weapons, and may not have any weapons or cartridges used by the services. This is one reason why almost all Italian pistols are available alternatively in 7.65 mm Parabellum caliber. This gives rise to very interesting possibilities, such as modern pistols for the 9 mm Steyr cartridge or the 9 mm x 21 IMI.

Benelli B 76

The Italian firm of Benelli Armi S.p.A. has long been known as a manufacturer of good rifles, and entered the field of handgun manufacture relatively recently. The result was a conception that could be put on what had become a heavily occupied market as both a police or military service weapon and a privately used weapon. This concept proved to be successful to only a limited extent. Other manufacturers marketed weapons with larger magazine capacities, and this very feature was for a time an important criterion for the acceptance of self-

Benelli Model B 76 in its normal form and with adjustable sights.

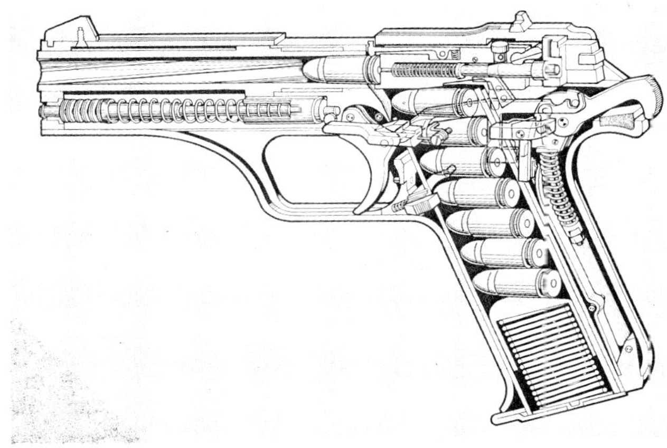

Diagonal drawing of the Benelli B 76.

loading pistols.

By lengthening the barrel and simultaneously adding extra weight, a large-caliber sport pistol was created that was improved yet again and marketed under the designation of MP 3 S in both 9 mm PARA and .32 S & W long WC calibers. The 9 mm PARA version in particular proved to have outstanding performance, and to date we have not been able at any time to achieve a similar

The same pistol, now with the grip, not intended for it, from the MP 3 S sport pistol with the same system. With its finger grooves, the weapon fits into the hand splendidly.

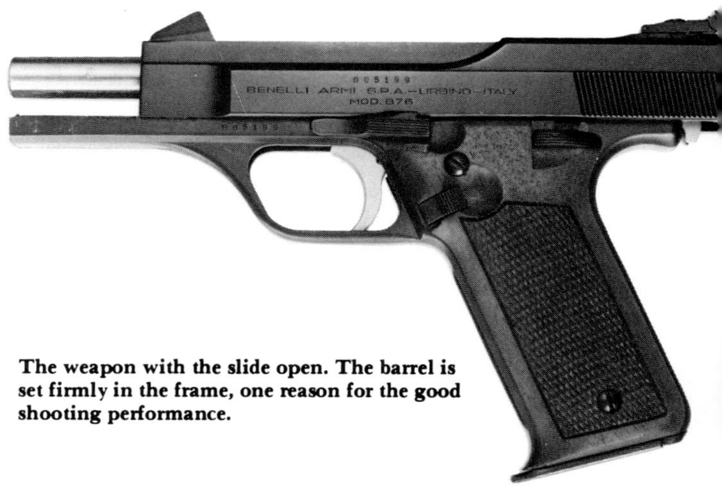

The weapon with the slide open. The barrel is set firmly in the frame, one reason for the good shooting performance.

The frame is neatly welded together out of two stamped halves, and is thus very stable. Additional braces stiffen the frame.

performance with any other pistol. Some features of the Benelli pistol are different from previous designs. First of all, the bolt system via a moveable support bolt is different.

With this system the Benelli does not bolt rigidly, but movably. A support plate (part 5 in the drawing on page 121) mounted at the rear of the breechblock achieves a non-rigid connection between the breechblock and the frame. In addition, the frame has a step against which the breechblock is braced. In the course of releasing the bolt, it lifts to some extent at the rear and can slide over the aforementioned step.

When the slide is drawn backward by hand, a bolt, conically shaped at the bottom, on the top of the breechblock fits into a matching cutout at the back of the slide, whereby it is lifted somewhat and then slides over the step. The 32-caliber sporting version does not have this function, but operates like a typical spring-mass breech.

Two advantages are in practice here: the barrel can be rigidly screwed into place, which was one of the reasons for the fine shooting performance, as no disturbances occur even with very lightly loaded pistols, while other systems no longer function properly under such conditions.

But it cannot be concealed that the functioning of the pistol over a period of time depends precisely on the maintenance of this sharp-angled step in the frame. If it suffers considerable wear, the Benelli becomes "faster", and the bolting no longer functions clearly. What would help would be a sintering or "armoring" of the step. With the use of a particular electrode, material of extreme hardness can be applied and protect it from any disturbances that might occur after heavy use.

The receiver is stamped out of 2 mm sheet steel, then welded and neatly reworked. Only internally can one notice after gaining some experience that the unification of the two halves must have been achieved that way. Further details become known over time and after dismantling, which can be described briefly here. After the magazine is removed and a safety check has been made, the slide is pulled back all the way and stopped at the back. In the process, one has to get used to a different type of magazine catch. It is not pressed into place, but pushed forward with the right thumb, after which the magazine section moves forward and is then stopped by a block. The slide has two possible positions in its rear position, one over the usual catch lever as well as a dividing rest behind it, into which the safety lever must be pushed. Here too a new technique must be gotten used to: the safety is pushed up vertically and not turned. With the help of the magazine base or a strong thumbnail, the two breech hooks are swung inward, after

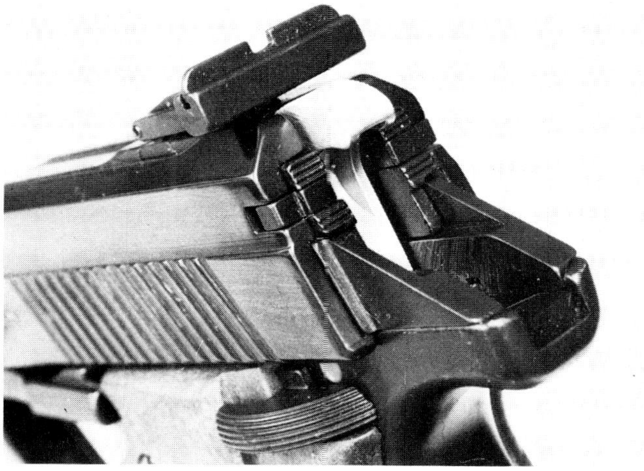

For dismantling, both hooks are swung out, which is not easy to do with this pistol.

View of the support flap, which forms a non-rigid link between the breechblock and frame.

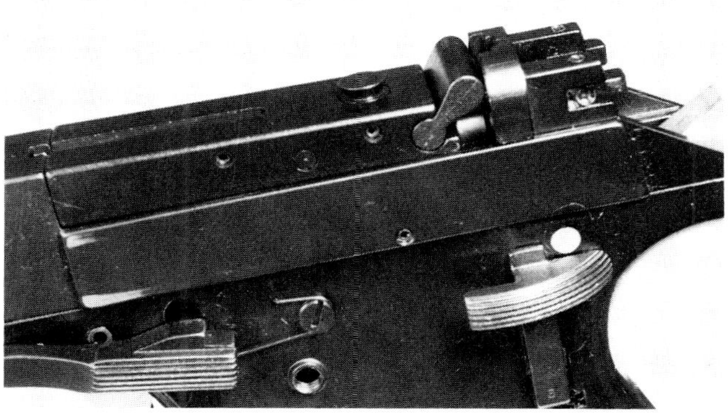

The receiver parts of the B 76 without the barrel.

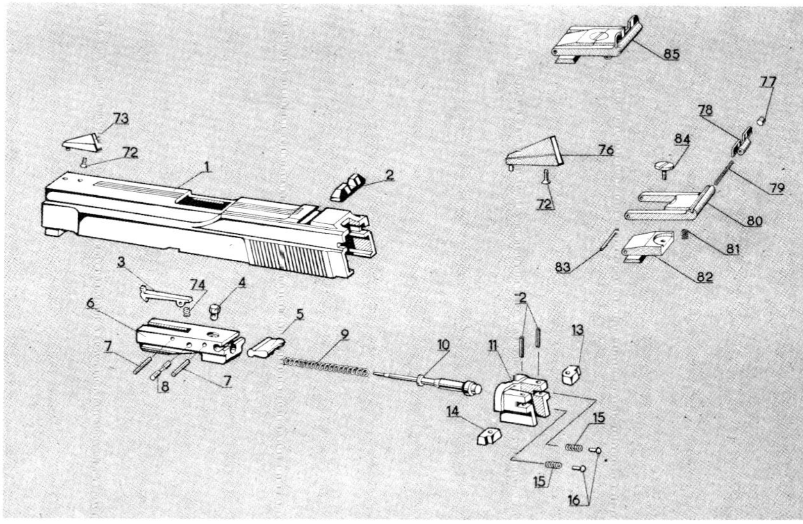

Parts of the slide, breech and sights.

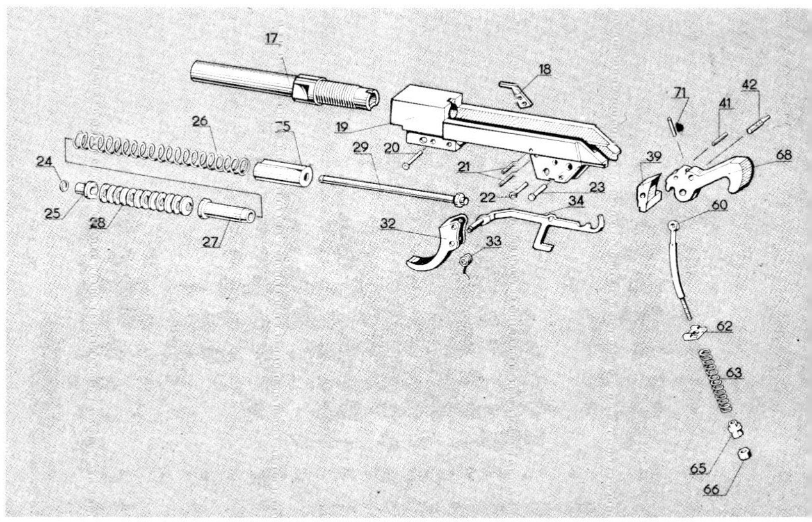

Parts of the barrel, grip inlay, buffers and trigger system.

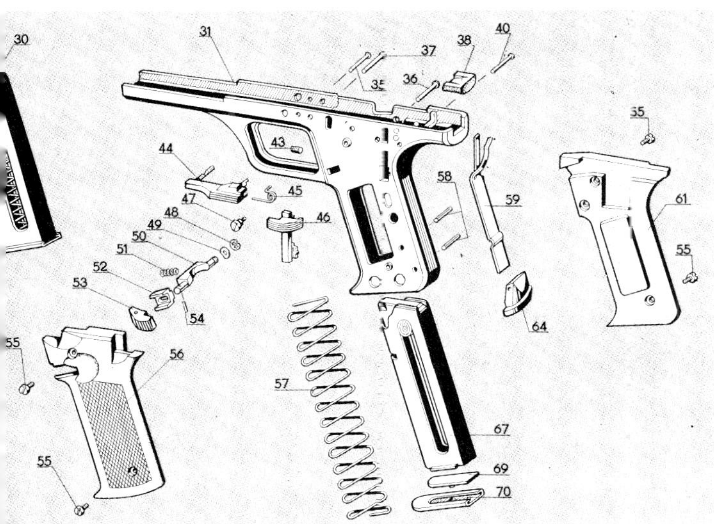

which, once the firing pin has been pushed in, the breechblock can be removed from the bottom of the slide. After that the slide is pushed out of the receiver to the front, and the recoil spring with its guides and the breechblock can be removed.

Only now can it be seen that the massive breech-guiding piece is linked to the receiver via the heavy cocking pins. The barrel is screwed into this guiding piece, and a size 14 wrench is required to remove it. This simple changing of barrels may be one reason why the pistol, with the same design, is available in 9 mm PARA, 7.65 mm PARA and 9 mm ULTRA calibers. On the

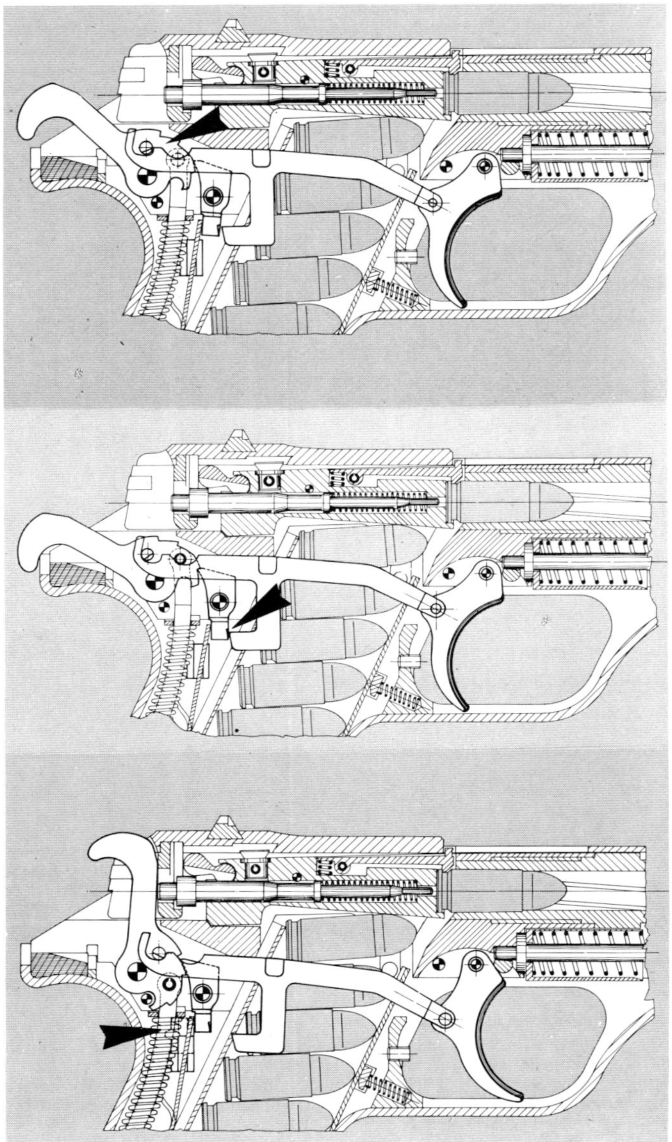

The individual trigger functions of the B 76.

The dismantled B 76. Note the unusual recoil spring with its encapsulated guiding rod.

other hand, the ease of changing the barrel may encourage the manufacturer to try fitting the pistol with a differently profiled barrel some day.

The lateral push safety works simultaneously on the trigger, hammer and slide. In addition, the hammer has a safety rest, from which it can be released only by the final cocking of the hammer.

The extractor is mounted at the top of the breechblock so that, when there is a cartridge or case in the chamber, it projects somewhat and indicates the condition of the weapon by showing its red front surface.

There are said to have been problems with the hammers of the first Benelli pistols, as they tended to break off. To counteract this, the improved version shown here has had a hammer buffer added at the back of the receiver.

The B 76 is marketed with a second magazine, a small Inbus wrench to adjust the trigger-stop screw, and a cleaning brush. The grip panels are made of walnut with a cleanly cut herringbone pattern, and the sport-model grip can be applied to all versions without any modifications.

Technical Data: Benelli B 76/MP 3-S Series

Version	B 76	MP 3-S	MP 3-S
Caliber	9 mm Para/7.65 mm	Ultra 9 mm Para.	32 S+W long WC
Magazine capacity	8	5	5
Weight empty	1000 grams	1170 grams	1170 grams
Barrel length	108 mm	143 mm	143 mm
Overall length	204 mm	235 mm	235 mm
Overall height	142 mm	142 mm	142 mm
Grip width	33 mm	50 mm	50 mm
Sights	adjustable	adjustable	adjustable
Sight line	153 mm	178 mm	178 mm
Trigger	double action	single action	single action
Bolt	support plate	support plate	none
Finish	burnished, matte	burnished/polished	burnished/polish

Beretta 1951 Model

Just after World War II, Beretta developed a self-loading pistol for the 9 mm Parabellum cartridge, and was officially adopted by the Italian Army and Navy under the designation of M 1951. In addition, this robust and easy-to-handle pistol was also put into service by Israel and Egypt. Another version of the pistol, with exactly the same construction, was made for the 7.65 mm Parabellum caliber; this was the Model 952. For sporting use, Beretta made the Model 952 Special, a weapon with a longer barrel, adjustable sights and a shaped grip. As it stood, the Model 1951 could no longer meet modern-day requirements. The trigger was designed only for single-action functioning — for the first shot, the hammer had to be cocked by hand.

The magazine, and the grip section is made of steel or, alternatively, aluminum, and holds eight cartridges in a single row. The magazine base is lengthened to the front and below, thus improving its handling considerably. Locking is done by a swinging bolt located under the barrel, in the same manner that was first used successfully in great numbers in the P 38. The swinging bolt has since been retained by Beretta, and can be found in the entire 92 to 92 F series.

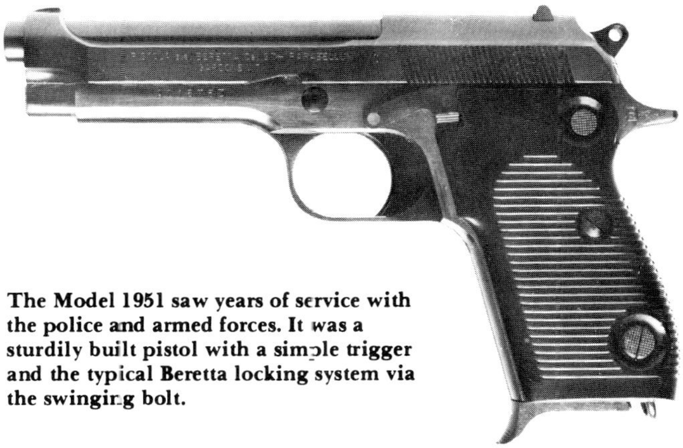

The Model 1951 saw years of service with the police and armed forces. It was a sturdily built pistol with a simple trigger and the typical Beretta locking system via the swinging bolt.

The trigger bar is situated on the right side of the receiver. The recoil safety works directly on this bar and, when the system is not completely locked, pushes it down out of its contact with the sear. The safety, a moveable push-button, is mounted in the upper rear of the receiver, and each of the plastic grip panels has a lowered orifice for it. When the cocked pistol is to be put on safety, the button is pushed from left to right, in which case the hammer is locked with the sear.

The magazine catch is located in the receiver so that a perforation in the left grip panel is necessary. The

Drawings of the Beretta Model 1951, showing the swinging bolt.

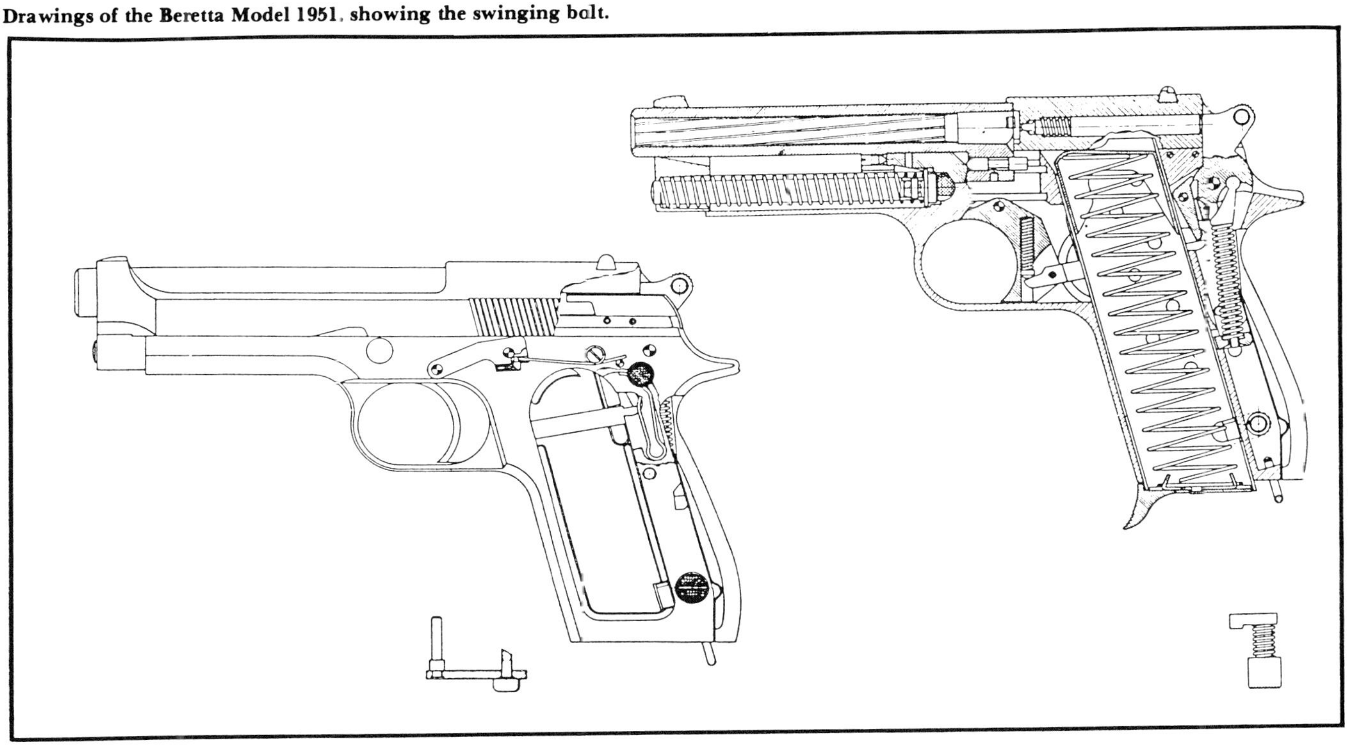

The same pistol dismantled. The frame is made of steel.

magazine is held completely fast by a hook.

As with all Beretta pistols, dismantling it is pleasantly simple. After checking the safety and removing the magazine, one pulls the slide back until the opening on the right side is directly over the dismantling lever located on the right side; this can then be turned. The complete upper section can then be pushed out of the receiver. After removing the recoil spring, which is controlled by a rod, the barrel can be lifted out of the slide. Further dismantling is unnecessary.

For military and police use (much as with a similar version of the Beretta 92), a version that could be switched to sustained fire was developed — at the time it was designated Model 951 "A Raffica." This pistol had a somewhat longer barrel and took magazines that held 10 or 15 cartridges. On the front of the receiver a folding handhold was attached, which was supposed to make control possible while shooting. The sustained-fire switch was located immediately above and behind the trigger on the right side of the grip.

The Beretta 92 Series

The Model 92, a pistol with a double action trigger, replaced the earlier Model 951 in 9 mm PARA caliber and the Model 952 in 7.65 mm PARA caliber. The preparation of a weapon with the same structure in 7.65 mm PARA caliber need not be ascribed to the good performance of this cartridge alone. In Italy, private ownership of any weapons and cartridges that are used by the military or the police is forbidden, and these are without exception weapons in 9 mm PARA caliber — it is also because pistols in the 9 mm caliber Steyr, were made especially for Italy. The concept of the 92 series was slightly modified several times. Of them, the 92 version remained the simplest in form. Aside from an identical bolt, the lateral safety is still at the upper rear of the receiver, and the magazine catch is mounted at the lower rear of the grip. The grip panels are made of wood, and the very small and deep-set sights are not adjustable. With 15 cartridges in a two-row magazine and one more cartridge in the chamber, the Model 92 was one of the first production weapons with this high magazine capacity.

The Model 92 S differs from the previous weapon in its placement of the side safety, which was now a turning lever mounted on the back of the slide. Former identifying marks remained unchanged.

The early Beretta 92 with its magazine catch down in the frame, and safety in the grip.

The Model 92 SB, featuring a magazine catch behind the trigger guard and safety high on both sides of the slide. Walnut grip panels are mounted.

The Model 92 SB is still up to date, and it is also on the market in shortened but otherwise identical form as the Model 92 SB Compact. The pistol is relatively large and heavy, but easy to hold and operate just the same. It is not meant to be carried under cover, but to be carried in a service holster. The grip is made of aluminum, finished in black and nicely worked, though the relatively short slide guide can be a disadvantage in terms of precision. The front and back of the grip are grooved lengthwise, not too sharply, and is quite an advantage, as the grip fits into the hand without slipping.

The magazine catch is normally inserted from the left, and is built so that it can be mounted on the right by a skilled owner or gunsmith.

Corresponding to present-day requirements for service weapons, the 92 SB has a complex safety system. The

Slide and barrel, showing the swinging bolt. Unlike many pistols, the slide of the 92 SB is open almost all the way.

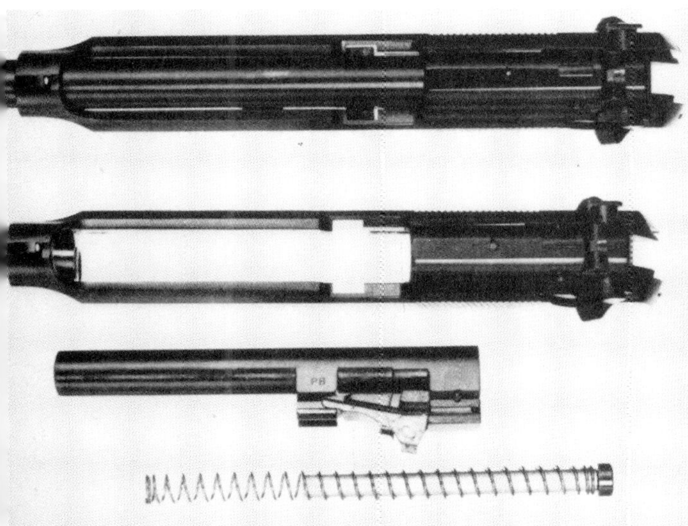

extractor projects visibly and tangibly from the slide when a cartridge is inserted, thus indicating the loaded condition — it is not possible to fire when the breech is not closed. When the side safety has been set, the trigger cannot be pulled, nor can the hammer be set in its resting position. When the safety is released, it can be set in its safety rest, from which it emerges safely when the safety is set. The cocked hammer can be decocked over the

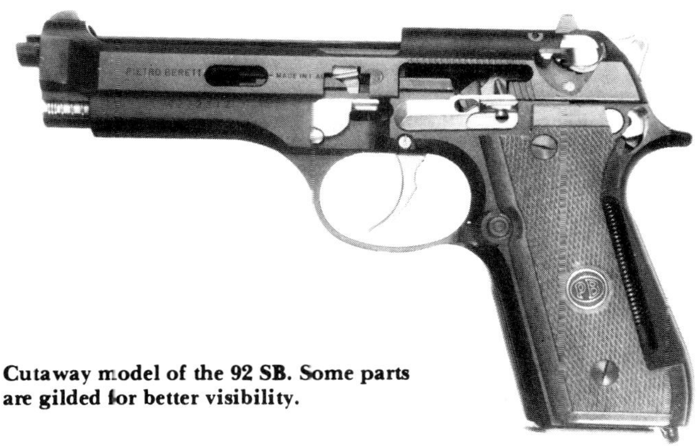

Cutaway model of the 92 SB. Some parts are gilded for better visibility.

safety, which is another modern requirement.

The short firing pin remains blocked until shortly before the shot is finally fired. During the last part of its movement, the trigger lifts a block vertically and thus releases the firing pin. If the weapon falls on its hammer, it cannot fire, nor can it if the trigger or hammer slides out of place. The lifted block emerges visibly some three mm out of the top of the slide, so that one can check the status of this system at any time.

The manual safety is set on both sides, though the lever on the right side is somewhat smaller.

Dismantling is simple, and is done almost exactly as with the Walther P 88, which arrived on the market later. After the magazine is removed and the chamber is checked, the locking button of the dismantling lever is pushed from the right, and then the lever is pushed downward 90 degrees. The whole upper part can then be pushed forward off the receiver. After the recoil spring is removed along with its guiding bar, the barrel can be pulled out of the sled to the rear. The bolt used in the 92 series is a blend of the Walther swinging bolt and the Browning spring support. As soon as the slide and barrel have moved backward some 8 mm, the pressure rod pushes below the swinging bolt in front of the grip and thus pushes the bolt down. In so doing, both of its

The cutaway model in detail: the contact of the external trigger bar with the sear, the contact of the recoil safety, and the blocking of the firing pin are easy to see.

Only when the trigger is pulled is the firing pin block lifted, coming out visibly and tangibly on top.

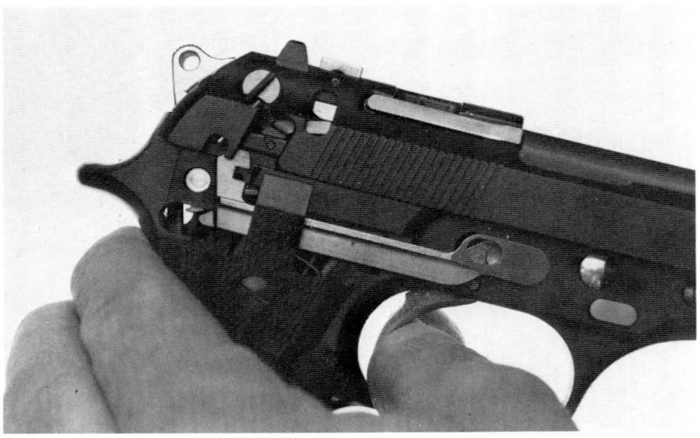

extensions move out of the cutouts in the slide, and the latter can move backward independently. Where the bolt strikes, no steel has been used — this was introduced in the P 38 to avoid misshaping of the material.

One can look into the bolt from above — as for why, it is neither logical nor beneficial. In the very area where the bolt turns into the slide, an additional step has been made. In any case, it would have made more sense to dispense with this step and leave as much material as possible there. Another problem is that, because of this open type of construction, the weapon is more inclined to pick up dirt.

The regular version of the 92 SB is sold with grip panels made of black plastic, but similar panels made of semi-dark stained walnut with a herringbone pattern are also available.

The 92 SB Compact model is slightly smaller in terms of length and height, and is presently available in 9 mm PARA and 7.65 mm PARA calibers. There are no other technical differences.

The Model 92 SB version has seen years of successful service in various police departments, including those outside Italy. In the USA it has been adopted by the police of numerous states, including the Connecticut and Wyoming State Police and the legendary Texas Rangers. Naturally, that is not exactly an unqualified joy for the local manufacturers, who have seen their own reputations sink more and more because of Italian developments. In spite of that, as renowned a firm as Colt has not yet been able to offer an up-to-date weapon that will satisfy the requirements of America's own armed forces and security agencies.

When a search for a new army pistol for the US forces was made, virtually all of the well-known manufacturers submitted their designs for testing. The winner of this competition was the firm of Beretta with its Model 92 F (F for Forces). The pistols to be delivered were manufactured partly in Italy and partly in a branch facility in Accokeek, Maryland, not far from Washington, D.C. Thus the problem of keeping domestic manufacturers employed was solved harmoniously for the most part, as the weapons are produced by American specialist labor there.

The Beretta Model 92 F differs only slightly in technical terms from the 92 SB and 92 SB Compact models. The receiver, though still made of aluminum, has a somewhat different shape, as does the magazine base that was made to fit it. The grooved trigger guard bends forward somewhat, and widens, as is generally required today for combat-ready pistols. The receiver does not run straight downward, but curves out slightly and thus cleanly fits into the hand. The surface is also different; it is no longer burnished to a high polish, but left completely matte and burnished a deep black. The grip panels are made of plastic with a pressed-in herringbone pattern and slightly roughened surfaces around it. The two-part safety, the simple dismantling and the magazine catch mounted high in the grip and capable of being inserted when needed have all been retained. The magazine holds 15 cartridges in two rows, and a sixteenth cartridge can be carried safely in the chamber.

For the civilian market, the F versions are alternatively available with walnut grip panels. Under the 98 F model designation there is also a version with the same construction, the 7.65 mm Parabellum caliber, which is made chiefly for private use in Italy.

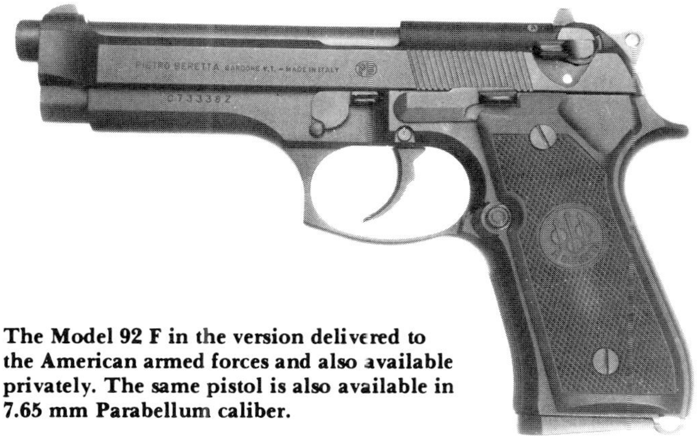

The Model 92 F in the version delivered to the American armed forces and also available privately. The same pistol is also available in 7.65 mm Parabellum caliber.

The 92 SB-Compact with the round trigger guard and wooden grip panels.

The Compact version holds 13 cartridges in the magazine and fires no worse than the longer version.

The slide is held back after the last shot in all models. The recoil spring is rod-guided.

Same technology but different grip sizes: At right the 92 F, at left the 92 F-Compact with the lengthened magazine base.

For the Beretta 92 there is a version that can be fired with an attached shaft. The picture comes from a Japanese kit.

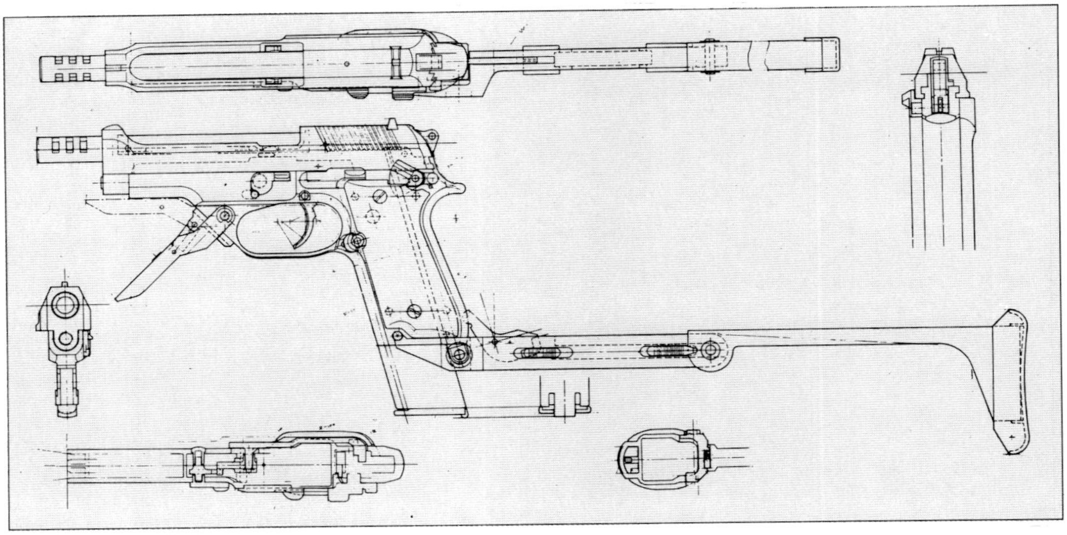

Mod. 92 S

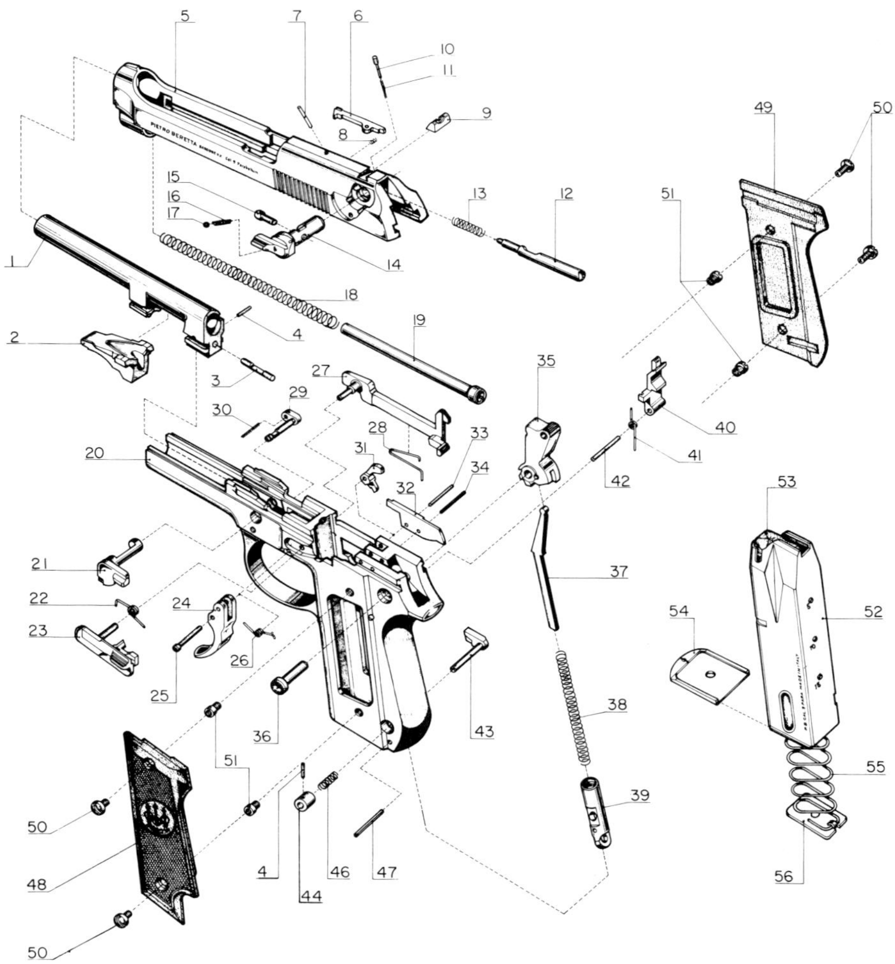

Parts of the Beretta 92 S; it has a manual safety high in the slide, and the magazine catch low in the grip.

Mod. 92 F, 92 F "Compact"

Parts of the 92 F and 92 F-Compact pistols for military use, with safety on both sides and magazine catch behind the trigger guard.

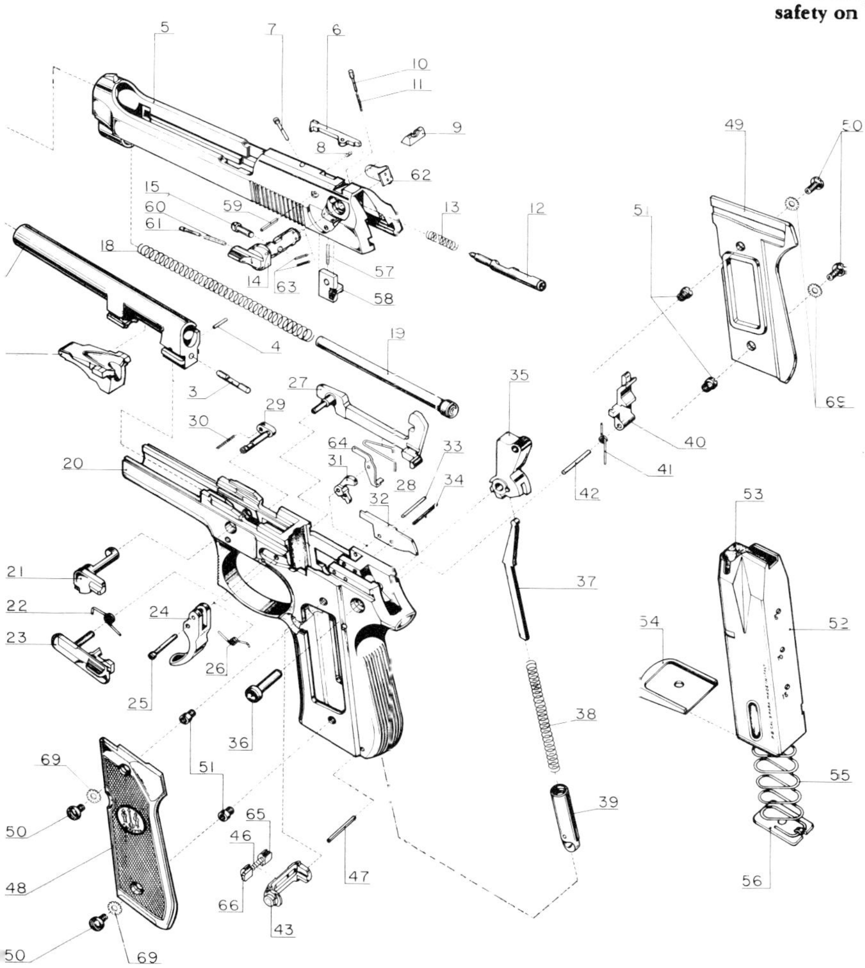

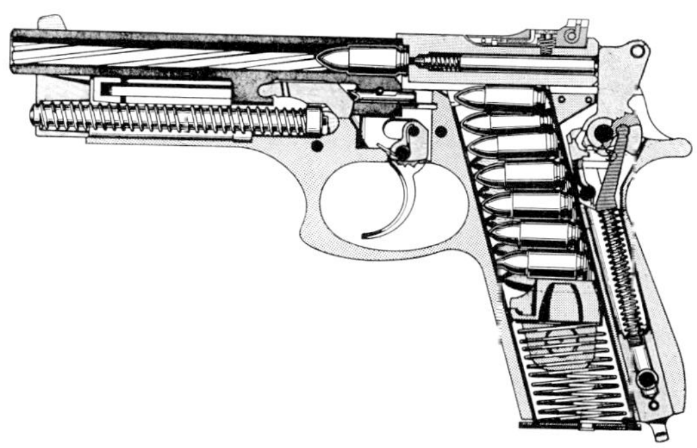

Cutaway of the early Beretta 92 with fixed sight and without the extra firing pin block.

Technical Data: Beretta 92 S and 92 SB Series

Type	92 S	92 SB	92 SB-Compact	92 SB-Compact
Caliber	9 Para.	9 Para.	9 Para.	7.65 Para.
Overall length	217 mm	217 mm	197 mm	197 mm
Height	137 mm	137 mm	129 mm	129 mm
Width	37 mm	37 mm	39 mm	39 mm
Barrel length	125 mm	125 mm	109 mm	109 mm
Sight line	155 mm	155 mm	147 mm	147 mm
Weight empty	975 grams	975 grams	885 grams	900 grams
Barrel profile	6 riflings to right, ca. 250 mm long			
Sights	Fixed, white markings on fore- and backsight			
Material	Aluminum frame			
Finish	burnished/eloxied			
Grip panels	plastic / wood optional / wood			
Safeties	Manual, both sides, firing pin, bolt, safety rest			

Bernardelli P 018/9

This is one of the developments which came into being on account of the search for a new self-loading pistol for police and military use. The trend inclined, among other things, toward a larger magazine capacity of 15 cartridges, a requirement that many of the new pistols are able to meet today without having grown into unhandy monsters.

The Bernardelli P 018/9, built by the Vincenzo Bernardelli s.p.a. in Gardone-Brescia, is now a part of a complete family of weapons. In Italy it is not legal for private owners to possess or fire cartridges that are in use by the police or the military, a limitation that is also law in other countries. Thus the P 018 was originally produced in 7.65 mm PARA caliber, and also made for export in 9 mm caliber. As a further alternative, the version with the rather smooth plastic grip is offered, plus a version with the same design with a wooden grip, and a version with decreased length, height and magazine capacity, designated "Compact" — this type holds one cartridge fewer than the basic version.

The P 018/9 has a very pleasant appearance, especially when one keeps in mind that in the last few years many pistols have shown an undeniable trend toward angular designs. The entire design is based on straight lines, however it is not angular in the sense of being uncomfortable or awkward to handle. The pistol makes a good first impression, the workmanship is neat, and the moving parts show almost no play. Naturally the pistol is not equal to the SIG 210, but is a very economical alternative to many a renowned American-made pistol with outmoded technology. The whole upper surface has a pleasant matte finish and is burnished a deep black. The operating levers are angular but not to the point where they cause disturbance or injury. The slide includes a sharp-angled handhold which bears a certain similarity to the Sig/Sauer pistols. The slide and grip are machined out of solid metal and neatly worked in every respect. This can be seen clearly when the weapon is dismantled to its smallest parts. Where other weapons have a thin, stamped trigger bar with insufficient stability against bending, here there is a bar more than 2 mm thick that can inspire confidence.

Dismantling is problem-free. After removing the magazine and checking the chamber safety, the slide is pulled back a few millimeters and then pushed out from the right to the left of the catch lever. The catch lever and

A little-known but well-made pistol: the Bernardelli P 018/9, also offered in the same form in 7.65 mm Parabellum caliber and as the shorter Compact version.

The right side of the Bernardelli pistol. The very straight lines contribute to the overall good looks.

The pistol dismantled for cleaning, without magazine or grip panels, which can be had in plastic or walnut.

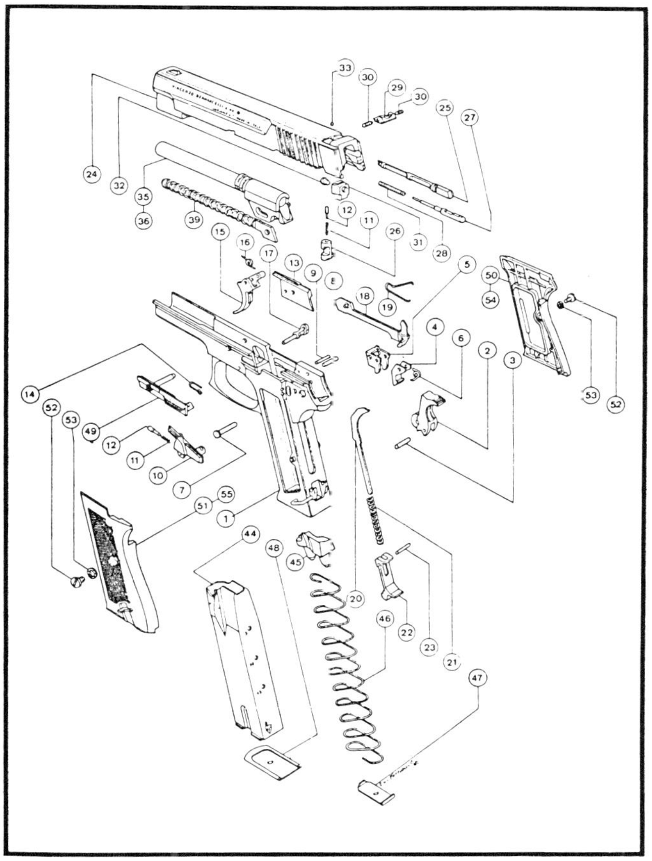

The parts of the Italian Bernardelli P 018/9.

slide each have a line marking for this purpose, and the lines must be made to match, though someone seems to have forgotten to mark the weapon at hand. The slide, along with the barrel, can be pushed forward out of the grip in the usual way, and the barrel can be removed after the rod-guided recoil spring is removed. The improved Browning-type bolt, with the inside guiding curve in the barrel attachment, is used. The barrel has two like formed cams on its upper surface in which it fits into corresponding grooves of the slide. The barrel has six riflings that turn to the right, with the typical profile for jacketed bullets. Its injection ramp has been smoothed by hand, insuring no disturbances in shooting.

When the slide is furhter dismantled and the firing pin, cover plate and extractor are removed, one notes a high degree of workmanship, which has not been the standard in pistols in this price range for years. The work has been done in such detail that a spring resting knob has been fitted in the cover plate of the firing pin to give added stability. This is not actually necessary in functional terms, as the plate is held sufficiently by the

A very stable steel frame. The trigger bar has been removed.

projecting firing pin. The firing pin is made of two parts with a firing pin section on the front, which is not surprising, as one would need three hands to assemble it otherwise. Assembly and dismantling can be done only while pushing in on the firing pin lock, which is pushed up over the trigger by the upstanding point of the sear immediately before firing. Thus despite its not exactly up-to-date safety system, the P 018 is a very safe pistol. In terms of safety, the hammer has a safety rest — the lateral manual safety acts as a rest and completely locks the sear , which is not a bad idea either. Safety systems of self-loading pistols, if they are the older lateral types, are more and more a thing of the past, yet the manufacturer has listened to the wishes of his official customers. This has led to positively astounding measures like the manual safety of the Astra A-90 or P 7 by Heckler & Koch —regardless of technology, business goes on.

The sights are only partially adjustable, and not at all in height, with only the backsight adjustable to the side. For this purpose the backsight block has an Inbus screw on each side, both of which must be loosened and then tightened after the sight is adjusted.

As for the remaining technology, the P 018 is not exactly filled with impressive new features. The system is very reminiscent of the Spanish Astra A-80, except that here a different manner of dismantling has been chosen, and there is no means of decocking the hammer.

The grip, made of injected plastic, has been criticized, as its surface outside of the rippled areas is simply too smooth to offer a sufficient handhold with long use, or a wet hand. The somewhat more expensive wooden grip is certainly the better choice. In practical testing the pistol

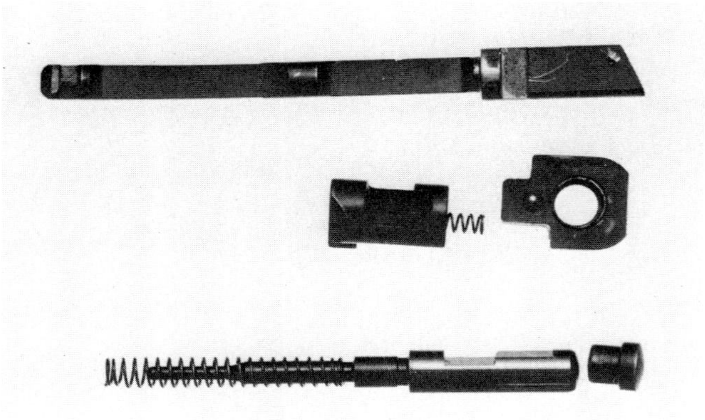

Moving parts of the slide. All parts are very well polished and fitted.

proved to be problem-free — too weakly charged cartridges that still function when fired from light pistols give problems here, though, and one has to come up with a good medium charge. The pistol was fired from a sitting position at a range of 15 meters, and with cartridges by GECO or Hirtenberger, the ten-point circle of the bull's-eye could be hit regularly with ease. The recoil was not great, being a weak push rather than the rough jerk given by many light pistols. There were no problems that could have been caused by the weapon, and a probable advantage in terms of shooting performance was the long movement of the slide on the grip, both pieces moving almost their entire length.

The trigger has been thoroughly was reworked. With a cocked hammer, it releases with hardly 3000 grams of resistance, and still has a rough path of more than one millimeter, after which it falls through a good 3 mm. This does not seem to change, for even if a too-short stop were applied, there would be problems in firing with the double action trigger, which has some 6000 grams of resistance but still stays within the bounds of normal values. Whomever does not just keep a pistol in a case and admire it joyfully once in a while, will want to subject the trigger to a thorough reworking. Some polish on the rests, a light shortening of the firing pin rest and a slight shortening of the hammer spring work at least minor miracles.

Tanfoglio Model 90 TA

In *Pistols of the World* by Hogg and Weeks, the firm of Tanfoglio is only briefly mentioned. In the 1940s they began to manufacture low-priced pocket pistols, which could be sold in great quantities in the USA at that time. In 1958 the firm went bankrupt, however it was soon brought back to life again under the name of "G. Tanfoglio Fabricca d'Armi." When strict provisions of the Gun Control Act went into effect in the USA in 1968, it struck Tanfoglio's low-priced weapons a hard blow, for they were as good as unsalable. Today this manufacturer is doing business under the name of "Fratelli Tanfoglio S.p.A. Gardone V.T. Italy", at least that is the inscription on the left side of the slide of the pistols shown here, which were first displayed to the general public at the IWA 86. Until that time, and for a time afterwards, little was heard of the pistols of the TA 90 series, as their importers wrapped themselves in silence. The situation improved only after the firm of E. Kettner had taken over their distribution.

In fact, pistols of the TA 90 series are not much more than copies of the Czech CZ 75, which has gained a good reputation in Germany. It was one of the first all-steel pistols in 9 mm Parabellum caliber with a 15-shot magazine. At closer inspection, several differences can be seen, some of which the CZ 75 ought to have. All in all, the Italian manufacturer has hoped for a good market in the USA, as in spite of everything, it is almost impossible to privately obtain weapons from the former eastern block. It is not surprising that the CZ 75 is offered for sale occasionally here, but at horrendous prices that have no real relevance to the product.

The similarity of the TA 90 to the CZ 75 in design goes

Technical Data: Bernardelli P 018/9 and P 019/9 Compact

	P 018/9	P 019/9 Compact
Caliber	9 mm Para. (7.65 mm P.)	9 mm Para.
Barrel length	122 mm	122 mm
Barrel	6 riflings, right	6 riflings, right
Overall length	213 mm	193 mm
Height	145 mm	139 mm
Grip width	35 mm	35 mm
Sights	Backsight laterally adjustable	
Sight line	160 mm	140 mm
Weight empty	ca. 998 grams	ca. 900 grams
Magazine capacity	15 + 1	15 + 1
Safeties	Firing pin block, bolt, manual, safety rest	
Material	Steel	Steel
Finish	matte burnished	matte burnished
Bolt	Browning, tipping barrel	
Grip panels	Plastic or walnut	Walnut

The CZ 75 could do well on the market. It is no wonder that it has been copied. Here are the CZ 75 and, in comparison, the TA 90 Baby.

to the extent that the barrels and slides can be exchanged, though without retaining the function of the decocking lever. In this respect the essential difference appears: The TA 90 has no manual safety on the side of the grip, rather it is on the upper left side of the slide, just behind the ridges of the handhold. The safety puts the trigger bar out of action and can always be applied whether the hammer is cocked or not. The hammer has a safety rest, and it can be decocked over this rest by setting the safety. When the hammer is decocked via the safety, the firing pin is first moved out of its effective area in the slide, and only then does the hammer move forward along with the trigger. The Czech pistol lacks this means of decocking the hammer, a trend of the times having been ignored.

The guiding of the barrel in the TA 90 is unlike that of its more or less distant model. A guiding casing has been screwed into the front of the slide with a long, thin screw. If need be, the casing can be removed and replaced by a very precisely fitting casing, a problem for gunsmiths. In addition, the TA 90 has a longer guiding rod for the recoil spring, which projects in front when the slide recoils. Many shooters complain that their CZ 75 becomes to hot after rapid firing and is inclined to jam — it is possible that this is a disadvantage of the closed slide. When a guiding rod is present, as in the TA 90, more cooling air can get into the weapon.

The sear is also different from that of the Czech pistol. It has a rounded decocking lever extending upward. When the safety is set, a small bar projects from the bottom of the slide, pushes on this sear lever and thus

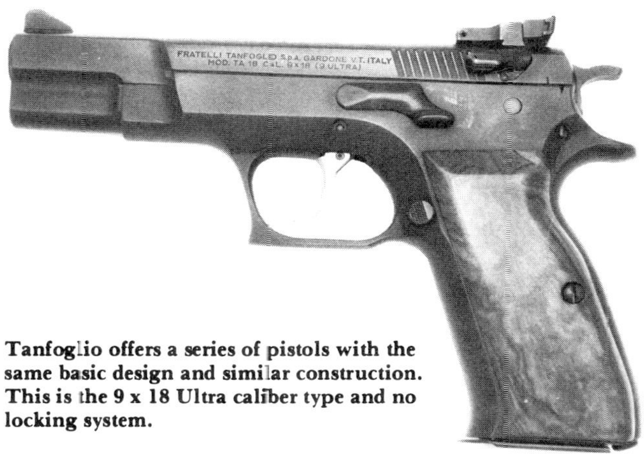

Tanfoglio offers a series of pistols with the same basic design and similar construction. This is the 9 x 18 Ultra caliber type and no locking system.

releases the cocked hammer. By this time, the firing pin has already been moved away.

Along with the normal 15-shot pistol, Tanfoglio has also brought out a smaller version, the TA 90 Baby. The magazine holds 12 cartridges, and the grip, slide and barrel have been decreased to a handy size. This little pistol is not notably larger than pistols in the particularly weak calibers, but its grip is clearly larger, and is made even bigger by the attached grip panels of steel-reinforced rubber. This compact weapon, with its trigger guard curved forward and ridged, fits into the hand particularly well and is certainly a sensible and also economical addition to what the firm marketed earlier. The sights are rimmed in white, the foresight is marked in white, the hammer has a shorter spur, and the barrel itself has only a ring-shaped bulge for bolting.

Unlike the Czech model, the Tanfoglio pistols have a rod-guided recoil spring. The grip panels are made of reinforced rubber.

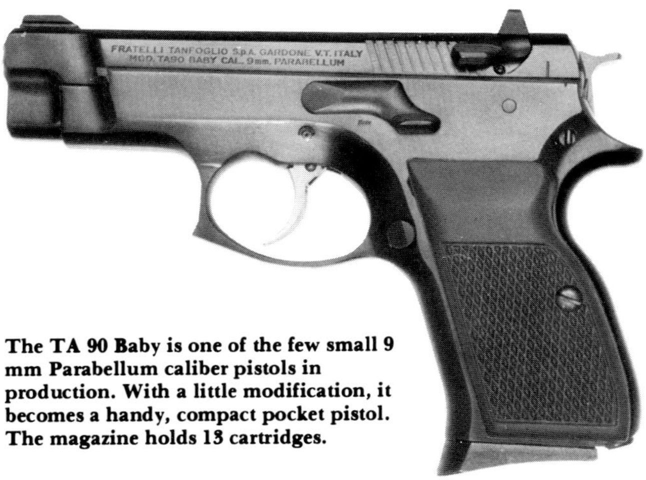

The TA 90 Baby is one of the few small 9 mm Parabellum caliber pistols in production. With a little modification, it becomes a handy, compact pocket pistol. The magazine holds 13 cartridges.

Technical Data: Tanfoglio TA 90/TA 90 Baby

Manufacturer	Fabricia d'Armi Fratelli Tanfoglio S.P.A., Gardone	
Designation	TA 90	TA 90 Baby
Caliber	9 mm Para*	9 mm Para*
Magazine capacity	15 cartridges	15 cartridges
Overall length	204 mm	175 mm
Height/width	140 mm/34 mm	125 mm/34 mm
Bolt system	Tipping barrel	Tipping barrel
Weight empty	1015 grams	850 grams
Barrel length	120 mm	90 mm
Barrel profile	6 riflings, right, 250 mm	6 riflings, right, 250 mm
Trigger	single/double action	single/double action
Sights	fixed/adjustable	fixed
Material/finish	steel/burnished	steel/burnished
Safeties	manual, uncocking lever, safety rest	

* Also planned: 9x18 Ultra, 7.65 mm Parabellum, 9x21 IMI

ISRAEL

After the founding of the State of Israel in 1948, no domestic weapons industry was developed at first. Revolvers made in England, with .38 and .455 Enfield calibers, were used as side arms, along with those from the USA and Italy. The M 1951 model by Beretta (9 mm Parabellum caliber, with single-action trigger and swinging bolt) was the official side arm.

The situation was similar for rifles, where, starting with the 98 Carbine, every imaginable western-world weapon was put into use. Only later was a domestic assault gun developed, the 7.62 x 51 caliber NATO made by Galil. The best-known weapon developed in Israel was the UZI machine pistol, named after its designer, Major Uziel Gal. It became the standard machine pistol of the Israeli armed forces and those of other lands, including the German Bundeswehr. Two slightly different versions were produced, one with a rigidly attached wooden shaft, the other with a folding metal shaft. The 9 mm Parabellum caliber UZI machine pistol features a design that is both simple and robust. The cartridge is activated when the forward position is reached directly on the barrel. When ready to fire, it is held under the pressure of the rod-guided recoil spring. Pulling the trigger releases the heavy breechblock and it rushes forward, introducing a cartridge from the magazine, inserting it in the chamber and igniting it. The breechblock is designed to enclose, the chamber of the barrel is fully enclosed in its forward position, which provides a considerable gain in safety for the shooter.

The UZI machine pistol became world-famous, not only in the Near East. It was accepted by the German Bundeswehr and used with two different shafts. The folding metal shaft is shown.

The UZI Pistol

Unlike other present-day machine pistols, the UZI has a grip safety. Only after pushing it in can the weapon be fired, either in single shots or sustained fire with a cadence of some 650 rounds per minute. The magazine holds two rows of cartridges, and there are magazines for 25, 32 and 40 cartridges, as well as clips that allow an angled combination of two magazines.

The Mini-Uzi is a very small, handy machine pistol for bodyguards and security forces.

On the basis of this successful design, the manufacturer, the Israel Military Industries, has built several variations, one of which is also available on the private market, though not in the countries in which such weapons are banned by the regulations of the war weapons control law.

The MINI-UZI is a near-perfect weapon for security forces. It is a robust design, simple and easy to operate, considerably smaller than the normal UZI, and yet its cadence is no slower — on the contrary, because of the lighter weight of the breech, it fires about 950 rounds per minute, with an average muzzle velocity of 352 meters per second.

Here too, the barrel is easy to remove after loosening the retaining nut under the pressure of the rest. In the muzzle area are two slits running diagonally forward and upward to dampen the muzzle movement. The cocking pusher does not go along when a shot is fired, but remains basically in the foremost position. Magazines holding 20, 25 and 32 cartridges are available, and the well-known grip safety is integrated into the grip. The shaft is different here, as it can be unfolded at the side. With its shaft unfolded, the MINI-UZI reaches a length of 600 meters, and when the shaft is folded in, the weapon, ready to fire, is only 360 mm long, with a barrel length of 197 mm.

The UZI pistol is truly an unusual weapon. In Germany it is subject to the strict regulations of the war weapon control law because of its resemblance to a fully automatic weapon, and would be of interest chiefly to specialist collectors, but without these rules, the situation in some Swiss cantons or other countries could be different.

One of its differences from the fully automatic machine pistol is its shape. For another thing, it bears more resemblance to the UZI carbine. Its operation and dismantling are as simple as they usually are for the UZI weapons group. After the casing top is removed, the breechblock and recoil spring can be removed. After loosening the retaining nut, the 115 mm long barrel can be pulled out of the casing from the front.

According to the firm's advertising, the UZI pistol is suitable for use by sport shooters, hunters and security forces. This may change however from one country to another.

An essential difference here consists of the breech type, and this can be substantiated, of course, only from the

The UZI pistol set up only for single action. In Germany it is banned from the private market because of its similarity to a fully automatic weapon.

firm's available information. The pistol, like the carbine, fires from a closed position and has a flying firing pin (closed bolt with floating firing pin). The firing pin is moved inside the breechblock where a case presses against the plate of the firing pin from the back, and an additional coil spring is activated inside this case.

The magazine, as is well known, is pushed through the grip from below, and holds twenty cartridges in two rows. The receiver contains the trigger assembly, and there the change from safety to firing takes place. Sustained fire is not possible. The sights are separately adjustable — the foresight can be adjusted vertically, the backsight horizontally. Both of the sights have white markings for better sighting in unfavorable light.

Technical Data: Mini-Uzi and UZI pistol

Manufacturer	Israel Military Industries, Ramat Hasharon, Israel	
Model designation	Mini-UZI	UZI Pistol
Caliber	9 mm Para.	9 mm Para.
Magazine capacity	20/25/32	20
System	Mass breech	Mass breech
Overall length	360 mm/600 mm	240 mm
Barrel length	197 mm	115 mm
Barrel profile	4 riflings, right, 233 mm	4 riflings, right, 180 mm
Sights	50 m/150 m	both adjustable
Night sight	–	Tritium (Beta) Light
Muzzle velocity	352 m/s	350 m/s
Rate of fire	950 per minute	single shot
Effective range	150 m	60 m
Material	Steel	Steel
Finish	burnished	burnished

AUSTRIA

Pistols in 9 mm Parabellum caliber were developed rather late in Austria, for the 9 mm Steyr cartridge had been the dominant military cartridge for a long time, and numerous pistols were built for it. This cartridge is somewhat longer, and could be described as 9 mm by 22 mm, as opposed to the 9 mm by 19 mm Parabellum. The bullet, weighing 7.5 grams, reaches a muzzle velocity of 335 meters per second, thus ranking below the values of the Parabellum cartridge.

Steyr Model 1912

The Oesterreichische Waffenfabrik Gesellschaft Steyr (later Steyr-Werke AG or Steyr-Daimler-Puch AG) has its headquarters in the city of Steyr. It was founded by Josef Werndl in 1863, and began to adapt large numbers of muzzle-loading rifles into breech-loaders. Just a few years later, the firm began to produce a wide variety of military weapons, and has continued to produce them to this day. Pistols like the Model GB, a rugged machine pistol, or the AUG rifle made for the Austrian Bundesheer, were produced along with outstanding hunting repeaters and rifles for sport shooting at 300 meters. In 1934 the firm merged with Daimler-Puch, resulting in the three-part name listed above.

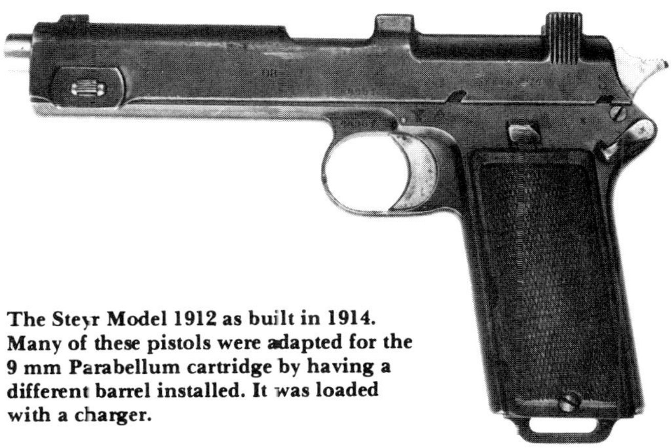

The Steyr Model 1912 as built in 1914. Many of these pistols were adapted for the 9 mm Parabellum cartridge by having a different barrel installed. It was loaded with a charger.

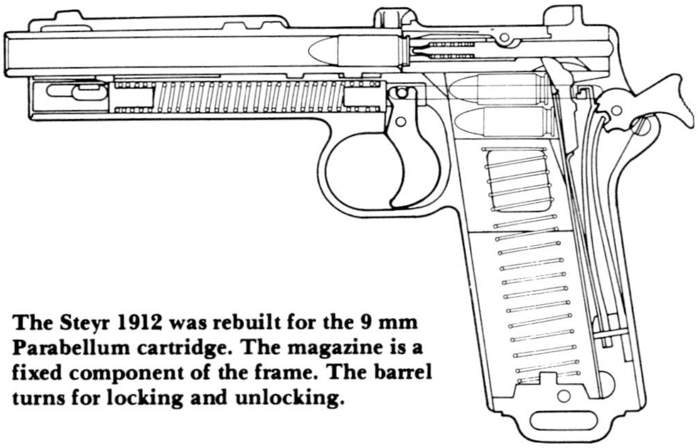

The Steyr 1912 was rebuilt for the 9 mm Parabellum cartridge. The magazine is a fixed component of the frame. The barrel turns for locking and unlocking.

The Steyr pistol in open position, plus a charger with eight 9 mm Parabellum cartridges and a box with 16 of them.

Pull back the slide, put in the filled charger, push the cartridges in with your thumb, and let the slide move forward again.

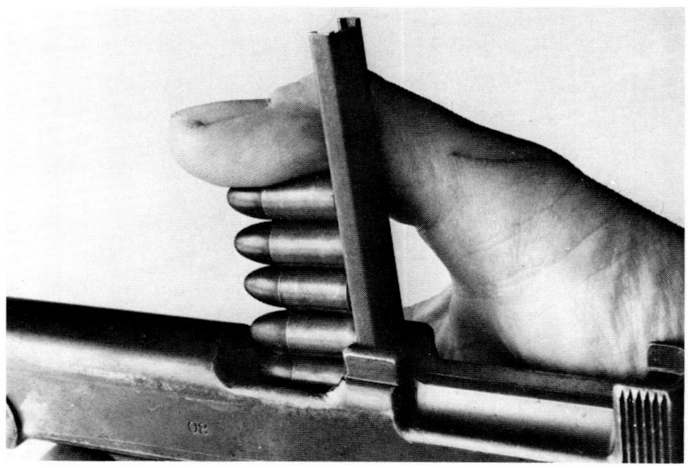

The firm's first pistol production is linked with names such as Roth and Krnka, who were able to come up with some very noteworthy designs.

The first successful military pistol was the Model 1911, whose concept is embodied in the patents Br Pat 29279/1911 and 8220/1912. The pistol has a steel slide which completely surrounds the barrel and lets it stick out only a little bit in the front. An interesting feature is the turning breech, in which the locking and unlocking of the barrel and slide are caused by a curve-guided turning of the barrel. This function is carried out with great precision, and for many years the Steyr pistol enjoyed the reputation of a reliable and accurate pistol. To be sure, its grip form was not especially suitable for rapid fire, but it had other noteworthy features to offer.

In the rear area of the barrel there are four knobs, the two upper fitting into the corresponding apertures in the slide. One knob is below, fits into a groove in the frame, and allows the back-and-forth movement of the barrel. The fourth knob is located somewhat diagonally between the others and, when the slide moves backward, activates the forced turning of the barrel by some 20 degrees, for which a recoil of some 8 mm for the still-locked system is required. During recoil, the barrel turns, as noted, some 20 degrees, whereby the locking releases the upper knobs inside the slide. Along with the end point of the unlocking, the fourth knob moves to the end of its groove in the grip and prevents the barrel from moving farther back. The released slide can slide backward against the pressure of the recoil spring, which is located in the front of the grip; in the process it extracts the fired case, ejects it, and cocks the external hammer. The hammer has a powerful leaf spring as its power source; the leaf spring in front of it (part No.11 in the drawing on page 139) functions simultaneously as a sear and sear spring; the third spring mounted in the grip operates the interrupter.

The magazine is a fixed component of the grip and is filled from above — the cartridges can either be pushed in individually or inserted from a filled charger. For danger-free loading, the slide is held in its rearmost position by the hook of the lateral safety, the charger with its cartridges is inserted into the opening on the upper rear by the ejection window, and the cartridges are pushed out of the strip and into the magazine by strong thumb pressure. After that, the empty charger is pulled out, the safety is released, and the slide can move forward again, which inserts the first cartridge. There is also a practical way to empty a filled magazine. The slide is

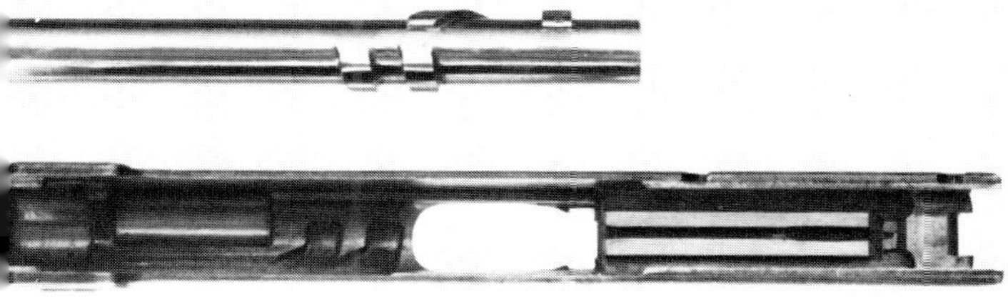

For unlocking, the barrel is turned along curves inside the slide, then stops and the slide moves farther back against the pressure of the recoil spring.

pulled back and hooked in its rearmost position. On the left side of the weapon, immediately above the grip panel, is a push-button (part 9 in the drawing) which is pushed down against the pressure of its spring. At this moment, all the cartridges still in the magazine move upward and out of the weapon. At the same time, this push-button, which has been pushed backward, can move forward again after the last shot.

The pistol was originally built to the 9 mm Steyr caliber. Considering the performance of this cartridge, it is all the more surprising that it did not gain widespread popularity and was built by only a few manufacturers.

Steyr delivered these pistols to the Austrian Army, where they were very popular among the officers. In all, some 250,000 of these pistols were built, with large numbers sent to Rumania and Chile.

When the German government more or less freely absorbed Austria in 1938, the Steyr pistol once again became of interest to the German or Austrian troops, as there was a veritably endless demand for pistols of all calibers. The German Wehrmacht did not want to introduce the Steyr pistol along with all the rest, and took a different course by fitting the pistols with a different barrel, made for the 08 cartridge. Some 50,000 pistols were modified in this way. The modified pistols are marked with the number 08 on the left side of the slide to show that they are made for the 08 cartridge, and the barrel bears the stamp of acceptance with the German eagle.

To dismantle the pistol, one must first empty the magazine and check the barrel. Then the slide is allowed to move forward again, and the hammer is decocked via the trigger. At the front, a spring wedge goes straight through the slide, spring case and receiver. This wedge is pushed out from left to right, for which a small screwdriver makes a handy tool. The slide can then be slid all the way back and lifted out of its guide rails. After that the loose barrel is taken out of its mounting.

For reassembly, the barrel is first placed on the receiver

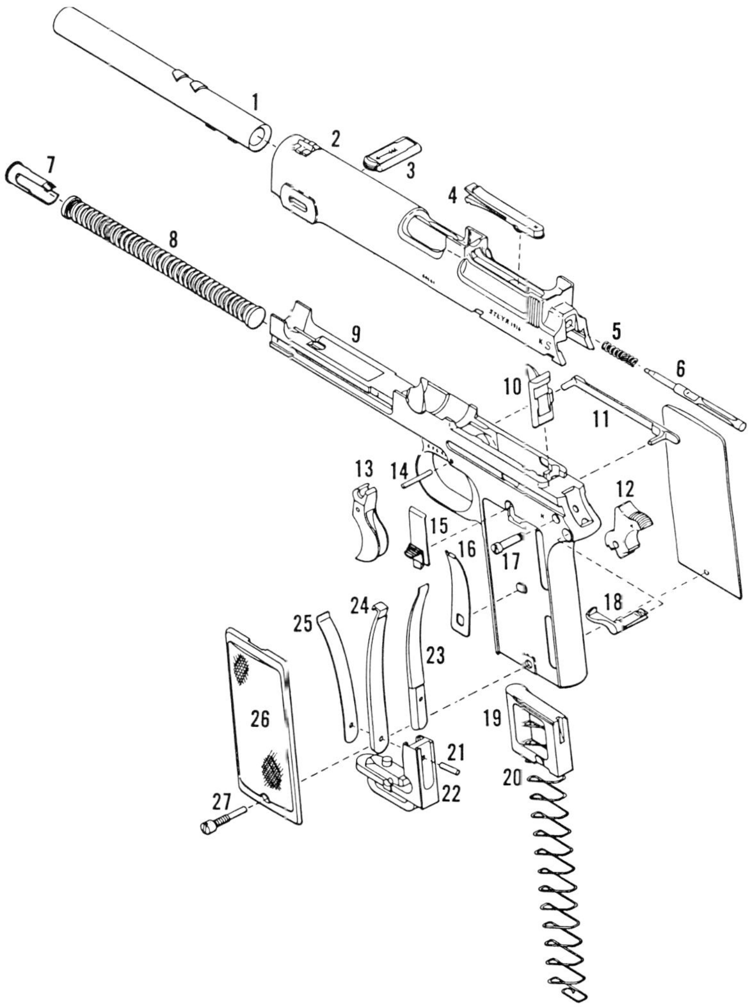

The parts of the Steyr pistol listed.

Steyr-Hahn
Model 1911 Pistol

1 Barrel
2 Slide
3 Slide Wedge
4 Extractor
5 Firing Pin Spring
6 Firing Pin
7 Recoil Spring Retainer
8 Recoil Spring with Caps
9 Frame
10 Ejector and Disconnector
11 Trigger Bar
12 Hammer
13 Trigger
14 Trigger Pin
15 Cartridge Release
16 Cartridge Release Spring
17 Hammer Screw
18 Safety
19 Magazine Follower
20 Magazine Spring
21 Spring Retainer Pin
22 Floorplate
23 Hammer Spring
24 Sear and Sear Spring
25 Disconnector Spring
26 Grip Panel
27 Grip Screw

with its knobs fitting into the apertures, and then pulled backward. After that, while pressing on the lateral lever (i.e., the magazine emptier or catch lever), the slide can be set in place at the back and pushed forward. Now the recoil spring is inserted with its cap (part 4 in the drawing), pulled back, and the cross wedge is pushed in from right to left, according to its markings, until it comes to a stop.

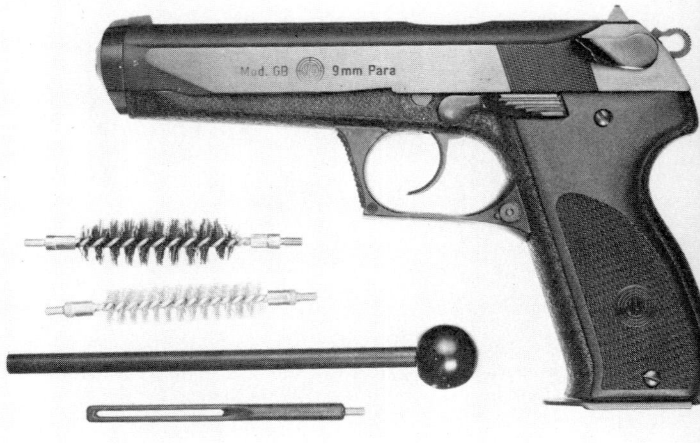

The Steyr GB with its cleaning equipment. This pistol has a gas-delayed mass breech and a barrel screwed in place.

Steyr Model GB

The world had to wait a long time for the GB, for it only

Technical Data: Steyr Model 1912

Manufacturer	Austrian Weapon Factory Company
Caliber	9 mm Parabellum (adapted)
Magazine capacity	8 cartridges via charger
Overall length	217 mm
Height/width	143 mm/30 mm
Barrel length	130 mm
Sights	Fixed
System	Turning barrel
Safety	Lever safety
Material/finish	Steel/burnished
Weight empty	ca. 960 grams

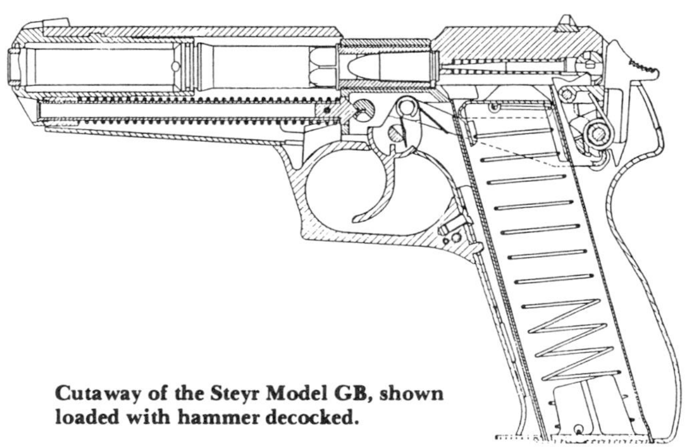

Cutaway of the Steyr Model GB, shown loaded with hammer decocked.

came into being when the Austrian Bundesheer needed a new service weapon. Steyr took part in the competition but did not receive the hoped-for benefit, as the firm of Glock, unknown until then, was chosen. This firm had offered a weapon of its own design and gained a lot of attention.

The GB is a big, heavy pistol meant to be carried in a holster, not a weapon to be carried under cover, which naturally limits its uses. On the other hand, it has theverynconsiderable advantage of a very large magazine capacity: 18 cartridges in the magazine and one more cartridge in the barrel.

The receiver is made of hardened sheet steel and is finished in rough-textured deep black paint to protect against corrosion, and at the same time provide a better hold and allow ridges to be dispensed with. The trigger guard, waffled at the front, is made of plastic and set into the grip. At its base is the holding knob for the magazine.

Not only is the design of the delayed mass breech a novelty, but so is the barrel. It is a triangular polygon

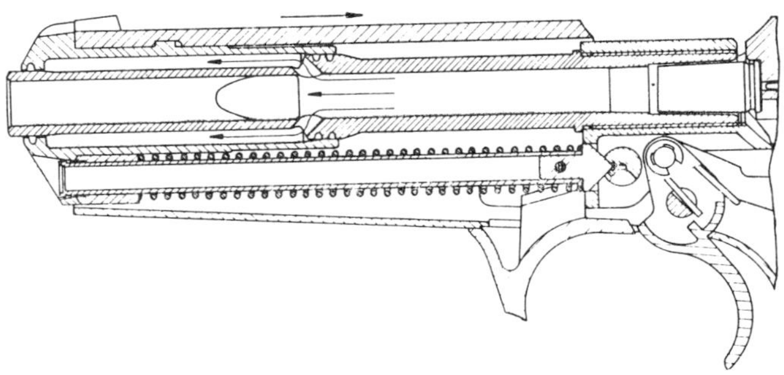

As soon as the bullet passes the borehole in the barrel, the powder gas can help dampen the recoil.

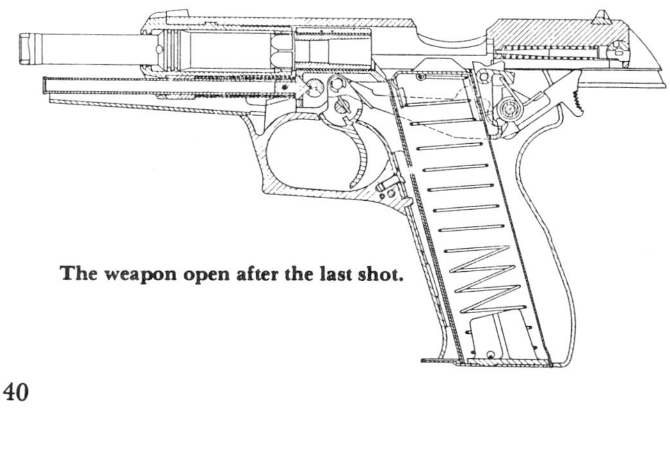

The weapon open after the last shot.

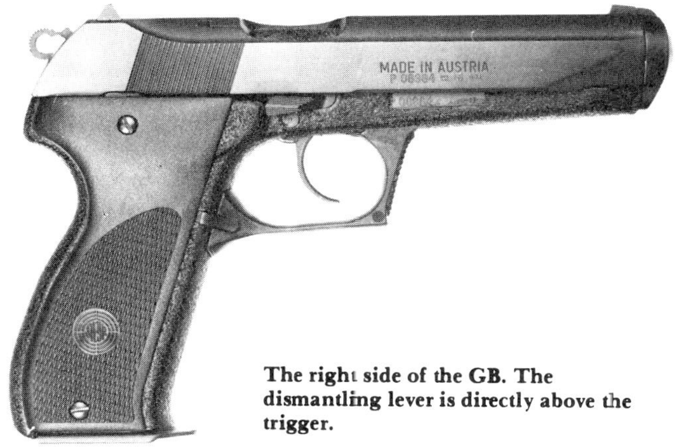

The right side of the GB. The dismantling lever is directly above the trigger.

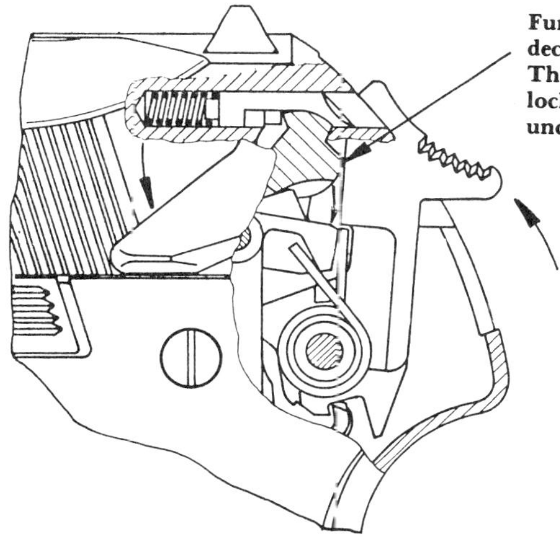

Function of the side decocking lever. The firing pin is locked when uncocked.

with all the advantages of this modern barrel profile. It is screwed firmly into the grip and hard-chromed inside and out. Further features of the GB include a double action trigger with a broad, ridged tongue, an external hammer operated via two torsion bars, a decocking lever to decock the cocked hammer safely, and simple dismantling without a tool.

In terms of design, the weapon has a gas-delayed mass breech that turned out to be quite big. When a shot is fired, a part of the freed gases is ducted through two holes in the area of the barrel thickening as soon as the bullet has passed through. The ducted gases enter a chamber formed from the barrel and the tube of the breech cap. Here it has a braking and delaying effect on the further recoil of the slide. This provides the advantage of a slightly decreased recoil, the total effect of which can be attributed to the size or weight of the weapon.

The other functions are as usual: the empty case is extracted and ejected, the hammer cocked during recoil and held in its resting place. The slide, when moving forward, brings the next cartridge out of the magazine. With its grip angle of 17 degrees, the GB fits into the hand nicely and can be aimed quickly. The fixed sights are equipped with points of light, one in the 3.5 mm bar foresight and two at the sides of the split backsight.

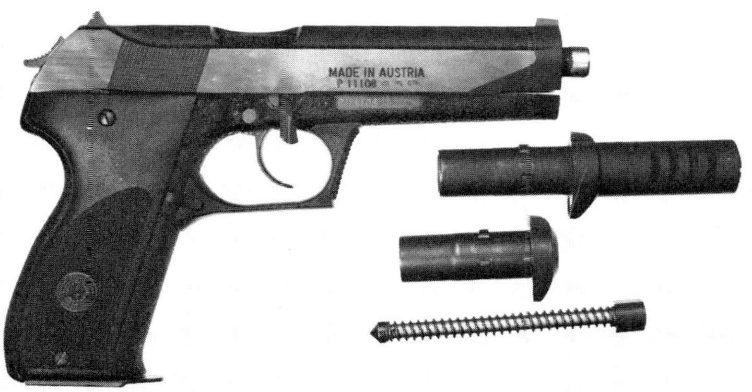

This was then just an experiment: the Steyr GB with an easily changed muzzle damper to provide somewhat softer shooting.

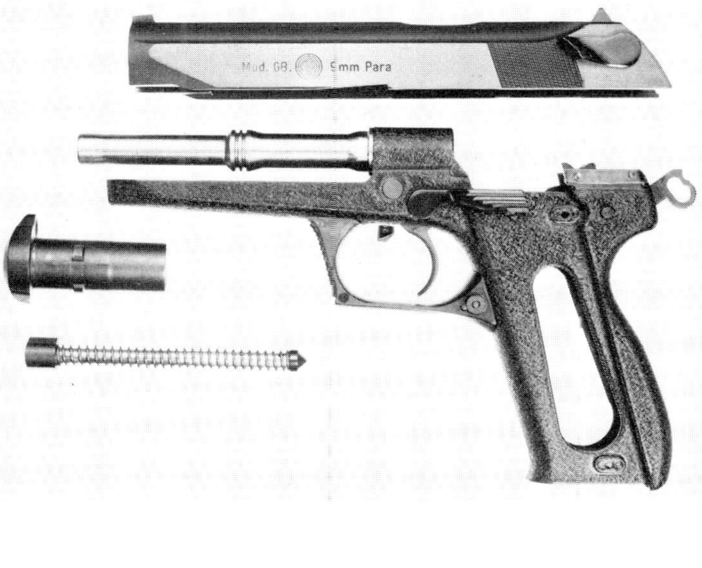

The GB disassembled for cleaning. The whole grip is coated with crinkled paint.

The GB is dismantled, as already noted, without a tool. After the magazine is removed and the chamber is checked, the spring-controlled dismantling lever on the right side of the weapon is swung downward 90 degrees. After that, the muzzle cap at the front of the muzzle can be turned 90 degrees to either the left or right. At that point it comes to a stop and can be pulled forward out of the slide.

After the muzzle cap is removed, the recoil spring with its bar falls forward out of the grip. Now the slide can be pulled backward a little bit and lifted off the grip, then pulled forward over the barrel and out of the grip.

This dismantling is sufficient for simple cleaning. The manufacturer encourages the owner to unscrew the barrel (#14 wrench) after a maximum of 1000 shots and thoroughly clean it on all sides, and then clean it again with polishing paste to remove any adhering bits of powder.

The same pistol, now with the added compensator.

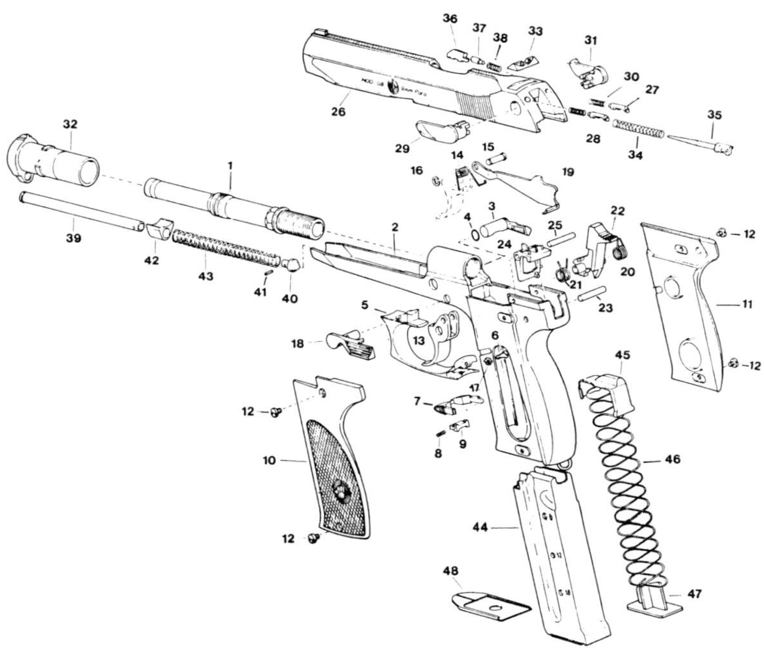

The parts of the Steyr GB with barrel unscrewed.

Technical Data: Steyr GB

Manufacturer	Steyr-Daimler-Puch AG, Steyr, Austria
Caliber	9 mm Parabellum
Overall length	216 mm
Height/width	142 mm/37 mm
Barrel length	136 mm
Sights	Fixed
Magazine capacity	18 cartridges
Weight empty	ca. 962 grams
Material/finish	Steel/burnished, painted
System	Gas-delayed mass breech
Safeties	Firing pin, falling, decocking

Glock 17 Army Pistol

When a new and modern self-loading pistol in 9 mm Parabellum caliber was sought for the Austrian Army, the firm of Glock, till then quite unknown, offered a very unusual design. It was no beauty in terms of outward appearance, nor was it conventional in terms of its chosen materials. Opinions of it were quite divided;

some found it exciting, while others rejected it as a "plastic pistol." Despite all that, it was able to take the wind out of the critics' sails, for it passed difficult testing and easily beat the competition. The durability of this "plastic pistol" must be tremendous. The weapon shown here, owned by M. Hugo, was under constant use at that time and had already fired some 20,000 rounds. No noticeable decrease in performance could be ascertained, nor could any signs of wear be seen. After 20,000 rounds, other (and better-marketed) pistols already show signs of rough use.

The Glock 17, a plastic pistol, as its opponents call it. But this pistol has numerous advantages to offer.

The Glock 17 has several features that make it very different from other weapons: the high magazine capacity of 17 cartridges, forming two rows, in a plastic magazine, the extremely low overall weight achieved by the use of plastic, the greatest possible safety for the shooter, who can fire a shot only by using the trigger.

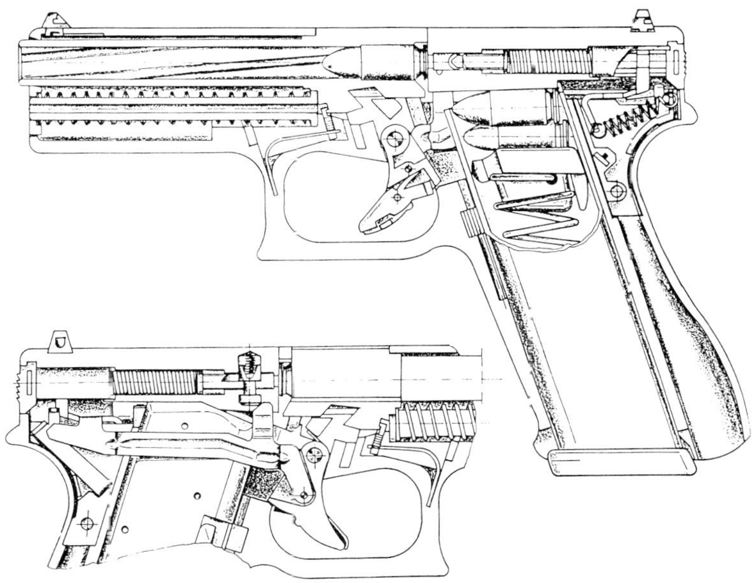

Cutaway of the Glock 17 with separate view of the trigger function.

The functioning principle is that of a mechanically locked recoil loader with a tipping barrel without a joint. In the Glock 17, the type of lock is essentially important; the pistol has no internal or external hammer, but instead a firing pin-lock, which is actually the exception rather than the rule today. In addition, it has an automatically acting firing pin and trigger safety, the Safe Action Trigger Safety, and also the unusual Safe Action Trigger System — these characteristics will be described in detail below.

The light weight of the pistol, and especially of the receiver is naturally surprising. Without a magazine, the Glock 17 weighs 620 grams in all, and the loaded magazine adds some 290 grams to that. The savings in weight is achieved through the use of a very light but very durable plastic, of which the receiver is injection-molded. The parts that guide the slide are cast, while other parts are held in place by removable pins. An unusual feature is the second "trigger" set in the trigger tongue, this is, in fact, the trigger safety, which is as simple as it is effective: a lateral, off-center pressure on the trigger cannot fire a shot, and only when the trigger safety is pressed at the same time is it possible to fire. The firing pin is partly cocked automatically and completely set on safety after every shot. Thus an unwanted shot, caused by a blow or a fall, for example, is not possible.

The Glock 17 open. It takes heavy use and features a refined and simple construction.

The functioning deserves to be described somewhat more precisely: in a loaded condition there is a cartridge in the chamber, the firing pin is partly cocked and on safety, the trigger is in its foremost position. If a shot is to be fired, one first pushes in the trigger safety with one's

The Glock 17 in detail: only when the small tongue in the trigger is pressed down can the trigger be pulled farther back. This makes the pistol fast and safe.

index finger, only then can the trigger be pulled. When the trigger is pulled back to the pressure point, the weapon's safety is released, that is, the trigger bar is in back of the safety ramp, the firing pin safety is released and the firing pin is cocked. When the trigger is pulled back farther, the trigger, by way of the control spring (part 24 in the drawing on page 142), releases the firing pin. As the shot is fired, the recoil causes the slide (part 1, called breech piece by manufacturer) to move backward; after moving backward about 3 mm, the lock between the slide and the barrel is released, the barrel swings down over the breechblock (part 22), and the slide moves back against the pressure of the rod-guided recoil spring. During recoil, as usual, the empty case is extracted and ejected.

The "coulisse" included in the slide activates the control spring and separates it from the trigger bar. It is thereby lifted by the trigger spring (part 25) and again moved into the course of the firing pin point. After this movement the breech piece moves forward again under pressure from the compressed recoil spring and moves the next cartridge out of the magazine and into the chamber. Here are the individual actions during the forward motion:

— the trigger bar is pushed onto the safety ramp by the firing pin,
— the firing pin safety is partly cocked,
— a cartridge is drawn out of the magazine,
— the barrel is locked with the slide (breech piece), and the weapon is again ready to fire and the safety is set.

After the last shot is fired, the slide is held back by the catch lever (part 27) and can be moved forward again by pressure on the handhold of this lever.

The Safety System

The Glock 17 has no external safety controls that can be wrongly or rightly operated by the shooter; all safety components operate without being activated by the shooter and offer, in their sensible combination, a high degree of real safety.

The *trigger safety* is built into the trigger as a lever (part 26), and when it is not pulled, it blocks the trigger's path backward. This safety is released only by being pushed in by the finger, so that the weapon is thoroughly on safety while being constantly ready to fire.

The *firing pin safety* is only released when the trigger is pulled. In its safety position, a bolt (part 9) extends into a cutout of the firing pin, under spring pressure, and blocks it.

An additional safety function is that of the *control block;* the firing pin (part 5), under the effect of the firing pin spring (part 7), pushes the trigger bar onto the safety ramp. In this position the firing pin cannot be released.

The Glock 17 dismantled for cleaning. The parts cast into the frame cannot be removed.

Dismantling the Glock 17

To dismantle the weapon for cleaning, it is sufficient to dismantle it into its main component groups; further dismantling of the receiver should be left to the specialist.

To dismantle the pistol, the magazine is removed and the safety of the chamber is checked. Then the trigger is pulled and the entire upper part is removed from the grip. To do this, the slide is pulled back some 3 mm and the bolt pusher (part 21) is pulled downward, after which the upper part can be pushed forward out of the grip. Removing the recoil spring and barrel is done in the same way as with the familiar pistols with a Browning-type breech.

If the slide is pulled back too far, the upper part cannot be removed. In this case, the trigger must be pulled again.

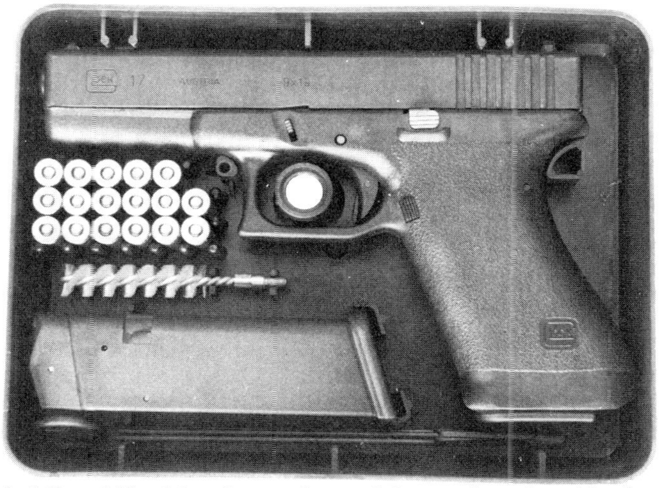

It is delivered like this: a dust- and watertight container of semi-hard plastic with space for a second magazine, cleaning tools and a load of cartridges.

What One Must NOT Do . . .

Every weapon has a few peculiarities which absolutely must be kept in mind during dismantling or when in a dismantled state in order to avoid damage to any parts. With the Glock 17, one must NOT move the trigger into its forward position by hand or move it otherwise when the upper part has been removed. The trigger can only be moved forward by pulling the slide back a short distance (ca. 15 mm).

When the slide has been removed, one must not push the firing pin forward by hand, as this could result in damage to the firing pin safety.

The covering plate (part 15) set into the rear of the slide may be removed, but not the steel inlay inserted there.

Technical Data: Glock 17

Caliber	9 mm Parabellum
Magazine capacity	17 cartridges
Overall length	188 mm
Overall height	131 mm
Grip width	30 mm
Sight line	165 mm
Barrel length	114 mm
Barrel profile	6 riflings, right, 250 mm
Weight - magazine	620 grams
Magazine, filled	ca. 250 grams
Muzzle velocity	ca. 360 m/s
Muzzle energy	ca. 500 Joules
Grip material	Plastic
Upper material	Steel
Sights	Fixed
Safeties	Safe-Action, firing pin, trigger safety

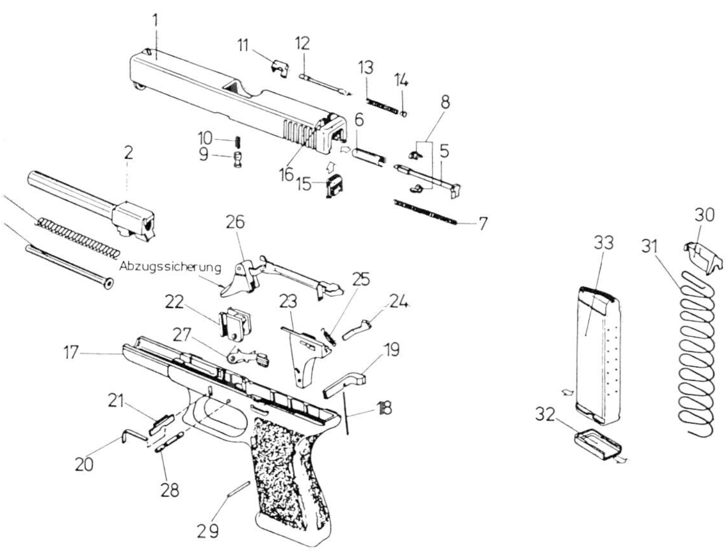

Parts of the Glock 17

1 Verschlußstück (Schlitten)
2 Lauf
3 Schließfeder
4 Schließfederführung
5 Schlagbolzen
6 Distanzhülse
7 Schlagbolzenfeder
8 Federteller
9 Schlagbolzensicherung
10 Feder zur Schlagbolzensicherung
11 Auszieher
12 Druckbolzen
13 Druckbolzenfeder
14 Federlager
15 Deckplatte zum Verschlußstück
16 Kimme
17 Griffstück
18 Feder zum Magazinhalter
19 Magazinhalter
20 Feder zum Verriegelungsschieber
21 Verriegelungsschieber
22 Verriegelungsblock
23 Steuerblock mit Ausstoßer
24 Steuerfeder
25 Abzugfeder
26 Abzug mit Abzugstange
27 Verschlußfanghebel mit Feder
28 Abzugachse
29 Stift zum Steuerblock
30 Magazinzubringer
31 Magazinfeder
32 Magazinboden
33 Magazinkörper

(Bezeichnungen laut Hersteller)

POLAND

Only for a short time was the Polish VIS pistol the Polish Army's official side arm, for just a few years after series production began, the country was invaded by German troops and all stocks were taken over by the German Wehrmacht as captured weapons. In all, some 380,000 VIS pistols were used by the German forces and officials, and accounts for almost the entire production.

The VIS wz 35 as made for the Polish Army before World War II, with the Polish eagle stamped in. The VIS wz 35 had some very modern features.

The version made during German occupation, with the P 35 and German acceptance stamps.

The same pistol open. The recoil spring is guided by a long rod with an added damper.

The design of the VIS was based on the Browning design that had been used for both the Colt Model 1911 and the FN High Power. Essential elements of both pistols are found in the Polish weapon, a few details were omitted, and others were added. In the process, the VIS, with its ability to let the cocked hammer move forward safely, possessed a feature that is found in almost all modern self-loading pistols.

The VIS-35 Pistol

The VIS pistol was a product of the Radom Weapon Works, the Fabryka Broni w Radomu, which was founded shortly after World War I and produced chiefly rifles, revolvers and weapon components, and was in fact the only Polish weapon factory that had any experience in the area of handguns. During the 1930s, great numbers of the Russian Nagant revolver were built — with its bullet fitting deep in the case and the forward motion of the cylinder when the hammer was cocked, was able to rank as the world's first truly gas-tight revolver. Some 20,000 of the Model Ng. 30 (a copy of the 1895 model) were produced for the troops, police and the Polish postal system.

At this time the Polish Army was equipped with a remarkable collection of the most varied weapons, and the urgent need for standardization was recognized along with that for armament with a more effective pistol. Originally the Polish government or its Department of Armament wanted to build the Czech CZ 25 under license, but both the designers and the military objected to this.

When this situation became known, Piotr Wilniewczyc offered to work out an independent design within a very short time and present it promptly in the form of drawings and calculations. The first advantage would have been that the high licensing fees of some $250,000 (1,300,000 Zloty) would not have to be paid to a foreign factory. While P.W. (his initials will be used here in place of his hard-to-pronounce name) was beginning the first of his design drawings, he was visited by one Jan Skrzpinski, the director of the Warsaw Machine Gun Factory. He was interested in the new venture, and the two men decided to work together and divide the fees to be won. But only as of the autumn of 1930 could the two of them devote more time to their enterprise, as necessary foreign trips and other work had kept them away from it earlier. The first production plans were finished late in 1930, and in February of 1931 the first prototype was finished; it was not yet burnished, but it fired. Its tests, held in the presence of the two designers and several officers, were more than encouraging. The Polish patent was awarded and given number 15567 on February 8, 1932.

The new pistol, known at that time as "Pistolet wojskowy wzor PWU 1928", was subjected to further tests and withstood even the hardest use without damage. Comparison shooting with one new pistol and one that had already fired 6000 rounds showed that the shooting performance had not decreased visibly. At 20 meters there was a dispersal circle of 55 mm with eight shots, an achievement that cannot be equaled by many modern pistols.

After tests were successfully concluded, the Department of Armament bought the pistol and paid a fee of 50,000 Zloty (at that time about $9650 or 23,000 Reichsmark). In addition, the two designers were to receive three finished pistols from series production, but this never materialized. Series production began in 1936, as did issuing to troops. Two essential changes had already been made at the request of the army officers who tested the pistol. Some of them wanted the rear profile of the weapon to be more rounded, while one from the cavalry wanted to be able to decock the hammer with his free hand while riding. A decocking lever was attached to the side of the slide for this purpose, when moved, first drew the firing pin back into its resting place and then released the cocked hammer safely by pressing on the sear. If the designer had included a double action trigger, which was discussed at the time, the VIS would have been the

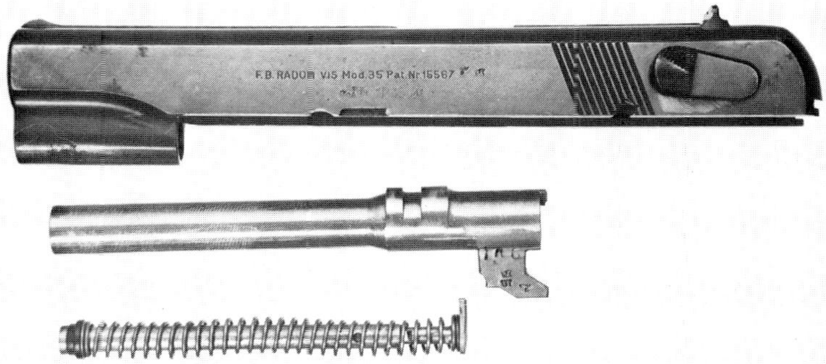

Slide, barrel and recoil-spring unit in detail, all parts with German stamps.

The same pistol dismantled for cleaning. This pistol is very well made and gives very good performance.

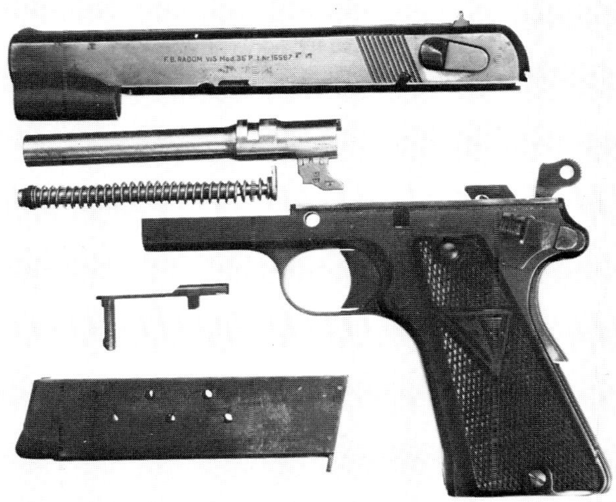

most modern design for decades, as present-day pistols do not offer more.

As for the name of VIS, it was said that the two designers simply wanted to combine the initials of their names, and in fact did so, so that the pistol was first called WiS. The Department of Armament changed this to VIS, the Latin word for power. Thus it was then called VIS, and often VIS 35 as well. The complete inscription on the left side of the slide is: "F. B. RADOM . . . . VIS wz 35 Pat. Nr. 15567"; there is also the Polish eagle emblem, under which some 49,000 weapons were produced before further production was continued under German-Austrian control.

As for the design of the VIS pistol, Piotr Wilniewczyc began where Browning had stopped and was able to

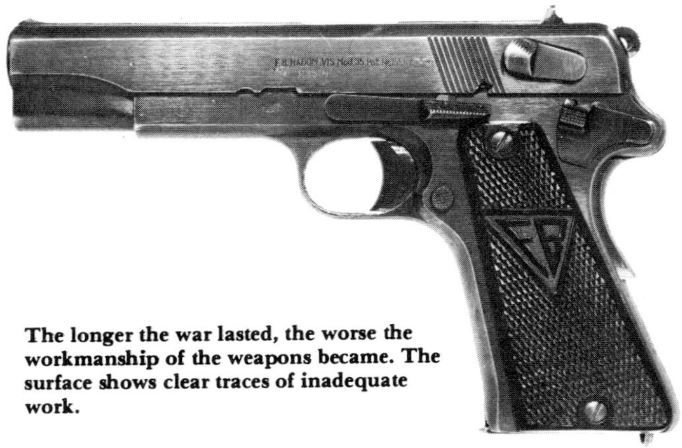

The longer the war lasted, the worse the workmanship of the weapons became. The surface shows clear traces of inadequate work.

include several practical improvements. Unlike the Colt 1911 model, there is no moveable chain between the barrel and grip; this simplified production and eliminated a source of faults. Instead, the barrel has the smooth angular form of the FN pistol, which has become more and more popular to this day (see SIG-210 or the SIG-Sauer pistols). The barrel is not placed in a housing at the front, for this is also not exactly an advantage for actually attainable shooting performance. The recoil spring was fitted with a guiding rod, making the pistol much easier to dismantle without a tool than is the Colt pistol. The guiding rod, though, is not merely a simple rod but has an additional internal spring. All of this is united to form a telescopic rod which also dampens its recoil when a shot is fired. Only at the end of the war was this type of guiding rod eliminated.

The designer originally did not want to include any kind of safety, but the officers, who were more inclined to trust an obsolete revolver than a self-loading pistol, made strenuous objections. As an acceptable compromise, a grip safety was installed, in addition, the wide hammer has a safety rest and the weapon also had a reliable recoil safety.

On the back of the grip there is a hook-shaped lever that allows easier dismantling. After removing the magazine, one pulls the slide back until the hook can be moved into its aperture, presses the catch lever out at the side and pushes the entire upper part forward off the grip. These too are all very modern features that could be applied to the Colt pistol only through costly rebuilding.

One small feature remained unexplained for a long time — the opening at the bottom rear of the receiver to hold an insertable shaft. There may have been a few tests using it, but a shaft of that kind was never put into production or introduced. In the process of simplification under German control, this aperture was later eliminated. All in all, the VIS proved to be a very neatly and admirably made weapon with a high degree of workmanship, and is especially true of the weapons with the Polish eagle. Under German control, production

The grip has an attachment for a shaft, but this was never added to the production type, only to a test piece.

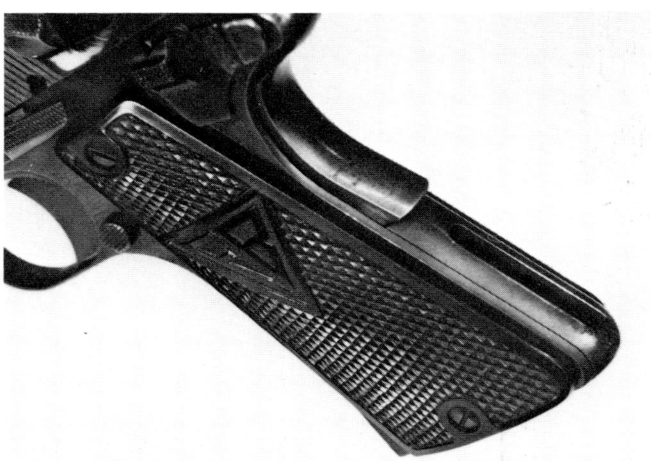

This type was made of remaining pieces toward the end of the war. The dismantling lever is omitted, simple grip panels of pressed resin have grooves and poorly phosphated surfaces.

quality remained high at first, but then sank to a lower level. Personnel declined, the shortage of materials became oppressive, and the constant demands for new weapons for the troops continued to grow. Thus there were numerous variations in which one can recognize this step-by-step simplification and drop in quality. First the neat polishing of the surfaces was eliminated, then came simpler grip panels of smooth wood, and the decocking lever was eliminated after the dismantling lever had been done away with.

The so-called K-series versions were especially simple. They were presumably assembled from parts at various facilities of the Steyr works at the end of 1944, after the factory was abandoned. One of these simple versions is shown here: it has simple grip panels of beechwood with grooves filed in, no dismantling lever, and a gray-green phosphatized surface.

Production in Poland was never resumed after the war, and the VIS remains a legend.

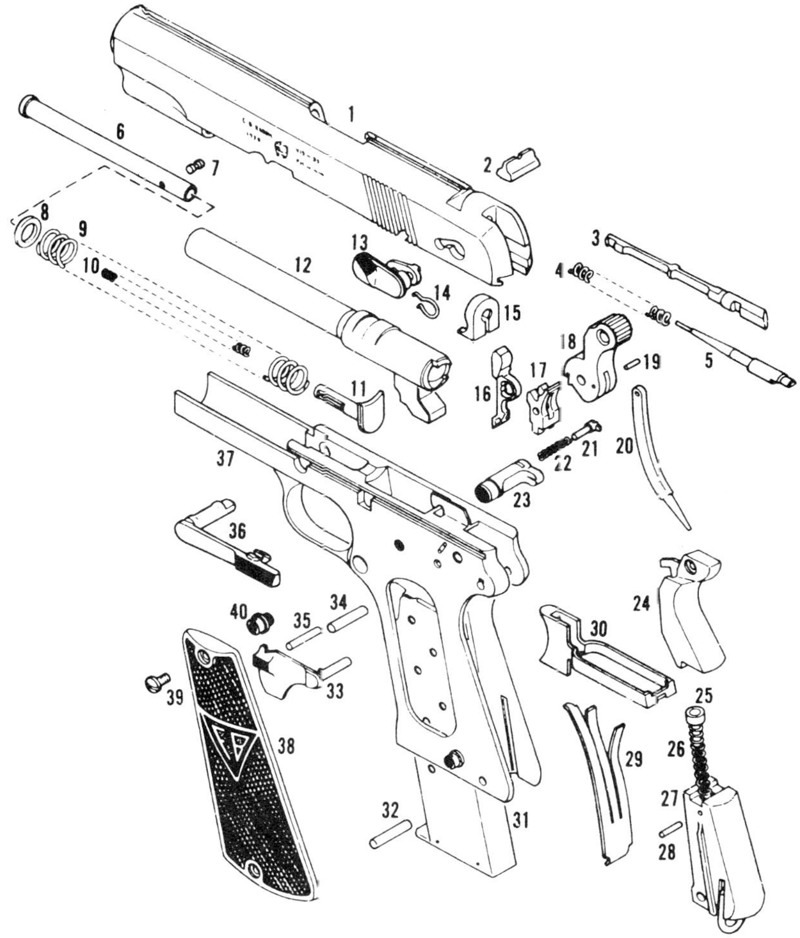

The Polish wz 35 in detail. Much of its technology resembles the GP 35 and Colt M 1911 pistols.

Technical Data: VIS WZ 35 Pistol

Manufacturer	Fabryka Broni Radom
Year made	ca. 1930-1935
Caliber	9 mm Parabellum
Magazine capacity	8 cartridges
Overall length	205 mm
Height/width	141 mm/34 mm
Barrel length	119 mm
Weight empty	1010-1030 grams
Sights	Fixed
Safeties	Grip and firing pin safety
Material/finish	Steel/burnished, phosphated
System	Browning-type tipping barrel

SWITZERLAND

Pistols from Switzerland — and there is actually just one, the well-known SIG-210 — are known for their high degree of workmanship, but also for their extremely high prices. If one wants to obtain a good weapon and does not mind paying the price, can get in the SIG 210, what is still the best-made self-loading pistol in the world. Today the simple SIG pistol has grown into a small family, for several different versions of the pistol have made it a suitable weapon for defense and for sport.

The SIG-Petter P 44/8; the number after the diagonal line shows the magazine capacity.

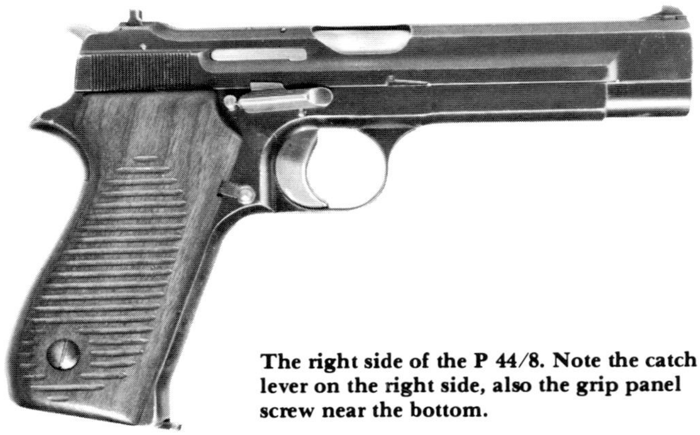

The right side of the P 44/8. Note the catch lever on the right side, also the grip panel screw near the bottom.

The SP 47/8 version, a pistol resulting from concrete suggestions from Sweden.

The SIG-210 Series

Before it was designated P 210 it was called "Neuhausen Self-Loading Pistol (Petter System)." This indicates its origin, as the present-day SIG pistol basically originated in a French development. In France a successor weapon to the venerable Lebel revolver was being sought. At the French firm of Société Alsacienne de Construction Mécaniques (S.A.C.M. for short), the engineer Charles Petter, who came from Switzerland, developed a self-loading pistol that was accepted by the War Ministry shortly thereafter and introduced officially under the designation of Mle 35 A. The pistol was built for the 7.65 mm long cartridge, a type whose performance was later recognized as no longer sufficient. Before German troops marched into France in 1940, some 25,000 Petter pistols had been produced, with the same number produced under German control. Petter had based his work on two well-known pistols, the Colt Government Model 1911 and the Browning GP 35, which was simply the right way to go about it at the time, and adopted some of their well-known characteristics.

The locking takes place via the tipping barrel with an intermediate chain. The mounting of the barrel in the front of the slide was a detail that Petter was able to improve.

One characteristic of the Petter pistol of those times is still used in the present-day SIG 210: the removable lock, which can be pulled out of the receiver in one piece.

In 1937 the Schweizerische Industrie-Gesellschaft (SIG) of Neuhausen obtained the right to manufacture and sell Petter pistols everywhere in the world except France. Thus in this rather laborious way the invention of a Swiss made its way back to Switzerland via France.

The first further development of the Petter pistol concerned its chief disadvantage, namely the too low-performance caliber. Thus the existing Petter pistol was enlarged somewhat and set up for tests with the 9 mm Parabellum cartridge. Since then, though, this statement has proved to be less than completely correct, for a plan has been found (see H.P. Doebeli, *Die SIG Pistolen*) that shows a Petter pistol in 9 mm caliber, signed by the S.A.C.M.

First Tests in Switzerland

In Switzerland it was intended to replace the Parabellum

An early version of the SIG 210-1 with unburnished grip. From here on the versions of the SIG 210 are all but identical and show only relatively small differences.

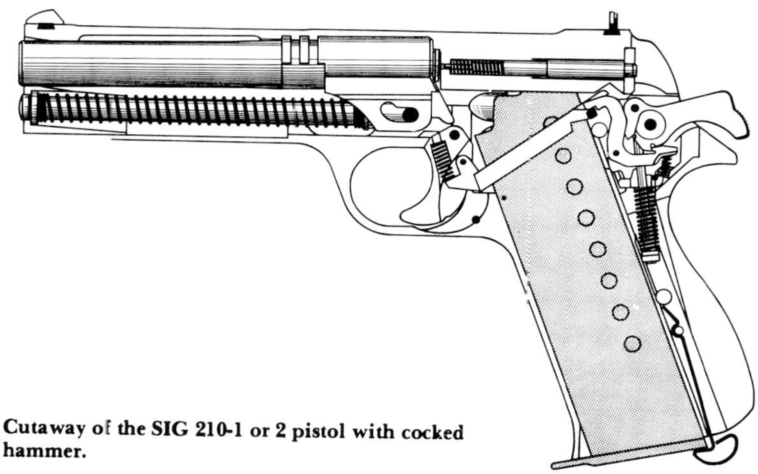

Cutaway of the SIG 210-1 or 2 pistol with cocked hammer.

The 210-2 version with matte surface, differing only in the walnut grip panels that afford a better grip.

Cutaway model of a SIG 210-2 with matte surface.

pistols that had seen service to that time with a better design. In this context, the firm of SIG was included by the Department of War Technology in the development of a new army pistol, which was already in progress. In the form of a manual, the request was made for the 9 mm caliber (suitable for pistols and machine pistols), a high degree of shooting precision, definitely safe operation, simple dismantling without the use of tools, and a magazine capacity of 8 to 12 cartridges.

The prototypes of this era differed more and more from the original Petter pistol. Only the locking system was retained, though without the chain. Both the improved mounting of the barrel forward in the slide and the elimination of the chain contributed very significantly to improving precision. The entire trigger and safety mechanisms were reworked. In 1944 ten prototypes could be turned over to the KTA for testing: they were the S.P. 44/8, S.P. 44/15 and S.P. 44/16 models, with the number after the diagonal indicating the magazine capacity.

In the chaotic era just after World War II, further developments came to a halt for a wide variety of reasons. New impulses came unexpectedly from Sweden, where the sport shooters' organization sought a successor weapon to the Parabellum pistol used until then. Inquiries from Sweden resulted in a model weapon that was designated the S.P. 47/8 SIG self-loading pistol. Swedish sport shooters had applied very concrete wishes to their search for a better sport pistol. The pistol was to be able to hold eight cartridges in its magazine, the trigger was to meet sporting requirements, and the possibility was to exist that, by changing barrels and recoil springs, it could fire both 9 mm Parabellum and 7.65 mm Parabellum cartridges. These requirements are still very important characteristics of the SIG 210 today. Shortly thereafter, in 1947, the Danish Army tested the S.P. 44/8 self-loading pistol for its suitability as a new army pistol, and introduced it officially as a service weapon a year later.

Now this pistol's success as a service weapon began.

For special occasions, SIG also turned out a very elegant weapon with deep engraving and carved grip panels.

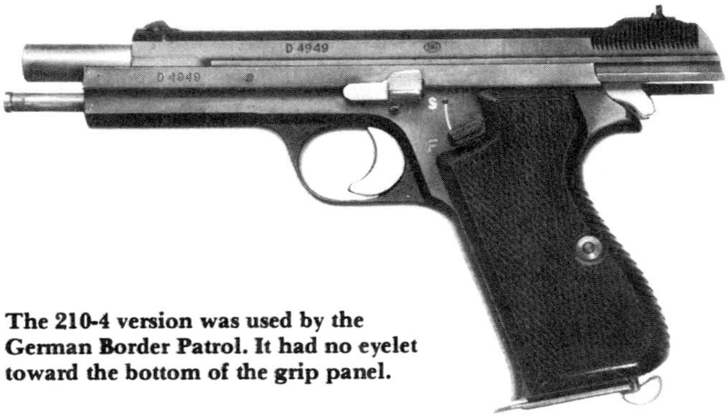

The 210-4 version was used by the German Border Patrol. It had no eyelet toward the bottom of the grip panel.

The special feature of the 210-4 is the loading indicator. As soon as a cartridge is inserted, the indicator sticks up out of the top of the slide.

The slide and barrel of the 210-4 version are no different from the other types from this perspective.

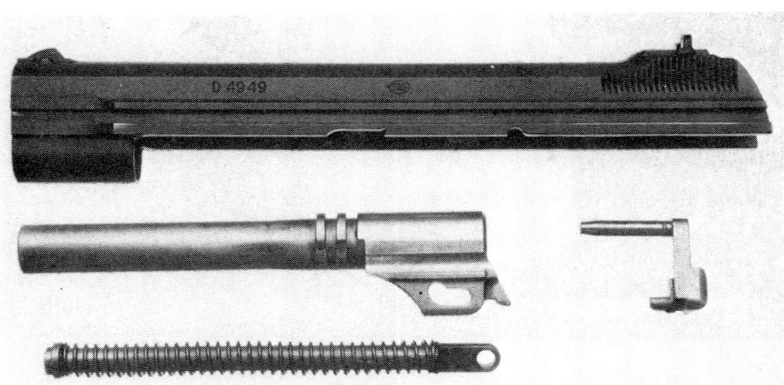

On October 24, 1948 the Swiss National Defense Commission announced the introduction of the SIG pistol as a new service weapon. It was introduced under the designation of "9 mm Pistole Modell 1949." In 1951, the German Federal Border Patrol introduced the same pistol as its service weapon. This was the P 210-4 version, recognizable by its full-size grip panels minus the strap cutout. The pistols for the Border Patrol were numbered from 0001 to 5000 and delivered between 1951 and 1954. In 1977-78 the first mustering-out of some 500 pistols took place — they were put on the civilian market and quickly became desirable collectors' items.

The SIG-210 Variations

The entire history of these excellent pistols is much too long to be told here. Like any other newly introduced weapon, it experienced several improvements and modifications in the course of time. The realm of SIG pistols has grown so extensive and complex through the years that several portrayals in book form have been devoted to it. An outstanding work in both text and photographic material was prepared by H.P. Doebeli, and is published by Motorbuch-Verlag under the title *Die SIG-Pistolen* — almost every variation known to date is shown here in detail, and within the firm's historical context.

Present-day production is oriented on the one hand to the continued manufacture of the SIG 210 as an "ordnance weapon", and on the other to the SIG 210 as a sport pistol easy to dismantle and suitable for everyone. This is a sensible program, as the firm's own research has shown, very few pistols are capable of attaining a degree of precision comparable to the SIG 210. The length of the barrel does not seem to play any decisive role in this, as one can regularly fire groups of ten shots into the inner circle, with its diameter of 25 mm, with the 120-mm long barrel. Several tests with the SIG 210 will be described in great detail in the appropriate chapter, so that a brief look will suffice here.

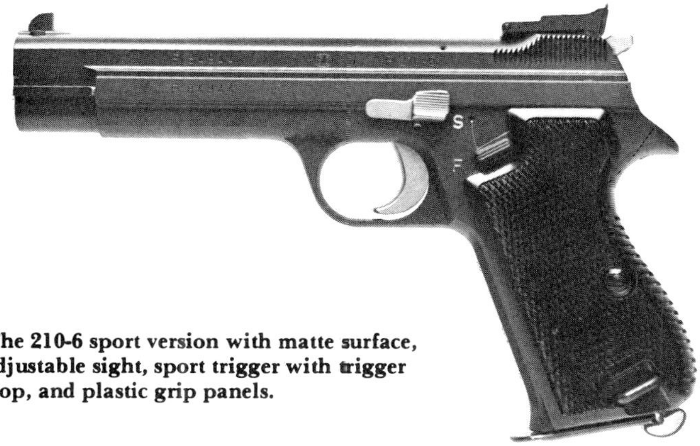

The 210-6 sport version with matte surface, adjustable sight, sport trigger with trigger stop, and plastic grip panels.

The following versions were on the market in mid-1986:

Model P 210-1
Caliber 9 mm Parabellum or 7.65 mm Parabellum, barrel length 120 mm, fixed sights, polished surfaces, strap ring and wooden grip panels.

The dismantled 210-6 without its grip panels.

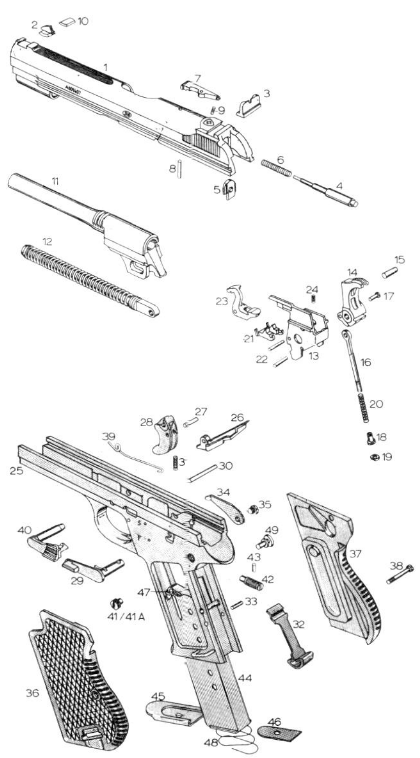

Model P 210-2
This is the so-called ordnance weapon; caliber 9 mm Parabellum or 7.65 mm Parabellum, barrel length 120 mm, fixed sight, sandblasted surfaces, strap ring and plastic grip panels.

Model P 210-5
The sport version, caliber 9 mm Parabellum or 7.65 mm Parabellum, barrel length 150 mm, micro-sight adjustable in all directions, sport trigger with trigger stop, sandblasted surfaces and plastic grip panels.

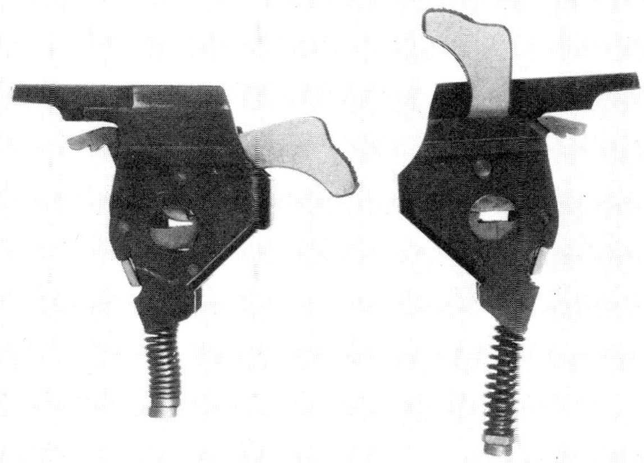

The lock is easy to remove from the grip. In sport pistols it is held by an additional screw and stays in its mount fully play-free.

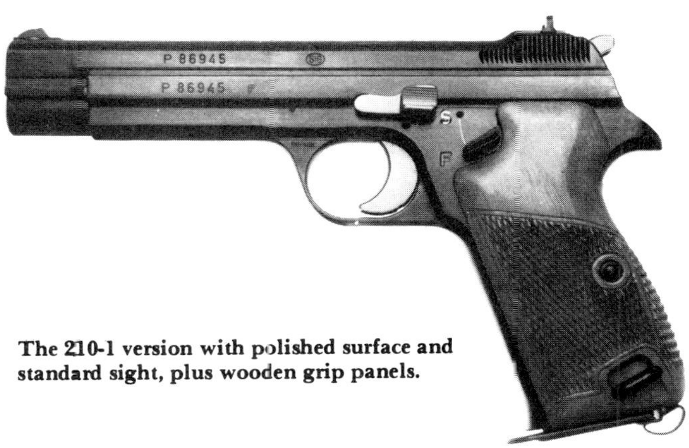

The 210-1 version with polished surface and standard sight, plus wooden grip panels.

Model P 210-6
Caliber 9 mm Parabellum or 7.65 mm Parabellum, barrel length 120 mm, micro-sight adjustable in all directions, sport trigger with trigger stop, sandblasted surfaces and plastic grip panels.

A weapon for sporting fans: polished surface, wooden grip panels and adjustable sights, with a barrel length of 120 mm.

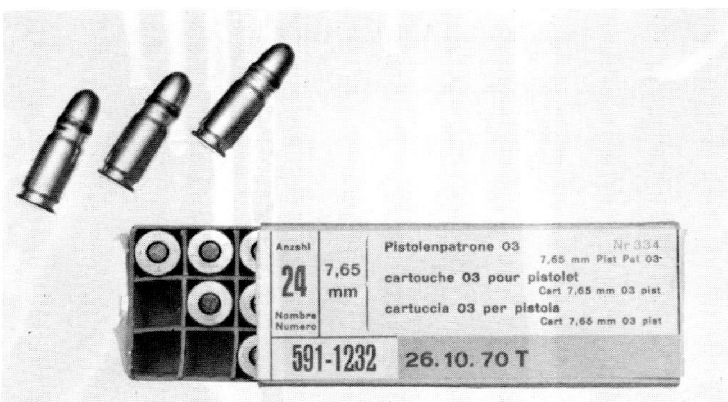

In addition, the manufacturer alternatively offers changeable grip panels made of wood, a changeable micro-sight and special hammer.

Changing to the .22 PR caliber is possible. The modification set includes the whole breech piece (slide) with the barrel, a different recoil spring and magazine. In addition, alternate barrels are available for use with lead bullets, both individually and in a complete modification system — the lock, hammer, etc., can also be switched. We cannot list all of these details here, however it can be noted that this pistol, expensive as it is to build, can always be modified to suit individual wishes. However, this is not cheap, as the sport lock alone costs 738 DM, the 150 mm barrel for lead bullets 925 DM, and the complete receiver 2300 DM.

Construction and Function

In terms of operation, the SIG 210 is a mechanically locked recoil loader using the locking principle of Browning. In a locked condition, the two ribs at the top of the barrel extend into the openings inside the slide. In that area, and in that of barrel guiding, the SIG 210 is made extremely tolerance-free, a very important basis for high shooting precision.

When firing, the locked barrel and slide move backward about 3 mm together, then the barrel moves diagonally downward and frees the slide for the rest of its recoil, and the empty case is extracted and ejected; the slide, moving backward, cocks the hammer and makes it settle into its resting position.

The SIG 210 has four independently acting safety systems. The safety lever blocks the trigger rail in its safety position when set at S, thus blocking the trigger. The release of the hammer is thereby prevented.

The *safety rest* on the hammer holds the hammer in case it should slip out of one's hand while being cocked. The function of the safety rest only takes place when the finger does not pull the trigger at the same time.

The *magazine safety* is a controversial feature of modern weapons; many shooters like it, while others reject it completely, for even with a cartridge in the chamber, a gun is worthless as a weapon if the magazine is lost. If the magazine is incomplete or not pushed in, this safety presses the trigger rail downward and separates it from the trigger bar.

The *recoil safety* interrupts the trigger function in the same way when the slide is not all the way forward and the weapon is not completely bolted.

Dismantling can be done in a few seconds without a tool. After removing the magazine and checking the safety, the slide is pulled back some 5 mm. In this position the breech catch (catch lever) is removed from right to left. The upper part can now be pushed out of the receiver to the front, and it is of note in this respect that the slide is not guided from the outside of the frame, but from inside the frame. This is also a reason for the

Technical Data: SIG-210 Series

Version	D 44/8	SD 47/8	210-1	210-4
Manufacturer		Swiss Industry Company, Neuhausen		
Caliber	9 mm Para.	9 mm Para.	9 mm/7.65 mm Para.	9 mm Para.
Magazine capacity	8 cartridges	8 cartridges	8 cartridges	8 cartridges
Overall length	213 mm	213 mm	213 mm	213 mm
Height/width	138 mm/35 mm	131 mm/31 mm	131 mm/31 mm	131 mm/31 mm
Barrel length	120.4 mm	120 mm	120 mm	120 mm
Weight empty	900 grams	990 grams	990 grams	995 grams
Sights	fixed	fixed	fixed	fixed
Safeties		Lever, magazine and closing safety		
Finish	burnished	burinshed	matte burnished	matte burnished
Grip panels	wood	wood	plastic, wood	plastic
Special features	Catch lever on right	–	–	Loading indicator, no ring for belt in grip

good shooting performance, for the slide thus moves on its rails without any play.

After the recoil spring along with its guiding rail is removed, the barrel can be lifted diagonally upward out of the slide. The dismantling of the sport model with its 150 mm barrel is somewhat different; before the barrel is removed, the foresight has to be unscrewed.

The Parabellum Pistol in Switzerland

Switzerland was the first country to introduce the new-type knee-joint pistol, based on the designs of Borchardt and Luger, as a service weapon. The DWM presented two pistols to the Swiss war materials administration in mid-November of 1898 which can be regarded as improved prototypes of the later Parabellum pistol. In Switzerland they were designated "Test Model III", while the Borchardt pistols offered earlier, in 1897, were called Test Models I and II.

According to what is generally accepted as valid today, Georg Luger did most of the work on the improved version, though concrete evidence for this does not exist. Luger's first pistol patent concerns an improved trigger mechanism and grip safety. In 1898 Luger had made a very important improvement to the breech. The free end of the two-armed rear joint used in the Borchardt pistol, with its friction rollers, had been replaced by two hinge buttons, by which the breech was guided on the curves of the high side shields of the receiver. The solution developed by Luger was simpler in its operation, plus more stable and easier to manufacture. Above all, the considerable shortening of the receiver was important, as the Borchardt pistol was simply too long and too unhandy.

Functioning of the Parabellum pistol made by the Weapon Factory of Bern in 7.65 mm Parabellum caliber.

A. Pistol at moment of firing, just before recoil.
B. Bolt has just been lifted, joint begins to bend.
C. Joint is completely open, empty case is ejected.
D. Next cartridge is inserted, system is bolted and cocked, ready to fire.

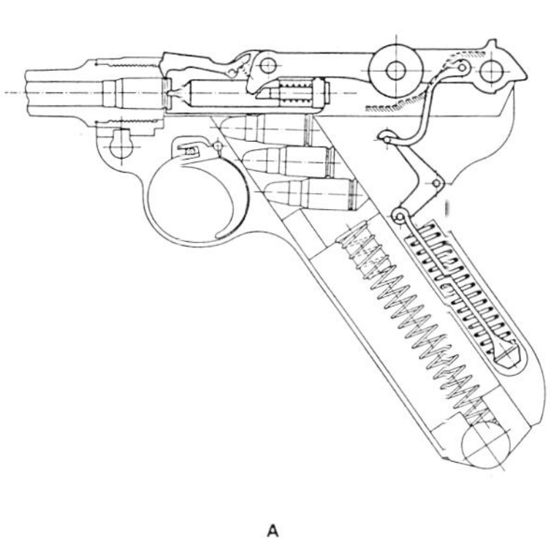
A

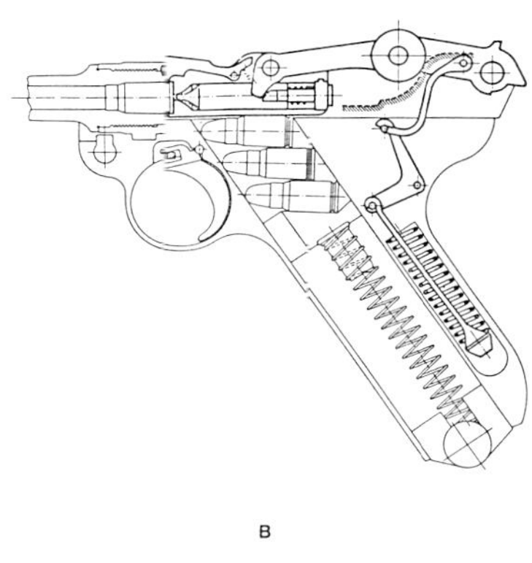
B

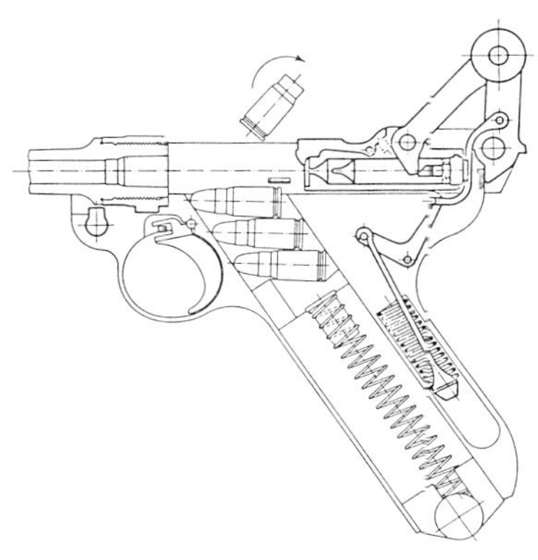
C

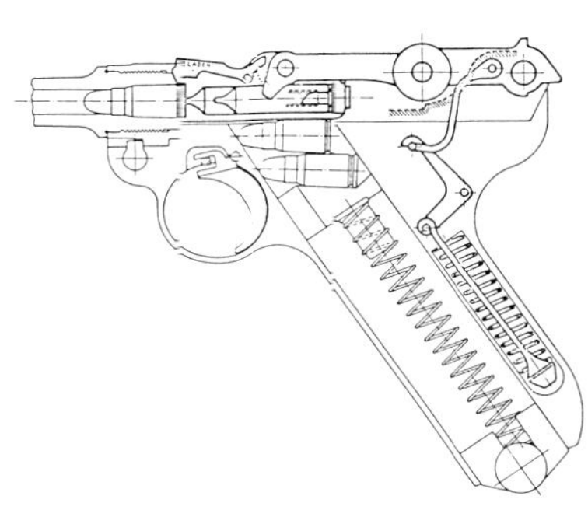
D

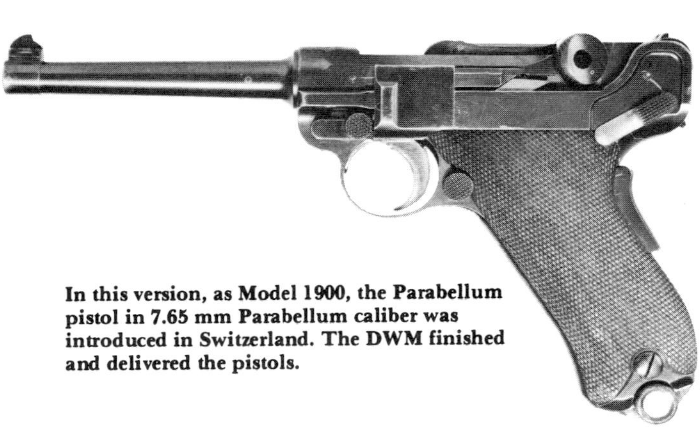

In this version, as Model 1900, the Parabellum pistol in 7.65 mm Parabellum caliber was introduced in Switzerland. The DWM finished and delivered the pistols.

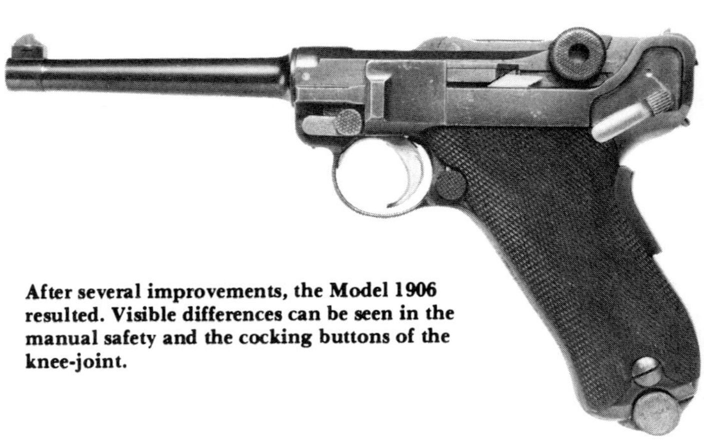

After several improvements, the Model 1906 resulted. Visible differences can be seen in the manual safety and the cocking buttons of the knee-joint.

The Parabellum pistol presented in Switzerland was already a typical specimen. The barrel and breech moved backward some 4 mm together, and then the external hinge knobs made contact with the guiding rails on the side shields and caused the system to open. The combined recoil was braked on contact, and the breech bent against the opposition of the leaf spring in the rear of the receiver. The contact of the spring and the nose at the bottom rear of the rear joint brought the bending to a stop. In its backward movement, the recoil spring stretched the breech again, and in the process a new cartridge was introduced from the magazine and the firing pin bolt was held before its compressed spring. The use of a bent leaf spring at the rear of the grip proved to be unfavorable under pressure, for the pressure of the spring was very slight on the last part of the backward motion. Then too, the knee-joint breech made the pistol sensitive to different loads: with both weak and overly strong cartridges, the pistol did not function perfectly. A high degree of quality in manufacturing the ammunition was required. The overall design of the 1898 weapon was already very similar to that of the later Luger pistols. The side shields of the receiver were different, the safety lever was still absent — it was added only in 1899 — and the prototype had only its automatically working grip safety.

The pistol as offered to the testing agencies in Switzerland was, with an empty weight of 990 grams, still too heavy, so that Luger was empowered to offer a lighter version.

The small bolt hook in the right cocking knob, which was supposed to prevent the breech from bending upward prematurely, proved to be superfluous. It was omitted from all pistols made from 1906 on.

In the earlier pistols, made from 1898 to 1904, one had to pull the hinge knobs back a little bit first before the joint was able to bend. From 1906 on a simple pull upward and backward was sufficient to open the breech. In addition, the 1898 and 1899 prototypes had grip panels on which the herringbone pattern was not cut all the way to the edge of the surface. Five examples of the 1898 Borchardt-Luger pistol probably went to Switzerland. In 1899 the prototype of an improved version was finished, and further tests of it were undertaken in Switzerland.

In 1899 new tests began in Switzerland, including the improved Borchardt-Luger, the Krnka-Roth, the Mauser C 96, the Mannlicher Model 1900, a design from the Fabrique Nationale in Herstal, and a design by the German Albert Huff. Only the Mannlicher and the Borchardt-Luger lasted to the final competition. The improved version featured a side safety at the rear of the grip, an improved breech, and a small reduction in the gross weight. In spite of this, the pistol was still regarded by the official agencies as too heavy. After the first successful tests, another twenty test models were ordered from Borchardt-Luger and issued to the troops, who were particularly enthusiastic about the good shooting precision. In March of 1900 the military urgently recommended to the Bundesart that the Borchardt-Luger be accepted. It was introduced by a declaration of the Bundesart on May 4, 1900 as "Pistole Ordonnanz 1900, System Borchardt-Luger." The first 2000 examples were delivered by DWM in 1901, the price at the time being 62 Swiss francs apiece.

The order to the DWM amounted to 5000 pistols, and another 1500 examples from this order went to the Eidgenössische Waffenfabrik in Bern, plus another 1500 dismantled pistols that were assembled in Bern.

After several modifications had been made to the pistol, it was renamed by an act of the Bundesrat on January 9, 1906 — the Model 1900-1906 was created, and

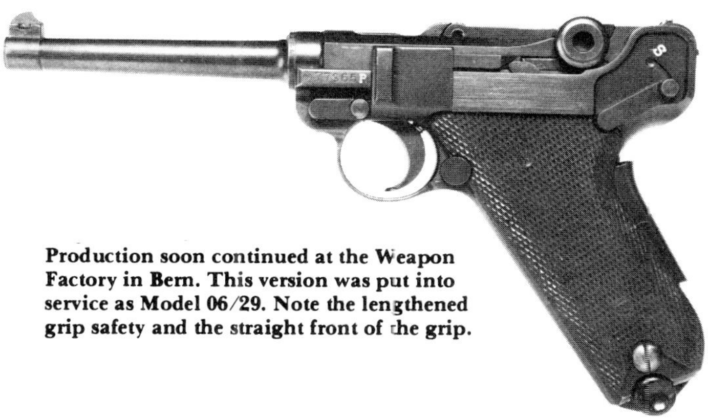

Production soon continued at the Weapon Factory in Bern. This version was put into service as Model 06/29. Note the lengthened grip safety and the straight front of the grip.

a total of 10,250 of them were delivered. During the first months of World War I the deliveries from Berlin were halted at once, and the Eidgenössische Waffenfabrik had to convert and produce the pistols. The first weapons produced there could be delivered as early as November 1918. Several attempts were made to simplify the costly and time-consuming production. The total of the modifications made in the process resulted in the Model 06/29, which was in production from June 1933 to November 1946.

For a long time the omission of the grip safety was a controversial point, however it was kept even when other countries used an almost identical pistol without the grip safety. The various simplifications were tested and calculations were made. The weapons factory in Bern was able to notify the KTA on August 28, 1918 that the production costs were to be decreased by some 30%. The price per weapon was then 170 francs including a reduction for 5000 or more pieces, or 160 francs with an order of 10,000, spread over a period of six years.

The visible modifications and simplifications in the new model included the straight front edge of the receiver, the cylindrically stepped fork housing where the barrel screwed in, the elimination of the strap loop, and the herringbone pattern on the locking piece, the safety, the hinge knobs of the knee joint and the magazine catch. In addition, simplified grip panels of pressed plastic were used instead of walnut. Only two spare magazines were delivered instead of the former three, and the surfaces were no longer prepared so well or so laboriously. The typical weaknesses of the Parabellum pistol were naturally a problem in Switzerland: the dependence on ammunition with an exactly correct charge, the high production costs, the sensitive individual parts, some of them filigreed. Last but not least, the effectivness of the 7.65 mm bullet did not remain over a period of time, thus at least 9 mm had to be used. In 1949 the 9 mm Parabellum cartridge was officially accepted, and along with it the pistol made by SIG-Neuhausen.

Technical Data: Swiss Parabellum

Version	Model 1900	Model 1906	Model 06/29
Manufacturer	DWM	DWM	Weapon Factory, Bern
Caliber	7.65 mm Parabellum	7.65 mm Parabellum	7.65 mm Parabellum
Magazine capacity	8 cartridges	8 cartridges	8 cartridges
Overall length	237 mm	234 mm	239 mm
Height\width	138 mm/40 mm	139 mm/39.5	138 mm/36 mm
Barrel length	122 mm	118 mm	120 mm
Weight empty	890 grams	890 grams	935 grams
Sights	fixed	fixed	fixed
Finish	burnished	burnished	burnished
Grip panels	wood	wood	Canevasite
Lettering	DWM	DWM	none
Safeties	lever & handball	lever & handball	lever & handball

SPAIN

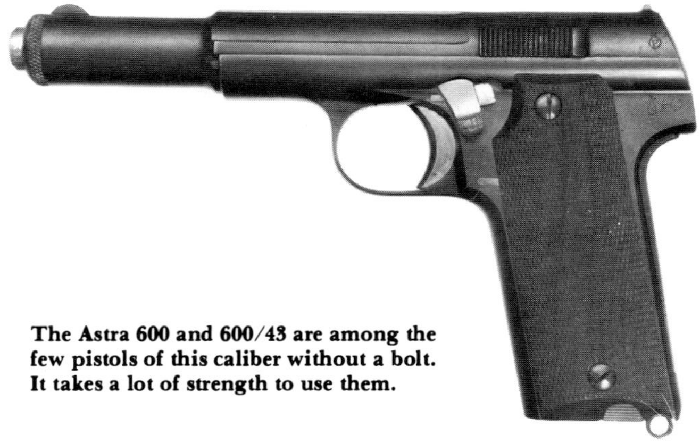

The Astra 600 and 600/43 are among the few pistols of this caliber without a bolt. It takes a lot of strength to use them.

Since the beginning of this century, a flourishing weapons industry has developed in Spain, chiefly in Eibar. It appears that one manufacturer must have had his premises right next door to another, and for many years they all did a good business. First of all the private market (in glaring contrast to the present day) could absorb many weapons indeed, and besides that, France and Italy had a great need for pistols — that need was met for the most part by Spanish manufacturers. Many of these small firms did not survive the chaos of the Spanish Civil War unscathed, and afterwars there existed only three large firms capable of producing handguns: Llama, Astra and Star. These firms still produce the weapons for the Spanish armed forces and police, and have succeeded in staying in business on a worldwide basis with modern designs.

Astra 600

The firm of Unceta y Cia was founded at Eibar in 1908 under the name of Pedro Unceta y Juan Esperanza. At first the firm made small pocket pistols, the best known of which was the "Victoria" model. In 1913 the firm moved to Guernica, the city where the German Luftwaffe thoroughly tested the effect of their aircraft and their armaments for the first time — with gruesome results. According to a government contract, the firm produced the Campo Giro pistol, from which the 300-400 and 600 series developed later. In 1914 the trade name of "Astra" was chosen for the firm's products, and it has been retained to this day, with the individual models also known by a number, such as this model, the Astra 600.

After World War I, Astra began to build the first pistol based on the "tube principle", and authors like to call attention to this fact, as these pistols look just as if they were put together out of several tubes. The Model 400, as it was called for the civilian market, was developed, and was adopted by the army and designated Model 1921. The pistol was made for the 9 mm Largo cartridge but can also fire other cartridges such as the 9 mm Parabellum, 9 mm Steyr, 9 mm Browning long and .38 Super Auto. The author has not been able to test them all, but the assertion made by American authors seems to be somewhat questionable, for the 9 mm Browning long would in any case not be strong enough to fulfill the function of the weapon.

The 1921 (or 400) model was introduced in the Spanish Army and remained in service for a long time. It was also sold to many other countries — even the French armed forces took it into their service. Some 106,175 of the Model 1921 were manufactured.

The Astra 600 is a shortened version of the Astra 400, made for the 9 mm Parabellum cartridge, with a 16 mm shorter the barrel. This version was produced as of 1943 under contract to the (friendly) German government, and the pistol is marked 600/43, and also bears the German test stamp and the name "Pist. Patr. 08", which is stamped on the barrel not far from the ejection window — a smaller quantity was made for the 7.65 mm

Excerpt from a German service manual for the Astra 600 pistol in 9 mm Parabellum caliber.

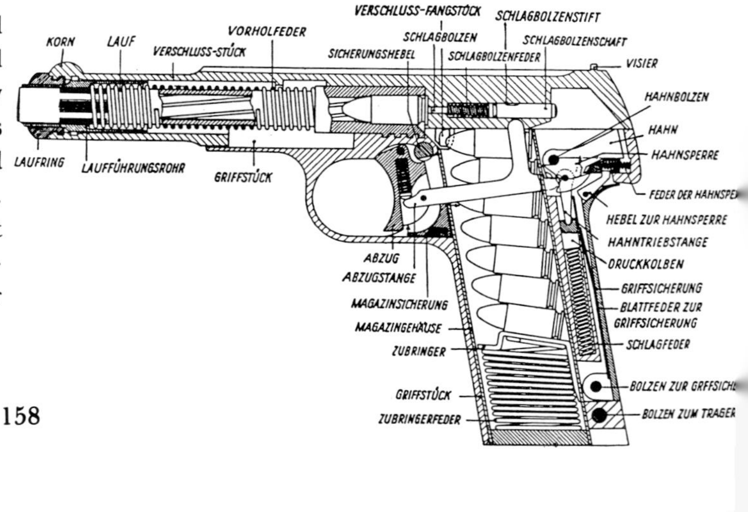

Right side of the 600 when open. As the P 4 pistol it was used for a time by German police units. When a barrel has grooves around it at the front, this always indicates that it has to be turned for dismantling.

The upper part with barrel and recoil spring is removed. With its comb on the bottom, the barrel attaches to the grip.

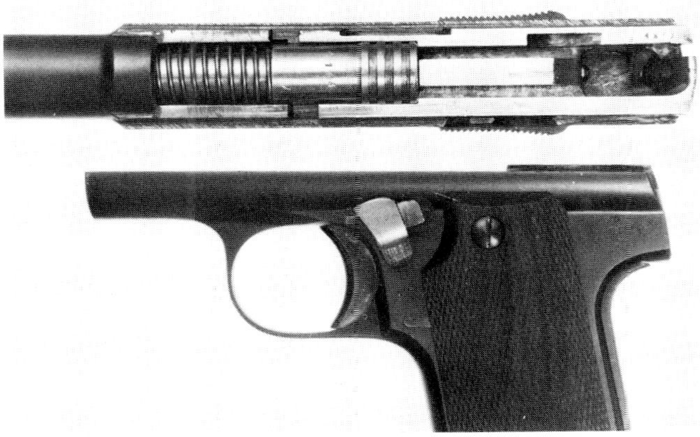

Parabellum cartridge. In all, 10,450 Model 600 pistols could be delivered to the German Wehrmacht by 1944, at which time the border between Spain and France was finally closed. Production went on after World War II — Germany ordered 14,000 pistols for police use, now bearing the designation of P 3. Exact production figures from this era are not available, but according to American sources, some 49,000 were made and sold, including 14,000 for the German police. At the time of World War II the Astra 600 sold for 43.90 Reichsmark, and the Model 300 in 7.65 mm short caliber for only 31.70 RM.

The Astra 600 is made completely of steel and is as cleanly made as it is sturdy. It has no locking system, but is one of the few pistols with an unlocked spring-mass breech. With the 9 mm Parabellum caliber, this requires a very strong recoil spring and a high breech weight, which is provided here by the closed slide. The safety systems make the weapon somewhat hard to handle by present-day standards, but it may well have lived up to the requirements of its day. The lateral wing safety blocks the slide and the trigger. When the safety is engaged, the slide can be moved only a little, but in heavily used pistols the safety may move out by itself so that it no longer blocks the slide. The grip safety locks the sear, when the grip safety is not pushed in, the hammer cannot be cocked, and the slide cannot move backward when the hammer is still decocked — this can only take place when the hammer is cocked. The magazine safety locks the trigger whenever the magazine is not entirely inserted. Its spring extension takes its place behind the trigger tongue so that no movement is possible. When a cartridge is inserted, the extractor, which is mounted on the side, sticks out a little further than usual, however this appears to be not enough of a control and, therefore, not safe enough.

For dismantling, it is best to pull the slide back while the magazine is still inserted and check the weapon for safety. Then remove the magazine — the magazine catch is located at the bottom of the grip. Then let the slide move forward a little and apply the safety lever so that the extension holds the slide.

Immediately behind the muzzle, the barrel is surrounded by ridges. On Spanish pistols and similar weapons this is always an indication that the barrel has to be turned for further dismantling. It must be turned (as seen from the front) 90 degrees to the left. In this position, its comb fits into a groove inside the slide and has come out of the matching comb-shaped cutout in the

The dismantled Astra 600 with grip panels still in place. It is a somewhat old-fashioned but very precisely and sturdily built pistol for its time.

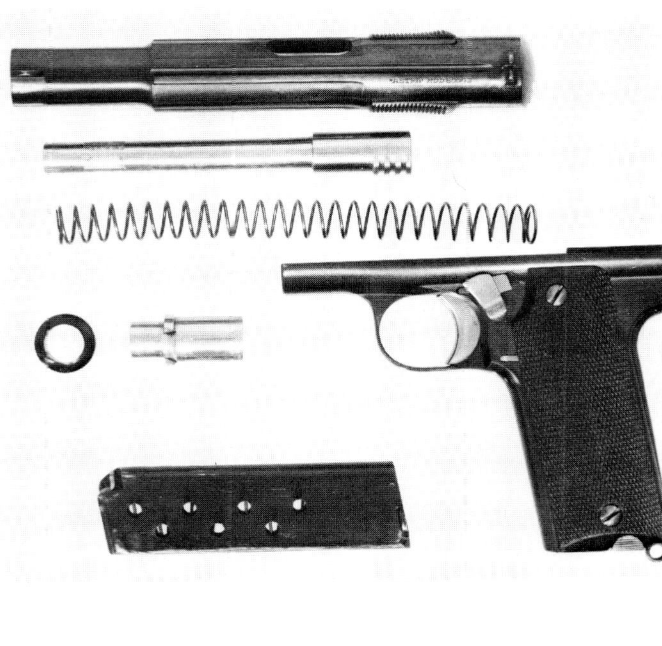

frame. This type of barrel mounting is reminiscent of many pocket pistols in which the barrel is fitted into the frame by a sort of comb, a connection that is not at all bad or injurious to precision. The upper part, with the projecting barrel, can now be pushed out of the frame at the front and dismantled further — with the great spring tension, one must always perform this step carefully. It is easier when the barrel is pushed back again far enough in the removed upper part so that its chamber can make contact with the contact base of the slide. To remove the barrel, the locking piece of the barrel guide housing is pushed in at the front with the help of the magazine base, after which the locking piece and housing can be turned and removed from the front of the slide. This must be done carefully, as everything is under the pressure of the strong recoil spring positioned around the barrel. Then the recoil spring is removed, after which the barrel is taken out and can be cleaned easily. This dismantling shows that one has not only a well-made pistol but also a sturdily constructed one in the Astra 600.

The 400 and 600 models barely differ in design, and the smaller version (Model 300, in 7.65 mm or 9 mm short calibers) is also built to the same design, but is simply smaller. There are differences in the various versions in terms of grip panels, the magazine catch, the strap ring at the bottom of the grip, and the magazine bottom.

On the basis of the design shown here, Astra has built further variations. The Astra Model 700 was a variant of the 400, made for the 7.65 mm cartridge. Another interesting version is the Astra 800 or Astra-Condor. The familiar technology was retained. One difference, though, is the external hammer with its long spur. The magazine catch was moved to the lower rear of the grip, and the grip safety was omitted. To increase handling safety, the Condor had a load indicator. The manual safety was moved to the back of the frame, and the grip is more curved to allow a better hold.

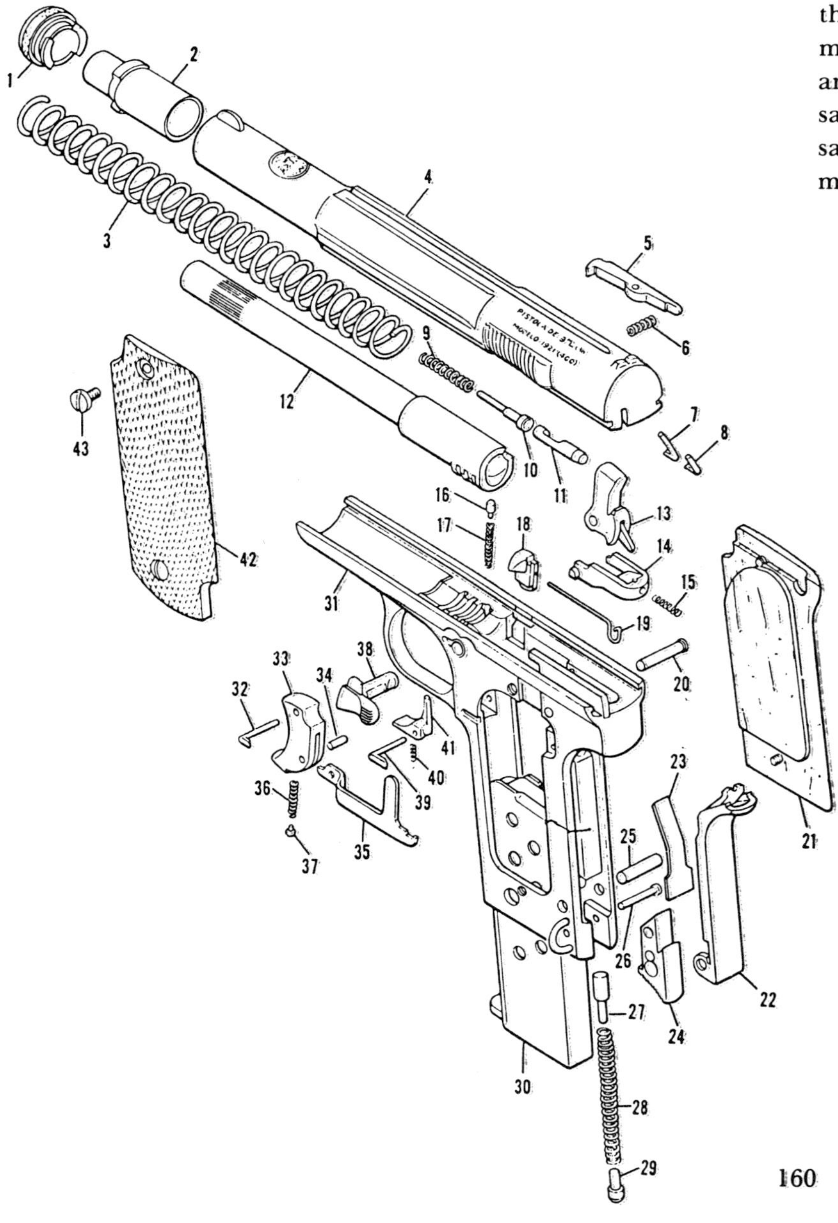

Parts of the Astra 400 (similar to 600)

Parts Legend

1 Barrel Bushing Lock
2 Barrel Bushing
3 Recoil Spring
4 Slide
5 Extractor
6 Extractor Spring
7 Firing Pin
8 Extractor Retainer Pin
9 Firing Pin Spring
10 Firing Pin
11 Firing Pin Extension
12 Barrel
13 Hammer
14 Sear
15 Sear Spring
16 Safety Catch Detent
17 Detent Spring
18 Slide Stop
19 Slide Stop Spring
20 Hammer Pin
21 Right Grip
22 Grip Safety
23 Grip Safety Spring
24 Magazine Catch
25 Grip Safety Pin
26 Magazine Catch Stop
27 Upper Spring Plunger
28 Hammer Spring
29 Lower Spring Plunger
30 Magazine
31 Frame
32 Trigger Pin
33 Trigger
34 Trigger Bar Pin
35 Trigger Bar
36 Trigger Bar Spring
37 Spring Plunger
38 Safety Catch
39 Magazine Safety Pin
40 Magazine Safety Spring
41 Magazine Safety
42 Left Grip
43 Grip Screw (4)

The Astra 800 (Condor) is made for the 9 mm Parabellum cartridge; its magazine holds eight cartridges, and the overall length of the weapon is 207 mm. It was first put on the market in 1958 and remained in production until 1969, by which time 11,400 had been manufactured.

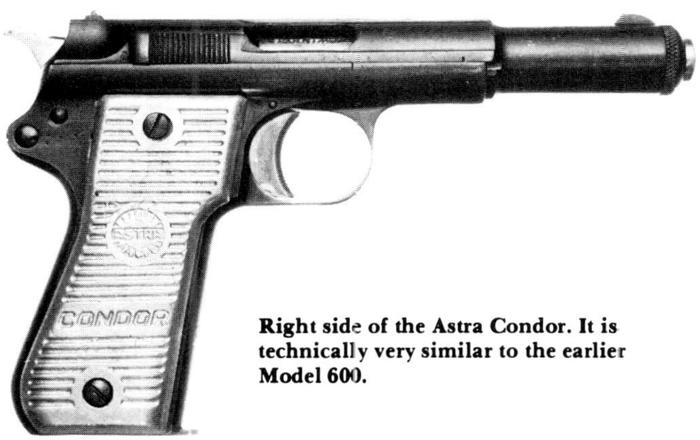

Right side of the Astra Condor. It is technically very similar to the earlier Model 600.

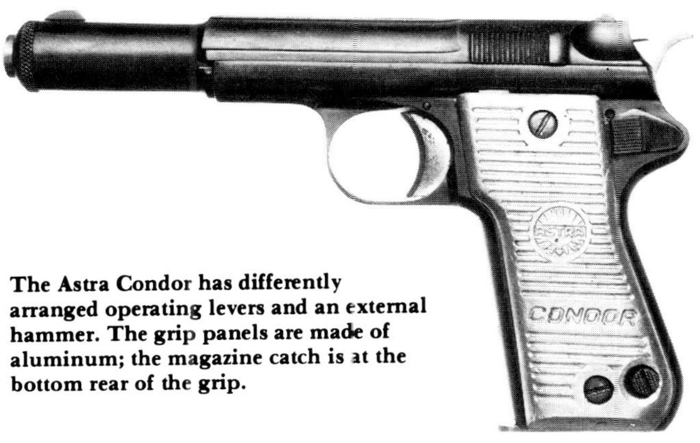

The Astra Condor has differently arranged operating levers and an external hammer. The grip panels are made of aluminum; the magazine catch is at the bottom rear of the grip.

Technical Data: Astra 600/43

Manufacturer	Astra Unceta y Cia, Guernica
Designation	Model 600/43
Caliber	9 mm Parabellum
Magazine capacity	8 cartdidges
Overall length	205-207 mm
Height/width	129 mm/30 mm
Barrel length	134 mm
Weight empty	1000 grams
Sights	Fixed
System/trigger	Unlocked/single-action
Material	Steel
Finish	Burnished
Safeties	Lever, magazine, grip

Astra A-80 and A-90

From time to time the market becomes very active. This is always the case when any government agencies or armed forces publish the specifications for a new and better pistol. At one time new weapons were being sought for the police, which were finally to be rearmed with the high-performance (and naturally also very penetrating) 9 mm PARA cartridge. This required pistols, for official (and later also for private) users, that had to measure up to the strict requirements in the specification book — exhaustive long-term tests showed every weakness and required the immediate elimination of every fault.

As the 1980s began, officials in the USA expressed a wish for a modern pistol in 9 mm PARA caliber. It was to have the best of safety systems along with a high magazine capacity. Despite the best lobbying, the government was not able to accede to these wishes, and alternatives had to be accepted. Both in the USA and in Europe, there soon appeared a number of new models, some of which had been derived from weapons already on the market. One such example was the SIG/Sauer P 226, which was derived directly from the P 225. Walther entered the competition with the P 88, deviating for the first time from the principle of the swinging bolt. In Europe too, there was a need for new developments when, for example, the Austrian Army wanted a better pistol. Steyr offered the GB with its gas-delayed mass breech, though without winning the military authorities' stamp of approval. A firm that had been almost completely unknown until then came on the market very

With the Model A-80, Astra was able to offer a very compact pistol with a 15-shot magazine. Much of it resembles, at least externally, the SIG-Sauer pistols.

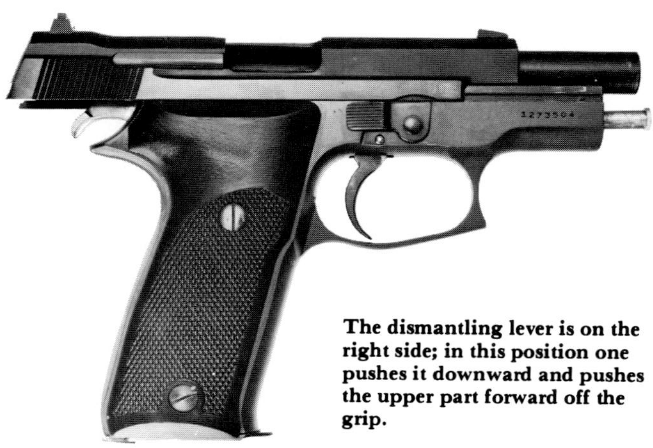

The dismantling lever is on the right side; in this position one pushes it downward and pushes the upper part forward off the grip.

quickly. The result was the Glock 17, a pistol whose technical design was as original as it was simple, and which became the Austrian Bundesheer's new pistol.

The Astra A 80 made by the Astra Unceta y Cia of Guernica likewise took part in this competition. It can hold 15 cartridges in its magazine and one more in the chamber, with which it can be carried in complete safety. When it appeared on the German market in 1983, its price was surprising — with a second magazine, it cost just under 1000 DM, although it is made completely of steel. Other similar pistols made by other manufacturers could not offer that. Either the designers from Guernica were inspired, or they had previously been in close touch with Eckernförde, for the A-80 is not only very similar to the SIG/Sauer pistol externally, but also has nearly the same design features in terms of its safety system.

Thus its designers were able, quickly and without a great deal of development, to offer a very compact and well-made pistol. The workmanship of the A-80 naturally cannot be measured by that of the SIG 210, but for its price it offers solid value. Its great firepower is unusually compact and handy, so that it could become a competitor to the new Mini-Gun made by Smith & Wesson.

Differing from the model (as this writer imagined it) is the magazine catch, which is inset at the bottom of the grip instead of right behind the trigger. That may disconcert some people, but with 15 cartridges plus one

The dismantled Astra A-80. The bolt is a further development of the renowned model. The whole weapon is made of steel.

in the chamber, it is not necessary to change the magazine every few seconds. The sights are fixed, though the foresight can be moved inside its cutout. Both fore- and backsight are marked in white, which is a considerbale advantage when targeting in poor light or against dark surfaces.

The hammer has a safety rest, in which it does not normally lie. It is held in this position when the decocking lever is moved while the gun is cocked. During the process, another safety function, the firing pin safety, comes into action. The firing pin is held by a cut-out block so that it can move forward only when this safety block is raised. For this purpose, the sear has an extension at the front with which it presses against the bolt and lifts when the trigger is pulled. Thus the A-80 is very safe and meets present-day safety regulations, which

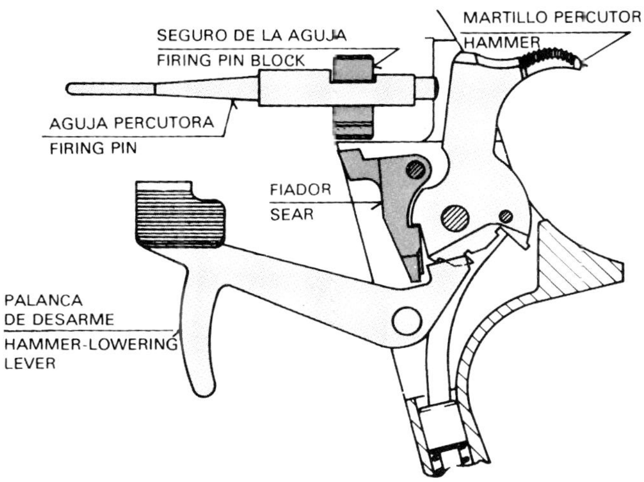

Trigger system of the Astra A-80 at rest. The firing pin is still cocked.

When a shot is fired, the firing pin block is lifted, the firing pin can move forward and ignite the cartridge.

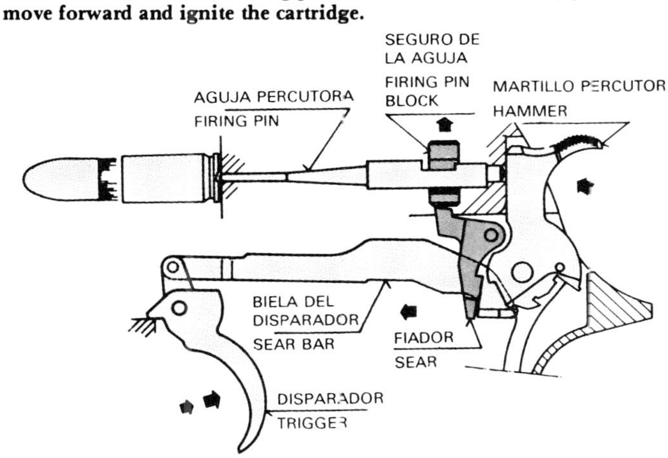

To modify the trigger one must dismantle all the parts from the grip. Only thus does one really get to know one's own weapon.

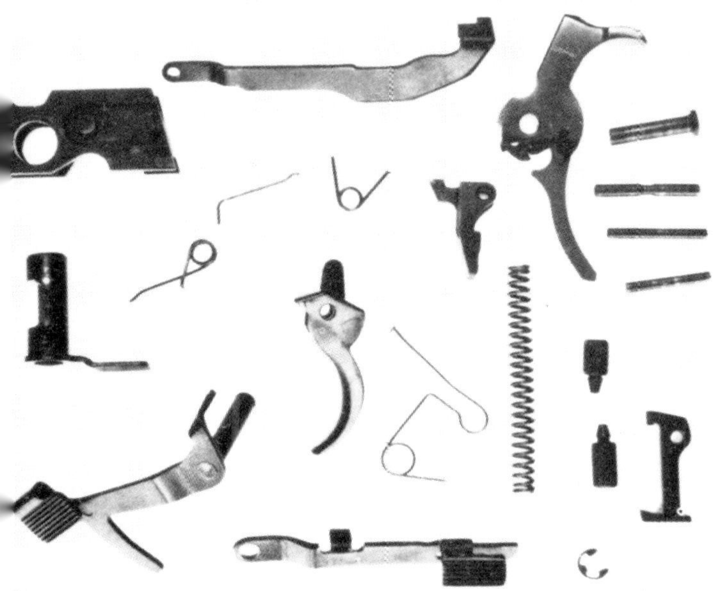

A weapon resulting from cooperation between Astra and Llama: the A-80 with a laterally adjustable sight.

Technically speaking it is nonsensical, but many major customers want it: the additional safety that blocks the already automatically blocked firing pin. The magazine catch is high in the grip, the sights are laterally adjustable, and the grip panels are made of walnut. This is the Model A-90.

have meanwhile become the norm.

The extractor likewise has a safety function. After a cartridge is inserted, it projects, clearly visible and tangible, at the side and indicates the loading condition — a red marking makes it easier to check optically.

The dismantling lever, which is simultaneously the catch for the barrel contact along with its inserting ramp, is located on the right side of the weapon. Dismantling is surprisingly simple: take out the magazine and check the chamber. Pull back the slide and hold it in place by pushing up the catch lever. Swing the dismantling lever forward 90 degrees. Push the upper part forward off the receiver. After that, the recoil spring with its guide rail can be taken out, as can the barrel with its powerful locking tab.

The shooting performance of the A-80 was tested numerous times while standing, both free-handed and one-handed. With the usual factory cartridges, groups of 70 to 80 mm diameters were achieved at a distance of 15 meters — this is thoroughly satisfactory performance for a defensive weapon. Not completely satisfactory, though, was the general nature of the trigger. For sustained fire, the trigger has to be pulled a long distance, and long fingers cannot bend that far. The single-action movement is long, and that cannot be changed, since the sear cannot be pushed far enough forward with a shortening of the rest to avoid unintentionally catching the hammer in the safety rest.

The A-80 is made in 9 mm PARA, .38 Super and .45 ACP calibers.

In 1986 several changes were made to the Astra A-80. At the request of several official clients, an additional manual safety was installed in the top of the slide, with it, the firing pin can be blocked by hand. Such a measure is technically nonsensical, but in similar fashion to the P 7 in its S version, the manufacturer had to take several major customers' wishes into consideration. The thus-modified pistol is sold under the designation of A-90. It also differs from the original A-80 in other features: the manual safety is located on both sides (very handy for left-handed shooters), the magazine catch was moved upward to the end of the trigger guard, and the sights can be adjusted laterally, as the foresight leaf can be moved between two screws that can be loosened.

Under the additional designation of INOX (as an abbreviation for inoxidable: non-rusting), both models, the A-80 and the A-90, have been made of stainless steel to the same design. Both pistols have a very tasteful appearance; their surfaces are satinized, with only the thin flank strips of the slide being polished to a high gloss.

Astra A-80 INOX in stainless steel.

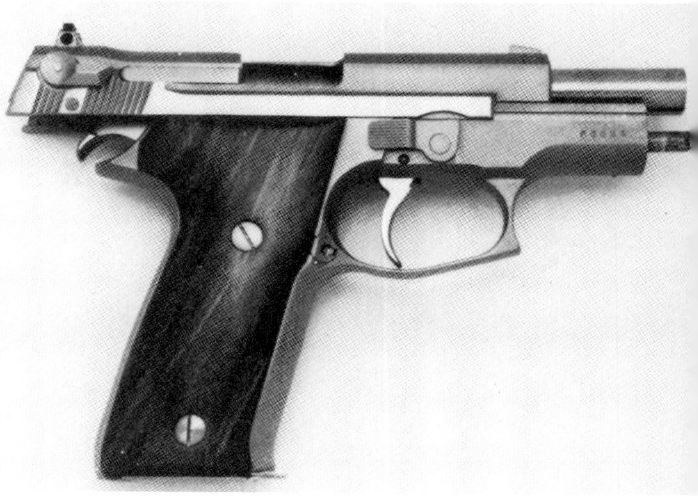

The right side when open. The Astra A-90 INOX has an additional safety.

No different technology, but the two makers' names: the Astra-Llama A-90 with burnished finish.

Both the Model A-80 and the A-90 are built in cooperation with the firm of Llama; the weapons resulting from this collaboration have both firm names on the slide, but without the place name that is otherwise found on Astra weapons.

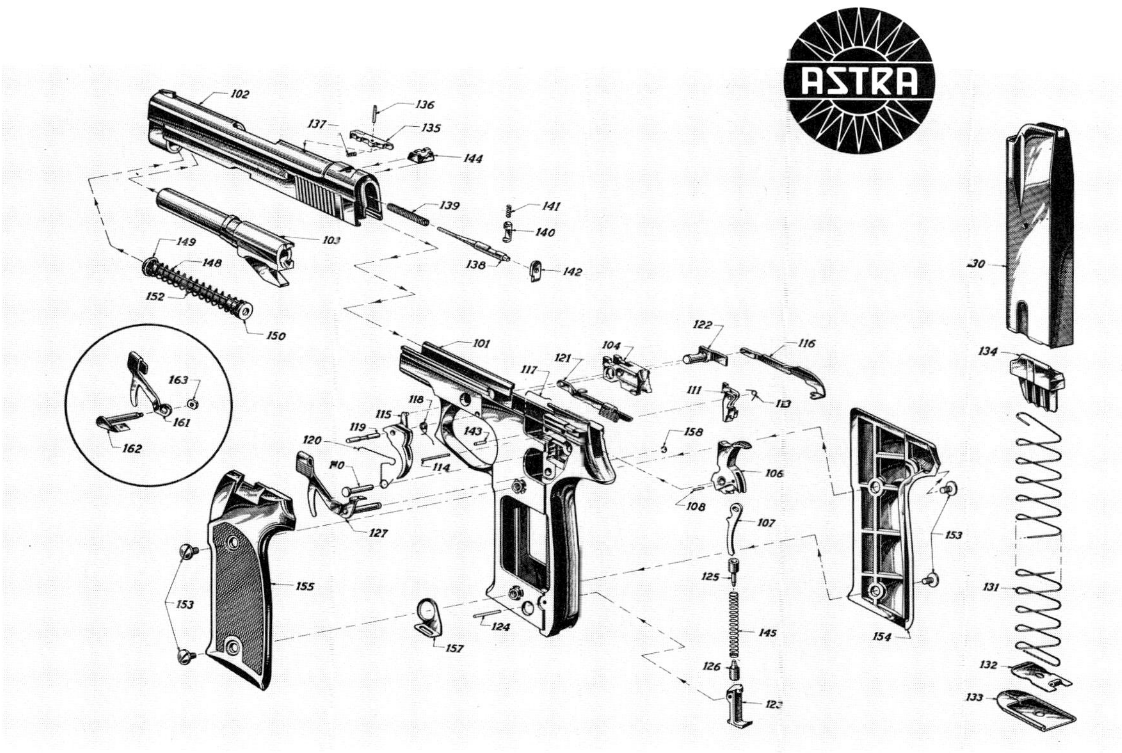

The parts of the Astra A-80.

Technical Data: Astra A-80

Caliber	9 mm Para.	.38 Super	.45 ACP
Overall length	180 mm	180 mm	180 mm
Height	142 mm	142 mm	142 mm
Width	36 mm	36 mm	36 mm
Barrel length	92 mm	92 mm	92 mm
Weight empty	985 grams	975 grams	955 grams
Magazine capacity	15	15	9
Sights	fixed	fixed	fixed
Prip panels	plastic	plastic	plastic
Finish	burnished	burnished	burnished
Safeties	decocking lever, firing pin block, extractor = loading indicator		

Llama 82

After gaining little commercial success with the somewhat wrongly made Omni II, the firm of Llama Gabilondo took its successful "big plunge" with the Model 82. This pistol became the service weapon of the Spanish armed forces, which is always encouraging for a manufacturer, for the high costs of preparing for series production can hardly be met by private sales today.

The Llama 82 follows the up-to-date trend of the 1970s and 1980s, in having a double action trigger and a high magazine capacity of 15 rounds in a two-row magazine. As for its system, it is based on the successful Beretta Model 92 which succeeded in winning the US Army competition.

The Llama 82 has a locking system with a swinging bolt, very much like that first introduced in grand style by the Walther P 38. The similarity to the pitol systems made by Beretta and Taurus (built under license in Brazil) is so great that the Llama barrel can even be used in the Beretta. The swinging bolt is, of course, somewhat thinner, which is one reason why this weapon's slimness

The OMNI by Llama has not been a great success. This is the .45 ACP caliber version, which does not differ essentially from the 9 mm type.

is so striking — its widest point on the slide measures only 27 mm. Before and behind that point the slide is only 24.5 mm wide, which is caused by the fact that only that area of the Llama 82 into which the cam of the swinging bolt fits has been made thick — it is the area of high stress. In the realm of the two-side safety too, the pistol's slide is not appreciably wider. The swinging area of the two side safety levers has been made deeper by cutting metal away, and the safety levers project only a little bit at the sides.

The modern styling is eye-catching. In fact, one might see a touch of streamlining in it. This makes the weapon very easy to carry in a holster, and can be quickly removed. The trigger guard is designed in steps to the front, and to afford a fingerhold in case of two-handed shooting, there is a handy grooving, but not so deep that

Llama supplied the Model 82 to the Spanish Army as its service weapon. A robust pistol with 15-shot magazine, swinging bolt, and safety on both sides.

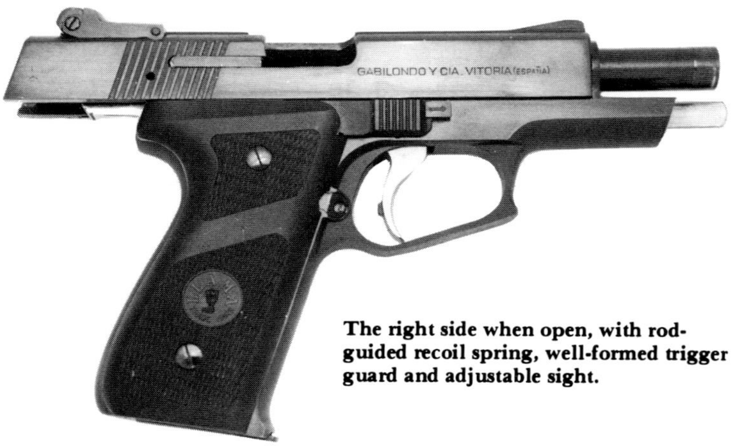

The right side when open, with rod-guided recoil spring, well-formed trigger guard and adjustable sight.

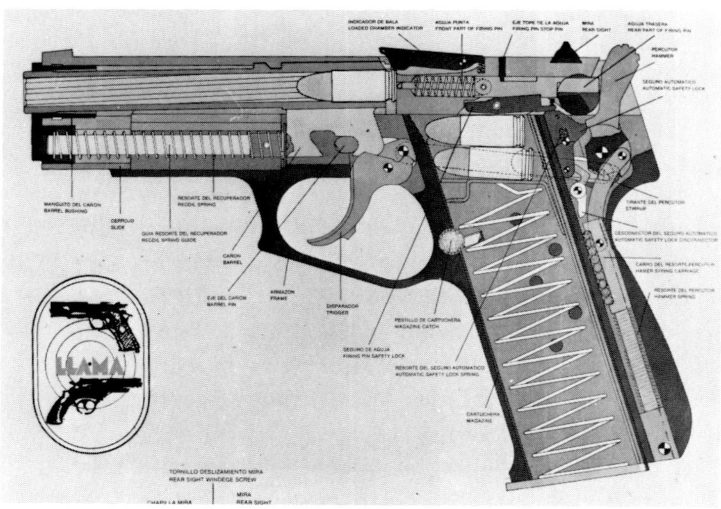

Cutaway drawing of the OMNI in 9 mm Parabellum caliber.

The right side of the Llama 82, with sturdy trigger bar, but also with very decorative grip panels.

Modern styling seems to please Spanish manufacturers. In front of the catch lever is the dismantling lever, which must be turned down 90 degrees.

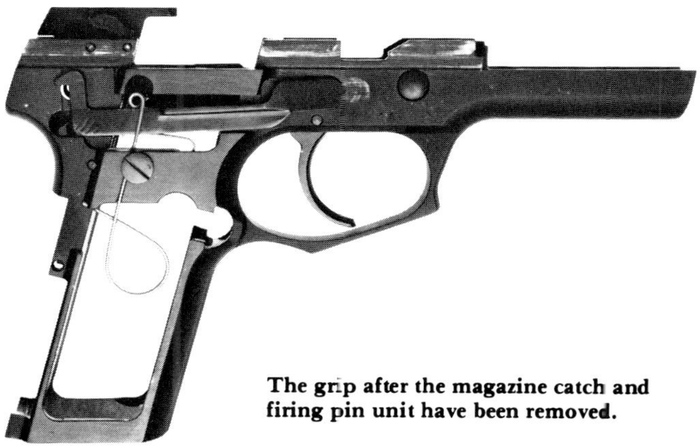

The grip after the magazine catch and firing pin unit have been removed.

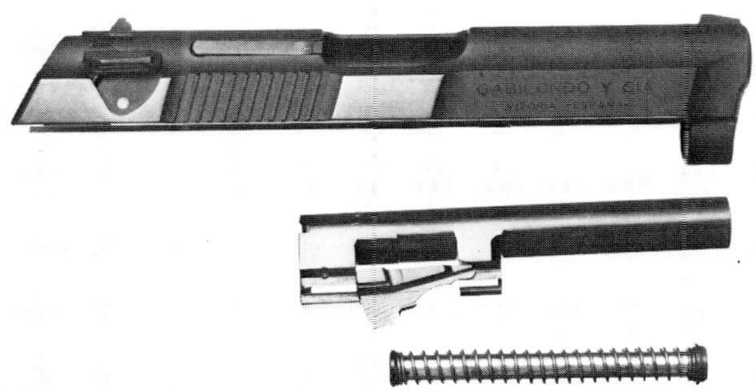

Unlike other bolted pistols from Italy, the slide is closed all the way and the recoil spring is in a capsule.

it hurts the finger with every shot. Just a few words now about the dismantling and operation of this pistol: After removing the magazine and checking the chamber, the slide is first drawn back until the two angle-like surfaces on the slide and the grip line up with each other. Now the dismantling lever, held in its resting position by a spring, is turned downward 90 degrees and the complete upper part can be pushed forward off the frame, in the process of which the rod-guided and encapsulated recoil spring falls out. The recoil spring with its capsule may be practical, but this author is inclined to see it as a disadvantage in terms of cleaning as well as dismantling and reassembly; a certain tension from the start, to keep it firmly in place, would have been better. For assembly, this type of recoil spring has the minor disadvantage that the slide has to be held with its underside upward, or else the spring will fall out.

Dismantling shows that the slide is guided along its whole length, mainly in the three areas of the grip, but also with the opposed mount of the recoil spring within two rails in the front part of the grip. Two notes about the slide and the grip: the slide, unlike that of the technically similar Beretta pistol, is closed along its whole length with the exception of the ejection window, which is an advantage for use in dirty surroundings. The grip is made of steel and is offered alternatively in aluminum, which makes a weight difference of some 235 grams. This is not a small difference if one has to constantly carry the pistol. The magazine catch can be moved from right or left without a tool, a consideration for the growing numbers of left-handed shooters. Appropriately, the magazine has a slit for positioning the catch on each side. Magazines are becoming more and more similar, and sometimes it is no longer possible to tell one from another without the weapon that goes with it. The magazines of the Taurus and Beretta pistols fit without modification and do not disturb the gun's operation.

Further dismantling can be done after removing the plastic grip panels, which are held, unfortunately, by only one screw apiece and therefore tend to break off in back by the short grip-horn. The back of the grip can be removed without a tool, and its sprung transverse bolt must be pulled back, after which the aluminum plate can be pulled downward out of its long grooves. The firing pin spring, also set in a capsule (here it is a real advantage), can be pulled out at the bottom. The axle of the hammer can be pushed to the side by pressing with the fingertip — the hammer, spring and back of the grip are now removed.

The Llama 82 has a whole series of safeties which, in combination, can scarcely let an unwanted shot be fired. After the magazine is removed, the magazine safety takes effect, a safety about which their is a worldwide difference of opinion. It takes effect when the magazine has been pulled downward a good 5 mm. The technical operation of this safety is original, and it can be removed easily if one wishes. On the right side of the grip there is a bent wire spring installed with its end section above the massive trigger bar. The magazine has a small bulge on its right side, and when pushed in, it lies under the end of the spring and thus pushes the spring up. As a result of this, a two-shanked wire spring under the trigger bar can push it up again and move it into the area of the sear; in an effective type of magazine safety, the trigger bar is not in the area of the sear.

The recoil safety likewise takes effect via the trigger bar. To the rear it has an extension that reaches up into the slide's course and is pushed down when the slide is in an unlocked condition. The result is like that of the magazine safety and the trigger bar is out of operation. Activating the manual safety has the same effect. When it is turned downward, a small bolt presses on the extension of the trigger bar and moves the trigger bar out of reach of the sear.

The magazine catch can be moved from right to left easily.

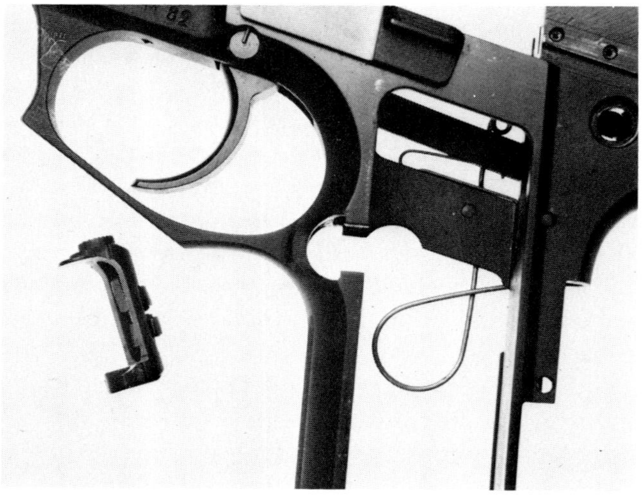

The barrels with swinging bolts. From top to bottom: Taurus, Llama 82 and Walther P 38.

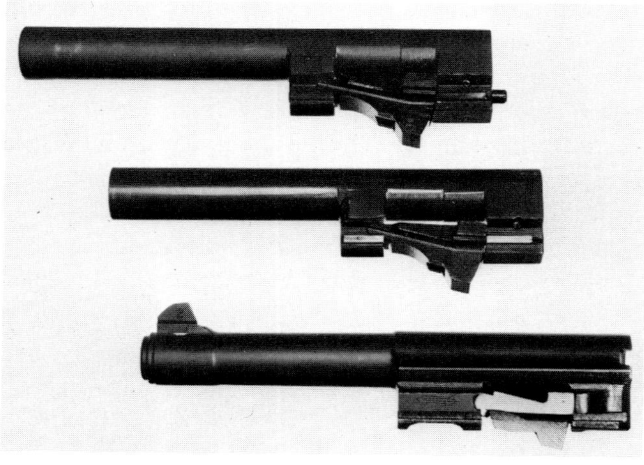

The cocked hammer can be decocked by using the manual safety without having to pull the trigger, and without the chance of an unintentional shot being fired. The firing pin has two parts — the rear part acts as a point of impact and transmits the force of the hammer to the front part. The rear of the firing pin is mounted in the shaft of the safety and is swung out of the hammer's reach when the gun is decocked. Only when that action is completed does an eccentric part of the shaft press an decocking lever mounted in the receiver and free the cocked hammer by pushing forward on the trigger bar.

Another means to safe pitol handling is the catching rest on its hammer, in which it is caught if it should chance to slip out of the hand while being cocked. It also fits into this rest automatically after being struck forward, where this also serves as the fall safety.

Whether a cartridge (or a case) is in the chamber can be determined by the position of the extractor, which then sticks out so far that it can be felt easily in this position, while it is otherwise even with the outer surface of the slide. A colored marking makes visual checking easier.

In terms of safeties, the Llama 82 is a very safe weapon to handle, even though it does not have a firing pin safety connected to the trigger — this would be one more step toward perfection.

The pistol proved to be a well-functioning weapon with various cartridges, and in the course of a short test there was only one failed shot, which could be disposed of via the cocking trigger. This must not necessarily be held against the weapon, as many cartridges have very hard percussion caps. Its shooting performance meets the requirements of a weapon for typical use — groups from 60 to 80 mm in diameter were achieved with almost all the cartridge types.

The magazine safety of the Llama 82. As soon as the magazine is inserted, the spring pulls the trigger bar down out of the path of the sear.

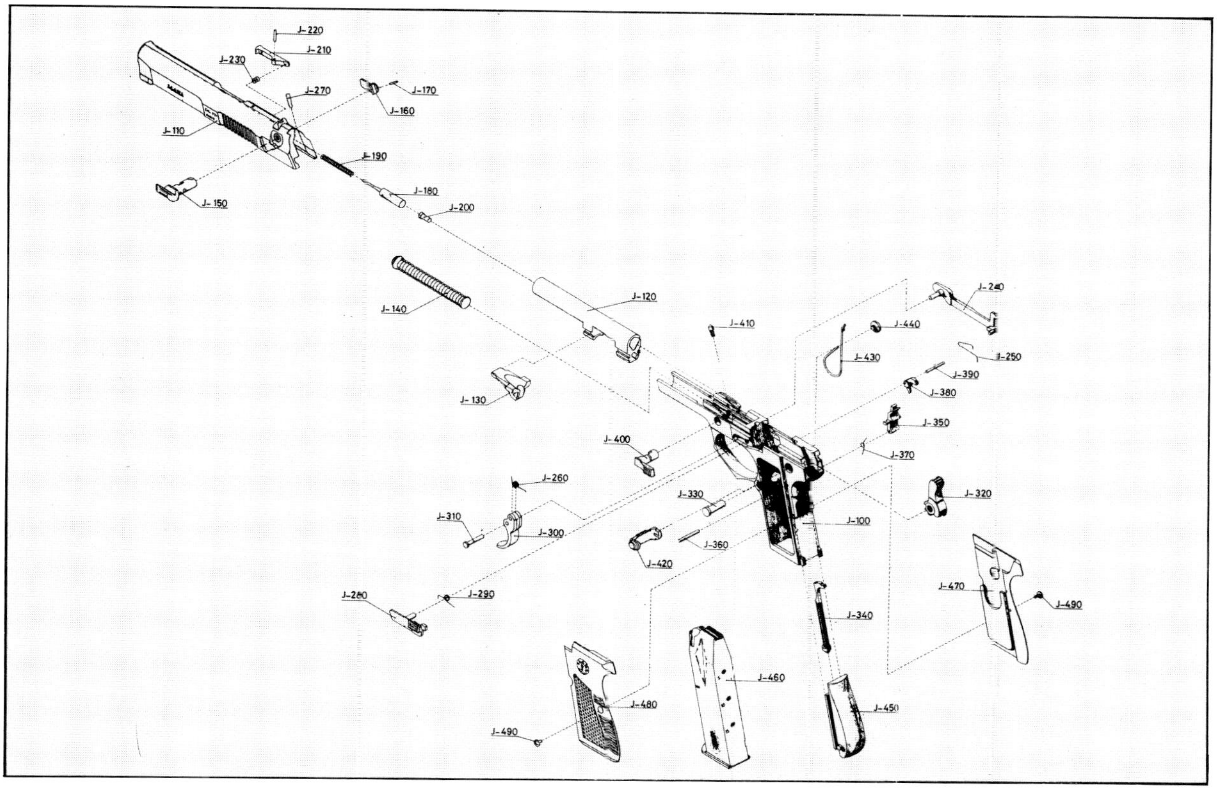

The parts of the Llama 82.

Technical Data: Llama 82

Manufacturer	Llama Gabilondo y Cia, Vittoria, Spain
Caliber	9 mm Parabellum
Magazine capacity	15 cartridges (15 + 1)
System	Swinging bolt, Beretta type
Overall length	209 mm
Overall height	134 mm
Grip width	35 mm
Barrel length	114 mm
Barrel profile	6 riflings, right
Weight empty, steel	1110 grams
Weight empty, aluminum	875 grams
Finish	Matte burnished
Safeties	Catch rest, uncocking lever, closing, magazine, manual safeties
Special features	Safeties on both sides, magazine holder insertable

Llama Model XI and XI-B

Llama always knew how to produce pistols similar to the government versions in a wide variety of types, and the choice of calibers extends from .22 LR through 7.65 mm, 9 mm short to 9 mm Parabellum and .38 Super, as well as .45 ACP. The technical conception differs only slightly, with either an unlocked mass breech of the well-known type or a bolt with a tipping barrel like that of the Colt Government model.

The resemblance to the original is great, though some details have been improved and other features simplified. For a long time the ventilated rail on top of the slide was a very typical feature. In the Model **XI-B** shown in the pictures here, this ventilation has finally been omitted, as it had no practical significance anyway, at least not in a pistol whose slide surrounds an internal barrel.

Because of the great similarity to the Colt Government pistol, a brief mention of the different features will suffice here. The barrel is guided inside a casing that resembles the earlier Colt bushing and contributes only a little to precision — quite the opposite, really, for such

A slightly modified copy of the American model: the Llama in 9 mm Parabellum caliber, also extant, almost identical, in .45 ACP caliber.

The right side when open. The grip has an unpleasantly sharp forward angle. The sight can be adjusted laterally between two small screws.

housings always fit into the slide with a lot of play at the front.

The top of the slide has a full-length rail with a transverse pattern of grooves that is interrupted only in the area of the ejection window. A foresight is mounted in the slide between two screws that allow it to be adjusted laterally, a very sensible arrangement that one wishes the original also had. While the Model XI has a loading indicator built into the slide in the form of a projecting flat piece, this was eliminated in the XI-B version. The XI-B type no longer has its spring housing, held by a pin, curving so far out to the back; it has by now become almost as flattened as the housing of a Gold Cup.

The inner construction in the area of the grip is like that of the Government: no parts that function differently are installed, and only the ejector is attached differently. A certain simplification is found in the attachment of the grip panels, which are finished in a herringbone pattern in some versions or made of smooth etched beechwood in others. No additional threaded screw-holes are installed in the grip, as the attachments for the holding screws are

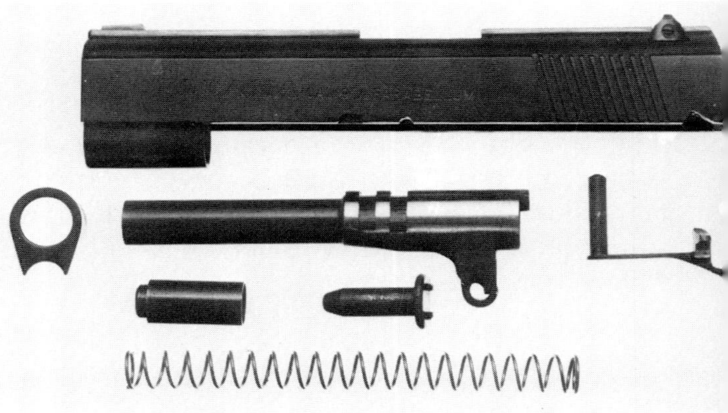
Slide and barrel plus recoil spring. Dismantling is like that of the Colt Government.

cut directly into the sides of the steel receiver itself.

Other well-known features of this series of Llama pistols include a side safety that holds both the hammer and the slide and a grip safety that must be pushed all the way in before a shot can be fired. The hammer has a safety rest, the firing pin is built, as it usually is, as a flying ignition pin, and the trigger cannot be pulled when the weapon is not locked. All of this has stood the test of time but no longer fits what is generally accepted as the standard today. One advantage is the ease of dismantling the magazine, the bottom of which can be pushed aside after a spring hook is depressed.

Additional simplification can be seen in the slide. The firing pin is not covered at the back by a separate plate, but is held by a vertically inserted bar so that it can move

The grip is all steel, the trigger bar goes around the magazine shaft on both sides.

within its functioning area. The extractor has likewise been kept simple and is mounted on the right side so that it can turn on a pin inserted from above. Because of the simplified construction described above, the slide remains quite massive at the rear, so that a backsight adjustable in all directions could be mounted here without causing any problems.

Technical Data: Llama XI and XI-B

Model	XI	XI-B
Caliber	9 mm Parabellum	9 mm Parabellum
Magazine capacity	8 cartridges	8 cartridges
Overall length	216 mm	200 mm
Height/width	137 mm/33 mm	138 mm/36 mm
Barrel length	128 mm	108 mm
Bolt	Tipping barrel, Browning type	
Weight empty	1187 grams	1045 grams
Sights	Laterally adjustable	Laterally adjustable
Material	Steel	Steel
Finish	Burnished, chromed, engraved, gilded with engraving, burnished with engraving	

The Model PD in 9 mm Parabellum caliber, likewise a slightly simplified Colt copy in the lower price range. A separate spring housing is not present here; it only looks that way.

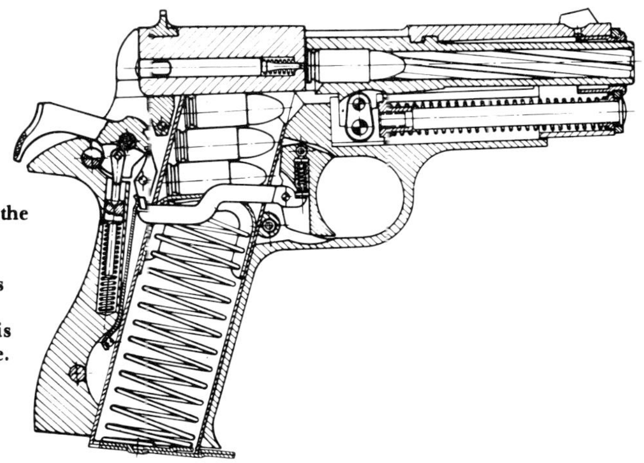

Cutaway drawing of the Star pistol. The main difference is the length. The pistol is ready to fire.

Star Model PD and BM

In both .45 ACP and 9 mm PARA calibers, the Spanish firm of Bonifacio Echevarria, using the brand name of "Star", has made several simplified copies of that famous American model, the Colt Government. Various barrel lengths are available, but their technology does not vary.

The mounting of the barrel is done in much the same way as in the early Colt bushing, which fits into the slide with a great deal of play and is one reason why the precision of such pistols, though sufficient for close ranges, cannot compare with modern designs. In similar manner to the Colt Government, though, very significant improvements have been made in the area of barrel mounting with very little effort, in order to improve the shooting performance.

The sights are fixed, and the little foresight is very small, and the backsight can, if necessary, be moved sideways (or be replaced by an adjustable sight).

The magazine has the same disadvantages as the original type: it is welded fast and is not at all easy to clean thoroughly. If it is very dirty, such a magazine is best washed thoroughly in cleaning gasoline and then sprayed with oil after being dried.

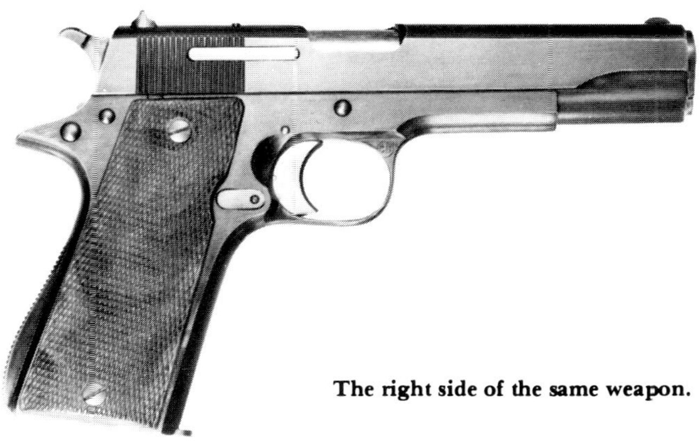

The right side of the same weapon.

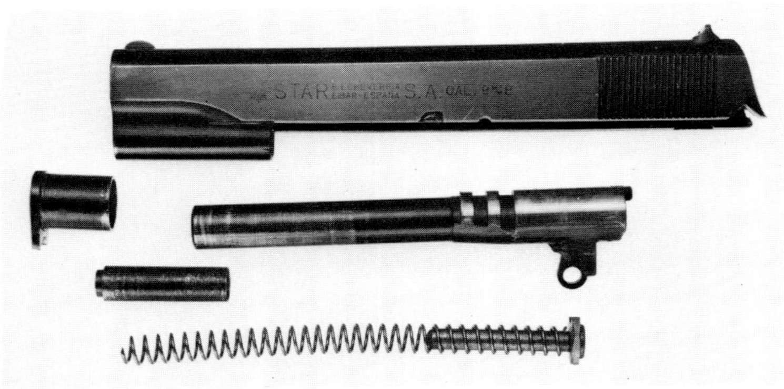

The slide and barrel of the Star Model PD. The guide housing at the front gives more play than guiding, a Colt fault that was retained here.

The receiver is neatly made of steel, and differs first of all from the original in having its rear panel in the form of a spring housing. This is the fixed component of the receiver, not being removable as in the Colt Government. Since the Star-PD has a simple single-action mechanism, it comes out with few moving parts. The trigger bar is a single one-sided piece and is guided on the right side, where it is located immediately in front of the sprung sear. The interrupter safety works from above, pushing the trigger bar downward when the breech is not completely locked and not allowing the sear to be pushed away. The lateral wing safety acts on the hammer and the slide, and is ready to be placed in its

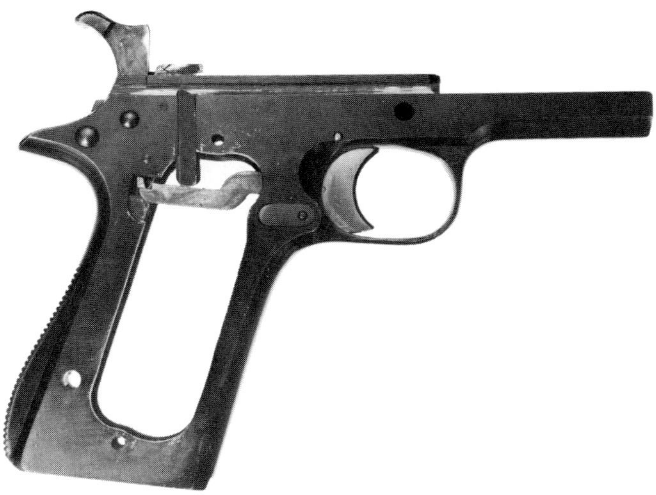

A small rail sticks into the slide's course and thus acts as a slide safety. When the slide is not forward in its bolted position, the trigger bar is pushed out of contact with the sear along the rail.

safety rest when the hammer is in position, and thus hold the slide immobile. From this position the safety must first be released, in order to either cock the hammer or pull back the slide.

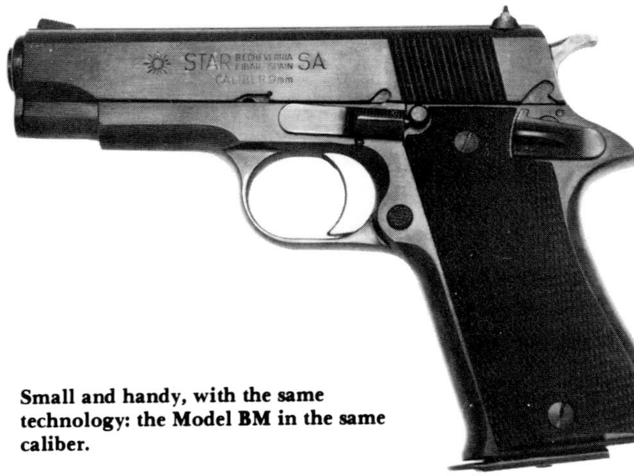

Small and handy, with the same technology: the Model BM in the same caliber.

The right side when open. Unlike its forerunner, its recoil spring is guided by a long rod.

All in all, we do not mean to put down the Star-PD as being of low value, but in its design it does not nearly represent what is presently on the market in the realm of modern self-loading pistols. Many of its details can be reworked to be more impressive — one thinks first of all of the badly fitting plastic grip panels. The weapon would make a better appearance if it were fitted with matte walnut grip panels. Workmanship is very solid, and the price is reasonable in terms of the weapon. On that basis, pistols like this might serve as practical starting points for various types of rebuilding.

Technical Data: Star Model PD/BM

Manufacturer	Star Bonifacio Echevarria, Spain	
Caliber	9 mm Parabellum	9 mm Parabellum
Magazine capacity	8 cartridges	8 cartridges
Overall length	216 mm	182 mm
Height/width	135 mm/30.5 mm	130 mm/32 mm
Barrel length	124 mm	99 mm
Weight empty	1050 grams	965 mm
Sights	Fixed	Fixed
Material/finish	Steel, burnished	Steel, burnished
Safeties	Magazine, safety rest, closing, manual	
System	Tipping barrel with joint	

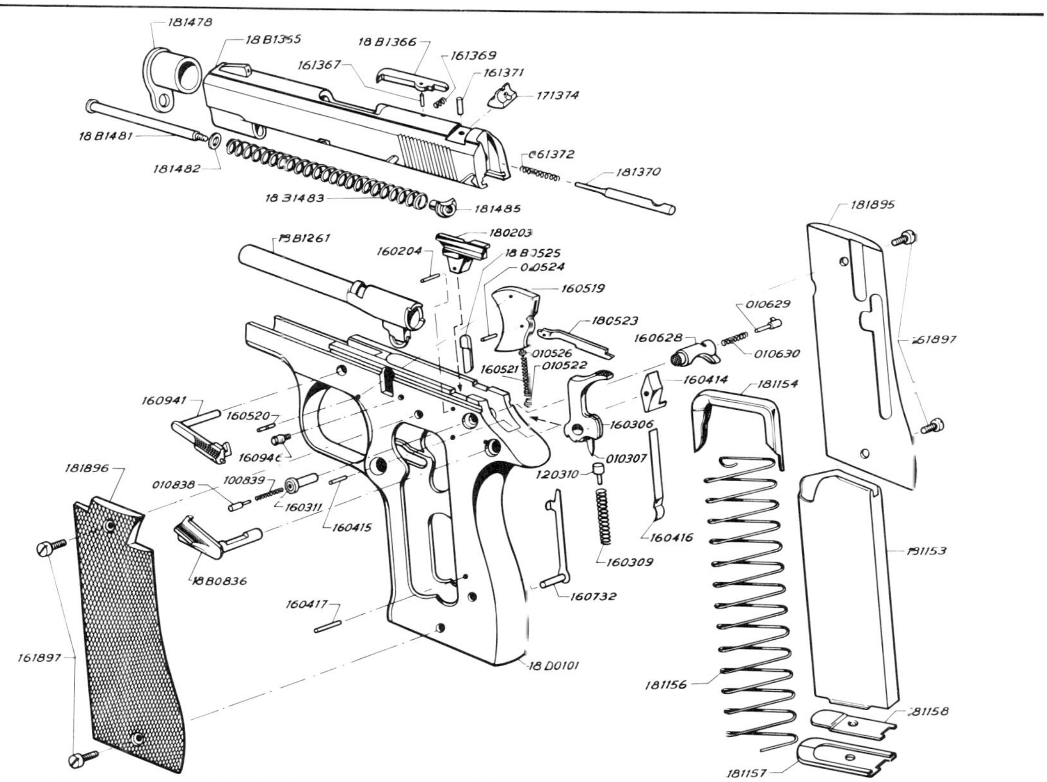

The parts of the Star BM.

Star Model 30 M and 30 PK

These two pistols are identical except that the PK version is somewhat shorter and therefore lighter. In Spain it became the official service weapon of the police and other security forces, while the 30 M version was intended more for the armed forces.

These pistols also follow the modern trend toward a somewhat higher magazine capacity with a simultaneously usable double action trigger and sights adjustable to suit the shooter, in that they are laterally moveable.

In many ways the 30 M resembles the SIG 210, sharing with it the long internal guide of the slide, which runs the entire length of the grip and surely enhances the expected shooting performance. In the USA this pistol, specifically the 7.65 mm PARA caliber type, was recognized as being "state of the art" by the specialist press, which particularly praised the problem-free operation and the technical conception, with the exception of the safety. Unfortunately, the Star pistols have not become very widespread in Germany, and for a long time lacked active importers and systematic advertising.

The Star 30 M is used in this form as a service weapon in Spain. It looks good, is well made and had a long slide course.

The Model 31 PK with an aluminum grip. This version still has its safety lever in an unhandy place; this was changed some time later.

The Model 30 P is not a production weapon, but was made up at the author's request, with the shortness of the PK pistol and a steel grip.

Right side of the 30 P type, externally identical to the 30 PK, which has an aluminum grip. The safety is on both sides.

Cutaway model of the 30 PK; all versions have a laterally adjustable sight.

The locking is done via the tipping barrel in the manner of the well-known Browning lock, which remains the most often-used principle in self-loading pistols. The 30 M has a lateral wing safety that immobilizes the firing pin and can be operated equally well from either side. A magazine safety separates the contact point from the trigger bar and sear when a magazine is not, or not completely, inserted. The hammer has a safety rest in which it is caught in case it should slide off. A further safety measure is the extractor which, after inserting a cartridge, projects visibly and tangibly from the slide. Its colored marking reinforces the visual determination of the loading condition.

A special feature of the 30 M is the removable striking assembly in the form of the entire back grip, thus servicing and tuning operations can be carried out with relative ease.

Dismantling for simple cleaning is reminiscent of the dismantling of the Czech M 75 pistol. After removing the magazine and checking the chamber, the hammer is cocked by hand. The slide is then pulled back until its marking lines up with the marking on the grip. In this position the catch lever can be pushed out the side and removed. After that, the entire upper section can be pushed forward out of the frame. Removal of the recoil spring and barrel are done as with similar pistols that have this type of lock.

A praiseworthy addition is the very detailed service manual, which describes the dismantling of the weapon to the last screw and pin very precisely in both words and pictures. This statement must be corrected here and now, as the 30 M does not have one single screw, not even for the grip panels, which are held firmly in place by the

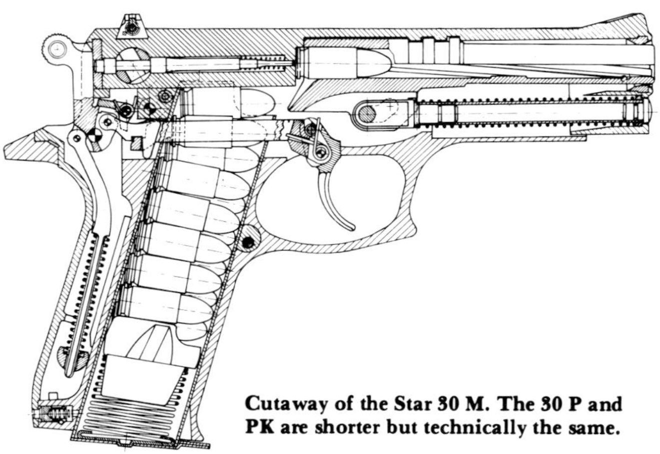

Cutaway of the Star 30 M. The 30 P and PK are shorter but technically the same.

The weapon with safety on. In this position the safety pivot pushes the firing pin into the slide and out of the hammer's reach.

The slide and barrel of the short 30 PK or 30 P version. The rod-guided recoil spring is in a capsule, an advantage for fast assembly. The point of the catch lever is a big help in dismantling Star pistols completely.

back of the grip. The pin of the catch lever with its rounded point serves as a tool for removing the firing pin assembly, which includes the hammer, the main-spring, the ejector, the sear, the interrupter and the hammer bar. After the firing pin has been removed, it is used to help remove the safety, and after the safety has been removed, the extractor can be taken out of the slide. The 30 M is very easy to service thanks to its construction.

The 30 PK version is 12 mm shorter and about 200 grams lighter as its receiver is not made of steel, but of aluminum.

The trigger bar on the Star pistols, with its two powerful side arms that go around the magazine shaft, deserves additional attention. When the hammer is cocked by hand, a hook attached to the hammer hooks onto the rear of the trigger bar and pulls it back. The trigger bar itself is the focal point of the safety system.

The magazine has a projection on the upper right side that, when fully extended and in its resting position, reaches under the trigger bar and lifts it a short distance against the pressure of a leaf spring (installed in the receiver). Only in this position can the trigger bar take effect on the sear, and only then can the hammer be released. The recoil safety is a small, insignificant eccentric piece at the right side of the firing pin unit. With its underside it lies against the trigger bar. If the slide is not far enough forward, the eccentric piece presses the trigger bar down and brings it out of the contact point on the sear.

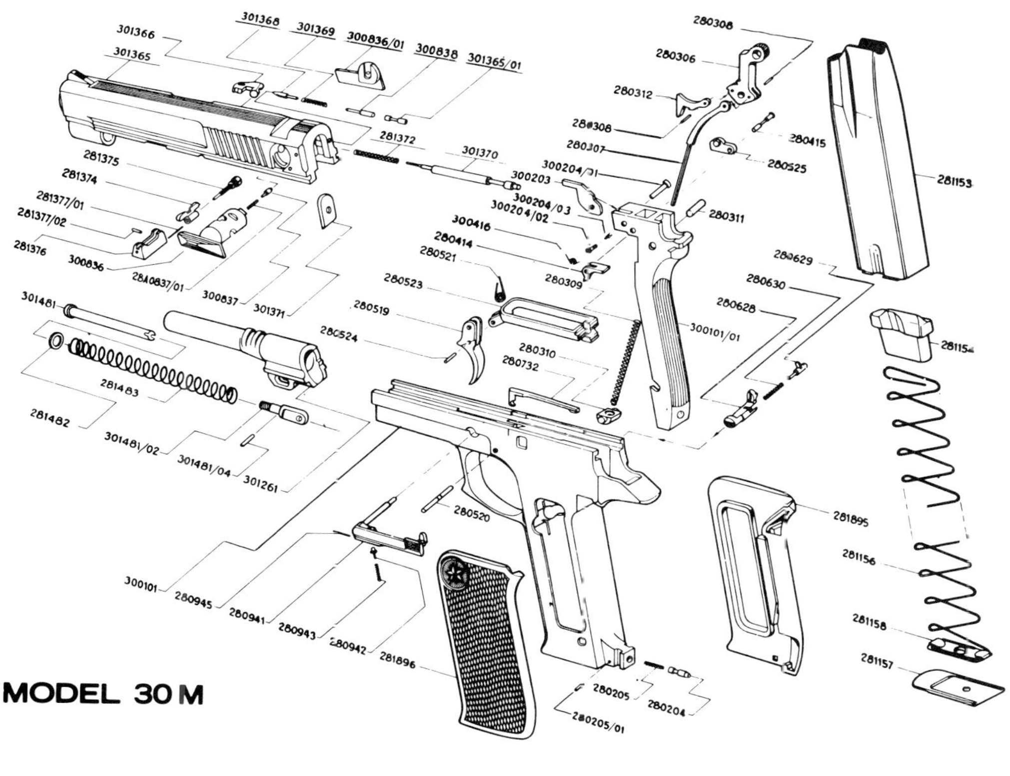

Parts of the Star Model 30 M.

MODEL 30 M

After pushing a spring bolt in, the whole firing pin unit can be lifted out of the frame.

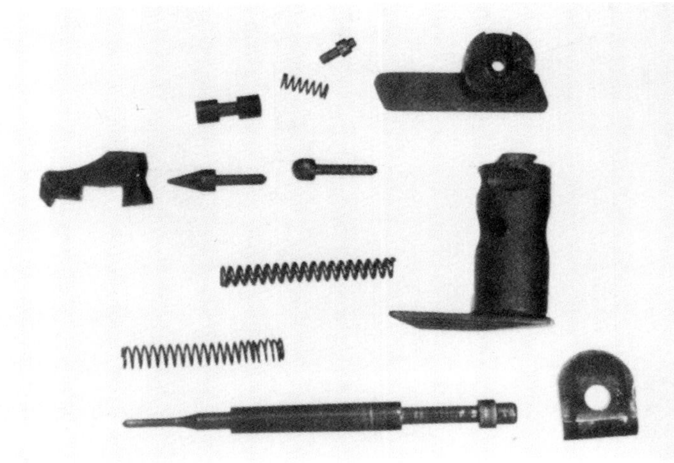

All parts of the slide, including the two-sided safety.

While in some pistols, like the Llama 82 or the Smith & Wesson pistols, the removal of the often unwanted magazine safety is easy to accomplish, it would require a considerable deal of effort in the case of the Star pistols. Here it would be better to avoid making a modification.

For those who enjoy reworking their triggers, the Star pistol is very advantageous. When the hammer is cocked, one can observe, with one look from the back, the contact point of the sear with the firing pin rest of the hammer. A slight shortening of the rest of the hammer and a careful smoothing of the sliding surfaces can make the already very quick-acting single-action trigger operate even more quickly and smoothly, but as is the case with self-loading pistols in general, caution is urged for work in this area as a matter of principle.

Technical Data: Model 30 M and 30 PK

Model	30 M	30 PK
Caliber	9 mm Parabellum	9 mm Parabellum*
Magazine capacity	15 cartridges	15 cartridges
Overall length	205 mm	193 mm
Height/width	135 mm/33 mm	135 mm/33 mm
Barrel length	110 mm	98 mm
Sights	Laterally adjustable	Laterally adjustable
Weight empty	1140 grams	860 grams
Material/grip	Steel	Aluminum
Finish	Matte burnished	Matte burnished
System	Tipping barrel without joint	
Safeties	Both sides, magazine safety, safety rest, closing safety, loading indicator	

* Also 7.65 mm Parabellum

SOUTH AFRICA

South Africa had no weapons industry of its own for a long time and limited itself to the use of weapons bought elsewhere, mostly from the western world. A pocket pistol known as the "Junior", in 6.35 mm caliber and made for a short time by the Pretoria Small Arms Factory in Pretoria, became known. Only in the most recent times did several in-house developments take place, brought about in part by the fact that more and more nations refused to deal with South Africa because of their apartheid policies.

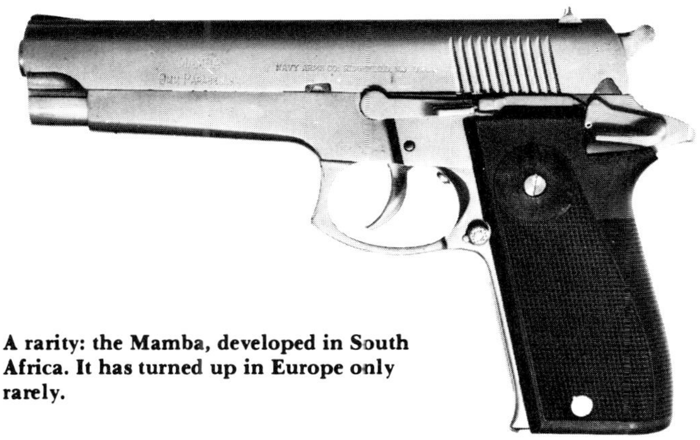

A rarity: the Mamba, developed in South Africa. It has turned up in Europe only rarely.

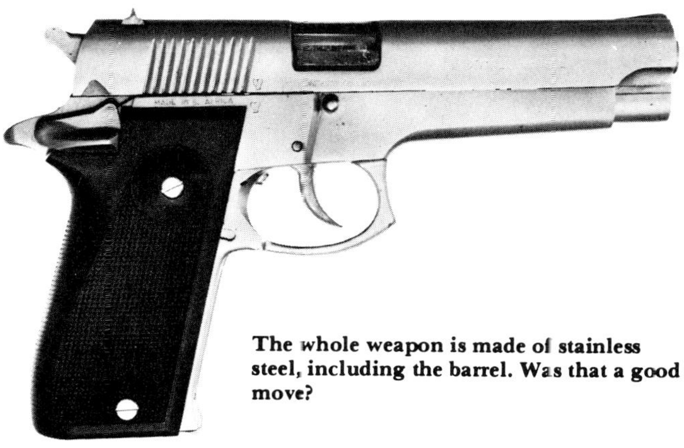

The whole weapon is made of stainless steel, including the barrel. Was that a good move?

The Mamba Pistol

The only self-loading pistol in 9 mm Parabellum caliber was known as the "Mamba", named after one of the most poisonous snakes on the African continent. The Mamba stirred up a brief commotion in Germany and then disappeared from the market just as fast as it appeared. It was conceived as a military and police pistol and made appropriately big and heavy.

After its development in Rhodesia, its further manufacture took place at Navy Arms in the USA, where efforts were made to improve the inherently good design further and make it a more marketable commodity.

The locking system operates by the tipping-barrel principle in a variation of the type we know from the HP pistol made by FN. There is one difference in the quick operation of the tipping movement. Not just after a certain recoil, but simultaneously with the recoil, the barrel and its attachments are steered downward. All the parts of the pistol are made of fine cast steel, even (and this is rather unusual) the barrel, into which the riflings are pressed. Further characteristics of the Mamba are the one-piece trigger as a component, a hammer-spring with adjustable weight, and the safety operating from either side — at that time, this had not yet become the general standard.

The pistol was marketed in a matte stainless steel version, or a deep black teflon finish. Navy Arms also put out a polished and burnished variety.

The first reports at that time (such as IWS No.5, 1981) attested to the Mamba's good shooting performance and dependable operation. The authors, though, agreed that the pistol had not yet been developed enough to compete with its competitors' products.

Technical Data: Mamba Pistol

Manufacturer	Partly by Navy Arms, USA
Caliber	9 mm Parabellum, 7.65 mm Parabellum
Magazine capacity	14 cartridges
Overall length	220 mm
Height/width	140 mm/34 mm
Barrel length	125 mm
Sights	Fixed
Weight empty, magazine	1125 grams
Trigger type, weight	DA 3.3 kp/SA 1.3 kp
Material	Stainless steel
Finish	Matte, burnished, layered

CZECHOSLOVAKIA

During and after the two world wars, the Czech weapons industry manufactured a large number of excellent handguns, most of them in the 7.65 mm, 9 mm short and 7.62 mm calibers. For a long time the 9 mm Parabellum cartridge, very widespread in the west, was not introduced. Czech pistols have always ranked above many other products for their quality workmanship on the one hand and their reasonable prices on the other.

One of the most successful self-loading pistols was the Model 75, which has been on the market a long time and is now available in various versions. This pistol, made completely of steel, is manufactured by the Presne

An early version of the CZ 75 with the flat slide and frame sides still extending far back.

Strojirenstvi Uhersky BROD, and is imported into Germany by Frankonia-Jagd of Würzburg, with the firm of Merkuria in Prague as its exporter.

The outward difference between the earlier and present-day versions is that the side surfaces at the front of the slide and on the grip extend farther back, with the newer versions a bit more filled-out in this area.

The Model CZ 75

This all-steel pistol is built to hold 15 cartridges, and a sixteenth cartridge can be carried in the chamber without diminishing its safety. The modern styling of the 75 model, with the holster-friendly rounding of its angles and edges, is as pleasant as its excellent workmanship in relation to its price. Thus it is not surprising that this weapon, made exclusively for export, has gained widespread success and only seldom given reason for objections, something that cannot always be said of imitations that have since appeared.

The CZ 75 in present-day form. The flat sides no longer go back so far, and there are grooves on the front of the frame and the trigger-guard attachment. The reliable technology was retained. The CZ 75 is still one of the best 15-shot pistols made completely of steel.

The slim slide is guided inside the grip for its entire length, a very important requirement for good shooting performance, and is supported by an easy adaptability to various cartridges and bullets.

Moving parts contribute to the favorable ergonomic form of the entire weapon. Both the catch lever and the safety are set flat against the grip and provide no danger of injury. On the other hand, they are easy to use despite their small size. The hammer has a safety rest, and when it is at rest, the side safety cannot be set — this can be done

The right side. This weapon's exterior has been sandblasted and burnished. The pistol is also available burnished to a high gloss, matte burnished, nickel-plated and painted as a so-called tropical version. What is under the paint remains unseen.

A braking piece is installed in the frame and also acts as a cover for the mainspring. The magazine moves forward a bit and must then be removed by hand. Many owners leave the piece in place.

The weapon when open. The slide is closed at the front. Shooters who expend much ammunition say the CZ 75 soon gets hot. A long guiding rod would be a help.

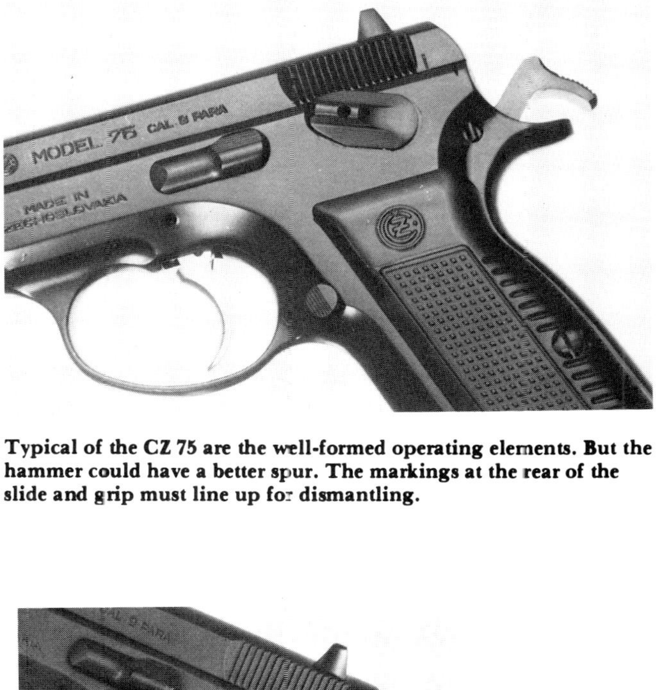

Typical of the CZ 75 are the well-formed operating elements. But the hammer could have a better spur. The markings at the rear of the slide and grip must line up for dismantling.

The slide and barrel of the CZ 75. The parts fit very well, the small guiding rod should be polished at once, for it abrades the recoil spring.

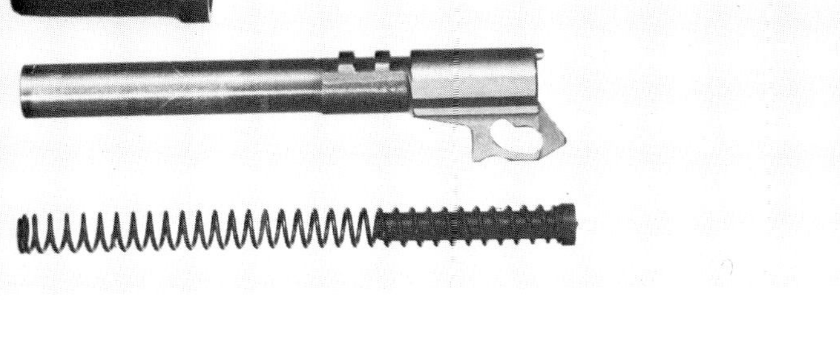

The magazine base with its extension. This is the sandblasted version with standard grip panels.

only when the hammer is completely cocked. The safety blocks the sear and can be pushed down comfortably with the thumb of the holding hand (unlike many other pistols). The automatic recoil safety functions via the doubly guided trigger bar, the two arms of which are pushed down through the lower course of the slide. The trigger bar is thus pushed under the sear and moves out of its area of operation. The CZ 75 has no magazine safety. Instead the magazine shaft has acquired a different mechanical device that should simply be removed if one wishes to. A long spring plate is built in to limit the main-spring, where it brakes the free fall of the magazine when the side-mounted magazine catch is activated. In this case the magazine moves a short distance out of the shaft, stops, and must then be pulled the rest of the way out by hand. This may be advantageous in individual cases, but shooters who value a quick change of magazines in sporting combat shooting shall, indeed must, remove this piece by simply pushing out the holding pin high in the receiver.

The lock functions via the tipping barrel in the manner of the improved Browning bolt, with a closed guiding curve into which the axle of the catch lever projects. In this area the workmanship of individual parts is trouble-free and shows no noticeable play. The slide itself is closed, for the CZ 75 has only a short guiding rail for the recoil spring, making it unsensitive to dirt in this area. Also, the sights are fixed, and the foresight designed more to be holster-friendly. When shooting in poor light conditions, the grooved ramp side naturally creates quite a disturbance. It is not possible to adjust the backsight block other than by driving it sideways inside the cutout mounting.

The pistol is regularly available with black plastic grip panels, whose patterned surfaces afford good gripping. Dismantling is very simple: after removing the magazine and checking the chamber, the slide is pulled back until the two markings toward the back of the slide and the grip line up with each other. Now the catch lever can be taken out, the upper part pushed forward, the spring removed and the barrel lifted out. The firing pin is held by a plate that can be pulled out as soon as it is pushed in a little bit. Some designers add particular details: here the thicker shaft of the firing pin has a small longitudinal groove which raises questions as to its sense and purpose. This author can explain its purpose only by suggesting that it conducts excess oil past the firing pin or is of use in the production of this part.

The CZ 75 has changed little by little, and today it is available in several slightly different versions, and all the handy accessories are also available, above all a good holster for any desired manner of carrying.

The painted version is known as the tropical type. It is not different technically or in its quality of workmanship, but unlike the normal version, its surface is not burnished, but rather has a satin-matte painted finish. This is intended to make it less sensitive to corrosion, though other surfaces do not rust quickly either.

The pistol becomes even more versatile through the availability of several modifications available from importers. It is possible to make the weapon somewhat more elegant with a hard nickel-plated grip, wooden grip panels with or without patterns, a backsight adjustable to the side, a Smith & Wesson sight (revolver sight), a trigger stop, and a reworking of the already excellent trigger.

The Peters Stahl firm of Paderborn also offers two modifying systems for the .22 LR cartridge (see there), which make economical training possible and equal the shooting performance of a good sport pistol with the right choice of cartridges. For some time Peters Stahl has offered interchangeable polygonal barrels, which fit neatly into the weapon and improve the verifiable precision markedly. Such barrels are available in the normal size as well as overlong and with a removable barrel weight.

Technical Data: CZ 75

Manufacturer	Presné-Strokirenstvi-Uhersky-Brod
Caliber	9 mm Parabellum
Magazine capacity	15 (15 + 1)
Overall length	203 mm
Height	138 mm
Grip width	33 mm
Barrel length	120 mm
Barrel profile	6 riflings, right
Sights	Fixed
Weight empty	1000 grams
Material	Steel
Finish	Burnished, painted, nickel-plated
Number of parts	55
Muzzle velocity	ca. 370 m/s
Muzzle energy	ca. 490 Joules

Variations on the CZ 75

Manufacturers have neglected to secure the patent rights to the basis of their design. Thus several imitations soon appeared, differing only slightly from the original. The Tanfoglio pistols are described elsewhere — here the Czech manufacturer's failure to develop a parallel compact version can be seen. With the TA 90 Baby, Tanfoglio has tried to fill this gap, and may succeed in doing so some day.

The Tanfoglio pistols differ only slightly in design. Their safety system is different, being mounted on top of the slide and capable of decocking the cocked hammer at the same time. This would also be a sensible improvement to the CZ 75. The shape of the catch lever is less favorable, which causes a noticeable disturbance in the smaller pistols in particular. The thumb of the holding hand can press too easily on the extension of the catch lever, as a result of which the slide is held back unintentionally in the middle of its operation, despite the still-full magazine. A further variation of a different type is the AT 84 built in Switzerland — it hardly varies from the original. Where the original bears the inscription "Made in Czechoslovakia" — the Swiss version is lettered "Solothurn Switzerland."

The Swiss manufacturer avoids most of the disturbing customs limitations that, with their high duties on products from the eastern world, make their sale in the USA as good as impossible. Thus in the most recent years a fine network of manufacturers under license has developed. Weapons are developed in one country and sold in another, generally for objective economic reasons. The firm of ITM (Industrial Technology & Machines) in Solothurn has contracted with the Czech manufacturer and quickly produced a small series of AT 84 pistols. The parts are received and assembled at ITM. Barrels and magazines from Czechoslovakia, grips and slides as fine-cast parts from Spain receiving their finishing touches in Switzerland, springs and small parts also from Switzerland.

The AT 84 was first marketed with painted or nickel-plated surfaces, followed shortly thereafter with a burnished surface.

The Model CZ 85

On the basis of the successful CZ 75, the Model CZ 85 was developed. The essential differences are the location of the operating devices on both sides, improved sights, differently stamped grip panels, the angular form of the operating devices, and a matte-finished top of the slide.

HUNGARY

Hungary found no access to the 9 mm Parabellum cartridge for its own use, typically of countries in the eastern military alliance. Until 1918 Hungary was part of the Austro-Hungarian Empire (the Imperial and Royal Dual Monarchy) and used weapons that were introduced within this empire without attempting to develop any of its own. The development of a Hungarian pistol began in 1912 with the Model 19 Frommer Stop, in 7.65 mm caliber. After World War I this was used by the Hungarian police and armed forces. It was followed by a pistol in 9 mm short caliber, which was not accepted by the military, as a pistol in this caliber is simply too weak in its effect.

In 1929 a different pistol was accepted, the model 29 in 9 mm short caliber. This pistol did not become very popular, because of its complicated construction. An improved version, the Model 37, was made for the 7.65 mm and 9 mm short cartridges and made in great numbers for the Hungarian Army. During German occupation this pistol continued to be made for the German troops, whose need for handguns of any kind was very great, but this version was also fitted with a manual safety at the left rear of the grip, and bears German acceptance stamps. After World War II, two inherently different Model 48 pistols were produced. The first Model 48, in 9 mm short caliber, is a somewhat lengthened copy of the Walther PP, which entered the civilian trade under the name of "Walam." In terms of design it is identical to the PP but is some 20 mm longer and differs somewhat from the original in its shape.

Model 58 Tokagypt

The second Model 48 is a copy of the Russian TT 33 in 7.62 mm Tokarev caliber. Its construction and operation are identical.

On the basis of the TT 33 pistol, a version in 9 mm Parabellum caliber was introduced. This was known as the Tokagypt 58, developed for the Egyptian Army. The Tokagypt 58 differs externally from the TT 33 in having its manual safety at the left rear of the grip, plus a lengthened magazine and a different type of grip panels, which are attached without screws.

At this time the Egyptian armed forces used almost exclusively weapons made in the western world — as of 1954 they switched to weapons from the eastern bloc. The reason for this was a western weapons embargo against Egypt. Shortly thereafter, Egypt had a weapons factory of its own built by Swedish technicians. The handguns produced there were almost all copies of well-known western weapons.

The stampings the impression that the weapon was made in West Germany. This was a minor sales trick.

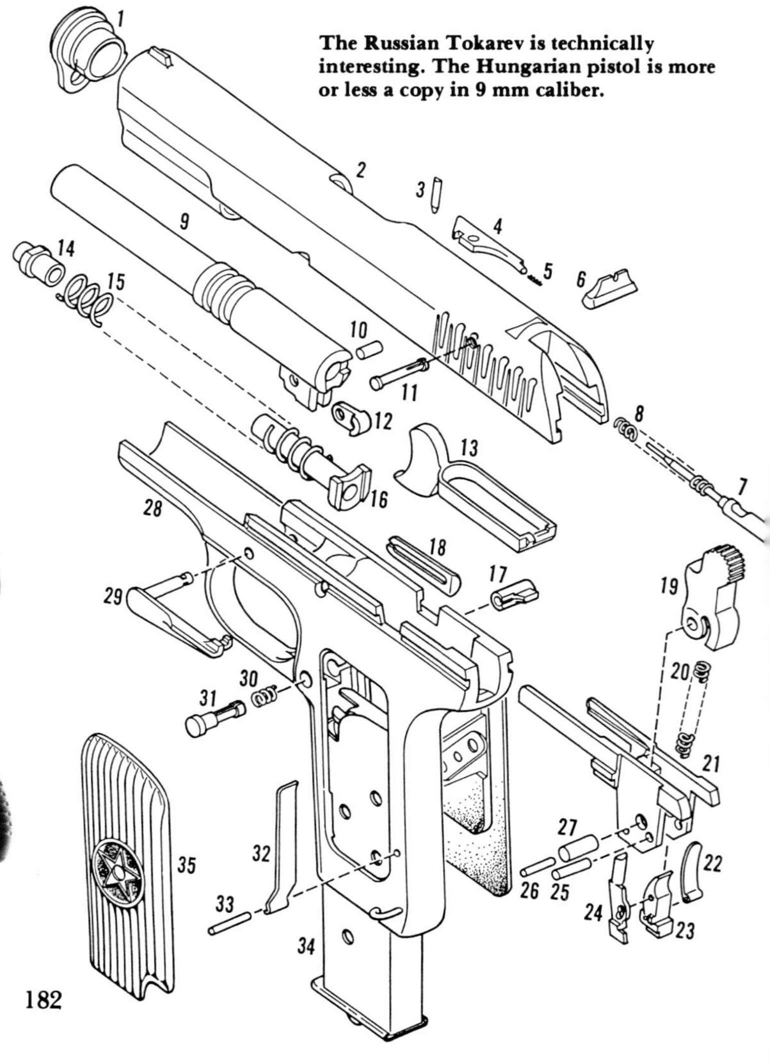

The Russian Tokarev is technically interesting. The Hungarian pistol is more or less a copy in 9 mm caliber.

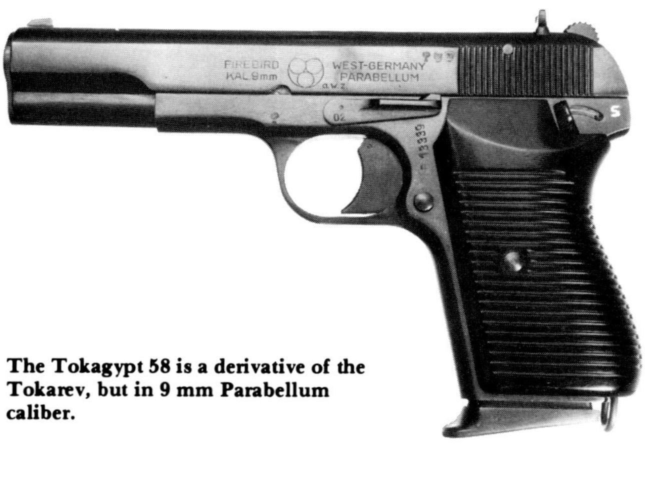

The Tokagypt 58 is a derivative of the Tokarev, but in 9 mm Parabellum caliber.

As for being equipped with handguns, the Egyptian Army originally used the British Webley Mark VI No.1 revolver in .455 caliber, as well as the Enfield No.2 revolver in .38 caliber. Egypt then introduced the 9 mm Parabellum cartridge and adopted the M 58 version of the TT 33 modified in Hungary. This pistol did not give great satisfaction, and the supplies that had been bought were turned over to the police — the army introduced the Beretta Model 1951, which then became the official side arm. In cooperation, a sporting version of this single-action pistol was also made, with a longer barrel and a grip that would fit into the hand better.

The Model 58 Tokagypt was also put on the civilian market under the name of Firebird. One seems to have had trouble coming up with lettering that would be accurate as well as stimulating sales. Despite its origin in Hungary, the pistol shown here is lettered on its slide

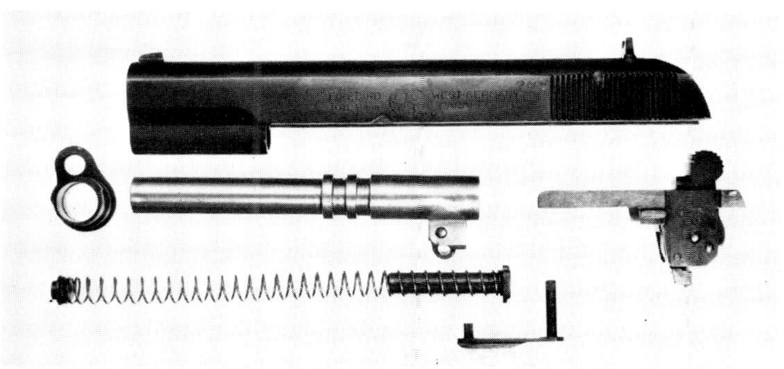

The locking over the tipping barrel, with its joint. The removable striker unit is a special feature, including the mainspring directly in the hammer.

"Firebird — West Germany — Kal 9 mm Parabellum — a.w.z." . . . note that it does not say "Made in Germany." There is also an emblem of one big cross and three small ones touching inside, which could be an imitation of the Rheinmetall trade mark.

As for this pistol's technology, it has the same type of lock as the Colt Government, except that here the barrel has its locking tabs all around and not just on top, as the Government does. This offers the advantage of greater stability ahead of the chamber as well as that of simpler manufacturing. The barrel fits into a housing in front, into the lower opening of which the plate of the recoil spring fits. This housing covers the entire forward part of the slide and stays in place there with very little play. For dismantling, the plate is pushed in with the point of a bullet and the guiding case is turned until it can be taken out of its position. Now the recoil spring is relaxed and projects out of the front of the slide. The catch lever is secured by an additional pusher. It is drawn back so that its holding tabs come out of the groove cut in the catch-lever pivot, and only then can the catch lever be pulled out of the grip to the left. At this stage of dismantling, the familiar details of the bolt system can be seen: two tabs with corresponding cutouts in the slide, connection by a chain piece, a short recoil-spring guide, the recoil spring with an end plate and a guiding casing mounted in the front of the slide and attached play-free by two tabs. The firing pin is held by a strong transverse rod that simultaneously limits its forward movement. The backsight is fixed in place, while the small foresight is an integral part of the slide. The arrangement of the recoil-spring guide on the mount of the chain is better here than in the Government. The two adjacent surfaces are made very precisely, so that the guiding rod cannot slide over this attachment place during assembly.

The receiver is machined out of steel, and the trigger presses against a leaf spring located in the back of the grip, with the lower part of the spring held in place by a pin. A special feature is the two grip panels of grooved black bakelite. A swiveling attachment is mounted on the inside of each piece so that its two arms fit into cutouts in the grip. One has to go to some trouble in working with a screwdriver blade inside the magazine shaft to detach the grip panels.

A practical feature which pistols made in the western world took on only later is the small lock which, after removing the slide, can simply be pulled out of the grip. Here too, the practical solution, actually a Russian development, is surprising. The wide hammer has a safety and a striking rest, into which the sear moves under the pressure of a leaf spring. The actual hammer spring is a powerful coil spring set into the hammer itself and braced against a transverse rod at the bottom. In addition, this removable lock still has an interrupter that moves vertically along the spring of the sear. The long extensions of the small lock deserve mention here; they function as "magazine lips" and make it easier to move a cartridge out of the magazine and into the chamber. The magazine itself has only extremely small lips that are not capable of doing their job in the traditional way. The side safety works directly on the sear, and this too can be seen only after dismantling.

It is remarkably easy to dismantle the magazine of both this pistol and the TT 33. A cover plate for the magazine spring fits, when bent slightly, into an aperture in the magazine base. If one pushes this cover plate in a bit against the pressure of the spring, the magazine base can be pulled out, making the other parts accessible for cleaning. Since the depth of the grip was actually planned for the longer 7.62 mm cartridge, a different magazine or a different magazine shaft would have been needed for the shorter 9 mm cartridge. The problem was circumvented here with a pressed-in sheet-metal insert on the rear wall of the magazine.

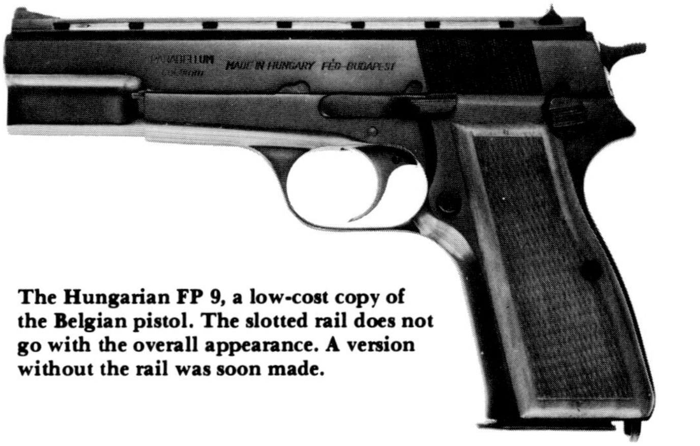

The Hungarian FP 9, a low-cost copy of the Belgian pistol. The slotted rail does not go with the overall appearance. A version without the rail was soon made.

Model FP 9

Another pistol made in Hungary for the 9 mm Parabellum caliber is the Model FP 9, which appeared on the German market in 1984, attracting no more notice then than it did when it disappeared a few years later. The price at that time, just under 700 DM for a pistol made completely of steel and including a second magazine, made the FP 9 a very interesting commodity.

It was and is manufactured by the FEG (Weapons and Gas Device Works) of Budapest. The Belgian FN pistol, known and respected throughout the world, was taken as a model — thus there are no essential differences from this well-known single-action pistol, which never went into production as an improved weapon with a modern double action trigger, in its technology and operation. Like its model, the FP 9 has a locking system with a tipping barrel and lacking a separate guiding casing at the front of the slide, plus an unfortunate magazine safety, a safety rest for the hammer, and recoil safety and manual safety on the side of the grip.

The overall workmanship is not as good here as in the FN pistol, and this may have something to do with the difference in price. But with some skill, a certain reworking could well be undertaken. The form of the hammer differs from the model too, as it has a long spur, unlike the FN, which has a perforated spur. The pistol was somewhat reworked by FEG later and gained not only another safety but also a simple type of hammer spur. The ventilated rail on the slide seems a bit strange, as it has no real purpose in a weapon of this type. After a great deal of criticism, the FP 9 was also marketed without this rail.

A reasonably priced pistol like the FP 9 would really benefit from a little reworking: polishing all the rests on the trigger, hammer and sear, decreasing the trigger's weight by installing a not so extremely ponderous

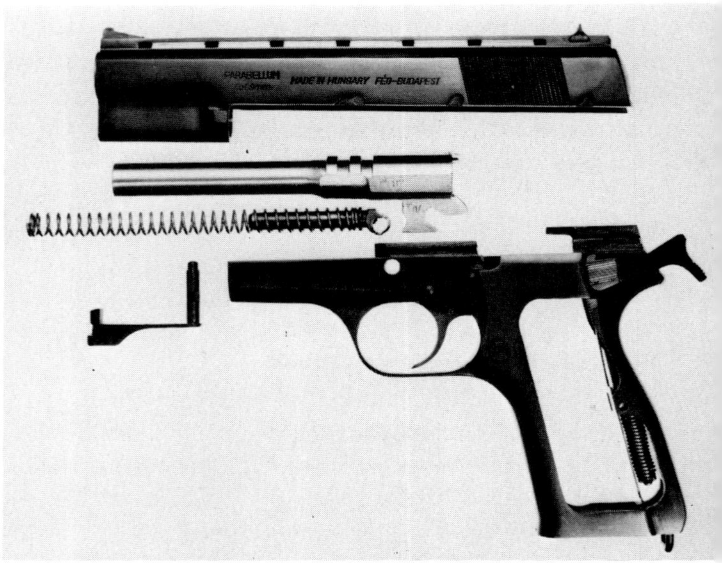

The dismantled FP 9 with its simple technology.

Cutaway drawings of the FP 9.

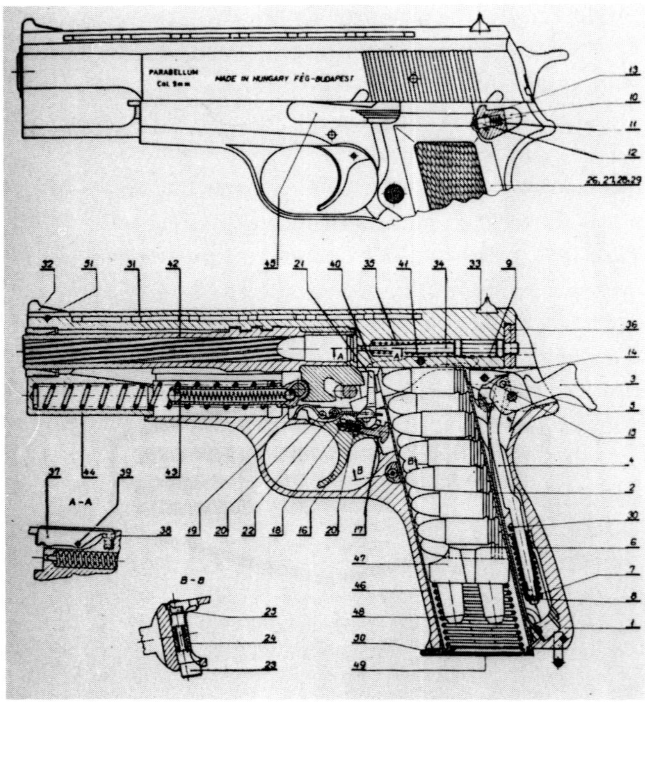

torsion spring and adding a stop-screw for the falling trigger tongue. In terms of shooting performance, though, the reasonably priced FP 9 was not far behind higher-priced pistols. Groups within the ten ring of the target at 25 meters from a sitting position, with the weapon supported, were easy to achieve.

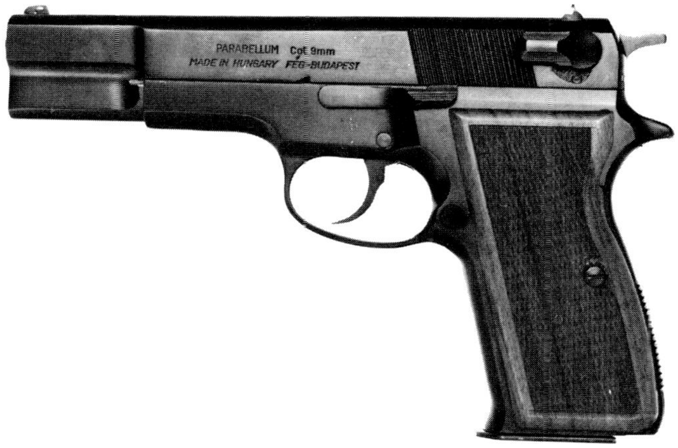

The P 9 R, another Hungarian pistol, has a modern double action trigger and an decocking lever on the slide. Here one finds many technical features of other pistols.

Technical Data: Tokagypt 58 Firebird

Model designation	Tokagypt 58 (Firebird)
Manufacturer	Feg-Budapest, Hungary
Caliber	9 mm Parabellum
Magazine capacity	8 cartridges
Overall length	197 mm
Overall height	135 mm
Barrel length	116 mm
Barrel profile	6 riflings, right
Grip width	34 mm
Weight empty	910 grams
Material	Steel
Finish	Burnished
Trigger	Single action
Sights	Fixed
Safeties	Safety rest, lever, closing

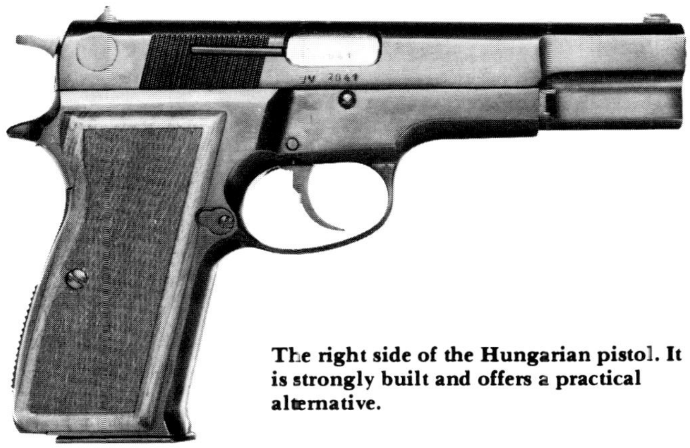

The right side of the Hungarian pistol. It is strongly built and offers a practical alternative.

Model P 9 R

It may be impossible to understand why the Belgians could not manage to put the successful High Power into production as a double-action pistol. The Hungarian manufacturer was in a position to do this very quickly, and just a year after the simple single-action pistol came on the market, it was joined by the improved P 9 R model. This is how an FN pistol with a double action trigger would have looked. The P 9 R is neither a modern, handsome weapon nor a weapon with striking new concepts, but it is very solidly contructed of steel, and will shoot very well after the trigger has been reworked and does not perform any worse than more expensive pistols.

The magazine holds 13 cartridges, the locking system works via the tipping barrel with the diagonally cut guiding surface on its underside and the addition of two tabs fitting into the cutouts in the slide. The guiding rod for the recoil spring is short and does not stick out the front when the slide recoils. Thus the pistol is a little less open to dirt on this side than others of its kind. The barrel is held in a stamped or crimped casing in the front of the slide — no play can be found here. All in all,

The dismantled P 9 R. For dismantling and assembly, the safety must be in the position shown here.

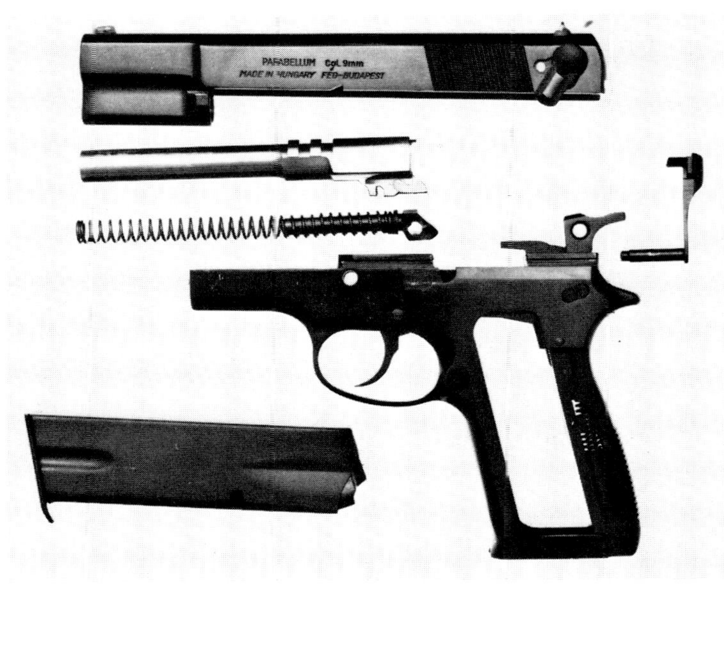

several design features of other pistols are found in this one with comforting modifications. The side safety decocks the cocked hammer, which has a separate safety rest. Simultaneously, with the setting of the safety, the surface of the safety spindle moves in front of the end of the firing pin so that It can no longer be reached by the hammer. Only in the "safety off" setting can the pistol be dismantled, and in the same manner as with similar designs.

The sights are fixed, the backsight block can be adjusted by knocking it to the side. The very small and also thin foresight is soldered into a small well on top of the slide.

The receiver is neatly made of steel, and is naturally as wide around the magazine shaft as a two-row magazine requires. In the back, an inset of darkened aluminum covers the grip and the mainspring, which is mounted there. A small rippled area affords a safer handhold. The trigger bar has two extensions that reach around the magazine shaft and pull the sprung sear out of its rest on the hammer when the trigger is pulled.

The shape of the trigger guard seems to have been borrowed from Smith & Wesson, likewise the shape of the trigger itself. What can be had here for relatively little money adds up to solid technology with workmanship that is more than worth the price. With lacquered grip panels of medium brown-stained hardwood, the grip is very wide, but it could scarcely be made any other way.

Technical Data: FP 9 and P 9 R

Manufacturer	Feg-Budapest, Hungary	
Model	FP 9	P 9 R
Caliber	9 mm Parabellum	9 mm Parabellum
Magazine capacity	13 cartridges	13 cartridges
Overall length	198 mm	200 mm
Height/width	130 mm/34 mm*	132 mm/36 mm
Barrel length	118 mm	118 mm
Weight empty	950 grams	1000 grams
Sights	Fixed	Fixed
Material/finish	Steel/burnished	Steel/burnished
Trigger	Single action	Single/double action
Safeties	Lever, magazine, lever, safety rest, closings.	Lever as decocking lever, safety rest, closings.

* Without trigger guard and sight

USA

In the United States access to the 9 mm Parabellum cartridge came only very late. The Colt M 1911 or M 1911 A 1 pistol was the official side arm almost since the beginning of the century, and today (early in 1987) the search for a usable pistol for the 9 mm Parabellum cartridge still has not been concluded once and for all, as will be explained in detail elsewhere. Two revolvers suitable for the .45 ACP cartridge were put into service, one type by Colt and the other by Smith & Wesson, both with modern double action mechanisms.

Attempts to introduce a different pistol or at least "make it palatable" always came to grief — the concept of the weapon designed by Luger was only one of many tests. Only after the end of World War II did intensive contact with the 9 mm Parabellum caliber and several weapons made for it take place, as pistols captured by American soldiers arrived in the States. Perhaps the mistrust of this caliber also originated at this time, for ammunition made toward the end of a war will not always function satisfactorily.

When NATO was founded, the 9 mm cartridge moved more an 156 re into the foreground, for it was the dominan ridge in the new alliance. Contracts for development were awarded and the search for a new service weapon began. In many cases the search and development did not lead to official contracts, but it was an advantage all the same: pistols like the M 39 and M 59 of Smith & Wesson originated at that time and could gain success on the civilian market; over the years there even developed a very successful and well-developed weapon family, down to the little Mini Gun with its twelve-shot magazine.

Nine-millimeter pistols found their way into police armaments, where this caliber was used for pistols and machine pistols. Today the 9 mm Parabellum (9 mm Luger) cartridge has already gained a high place in the USA and can no longer be left out of what is on the market there. Not as many pistols by far are built in this caliber in the USA as in Europe, but pistols shipped in from Europe meet the needs completely and with much variety.

Pistols by Colt

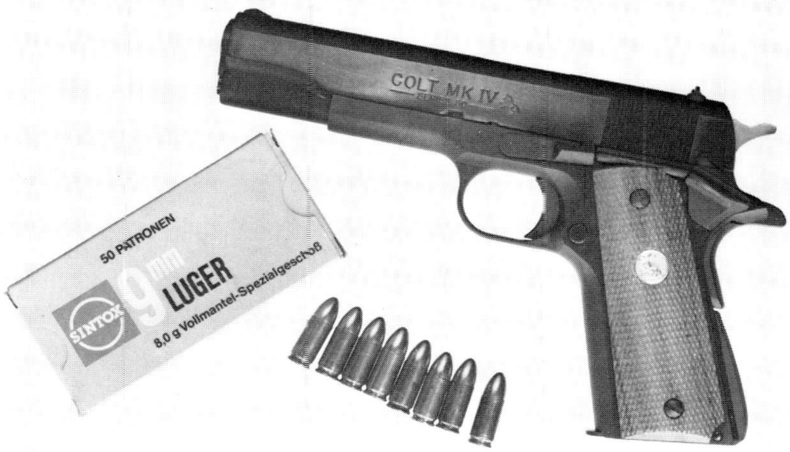

The Colt Government in 9 mm Parabellum or Luger caliber, as it is called in the USA. This weapon comes from the 80 series and already has a firing pin safety.

The right side when open. The bulge on the barrel in the muzzle area is typical.

The versions of the Colt Government in 9 mm Parabellum caliber to be noted here, and the Commander pistol, were based on the Colt 1911 or 1911 A 1. This pistol basically was and still is the best and most important development of the Colt firm. Colt stuck with a single-action trigger despite all the requests from the civilian market, even after a search was being made for a new and, above all, modern service pistol at the beginning of the 1980s, and even before, Colt could not offer a well-functioning prototype.

The pistol developed by J. Browning has now been in service for some seventy years, and almost three million pistols in .45 ACP caliber have been made by the Colt firm or under license from it. Thus the Colt pistol has become a worldwide bestseller and remains so today, concrete proof that one can do good business with simple and even outmoded weapon technology. Over the years the pistol has undergone several changes, and the privately marketed Government and Commander models can scarcely be improved. Only with the 80 Series could the internal safety of the pistols be improved — a firing pin block holds the firing pin immobile when the trigger is not pulled.

In its technology the pistol is simple and robust, one reason why many tuning experts are happy to work on it and make improvements. The locking system is found here in its most original form: a rear-tipping barrel with a joint that is held by the axle of the catch lever. This very area offers sufficient potential for improvement, as much play in this area results in insufficient shooting accuracy.

The barrel is set in a removable housing at the front of the slide; the housing was improved for the Series 70 models and has since consisted of a sprung basket that reaches around the muzzle and thus holds the barrel to prevent play. The mounting of the guiding housing inside the slide, though, is not play-free, and this is the subject of constant criticism and technical improvements. The receiver is made of steel, and the Commander is also available, as the "Lightweight Commander", with an aluminum frame, which makes a difference of 250 grams or more in weight, an important consideration for someone who has to constantly carry the weapon.

The sights are fixed, and the foresight is very small and thin — here too, modifications absolutely need to be made for effective use. The parts trade offers numerous replacement sights, the simplest of which can be inserted directly into the existing apertures. But then the sight is high above the level of the hand — it is more effective to install a low-level sight such as, for example, the Peters sight, which is adjustable in all directions. The trigger is a single-action type. It offers no possibility of modification. It can, though, be replaced by a trigger with a surface that projects further, the so-called combat trigger, which is much easier for shooters with long fingers to operate. It has a trigger-stop screw which presses backward against the pivot of the sprung magazine catch. The triggers of the Colt pistols simply must be reworked, and can be smoothed easily by gunsmiths, as well as reduced in effective weight — along with the stop screw, an excellent trigger adjustment is easy to attain.

The grip safety is characteristic of these pistols. Only when the safety is pushed in is it possible to pull the trigger. Here too, the situation can be improved with available accessories: the normal grip safety has a very

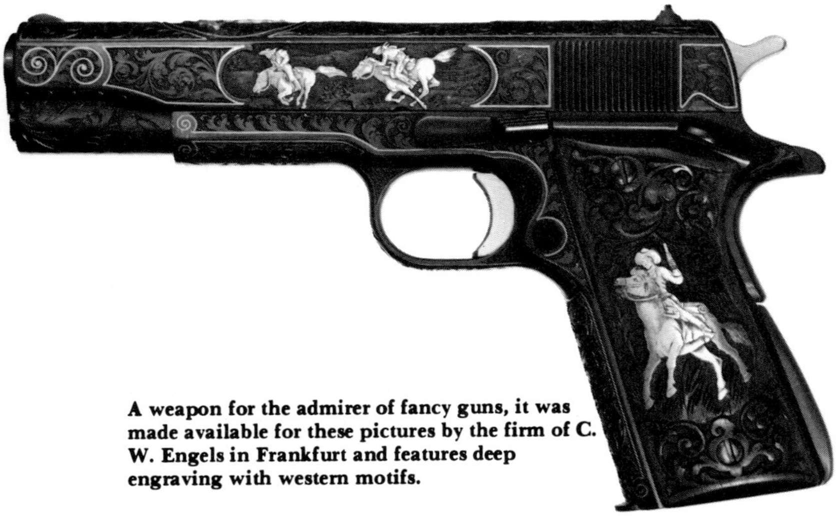

A weapon for the admirer of fancy guns, it was made available for these pictures by the firm of C. W. Engels in Frankfurt and features deep engraving with western motifs.

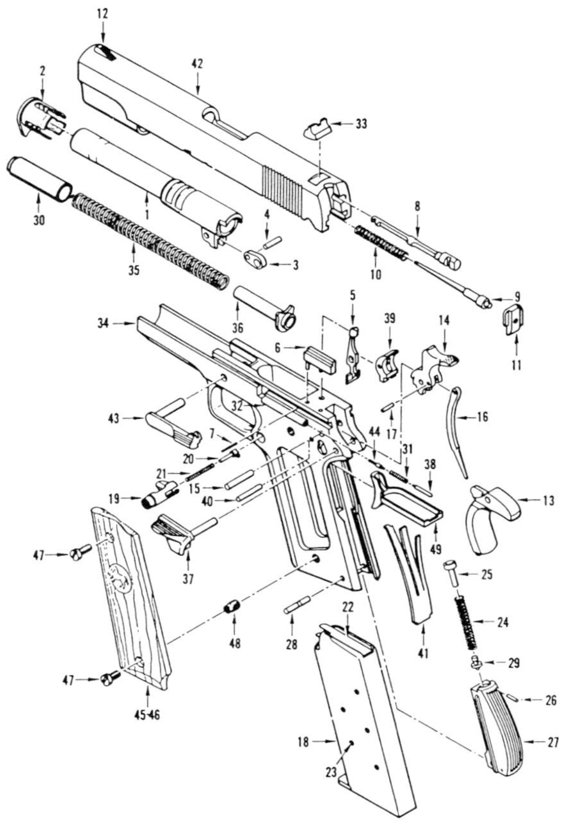

1 Barrel
2 Barrel Bushing
3 Barrel Link
4 Barrel Link Pin
5 Disconnector
6 Ejector
7 Ejector Pin
8 Extractor
9 Firing Pin
10 Firing Pin Spring
11 Firing Pin Stop
12 Front Sight
13 Grip Safety
14 Hammer
15 Hammer Pin
16 Hammer Strut
17 Hammer Strut Pin
18 Magazine Assembly
19 Magazine Catch
20 Magazine Catch Lock
21 Magazine Catch Spring
22 Magazine Follower
23 Magazine Spring
24 Main Spring
25 Main Spring Cap
26Main Spring Cap Pin
27 Main Spring Housing
28 Main Spring Housing Pin
29 Main Spring Housing Pin Retainer
30 Recoil Spring Plug
31 Plunger Spring
32 Plunger Tube
33 Rear Sight
34 Receiver
35 Recoil Spring
36 Recoil Spring Guide
37 Safety Lock
38 Safety Lock Plunger
39 Sear
40 Sear Pin
41 Sear Spring
42 Slide
43 Slide Stop
44 Slide Stop Plunger
45 Stock (Left Hand)
46 Stock (Right Hand)
47 Stock Screws (4)
48 Stock Screw Bushings (4)
49 Trigger Assembly

The parts of the 70 series Colt Government. This version does not yet have a firing pin block.

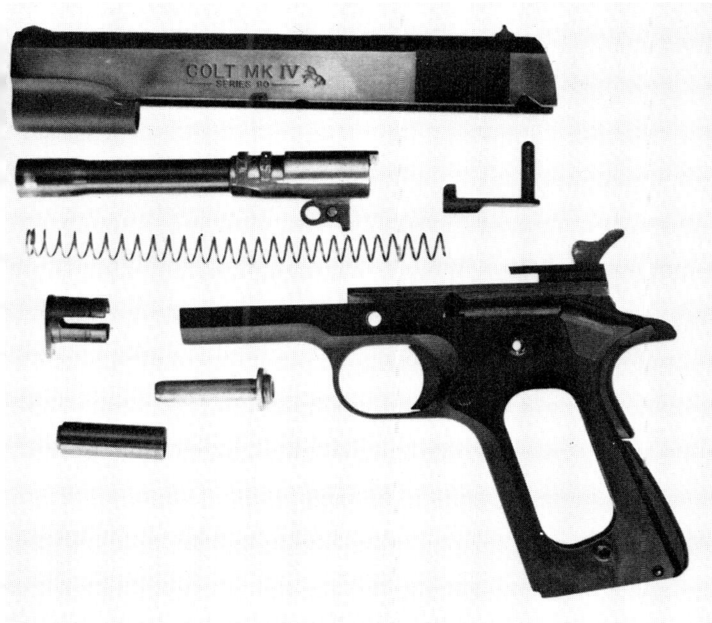

The dismantled Colt Government in 9 mm Luger caliber. The frame is made of steel. Despite its not overly modern technology, it is still a bestseller among handguns.

small, short spur that pushes unpleasantly into the shooter's hand in long series of shots. It can be replaced by a safety that includes a longer spur with a wider surface.

In all, there are four independently working safety systems in the Government and Commander pistols: the grip safety, the safety rest on the hammer, the recoil safety, and the manual safety on the left side of the grip. In addition, the Series 80 models also have a firing pin block. Thus the pistol is as simple to handle as it is safe, even though the cocked hammer cannot be decocked safely by a special apparatus in the manner of modern pistols. A few details as to dismantling: after checking the chamber and removing the magazine, pull the slide backward a little bit. Press the spring housing in lightly and turn the guiding housing of the barrel to the left, as seen from the front, then remove the spring housing completely from the slide.

Now pull the slide back until the nose of the catch lever is under the aperture on the underside of the slide, and push the catch lever out of the grip from right to left. The slide, with recoil spring and barrel, can now be pushed forward out of the frame. After that, the guiding housing can be turned to the right until it can be removed, after which the spring is pushed out to the front, the joint of the barrel bent forward and the barrel

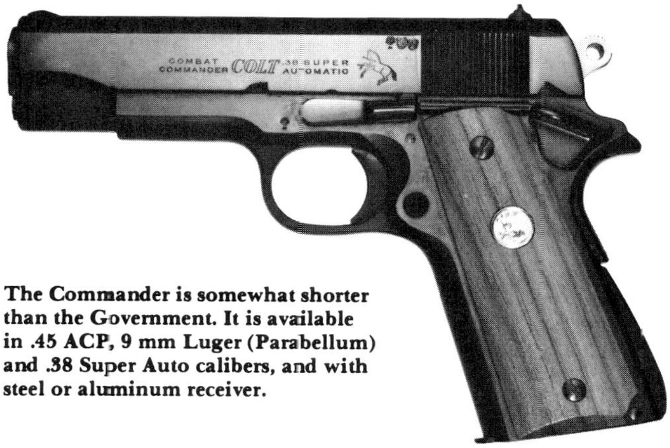

The Commander is somewhat shorter than the Government. It is available in .45 ACP, 9 mm Luger (Parabellum) and .38 Super Auto calibers, and with steel or aluminum receiver.

pulled out of the slide.

Pictures often show a rebuilt version in which shooters have had a guiding rod for the recoil spring installed. In this case the spring housing has to have a hole bored to allow the guiding rod to pass through it when the slide recoils. When this modification has been made, dismantling is much easier. It is sufficient to pull back the slide and remove the catch lever. After that the entire upper part, including the guiding housing, recoil spring and barrel, can be pushed out of the grip as a complete unit.

On the constructive basis of the Colt M 1911 A 1 or the Government, several variations were made, as well as almost identical copies by other manufacturers, using the same mechanics but often with poorer material and workmanship. In 1949 a shorter and lighter pistol for the .45 ACP cartridge was made and named "Commander

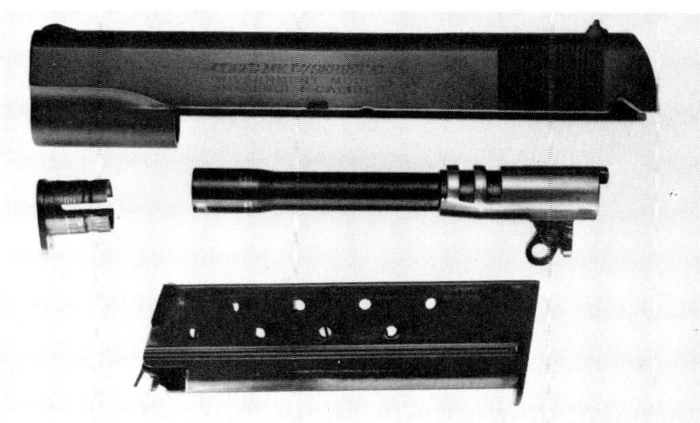

This switching kit converts the Government from .45 ACP to 9 mm caliber. The different ejector, already installed in the grip, is not shown.

Model." The grip was shortened, and so were the barrel and the slide. This shorter pistol gained success on the market and was soon offered in .38 Super and 9 mm Parabellum calibers, as well as 7.65 mm Parabellum caliber for Italy.

Hardly any other pistol has so many accessories, replacement parts and tuning equipment. Many a clever manufacturer has tried to capitalize on its lack of precision. The Government has only moderate accuracy, especially in the 9 mm caliber, but many of the "improvements" do not live up to what is claimed in their advertisements. In many cases, rebuilding measures go so far that they cost more than a modern double action pistol, which does not always make much sense. Improvements can be made in the areas of the simple sights, the trigger, and perhaps in flattening the curved mainspring housing. A real increase in accuracy can be shown with the installation of the Peters Steel polygonal barrel, and the play between the slide and the grip could be decreased, which would make even more sense.

The firm of D. Ehrenreich GmbH, located at 8459 Neukirchen (Holnstein 28-29) Germany, sells the original accessories for the Colt pistols, made by Federal Ordnance. The accessories are available in sets according to the desired level of rebuilding, and can be installed at

The Officers ACP in .45 ACP caliber, a short pistol for officers and private owners. One hopes it will also be available some day in 9 mm Luger (Parabellum) caliber.

The Randall pistol is a typical Colt copy, made of stainless steel. This is a .45 caliber pistol; it is available in 9 mm caliber but otherwise unchanged. A special weapon for left-handed shooters, with all moving parts reversed.

The author's highly modified Colt Government in its holster.

Several modifications have been made: the rear (spring housing) ground down straight, the grip roughened in front, a lengthened grip safety, a longer Combat trigger and the hammer from a Commander.

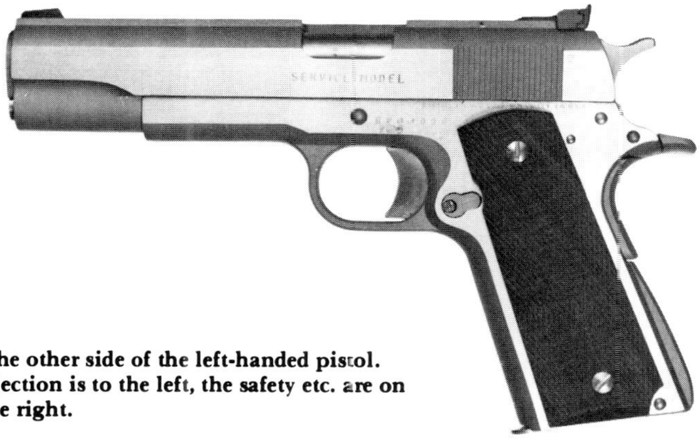

The other side of the left-handed pistol. Ejection is to the left, the safety etc. are on the right.

The Randall pistol when dismantled. Removing the barrel is unnecessarily complicated not impossible without a special tool.

any time without going to a gunsmith or reworking parts. The following possibilities exist:

Level 1: Slide catch lever long and safety long.
Level 2: Slide catch level long, safety long, magazine catch long and grip safety large.
Level 3: Slide catch lever two-sided and safety two-sided.
Level 4: Slide catch lever two-sided, safety two-sided, grip safety large and magazine catch long.

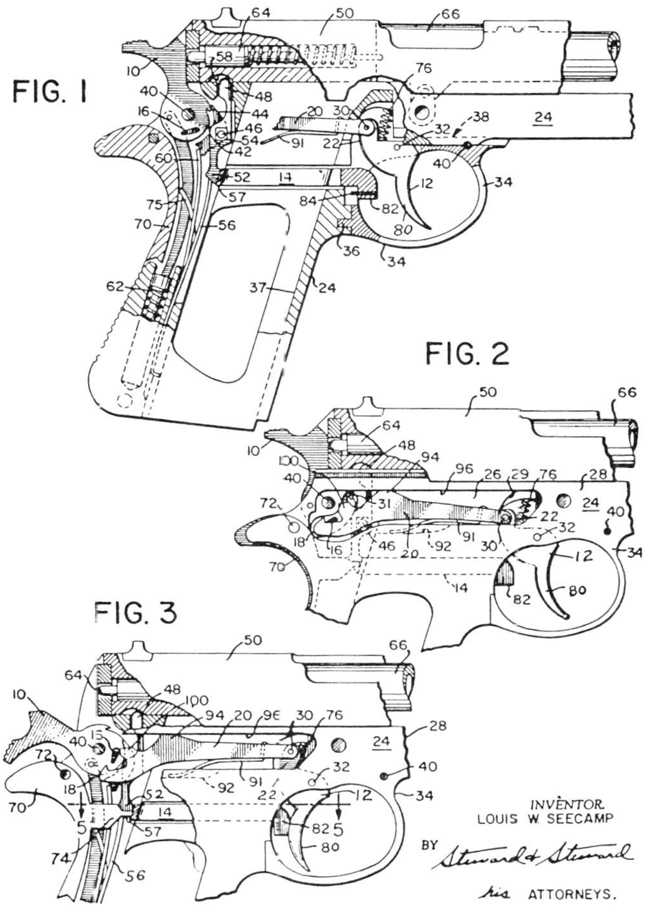

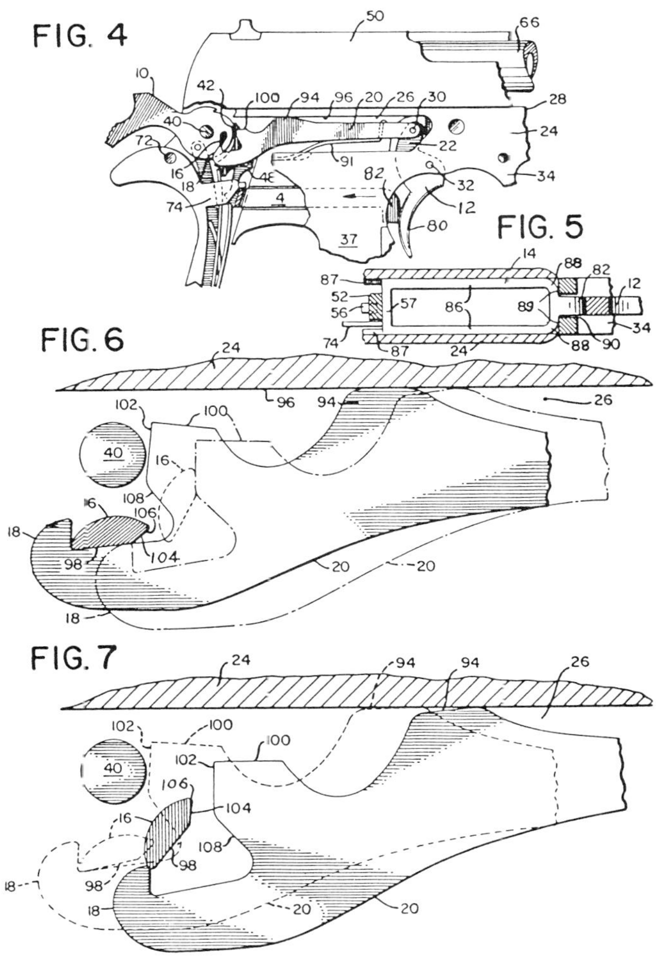

Upper right: L.W. Seecamp was untiring in his attempts to equip the Government with a double action trigger. An excerpt from his patent drawing.

Lower right: Details of his patent drawing showing operation of the trigger bar.

The two-sided parts also include the lengthening.

Both pistols can be obtained in any caliber, and a rebuilding kit to turn the .45 Government into 9 mm Parabellum caliber can also be had. It includes a different slide, the barrel, the magazine and a flatter ejector, which must be changed whenever the pistol is switched.

Technical Data: Colt Pistols

Manufacturer	Colt Patent Firearms Mfg., Hartford CT	
Model	Government	Commander
Caliber	9 mm Parabellum*	9 mm Parabellum*
Overall length	215 mm	203 mm
Height/width	140 mm/31 mm	140 mm/31 mm
Barrel length	125 mm	108 mm
Weight empty	1100 grams	994 grams (767)
Magazine capacity	9 cartridges	9 cartridges
Sights	Fixed	Fixed
Material/finish	Steel/burnished	Steel/burnished
Safeties	Safety rest, grip, closing, manual; as of Series 80 also firing pin safety	

* Also .45 ACP and .38 Super

The Ruger P 85 Pistol

It was said for a long time that Ruger was working on a self-loading pistol in 9 mm Parabellum caliber, and so-called project studies were displayed again and again at exhibitions. In mid-1986 the first weapons appeared on the private market, after which there was again complete silence about this new pistol. One has to view them with the background in the USA at that time in mind. The first US Army testing saw the Beretta 92 F come through the stringent tests in first place, very much to the annoyance of the domestic manufacturers, who subsequently tried to take legal action to change this decision. Thus the firm of Ruger can feel that it has a very good chance, and things finally went so far that the firm built a new factory in Arizona to produce the P 85. The P 85 makes no effort to win a beauty contest, nor is it particularly suitable for use as a match weapon. All publications to date, especially in the USA, attest that it has good shooting performance, trouble-free use with a wide variety of cartridges, and great handling safety. Ruger gave preference to the use of new and economical manufacturing technology, for to have any hope of winning a government contract, the new pistol had to be reasonably priced, more so than the competing weapons from the other manufacturers. Thus many parts were made of fine-cast steel, including the slide, the small parts of the system, and the block at the rear of the barrel, into which the barrel itself is simply pushed. The frame is made of an aluminum alloy, likewise produced by the fine-casting process, and hardly reworked.

The system of the locked P 85 is a mixture of tried and true techniques. As with the pistols made by SIG/Sauer, the barrel is situated in the window of the slide, and like Colt pistols it has a chain under the barrel, through the lower aperture of which the pivot of the catch lever passes.

The magazine holds 15 cartridges in two rows, and another cartridge can be carried in the chamber without any loss of safety. The combination of the individual safeties corresponds to the status generally expected today. Along with the usual recoil safety, the P 85 has a manual safety at the upper rear of the slide, with which the cocked hammer can be decocked harmlessly. While decocking, the firing pin is simultaneously held in its longitudinal position and the trigger bar is moved out of its holding position. The Ruger pistol does not have a true loading indicator, but it can be felt by the somewhat projecting extractor whether there is a cartridge or a case in the chamber.

The grip panels of black plastic are each held with a single screw, and their grooving is somewhat reminiscent of the early P 38 made by Walther.

Dismantling the P 85, though, is rather unusual. After removing the magazine and making the usual safety check, the slide is locked into its rearmost position with the catch lever. Then one must reach into the ejection opening with one finger and push the ejector down until it stops. During the process, the firing pin block is pushed downward and the slide's path forward is opened. Then one lets the slide move forward until the catch lever can be pulled out on the left, and from there on, the further dismantling proceeds as usual.

In terms of total constitution, the P 85 should be a simple, robust and reasonably priced weapon for service use. The safety or decocking lever is mounted on both sides, and the magazine catch can also be operated from either side. The trigger guard extends a long way to the front, and this too corresponds to the military requirements, as one must be able to operate the pistol while wearing heavy gloves. The interrupted guiding of the slide may seem somewhat unconventional, as it sets on the frame with a lot of play. The sights are marked in white, and the foresight can be replaced, so that it is possible to change its height.

Technical Data: Ruger P-85

Manufacturer	Sturm, Ruger & Co. Inc., Southport CT
Years made	ca. 1984-86
Caliber	9 mm Parabellum
Magazine capacity	15 cartridges
Overall length	200 mm
Height/width	143 mm/39 mm
Barrel length	115 mm, 6 riflings, right
Sights	Fixed, foresight exchangeable
Safeties	Firing pin block, decocking lever, closing safety
Material	Fine casting, aluminum grip
Finish	Matte burnished, phosphated
Total weight empty	1100 grams
Weight empty	ca. 940 grams
Weight loaded	ca. 1120 grams

Cutaway view of the new Ruger P-85, a weapon with unique technology.

Detonics Pocket 9

The desire to have as small a pistol as possible for the 9 mm PARA cartridge could previously be met satisfactorily for the most part only by tuning experts. To do this, one took time-tested designs and shortened them wherever possible. Sometimes such rebuilding also gave rise to production weapons, as has been seen in the Mini Gun by Smith & Wesson, which is basically a factory-made Devell rebuilding, simply produced in large numbers.

The Detonics Pocket Power 9 is probably the smallest pistol with a cocking trigger. It locks via a delay of the movement in the chamber, a technically very interesting but not always dependable process.

The Pocket 9 by Detonics may be by far the smallest self-loading pistol in this caliber. As small as it is, some of its design features are quite interesting. The measurements of this pistol are: Overall length 150 mm, height 104 mm, width 28 mm, barrel length 80 mm, and unloaded weight 790 grams. The magazine holds six cartridges, and another can be carried in the barrel without danger, for the firing pin is held fast by the safety and cannot move forward even in the pistol is dropped.

The Pocket 9 has no locking device in the usual sense, but works with a delayed mass breech. When fired the recoil is correspondingly heavy, and feels harder than that of a larger pistol.

There is an outward bulge all around the front third of the chamber. The cartridge case spreads when a shot is fired and thus makes it deliberately hard to extract, for it pushes itself into this bulge. This is naturally playing with fire, for the extent of the delay depends directly on the spreading properties of the cartridge case. Thus it does not function the same with all cartridges and will probably react more strongly to cartridges producing less gas pressure. The shooting performance of the little

The barrel is mounted firmly in the frame, the recoil spring is wrapped around the barrel. All the parts are made of stainless steel.

The left side of the grip. In some versions another spring is added to lift the ejector so it can act as a slide catch.

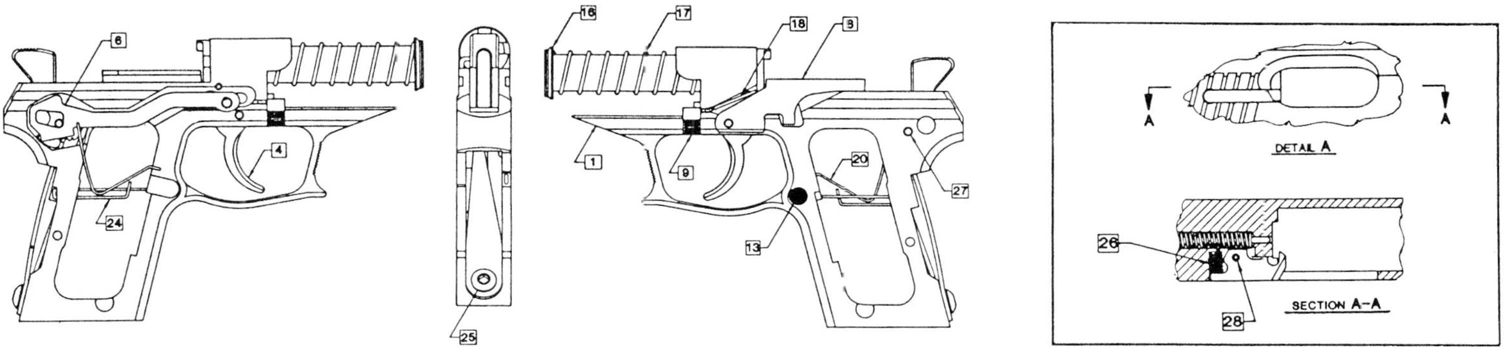

Detonics Pocket Power.

1 Griffstück mit Lauf
2 Schlitten
3 Stift zur Schlittensperre
4 Abzug
5 Hahn
6 Unterbrecher-Einheit
7 Auszieher
8 Schlitten-Sperre (Fanghebel)
9 Sperrschieber
10 Sicherung links
11 Sicherung rechts
12 Schlagbolzen
13 Magazinhalter
14 Schlagfeder
15 Abzugstollen (Feder)
16 Lauf-Führungsteller
17 Schließfeder
18 Feder zum Fanghebel
19 Feder zur Schlittensperre
20 Unterbrecher-Feder
21 Lauf-Federring
22 Schlitten-Federring
23 Schlagbolzenfeder
24 Magazinhalter-Feder
25 Schraube zur Schlagfeder
26 Auszieherfeder
27 Hahnachse
28 Auszieherstift
29 Griffschalen-Schraube
30 Griffschale rechts
31 Griffschale links
32 Magazin, kompl.

(Anmerkung: Das in der Zeichnung mit Nr. 8 gekennzeichnete Teil ist bei der jetzigen Pocket Power anders geformt. Es fungiert nur noch als Auswerfer, nicht hingegen als Kammerfang. Dabei entfällt auch die Feder Nr. 18, eine kleine Drahtfeder, die Teil 8 gegen den Druck des Magazinzubringers nach unten drückt.)

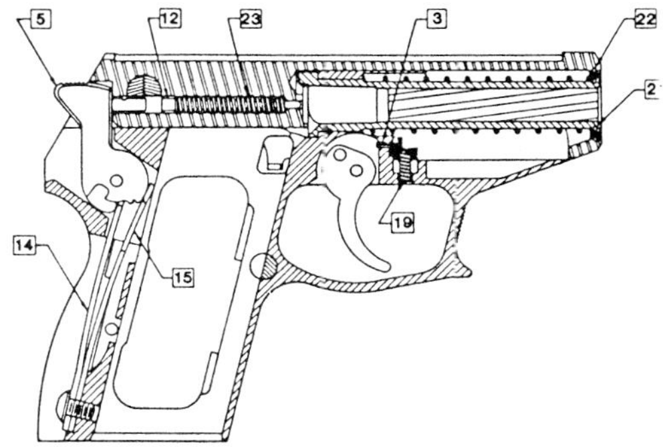

Technical details of the Detonics Pocket Power. It is presently the smallest 9 mm Parabellum pistol with a double action trigger.

pistol proved to be irregular, with the best results scored while using cartridges made by GECO: about 80 mm diameter for groups of ten at a range of 15 meters. Other cartridges, such as those made by Sako, Norma, Winchester or Hirtenberger, scored progressively worse at longer ranges, and sometimes cases got stuck and had to be pushed out frontward. In this case the choice of a cartridge and the behavior of the case are of decisive importance for problem-free functioning.

The Pocket 9 is made of stainless steel, and the grip and slide are cast, as is very customary today, and prepared cleanly in all important functioning areas. The surfaces are satin-matte, and the overall workmanship is pleasing and appropriate.

As in the well-known Walther PP pistols, the barrel is pushed firmly into the grip and additionally secured by a transverse rod. Dismantling is also similar, though not easy at first, because of the powerful recoil spring and very small manufacturing tolerances. One removes the magazine, checks the chamber and pulls the locking piece down in front of the trigger — it can get stuck easily and absolutely must be pulled down equally on both sides. After that the slide is pulled back, lifted off from the rear and pushed out of the grip at the front.

During assembly it must be remembered that the guiding plate of the recoil spring must be situated far enough ahead of the steel ring at the muzzle of the barrel. Special attention should be given to the grip panels, which are made of black-epoxied NE-metal. They are pushed into the receiver, for which they have special guiding surfaces, and screwed completely tightly — of course the form springs and the trigger bar have to stay in their positions.

As for springs, Detonics has taken an original approach that is simultaneously effective and space-saving. The hammer activates a leaf spring low in the receiver, and another leaf spring pushes on the sear. A form spring made of spring wire and mounted at the side pushes the trigger bar up and simultaneously secures the magazine catch, which is also sprung by it.

The sights are rigid and set inside a groove machined into the slide, so that the foresight necessarily is in shadow. Both the deep-set sights and the shape of the hammer see to it that the pistol cannot get snagged in the holster. The safety, operable from either side, holds the firing pin fast and locks the hammer.

The Smith & Wesson M 39 in its early form, with laterally adjustable sight.

Pistols by Smith & Wesson

Smith & Wesson, as a manufacturer of handguns, has become as much of a concept as the firm of Colt in the USA or Walther or Heckler & Koch in Germany. When one mentions a Smith & Wesson, it goes without saying that one refers first of all to a revolver, for in the realm of the revolver, this manufacturer can offer an array in all possible calibers that could hardly be enlarged. In addition, Smith & Wesson has done well as a manufacturer of self-loading pistols and, despite the American fondness for the Colt Government and its .45 cartridge, been able to carve out a sufficiently large niche in the hotly-contested market with the 9 mm Parabellum (still called the 9 mm LUGER in America). In addition, Smith & Wesson produces, has produced or markets under its own name very different weapons: repeating rifles for hunting and sport, self-loading and pump rifles, plus numerous knives, holsters and accessories.

With its first self-loading pistol, the early Model 39, the manufacturer offered for the first time a pistol for a cartridge regarded as small in the USA. This model was more like a sideline development, the sale of which on the private market was not foreseen at first. On the basis of war experience, it was proclaimed that a lighter pistol with modern technology, somewhat larger magazine capacity and a laterally adjustable sight was wanted. Such prototypes were built in hopes of large-scale contracts from the Defense Department, but nothing came of it in the end. A different viewpoint prevailed and the venerable Government, in .45 ACP caliber, was retained. Smith & Wesson swallowed its hopes and its developmental costs, and then put the Model 39 on the market in 1954 as a civilian pistol. The same thing happened to numerous pistols in recent years when they were not accepted by the U.S. Army, with the Beretta Model 92 F, as can be read elsewhere, having won the competition.

The Model 39

Today the Model 39 is no longer produced in its original form, having been replaced by several technically similar weapons. The basic technology, though, has remained and can be described concisely here. The locking of barrel and slide functions in the familiar Browning principle, which was changed only slightly, and it differs from the Colt pistol in being somewhat easier to operate and dismantle. The barrel is mounted at the front in a separately removable housing, which stays in place very snugly and has scarcely any play under the pressure of the rod-guided recoil spring. The trigger is designed as a cocking trigger, and both its ease of movement and its usefulness as either a single- or double action trigger are typical of pistols made by this firm, even though a little bit of reworking, as with many pistols, will afford the private user greater accuracy.

The aluminum receiver, caused problems for many combat shooters, and also cost a lot to combine the "Master" grip, made of steel, with the slide of the M 39. At that time, ambitious small-scale producers did the same thing and offered alternative frames made of steel or stainless steel, to which all the parts of the original frame could be attached without any technical difficulties. Today the steel grip is in regular production, so that modifications of this kind are not necessary.

The safety is designed for hard use. The lateral wing safety holds the firing pin fast, the magazine safety interrupts the trigger mechanism as soon as a magazine is either absent or not completely inserted. The cocked hammer can be decocked by using the safety lever, and

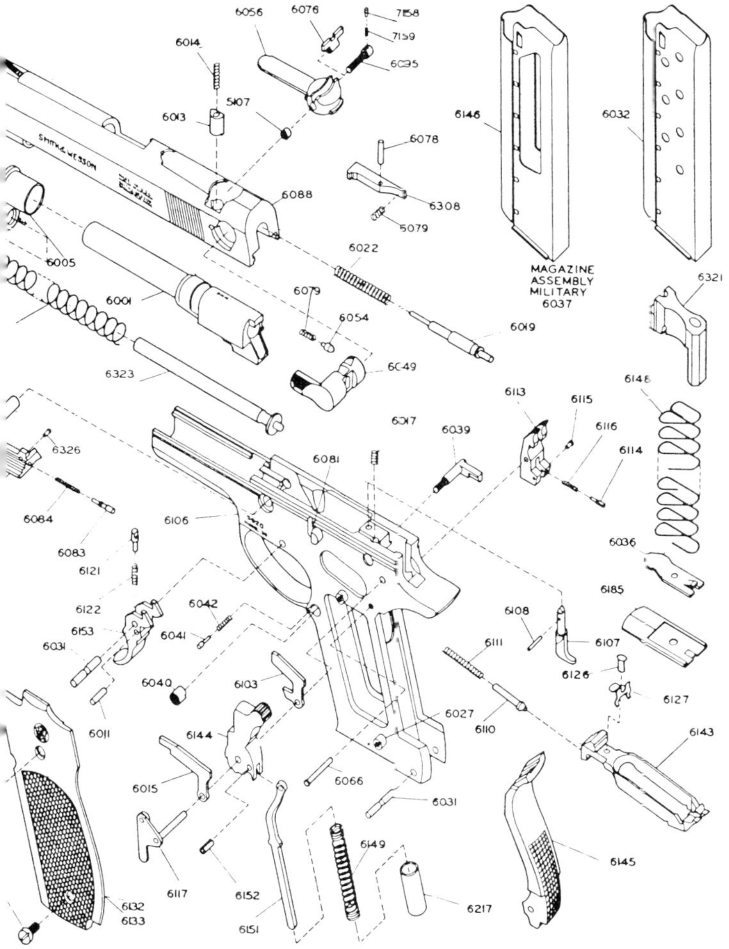

Parts of the Smith & Wesson M 39. The drawing shows the early type with laterally adjustable sights lacking protective flanks.

the trigger is immobilized when the safety is set.

The magazine, neatly made and able to be dismantled for cleaning, has a plastic follower with long arms that provides trouble-free cartridge insertion. It holds eight rounds and shows how many are present through the view holes on the side.

Model 59

This version is actually not a new pistol, but only a form of the successful basic pistol modified in the frame and magazine. The magazine holds a total of 14 cartridges in two rows, which naturally results in a somewhat thicker grip. This presumed disadvantage is equalized by very cleverly attached grip panels of black plastic, made only a few millimeters thick to help minimize the real breadth of the grip. Many parts of the two pistols are interchangeable. The Model 59 was first exhibited in November of 1972, before which its development, according to the firm's announcement, took all of four years.

Over the years, other variations followed, based on the 39 and 59 models, while the early versions were no longer officially included in the manufacturer's offerings.

The early Model 59 pistol, made to hold 14 cartridges.

Model 439

The aluminum grip has remained, but the sights, the firing pin, the safety and the extractor, the dismantling of which has been simplified, have been changed. The firing pin safety secures or blocks the new-type firing pin until the trigger is pulled back all the way, and the magazine safety, not at all appreciated by many owners, has been retained, making an otherwise operable pistol

The M 539 frame. The inlay in the back is made of darkened aluminum and covers the mainspring.

The M 439 (aluminum frame) and M 59 (steel frame) types have vertically and laterally adjustable sights, an improved extractor and the typical protective sight flanks.

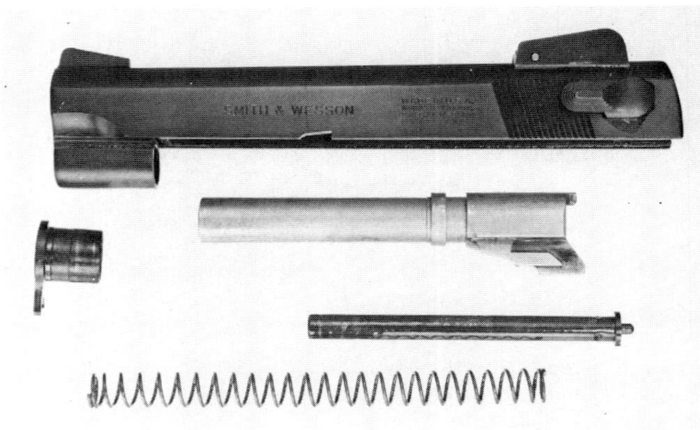

The same technology in all pistols of this series: slide with removable barrel, recoil spring, guiding rod amd housing.

useless if the magazine is lost, since it can only be fired then if one pushes a screwdriver through the empty magazine shaft against the sprung lock in the lower rear of the slide. This author regards such a safety as very risky and prefers to remove such superfluous parts. In any case, severe damage to the magazine would give the same result as the loss of the magazine.

To remove the magazine safety, (parts 8 and 9 in the drawing on page 197), the sight is removed, which is made easy by pushing in its two push buttons (parts 50 and 51). After loosening screw #49, the sight carrier #48 can be pushed sideward out of its position, and the part in question can then be removed, along with its spring, from the left opening (as seen from the rear), after which the sight can be replaced in the opposite order.

For all the newer models, a safety can be ordered that is operable from either side. One can either order it factory installed or install it later as an alternative part. The removal of the safety pivot after pushing the firing pin can be done in the intermediate position between safety on and safety off, and takes only a few minutes.

Model 539

This is the otherwise identical version with a steel grip, which raises the empty weight from 765 to 1021 grams. This version came into being in an unusual way. For years there were requests for a version with a steel grip, and they could not be ignored — thus only an aluminum grip with a grid pattern is still in production. No sooner had the new version become available than the dealers

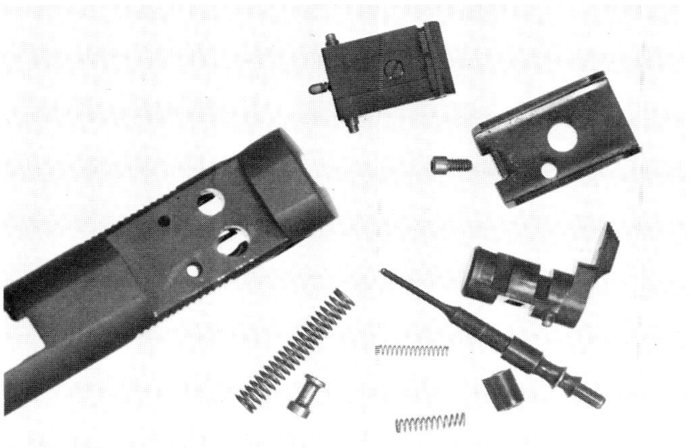

Safety, sights and firing pin are removed. It is easy to disconnect the magazine safety of a Smith & Wesson pistol.

Those who shoot a lot will appreciate a Pachmayr rubber grip. The weapon fits well into the hand.

complained that this pistol was hard to sell, for scarcely anybody wanted it. It sold like the proverbial "sour beer" in the mid-1980s, and at prices that nobody could have imagined, on account of the high exchange rate, the difference between it and the aluminum version reaching 40% at that time. The author prefers a weapon with a steel grip, for he does not have to carry it, other than, well protected in its case, on the way to the shooting range. A heavy pistol is inherently more pleasant to use, because its recoil is not nearly as hard. But another problem appears in a comparison: loaded with cartridges that are a little too weak, the heavy version does not function without problems, while the same cartridges cause no trouble in the lighter pistol.

A good and well-formed holster is practical. This one is made by Bianchi.

Model 639: Adjustable Sight

This is identical to the previous model but made of stainless steel. It appeals chiefly to the admirer of bright shiny weapons, as a stainless-steel weapon looks much more elegant than the nickel-plated version that is also available. For one who does not enjoy cleaning with oil and must often carry the pistol in a holster, this version is surely a sensible and appropriate alternative.

Model 639: Fixed Sight

This version lacks only the vertically and laterally adjustable sight with its protective side panels. These pistols with fixed sights have been offered by Smith & Wesson in both aluminum and stainless steel.

The Model 639 is the same weapon in stainless steel. Weapons of this material may be somewhat easier to maintain.

The M 639 when open. After the last shot, the slide is held back, moving forward after the slide catch is moved.

Model 459

Based on the already described Model 59, this has the protected, vertically and laterally adjustable sight, otherwise there are no noteworthy differences. With the same model designation, it is also available with a fixed sight and is listed in the catalog with the added designation "Fixed Sight."

Model 559

This version has a steel grip but no other differences.

Model 659

This is a stainless steel version with no other technical differences. With the added designation of "Fixed Sight", the same pistol is offered with a non-adjustable sight.

The Model 659 made of stainless steel, with fixed sight and 14-shot magazine.

The grips of the M 639 and 659 for comparison. The shape of the trigger guard was improved for the 659 series.

The two slides with barrels. The two-sided safety can be modified.

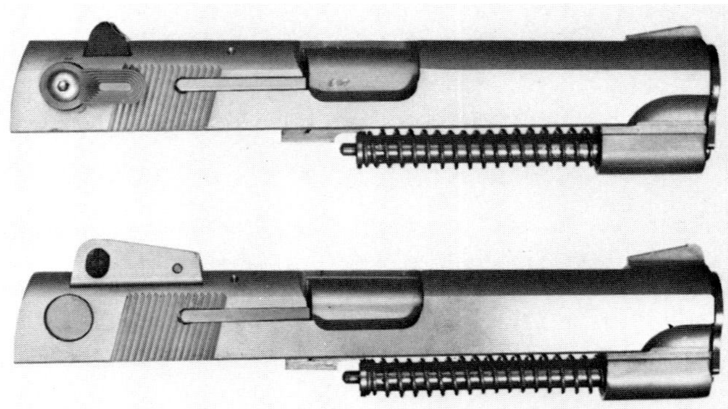

The dismantled M 659 without grip panels. Smith & Wesson pistols are well-built and enjoy worldwide popularity.

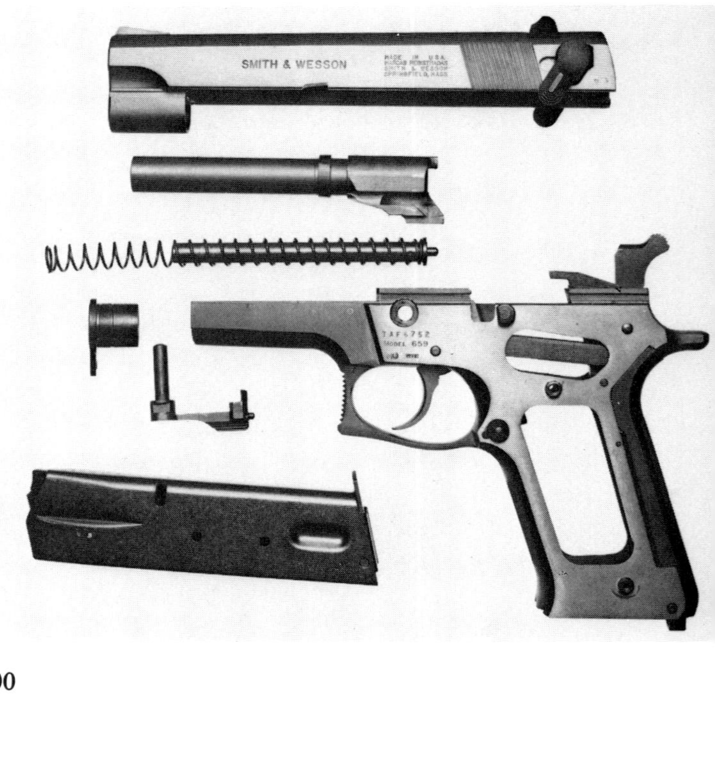

Model 469 "Mini Gun"

This is the firm's newest creation, and deserves a special attention here.

The pistols made by Smith & Wesson enjoy great popularity now as before, for they are neatly and solidly built, give good shooting performance and are easy and safe to handle. Naturally there are two schools of thought on the problematic magazine safety, but one need not take this safety into consideration when making a decision. The two-sided safety offers an added alternative for the left-handed shooter. The shape of the M 39 has changed just as little as that of the M 59, both being, in a certain sense, timeless.

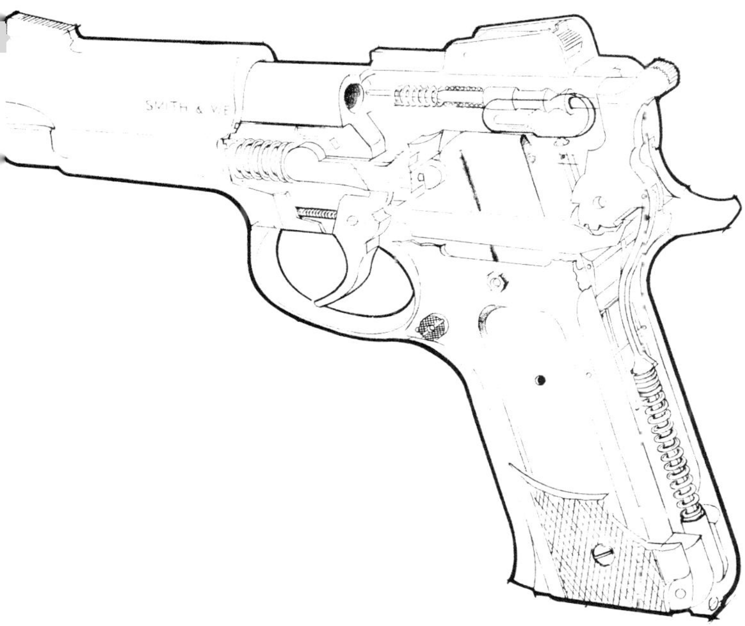

1. A firing pin safety blocks the firing pin until the shot is fired.
2. Rugged, protected sights are vertically and laterally adjustable.
3. With the safety on, a massive steel arm extends over the firing pin. At the same time, the hammer can move forward.
4. A magazine interruptor prevents the weapon from firing without a magazine in place.
5. The double-action mechanism allows the first shot to be fired without manually cocking the hammer. Pulling the trigger cocks the hammer for the first shot, and the system cocks the hammer for additional shots.

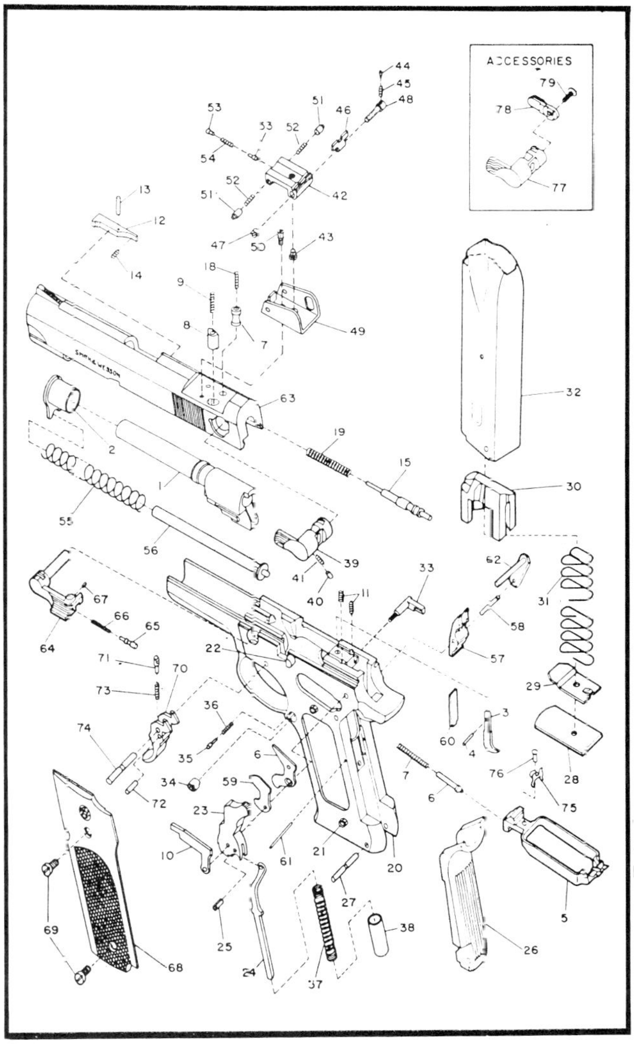

The parts of the M 659, identical to the M 459.

Smith & Wesson Pistols with adjustable sights

Model	439	539	639	459	559	659
Caliber	9 Para	9 Para	9 Para	9 Para	9 Para	9 Para
Magazine capacity	8	8	8	14	14	14
Barrel length	102 mm	102 mm	102 mm	102 mm	102 mm	102 mm
Overall length	189 mm	189 mm	189 mm	189 mm	189 mm	189 mm
Weight empty	822 g	1021 g	1021 g	850 g	1134 g	1134 g
Slide material	Steel	Steel	Stainless steel	Steel	Steel	Stainless steel
Frame material	Aluminum	Steel	Stainless steel	Aluminum	Steel	Stainless steel
Finish	Burnished*	Burnished	Satin	Burnished*	Burnished	Satin
Grip panels	Wood	Wood	Wood	Plastic	Plastic	Plastic

* alternatively burnished or nickel-plated

Smith & Wesson Pistols with Fixed Sights

Model	39	439	639	59	459	659	469	669
Caliber	9 Para	9 Para	9 Para	9 Para	9 Para	9 Para	9 Para	9 Para
Magazine capacity	8	8	8	14	14	14	12/20	12/20
Barrel length	102 mm	102 mm	102 mm	102 mm	102 mm	102 mm	89 mm	89 mm
Overall length	189 mm	189 mm	189 mm	189 mm	189 mm	189 mm	175 mm	175 mm
Weight empty	760 g	765 g	1021 g	790 g	794 g	1134 g	728 g	735 g
Sights	Laterally adjustable	Fixed	Fixed adjustable	Laterally	Fixed	Fixed	Fixed	Fixed
Slide material	Steel	Steel	Stainless steel	Steel	Steel	Stainless steel	Steel	Stainless steel
Frame material	Aluminum	Aluminum	Stainless steel	Aluminum	Aluminum	Stainless steel	Aluminum	Aluminum
Finish	Burnished*	Burnished*	Satin	Burnished*	Burnished*	Satin	Burnished**	Satin
Grip panels	Wood	Wood	Wood	Plastic	Plastic	Plastic	Delrin	Delrin

* Alternatively burnished or nickel-plated
** Alternatively burnished or matte nickel-plated

Model 469

With this small pistol in 9 mm PARA caliber, the firm of Smith & Wesson joined a timely trend, which was a very sensible business policy. In the USA, the firm of Devel marketed very good small versions of the Model 39 and 59 pistols, which were made smaller whenever possible. They were handy weapons for high-performance cartridges.

With the Model 39 the manufacturer had recognized the requirements of the market. It possessed Browning-type locking along with modern safety systems and a double action trigger, already familiar in Walther pistols. A short time later, the Model 39 evolved into the Model 59 with its larger magazine capacity. It carried 14 rounds and corresponded completely to the previous model technically. Later other modifications were made to the model in terms of the sights and an improved extractor, while both pistols were finally offered alternatively with steel receivers or made completely of stainless steel, like the Model 639, but otherwise technically identical.

The little Mini Gun is a production alternative to the tuned pistols. The hammer has just been cocked. The magazine holds 12 cartridges.

The right side of the same pistol. At rest, the hammer does not stick out of the slide; only when on the safety rest does it project somewhat.

The mechanics of the Mini Gun are no different from

The dismantled Mini Gun. The grip panels of textured neoprene are held on without screws.

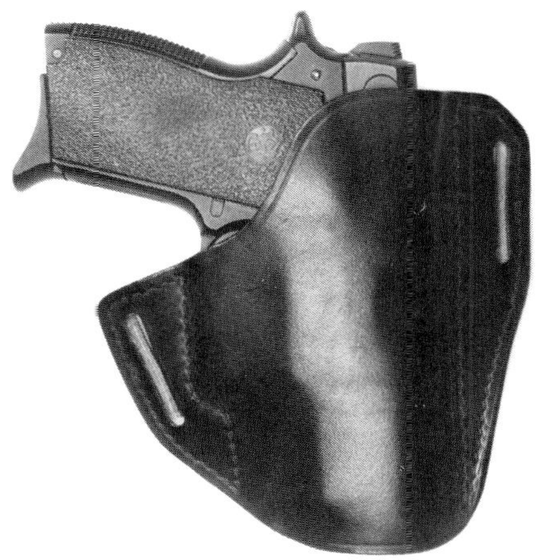

In its holster, the weapon does not protrude much; it is almost ideal for concealed carrying. The hammer is on the safety rest.

those of previous pistols. The mounting of the barrel in the front of the slide, though, is different. The problematic guiding housing has finally been eliminated, and the barrel passes instead through the exactly fitted opening in the slide. For this purpose the barrel has not been made cylindrical all the way to the muzzle, but has rather been turned with a bulge so that it can always fit into its mounting without problems. The receiver (made of aluminum) has been shortened, so that only 12 cartridges will now fit into it. But the magazine base has a wide, curved extension to fit into the hand, and the pistol fits into a large normal hand very well.

The trigger guard was bowed slightly, and its front is equipped with a very sharp-angled grid pattern to give a finger a secure hold. It is somewhat too sharp-angled for an ungloved hand, and will cause discomfort to the finger that rests on it with every shot.

New trends were also kept in mind when the trigger tongue, which is about 10 mm wide, was designed. It is no longer grooved, but pleasantly smooth. The trigger itself has a rather long but not necessarily squeaky working path. In any case, some careful work by a gunsmith would do well here.

The most notable feature of the Mini Gun is its hammer, which might be better called a striking-piece. It has no spur and fits smoothly into the rear of the slide so that it cannot hook on anything when the gun is drawn. It would be necessary to fire the first shot by using the double action trigger, which can be done if time is short. Whoever would still like to cock it can use a little trick. One pulls the trigger back a little way until the striking-piece stops at the safety rest. Now, since it is well ridged, one can grasp it with a finger and cock it completely.

To keep the grip from getting too thick, screws for the grip panels have been eliminated. The very flat panels with their too-smooth textured surfaces clamp over the receiver. For the admirer of well-finished walnut wood this means that such grip panels can be made for the Mini Gun only with a great deal of effort, if at all.

By mid-1984 the first additional variations of the Mini Gun had been announced. Smith & Wesson produced a small series with expensive engraving and a matte nickel-plated finish. For 1985 another version, with a steel receiver, was announced in the specialist press. This

The matte nickel-plated version with TAC preceding the number. It was soon followed by a version with a stainless steel slide. After this is printed, there will definitely also be a version made completely of stainless steel.

The Mini Gun when open. Note the bulge around the muzzle. Unlike the other pistols, the Mini Gun has no additional barrel housing at the front of the slide.

was a sensible alternative, for not all shooters like aluminum, on the one hand because of the likelihood of abrasion in case the material is not hardened enough on the surface, and on the other because these small, light pistols have a hard recoil that slams them into the hand with every shot.

Before the end of 1985 another variation of the little Mini Gun appeared. Under the model designation of M. 669, the pistol was offered with a stainless steel slide and a receiver with a matte nickel-plated finish. In optical terms this is not very striking. Up to this point, many shooters were still hoping for a rust-free all-steel pistol in this handy size. The safety is located on both sides of this new version, and is assembled from the already mentioned available parts, which can also be added to other S&W pistols with little effort. Whether it will go into series production one day is not yet known, which also applies to a 20-shot magazine for the M 469/669.

Also of interest are the letters that the manufacturer stamps on these pistols in front of the numbers. TAB is found before the number of a burnished version with aluminum frame, TAC before the number of a matte nickel-plated version, also with an aluminum frame, and TAE on the version with the satin-finished aluminum frame and the stainless steel slide.

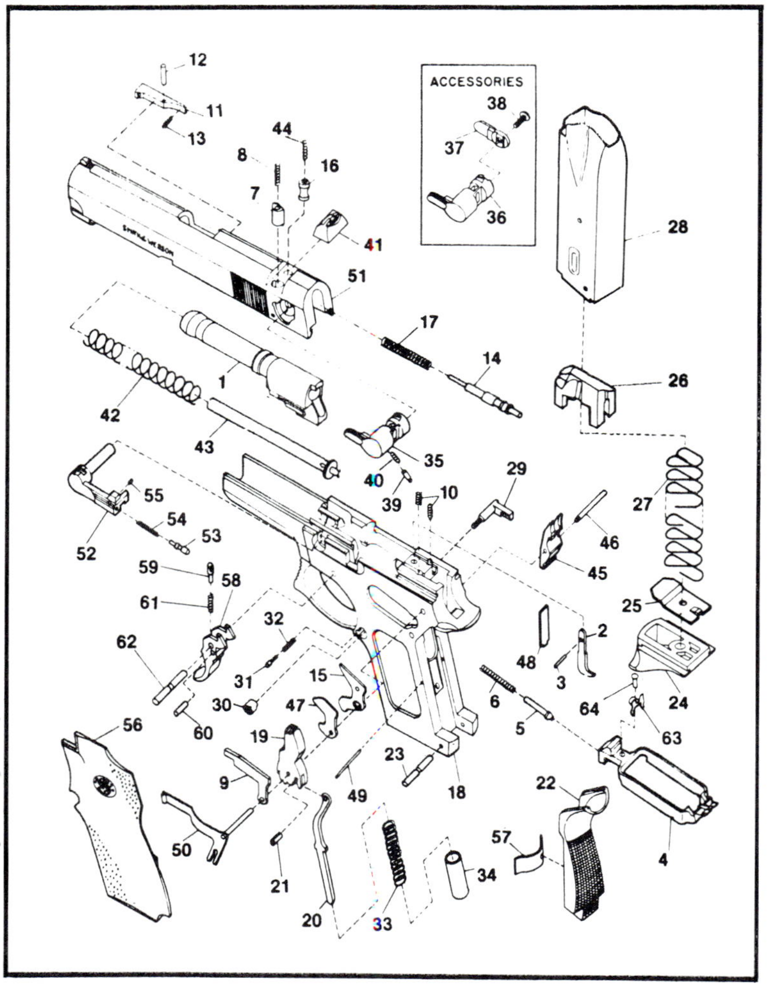

Technically the Mini Gun is very similar to the M 459, but the hammer and type of grip panel attachment are different.

9 mm PARABELLUM SPORT PISTOLS

Sport shooting with pistols or even revolvers in 9 mm Parabellum or 7.65 mm Parabellum caliber was formerly not very widespread in Germany. Very practical problems, in part, stand in the way, for participation in sport shooting exclusively in these calibers and training regularly in advance would certainly be too much of a financial burden for many shooters. Aside from that, one would not expect such high scores from oneself and such a weapon as from someone with a weapon in .22 LR caliber, for the latter weapon only starts to perform really well after 10,000 rounds, or at least this is the opinion of numerous large-caliber shooters. In modern times as well, it cannot be denied that considerations as to the users of shooting ranges and damage to the environment have become a further problem. Therefore it makes sense to get involved in sport shooting by doing the greatest part of one's technical training in the smaller calibers. Pistols in 9 mm Parabellum caliber are not welcomed at many shooting ranges — there shooters are inclined to be thankful that they can shoot in peace and without restrictions with small-caliber weapons. Thus such groups and organizations can rarely offer any help in trying to obtain official permission. In many places too, the firing of jacketed bullets at shooting ranges is forbidden, though it does not always make sense, probably only when one considers the heightened danger of ricochets. The 9 mm Parabellum is after all a cartridge with a jacketed bullet, and all the tests with lead bullets have not had much effect. With lead bullets, excellent precision can be attained with a good weapon, but always only for a short time, until the barrel is badly leaded up. Somewhat better results can be attained with a barrel that is designed and built for lead bullets, but this is not a cure-all, as leading-up takes place with some delay, but it does take place.

The cartridge is still beset with an unproved prejudice: that it is only a military cartridge and, as such, is not inclined to provide sporting precision. That is certainly true when it refers to older supplies of ammunition that were not made according to present-day norms. It also applies without reservation to many of the pistols that were simply not made for such precision or that were good enough when they were new but are now more or less worn out. If one takes as an example a high-priced pistol, one of them being the SIG 210, and fires several cartridges of present-day production from a shooting machine at a target from a range of 25 meters, one will find out that with many types the ten circle will always and the inner circle will often be hit, based on series of ten shots apiece under unchanged conditions.

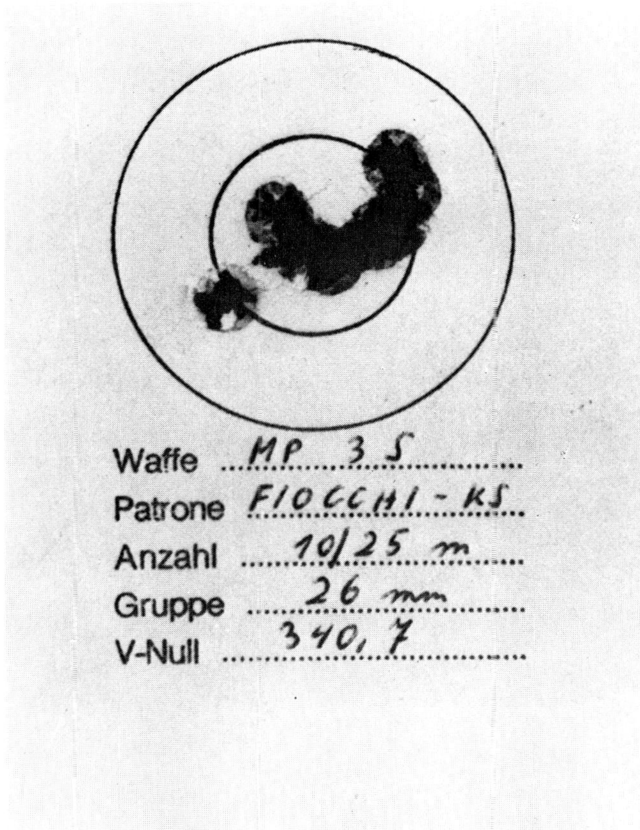

Sporting performance in 9 mm Parabellum caliber is attainable with many cartridges and several weapons. The picture shows ten shots from a Benelli MP 3 S, fired from a shooting machine at 25 meters.

Further attempts with self-loading cartridges, as well as tests with the Benelli MP 3 S sport pistol, will surely attest to a high level of performance with this cartridge, but the weapon must be a good one, or it must be suitable for sport shooting. While an improved grip, a polished trigger with a trigger stop, and an adjustable sight may possibly create an atmosphere of sportiness, they do not necessarily create a high-performance sport pistol. As for the possible shooting performance, the prejudice against the cartridge may have been superseded by now. The same is true of the 7.65 mm Parabellum, which can provide excellent scores with pistols made for them.

Large-caliber sport shooting was limited too long to the concept of the .45 ACP caliber and originated in an era when there was scarcely a pistol available except the tuned Colt Government or the production Gold Cup. Today large-caliber sport shooting, at least under the aegis of the Deutsche Schützenbund, has developed in the direction of the .32 caliber Smith & Wesson long Wadcutter, while the .38 SPL caliber has become less and less important. But shooting by the rules of the Schützenbund is only one part of the existing possibilities, for there are also other organizations that offer interested shooters the opportunity, for in the end, shooting can and does (sometimes) offer pleasure. It is a pleasure to see with what an easygoing and comradely atmosphere other organizations conduct their events without having to make any compromises for safety's sake.

Target for pistols, 25-50 meter range

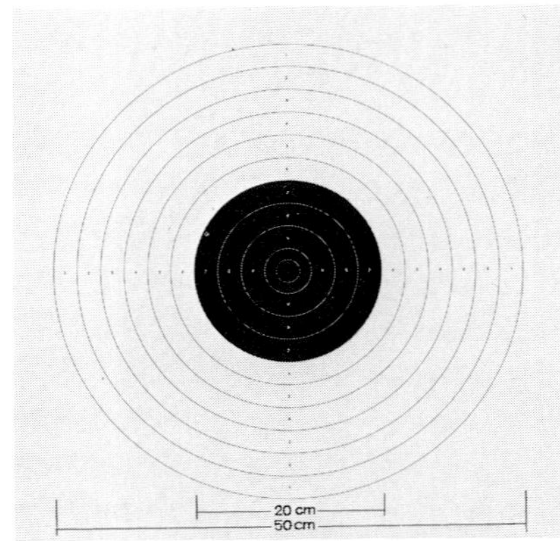

Pistol target, 25-50 meter range, to the standards of the International Shooters' Union and the sporting rules of the German Schützenbund.

Format: 55 x 55 cm Circles: 10 Total diameter: 500 mm Ring diameter: 200 mm Diameter of 10 ring: 50 mm Diameter of "Mouche" in 10 ring: 25 mm Ring 1-9 width: 25 mm each

Shooting by Deutsche Schützenbund Rules

Revolvers or self-loading pistols in 7.62 mm to 11.5 mm (.32 to .45) calibers are allowed if their unloaded weight including magazine and case-collecting systems (such as GSP) do not weigh more than 1400 grams. The trigger resistance at the moment a shot is fired may not be lower than 1.36 kp. Including accessories (other than the case-collecting system) must fit into a case with the internal dimensions of 300 x 150 x 50 mm. Up to .38 (9.7 mm) caliber, the maximum barrel length is 153 mm; for .44 and .45 (11.0 and 11.5 mm) calibers the maximum length is 166 mm. A minimum barrel length for revolvers is also stipulated; they may not be shorter than 100 mm. Thus the Schützenbund has finally recognized reality.

Regulations for ammunition are: Central-fire cartridges only with lead bullets. Jacketed and semi-jacketed bullets are not allowed. The shooting program consists of two parts, precision shooting and duel shooting. One shoots in a one-handed standing position, at a distance of 25 meters, at a ring target or the central part of a figure target, which has been used exclusively since January 1, 1985.

Precision shooting includes individual series of five shots each in six minutes. According to one's class, it can be 15 or 30 rounds. The duel shooting has strict time limits. The targets turn toward the shooter for a space of three seconds and then turn away for a pause of seven seconds. The shooter fires at only one target (unlike rapid-fire pistol practice) and has only three seconds of time in all. This is a type of shooting for mixed temperaments, and since both parts are counted in the score without differentiation, a shooter can make up for a poor score in precision shooting with a good one in duel shooting, or vice versa.

Shooting by BDS Rules

The BDS — Bund Deutscher Schützen — is a specialist organization for large-caliber sport shooting, has worked out its own program and set up regulations that are as complex as they are incomprehensible. For lack of space, the full extent of their possibilities cannot be given here.

Interested parties may apply to the appropriate business offices, for it appears today that all their rules are in a state of flux and have not yet taken their final form. In any case, an additional opening for sport shooting with large-caliber pistols is available, with shooting divided by caliber groups and types of ammunition, such as Magnum ammunition, reloaded Magnum cartridges, normal types or special ammunition. In any case, the interested party can make rewarding contacts with the groups and units of the BDS.

Shooting by BDMP Rules

The BDMP — Bund der Militär- und Polizeischützen — has set up a well-balanced program for the sporting use of rifles, pistols and revolvers and conducts well-organized shoots on national and international levels. Activities are provided for service pistols (DP 1 and DP 2) and sport pistols (SP).

Service Pistol 1

All unmodified service pistols are allowed. No adjustable sights, trigger weights not under 1360 grams, no shaped or combat grips. Calibers from 7.62 mm to .455. All standard production ammunition is allowed, with all types of bullets, including bullets with full jacket, semi-jacket, or galvanized coating.

Not allowed are Wadcutter cartridges — the charge may not be so weak that the repeating function fails.

Shooting may be done with one or both hands, from a distance of 25 meters, at the UIT ring target, with a shooting score of 15 shots in three series of five shots apiece in six minutes.

Service Pistol 2

All service pistols are allowed, with and without technical modifications. The sights may be adjustable, and contrast sights are allowed. The minimum trigger weight is 1360 grams, and a trigger stop is allowed.

The production grip panels may be replaced by better ones, though sport grips (with adjustable handholds) are not allowed. The calibers range from .32 to .455, and all types of bullets except the Wadcutter are allowed.

As in the Service Pistol 1 class, shooting is done from a distance of 25 meters at the UIT ring target, with 15 shots in three series of five shots each within six minutes.

Sport Pistol

All pistols and revolvers from .32 to .455 calibers are allowed. The weapons may be set up like sport pistols or revolvers according to the rules of the Deutsche Schützenbund — this applies to the type of sight, grip and barrel length (to a maximum of 153 mm). With an unloaded magazine the weapon may not weigh more than 1400 grams, and the grip may not be wider than 50 mm.

Benelli MP 3 S

On the basis of the Model B 76 pistol, Benelli developed two sport pistols, one in 9 mm Parabellum caliber and the other in .32 S&W long WC. The two weapons can barely be told apart externally, as only their locking systems are different. The .32 caliber version can get by with an unlocked mass breech, but the version in 9 mm caliber has the typical Benelli locking system using the swinging bolt at the top.

A pistol built on this basis has a very noteworthy advantage for the sport shooter or reloader who strives for the highest precision: The barrel is screwed fast in the receiver, and any play between any parts of a bolt system cannot work itself out, as such parts are not necessary. Tests with a shooting machine were able to prove precisely this, for even with an SIG 210 such a remarkable achievement is scarcely or not at all possible. Of all the weapons tested to date, the MP 3 S sport pistol in both calibers has shown the best performance. Only in .32 caliber has the sport pistol by Erma of Dachau been able to attain closer groups.

The entire problem of whether or not to use a lead barrel can be ignored here for the most part. The barrel profile is laid out, and the workmanship on the inner surfaces is so good that, even after shooting long series of lead bullets, no lead deposits were visible or measurable. The target pictures shown for the 9 mm version were all attained with lead bullets — with jacketed bullets the groups were not quite so close, though in many cases still within the area of the inner ten, the "Mouche." Since the barrel with fixed mounting also offers no further sources of error in testing, it will be referred to again in the "Reloading" chapter in order to show how great the difference in performance ultimately can be in conjunction with types and quantities of powder.

Back to the barrel with fixed mounting. It is screwed into a carrier piece pinned to the receiver, and a wrench

The Benelli MP 3 S with added shaped grip without handhold attachment. The finger grooves are allowed again, after many years.

The right side of the MP 3 S, an elegant pistol in typical Italian style.

with a width of 14 mm is needed to remove it. Without any great effort, the installation of a differently profiled barrel or a 7.65 mm Parabellum caliber barrel would be possible at any time. The barrel is "only" 143 mm long and does not utilize the whole allowable maximum length.

Over the part of the barrel that extends up out of the closed slide, a muzzle weight has been pushed and held in place with a set screw. Two small extensions on its underside reach under the front of the receiver and provide for correct centering during assembly. At the same time, the front weight carries the bar foresight, lightly cut at the rear; there is no way to change the foresight. It has been sacrificed for the advantage of a good view all around.

The trigger, which is limited here to the single-action function, is different from that of the normal B 76. The hammer has such a flattened safety rest that the sear can slide out of the position when the trigger is pulled. This does not appear to be advantageous, but anyone who practices regularly can use this trigger, with its release from the former safety rest, very well for dry practice.

The MP 3 S has a relatively steep grip, set at an angle of 65 degrees, which is no different from the grips of many other typical pistols. A shaped grip with clearly formed finger grooves and a sufficiently wide thumb groove has been attached. With this grip one does not have the comfort of a weapon with an adjustable grip, but in spite of that the grip offers a good and slide-free handhold. The manufacturer alternatively offers a prepared raw component that can be made into a very personal grip which will fit ideally with a bit of skill.

The trigger can not be modified in terms of weight, and at 1500 grams it operates quickly and smoothly — one should not only regard a trigger with finely adjustable weight as an advantage, as a pistol in this caliber should not have too light a trigger. Its clean, frictionless functioning and effective stop-screw are much more important. The stop-screw installed here is somewhat heavy and hard to adjust, since it is not secured further, it must be affixed with adhesive after the right setting has been found and tested.

The MP 3 S fits nicely in the hand and is more than friendly when firing. There is no hard blow on the hand, and the pistol fires remarkably softly. It is remarkable too that it still functions well when very light charges are fired, so light that they will quickly cause other pistols to stop operating reliably.

With self-loaded cartridges, groups of ten shots can be fired with the machine down to 16 mm (with the caliber reduced from 9 mm). The tests with factory-loaded cartridges, all with jacketed bullets, gave similarly good results: GECO FJ (Full-Jacketed) with 36 mm at 356 m/s, Winchester FJ with 49 mm at 351 m/s, Hirtenberger FJ with 57 mm at 344 m/s, and Flocchi FJ-conehead with 26 mm and 28 mm at 340 m/s. These are results that effectively contradict all earlier objections to the performance potential of the Para cartridge.

Improvements could be made to this pistol's sights, which appear to be rather decorative and filigreed.

The dismantled MP 3 S. The fixed barrel is a great advantage for good and reliable shooting performance. First-class results in tests were obtained with this pistol.

Whether they are still sturdy after long series can be shown only after long experience with this otherwise quite good sport pistol.

Technical Data: Benelli MP 3-S

Caliber	9 mm Parabellum/.32 S & W long WC
Magazine capacity	5 cartridges (with limiter)
Overall length	235 mm
Height/width	142 mm/50 mm
Barrel length	143 mm
Sight line	178 mm
Material/finish	Steel/burnished
Trigger	Single-action only, ca. 1500 grams
Grip panels	Shaped walnut
Accessories	Case, magazine, tool, cleaning rod, brushes

FN-GP Competition

In 1977 news of a GP modified for sporting use first became public. The manufacturer thereby followed a path that was as effective as it was economical, for it was based on the reliable High Power, with only its sights, barrel and side safety changed.

The barrel is 150 mm long and bears a removable weight at the front, held in place by two set screws on the sides. The front weight is simultaneously the base of the bar foresight fixed to it. The adjustable sight is taken from the small-caliber "International" sport pistol and is mounted advantageously deep in the slide. There has always been criticism that this sight was scarcely more than an adjustable sheet-metal hook, but as always, the sport version of the GP thus fits very deeply in the hand, and the distance between the back of the hand and the sight has been kept as small as possible.

The side safety has been improved, as its lever has been extended further to the front.

The sport version of the FN High Power with a 150 mm barrel and added front weight, plus deeply inset adjustable sight.

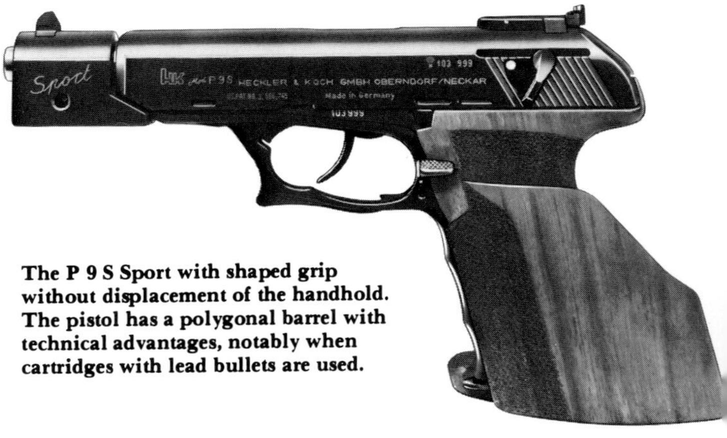

The P 9 S Sport with shaped grip without displacement of the handhold. The pistol has a polygonal barrel with technical advantages, notably when cartridges with lead bullets are used.

This pistol has not become very widespread in German-speaking areas, however in France and Belgium it enjoys a much greater popularity. Sport shooters who have had the opportunity to use it judge it to be well-balanced and precise-shooting, plus well-made and pleasant to shoot with.

The pistol reaches an overall length of 230 mm, is 128 mm high including the sight, and 35 mm wide at the grip. The magazine, like that of the normal GP, holds 13 cartridges in two rows. The sport version weighs only 980 grams when unloaded.

P 9 S Sport

For some years Heckler & Koch has offered a sporting version based on the P 9 S in 9 mm Parabellum caliber. The technology and the type of locking system have already been described elsewhere, so that we need only note the differences here. In various production lots there have been sport pistols with a longer barrel, a slide without a foresight but with an adjustable sight and a well-formed sport grip that makes an adjustable hand-hold unnecessary. It fits into the hand very well and can be supplied in three different sizes.

In greater quantities, the sport pistol still has a normal slide with fixed sight and a 102 mm barrel — the combat grip panels made of plastic are provided for this version.

The barrel of the sport pistol is 140 mm long and has a 190 gram front weight with foresight mounted on it. It is adjusted with the help of an adjusting tool that comes with it, and sets it firmly by tightening the screw at the bottom of the barrel weight. Even after long series of shots, no loosening of this type of attachment has been found. In the trigger guard, similarly to the early P 9 with single-action trigger, a trigger stop, called the "Abzugstopper" (trigger stopper) by the manufacturer, has been installed. If one wants to use a double action trigger, then the trigger stopper must be swung out of the way, thus providing a longer path for the trigger tongue to follow. Its adjustment is problem-free and is done by using a set screw at the side, and after the stopper has been put into its position, it is screwed fast.

For further fine adjustment, and not for regulation of the trigger weight, a fine adjustment can be installed in the receiver. For this modification, a different interrupter (part 44 in the P 9 S drawing on page 39) is needed. Up in its transverse step there is a fine-threaded screw inset, which when screwed down presses on the rest lever (equivalent to the sear, part 42) and moves it forward slightly. Thus it does not reach quite as far into the striking rest of the hammer, and the trigger can be released more quickly. An adjustment in this area is not without danger, for if it adjusted too narrowly, the weapon can and will double. The grip of the rest lever on the rest of the hammer is reduced by turning it to the right and increased by turning to the left.

Sport Parabellum by Mauser

After the production of the legendary Parabellum pistol had resumed successfully at the Mauser works in Oberndorf, and in answer to great popular demand, various experiments began at the beginning of the 1970s. At this time prototypes of "pocket pistols", shortened pistols with otherwise unchanged mechanics, were made. Around 1973 the first sport pistol was ready for public showing: the Mauser-Sport in 9 mm Parabellum caliber. The high precision inherent in this design was well known. Tests of the Model 06/29 in Switzerland gave the best and most encouraging results. During and after the war, the Parabellum pistol had been able to score spectacular performances again and again, and in 1949 it was used by Swiss sport shooters in the world championship. At first it was attempted to preserve the 120 mm barrel length, and the pistol was given different sights, but that was not enough to meet sporting requirements. The Mauser-Sport was equipped with a receiver without a grip safety, a slightly modified fork housing and a thick cylindrical barrel. The slightly less powerful 7.65 mm Parabellum cartridge does not perform without problems in such a weighty barrel, for the recoil is influenced by the mass of the barrel. This version has a barrel flattened on the sides, and in both pistols the barrel is 110 mm long, thus well below the usual barrel length of sport pistols.

An adjustable sight was carefully added to the rear joint, and the trigger was reworked. The trigger tongue has two small screws in its upper extension, allowing an exact adjustment of the two side paths, but not allowing an exact and, above all, play-free setting required for sport pistols. The easily adjustable trigger can only be seen as a makeshift solution. It is the trigger of the Parabellum pistol that stands in the way of sporting use, for it is imprecise and indefinable in character. This is brought about by the transition of the horizontal movement into a vertical-lateral pressure to free the firing pin. The trigger can be improved only slightly, however modification in the nature of a real sport trigger is barely possible.

Another handicap of this sport pistol is the attachment of the sights. Many shooters have doubts about their weapons when the sight line is interrupted while shooting. This interruption results when the sight is mounted on a part of the weapon that moves when a shot is fired. This is exactly what happens here, for the rear

The Mauser Sport in 9 mm Parabellum caliber, with a thick round barrel. It is long since a thing of the past.

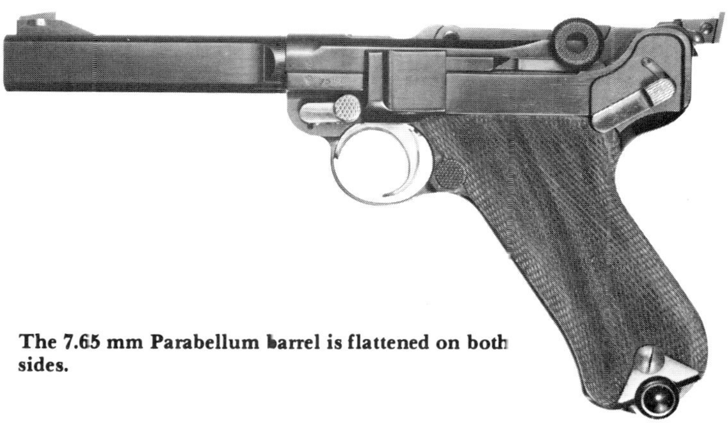

The 7.65 mm Parabellum barrel is flattened on both sides.

The sight is mounted in the rear joint. Such an interrupted sight line is generally regarded as a disadvantage.

joint makes a horizontal movement first and then a vertical one.

Thus the Mauser-Sport should not necessarily be regarded or used as a sport pistol. It is simply too delicate for regular use, and whoever owns one of these rare pieces today would do well to maintain it as a valuable collector's item. The version shown here, in 7.65 mm caliber, could be bought at the end of 1975 for a price of just over 2500 DM, and was the last pistol of its kind from the Oberdorf works. At that time a normal Parabellum pistol cost some 1200 DM, today the normal version is available for prices just under 4000 DM. So a Mauser-Sport is just too valuable to shoot with.

The Peters Multical 07 prototype, a pistol for firing several calibers. The barrel utilizes its full length. This is a high-performance weapon.

Peters Multical 07

During the past years the firm of Peters-Stahl in Paderborn was always offered a few technical surprises. Among the firm's products are the switching systems described elsewhere, that turn a solid basic weapon into a high-performance sport and training pistol. They include alternate barrels for numerous production pistols, plus tuning parts such as the fine-adjustment Peters sights with their notably low installation height.

Before the Multical 07 went into production, the locking principle used in it had already been tested in

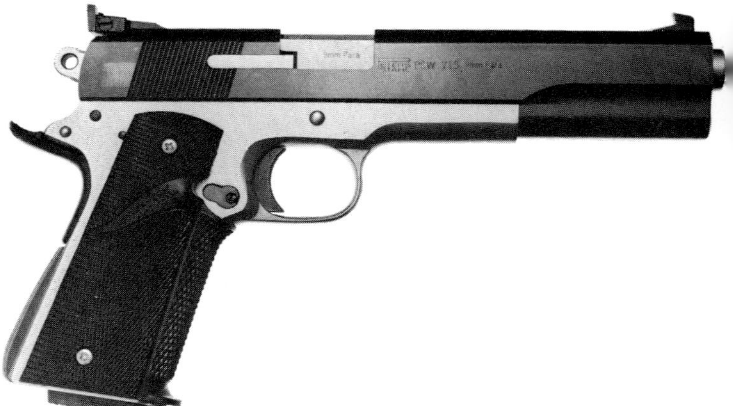

The right side of the Multical 07. Almost all the weapon's parts are made or at least considerably modified by Peters-Stahl.

The SIG-Hämmerli P 240 can be modified to 9 mm Parabellum caliber with the PSW I-S.

The Multical 07 when open. The lengthened moving parts and grip safety are advantageous.

another weapon and offered for it as a self-contained system.

One of the pistols highly prized by active sport shooters was and still is the SIG-Hämmerli P 240 in .38 SPL-WC or .32 S & W long WC calibers, and there is a switching system available for the .22 LR cartridge. The switching system made by Peters for the P 240 allows the 9 mm Parabellum cartridge to be fired with acceptable sporting precision. As marketed, it consists of a slide that fits the weapon precisely, with an overall length of 235 mm, a well-fitting barrel with a length of 148 mm, an encapsulated recoil spring with its guiding rod, and a magazine suitable for 9 mm Parabellum cartridges, plus an additional breech-holding lever that is used in making the switch. The close tolerances make fitting to the weapon in question or to its receiver necessary, a task that is carried out at the Peters-Stahl factory. Simply buying it "off the rack" is neither sensible nor, when buying new, possible.

The barrel with its rounded hexagonal polygon-profile has a heavy block at its rear to lock it to the slide; the locking areas in the slide as well as on the barrel itself are kept at angles, which counteracts any possible twisting of the barrel during firing. This specialty, along with the basis of shooting performance, is found in the switching system here, as well as in the Multical 07, in

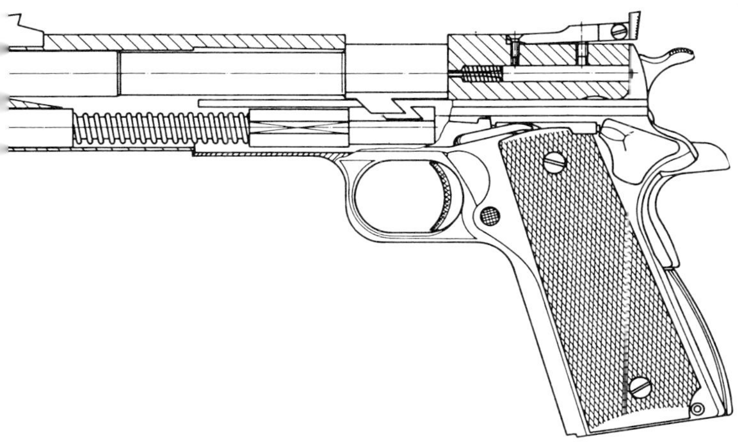

Cutaway drawing of the Peters Multical 07 with its improved barrel guide.

the manner of guiding the barrel and the sinking of the barrel to initiate unlocking, which takes place only when the bullet has actually left the barrel. The guiding rod of the recoil spring is fitted into a block which is mounted snugly in the receiver and held there by the pivot of the catch lever. At first the barrel and slide glide backward together in a straight line, but then the angled surface of the block pushes the barrel downward over its hook, the system unlocks, and the slide goes farther back as usual. The advantage is provided by the high degree of precision in production; only in this way can the expected performance actually be attained, for it is the play in the parts involved in locking inside a production self-loading pistol that is a major cause of insufficient shooting performance.

The locking principle of the Multical 07 is not different. What is new is that the shooter has a variety of calibers to choose from, and yet the weapon itself is marketed in only one caliber. One must also but the desired adapting set. Using the same frame and slide, it is possible to use .45 ACP, 9 mm Parabellum, .38 Super and .38 SPL WC cartridges.

It is not at all easy to find a system that, while using the same slide and recoil spring, will compensate for the completely different gas pressures of the various cartridges. Peters tries to do this by using locking times of varying length. The hook under the barrel is different, being longer for the .38 Super and 9 mm Parabellum calibers and shorter for the .45 ACP barrel. Thus the longer hook reaches the deflecting angled surface sooner and the locking time is therefore shorter. The situation is very different for the .38 SPL cartridge, where a spring-mass bolt is sufficient. This barrel has an even longer hook and thus depends only on the guiding surface without being guided downward.

A further problem is that of differing diameters of cartridge-case bases. With a fixed strike plate no adaptation is possible. In addition to the usual extractor hook, Peters also gave the system a so-called multi-claw, which attaches to the various strike plates under the pressure of a spring. All the barrels for the Multical 07 have a uniform length of 152 mm and the polygonal profile introduced by Peters, which has six segments and a rifling length of 450 mm, turning to the right. They are hardened by a nitrate bath, their workmanship is excellent, and so is their shooting performance.

The receivers correspond to those of the Colt Government and are made out of raw castings, finished to be tolerance-free and neatly turned out. The moving parts are obtained from various manufacturers and finished. The impressive pistol is marketed in either a burnished finish or with a stainless steel grip, the latter

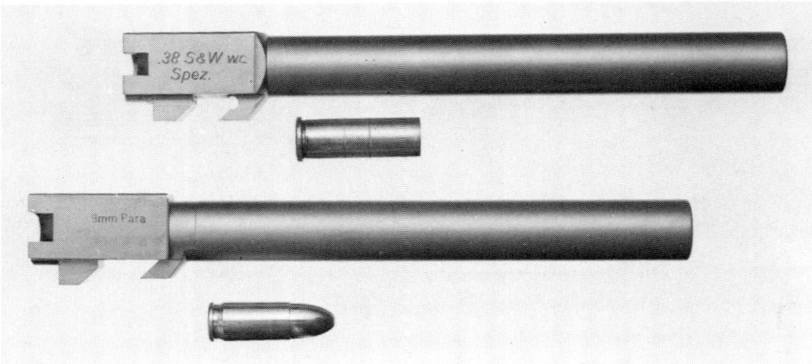

The barrels are made to the smallest tolerances and bolt neatly into the slide with their angled end-pieces.

at no extra charge.

The magazines are made by Colt as long as they are for the .38 SPL cartridge; the other magazines are obtained from suppliers. According to caliber, they hold five (.38 SPL), seven (.45 ACP) or nine cartridges. The pistol has an overall length of 242 mm and weighs 1290 grams unloaded in .45 ACP form; it is not a light weapon, but is a solid sport pistol. It is optionally available in production form with several other improvements, such as a lengthened safety, lengthened catch lever, round Commander hammer and lengthened grip safety.

SIG 210

The name of SIG 210 is linked with the concept of the large-caliber pistol with sporting potential. In all versions, and also in both calibers, the 210, even with the original barrel, gives such excellent shooting performance that it can be put to sporting use unconditionally. The reason for the tremendous shooting potential is the precise preparation, above all the tipping of the barrel, which works so favorably that no disturbance of the bullet's trajectory is possible in any case. In practice this means that one can load cartridges for the 210 down to the lower limit. Thus good precision is achieved which does not result in the elimination of the repeating function, whereas other pistols no longer function with such weak charges.

The version with the 120 mm barrel (made for jacketed bullets) is optionally available with fixed sights or the added adjustable sight. In this version, depending on the cost of the surface preparation, a relatively economical entry into large-caliber shooting is possible.

The 210-6 version, with a barrel length of 120 mm, is somewhat more comfortable. This version has the sport trigger with trigger stop, the lock is held play-free in the frame by an additional screw, and the sight is adjustable in all directions. The adjustable sight, raised in a simple manner, does not really live up to either the quality nor the price of the weapon. Any other manufacturer would disapprove of such an unesthetic and sportingly unfavorable solution, but here it is part of a "legend in steel" and is willingly accepted.

The SIG 210 with its 150 mm barrel offers superb performance in 9 mm Parabellum caliber. The "Target" version shown here was made only in small numbers.

An older 210-5 in 7.65 mm Parabellum caliber.

The type most thoroughly prepared for sporting use is the 210-5 version, with its 150 mm barrel and customary adjustable sight. The somewhat longer barrel adds a barely discernable gain in precision, however the balance of the weapon is improved by it, and the sight line is favorably lengthened. The barrel has threading around the muzzle area, and the center ring with its exchangeable bar sight is held here between two screwed-on rings held in place with set-screws. A steel wedge inserted from the side prevents play or unwanted twisting of the foresight ring. This solution is technically simple and effective, and a more complex one is not necessary.

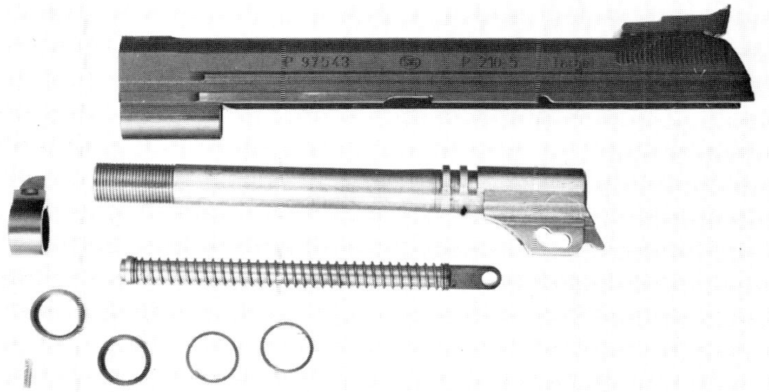

The slide and barrel of the SIG 210-5 Target sport pistol.

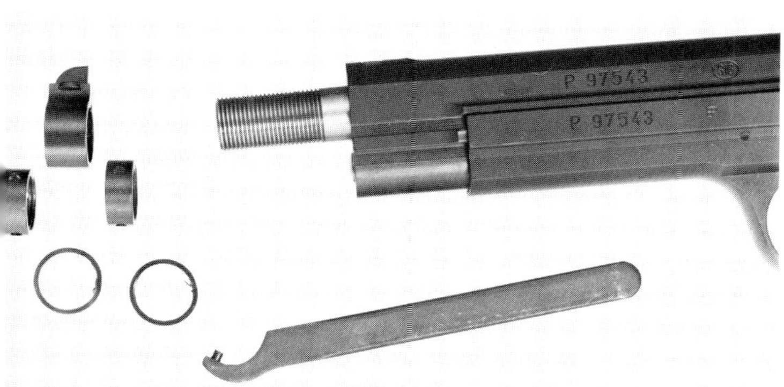

Before removing the slide, the foresight must be removed. With its screws, it is absolutely fixed to the barrel.

The character of the sport model is emphasized by the availability of effective additional components. The shooter who wants to use lead bullets often can obtain a special barrel for this type of bullet. The parts of the sights, wider leaves for the sight and various foresights in a succession of heights, are exchangeable, thus any personal adjustment of the sights is possible.

An interchangeable system for use with the .22 LR cartridge is available. It is not only as expensive as a good complete sport pistol, but it also delivers comparable performance. Thus the owner of a 210 equipped with an adjustable sight and an interchangeable system can take part in all kinds of sport shooting without having to accept a decrease in shooting performance.

The alternative barrels made by the firm of Peters-Stahl are described elsewhere. They show a clear improvement to the already excellent shooting performance and, above all, offer an economical alternative.

This SIG 210 was modified by Oschatz for sporting combat shooting (photo by S.F. Hübner).

Sport Revolvers for 9 mm Parabellum

The availability of revolvers for the 9 mm Parabellum is limited, with a few models being on the market, presumably for defensive use. Sport revolvers exclusively for the 9 mm cartridge have not been made to date, as there seems to be a lack of confidence in their performance potential.

The author's own tests (see revolvers) of a Combat Magnum Model 19 with an added cylinder from a 9 mm caliber revolver showed that the attainable performance is not at all bad. It is surprising how pleasantly and softly the cartridges could be fired from a revolver with a six-inch barrel. Then too, a reloader has an added advantage, for one can easily fire wrongly, and too weakly charged cartridges from the revolver.

Tests of a Korth .357 Magnum caliber revolver with an added 9 mm Parabellum changeable cylinder also showed good performance, though no groups were attained such as can be attained with weakly-loaded .38 WC cartridges. At a distance of 25 meters, factory-made cartridges such as the GECO FJ, the Hirtenberger Combat FJ and the Lapua FJ repeatedly scored groups between 26 and 38 mm. This is quite sufficient for sporting use, even if the performance-oriented shooter will and must regard that as a mere borderline case in shooting technology. The 9 mm cartridge offers no particular advantages. A revolver with an changeable cylinder for the purpose will basically enhance only the weapon's versatility.

Manurhin produces a wide assortment of revolvers for sport and defense on the basis of the MR 73 system. In so doing, Manurhin has become the first manufacturer to get away from the six-inch barrel, so as to give the shooter somewhat more freedom in the formation of the shaped grip. Of course revolvers with six-inch barrels are also offered, but the barrel lengths of 5.25 and 5.75 inches are intended more for the sport shooter, and the small differences in length do not make any noticeable difference in the attainable shooting performance. The technology of the MR 73 series is described elsewhere; a table here sums up the presently available variants.

Sport revolvers in 9 mm Parabellum caliber are not only a new alternative for the performance shooter, but even more of a sensible expansion and enrichment of what is presently available.

Modelle		Kaliber	Wechsel trommel	Gewicht ungeladen in g	Gesamtlänge der Waffe in mm	Lauflänge in mm	Drall in mm	Visier	Visierlänge in mm	Abzugsgewicht single Action in g	Abzugsgewicht double Action in g
MR 73 «POLICE» ET «DEFENSE»	2''1/2	.357 Mag .38 Sp	9 mm Para.	880	195	63	400	Fest	100	Maxi 2800	Maxi 4900
	3''			890	205	76	400		115		
	4''			950	233	102	400		140		
MR 73 «SPORT»	4''	.357 Mag .38 Sp	9 mm Para.	970	233	102	400	Einstellbar	142	Mini 1360	Maxi 4900
	5''1/4	357 Mag .38 Sp	9 mm Para.	1050	264	133	400		174		
	5''1/4	.32 Lg	—	1050	264	133	480		174		
	6''	.32 Lg	—	1070	283	152	480		193		
	6''	.357 Mag .38 Sp	9 mm Para.	1070	283	152	400		193		
	8''	.357 Mag .38 Sp	9 mm Para.	1170	334	203	400		250		
MR 73 «GENDARMERIE»	3'' à 8''	.357 Mag .38 Sp	9 mm Para.	ÄHNLISCHE TECHNISCHE DATEN WIE DIE «SPORT» MODELLE, MIT SCHMALES UND SEITLICH ABGERUNDETES KIMMENBLATT UND MIT SCHRÄGES KORN							
MR «LONG RANGE»	9''	.357 Mag .38 Sp	—	1300	360	229	476	Einstellbar	293	Mini 1360	—
MR «SILHOUETTE»	10''3/4		—	1428	424	273	476		337		
MR.32 MATCH	6''	.32 Lg	—	1080	275	152	480	Einstellbar	209	Mini 1360	—
MR.38 MATCH	5''3/4	.38 Sp	—	1080	276	146	476		210		

A chart offered by the Manurhin firm, its contents not corrected.

CONVERSION AND REDUCING SYSTEMS

The option of offering reducing systems for pistols in service, private or sporting use is very old, and for the 08 pistol in particular there have been numerous systems for 4 mm M 20 and .22 LR cartridges. Today too, a small-caliber conversion system is still a sensible alternative, for first of all, it allows economical shooting and thus far more frequent use of the weapon at a much lower cost for ammunition and with less mechanical damage to the weapon. When it is set up for the .22 LR cartridge, it can be fired on the usual ranges at distances up to 25 meters, and special safety provisions are not necessary, beyond the maintenance of generally good condition. At this time the question of noise also plays a major role, and some shooting ranges have had pressure put on them in the form of partially unjustified limitations on account of the emissions produced. Here the move to a smaller caliber can be a beneficial alternative, even though it has the disadvantage of changing the whole operation of the weapon and its shooting behavior.

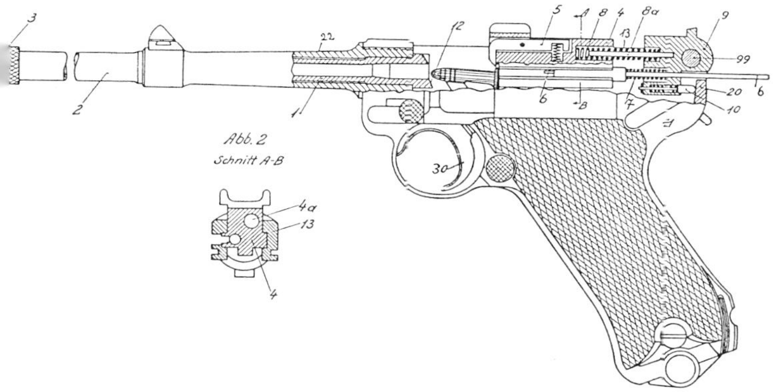

The ERMA factory, among others, made small bore conversion systems for the 08 pistol.

Drawing of the small bore conversion system of the 08 pistol, showing the wooden case and what is delivered in it.

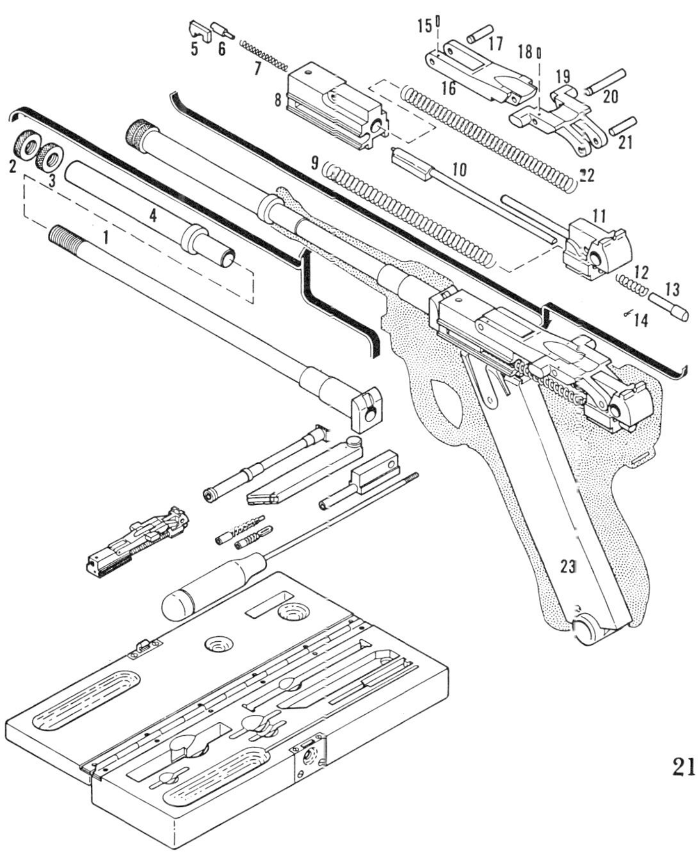

Systems for the Walther P 38

The P 38 can be used either as a production weapon or with an added conversion system, and no changes to the basic weapon are required to equip it for the smaller caliber. Externally the conversion system, and this applies in the same way to the standard .22 LR caliber P 38 pistol, can be recognized by the markings on the slide and the pierced bridge. What is different here is the cover plate, visible from above, which in this case is made

A .22 LR caliber P 38. This pistol has no signal rod, and the bridge on the slide is pierced.

somewhat shorter, and the safety indicator over the signal rod — the signal rod has not been built into the slide of the .22 version. The cutaway drawing also shows the different shape of the firing pin, as well as the loss of the swinging bolt.

After the system has been installed, the barrel is fixed in position, and only one of the two lateral recoil springs is used, which is why one of the guiding tabs at the bottom of the slide has been machined off.

The testing of a proven system shows it to be very good. From a sitting position at a distance of 15 meters, the ten circle of a customary ring target could always be hit with all the cartridges tested, a performance that corresponds sufficiently to the utility of such aids. Trouble-free functioning, though, is another matter. One cannot use any available .22 cartridge, for many of the specifically sport cartridges have charges that are much too weak. This is shown by a quick comparison of the weights or masses of the effective breech components or slides, as these systems naturally do without any kind of a bolt and get by with the unlocked spring-mass breech. The breech mass of a Walther GSP sport pistol is all of 135 grams, the slide of a .22 caliber Walther PP weighs 175 grams, and the slide of a small-caliber P 38 weighs 230 grams. Shooting is correspondingly disturbed as soon as too weakly charged cartridges are used, in which case the empty case is ejected but the next cartridge is not inserted. With strongly charged cartridges, particularly the so-called HV types or the Stinger, these disturbances did not take place.

During the 1960s, Walther prepared a somewhat differently designed system for the "Federal Minister of the Interior." The quantity of these weapons produced could not have been very high and adds up, according to the manufacturer's information, to some 300. The slide in this system differs from present-day Walther production only in terms of the lettering on its side: on the left side there is a polished field in which, along with the Walther emblem, the inscription "Carl Walther Waffenfabrik Ulm/Do. P 38 Cal. 5.6 mm" is etched. The kit for this system is composed of an insert barrel, two magazines and the special slide, all packed in a neatly made case of light-colored wood.

The insert barrel is 132 mm long, with 118 mm devoted to rifling. It is pushed into the existing 9 mm barrel and stays there without any noticeable play, for its thickened rear area fits exactly into the slightly conical cartridge chamber. The barrel ends in a wide plate into

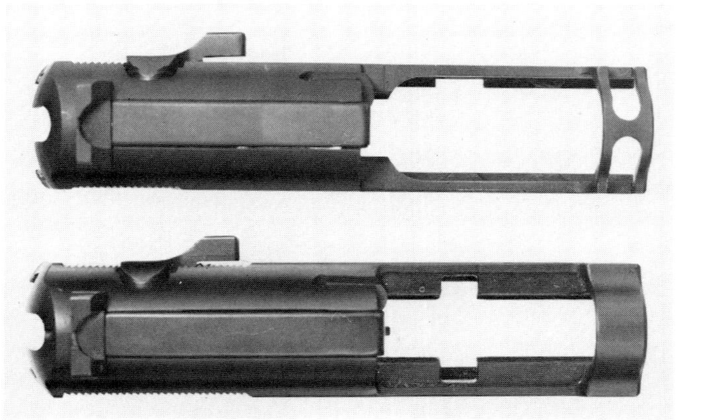

Two slides: P 38 in .22 LR and P 38 in 9 mm Parabellum calibers. The latter has two perforations for attaching the swinging bolt.

The conversion system made for the authorities by the C. Walther firm in Ulm. The small-caliber barrel is pushed into the 9 mm barrel and attached at the rear. The slide that goes with it is some 6 mm shorter in the area of the strike plate.

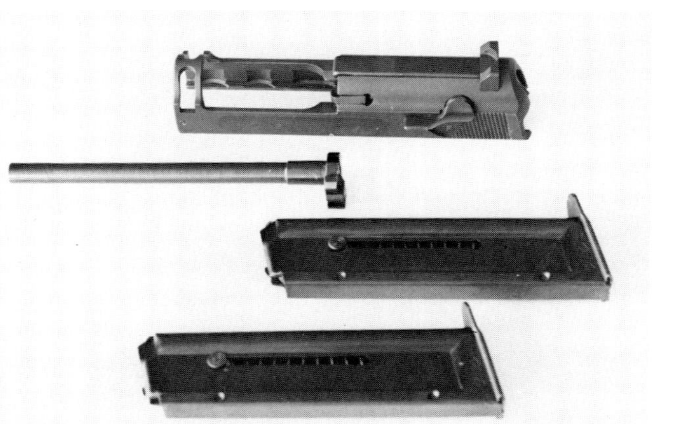

A normal frame with an added official system. This version has the polished sides of its slide marked "P 38 Cal. 5.6 mm."

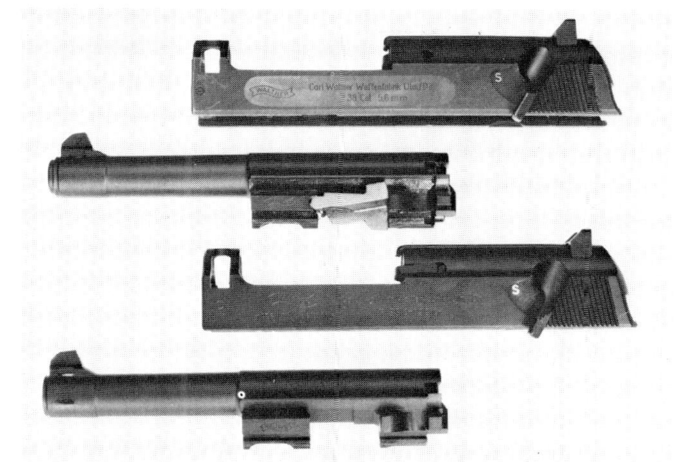

The official system (above) with the barrel already inserted, below it the slide and barrel of the normal conversion system for the P 38.

which a small ramp has been cut.

Along with the appropriate slide, the unit thus composed is pushed into the receiver. The swinging bolt is not removed and remains held in its upper position, so that the slide can move against the pressure of one of the two recoil springs without moving the barrel. This system fits weapons of various manufacturers and causes the user no differences in handling.

Systems by Peters-Stahl

The firm of Peters-Stahl, located in Paderborn, Westphalia, has meanwhile produced a large assortment of small-caliber conversion systems, offering a suitable system for almost every 9 mm PARA or .45 ACP caliber pistol on the market. The manufacturer has thereby spotted a hitherto unfilled gap in the extensive weapons market and filled it. The goal of the firm's work is obviously to give the owner of a large-caliber weapon the chance to make an economical and simple change, as well as to appeal to the sportingly inclined shooter. Thus the promise of sport-pistol performance is certainly worth being put to a concrete test. The target pictures shown are the best of an extensive testing with commercially available types of cartridges: the systems, especially the longer systems with the added S designation, really attain the level of good sport pistols, and with some types it has been possible to shoot truly excellent groups. The test of such a system on an SIG 210

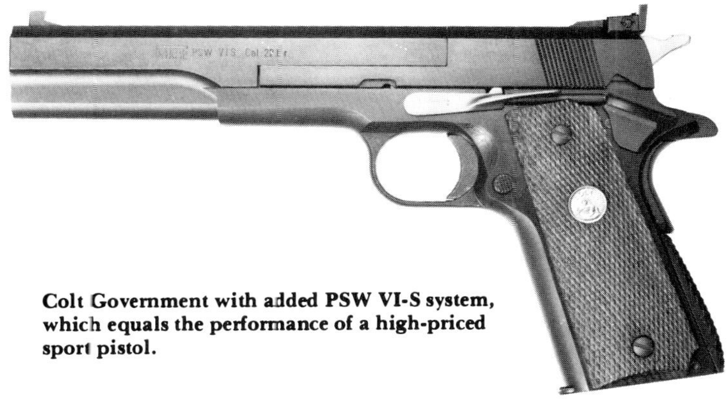

Colt Government with added PSW VI-S system, which equals the performance of a high-priced sport pistol.

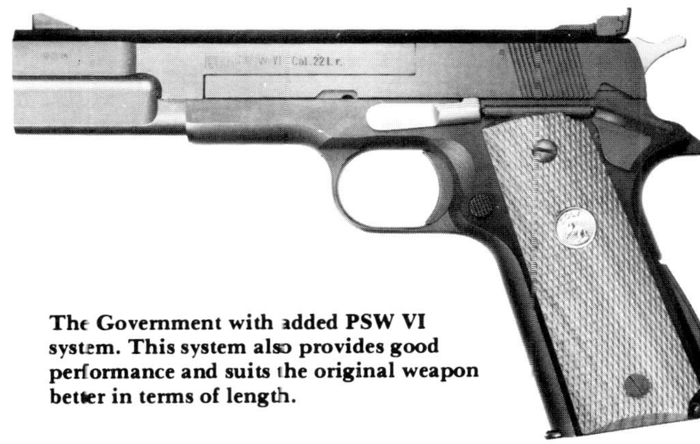

The Government with added PSW VI system. This system also provides good performance and suits the original weapon better in terms of length.

The shorter PSW VII system is practical for use on weapons like the Colt Commander. The system must be fitted to the basic weapon by the manufacturer in any case.

is of special note, as its best group after the caliber change had a dispersion of only 6 mm in a group of ten.

Peters itself produces nearly of all the parts for its systems, using the most modern production machinery for 35 work processes. The basic material is C 45/50 CrV 4 steel, which is heat-treated, polished and burnished a deep black after the parts have been made. The barrels

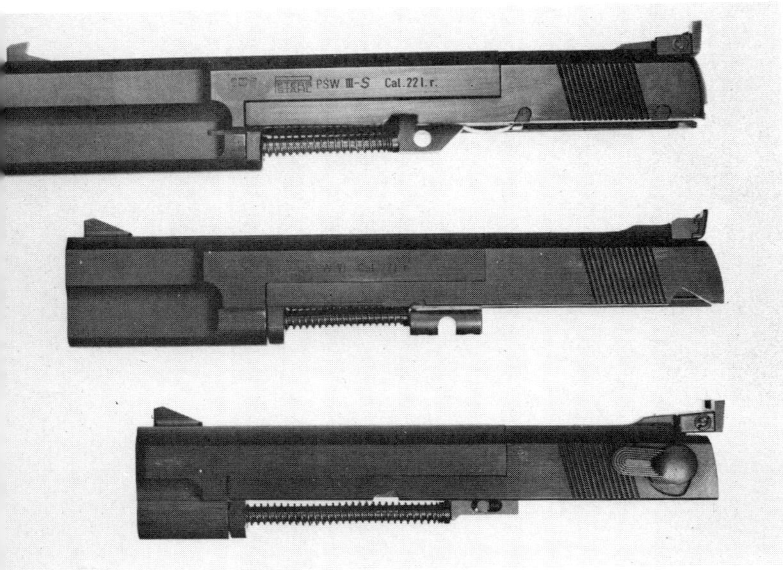

The three basic lengths of the Peters system. Note that each underside requires a different type of play-free attachment.

are manufactured in Belgium by the firm of Delcour, a highly respected producer of gun barrels. Peters modifies the raw barrels to the required external thickness and attaches them to its systems with Loctite adhesive, which bonds permanently after heat treatment.

An independent, partially patented means of attaching and play-free anchoring of the system to each basic weapon has been developed, including equally quick dismantling. In every case, a play-free seat for the system must be created on the basic weapon, which is easy to say because a systems should fit onto a brand-new Colt Government just as well as onto a worn-out war veteran, in whose grip an added trigger stop was meant to add a touch of sportiness.

The basic construction will be described here, using the PSW VI S system with a barrel length of 150 mm as an example.

The weight front part of the system, the complete system weighing some 720 grams without a magazine, includes the pushed-in and glued-in barrel, with its muzzle set back a good millimeter for protection. Over it, a bar foresight, sharply cut to the rear, is pushed into a

The PSW III-S system on an FN pistol, with Pachmayr grip panels. With a well-tuned trigger, this is a superb combination.

A dismantled system that fits the Colt pistols. Here the block must be fitted exactly to height by inserting steel plates of various thicknesses. Every system has an adjustable sight.

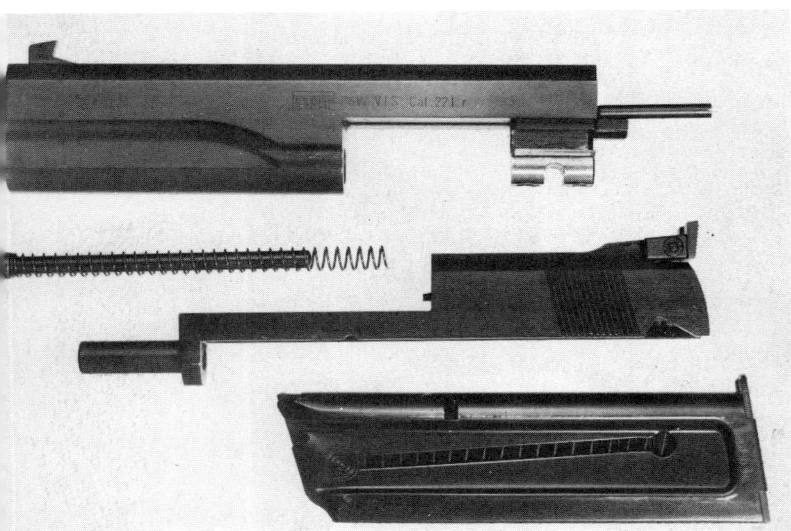

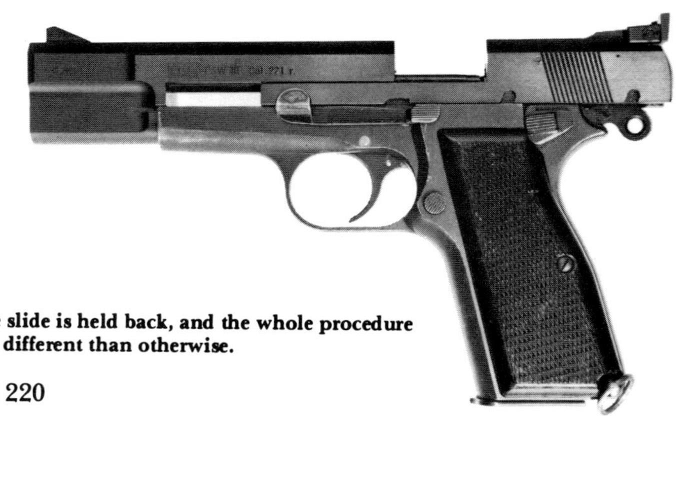

After the last shot, the slide is held back, and the whole procedure with this system is no different than otherwise.

machined-out space and pushed in from the front by a small screw. A sliding foresight is included in the usual package and can be inserted when needed. The supplying ramp is part of the front of this system, which is strongly made and well polished — no problems of any kind showed up there during practical testing. Right next to the ramp a rod is installed, where its lateral extension serves as an ejector. Corresponding to this, the moveable breechblock has a bored-out hole into which this rod projects.

Under the cartridge chamber is the mounting block, this being the part by which the system is made to fit exactly into any receiver. To make for a really good fit, it is necessary to send the weapon and system to the manufacturer for their first fitting. The author has often heard complaints about improperly functioning systems

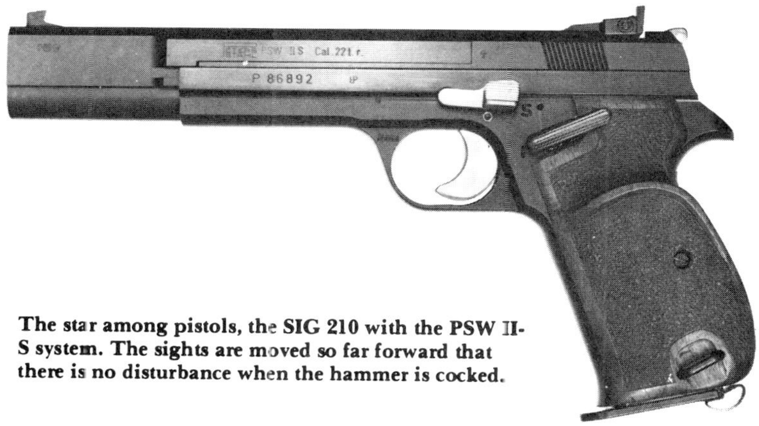

The star among pistols, the SIG 210 with the PSW II-S system. The sights are moved so far forward that there is no disturbance when the hammer is cocked.

The system for the Star Model 28 (predecessor of the M 30 series) shows how well the lines of system and weapon blend.

Technische Daten / Technical data

W No.	passend für Usual for	Gesamtlänge Overall length	Visierlinie Sight radius	Gesamthöhe Overall height	Lauflänge Barrel length	Magazinkapazität Magazine capacity	Kaliber
SW I	SIG P 240	265 mm	220 mm	150 mm	150 mm	10	.22 L.R.
SW IS 9P		248 mm	210 mm	136 mm	150 mm	8	9 mm P.
W II	SIG P 210	199 mm	172 mm	137 mm	115 mm	10	.22 L.R.
W II S		223 mm	200 mm	137 mm	150 mm	10	.22 L.R.
W III	F.N.G.P/H.P.	184 mm	167 mm	133 mm	114 mm	10	.22 L.R.
W III S		212 mm	200 mm	133 mm	150 mm	10	.22 L.R.
W IV	S&WM 39, M59 M 539 etc.	192 mm	164 mm	144 mm	110 mm	10	.22 L.R.
W IV S		214 mm	176 mm	144 mm	138 mm	10	.22 L.R.
W V	Brünner.M75	198 mm	170 mm	135 mm	117 mm	10	.22 L.R.
W V S		220 mm	205 mm	135 mm	150 mm	10	.22 L.R.
W VI	Colt Government Combat Commander Handballer etc.	194 mm	185 mm	144 mm	123 mm	10	.22 L.R.
W VI S		221 mm	212 mm	144 mm	150 mm	10	.22 L.R.
W VI S 9P		220 mm	210 mm	145 mm	150 mm	9	9 mm P.
W VII		174 mm	165 mm	144 mm	103 mm	10	.22 L.R.
W VIII	Star Mod. 28 etc.	180 mm	166 mm	130 mm	112 mm	10	.22 L.R.
it Lieferzeiten muß gerechnet werden							

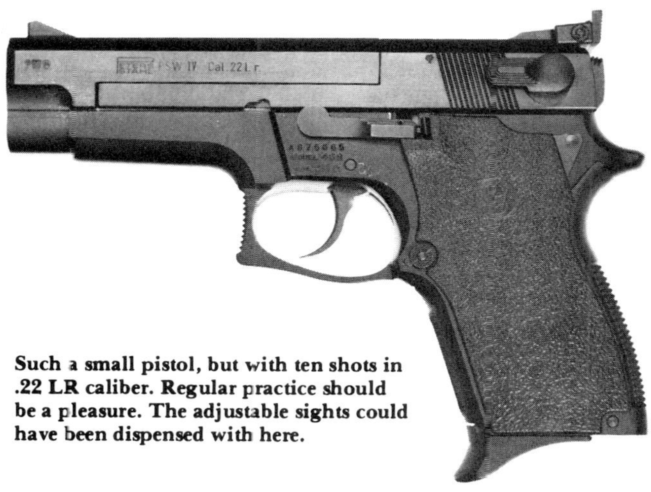

Such a small pistol, but with ten shots in .22 LR caliber. Regular practice should be a pleasure. The adjustable sights could have been dispensed with here.

because almost every shooter has tried to do the fitting himself with simple and sometimes wrong tools.

The cross-section of the block is round with a machined flat surface above and below, and the rounded outer diameter is made to fit inside the Government receiver. According to tolerances in the frame, the system must now be made somewhat flatter or higher. To accomplish this, flat pieces of different thicknesses are placed in between, and any distance can be attained by a combination of the individual plates. Two M-5 screws hold this block fast from below — it must be checked now and then to see whether they have become loosened by shooting. Another hole is bored diagonally through the mounting block with the diameter of the catch-lever pivot. After pushing the system into place and inserting the pivot of the catch lever, it stays firmly in place on the grip.

The breechblock has two extensions at the front that are linked over a step — a tubular piece has been welded electrically into the step and serves to guide the rod-supported recoil spring.

The breechblock, with its extensions, slides under the front of the system, and to the rear of the breechblock its guiding grooves fit onto the matching rails. Under the best of conditions this takes place nearly play-free, but in the end it is somewhat dependent on the condition of the receiver.

All systems have an adjustable sight, though earlier systems are still equipped with the American Milett sight, while new systems have the Type S 1 sight, which Peters has manufactured according to its specifications and then assembles. The adjustment is made in small steps, and the backsight leaf, tilted slightly backward, provides unobstructed visibility. It may be of interest that this sight can also be mounted on other weapons, and the Peters firm does the necessary fitting work itself.

Magazines for the different systems vary. In part, such as for the Government model, one can use the original magazine, but other systems use original magazines into which a suitable small magazine has been inserted, always keeping the capacity at ten cartridges. One magazine is made by Peters itself and gives no cause for complaint.

To what extent a weapon or a system will prove to be stable over a stretch of time is mostly speculation. According to information from the manufacturer, a system rigorously tested with normal cartridges showed no damage after firing 30,000 rounds, nor after firing 1000 test cartridges made by the Remington firm with a more powerful charge.

The target pictures shown here were achieved with the use of a Ransom Rest, always in groups of ten at a distance of 25 meters. Both of the shorter systems show less precision than the longer systems, but with a suitable cartridge they easily equaled the performance of many commercially available sport pistols, which often do not function with so great precision either. Disturbances occurred only with the short systems, and then only while they were being handled in the shooting machine, but not when fired from the hand with the same cartridges. The fact that one must always seek and find the proper cartridges for a sport weapon is illustrated

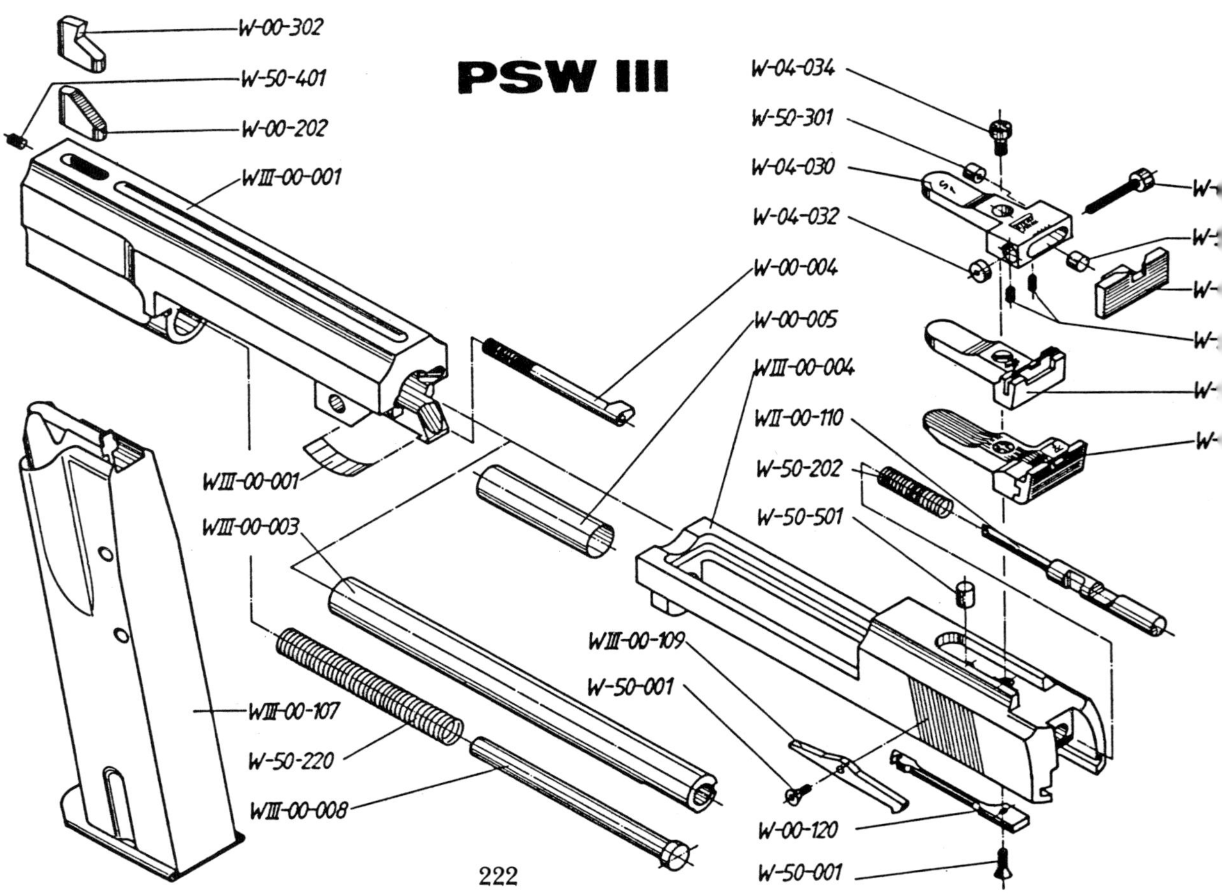

The parts of the Peters PSW III system. The systems differ from one basic weapon to another in the way they are attached.

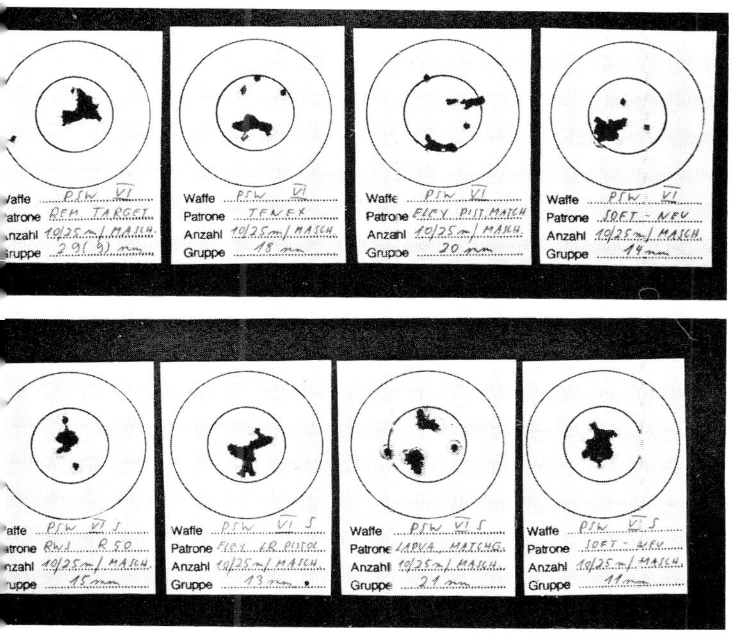

The manufacturer promises "sporting performance", which can be confirmed without reservation by one's own tests; one need only find the right .22 caliber LR cartridge.

Comparative cutaway drawings of the extant Peters systems.

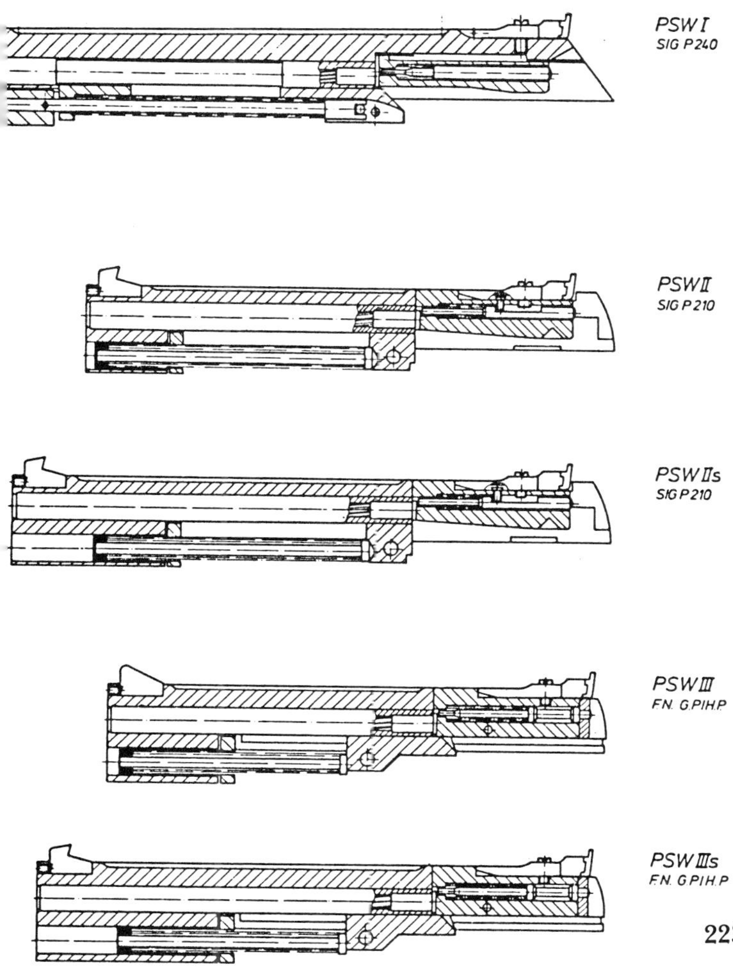

by a comparison with the PSW VI S system: an 11 mm dispersion circle with the lightly charged SOFT and a 50 mm circle with the more heavily charged FIOCCHI MAXAC.

The Furter System

A noteworthy conversion system for the SIG 210 was developed by the Swiss gunsmith K. Furter (Jurastrasse 10, 4600 Olten, Switzerland). It is made for the .22 LR cartridge and is designed for single shots. This system deserves to be recognized for its concept, its practical construction, and also its shooting performance.

The set includes the actual system and a wooden magazine; this is required to disengage the magazine safety of the SIG 210. The wooden magazine, made of oiled walnut, is somewhat shorter than a normal magazine, and is closed at the base by a screwed-on sheet-metal plate.

The system itself is constructed like a slide for the pistol and is simply pushed into the guides. There it stays firmly, and it is surprising to see what solid precision is attainable for both the pistol and the system. It also fits every bit as perfectly into other SIG pistols. It is attached by means of the catch lever, the pivot of which passes through a hole bored at the bottom of the system.

The 135 mm round barrel is flattened on the sides and mounted movable in the "slide" at the front, supported

The SIG 210 with the Furter system; the pistol, of course, remains a single-shot type. The shooting performance of this system is more than excellent.

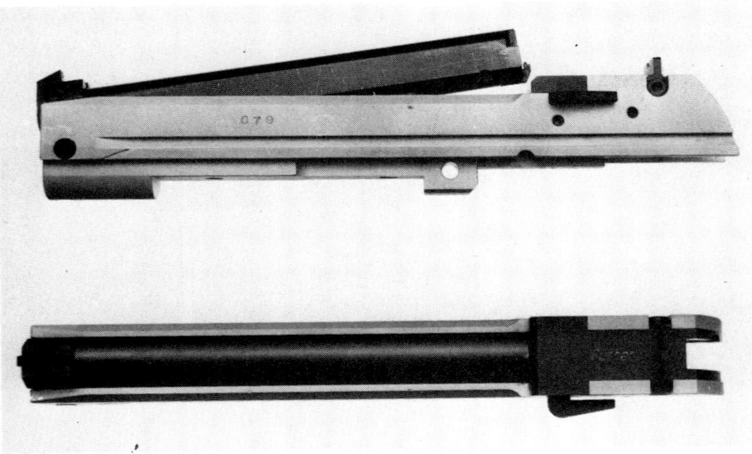

The barrel is folded up for loading. The sight is separately adjustable vertically and laterally.

by a spring. After light pressure on the locking lever on the left side of the system, it springs up and can be supplied with a cartridge. Under the cartridge chamber an extractor is mounted under pressure from a spring. When the system is opened again after firing, many cases fly gently out of the chamber, while others are pushed far enough forward and can be grasped easily with the fingers.

The barrel is mounted at the front, rests in place at the rear, and also has a rod at the bottom that fits into an extension of the "slide" — this is a fully play-free mounting, and practical testing with a shooting machine shows the high degree of workmanship.

The "slide" is machined inside to its full length, and the firing pin as well as the sights are held in an inset piece that is fastened with two strong high-tension pins. The firing pin is located a bit to the right side, where its chisel-shaped point gives the cartridge a strong impact that assures ignition.

The sight is laterally adjustable between two Inbus screws, and the foresight is adjustable. The attachment of the foresight is firm — a small tension pin keeps it from getting lost and allows it to turn, and an Inbus screw holds it firmly in its mount. The fore- and backsights have a good width for sporting targeting, and both have white markings that can be done without. All in all, the Furter system makes a very good impression. While the barrel is burnished, as are the parts of the sight and the inlaid piece at the back of the slide, the whole system is matte nickel-plated. It harmonizes well with the design lines of the SIG pistol and does not cause the shooter any great changes in terms of either weight distribution or handling.

It was fired from a Ransom Rest at a distance of 25 meters, in four groups of ten rounds apiece. The results achieved were: Soft 12 mm, Soft-Match 11 mm, RWS Pistol Match 18 mm and RWS-Subsonic 13 mm. This is more than satisfactory performance which is scarcely equaled by many sport pistols. Unfortunately, this system has been made so far only for the SIG 210 pistol.

The Colt Government CO_2 System

For the Colt Government, in either .45 ACP, .38 Super or 9 mm Parabellum caliber, there appeared in mid-1968 a switching system that fired the usual 4.5 mm (.177) Diabolo bullet with carbon dioxide gas from a small replaceable capsule. There also appeared an additional system for a pistol for which there are more exchangeable systems available than for any other weapon on the market. The system shown here is manufactured by the firm of Blaser, located in Isny in the Allgäu, and is based on a design by a gunsmith named Idl which contributed significantly to the development of the new air pistol made by the firm of Carl Walther. The name of Blaser is more closely related to the production of the finest and best-made, and highest-performing hunting weapons.

To use it, one needs only the receiver and catch lever of the basic weapon — the latter's pivot holds the installed system in place. The magazine is removed, the catch lever is installed, and the system placed on top of the receiver. Through the empty magazine shaft, a long

The Blaser system with 12-gram CO_2 capsule.

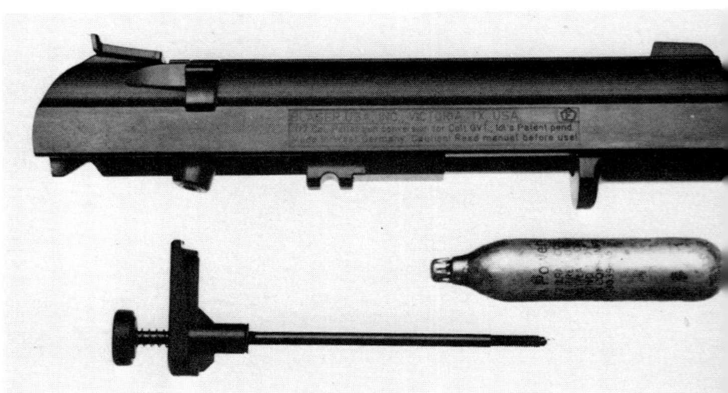

The Government can now be an air pistol as well.

screw with a spring holds the system fast to the grip, where it stays in place fully play-free. This system differs from the original Colt system in this respect. The one is play-free, the other is not. It is a wonder that no other pistol has been modified as often as the Colt Government and its variants.

The 140 mm barrel (which has 12 very fine riflings) is pressed into the upper part, made of non-iron cast metal and held in place at the front by an encircling nut. In the bottom of the system one inserts a capsule containing 12 grams of the liquid propellant gas, this quantity being sufficient for 80 to 90 rounds, and it is impossible to put the gas in incorrectly. Despite this structure, the conversion system with its sight does not rise particularly high above the shooter's hand. At the same time as the retaining screw of the capsule is tightened, the capsule is punctured from the rear, and the gas is now at the vent, ready to be utilized. To fire, the loading lever is pushed forward to the side, a bullet is inserted, the lever is pulled back again and the hammer is cocked. The hammer strikes on the sprung valve rod so that a small amount of gas is now freed. According to the bullet type, shot velocities (measured with the VM 25 device made by the firm of Weinlich) are from 112 to 108 meters per second.

The sight can be adjusted in height to a small degree on a slanted ramp, and a smaller lateral adjustment is also possible. No changes in handling need to be made. All the safety systems in the grip remain as they were except the recoil safety, which is not needed here.

The shooting performance is not bad, though one should not expect the impossible. At distances of six to seven meters, groups with diameters of 10 to 12 mm could be attained with the system mounted on the weapon, and this comes very close to meeting the actual needs of a utilitarian weapon.

The Colt Conversion System

The conversion system for the Government made by Colt, designed for the .22 LR cartridge, is offered as a separate system or as a complete weapon, the latter designated Colt-ACE. The set is composed of a light slide with adjustable sights like those of the Gold Cup and a higher bar foresight, a recoil spring with a short guiding rod and enclosing housing, an unsprung guiding housing for the barrel, the barrel with a moveable chamber, an ejector and a magazine that holds ten cartridges.

The system is mounted in the usual Colt manner, with the pivot of the catch lever passing through a hole bored in the extension under the barrel. Typical of this system is the so-called Floating Chamber, a chamber that is moveable to the rear, such as is found in, for example, the PT system of the P 5 pistol by Walther or the small-caliber version of the P 7 by Heckler & Koch. The chamber moves backward a bit while a shot is fired and thus delivers a heftier impact, which is necessary to move the slide. The shooting performance of the Colt system is regarded as only moderately good and has no valid relation to the price. The system is suitable for use in practice but is not capable of providing satisfactory sporting performance. The single-row magazine of this system will appear again elsewhere, as it is used for the Peters system whenever that is applied to a Colt Government or Gold Cup.

The Kart System for Colt Pistols

The highest-performance switching system for the Colt Government (except the Peters system) is made by the firm of Kart-Sporting Arms. It gives such good performance that, with a well-tuned trigger, it can be put to sporting use without limitation. To be sure, it requires a well-adapted trigger and the addition of better grip panels, preferably panels with adjustable handholds.

The front part of the system is attached to the grip rather firmly by the pivot of the catch lever and a set-screw. The effective breech mass slides under the rails of the upper part and causes no disturbance during targeting. A sight that is adjustable by small steps in all directions and meets the highest demands is installed. After installing the catch lever that goes with the system, functioning with an attached switching system is no different from that of the basic weapon.

The Kart system was a longtime bestseller. It is rather difficult to mount, but gives excellent performance.

Insertion Barrels by Lothar Walther

The firm of Lothar Walther, located in Königsbronn, Württemberg, has won a good reputation in recent years as a manufacturer of high-quality barrels for all imaginable types of firearms. In addition, the firm has been producing numerous reducing systems for many years, making it possible for the owner of a large-caliber weapon, whether revolver or pistol, to practice and shoot at short ranges. From pistols in 9 mm Parabellum caliber, depending on the system or inserted barrel, cartridges of 4 mm M 20, .22 short or .22 LR calibers can be fired, and very good and, above all, realistic groups can be shot from 5 to 15 and 25 meters.

The attraction consists, for one thing, of allowing one

The dismantled Kart system with receiver and magazine.

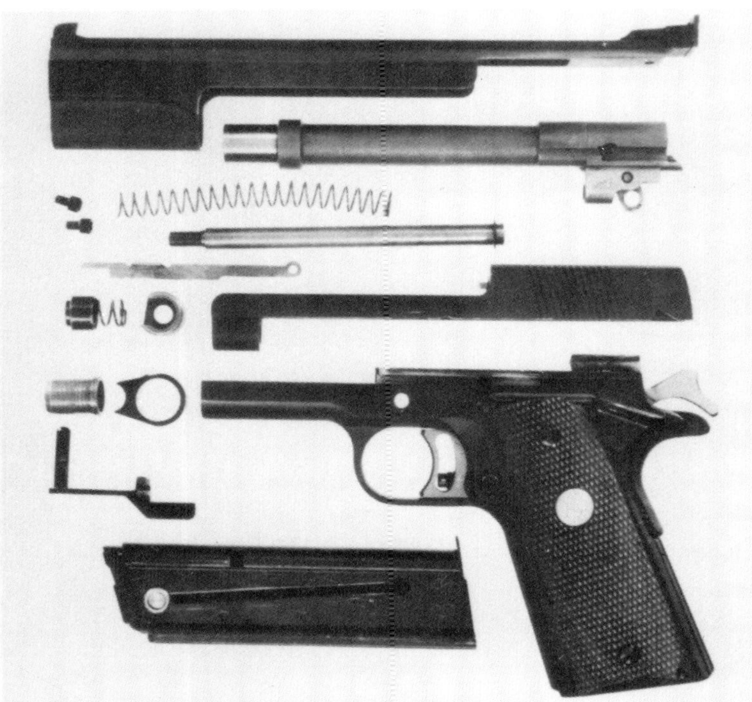

The P 38 with insert barrel by L. Walther, made for the small 4 mm M 20 cartridge. It can shoot up to five meters. The small cartridges are inserted in steel loading cartridges.

An insert barrel has now been installed in the P 38; it has its own chamber. Ignition is done by an intermediate piece adapted for rim ignition.

The 08 pistol with insert barrel for .22 short cartridges. With this too, good performance is possible. The short cartridge comes inside the loading cartridge; the igniter piece is behind it.

Insert barrel with loading cartridges for the .22 short cartridge, shown in detail.

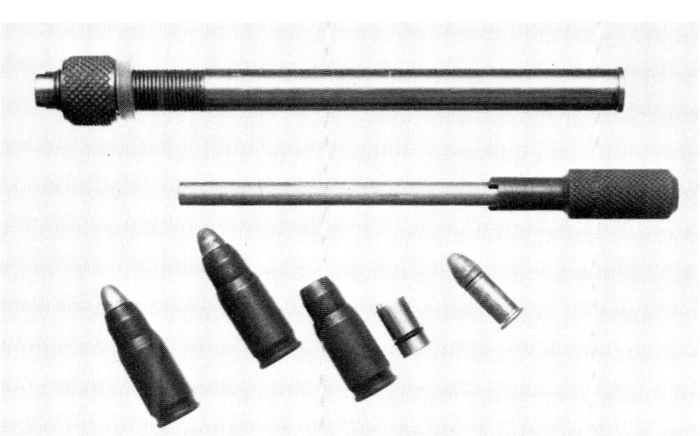

to practice at low cost and with low noise, and for another, it is a pleasure to take an older weapon out of a collection and fire it now and then. No modifications to the weapon are necessary, and no particular pressure or damage occurs. Between the 4 mm M 20 and the .22 caliber types there is a technical difference in terms of ignition. When one has a system for the small 4 mm cartridge, one can do without an intermediate percussion piece, for this midget cartridge also has central ignition. The insertion barrels are available in different lengths for 9 mm Ultra, 9 mm Parabellum, 7.65 mm Parabellum and .45 ACP weapons. But all of them operate in the same way. The barrel is inserted into the barrel of the pistol and screwed on at the front. It is thus reinforced in the cartridge chamber and is held fast at the muzzle by a heavy encircling nut plus an intermediate piece made of plastic. In spite of this, one should check the screw for tightness now and then between series. The small 4 mm cartridge is inserted in a special loading cartridge made of steel, three of which are loaded into the magazine. The repeating function of the weapon is naturally not maintained, thus every cartridge must be loaded by hand via the repeating mechanism and also removed, in the process of which a soft bottom should receive the loading cartridge so that it is not permanently damaged.

Good shooting performance; only the point of impact is different. This target was shot at from a sitting position at 15 meters.

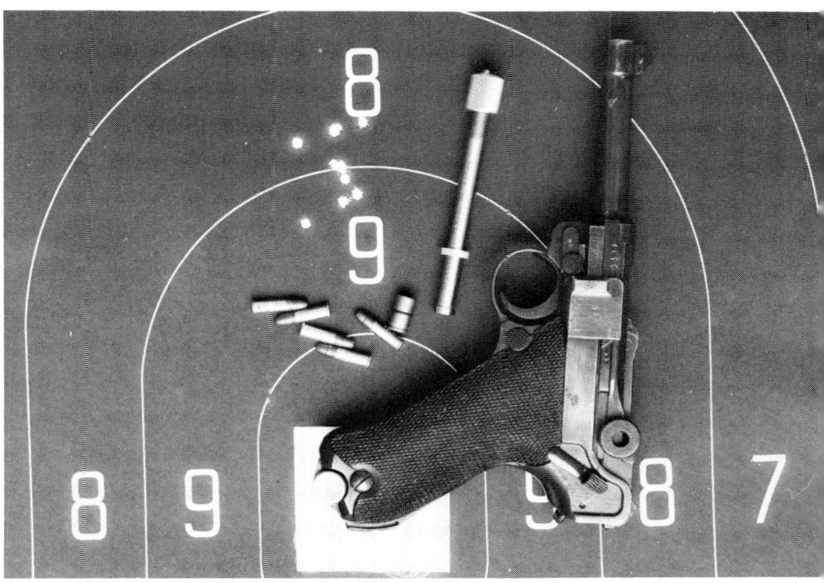

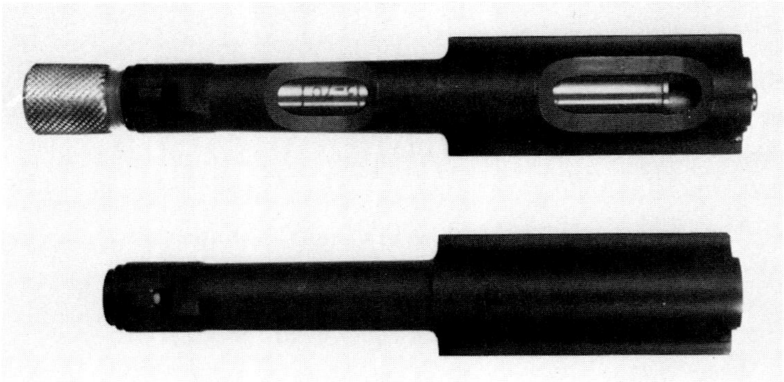

The insert barrel for the P 38, shown in the barrel of the cutaway model. It fits snugly into the step of the barrel's own chamber.

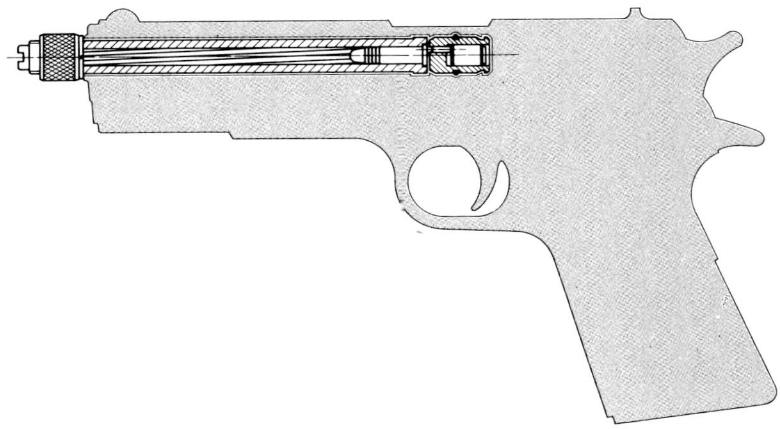

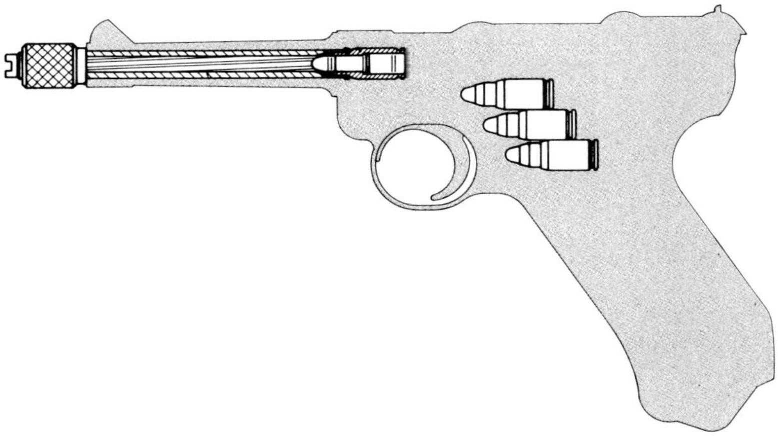

Using the insert barrel made by L. Walther of Königsbronn, low-cost training in .22 caliber with good results is possible.

The insert barrel has an advanced cartridge chamber into which the loading cartridge fits. The rotationless flight of the small round bullet is short.

At a distance of five meters, groups up to 20 or 25 mm in diameter can be fired, and for this purpose there are special practice targets, like customary figure targets but with reduced dimensions. Since the manufacturer made the forward threads very long on purpose, one insert barrel can fit several different weapons. The handling of the insert barrel for .22 caliber cartridges, though, is somewhat different.

These cartridges have rim ignition, however an intermediate percussion piece must provide ignition at the rim, which works without problems in normal weapons with a not overly weak firing pin.

The set includes three loading cartridges, which simultaneously form the cartridge chamber, and one percussion piece for every cartridge. First one inserts the 22 caliber cartridge into the loading cartridge and puts the percussion piece, secured by a small rubber ring, behind it. These combined "cartridges" are also inserted singly by hand and then removed easily.

Shooting performance is remarkably good, with shooting behavior more than pleasant. Only the targeting points must be chosen differently than when shooting original cartridges. With an older 08 fired from a sitting position at a distance of 20 meters, groups from 30 to 40 mm in diameter were achieved regularly, and with a .22 cartridge that would fit the barrel even better, the results could become better — or worse.

Insert barrels of this kind do not compete with self-loading conversion systems, nor are they intended to. Their handling, though, is not too complicated, the price is reasonable, so is the workmanship, and the results are not disappointing.

REVOLVERS

Even though the 9 mm Parabellum cartridge is a classic pistol cartridge, several revolvers have none the less been produced to use it. In terms of performance, the 9 mm cartridge ranks somewhere between a medium .38 SPL and a normal .357 Magnum. For police use when fired from a handy revolver with double action mode, it offers the advantage of uniformity, as it is not necessary to

Pistol and revolver in 9 mm Parabellum caliber. A modern pistol like the P 226 holds 16 cartridges, but a revolver with the same design and barrel length holds only six.

constantly keep several types of cartridges on hand.

The necessary modifications to the weapon for this purpose are not too difficult, for the external diameters of the cases are similar and the actual bullet calibers are almost the same. The differences in barrel dimensions, aside from the different formation of the profile and the rifling length, are likewise small and are measured in terms of hundredths of a millimeter. The performance of a revolver set up for 9 mm Parabellum cartridges need not be inferior to that of a good self-loading pistol. A revolver made by Smith & Wesson (Model 547, with 4-inch barrel) was used to achieve equally good results to the Model 539 or 659 pistols made by the same manufacturer.

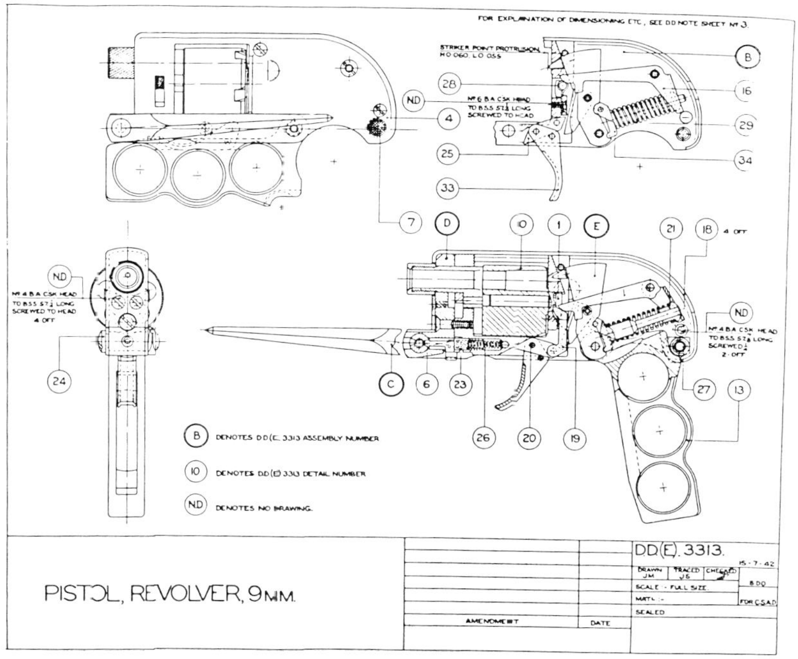

Design for a 9 mm caliber British army revolver. It encloses a sword blade and can also be used as a blunt instrument.

Single-Action Revolvers

There are very few such revolvers on the market, and at the moment there are only two versions of the Ruger Blackhawk, with the model designations of BN 34 X and BN 36 X. Ruger calls its revolvers "convertible", which tells a lot about the solution of the technical problems. Convertible revolvers can be used with the 9 mm Parabellum cartridge as well as the .357 Magnum (and

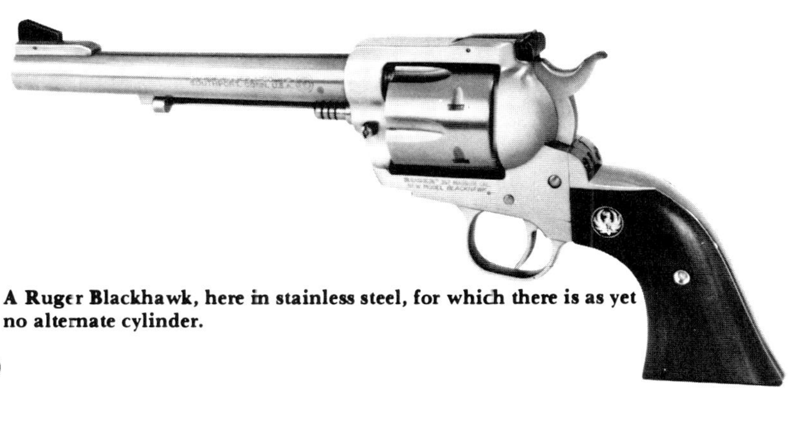

A Ruger Blackhawk, here in stainless steel, for which there is as yet no alternate cylinder.

naturally all versions of the .38 SPL cartridge). For this purpose they have a changeable cylinder for each of the two cartridges, and can be easily changed by hand, without tools and without making changes to the weapon itself.

The unusual characteristic of having no rim at the base of the cartridge causes no trouble here. All of the holes bored into the cylinder correspond exactly to the lengths of the Parabellum cases, and the cartridge lies in the hold up to the mouth of its case and finds sufficient support. The removal of the used case is done individually by hand with the help of the spring ejector — nothing else is necessary, and all the handling is simple and not prone to disturbances.

The Ruger revolvers stand out for their robust and yet pleasant workmanship. With their distant ancestor, the Colt Single Action Army, they have at best only their approximate external form in common — their inner structure is completely different. Ruger prefers to use coil springs made of piano wire, whereas leaf springs are not used with the exception of a double-shanked form spring. This principle applies to even the smallest springs. The models in the "Blackhawk" series are available in the actual revolver calibers, as well as with different barrel lengths in burnished or stainless steel versions. The Convertibles are an exception, as they are available only in burnished finish.

The first striking characteristic is the single rest for the hammer, while other single-action revolvers have at least two and usually three rests. The Ruger revolver has only the striking rest, from which the cocked hammer is released. The cylinder gate, though, has been given a special function. An inner arm of the loading gate works on the cylinder stop. As long as the gate remains closed, the hammer can be cocked by hand and the cylinder can be turned further. If the hammer is in its foremost position, then the gate can be swung up for loading or unloading. In this position the cylinder stop is disengaged, the cylinder can be turned, and to guarantee complete safety during loading, the hammer cannot be cocked when the gate is open, while the gate cannot be raised when the hammer is cocked.

In crass contrast to the "genuine" Colt revolvers and their imitations, the Ruger revolver is quite safe. If the weapon should fall on its hammer, the hammer's spur could well be damaged, but a shot cannot be fired. The weapon can be fired only by uninterrupted pulling of the trigger, to which the so-called transfer pin — a trans-

The transfer bar lever is in front of the firing pin; only thus is ignition possible. The revolver gains a high degree of safety.

mission lever — is attached. When the trigger is pulled back, this transfer bar is pulled back over the ignition bar that is mounted on a spring in the frame. The hammer has an extension on its inside which can be filled out by the transfer bar above it, and this position is necessary to cause ignition. If the finger slides off the hammer during the cocking process, then the transfer bar remains below and the head of the hammer hits against the frame without being able to reach the firing pin at all, however all of this functions only in the described manner when one does not have a finger on the trigger during cocking.

Still another safety is activated by the transfer bar. It is constantly pushed back by a small sprung rod at the end of the cylinder pivot. Only under this pressure can it push past the slightly projecting firing pin when the trigger is pulled. If the cylinder pivot is not completely pushed in until it is bolted, then the transfer bar pushes against the now-absent reverse pressure. moves under the firing pin and blocks the further cocking of the hammer. The shooter thus has an immediate indication that the pivot of the cylinder has been pushed in wrongly and incompletely.

With the Blackhawk Convertible in .357 Magnum and 9 mm Parabellum calibers, the manufacturer has created an ideal side arm for all those who need to go hunting in inhospitable areas. The weapon itself is safe and no problem to handle, if one hand is injured, it can be made ready to fire with one hand, and it shoots cartridges that can be bought all over the world.

A similar convertible revolver was made by the German firm of Sauer & Sohn a long time ago, particularly for export to the USA. This was the Sauer Western Six-

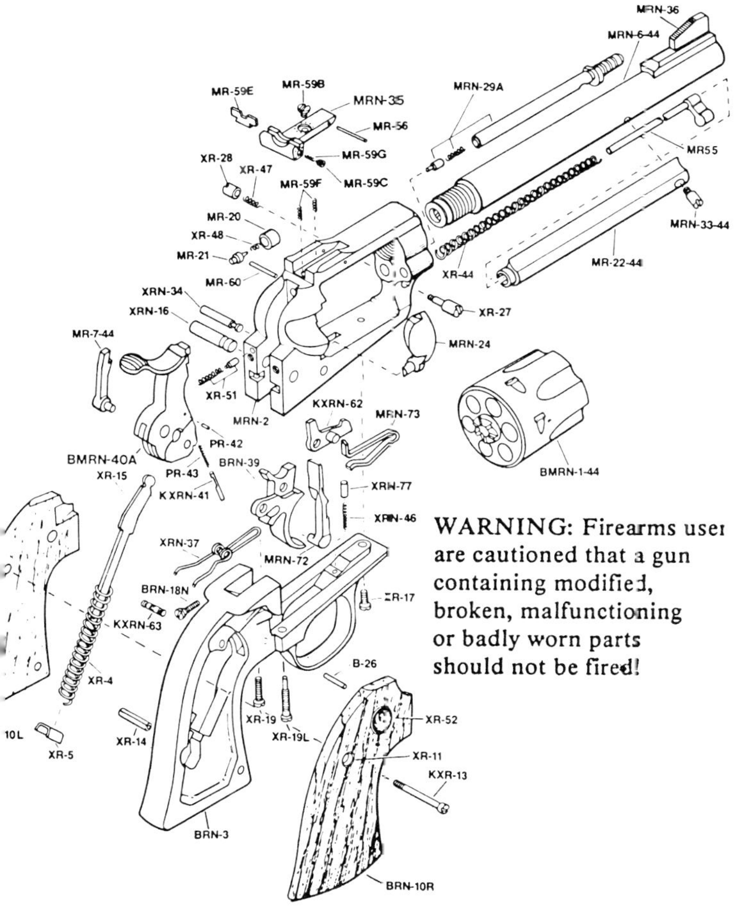

Ruger made the single-action revolver thoroughly safe. The various models are built according to the principle shown here.

shooter, the production of which was given up at the beginning of the 1970s. The Sauer Sixshooter was made in .45 Long Colt, .44 Magnum and .357 Magnum calibers, and a changeable cylinder for 9 mm Parabellum cartridges was available. Production by Sauer ended when the manufacture of the SIG-Sauer 220, 225 and 226 self-loading pistol models began and its export could no longer bring in sufficient profit. The tools for the revolvers were sold to the firm of H. Weihrauch in Mellrichstadt. The Western Revolver produced by Weihrauch are physically identical, but to date the firm has not offered an alternate cylinder.

Double-Action Revolvers

Utilizing the Para cartridge in a revolver with a double action trigger and swinging-out cylinder is not at all simple, and the solutions to date have been less than satisfactory. The seating of the cartridge against a step in the cylinder bore causes no problems, but the error-free extraction of the fired cases causes all the more. The more strongly the cases are lodged in the bores, the more difficult it becomes, which means that one should not necessarily use heavily charged cartridges, depending on the revolver.

The Astra "Police"

Along with self-loading pistols in various calibers, the Spanish manufacturer Astra-Unceta Y CIA produces a whole series of revolvers in .38 SPL, .357 Magnum and .44 Magnum calibers. All have the same basic lock and differ only in size and material, for the so-called INOX models, which are made of non-rusting material, and have been available for some time.

The Model 357 is available with four-, six- and eight-and-a-half-inch barrel lengths, as well as with a changeable cylinder for 9 mm Parabellum or 9 mm Steyr cartridges, whose cases are somewhat longer. The "Police" model was developed from this model and is made with three- and two-inch barrel lengths. The cylinder holds six cartridges, the overall length is 212 mm, the empty weight is 1040 grams. It is not a very light revolver, but rather a powerful weapon for hard use.

The lock itself is similar in construction to that of the S & W revolver, which has been taken as a model all over

The Astra Police in .357 Magnum caliber, with an exchange cylinder for 9 mm Parabellum caliber. It is loaded with clips of six.

Individual parts of the Astra Police, which can be used in .357 Magnum and 9 mm Parabellum calibers.

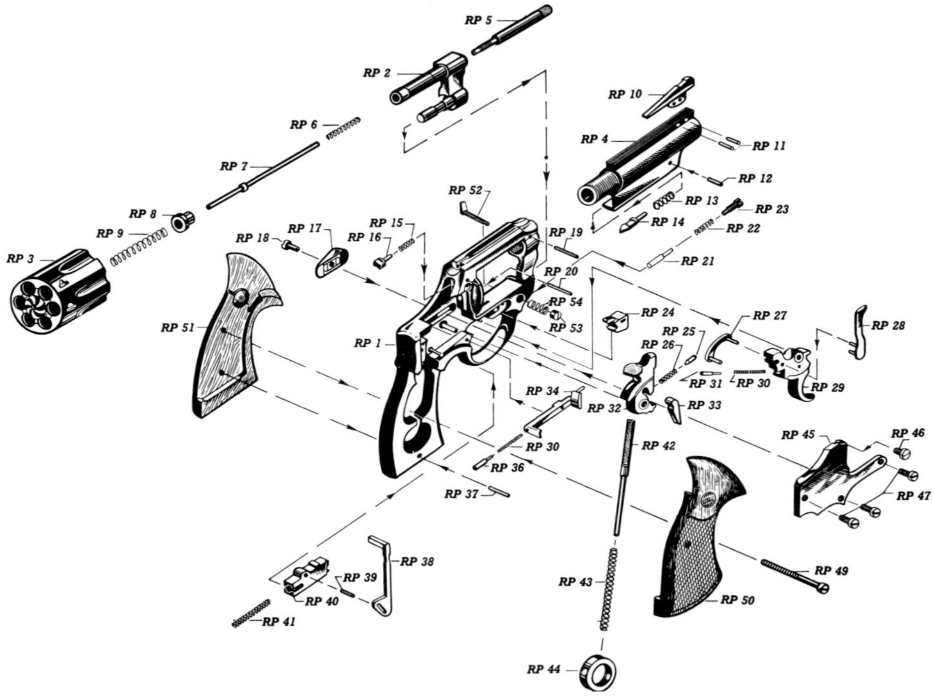

the world. But here a coil spring has been chosen as the hammer spring and an effective means of displacing this spring has been created. Installed in the grip there is a so-called regulation ring with four holes of different depths. The coil spring is set in one of these holes. If necessary, one can select a hole with a different depth, thus giving the coil spring more or less initial tension, which results directly in a more or less strong strike by the hammer.

The cylinder can be changed without a tool. Development of this new feature seems to have been based on the Korth revolver, as it is no different. One pushes down the sprung push-button at the right front of the frame when the cylinder is swung out to the side and pulls the cylinder forward out of the frame, along with the crane. All that is actually changed is the cylinder with its pivot, whereas the crane is also changed in the Korth revolver.

For the Astra revolver one needs clips that hold six cartridges in their grooves. One pushes the cartridges singly into the filler and can always load or unload them together, a small disadvantage, to be sure, but a clearly functioning principle.

The Korth Revolver

The revolver from Ratzeburg, available in .357 Magnum, .22 LR and .22 WMR as well as with a changeable cylinder for 9 mm Parabellum cartridges, enjoys a worldwide reputation of being one of the best of all revolvers. Only materials of extreme toughness are used, and after the final work processes are done, they are hardened additionally on their outer surfaces. This creates almost the hardness of glass to the surfaces that are exposed to wear, and a certain elasticity to the parts themselves. The chromium-manganese steel is guaranteed to have a tensile strength of 130 to 140 kpm, and these values exceed those of the steels used in many other weapons.

The barrel is not drawn to eliminate chipping but rather hammered cold — formerly this may have been an outstanding characteristic, but now it has become the norm for quality weapons. After hammering, the material takes on an additional thickening. The barrel is mounted in a hardened barrel- and breech-cylinder that is drawn out toward the muzzle as is the Colt Python. This gives the revolver a practical front weight, for one thing, and also makes its overall design look better. The barrel jacket has an integrated valved rail with a drag foresight set into it and a longitudinal groove on the top.

The unbolting of the cylinder deserves special emphasis here, as it is bolted via its pivot in the back of the strike plate and under the barrel in front. The unbolting lever or push-button is not mounted on the side of the frame, but in the back of the frame on the right side of the

The Korth revolver, a finely engraved version with an exchange cylinder. The cylinder of a Korth is removed along with the crane.

Every Korth revolver is made precisely in every detail. In this respect it cannot be excelled.

The matte burnished Korth Profi with a three-inch barrel. A very good feature is the broad grip with finger grooves.

hammer. One pushes the easily reachable button forward and swings the cylinder out to the left side by simultaneously pushing on it. If the cylinder is to be removed, either for cleaning or to be replaced by a cylinder for a different caliber, then the locking knob on the right side of the grip is pushed in and the cylinder, complete with crane, is pulled out of its guides. If a change to a different caliber is being made, the cylinder is replaced along with the crane, and this complete unit is naturally included in the marketed set.

The illustrations show the three-inch Combat version with striking engraving and gold inlay, a treasure for fans of well-developed, finely built and not exactly low-priced weapons. The sight of this version can only be adjusted laterally, and the massive backsight leaf is easier to push sideward between two side screws.

The trigger offers a wealth of possibilities for modification and stands out in both types of handling for its soft and even movement. The Korth revolver has a double action trigger with pressure-point regulation; this regulation is done by changing the small wheel that is mounted on the upper arm of the trigger. These wheels are numbered, bearing easily visible numbers from 1 to 4, while the number 5 wheel is installed in the standard version. When the hammer is forward, this wheel is directly under the catch of the hammer, and when the hammer is pulled back, the catch moves away over the wheel. The result of this is that after the wheel is in place, one feels no increasing resistance at all. This setting is particular optimal with the number 5 wheel.

The trigger weight can be adjusted from outside without dismantling the gun. At the factory, the trigger for single-action is set at a weight of some 1400 grams, and adjustments from about 1000 to 2000 grams are possible. The adjustment is made by using the screw immediately behind the root of the trigger guard, where a spring-tension bolt with a torsion spring around it is mounted in the frame. Before adjusting it, the counter-screw on the opposite side is loosened, and after the adjustment is made, it is tightened again. Because of the extremely thin slit of the screw, this can be done only with screwdrivers made especially for the Korth revolver.

A view of the cylinder, loaded with 9 mm Parabellum cartridges.

The small cutouts on the star are easy to see. The fit into the groove at the bottom of the case.

Cartridge cases can be ejected by using a little trick which is based directly on the shape of the ejector star. The segment of the ejector star that lies directly under a case or its groove has a sickle-shaped cutout. When the star is raised, this moves forcefully further into the groove of the cartridge base and thus moves the case upward. The first effect of this principle is seen when the cylinder is being loaded, as every cartridge fits into place audibly and tangibly.

The choice within the model range has grown greater regularly, indicating that the demand for revolvers of high value throughout the world has not decreased. A noteworthy revolver is the so-called Korth-Profi, actually a type of low-cost revolver with little work put into its surface preparation. The entire surface has been burnished to a silky-matte finish. Such weapons are much easier to take care of, for fingerprints cannot be seen on them. What is offered in terms of grips has also been designed wisely to fill the latest demands, especially for the short-barreled revolver, where the uncut grip with the finger grooves at the front is optimal. Whomever shoots several series of heavily charged cartridges will be happy to exchange the herringbone grip for the Profi grip.

In all, the Ratzeburg factory offers three different sights, depending on the version: the Combat sight, somewhat adjustable in height and to the side, the earlier Sport sight, and the big Match sight with the changeable backsight leaves.

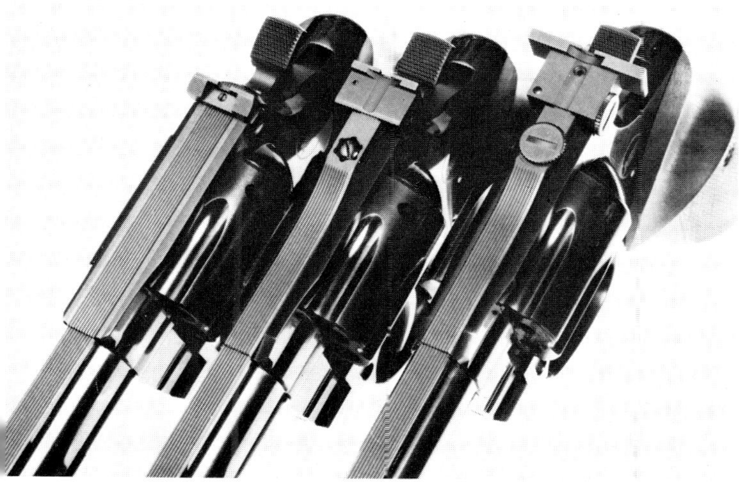

The three Korth sights. From left to right, Combat, Sport, and Match sights, the last with a changeable backsight plate.

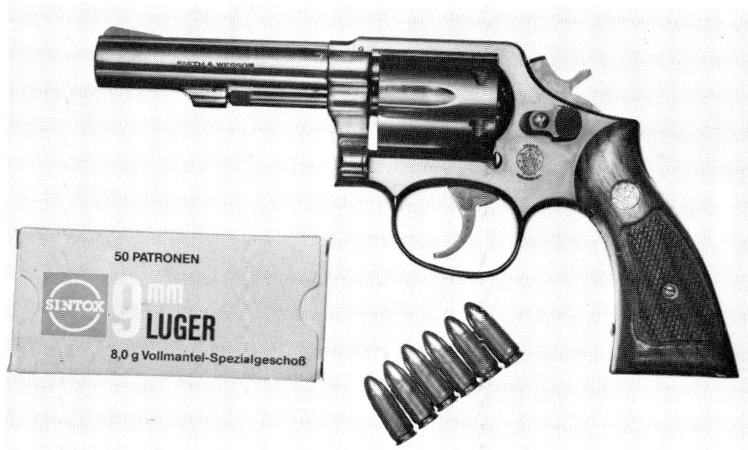

The Smith & Wesson Model 547 is no longer in production. The barrel is four inches long, the K-frame has an angled grip.

Smith & Wesson Model 547

Smith & Wesson offers a very thorough selection of revolvers made for every cartridge currently on the market.

In principle, the same lock design is always used, however it is adapted in size to the design of the individual model. Further variations can be created by changing the barrel length, the material and the frame. Smith & Wesson has marked the frames with letters and varies them in many models according to the type of grip: the round butt with a rounded grip or the square butt with an angular grip. The J frame is for the small revolver, the K frame for the medium type, likewise the new L frame, while the N frame is used for heavy versions in calibers such as .45 long Colt or 44 Magnum.

The Model 547, which is no longer produced, was available at very reasonable prices from the middle to the end of 1985. Some day there will be a proverbial run on well-kept collectors' pieces.

Two slightly different versions were available: one with a three-inch barrel and rounded grip, and one with a four-inch barrel and angular grip, the type shown here. The small Service grip can be substituted for the larger target grip or the grips made by other manufacturers.

Externally the Model 547 corresponds exactly to the successful Smith & Wesson Model 10 Military Police with its thicker barrel, the so-called bull barrel. The hammer spur is different, and has been shortened

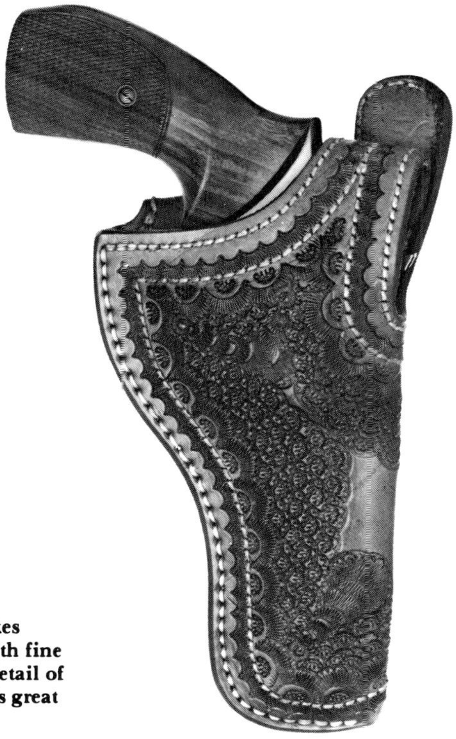

Harry Maacken makes excellent holsters with fine decorations. Every detail of the holster shows his great ability.

The hammer has no ignition pin, the firing pin is set into the frame, and the sight is fixed.

Small rods reach into the grooves of the 547's cartridge bases. Problems occur only with very strongly charged cartridges, for their cases press too strongly against the walls in the cylinder.

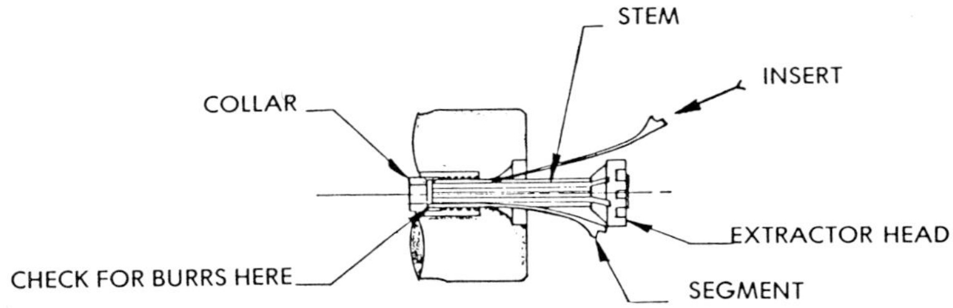

In the Smith & Wesson revolver, clawlike rods reach into the grooves on the cartridge bases.

slightly on the Para-revolver, and the hammer itself is also different, having no inset ignition pin. Ignition of the cartridge is done by the ignition pin which is either sprung or mounted high in the frame under the sight groove. Two pins are mounted there; the lower one ignites the cartridge, while the upper one pushes the cartridge forward or holds it in place so firmly that it stays with the mouth of its case at the edge of the cylinder hole. Fired cases thus show two punctures: the stronger puncture in the percussion cap and a lighter marking made by the limit pin (part 34 in the drawing on page 237). The two pins are held in position by a cover plate and can be removed from their holes at the back when the plate is removed. The revolver is safe to handle; a fall on the decocked hammer with a cartridge in place cannot cause a shot to be fired. Firing only occurs when the trigger is in its rearmost position and, in this position, the hammer block (part 54) is pulled down. Smith & Wesson has remained loyal to the old, time-tested leaf spring as a mainspring for the hammer. Its pre-cocking

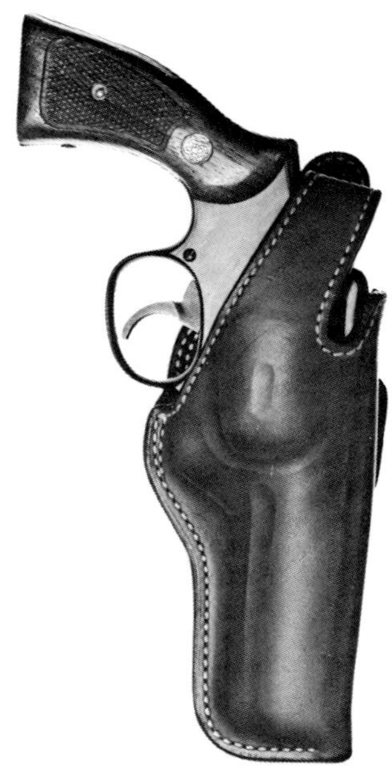

The appropriate holster goes with the revolver; this is a simple holster made by Bianchi.

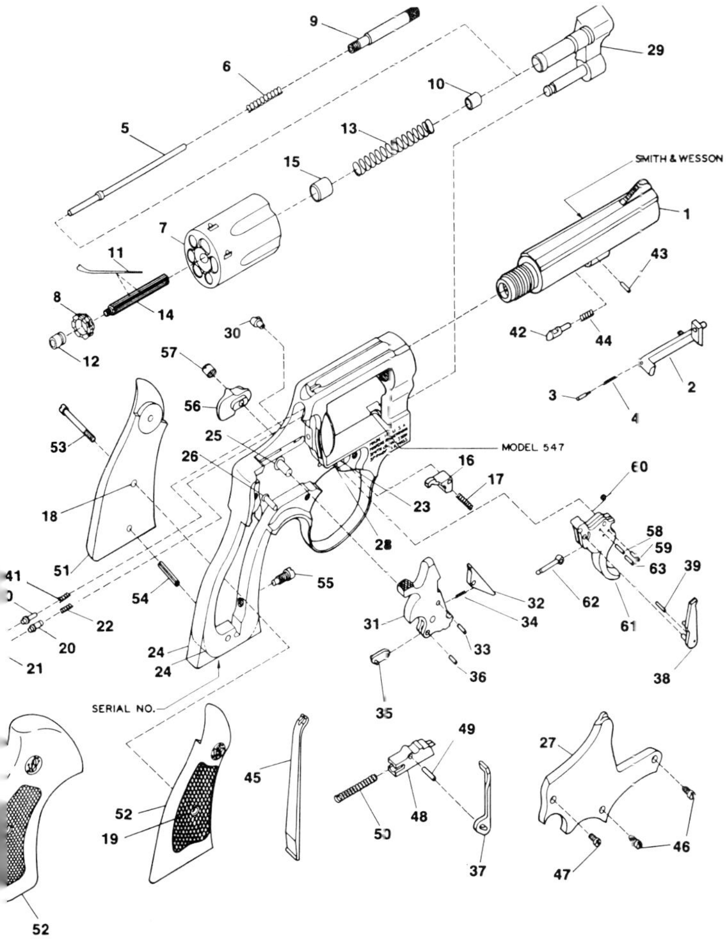

The parts of the M 547, which was made with three- and four-inch barrels. The differences mainly involve the cylinder and ignition.

can be weakened or strengthened by means of the small screw set low in the grip. An overly weak setting obviously decreases the tangible trigger weight somewhat, but in opposition to that, it makes ignition unsafe depending on the hardness of the percussion cap.

The extraction of loaded cartridges or fired cases is planned so that it does not cause problems in practice. They used to occur only when strongly charged cartridges were fired and their cases stuck fast in the holes. In the pivot of the extractor there are six longitudinal grooves, matching the six holes in the cylinder, into each of which a segment of the extractor (part 19) fits. The six segments are mounted snugly inside the pivot grooves and surrounded by coil springs. They themselves cannot give way either forward or backward. When cartridges are loaded into the cylinder, the small point of the sprung segment moves into the groove on the base of the cartridge and pushes just slightly against it. With pressure on the cylinder pivot, the cases are pushed out some 13 mm and fall out of the holes by themselves when the revolver is held at an angle.

The technical design by Smith & Wesson is original and safe for handling. It does, though, have two typical weaknesses that should be mentioned. The grooves on the cartridges must be sharply angled at the rear. If one uses worn cases already damaged at the rear, the small point of the segment cannot fit in reliably. As long as normal cartridges are used, this disturbance does not occur. The small points of the segments absolutely must not be rounded — this can happen less often through wear than through too-frequent cleaning of the cylinder holes with sharp metal brushes.

The shooting performance of the revolver (with four-inch barrel) is notably good. With a variety of cartridges it was possible to achieve groups of ten from 60 to 100 mm from a sitting position at a distance of 15 meters. This performance might even be beaten by using self-loaded cartridges with the right balance of bullet and powder charge. This handy revolver in 9 mm Parabellum caliber also spares a reloader a good deal of work. If one has loaded charges that are too weak for the self-loading pistol in question, they do not necessarily have to be unloaded but can be fired easily from the revolver.

Manurhin Model MR 73

In 1972 the French manufacturer Manurhin (Manufacture des Machines du Haut-Rhin S.A.) began to

Model MR 73 with three-inch barrel and fixed sight, plus the cylinder for 9 mm cartridges. The MR 73 has an excellent double action trigger.

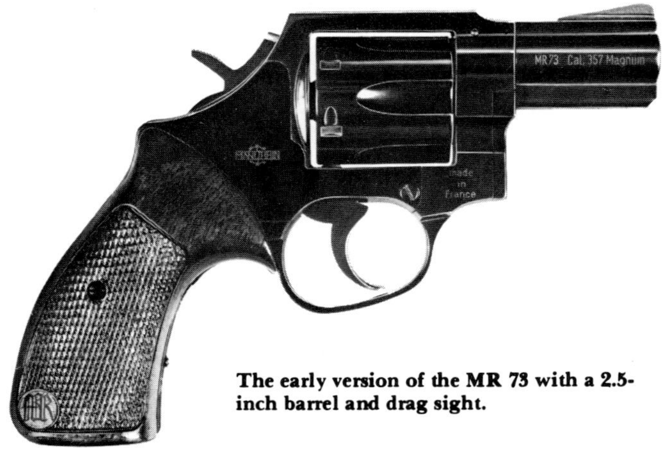

The early version of the MR 73 with a 2.5-inch barrel and drag sight.

Model MR 73-Sport with adjustable sight, four-inch barrel and added rubber grip, which affords a very good, firm hold.

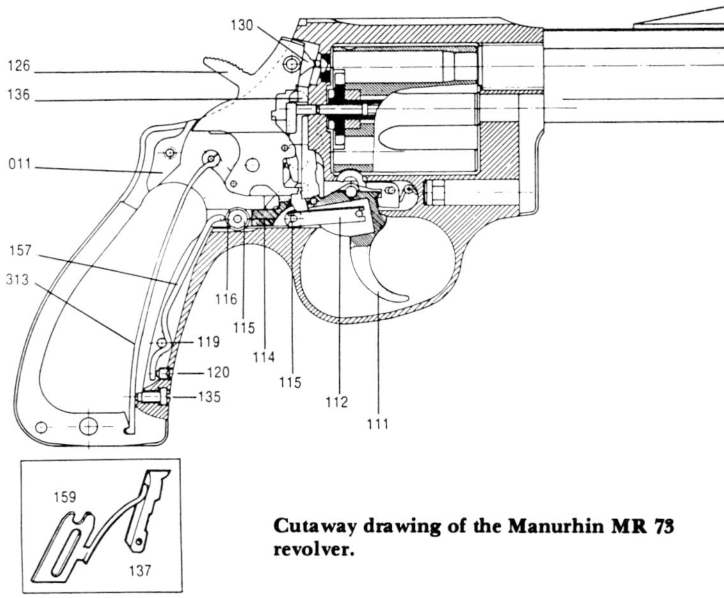

Cutaway drawing of the Manurhin MR 73 revolver.

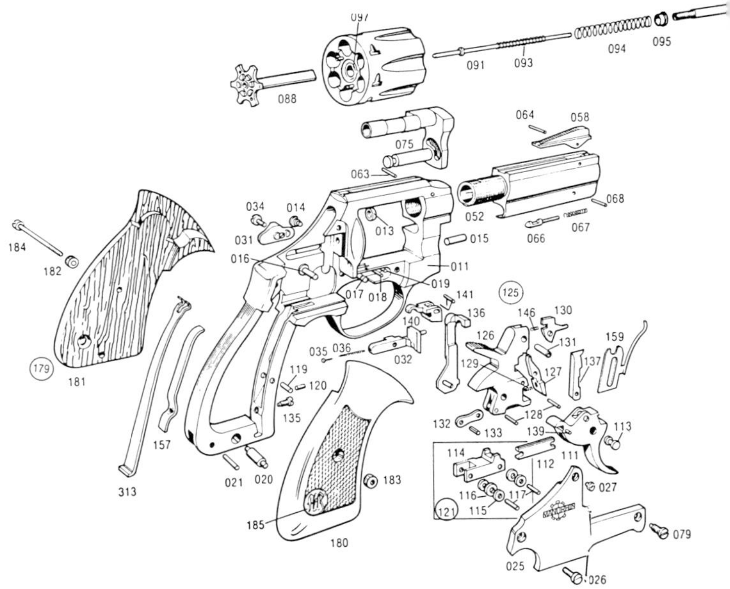

The parts of the MR 73. Scarcely any other revolver can offer so highly-developed technology.

develop its own revolver. Manurhin is not a newcomer in the field of weapon production, as the firm has built several pistols under license from Walther for a long time.

With its revolver, which has grown meanwhile into a whole family of revolvers, Manurhin offers several new developments that indicate much research into the problems of firing the first shot over a double action trigger. The revolver is available either with or without an adjustable sight, and the pure sport revolvers have a sport sight with steps to the rear. The modern barrel lengths from 2.5 to 8 inches are available, or even 10.75 inches in the case of the Silhouette revolver. A changeable cylinder for the 9 mm Parabellum caliber is available for the revolvers in .357 Magnum and .38 SPL calibers, and it is changed easily after the set-screw at the front of the frame is removed. The crane is the same for both cylinders, and it has not been made in such costly form here as in, for example, the Korth revolver.

The lock construction has changed slightly in the newer versions, concerning essentially the spring of the cylinder-transporting lever. The patented double action trigger has remained, and its characteristics will be briefly described here. When pulled it is noticeable that there is hardly any increase in resistance as it is pulled back. This is a very special characteristic of the MR 73. An experienced shooter can shoot better with a double action trigger than with a pre-cocked hammer. The sliding part runs on four rollers mounted on pins, and has a fifth wheel, the trigger-spring roller (part 116 in the drawing on page 238), on its rear axle. The trigger spring, mounted in the grip frame so it can turn, pushes against this wheel. The spring's shape has changed

Manurhin also offers an extra cylinder for the long-barreled versions.

The dismantled MR 73. The mainspring and trigger spring can be switched low on the frame.

slightly in recent years. Pre-cocking the trigger is varied by an Inbus screw set in the grip, and this immediately changes the trigger weight as well.

When the trigger is now pulled, it pushes the roller-mounted sliding piece backward, and the (number 116) roller pushes against the projection of the spring. With that the front part of the spring "clatters" right up onto the roller, and the spring pressure that occurs in the process of this "clattering" is no longer directly related to the pressure of the finger on the trigger. The result of this is that the hammer is cocked and can strike without any tangible increase in pressure.

Between the hammer and the grip there is an internal safety (part 136) which prevents the hammer from striking the ignition pin without activating the trigger. In this respect the MR 73 lives up to the safety regulations that apply to modern revolvers.

Toward the bottom of the frame there are two adjustment screws, the upper one of which affects the already mentioned trigger spring. The adjusting screw under it affects the mainspring, more or less as in the Smith & Wesson revolvers, by strengthening the pre-cocking when tightened and decreasing it when loosened. The

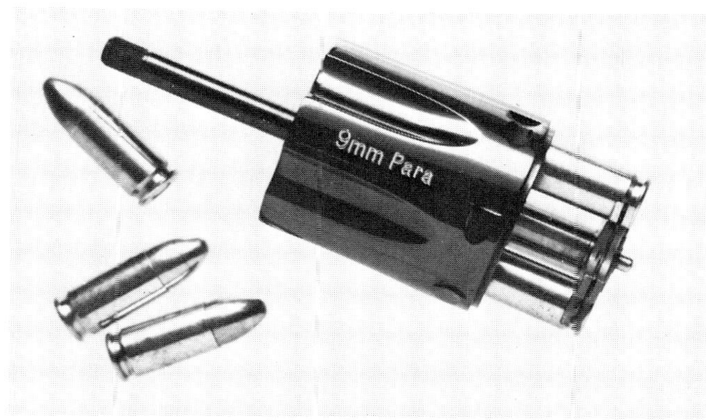

The earlier 9 mm Para cylinder was marked as such; this was omitted later.

The ejector star of the MR 73 in detail: the small segments of steel wire hold the cartridge safe and sound. No disturbances occurred during testing.

pre-cocking must not be made too soft, otherwise not all the cartridges will ignite, as some of them have very hard percussion caps.

The trigger itself is grooved and equipped with a stop screw which is simply set into the tongue. Its attachment there is not particularly easy, but its effect is best.

The version shown in the pictures does not have an adjustable sight; one aims over the sight groove cut on top of the frame. Its curve at the rear keeps the notch well in shadow.

All in all, the MR 73 is characterized by very neat and high-quality workmanship with an appropriate price; along with an alternate cylinder, it costs almost 2000 DM, which is a rather high price for a small device in series production.

The changeable cylinder in 9 mm Para caliber utilizes a simple principle that is not very different from the system of the basically similar Ruger revolver. The holes

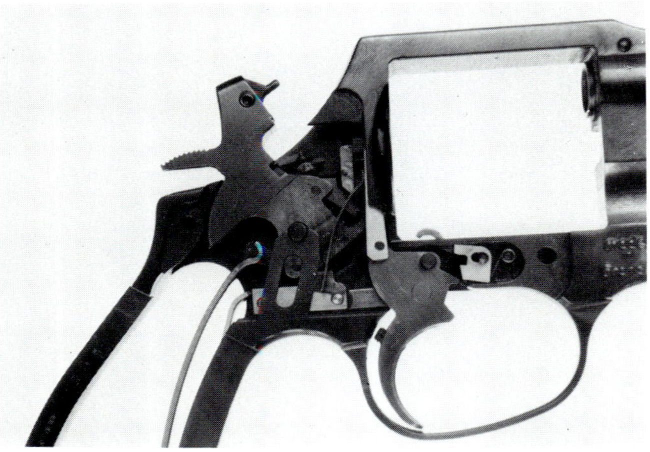

The open lock of the MR 73 with the hammer cocked. Here the position of the two leaf springs can be seen clearly. The sliding piece runs on small rollers.

The Special Police revolver was built in collaboration with Ruger. The type shown here has a trigger guard that is removable from below.

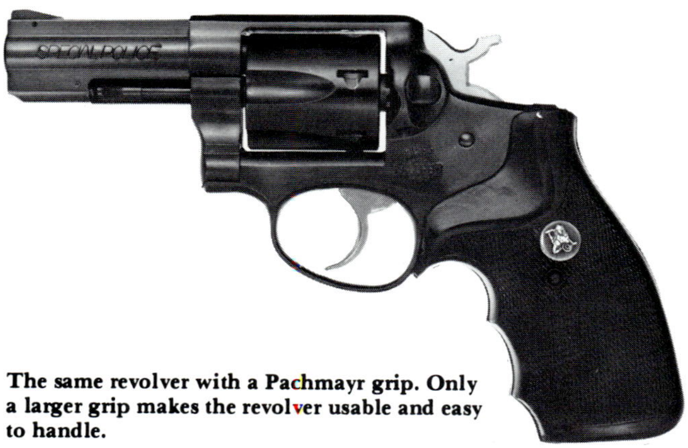

The same revolver with a Pachmayr grip. Only a larger grip makes the revolver usable and easy to handle.

have the usual steps on which the inserted cartridges rest. The ejector star, which is made very strong, includes a semicircular spring piece for every cartridge, with their two outside sections standing out slightly. When a cartridge is inserted, the ends of the spring piece fit into the groove at the base of the cartridge and hold the cartridge fast. This principle makes sure that even in the weapon is held at an angle, the already inserted cartridges will not fall out of the cylinder — an advantage that other revolvers do not offer. Fired cases can be removed without difficulty, so that the MR 73 can be described as problem-free in this respect. Its shooting performance, in both .357 Magnum and 9 mm Parabellum calibers, is also satisfactory.

Manurhin Special Police F 1

In collaboration with the American firm of Ruger, Manurhin has developed a revolver with a simplified construction, designed especially to satisfy the requirements of the French police.

There were formerly two somewhat different models, the "Special Police" and the "Special Police F 1« (or X 1 in stainless steel). The typical design feature of the Ruger revolver is the trigger unit which can be removed from below. After the grip panels and the mainspring are removed, the latter by pressing on a sprung bolt, it can be taken out. This is advantageous for dismantling, and the inclusive frame is an advantage in itself, however this should not be overemphasized, for open frames are durable enough. Another identifying mark is the transfer bar, which is attached directly to the extension of the

The Special Police dismantled. At the rear of the trigger is the spring bolt which has to be pushed in to remove the trigger unit.

trigger. Only when the trigger is pulled and remains back does the transfer bar lie in front of the firing pin, which is set into the frame, so that the latter can receive the impact. If the finger slips off the trigger, the transfer

The Special Police X 1 in stainless steel. This version has a removable side plate.

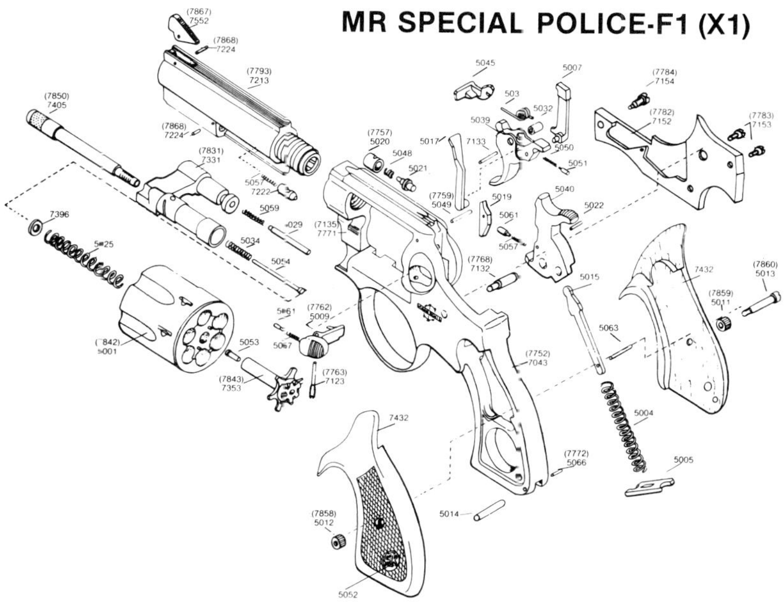

Loading is done with clips, several of which can be kept in a small pouch. One can load a clip revolver quickly but has to depend on the clips.

bar is pushed forcibly downward and the firing pin cannot be struck by the hammer. Only the combination of the hammer surface and the transfer bar can make ignition possible, a very effective safety against falling and being struck too.

The removable trigger unit was created for the "Special Police" version, which is no longer in production. It was followed by the "Special Police F 1" revolver with the same lock but with a plate attached at the side and held by three screws. Thus the lock is basically easier to reach, and the crane, along with the cylinder, easier to exchange. A separate cylinder is available for use with 9 mm cartridges, and here the problem of a rimless bottom has been dealt with simply in the grip: the cylinder is loaded with clips; three cartridges are set in a half-moon steel clip, as shown in the picture. The clip is both an advantage and a disadvantage, for it causes a certain dependence in terms of supply. On the other hand, one has the undisputed advantage of being able to load the cylinder very quickly with two clips.

The two revolvers shown here are already things of the past, but they are available in great numbers. Their workmanship is good and solid, the locking is excellent and so is the double action trigger. Accessories include holsters, pockets and various grips. The cylinder turns and opens to the left, and every version holds six cartridges; the available barrel lengths are 2.5, 3 and 4 inches, with weights of 918, 950 and 1005 grams.

Cutaway drawing of the Special Police F 1 or X 1. This revolver shows Ruger technology but departs from it in having a removable side plate.

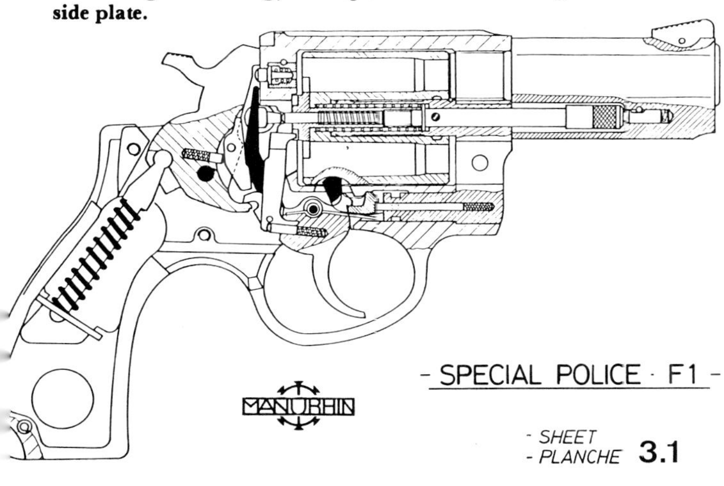

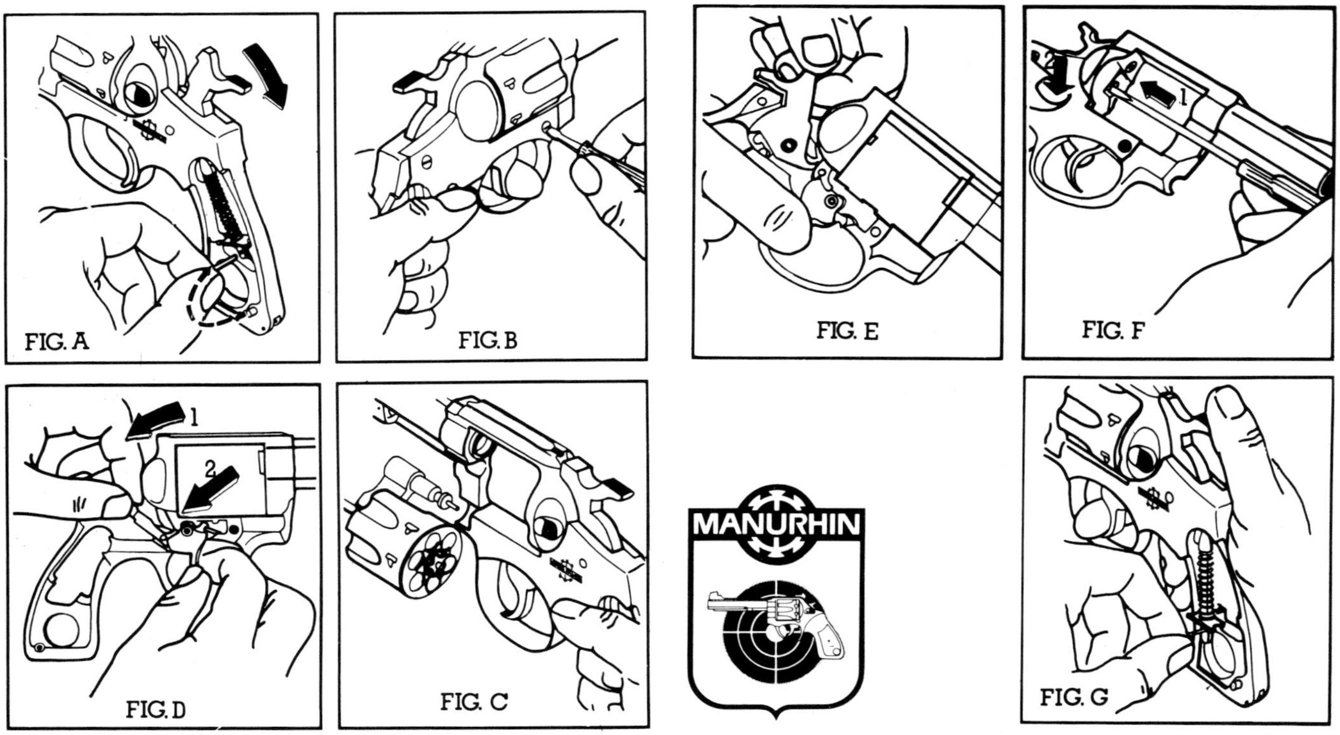

Dismantling and assembly of the Special Police F 1 and X 1.

Revolvers by Ruger

The American manufacturer, Sturm & Ruger, of Southport, Connecticut, has been active since 1949 in the production of revolvers, pistols and rifles. The firm has produced very impressive high-performance weapons that stand out just as much for their superb workmanship as for their excellent shooting performance. A surprising feature of Ruger weapons (which are imported and distributed in Germany by Frankonia-Jagd of Würzburg) is the favorable relationship between quality and price. Ruger was the first manufacturer to use stainless steel to a great extent in the construction of handguns, and without astronomical prices at that. Revolvers made by Ruger enjoy a good reputation . . . and one can really afford them.

For defense, hunting, service and sporting use, Ruger offers a wide selection in present-day calibers, including a revolver for the 9 mm Parabellum cartridge. A changeable cylinder is not offered, instead the 9 mm Para version is a complete weapon. The two models in 9 mm Para caliber are the POLICE SERVICE SIX and the SPEED-SIX, both made with a fixed sight in the manner typical of such revolvers.

The Ruger Service Six in 9 mm Parabellum caliber. It was never able to do well in the market.

The revolvers made by Ruger differ very noticeably in construction from previous designs. They dispense with an unscrewable side plate, and all moving parts are arranged on the powerful trigger guard so they can be taken out the bottom of the frame complete. This is practical, for one thing, and for another, it has the advantage that the frame offers great strength, as it lacks the weak points in the area of the removable side plate.

After the grip panels have been removed, the mainspring can be reached. To remove it, it is cocked, and then a hole bored in its guiding rod becomes visible, into which a nail or pin is inserted, then removed.

The trigger guard and its adjacent moving parts are

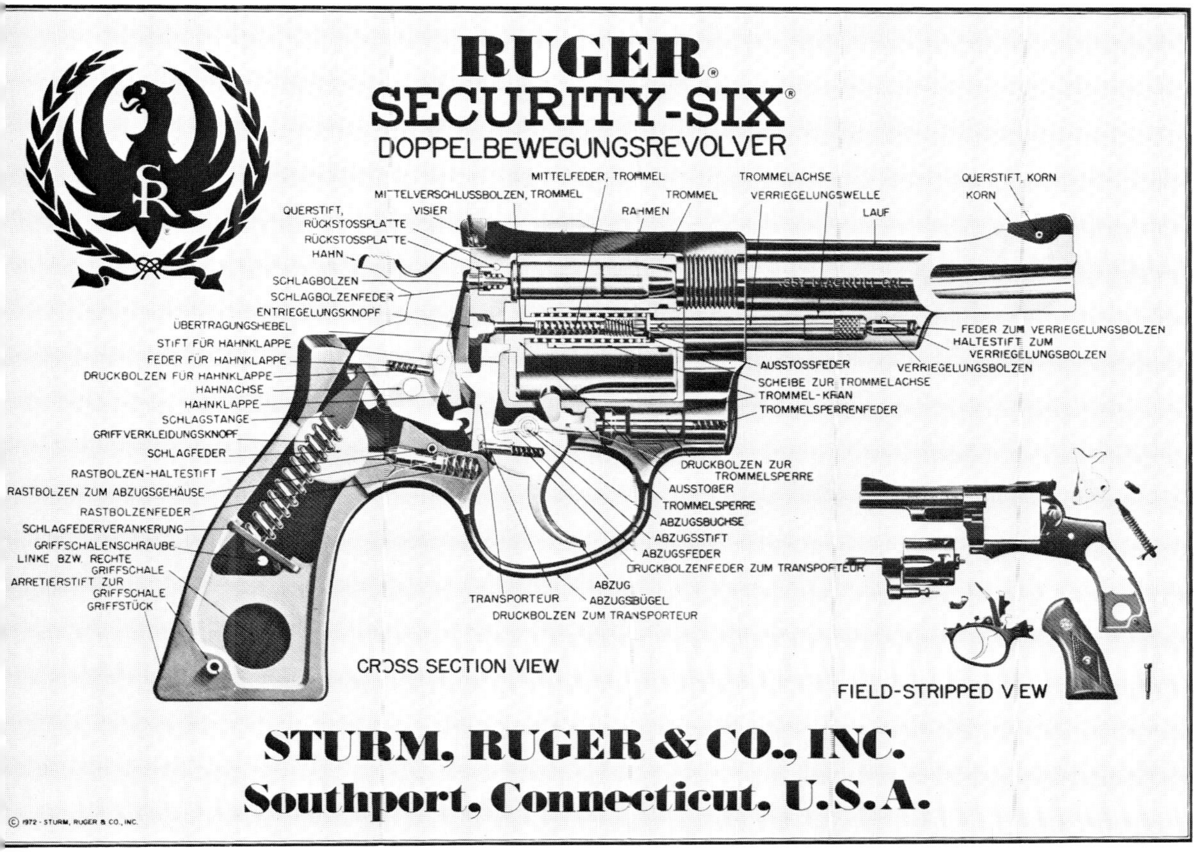

The typical construction of the Ruger double-action revolver. They are well-built, robust, and capable of good performance.

A small ring of spring wire fits into the groove on the base of the cartridge.

inserted in the forward part of the frame and held in the rear by a strongly sprung bolt. The bolt is pushed in and the complete trigger unit is swung down out of the frame. Another specialty is the locking knob for the cylinder, which swings out to the left. It is not a lever in the commonly used manner, but more of a well-shaped push-button which, when pushed, releases the cylinder.

The version made for the 9 mm Parabellum cartridge has a patented so-called rimless extractor. A ring of steel wire has been set in the extractor star and fits into the groove of the cartridge base when the cartridge is loaded. This functions well but does not inspire nearly as much confidence as the star of an earlier .357 cylinder can.

The revolvers made by Ruger are completely safe to handle. Safety is attained here similarly to the single-action revolvers, with the help of the so-called transfer bar. This transfer bar is mounted movably on the trigger and only moves into its functioning position when the trigger is pulled. It then lies in front of the hammer so that the connection between the hammer and transfer bar creates a unit that can reach the mainspring, which is mounted in the frame with a spring. The hammer has a cutout and would strike high on the frame if it were not for the raised transfer bar — a blow, bump or fall here could not in any way cause an unwanted shot.

The M 19 Combat Magnum as a sport revolver. Revolvers are becoming more versatile today thanks to the available grips.

A Different Caliber Change

A change in calibers and cartridges in normally a change between 9 mm Parabellum and .357 Magnum, as the actual bullet diameters are as good as identical.

For the tests described here, the author used his own Combat Magnum (Model 19) with a six-inch barrel and a Model 547 with a four-inch barrel in 9 mm Parabellum caliber. Initial tests showed that the cylinders were interchangeable, though not limited to the cylinder alone, but including both cylinder and crane. The two revolvers have slightly different cranes, on account of the further central hole bored into the Para cylinder. At first the cylinders fit with some difficulty after being switched, but improved from cocking to cocking and later from shot to shot. In front, where the surface of the crane touches the corresponding surface of the frame, the two parts do not fit together completely, however this does not necessarily have to disturb the functioning. Whomever is planning to make a serious exchange in the manner shown here would do well to have the two cylinders fitted by a capable gunsmith, and also fired in properly by him. The cylinders themselves fit, each having a length of exactly 42.60 mm. The ignition also works properly, although considerable technical differences exist. The revolver in .357 Magnum form uses the ignition pin set in the hammer to ignite the cartridge, while the Para revolver had an ignition pin set in the frame with a spring. No problems occurred here during testing.

It is possible to exchange cylinders between the M 19 Combat Magnum and the M 547. Switching results in a short .357 Magnum, .38 SPL and 9 mm Parabellum revolver. The cranes are changed along with the cylinders.

Shooting performance is naturally of interest. Only groups of ten were fired from a sitting position, and only some of the possible tests were made. Shooting was done at a distance of 15 meters, which is much more than the actual range at which such weapons are used. The distance of 15 meters in shooting from a sitting position shows almost the same results as shooting from a Ransom Rest at a distance of 25 meters.

First the results of the six-inch version, reequipped for the 9 mm Parabellum caliber. With the Hirtenberger Combat, a group of about 80 mm diameter was achieved, during which one stray shot spoiled the otherwise good group — the other nine shots were in a circle of barely 55 mm diameter.

With the Para cartridge imported by Kettner of Cologne, an excellent group of 40 mm diameter was achieved. Subsequent groups of five attested to this good performance again and again. Here, then, is a very good combination of weapon and cartridge. The group fired with self-loaded cartridges stayed within a diameter of 55 mm, again two stray shots away from a very close group. The cartridges included a fully jacketed bullet by Hirtenberger, a case by Geco and 4.8 grains of P 805 powder by Rottweil.

Now the results with the Para revolver refitted for the .357 Magnum caliber. The first group was still fired in 9 mm Parabellum caliber, but with the author's own loading as described before. The group of ten had a diameter of 60 mm, not bad for this cartridge and a weapon with a short barrel as well as not particularly favorable targeting visibility.

After changing the cylinder, the .38 SPL by Geco was fired, a version with a full jacket, and was not much more gentle than the same manufacturer.s .357 cartridge in recoil and muzzle flash. The performance was surprising:

a group with a diameter just under 50 mm, with all the shots other than two exceptions close together.

The .357 Magnum made by Geco, in a version with partial jacket and flat head, showed an even better performance potential: 45 mm with one stray and about 28 mm not counting it. Here too, the performance is more than satisfactory.

SPECIAL WEAPONS

The UZI Carbine

A country like Israel is constantly under threat from its neighbors and dissatisfied groups of its population. Power struggles, bloody attacks and the like are everyday events. Thus Israel must have powerful troops ready, however that is only a part of its security policy. The protection of remote areas, kibbuzes or farms is only possible with the help of involved citizens. Thus it is no surprise that weapons are available to private individuals in Israel that cannot be obtained here.

On the basis of the familiar UZI type machine pistol, Israel Military Industries has developed a smaller version, plus a so-called UZI pistol and a handy UZI carbine with a 410 mm barrel, in 9 mm Parabellum caliber. The choice of caliber was based on both the good results given by this cartridge and its availability.

Externally, the UZI carbine looks just like the machine pistol except that it has a longer barrel and has no switch for sustained fire. The carbine is a self-loader with an unlocked mass breech and flying firing pin, made exclusively for single action. The magazine holds 25 cartridges, and another magazine for 32 cartridges is available as an accessory, plus a clip that forms an L-shaped link between the two magazines.

According to its advertising, the weapon is intended for hunters, sport shooters and collectors, and is also supposed to be safe from misuse by children, as it is impossible to fire it without pushing in the grip safety, as children's small hands cannot operate the safety and trigger at the same time.

The UZI carbine as a "sport weapon." And though it can be done in other lands, the world does not always end.

The UZI carbine in 9 mm Parabellum caliber; with the same construction, it is also sold in the USA in .45 ACP caliber. It can only fire single shots.

The production carbine has a folding metal shaft which makes it look quite "military", and a wooden shaft that can be screwed on, like that of the machine pistol, and is available as an accessory. The shooting performance is stated by the manufacturer as attaining groups of 7.6 cm at 100 meters, which would be an outstanding performance, but we cannot test it in Germany, for the carbine is not available here because of its appearance as an automatic weapon. The Israelis, on the other hand, do not regard the safety of their country as being endangered by having such weapons owned by the populace. On the contrary, this is seen as providing extra security. More of such and similar weapons are in the hands of the law-abiding citizenry, the harder it is to attack them. In addition, there was at one time a well-built defense-sport carbine available to interested civilians in Germany, and trained shooters are always available, a very important point in crisis areas. The manufacturer packs this impressive carbine in disassembled form in a handy carrier bag that holds the weapon without its barrel, the barrel, the belt and the magazine. With its shaft folded up, the whole carbine is only 610 mm long, and with the shaft folded out it measures 800 mm, with a weight of 4.3 kilograms including a magazine filled with 25 cartridges.

A short list of available accessories may be of interest: an alternative wooden shaft to replace the folding shaft, a tool for adjusting the sight, a handy device for loading and unloading the magazine, magazines from UZI production and holding 32 or even 40 cartridges, cleaning devices and "display barrels." A display barrel is a barrel of the same length as the machine-pistol barrel and can be substituted for the long barrel but cannot be used for shooting — it simply makes the carbine look like a machine pistol without being one. For training purposes the manufacturer has recently begun to offer a switching system in .22 LR caliber. It includes a 150 mm length insertion barrel, a magazine with an inserted .22 magazine, and an alternate breechblock including firing pin and ejector. The barrel is pushed into the existing barrel, the original breechblock with mainspring is removed and replaced by the new breech, and the magazine is

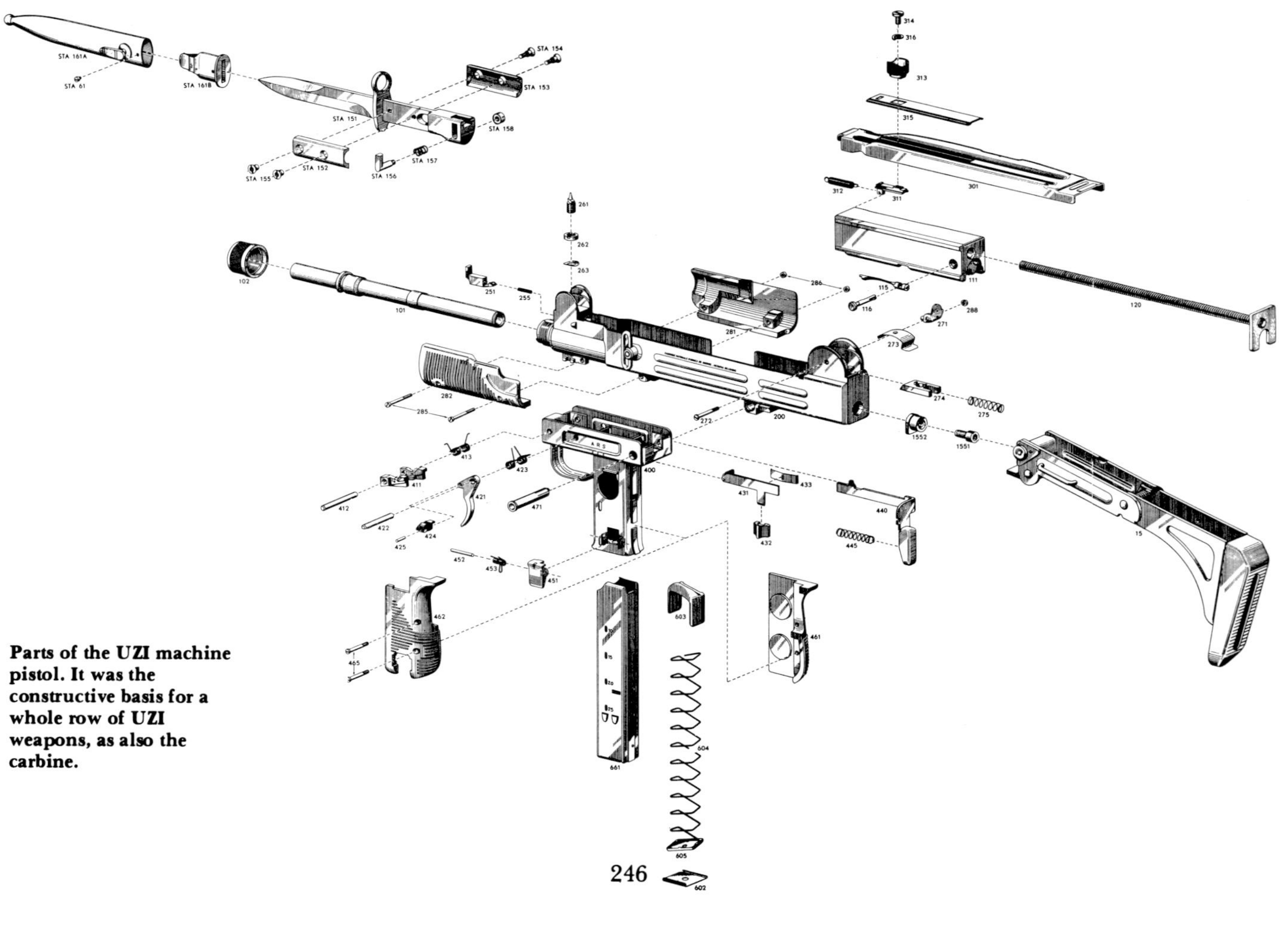

Parts of the UZI machine pistol. It was the constructive basis for a whole row of UZI weapons, as also the carbine.

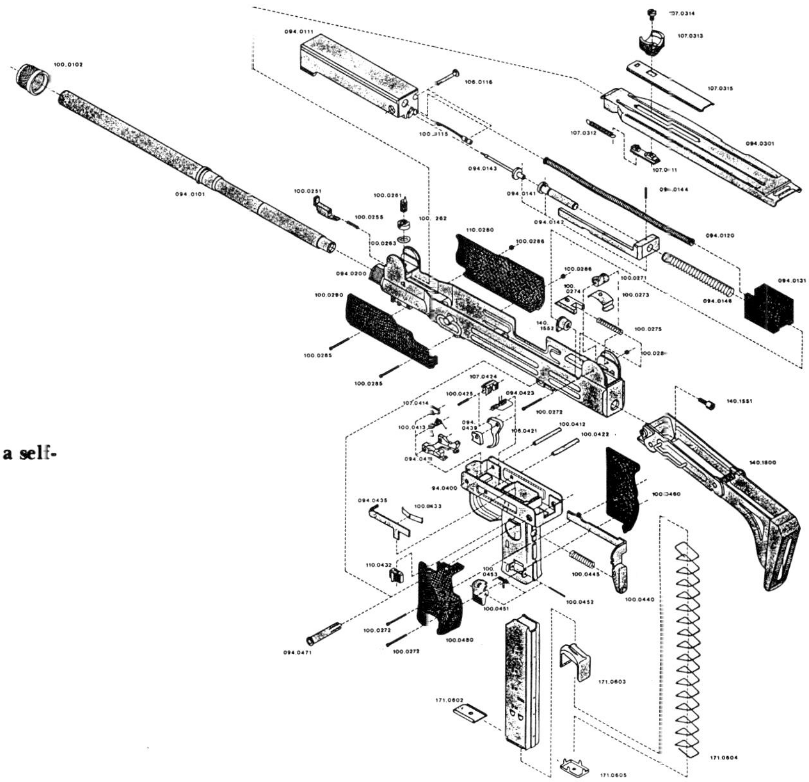

Parts of the UZI carbine in 9 mm Parabellum caliber, as a self-loading semi-automatic weapon.

simply switched. The operation is unchanged, just set up for the small rim-fire cartridge and for shooting at shorter ranges. The complete system weighs 580 grams, and thus the reequipped carbine has an overall weight of 4.4 kilograms without a filled magazine.

Technical Data: UZI Carbine

Manufacturer	Israel Military Industries
Caliber	9 mm Para (also .45 ACP)
Magazine capacity	25/32/40
System	Mass breech, single action
Overall length	610 mm/800 mm
Barrel length	410 mm
Barrel profile	4 riflings, right, 1 x at 245 mm
Sight line	309 mm
Sights	Fore- and backsight sepa rately adjustable
Material/finish	Steel/burnished
Weight empty/loaded	3.8 kg/4.3 kg
Muzzle velocity	380-460 m/s

The Camp Carbine by Marlin

The Camp Carbine is the first purely civilian self-loading weapon made for the 9 mm Parabellum cartridge. In the same form, it has also been marketed for some time for the .45 ACP cartridge, both being very

The Marlin Model 9 Camp Carbine; it is also available in .45 ACP caliber. An impressive and handy weapon of a very different kind.

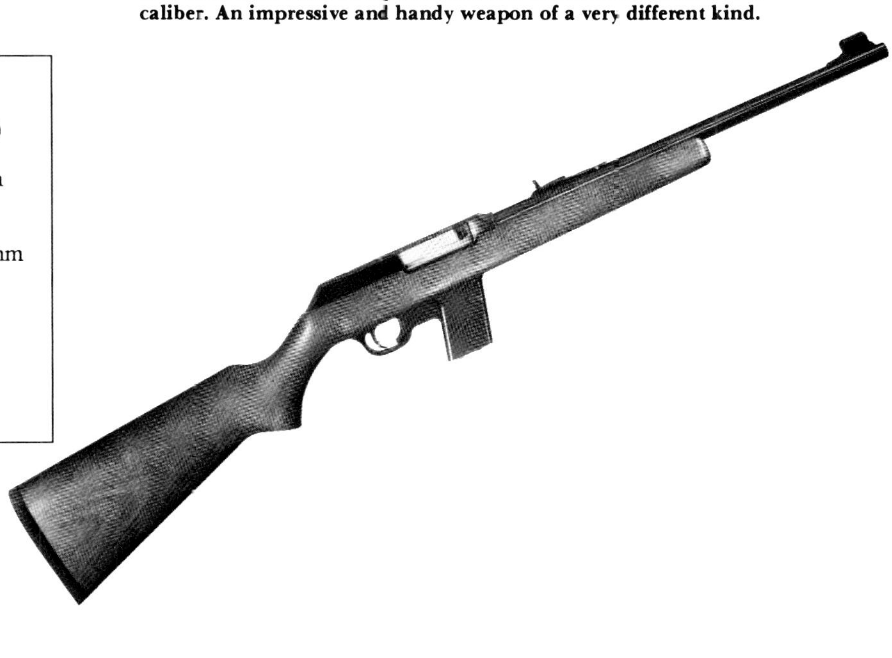

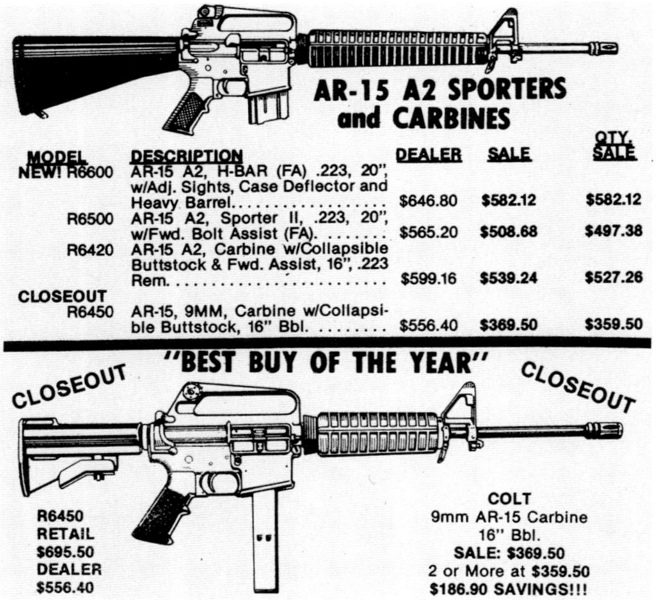

Excerpt from an American advertisement showing the Colt AR-15 in 9 mm Parabellum caliber with push-in shaft.

popular cartridges in the USA as in Europe. With this small, handy gun — its standard magazine holds 12 cartridges, and a 20-shot magazine is available as an accessory — the manufacturer is following a very up-to-date trend, offering a self-loader, for use in open country, that fires the same cartridges as an obtainable pistol or revolver in this caliber. Similar combinations have existed for some time: bottom-lever repeaters in .357 Magnum or .44 Magnum/.44 Special calibers.

Marlin is best known as a manufacturer of well-built rifles, and the Camp Carbine is advertised with emphasis on its excellent ballistic values: the 9 mm cartridge fired from the carbine offers up to 22% higher muzzle velocity and up to 50% more muzzle energy than a weapon with a 4-inch barrel. These values could be confirmed with the Weinlich VM-25 where the bullet attains a velocity of 390

The manual safety is at the front of the trigger guard and can be reached quickly by stretching the trigger finger.

The barrel and cover are removed; under them is the trigger housing with the plastic magazine shaft.

to 400 meters per second, as compared with "only" 340 to 350 m/sec from an ordinary pistol.

The small Camp Carbine is only 895 mm long and weighs barely 3000 grams unloaded and without a telescopic sight. With the Leupold scope, offering sixfold magnification, plus the Weaver mount, the unloaded weight is about 3300 grams, which is not much at all, and handling the weapon is practically child's play. The barrel is screwed into the system housing, which is machine out of solid material, and as one would expect from Marlin, it has twelve fine micro-riflings, which should inspire caution in those who like to use lead bullets. The author has limited himself exclusively to tests with VM or TM cartridges, so detailed performance figures will follow shortly.

The sight can be adjusted for height by using the stepped backsight, and the backsight leaf itself can be folded forward if a scope needs to be set particularly deep.

In its shaft form, the self-loader is somewhat reminiscent of the other Marlin self-loaders, and these in turn are rather similar to the optical model of the M 1, which is highly regarded in the USA. There are no herringbone or otherwise roughened surfaces, nor is their a cheek, which makes it appear to be equally handy

The complete mass breech with cocking lever, recoil spring and guiding rod.

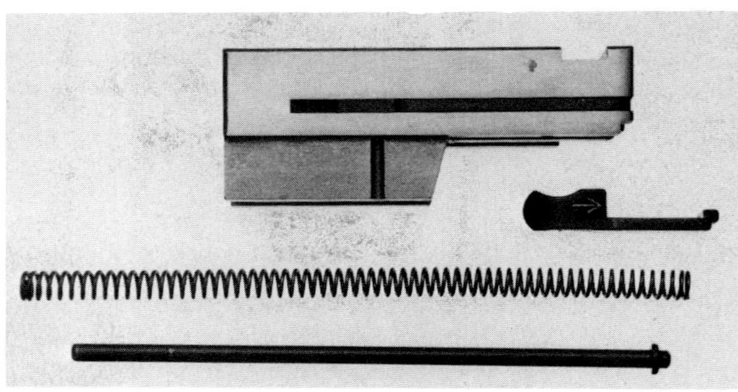

A Leupold Compact with sixfold magnification was mounted here. A Weaver mount was used with it, though it had to be shortened at the front so as not to overhang.

for left- and right-handed shooters to use. The front shaft, with its rounded cross-section, extends more than half the length of the barrel, and the system is held tightly together by two screws that cannot be lost These screws came loose easily during shooting tests and caused very irregular shooting results, and only after countermeasures were taken could the shooting performance of the weapon and cartridges be confirmed.

A weapon for use in open country neither can nor should lack an effective safety system, and the carbine has several of them, which combine to make the weapon safe to handle. In the trigger unit, which is made of reinforced black plastic, there is a so-called Garand-type safety mounted in the trigger guard, similar to that of the Garand rifle that was once in official use. In a safety position, the safety wing extends into the trigger guard. A small push with a finger makes the weapon ready to fire, and does so quickly, without any fumbling. The safety works directly on the trigger by blocking it.

A magazine safety allows the trigger to be pulled only in the event that the magazine is completely inserted and held in place. Its arm reaches into the magazine shaft and is pushed in by the back of the magazine.

The carbine does not have a shooting safety of the type used in pistols, and thus the cocked hammer can be decocked gently when the breechblock is not all the way forward without having it strike the firing pin too hard. A loading indicator, though, is installed. As soon as a cartridge is inserted, an indicator sticks out, easily visible and tangible, immediately behind the extractor. The extractor pushes against its short shank, which improves its effect even more.

The high trigger weight is also related to the safety factor, as a branch that hits the trigger by accident cannot easily cause an unintentional shot to be fired. The sunken magazine catch is built in a similar way. As it is intentionally difficult to reach, it frees the magazine only slightly, after which one has to pull it out of the shaft by hand.

The functioning principle is remarkably simple, and an unbolted mass breech is sufficient. Inside the breech housing, which is machined out of solid material, the breechblock, weighing some 380 grams, slides against the pressure of the rod-guided recoil spring To the rear, a nylon buffer limits its path and makes itself pleasantly noticeable when shooting.

The entire trigger unit is made of plastic, enclosed by two side plates of steel which also form the sliding rails for the breechblock as well as the mounts for all the pivots. During recoil the hammer is cocked and caught in its rest. The whole unit can be removed quickly by loosening only one spring clip. A special feature is found on the ramp to the barrel. It is not a part of the screwed-in barrel, but sits movably on the trigger unit. One must push it back a bit during assembly, after which it straightens out again.

The sight is, as already noted, adjustable in height by means of a stepped wedge. The brass foresight is well protected inside a removable tunnel.

A Leupold scope with sixfold magnification was mounted here. As a so-called compact-glass, its short length fits the small weapon well. The top of the housing has four holes bored and threads cut in. The Weaver mount and the Weaver rings that go with it fit here. The rail was too long in its original form and stuck out at the front, so it was shortened slightly, and the grooves that let the holding screws pass through had to be relocated accordingly. The Leupold scope affords an extremely bright and sharply defined picture.

The handyman still has a chance. This is an adjustable folding bipod that can be taken from the front shaft at any time.

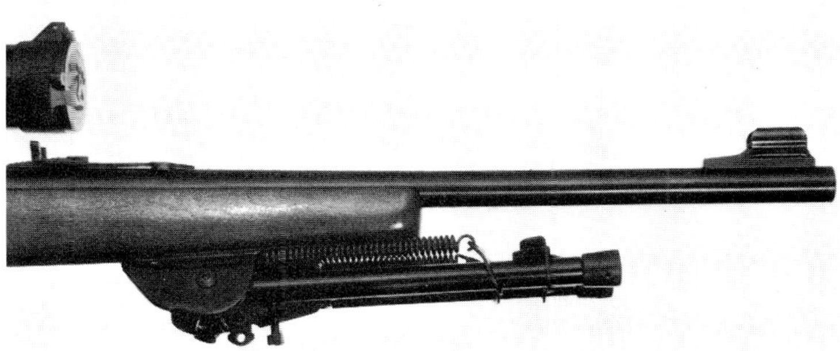

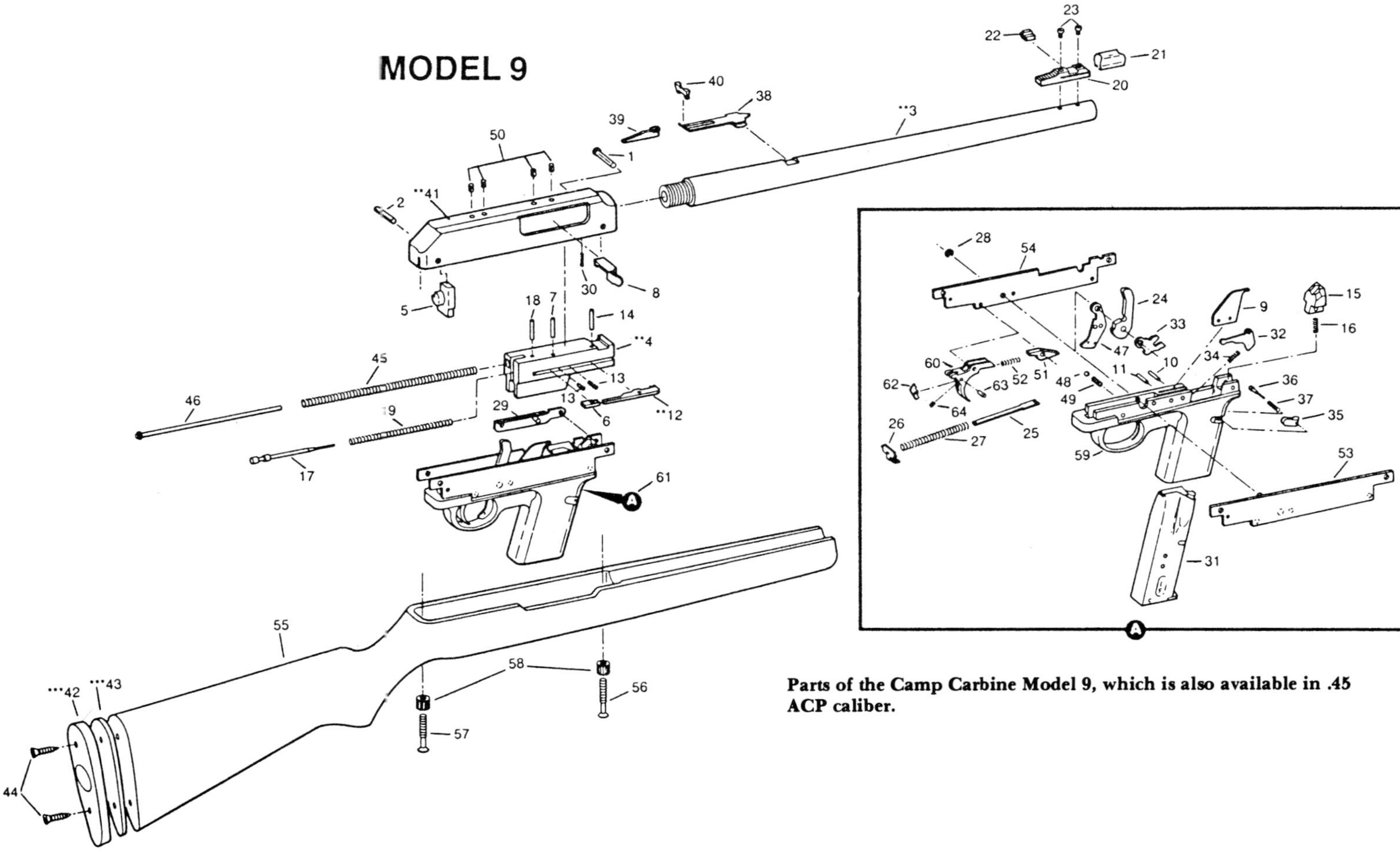

Parts of the Camp Carbine Model 9, which is also available in .45 ACP caliber.

The shooting performance of the Camp Carbine is "mixed", as it does not fire well with all cartridges, and in particular, the varying results of the individual types of cartridges should definitely be regarded and evaluated as experimental. During the author's tests, it fired best with semi-jacketed Geco cartridges, achieving groups of five the size of a five-Mark coin at a distance of 50 meters repeatedly, with good results.

Derringer

The Derringer (correctly spelled "Deringer" with only one r) won its first sad renown when President Abraham Lincoln was assassinated. Now as then, it is a short weapon that can be carried inconspicuously and is very effective at short range. Derringers, or at least similar weapons, haveall matter of ignition systems. However, they became popular only with the percussion cap, and are easier to handle with metal cartridges.

The Derringer shown here is made for the 9 mm Parabellum cartridge. This caliber in such a weapon can be regarded in itself as unusual, as they are otherwise especially made for cartridges with rims, if such a simplification is allowable here. The manufacturer, the Derringer Corporation of Waco, Texas, USA, has set out to offer a double-barreled Derringer for any imaginable cartridge.

The market for such midgets exists. Some want one as a nostalgic collector's item, while others regard it as a

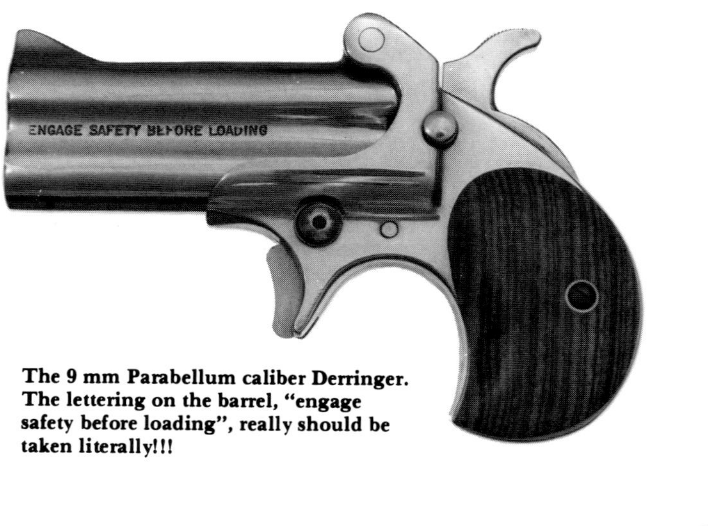

The 9 mm Parabellum caliber Derringer. The lettering on the barrel, "engage safety before loading", really should be taken literally!!!

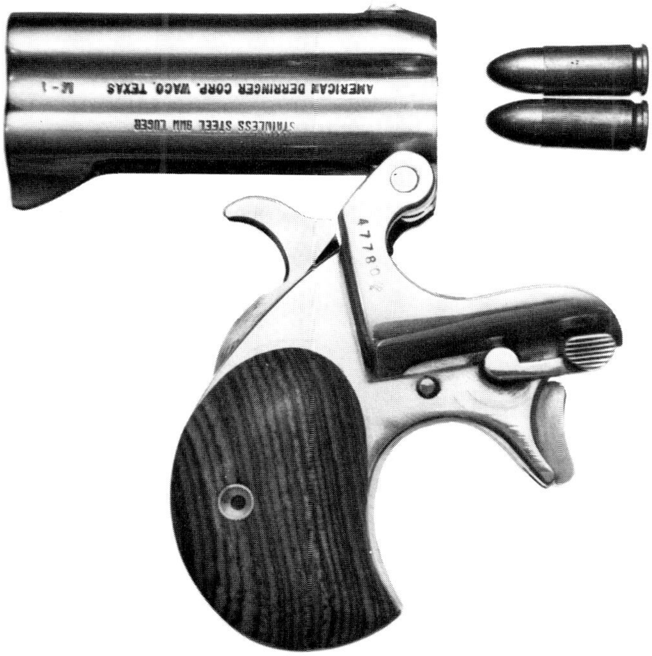

Fold up the barrel and insert two cartridges, then close, bolt, cock the hammer and shoot.

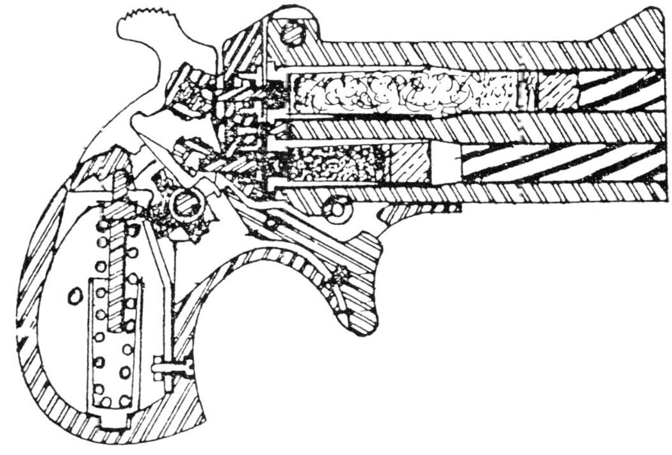

Above and lower left: Cutaway and parts of the Derringer made by the American Derringer Corporation.

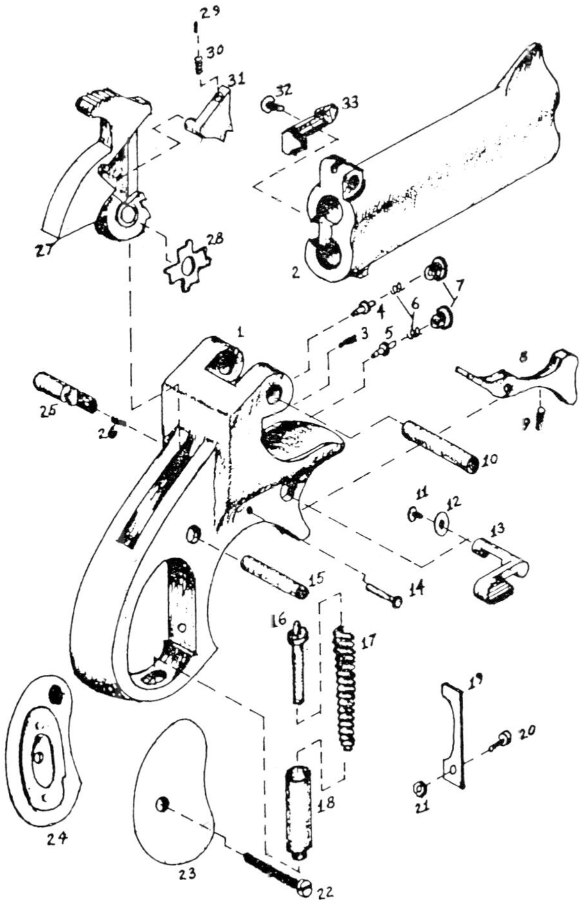

Individual Parts, American Derringer (Not all the parts shown here belong to this weapon; some are for a different though similar version.)

1 Rahmen (Griffstück)
2 Lauf m jeweiligen Kaliber
3 Stift zur Sicherung
4 Oberer Schlagbolzen
5 Unterer Schlagbolzen
6 Schlagbolzenfeder
7 Schlagbolzenhülse
8 Abzug
9 Abzugfeder
10 Lauf-Achsstift
11 Schraube zur Sperre
12 Feder zur Sperre
13 Lauf-Sperre
14 Abzugachse
15 Hahnachse
16 Hahnstange
17 Schlagfeder
18 Schlagfeder-Hülse
19 Wahlscheibenfeder
20 Schraube zu 19
21 Mutter zu 20
22 Griffschalenschraube
23 Griffschale
24 Griffschale
25 Sicherung
26 Sicherungsfeder
27 Hahn
28 Wahlscheibe
29 Stift zum Schlagstück
30 Feder zum Schlagstück
31 Schlagstück
32 Schraube zum Auszieher (entf.)
33 Auszieher (entf.)
34 entf.

final defense in critical situations, perhaps as a second weapon concealed on the body.

The manufacturer presently offers seven different versions in a total of 26 different calibers, the strongest of which can barely be controlled and almost always cause bodily damage to the shooter. Firing powerful cartridges from an extremely short and thus light weapon is not much fun, and the manufacturer is not exaggerating when he says in his thoroughgoing service manual that only a few shots of this kind should be fired per day. Injuries to hand joints cannot be ruled out, and the question of sense and purpose can rightfully be raised.

Shooting the 9 mm Parabellum caliber is less dangerous — of course there is a strong blow to the hand, but that can be endured. Technically, the rimless cartridge requires a compromise: the Derringer in this caliber has no extractor. One pulls the empty case out of chamber with a fingernail or, if time allows, uses a rod to push it out frontward through the muzzle. When just a few shots have been fired and the two chambers are still clean, the fired cases can still be removed easily with a fingernail. In the case of heavily charged cartridges or frequently used cases, it is best to unload through the muzzle.

The construction of the Derringer is very simple. The double barrel is made of one piece and attached so that it pivots high on the frame (or grip). As a matter of principle, one should avoid removing this pivot, because it is pressed in snugly and cross-hatched on both ends. The inside of the barrel is not much to look at. The

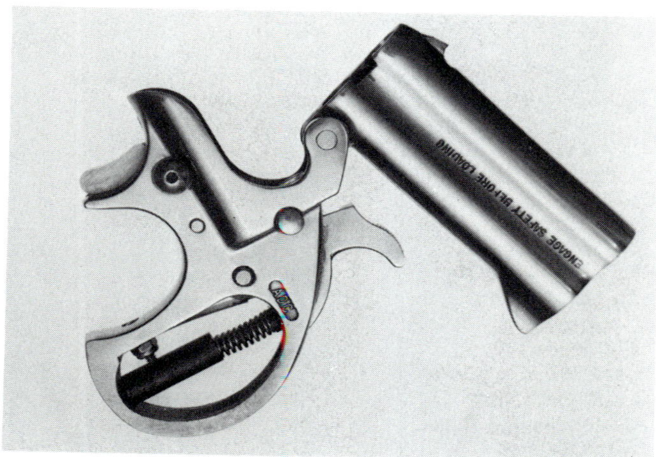

After removing the grip panels, the mainspring can be seen inside a casing.

The two strike plates with their firing pins are dangerous if one handles the little weapon the wrong way.

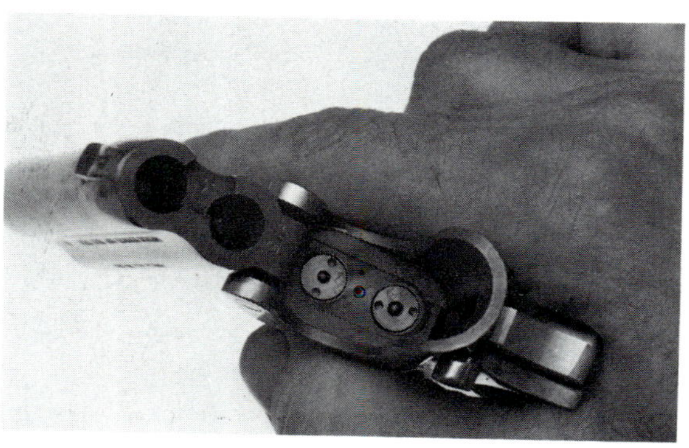

riflings are rather crudely made, and the chambers could have been made considerably better in view of the high price tag. A spring block holds the barrel firmly in the frame, and the tangible play disappears completely only when two cartridges are inserted.

The way the two cartridges are ignited with only a single hammer is interesting. On its right inner surface, the hammer has a firing pin installed, under spring pressure. It is switched by a four-pointed star every time the hammer is cocked. Thus a Derringer made in this manner does not necessarily fire first the upper and then the lower barrel, but first the one and then the other, depending on which barrel's turn it is. Two firing pins, working independently of each other, are mounted in the strike plate, where the hammer strikes either the one or the other. The two barrels, incidentally, shoot not too far from each other, and after several shots from a distance of five meters, the two groups of shots were mixed inside a circle about 100 mm in diameter — cartridges by Geco, Norma and Winchester were used.

The trigger is a single-action type of the simplest construction. It extends into the hammer rest, stays there under the pressure of a small coil spring, and releases smoothly.

It is no exaggeration to say that Derringers are not very accurate weapons — the manufacturer does not deny this, but rather warns the user of possible operating errors. Not without reason are the words ENGAGE SAFETY BEFORE LOADING clearly stamped into the left side of the barrel!

The safety is a strong transverse bolt that one can set immediately after it passes through the safety rest of the hammer. The hammer and the safety both have cutouts for this purpose, so that the two parts can link solidly together. Only when the hammer is pulled into the firing pin rest does the safety spring out and open the hammer's path to the firing pin. One should not in any case rely only on the effect of the safety rest, for a break can take place there, and a fall on the hammer would lead to an unwanted shot being fired. In any case, the safety should be set first, after which loading or unloading can be done.

A further safety problem is the type of firing pins, which are not constructed here as short firing pins. If the hammer is driven forward, its striking piece is always behind one of the pins, which then projects. If the pistol is now loaded and the barrel is swung back vigorously, then it will, in fact must, result in a shot being fired.

All of this sounds rather discouraging, for one would rather not have or use an unsafe weapon. But it should be considered that the best will in the world cannot build any more safety devices into such a small space, and with proper handling (always set the safety first), very little should go wrong. In this respect, the little Derringer made by the American Derringer Corporation is an impressive, reliable small weapon. Made completely of stainless steel, neatly worked and well polished, it deserves criticism only for the workmanship inside the barrels. Just a few words about its technology: After removing the two rounded grip panels, one can see the mainspring, a guided coil spring inside a casing that is braced low in the frame. After the block has been removed, the trigger pivot can be driven out, then the mainspring, the leaf spring for the guiding piece, and finally the hammer can be removed. There simply are not very many parts.

RELOADING

The whole realm of reloading has been able to become more and more widespread and popular of late, and there are many good reasons for it. For the frequent shooter, the cost has become a serious problem, and linked with that is a certain annoyance at having to scrap an empty cartridge case that has only been used once — the case is the most expensive part of the cartridge. Viewed exclusively from the standpoint of cost, reloading is beneficial, and the more cartridges are reloaded and reused, the more favorable it becomes. Many good books have been written on this subject, many good and "quick" devices are on the market for the well-versed reloader.

Reloading the 9 mm and 7.65 Parabellum cartridges is relatively free of problems, for in the 9 mm realm in particular there are many good components available. Almost every manufacturer of cartridges markets his components as separate items for the reloader. The choice of suitable types of powder is satisfactory, percussion caps are available in sufficient variety, and the cases last fairly long, for one need not and must not crimp their mouths by rolling them, which considerably affects how long they will last.

Cleaning

This subject will be treated only briefly, and a few tips learned in practice will be offered. One small detail should be dealt with at once: that of typical dirt. Depending on the weapon, the cartridge case will get more or less dirty when fired, and this is affected by the type of chamber and how well the expanded cases contract again in it. If the contraction at the mouth is not complete, then the cases will be thoroughly enveloped by flaming powder gases and will come out of the chamber besmirched. Additional cleaning is more necessary here than for Magnum cartridges fired from a well-kept revolver, and the situation (always directly dependent on the weapon, the charge and the type of powder) can even go so far that a case must be cleaned thoroughly every

Upper left: a borderline attempt. Two separate contacts on the slide and grip close the circuit for the electric flash. The bullet could not be made visible; only the burned powder behind the bullet can be seen.

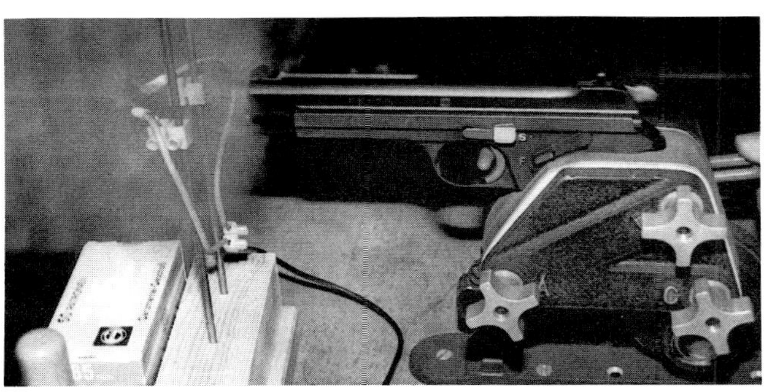

Lower left: Here the contact is some 5 cm in front of the muzzle. As soon as the bullet flies through the two metal brushes, the contact for the flash is closed. The slide has just begun to recoil and at this moment has already moved back some 5 mm.

In devices such as the Turbo 1200 shown here, the cases become even cleaner than at the factory. The granulate, when stretched with rice grains, will clean at least 4000 cases.

time it is reloaded. Cases with dirt stuck to them get even dirtier with the next shot. This can lead to problems while loading in the press and disturbances on the way from the magazine to the chamber.

Practical chemical cleaning, using immersion baths, can be used, and so can a simpler mechanical cleaning in a device made for the purpose. Here the empty cases are shaken in a granular abrasive, and after one or more hours most of the cases look better than cases fresh out of the factory. This mechanical cleaning allows great quantities to be cleaned at low cost — with one kilogram of abrasive, and without losing any effect, up to 4000 Para cases can be cleaned thoroughly. One can even "stretch" the abrasive by adding scaled rice, but this can cause problems with defused cases, as the rice grains easily get stuck in their cap chambers.

Cleaning with chemical also gives good results, even though the cases do not take on the highly polished look produced by the mechanical cleaning process.

Cartridge Lengths

The length of the finished cartridges, and the length of the cases to be loaded previous to that are an important standard, especially for the 9 mm Parabellum cartridge. Every deep placement of a bullet leads to large-scale increases in pressure, which do not do either the proper functioning or the weapon's precision much good, and in extreme cases can result in extreme risks for the weapon and the shooter. The exact length of the case is 19.15 mm, a dimension that should always be checked BEFORE loading. Too-short cases (they are the exception) are unusable, and too-long cases have to be trimmed to the proper length, which means turning them at the front with a simple tool.

If the ejected cases fly different distances out of the weapon despite presumably equal powder charges, this is a first sign of differences in pressure. It can also indicate a difference in firmness with which the bullet sits in the case.

The installations on the matrices are oriented to the outer dimension of the cases and do not take any possible differences in the strength of the case material into consideration. Whether a bullet is set firmly enough is

For 9 mm Parabellum cartridges, equal bullet length and equal depth in the case are very important.

shown by a simple test: One presses the finished cartridge with the bullet on the surface of a personal scale until the scale shows a "weight" of 25 to 27 kilograms. Up to that point, the bullet should not push deeper into the case. Uneven setting of the bullet brings the danger of malfunctioning, as when a shot is fired, the bullets of the cartridges still in the magazine are displaced and hinder their movement into the chamber. In case of incorrect loading, this can even cause the bullet to get stuck at the front of the chamber when the weapon is loaded by hand.

Strong charges should also be uniformly treated with rim paint for adhesion. In practice one should keep in mind not to load mixed cases, but always cases from the same manufacturer and, if possible, from the same lot.

In the Lee Progressive 1000 there are always three cases being worked on. With every lever stroke, a finished cartridge comes out of the machine, at a rate of some 400 per hour.

Typical Charges

One should not place too-high hopes in an ordinary charge in terms of precision; not every pistol shoots like an SIG 210. The author's own tests (published in the journal *Internationaler Waffenspiegel,* issues June 1984, and January 1985) show that dispersion almost always increases with heavier charges. A typical charge should be envisioned first of all so that the functioning of the weapon is maintained, with a certain functioning reserve left, and that the effect on the target is in agreement with the bullet used.

It is not possible to specify one very definite charge that will provide the required safety for every weapon. Cartridges with medium charges, according to the powder manufacturer's data, can cause problems when fired from various pistols, and result in an unsatisfactory slide recoil, as well as disturbances in cartridge insertion.

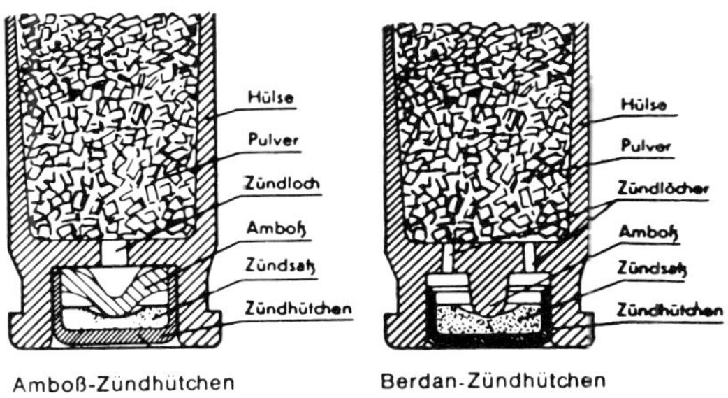

These are the two basic types of ignition, the anvil type at left and the Berdan type at right.

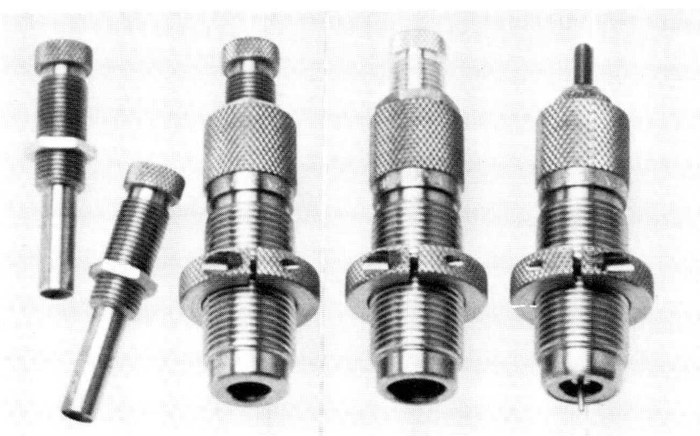

A typical set of matrices used for reloading.

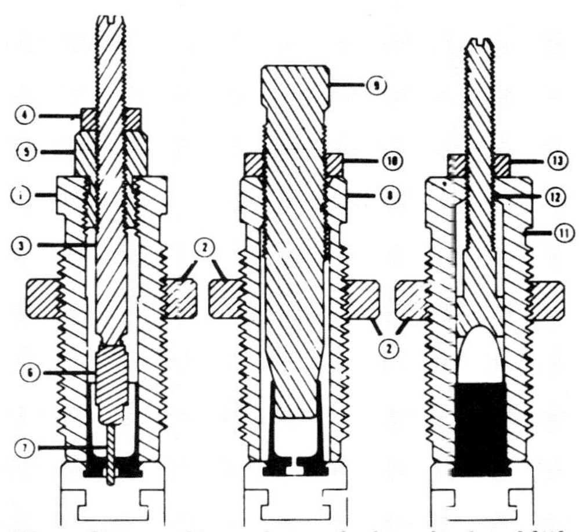

Dreiteilige Sätze für schwach konische Hülsen
(Gruppe C, F, I und L)
1 Kalibriermatrize — 2 Gewindering — 3 Gewindestange — 4 Kontermutter — 5 Buchse für Gewindestange — 6 Überwurfmutter für Ausstoßer — Zündhütchenausstoßnadel — 8 Trägerbuchse des Aufweiters — 9 Aufweiter — 10 Kontermutter für Aufweiter 11 Setzmatrize — 12 Setzschraube — 13 Kontermutter für Setzschraube

If one has loaded a cartridge for precision and still guaranteed its functioning safety, this is always risky and questionable. Here are a few concrete examples. For a Parabellum pistol one needs a truly medium load, and if one goes over or under it, it soon malfunctions, in fact, the weapon "swallows itself" from heavy charges. If a cartridge for an M 39 with an aluminum grip is being used, then the functioning of the cartridge in the same pistol with a steel grip is at least questionable, if not downright disturbing. The same charge would cause considerable disturbance in a P 38, as it would be somewhat weak. A cartridge with a medium load, as a feasible compromise, would hardly function with the switching system of a Colt Government, and on the other hand, a Benelli MP 3 S will fire even the lightest charges without malfunction.

The Lahti pistol, for example, requires a charge verging on the maximum or it will crush any cases to be ejected, making them unusable. The replacement barrels made by the firm of Peters-Stahl should also be used only with a strong charge, as experience has shown. With a medium charge, the weapon will misfire immediately.

The manner in which one shoots also makes a difference when trying to attain very high precision. If the pistol functions properly in the shooting machine but does not function right with the same charge when fired by hand, the effect will be smaller for stabilized shooting with the weapon held fast.

Thus a customary charge must never be used if it will create a danger at the lower limit of functioning. There is nothing wrong with testing this limit for the weapon in question instead of adopting another shooter's successful recipe untested. It is also important to decide on a definite distance for a customary charge and to know exactly what results are attained with this cartridge fired from this weapon at this distance. The horizontal and vertical variations depending on powder type, powder amount and bullet can be astonishing and definitely require a critical observation.

Wrongly loaded cartridges are usually unloaded again, a job that one can spare oneself if one has a 9 mm caliber revolver — for training purposes, such wrong charges are still usable.

Choice of Components

From a combination of the individual components such as powder type, powder amount, percussion cap, bullet and case, one can create so many different charges that a single "reloader's lifetime" would not be long enough to experiment with them all. Simplified patent recipes are thus to be forbidden. Only a few tips can be offered.

A jacketed bullet (full jacket) with a weight of 8.0 grams is customary. Bullets with semi-jackets or lead bullets, in different shapes, are possible. There are considerable performance differences in terms of provable precision when, with otherwise equal charges, the FJ bullets made by different manufacturers are used. In each case it is practical to settle on one specific brand and then choose the other components to suit it.

This is also more or less valid as regards a choice of

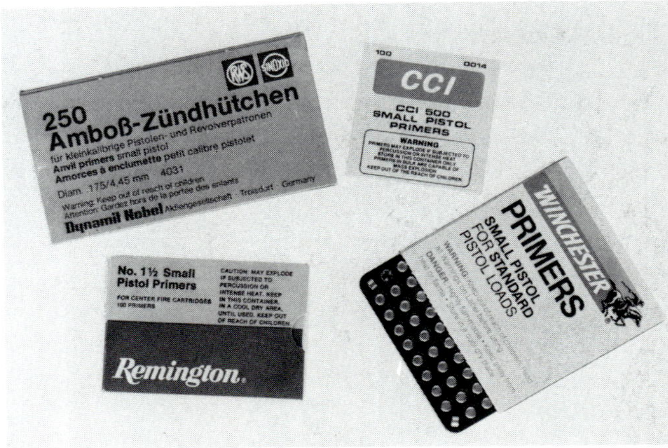

Percussion caps by various manufacturers. The caps show no differences worth noting for ordinary use.

powder type. Even when, according to measurement, two different types show the same bullet velocity, this is far from proving that the precision is equal — this point is especially important in charges for sporting use. Differences in ignition, on the other hand, seem to be only slight or even almost unprovable when the normal and intended percussion cap is used.

A more important factor is the choice of cases, or at least a certain uniformity in workmanship. If one has large quantities available, one should store and load the cases separately according to their manufacturer and preparation.

Sporting Loads

It is not correct to attribute insufficient verifiable sporting performance to the 9 mm and 7.65 mm Parabellum cartridges — this appears to this author to be an often-repeated prejudice. Many weapons of these calibers simply are not inclined to give first-class performance on account of their construction and assembly tolerances. Nor do they need to, for many of them are weapons made for use at relatively short ranges — it will always be sufficient to put five shots into a circle eight to ten mm in diameter at ten meters. Most of the better-known pistols and revolvers, though, shoot better.

Repeatable and verifiable sporting performance can be attained only with a few self-loading pistols — examples attained with an SIG 210 and a Benelli MP 3 S are shown here. They do not reflect the whole spectrum of possible combinations, but they show clearly what kind of performance one can attain with careful work.

The ambitious sporting reloader can go down to the minimum charge without taking personal risks. The muzzle velocity can thereby be lowered until the functioning is just barely maintained, at a velocity of 260 as opposed to the normal 320 meters per second. What must be taken into consideration is that the conclusion will almost always be drawn that precision gets worse with increasing charge and speed, and the general

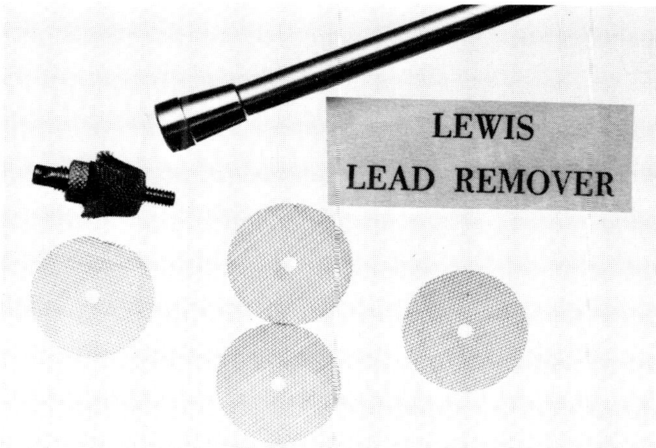

Only with Lewis Lead Remover does one really get the lead out of the barrel.

The barrel must not be oiled. Cleaning is always necessary between series of lead bullets.

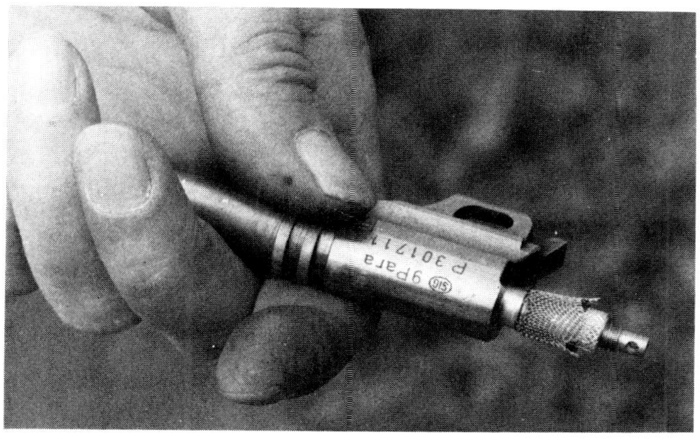

dispersion increases too. Somewhere on the long path between minimum and maximum, a particularly good group of shots will appear, and tests with still smaller differences in the amount of powder can be made around this point. If one repeats a good group of shots several

Measuring the muzzle velocity with the Weinlich VM 25, a very practical and rugged device.

times, then that is the optimal charge with the chosen components for the weapon in question.

Sometimes the attainable optimum is at another point. Tests of the SIG 210 fired from a shooting machine, and using Kemira N 330 powder and Hornady VM bullets, gave acceptable performance only with stronger charges. The bullet, which weighs 5.1 grams, is simply too light and requires a strong charge that gives velocities of 400 meters per second and more.

A special problem is caused by lead bullets, which are the only pistol bullets allowed at many shooting ranges. The available loading data are not essentially different, and the precision for the SIG 210 and the MP 3 S is excellent. Here too, there is a clear connection between decreasing performance and stronger charges.

Bullets made of lead cause problems in other ways, for they smear the barrel and quickly decrease performance. This depends directly on the charge and the velocity — weaker charges with lower velocities increase the deposit of lead somewhat, while faster charges leave a normal barrel unsuitable for use only after sixty or more rounds. In this case, only a stiff mechanical cleaning will help.

When lead bullets are to be used regularly, it is advisable to reequip with a special lead barrel. It has differently shaped riflings, and though lead is deposited, it comes later. Practically no leading was shown in tests of the MP 3 S barrels, which could be used regularly without being cleaned in between, and there was no discernable leading in the Peters barrels which were installed in the weapons in exchange.

Loading Data, 9 mm Parabellum; Bullet Weight 7.8-8.0 Grams

Powder	Grams	Grain
Rottweil P 801	max. 0.260, min. 0.220	max. 4.0, min. 3.4
Rottweil P 804	max. 0.325, min. 0.265	max. 5.0, min. 4.1
Rottweil P 803	max. 0.330, min. 0.265	max. 5.1, min. 4.1
Rottweil P 805	max. 0.325, min. 0.260	max. 5.0, min. 4.0
Kemira N 330	max. 0.260, min. –	max. 4.86, min. –
Dupont 700 X HI Skor	max. 0.260 by "DEVA"	max. 4.0 by "DEVA"

Loading Values, MP 3-S 9 mm Parabellum (with KS bullets)

Powder	Bullet	Charge grains	Group mm	Vo m/s
Rottweil P 805	KS greased	4.0	48/52	246
	KS greased	4.2	16/21	259
	KS greased	4.3	27	279
	KS greased	4.4	30	284
	KS greased	4.5	47	300
	KS greased	4.6	53	309
	KS layered	4.2	38/42	261
	KS layered	4.3	38/46	275
	KS layered	4.4	47	285
Kemira N 330	KS greased	4.0	34	279
	KS greased	4.3	20/20	309
	KS greased	4.5	52	321
	KS greased	4.7	52	328
	KS layered	4.0	54	289
	KS layered	4.3	39	321
	KS layered	4.5	54	338
	KS layered	4.7	51	341
Dupont 700 X	KS greased	3.8	41	258
	KS greased	4.0	32/24	281
	KS greased	4.2	49	293
	KS layered	3.8	40	270
	KS layered	4.0	18/21/26	281
	KS layered	4.2	36	286

REBUILT PRODUCTION PISTOLS

Often pistols in series production are made so much smaller by clever gunsmiths that they have unhandy dimensions despite their high-performance caliber. This does not always work out well for those who do such work, if one may cite the example of the Devell firm in the USA. This firm specialized in making very small pistols on the basis of the Smith & Wesson Model 39 and 59, with their barrels, slides and grips made shorter or smaller. Then Smith & Wesson got the idea of putting a similar pistol on the market themselves. It is now known and treasured as the "Mini Gun" model, and still has a magazine capacity of twelve cartridges. The demand for the production weapon was great, but for the Devell firm it pointed the way to bankruptcy.

The P.C. Super

The firm of Detlev Joniskeit, located in the valley town of Allersbach, Germany, had already made a name for itself on numerous occasions with its own developments or clever conversions of weapons. In this case it is a general shortening of a Walther P 4 pistol which, after the work was done, had a length of 156 mm, not much longer than a typical 7.65 mm or short 9 mm caliber pistol. Externally the P 4 looks remarkably like the time-tested and venerable P 38, however it differs by not only having a somewhat shorter barrel, but also a different arrangement of the safety system. The side safety lever is under the pressure of a bent spring and automatically raises again after being activated. When the weapon is cocked, the hammer goes forward again while the firing pin remains secured, and the trigger moves forward.

To shorten the grip, it was cut down to about half its height and welded back together after a piece was taken out. The work was done neatly and left no recognizable traces behind. This shortening, of course, reduces the magazine capacity from eight to seven cartridges, and the original magazine is also shortened to fit. Expectedly, this makes it fit into the hand a little less comfortably, but one can put one's little finger under the base of the magazine comfortably and safely.

The barrel and slide are made by the firm, with the slide minus the step that is typical of Walther pistols. In order to have enough stability all the same, the flanks of the slide are made stronger. A light strike on one of the flanks makes the slide swing like a tuning fork. Despite its stronger side flanks, it does not necessarily look misshapen, as this is counteracted by its cut away to the front on both sides. The barrel jacket, arched at the top, is likewise made by the firm, and the barrel, which is only 70 mm long, is pushed into it, though not as smoothly as in the original Walther product. The bolt and other moving parts are retained, and users of the original weapon need not make any adjustments. The sight of the weapon at hand is fixed, but unlike it, other versions have a laterally adjustable backsight. The backsight is marked in white under its notch, the drag foresight comes from a Dan Wesson revolver and has a white plastic inlay, which makes for easy targeting against a dark background.

The little P.C. Super is nicely turned out in every way. The trigger is far better than that of the production weapon. Only the grip panels of oiled walnut, minus

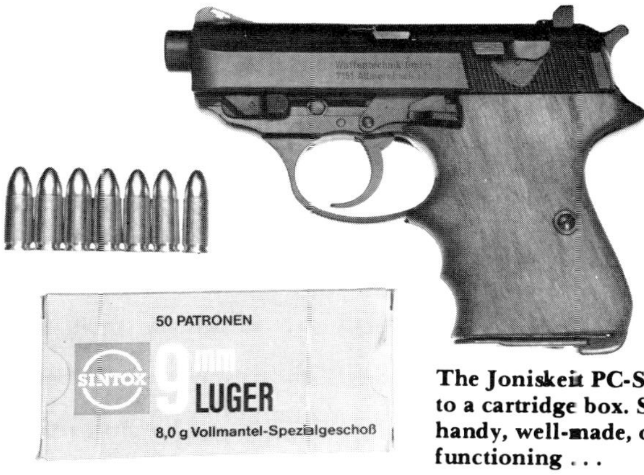

The Joniskeit PC-Super compared to a cartridge box. Small and handy, well-made, only its functioning . . .

PC-Super and normal P 38 compared.

Smooth surfaces prevail on this rebuilt pistol. The sights of the version shown here cannot be adjusted.

The same pistol open. The swinging-bolt system was retained.

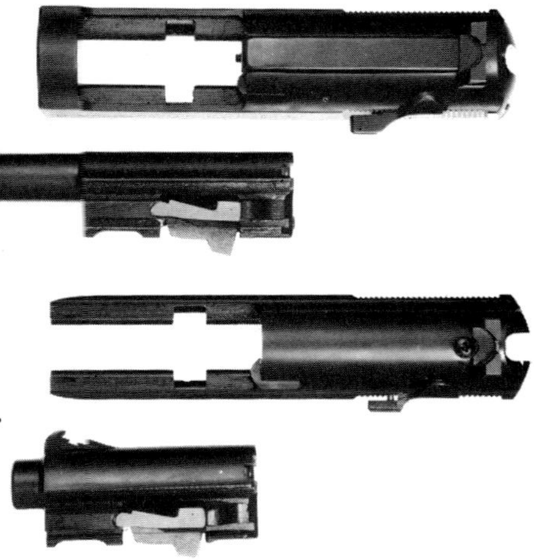

The system of the rebuilt pistol is based on the P 4; there is no real safety, just an decocking roller, and no lid up in the slide. The slide is open at the front, resembling a tuning fork.

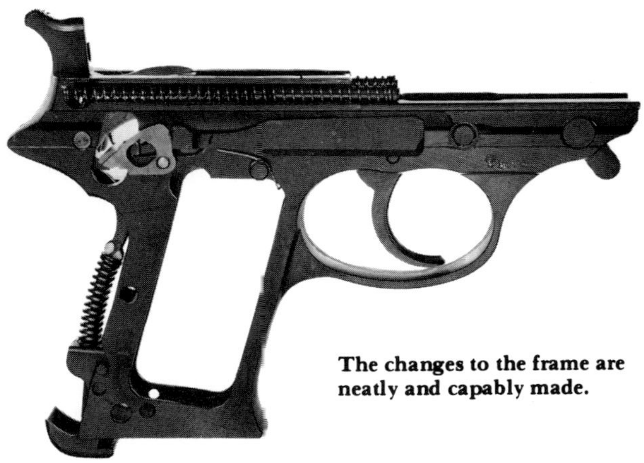

The changes to the frame are neatly and capably made.

other coloring, are less attractive. Naturally they are made very flat and thus presumably go without a slight recess for the thumb, however this is an advantage in the end, since they are equally suited to use by left- and right-handed shooters. The shooting performance of the P.C. Super is not bad, and the low shooting which the author has experienced may be a personal error, for other shooters have gotten better results in terms of height. Fired seated and steadied, at a distance of 15 meters, groups of 60 to 80 mm were attained, and no particularly clear differences between cartridges made by different manufacturers became noticeable. Trouble-free functioning, to be sure, was a different matter, and the available weapon could not win the proverbial laurel wreath. After almost every shot, the case still in the extractor jammed diagonally in the ejection window. At this point the next cartridge was already halfway inserted. This malfunctioning was not limited to any particular brand of cartridge, but occurred with all brands with no relevance to the strength of their charges. Both extremely weakly and heavily charged cartridges loaded by the author made no improvement.

This might also be possible: the upper part of the PC-Super and the grip of the P 38 or P 4.

Technical Data: Joniskeit P.C. Super

Caliber	9 mm Parabellum
Magazine capacity	7 cartridges
System, bolt	Walther, swinging bolt
Overall length	156 mm
Overall height	120 mm
Grip width	28 mm
Slide width	31 mm
Safety width	35 mm
Weight empty	760 grams
Weight, upper part	460 grams
Grip material	Aluminum
Upper part material	Steel
Muzzle velocity	ca. 330 m/s*
Muzzle energy	ca. 420 Joules*

* Depending on cartridge and bullet

The Life Expectancy of a Weapon

The question of how long a life expectancy a weapon, and in this case a self-loading pistol, has cannot be simply answered. Little information on the subject, based on actual tests, is available in print, and beyond that silence. The question of life expectancy can extend into two very different areas: the maintenance of a barrel in terms of its precision and/or the sturdiness of a frame and the moving parts built into it. The requirements of police testing centers are based on the results of 10,000 shots with standard ammunition, during which individual parts have to be replaced. However, this does not say anything as to whether the weapon still gives sufficient shooting precision.

The life of a barrel depends chiefly on what type of bullets are fired and with what charges. Jacketed bullets wear out the barrel faster than lead bullets, and cartridges with strong charges cause wear sooner than cartridges with weaker charges, but play is usually slight then, for the self-loading function must be maintained.

If we consider the wear on a large-caliber revolver, it can stand tens of thousands of shots of lead bullets with moderately heavy charges — very heavy charges will lead to considerable wear on the barrel and frame.

Most self-loading pistols in calibers from 9 mm up are designed for at least 5000 shots, based on ammunition to NATO standards in type and charge. Weapons with an aluminum frame sometimes show serious damage after 2500 to 3000 shots, and very few pistols with an aluminum frame last much beyond that. The German manufacturers can point to weapons that are still functioning after 30,000 to 40,000 shots, but to what extent these are individually made weapons is not known. In principle, official agencies that require at least 10,000 shots are not making any unrealistic demands. One can regard today's pistols in the light of these standards.

As for the precision of a 9 mm Para barrel in sporting use, well-known ammunition manufacturers accept the premise that a barrel will no longer show its best performance after about 3000 shots.

Tuning by Oschatz

The master gunsmith Oschatz of Stuttgart, Germany has been able to make an outstanding name for himself in recent years one who does not work on any handgun without studying it first, and who personally produces adapted means of tuning all available models. Thus the extent of his work depends essentially on the wishes of his customers, each of whom acquires a very personal weapon.

One of the most often tuned pistols is the popular CZ 75 model, which is also offered in modified form by Frankonia-Jagd, among others.

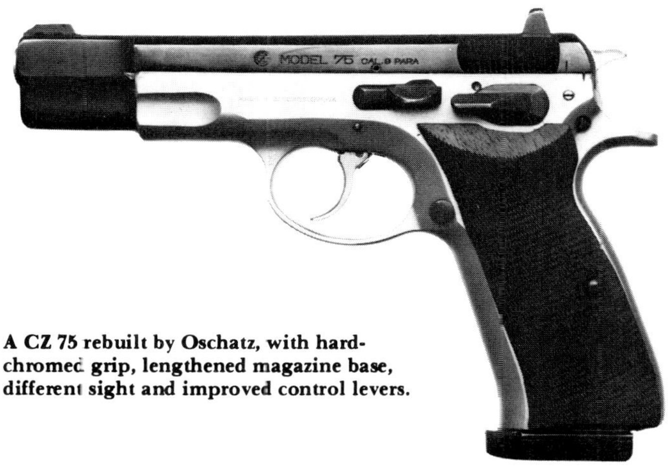

A CZ 75 rebuilt by Oschatz, with hard-chromed grip, lengthened magazine base, different sight and improved control levers.

The version shown here looks quite different from the production weapon. The frame is matte chrome-plated, and the chrome is so durable that no traces of wear can be seen on it even after long use. The pistol shown here still bears one of the small-series numbers and was in use for at least five years. The magazine base has been fitted with an extension made of black plastic, and the braking plate inside the magazine was fastened down and serves only as a rear limit. The attached grip panels are made of walnut and cover the grip completely and well. The herringbone pattern is neatly cut by hand and noticeably improves the way the weapon fits into the hand.

The magazine catch is unchanged, though light pressure is sufficient to make the magazine fall out of the weapon into one's hand. The trigger has had all its rests smoothed and slightly inset, so that it pulls cleanly and without any noticeable resistance. An additional trigger-stop was built in, a measure that, in principle, should

The improved control lever in detail. The lock is held play-free by two set screws at the sides.

not have been taken with the CZ 75, for despite the good movement, the trigger subsequently drops a bit, with the visible result of shots that pull to the right.

For play-free functioning and protection against corrosion, all the parts inside the frame are likewise matte chrome-plated, with the exception of the sear.

The somewhat decorative-looking ejector can become a weak point, as Oschatz has lengthened the ejector. This lengthening is secured by a pin at the rear and electrically welded to a neatly attached point in the front. Breaks here, though, seem to be ruled out for some time.

In the CZ 75, the ejector is a complex part with several functions, such as providing a mount for the sear. Any play there is a disadvantage to good trigger functioning. Oschatz added a screw on each side in the back of the grip, and the moving part "ejector" now sits completely firmly and wobble-free between them.

To remain in the receiver: whoever uses a CZ 75 will be bothered by the scratching sound of the guiding rod with the recoil spring. The guiding rod was polished and matte chrome-plated, which eliminated the scratching. The barrel has not been reworked internally, but its outside was likewise matte chrome-plated, so that everything makes a very good appearance together. Immediately over the muzzle there are four holes bored in the manner of a Magna-Port; corresponding to this, the slide has six somewhat larger holes bored in the area of the foresight. This modification did not show any remarkably great effect, and in any case the heavy CZ 75 lies in the hand rather quietly when shooting.

The sights were improved for shooting in unfavorable light conditions. A higher backsight block with a wider notch was installed, a white plastic inlay was added under the notch, a longer, wider and also higher foresight with a white longitudinal inlay was mounted. With the sights in this form, targeting is considerably easier in a poor light.

Other changes include the operating levers, both of which were enlarged and cross-hatched on top, another major improvement when the pistol has to be used quickly. The somewhat long spur of the hammer was shortened and cross-hatched on top, and finally matte chrome-plated. Along with its shorter surface and the cross-hatching of the back of the slide, this eliminates almost all disturbing reflections in the area of the sights. All in all, a pistol reworked in this way makes a good impression, and becomes even better the more one uses it. Everything somehow works more lightly and cleanly, just as production weapons may have functioned in the "good old days." Naturally, such modifications are not exactly cheap — the same price would buy two more production pistols.

Installing Polygonal Barrels

Replacing the barrel of a weapon is not unusual, however it is a job for the specialist and not for the hobbyist. Many problems can arise when a pistol is basically well-built, however the manufacturer did not produce a highly precise barrel. In the realm of .22 LR caliber sport pistols, such work is easily done by the specialist: if the basic weapon has a thick barrel, it is bored out larger while carefully secured, and a suitable barrel liner is glued and/or riveted inside this bored-out space. Pistols by High Standard, Ruger or FN are well suited to such reworking. One must only install a really good barrel, and this new barrel must also produce truly improved performance.

In the realm of the 9 mm Parabellum caliber, the desire for better shooting performance is often understandable, as the barrel is often worn or shot out, and no longer stays satisfactorily in place nor gives satisfactory performance. For this situation the firm of Peters-Stahl in Paderborn offers an interesting alternative, namely the replacement of the barrel by a polygonal barrel made by the firm. Peters is trying primarily to accommodate those shooters who want to make sporting use of their pistols and thus are dissatisfied with the existing shooting performance. Peters builds a barrel with a patented hexagonal polygon cross-section, however a look through the barrel gives the impression that one is looking at a worn-out or ground-down rifled barrel. The barrels installed by Peters are obtained as raw material and prepared further, which includes trimming to the

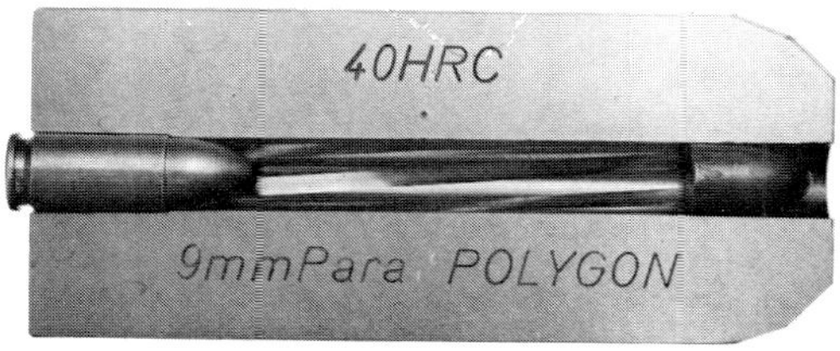

The hexagonal polygon profile, as used in the Peters barrels.

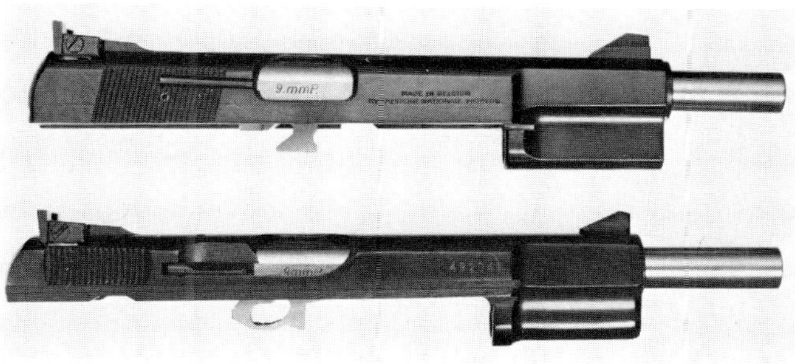

Slides with attached Peters barrels. FN High Power above, CZ 75 below. Both slides have Peters-Stahl sights, which can be adjusted very finely.

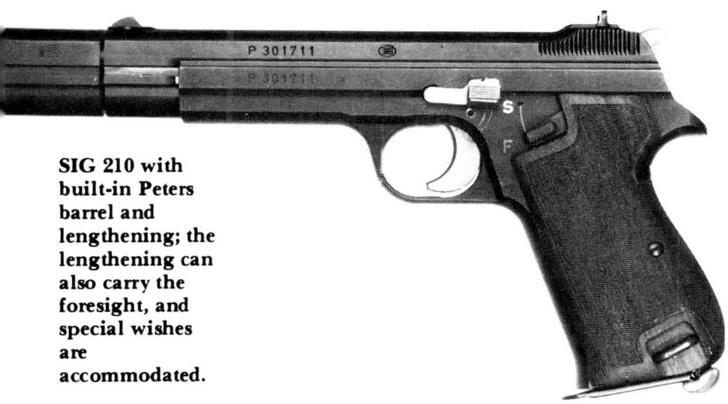

SIG 210 with built-in Peters barrel and lengthening; the lengthening can also carry the foresight, and special wishes are accommodated.

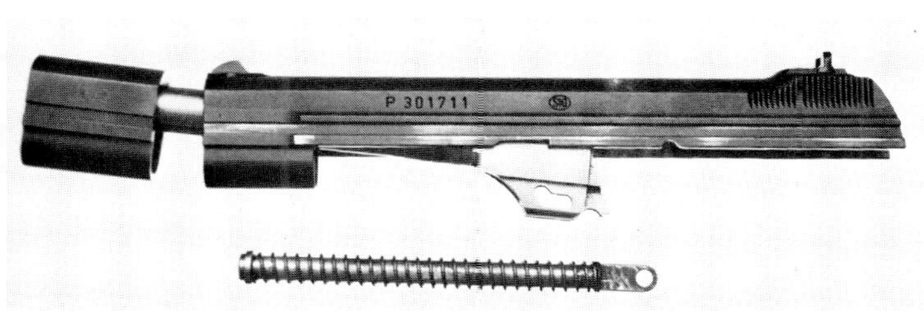

Before the barrel is removed, the front weight has to be taken off, but the barrel can be cleaned very well in place too.

A venerable High Power with a new barrel that almost makes it usable for sports.

desired length, installing the chamber, attaching the bolting mechanism and, above all, heat-treating and hardening all surfaces. This rebuilding must absolutely be done by the manufacturer, for Peters fits and cuts every barrel to fit the individual pistol exactly. So one cannot buy such barrels from the rack and simply install them, as this would lose much of the gain in precision. The barrels are longer than the production barrels but remain within the limit of 150 mm including chamber required by the sporting regulations. One can optionally allow the barrel to project from the slide, or one can take a barrel weight that fits the slide and remains removable thanks to a refined clamp mechanism. The barrel weight can carry the foresight, but the foresight can also remain on the slide, as the owner wishes.

Three such barrels were tested here for this description, and the results were noteworthy, showing that rebuilding is always really worthwhile when the shooter wants better performance and has also had trouble with dirt in the original barrel. This becomes very easy to see when lead bullets are fired from an older-type barrel. After 50 to 60 shots at most, the lead build-up is so great that decent shooting at 25 meters is no longer possible. So-called lead barrels put off the problems a bit, letting one shoot about twice as many lead bullets. The polygonal barrel made by Peters is different. After 250 shots with lead bullets, and without any intermediate cleaning, a test series was fired. The results were better rather than worse. There was no discernible build-up of lead in the barrel. The gain in muzzle velocity is not significant, thus a direct comparison is not completely exact, for the Peters barrel is longer than the weapon's original barrel. Measured with the FMJ 25 made by Weinlich firing cartridges by Remington, the 9 mm Para barrel of the Government gave an average for ten measurements of 339.8 meters per second, and the Peters barrel 344.8 m/sec. The longer barrel generally gives a higher velocity, but the friction between barrel and bullet is more intensive, so that a part of the energy is consumed there.

The first weapon to be tested was a Government model equipped with a 9 mm Parabellum caliber switching system from the manufacturer. Fired from a Ransom Rest shooting machine at 25 meters, it gave shocking results, just what one would expect from a Government in 9 mm caliber. Groups of ten were shot, first with the original barrel, then with the Peters barrel. The results with the Peters barrel are given in parentheses after the

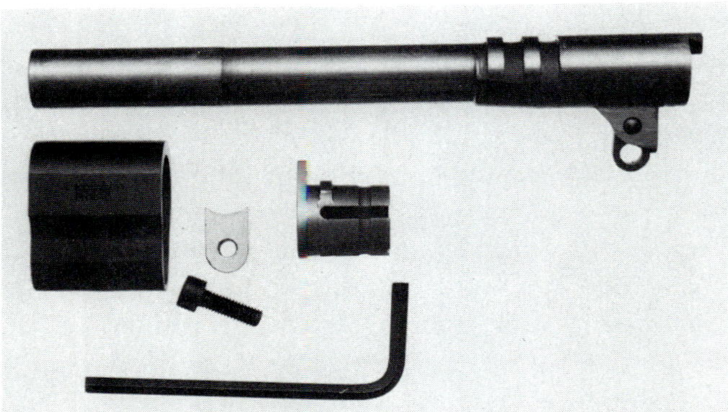

A spring casing is available for the Colt Government. The front weight is held fast with a clamp.

The author's pistol as a "building site." Even a guiding rod for the recoil spring will not collide with the front weight.

others. Norma-FMJ (Full Metal Jacket) with 152 mm (108 mm), Winchester FMJ 152 mm (108 mm), Hirtenberger-Combat 98 mm (62 mm), and Lapua FMJ 150 mm (58 mm). This shows the clear superiority of the polygonal barrel, however it should be known that a pistol like the Government is hard to evaluate in this manner when fired from a shooting machine with tension on the grip because of the considerable play between the frame and the upper part. Tests with steadied weapons, aimed with unchanged sights, prove this suspicion. In this case the Peters barrel was still clearly superior, but the differences were no longer so glaring.

The second weapon tested was an HP pistol made by FN during the war. Here better possibilities for comparison were at hand, as this was a tuned weapon whose play between frame and upper part had been eliminated. The bolt of the FN is better, as the moveable link as a source of doubt is not included in the design. The results from the shooting machine, with the values of the Peters barrel in parentheses: GECO FMJ 45 mm (28 mm), GECO lead bullet 51 mm (44 mm), Norma 44 mm (29 mm), Winchester 56 mm (36 mm), Hirtenberger-Combat 63 mm (24 mm), and Lapua 54 mm (43 mm). Again the improvement is clear to see.

The results obtained with the SIG 210 were even more decisive. This is, after all, a pistol with quite negligible play between the upper part and the grip, and here the slightest differences show up when, for example, reloaded cartridges are used. The values of the individual series: GECO FMJ 25 mm (27 mm), GECO lead bullet 33 mm (21 mm), Norma 37 mm (23 mm), Winchester 33 mm (27 mm), Hirtenberger-Combat 30 mm (26 mm), and Lapua 37 mm (18 mm). The only exception was the cartridge by Sellier & Bellot: SIG original 33 mm, Peters barrel 46 mm.

Several series fired with self-loaded cartridges using P 804 powder and Norma cases and bullets corroborated this. The SIG original gave groups of 33 and 22 mm, the Peters barrel groups of 24 and 15 mm.

Tests of this kind can always tackle a problem but never completely dispose of it. But one thing is clear after just a few series: by replacing the barrel, a better performance can be gotten from the pistol. A decrease in performance can occur, but it remains the exception in an individual case.

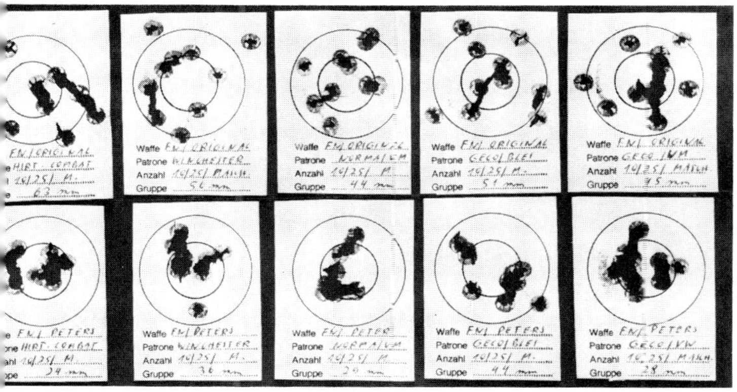

Targets hit by the High Power from a shooting machine. The upper row with the original barrel, the lower with the Peters barrel.

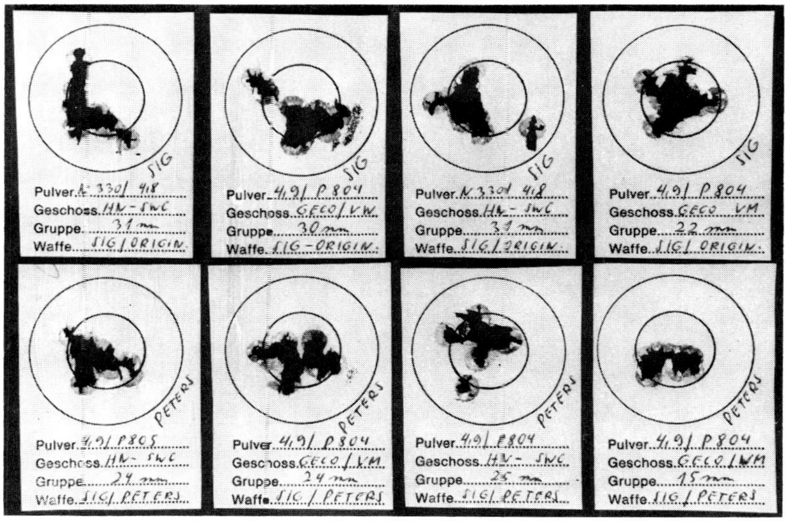

Another performance comparison. Above the SIG 210 barrel, below the Peters barrel, both of which shoot extremely well.

FINDING, CHECKING AND TESTING

Weapons of all kinds are thoroughly tested by the customer in some way before being officially accepted. In recent years, statements and information on this testing is made public much more than may have been the case in the past. For the private user of a pistol, this has very definite advantages, for one thing, onw also obtains, in this manner, a fully developed design based on the most modern technology, and for another, one can rely on these tests for data on performance capability and durability. Last but not least, many pistols presently in private hands were the results of official or military contracts and developments, so that at this point it may be of general interest to get to know some of the selection processes and their results somewhat more thoroughly.

One of the internationally respected long-term tests came about in connection with the search for a high-performance pistol for the German police. Several good pistols owe their existence to this search.

The Search for a Police Pistol

Though the German police was formerly equipped with weapons just as the manufacturers offered them, this time another way to do the job was tried — and succeeded. The official police agencies put together a

The Walther PP and PPK models were typical German police pistols for decades.

catalog of requirements, and the manufacturers who took part had to develop a weapon that measured up or modify an already designed weapon to comply. Until then the PP or PPK pistols made by the firm of C. Walther in Ulm were generally made for the 7.65 mm caliber, but the less than satisfactory effect of these cartridges became better and better known, and was made even clearer by the assassinations committed by German terrorists. The police forces of the German states, as well as a good part of the Federal Border Police, were equipped with the P 1 (P 38) pistol in 9 mm Parabellum caliber.

In 1974-75, Arbeitskreis II, as a result of a decision by the Technical Commission of the Interior Ministers' Conference, formulated the so-called "Catalog of Requirements for Handguns." In this catalog the requirements that had to be fulfilled by the new pistol were set forth. The most important requirements in the catalog were as follows:

Caliber 9 mm
Muzzle energy 500 Joules
Overall length ca. 180 mm
Overall height ca. 130 mm
Overall width ca. 34 mm
Weight with filled magazine not over 1000 grams

Constant readiness to fire:
The weapon must be capable of being carried and drawn safely in a condition of heightened readiness to fire. Instantaneous firing without additional manipulation of operating levers (safeties) must be possible by pulling the trigger.

Falling safety:
Also if the weapon falls or is struck, this must not cause a shot to be fired.

Lifetime:
The main parts, such as the barrel, breech, frame, recoil spring and mainspring must withstand the effects of 10,000 shots. Parts that experience wear, such as the firing pin and firing pin spring, must withstand 5000 shots.

Testing:
In the catalog the testing is described in detail, with the type and extent as well as the duration of the individual tests being specified precisely.

Four well-known German manufacturers took part in the competition: the firms of Heckler & Koch with their PSP pistol, the Mauser firm with the Model HSP, the firm of Sauer & Sohn with the Model P 6 and the firm of C. Walther with the Model P 5, all in 9 mm Parabellum caliber, for only this cartridge could supply the required muzzle energy of 500 Joules.

The new pistols, according to the criteria in the catalog, were to be tested with 10,000 rounds, however none of the weapons could stand the stress of this burden, which was no cause for concern for a new development. Several tests had to be made before the requirements could be met.

The third test in this series was carried out at the Border Patrol School in Lübeck from March 21 to May 12, 1977. Once again, a work group was formed, composed of police officials from the federal government (BGS and BKA) and the states of Baden-Württemberg, Bremen, Hamburg, Niedersachsen, Nordrhein-Westfalen and Schleswig-Holstein.

Some of the tests were not possible in Lübeck and were carried out at Test Center 91 of the Bundeswehr in Meppen. These tests concerned the stress on the weapons caused by temperature, dust, mud and rain, plus an immersion test. On the basis of this testing, the P 6 pistol made by Sauer & Sohn could be most highly recommended by the work group for general adoption. The introduction of a single weapon for the whole country was rejected, and problems of workplace security surely must have played a justified role.

After the tests were concluded, the three pistols suggested for adoption (the Model HSP by Mauser was withdrawn at the beginning of the tests) were divided among the German states as follows:

Federal Border Patrol: P 6 (Bundesgrenzschütz
Readiness Police: P 6 and P 5 (Bereitschaftspolizei)
Schleswig-Holstein: P 6
Hamburg: P 6
Niedersachsen: P 7 (formerly PSP)
Bremen: P 6
Nordrhein-Westfalen: P 6
Hessen: P 6
Rheinland-Pfalz: P 5
Baden-Württemberg: P 5 and P 7
Bavaria (Bayern): P 7

These are the present-day police pistols P 7, P 5, and P 6 (photo by P. Weinreich).

Saarland: P 9 S
West Berlin: P 38 (made by Manurhin)

No criticism of the quality of these decisions can be given here, as all three pistols proved in the following years to be very rugged designs, even if one or another minor modification remained to be made. In any case, since this time the German police has used modern, high-performance self-loading pistols that offer a high degree of safety to the shooter and yet are ready to fire quickly.

Details of Testing

Immediately after the introduction of the new pistols, favorable articles appeared in several police journals for the purpose of inspiring concerned officials to feel trust and assurance in their new service weapons. The details repeated here are taken from a work by PHK Manfred Schulte, and a plethora of technical details has deliberately been avoided.

After a pistol has been determined to be basically developed enough to see service, a pilot-lot test still has to be carried out before series production begins, and during series production, quality tests are carried out constantly. For this purpose, the federal government sends qualified officials who go to the factories and supervise the maintenance of technical requirements for delivery to the Federal Ministry of the Interior and other applicable offices. Independently the manufacturer's constant checking goes on, which includes regular tests after delivery of raw materials or small parts made outside the factory. Observing such tests on the spot, one can obtain and regularly use one of these weapons with great confidence.

The tests carried out by the officials begin with the *pilot-lot test,* and only after its satisfactory conclusion does series production begin — and only after that is the weapon accepted by the federal or state government. For this purpose the manufacturer turns out a series of 100 pistols, five of which are chosen at random. Then two of the weapons are used for functional shooting tests, one for falling safety tests, and two for endurance shooting. To prepare them for functional shooting, a magazine filled with eight cartridges is inserted into each of the two chosen pistols, a cartridge is put into each chamber, and the hammer is then decocked. Two weapons are now put into the cooling chamber and left for 24 hours at a temperature of 240 degrees Kelvin. Removed from the cooler, the pistols immediately ice up from the surrounding air. Now a shot is fired from the first pistol by pulling the trigger, and from the second pistol via the pre-cocked hammer. Both weapons must shoot at once, and no movement of the slide to make them work is allowed.

If both pistols fire without problems, this test has been passed. If functional problems appear, then the test is repeated with twice the number of pistols, and if problems occur again, then the test is considered to have been failed and the whole lot of pistols is rejected.

Next comes the *falling safety* test. One pistol is loaded with seven live cartridges in the magazine, and one cartridge without a propellant but with a live percussion cap is loaded into the chamber. After loading, the pistol is decocked via the device at hand (the decocking lever), and the hammer is in its foremost position. From an apparatus prepared for the purpose, the pistol is now allowed to fall from a height of two meters onto a steel plate 10 mm thick, so that it falls directly onto its decocked hammer. The same falling test is made with a "falsely" decocked hammer, which is then, as with a revolver, allowed to move forward over the trigger with the help of the thumb.

The falling test is regarded as having been passed when no visible impression of the firing pin on the percussion cap is recognizable after either test.

The third and last test is the *endurance firing,* which is performed with two pistols. The two pistols are first precisely measured and thoroughly inspected. Subsequent endurance firing includes 10,000 rounds in series of 1000 rounds each. At the beginning of the first series, a target pattern is shot and the muzzle velocity is determined. After every series of 1000, the pistols are dismantled, examined for cracks and the like, and measured. The endurance shooting is regarded as having been passed when:

1. no cracks or breaks appear in major parts and the natural wear of the moving parts has not led to operating disturbances.
2. the occurring functioning disturbances have not exceeded the limit value of 21 (two per 1000), meaning 20 in a total of ten thousand rounds. Singly occurring disturbances are not counted.
3. the breech gap is not greater than 19.50 mm (meaning that no material stretching has occurred in the weapon).
4. after eight shots have been fired by hand, five of them must have hit the bull's-eye of the target from a distance of 25 meters.
5. the muzzle velocity does not fall 5% or more below the value stated by the factory.

This has to be given special attention: the stable and technically problem-free design of the pistol used. Half-hearted solutions have no hope of success.

If *one* of these conditions could not be fulfilled, regardless of whether by one or by both weapons, then the endurance shooting may be repeated with two other pistols. If faults appear, the manufacturer is given the opportunity to make modifications, and if the next endurance shooting is failed, the whole lot is rejected.

Only when all of these tests have been passed may series production for the agency that placed the order commence. Before the finished weapons are then accepted, they must be subjected to a *quality test,* in which all the pistols are tested, with the individual parts tested at random. The following tests are to be carried out:

Material testing
Hardness testing
Spring testing
Assembly observation
Testing of external condition
Testing of conformation to standards
Operating and functioning testing
Testing the interchange capability of parts
Firing
Functional and target shooting
Measurement of muzzle velocity

During *material testing,* the tester has to check the test certificates of the manufacturer to determine whether they correspond to the appropriate "NATO requirements for an industrial testing system."

In the *hardness test,* certain parts are tested at random for retention of hardness. Testing is also done at random and involves testing the retention of form and loss of spring power. The springs are put under functioning pressure for 24 hours. All measured functional values must remain within the tolerances listed in the technical drawings.

In *firing,* two shots are fired from each pistol, using special cartridges with extra-heavy charges and following particular safety precautions. This allows durability to be tested, and the pistol is stamped on its error-free parts as proof of having been fired. To simplify the process, and above all to handle the usually large numbers of pistols, the state examiners have set up their own closed department at the factory, so that the process of manufacturing will not be delayed essentially by their testing. The *target shooting* could also, under certain conditions, be regarded as functional shooting. Firing is done at the usual target from a distance of 25 meters. Eight shots per pistol are fired, and all eight must be within a 16 cm circle if the weapon is fired by machine. When firing by hand, only five of the eight shots must be within a circle 16 centimeters in diameter. Under the following conditions it can also be regarded as functional shooting: first seven shots are fired by hand, after which the hammer, as prescribed, is decocked using the decocking lever and the eighth shot is fired using the double action trigger. If there is no malfunctioning in all of this, then the functional shooting is regarded as having been passed.

Another functional shooting test also takes place under more stringent conditions. Under the following conditions, the following types of shots must be fired with one pistol per lot:
— barrel inclined 75 degrees downward
— barrel inclined 75 degrees upward
— barrel in a horizontal position
— barrel horizontal, but pistol cooled to 249 degrees Kelvin for six hours.

After the tests described above have been completed, the pistol is dismantled and cleaned, and at the same time its outward appearance, technical composition and correct procedure in all work processes according to the requirements of the technical conditions for delivery are examined.

Then measuring tests are made on and in the barrel, of the breech gap, the firing pin in front and rear positions, and the trigger resistance in both types of its functioning. The dropping path of the trigger is checked, as well as the functioning and smooth operation of the parts, with all movements tested and measured.

The required shooting performance must be documented by the manufacturer with factory targeting results. If one shoots sitting down at the same distance, one should get much better results.

To test *interchange capability,* five pistols are chosen at random from each lot and dismantled. With a random mixture of frame, barrel, recoil spring, guiding tube and magazine, they must all function without trouble.

Testing *muzzle velocity* with one pistol per lot is a binding requirement. If the velocity falls below the required minimum value, then the measurement must be repeated with five other pistols from the same lot. Before the lot is rejected after a second negative test, it must be determined whether the ammunition is at fault in this case.

These procedures show clearly with what care the testing of weapons for service use is carried out today, a fact that can and must provide assurance to everyone whose life may one day depend on the safe functioning of their weapon. It may be that a weapon bearer never in his life will get into a situation where he must defend himself, or it may be that over the course of decades he needs to fire only one shot under such conditions, but he must be able to fire that shot unconditionally, and these regulations and regular tests give him that guarantee.

Austrian Army Testing

After exhaustive comparisons and stringent tests, the Austrian Army decided to use the Glock pistol, introduced there under the designation of "Pistol 80." Since its introduction, the pistol, made at Deutsch-Wagram, Austria, has stirred up quite a storm, for many people have spoken out against a "weapon made of plastic." In this respect it is necessary to dispose of a prejudice, as in our own tests we tested a Glock 17 that had already fired more than 20,000 highly-charged self-loaded cartridges. Traces of wear were not yet visible in the steel parts bedded in plastic, and even the steel parts that moved against each other looked like those of a newly purchased weapon fresh from the factory.

The second point of contention for or against the Glock 17, and a very important selling point, was that it was ideal for use as a terrorist weapon, for on account of its plastic parts it can be brought through X-ray devices at airports unspotted. This rumor was first spread by Jack Anderson in the Washington Post, after he claimed to have brought a normal pistol and a "plastic pistol" of the Glock 17 type through a checkpoint simultaneously. Siegfried F. Hübner took this as a reason to make a test himself after having a talk with the manager of a large civil airport. He dismantled his own Glock 17 and packed the pieces separately into his luggage and camera case. Despite the photographic equipment in the latter, the breech (slide) of the Glock 17 was spotted at once, and so was the magazine with its steel spring, as well as the cartridges in the magazine. Even the frame with its cast-in steel parts was visible in the scanner or spotted on his body by the usual metal detector. Thus an evil rumor was started, and who knows what purpose it was actually to serve . . . in the USA the original pistol from Austria became quite well known.

But back to the Austrian Army's search and the requirements it set up. Here too, they did not want to buy whatever was on the market, but wanted a pistol made to fit their own demands. For the evaluation they set up a series of so-called borderline criteria. Non-fulfillment of them characterized the failure to measure up to the most important requirements, which in individual cases even ruled out the "PISTOLE" system from future acceptance by the Bundesheer. Proposed or tested pistol designs were — if they did not fulfill *all* of the borderline criteria — eliminated from the testing process regardless of how well they fulfilled the normal criteria and possible

Bedienungssicher

Alle Bedienungselemente sind für bequeme Einhandbedienung angeordnet. Nach der Ladebewegung kann der Schlaghammer mit dem Entspannhebel sicher entspannt werden, dabei bleibt der Schlagbolzen immer gesichert.

Fallsicher

Ein wesentliches Merkmal der P 226 ist die Fallsicherheit. Ob gespannt oder entspannt kann sich – dank der automatischen Schlagbolzensicherung – kein Schuss lösen.

Unempfindlich gegen Schmutz

Die geschlossene Konstruktion der SIG-SAUER Pistole P 226 macht die Waffe unempfindlich gegen Verschmutzung. Die wartungsfreundliche, ohne Werkzeuge zerlegbare Waffe gestattet eine leichte und schnelle Reinigung.

Excerpt from a Sauer & Sohn advertisement: safe if it falls, safe to operate and insensitive to dirt of any kind; this is required and delivered.

"economic advantages." (The above is taken from the introduction to the Austrian test report.)

Borderline Criteria

1. The system must be a self-loading pistol.
2. The pistol must be able to fire the 9 mm 08 (Parabellum) cartridge.
3. It must be possible to fill the magazine with cartridges without special means.
4. The magazine must, when functioning properly, be able to hold at least eight cartridges.
5. All operations in preparing to shoot, shooting and maintaining the weapon after shooting must be performable one-handed with either hand, so that they can be carried out with either the right or the left hand.
6. The technical safety of the weapon must be guaranteed unconditionally in case of being struck, hit, or falling onto a steel plate from a height of two meters.
7. The weapon must be capable of being dismantled for basic cleaning and reassembled to a functional state without the use of tools.
8. No tool must be necessary for maintenance and repair.
9. The weapon may consist of, at most, 58 individual parts (this corresponds to the Pistol 38).
10. Instructional measuring and testing devices must not be necessary for the activities of the "troop material maintenance" stage.
11. The supplier must provide at least one complete set of drawings and exploded drawings to the BMLV at least before the acceptance of the pilot series. The drawings must include dimensions, tolerances, materials used, surface treatment and information on other operations essential to production.
12. All individual parts must be interchangeable in the system without reworking.
13. With the firing of the first 10,000 shots (with ammunition corresponding to requirements), no more than 20 jammings may occur, even if they may be set right without tools.
14. All main parts must be made so that, after 15,000 shots with normal ammunition and additional stress firing, the further use of the weapon will be guaranteed with technical and functional safety. The additional stress firing will be done according to TP 1005 requirements as they are applicable, with 6000 bar.
15. The shooter must not be endangered under any conditions by the case ejection during correct weapon handling.
16. The muzzle energy must, when firing the HPAG-manufactured 9 mm 08 cartridge, amount to at least 441.5 Joules.
17. Pistols that attain fewer than 70% of the highest possible points for usable value will not be released for use by the Bundesheer.

To sum up . . . the Glock 17, alias Pistol 80, attained a total score of 88.7% of the maximum attainable points for usable value and thus became the winner of the test. Since the Pistol 80 and the results of its evaluation were not subjected to any publishing or secrecy limitations by the BMLV, the public was able to learn all the details.

The calculations of the velocity values as V5 were based on a measurement five meters before the muzzle with the 9 mm P 08 cartridge made by Hirtenberger, ammunition temperature plus 20 degrees Celsius. The average for the first series (after 32 shots) was 348.4 meters per second, the value for the second series (after 10,000 shots) was 343.6 m/sec, and the value of the third series (after 15,000 shots) was 346.4 m/sec. Thus despite the considerable stress on the barrel, the muzzle velocity was almost unchanged.

Some of the tests will be cited here in abbreviated form; they show clearly to what great stresses a "pistol" system created for the armed forces is exposed.

Type Test

This tests the interchange capability of the parts without reworking. Six weapons are dismantled and reassembled with exchanged parts, after which there must be no failures to function.

Shooting Program
The endurance shooting includes a total of 15,000 shots with normal cartridges. Here the durability of the moving parts is tested. From 10,000 shots on, the technical and functional safety systems are also tested. The weapons are simultaneously tested under more severe conditions for functioning and handling safety.

Sand Test I
A sandstorm is imitated, in which the weapon is sprayed for five minutes with crushed quartz sand with a grain size of 0.25 mm. Immediately afterward, the functioning safety is tested.

Sand Test II
The weapon is made very dirty with sand and then its functioning is tested.

Mud Test I
The weapon is shaken in a special shaking machine for five minutes, then dirtied with mud and fired.

Mud Test II
The weapon is strongly dirtied with thinned mud and then its functioning is tested.

Rain Test
The weapon is exposed for five minutes to an imitation spray of rain and cooled off, then its functioning is tested.

Coldness Test
The weapon is exposed to a temperature of -40 degrees Celsius for twelve hours and then immediately fired.

Heat Test
The weapon is exposed to a temperature of +50 degrees Celsius and then fired.

Ammunition Suitability
Cartridges made by various manufacturers and with varying charges are fired. The weapon must fire with less than five malfunctions per thousand and fire cartridges with hollow-tip bullets, conical-tip bullets and semi-wadcutter bullets.

VTV Test
Here functional capability under strong temperature changes is tested. The weapon is cooled to -40 degrees for 12 hours, then raised to +21 degrees for 3 hours, and then again cooled to -40 degrees for 12 hours.

Fall Test I
From a height of two meters, the cocked weapon is allowed to fall onto a steel plate so that it sometimes falls on the muzzle and sometimes on the hammer (in every

The frozen pistol is fired, which one would not try with one's own weapon, but it stands the test. The Glock is seen here during Austrian Bundesheer testing.

hammer position). In none of the tests may a shot be fired. The test is repeated ten times.

Fall Test II
The weapon falls from a height of two meters, in any position, on a surface of crushed stone; it must not fire a shot.

Performance Test
Here the target results under both use-simulated and technically standardized conditions are examined. *First-shot targeting:* two-handed firing, 7 meters from the target. The target is a full disc that appears unexpectedly. The time allowed for drawing and shooting is two entire seconds. Ten shots per shooter are made three times. Each time, seven trained and seven untrained shooters

are allowed to shoot.

Follow-up targeting: two-handed firing, ten meters from the target. The targets are three half-discs at two-meter intervals, appearing unexpectedly. Shooting time is six seconds. Again seven trained and seven untrained shooters shoot in five series of six shots each. Also tested are the dispersion in the combinations of weapon-man and weapon-cocking process.

Other pistols also took part in the Austrian army tests: the Beretta 92 SB in two versions, the SIG-Sauer P 220, P 225 and P 226 in one version each, the Heckler & Koch P 7 (PSP) in one version, the Steyr GB in one version, the Glock P 80 in one version and the Voere P 80 in one version. As already mentioned, the Glock P 80 (Glock 17) scored best, above all in fast drawing and shooting on account of its safe-action trigger, and was clearly superior to the other weapons. It has a favorable grip angle, so that even untrained shooters can aim quickly, and also has a considerable firepower, having 17 cartridges in its magazine. Its functioning safety was surprisingly good — in one of the tests it fired, with breaks for cooling, 10,000 shots within four hours without any malfunction.

Tests in the USA

For seven decades, the Colt M 1911 pistol in .45 ACP caliber was the official side arm of the American armed forces. For a long time there was no thought of ever putting a different weapon into service, but this way of thinking changed more and more, just because of the caliber, when the North Atlantic Treaty Organization (NATO) was formed after World War II. 2.4 million pistols of this type were made for the U.S. Government alone, however today the government no longer buys them, and it is the civilian version, the Colt Government, that remains a successful seller on the US market as before, and not just there.

In the years between 1946-1955, the procurement officials of the Army Ground Forces began to look, for the first time, for a new and different handgun. The first specifications from the Ordnance Technical Committee of 1947 established the value limits for the future weapon: weight not over 710 grams, overall length not over 178 mm. In comparison, the M 1911 A 1 weighed some 1130 grams and had an overall length of 219 mm.

The future weapon was to have new features including a double action trigger like that of the Walther P 38. Its caliber should be approximately .35 to 9 mm, by which the Parabellum cartridge was meant, as it was used by most of the European countries who were then known to be the future partners in NATO. A resulting decision for the Parabellum cartridge was only logical and would cause fewer logistic problems.

On the basis of these specifications, three well-known manufacturers submitted their designs: they were the firms of Colt, High-Standard and Smith & Wesson.

Colt and High-Standard submitted their designs quite soon, while the firm of Smith & Wesson held back somewhat. After all, it was an established maker of revolvers. Pistols were an unknown new venture. Colt offered a shortened version of the M 1911 A 1 in .45 ACP and 9 mm Parabellum calibers, plus a Type T 4 weapon in 9 mm Parabellum caliber. The High-Standard T 3 pistol was made to the same caliber. At this time, several light versions of the High Power Pistol made by Inglis and based on the Browning concept were tested. From this era came the well-known Colt Commander and the later Smith & Wesson M 39.

The first tests with an aluminum frame began in 1947 in collaboration with the Forgings & Castings Laboratory of the Sales Development Division of the Aluminum Company of America (Alcoa). By 1948 suitable frames were available, and thus in 1950 the new, smaller, lighter pistols in .45 ACP, .38 Super and 9 mm Parabellum calibers could be put on the private market as the Commander model.

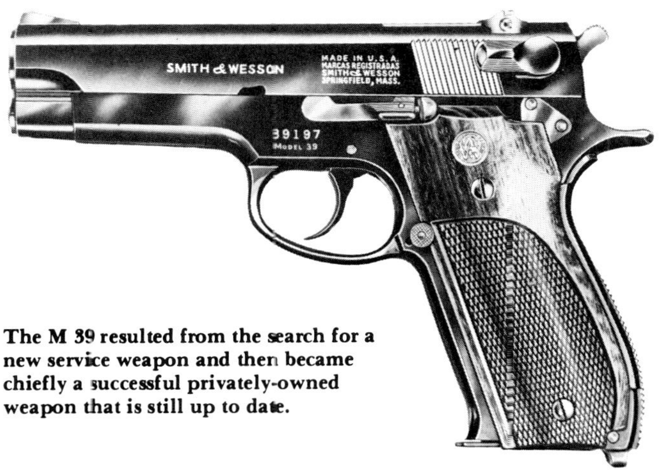

The M 39 resulted from the search for a new service weapon and then became chiefly a successful privately-owned weapon that is still up to date.

At Smith & Wesson the work began in 1946, after C.R. Hellstrom became the president of the firm. The first prototype was a design from the department led by Joe

Norman; thus the Model 39 X, which was introduced on October 28, 1948, was created. During manufacturing this weapon was known by the factory designation of X-46 — it had a cocking trigger, an aluminum frame, and the unusual grip angle of 25 degrees. Later pistols had an angle of only 15 degrees. Between 1948 and 1954 a whole series of X pistols was built, chiefly as factory project studies, with and without a double action trigger and with various grips and different types of bolts. The final series production of these self-loading pistols began in 1954, and only in 1957 were the pistols given the designation of Model 39, for only then did the firm begin to give the individual weapons model numbers. The Model 39 became a successful design that won acclaim particularly for its timeless form and good workmanship. To this day the firm has built a series of additional successful versions. In 1971 the extractor of the Model 39 was improved. The extractor of the earlier versions, in the form of a long spring, broke easily and did not prove itself. The pistols of the old type have been designated as 39-1, the pistols with the improved extractor bear the number 39-2.

The US Army began its tests with the Colt Commander and the Smith & Wesson M 39 in 1955. At this time the Deputy Chief of Staff of the Army for Logistics officially determined that there were still very great numbers of usable Colt M 1911 A 1 pistols available among the troops and it was unnecessary to introduce a new one. Thus a new pistol in 9 mm caliber was not introduced, but the private market and several police departments were happy to put the new pistol with the handy caliber into use. The U.S. Army stuck with its old but very popular Colt M 1911 A 1.

In the mid-1970s the M 1911 A 1 acquired a companion in .45 ACP caliber: the M 15 General Officers Pistol. The M 15 was a modified version of the National Match (similar to the Gold Cup) in .45 ACP caliber. Until then the officers from the rank of brigadier general (one star) up were issued a pocket pistol in .32 or .380 caliber. The number of them in use was rather large, and from 1941 to 1945, a total of 17,330 pistols in .32 caliber and 1113 pistols in .380 caliber had been ordered from Colt. After they were removed from active service, the higher officers were allowed to keep their former service pistols.

Between 1965-1967 the idea of issuing a pistol in 9 mm Parabellum caliber to generals was considered. The P 38 pistol by Walther, the Hi-Power by FN, the Colt Commander and the M 39 by Smith & Wesson were once again placed on the short list. Instead, the Rock Island Arsenal made a different choice; it was thought that the American generals had to have something special as a side arm. Colt offered a version in 9 mm caliber, the M 1969 General Officers Pistol, but the army officials stuck with the familiar .45 ACP caliber.

In summer 1972, series production of the M 15 for the generals began, though it was more like handwork, carried out by a few specialists at the factory. The frame came from the M 1911 A 1 and was shortened more than that of the Commander, the slide was likewise taken over from the M 1911 and shortened considerably. A different recoil spring and a different guide were needed. The resulting pistol much resembled the Officers ACP, available on the private market, which is shown here. The M 15 weighs 64 grams less than the normal M 1911 A 1 and is an independent special product. The Model 59 by Smith & Wesson is another pistol that was originally developed not for the private owner but as a result of a military request or wish. During the Vietnam War, the US Navy Seal (Sea, Air and Land) Teams wanted a self-loading pistol with a silencer. Smith & Wesson offered several M 39's with a steel frame and changed this pistol so it could take a silencer. After testing this prototype, the Navy asked Smith & Wesson for several pistols with a 14-cartridge magazine; the first prototypes had already been made at the factory several years before, so that these wishes could be fulfilled quickly.

In 1968 the manufacturer delivered some of these silenced pistols under the designation of Mark 2, Mod. O Silenced Pistol. The troops soon gave them the nickname of Hush-Puppy. The silenced Mark 2 had an additional locking lever of the left side of its slide, so that the slide could be locked in place. A slide that would recoil as usual would have prevented the silencing principle from working.

The Mark 2 Mod. O differed from the other pistols in terms of material, for both the frame and the slide were made of stainless steel. It fired a special cartridge with a bullet weighing 10.2 grams — its muzzle velocity was decreased to about 274 meters per second, thus below the speed of sound.

Encouraged by the success of their Hush-Puppies, Smith & Wesson thereupon extended their program in the 9 mm Parabellum caliber and produced a smaller lot of Model 59 for troop testing. The Model 59, likewise a very desirable pistol today, holds 14 cartridges in its magazine and scarcely differs in design from the Model

39. The frame is likewise made of aluminum (or alternatively of steel today), the grip is somewhat wider (25 mm, instead of the M 39's 19 mm), and the entire pistol is somewhat heavier (the M 59 weighs 57 grams more than the M 39 when unloaded).

Neither the M 39 nor the M 59 was introduced officially, but two more good pistols were available to the police and to private owners.

The U.S. Air Force

The Air Force had introduced the Smith & Wesson Model 15 revolver in .38 SPL caliber as a light side arm for their personnel; in addition, the Colt M 1911 A 1 was also used. In August of 1977 the U.S. Air Force Armament Laboratory at Elgin Air Base began to consider how the revolver might be replaced by a 9 mm caliber pistol. Contacting the well-known manufacturers, Dale M. Davis, the Technical Director of the Department of Guns, Rockets and Explosives, told them of this intention. Shortly thereafter, this resulted in the arrival of the pistols to be tested and compared, all in 9 mm Parabellum caliber:

Beretta Model 92 S-1
Colt Stainless Steel Pistol (SSP)
Browning Hi-Power made by the Fabrique Nationale (M 1935)
Modified Hi-Power "Fast Action" by the Fabrique Nationale
P 9 S by Heckler & Koch
VP 70 by Heckler & Koch
PSP by Heckler & Koch
Model 459 and Model 459 A by Smith & Wesson
Model 28 by Star of Spain

(The pistols made by Smith & Wesson had an improved extractor, a new firing pin safety and a modified sight with two protective side panels. The Star pistol, which had just come onto the market then, was a double-action pistol with a fourteen-shot magazine and safeties on both sides with removable firing pin assembly).

With the exceptions of the pistols from the Fabrique Nationale (FN), all the pistols at hand had a double action trigger, and the VP 70 had a trigger that could be used exclusively as a cocking trigger. The principle of the Fast-Action trigger in the modified Hi-Power pistol was new, a transition piece between the simple single-action trigger and the modern double-action type. The hammer can be cocked and released with the thumb, which is said to allow very fast first shots with high targeting safety after some practice. FN had also improved the Hi-Power in other ways, with a lengthened safety for use from either side as well as a combat sight. The pistol with the new type of trigger was still being tested by several armed forces and police departments in Europe at that time, but had not been accepted. Thus FN quietly withdrew the Fast-Action pistol and subsequently refrained from publication of any kind; in similar manner, all became quiet as concerned a double-action FN pistol several years later, when there was no hope of large-series production in a more than saturated market.

Colt had offered the Model SSP as a practical alternative to their outmoded Government, but here too there was silence about its actual design after a time. The SSP was a design by Robert E. Roy, who finished his work on it at the end of the 1960s. It was then supposed to be introduced as Colt's Model 1971 Double Action Pistol, but the good designs were left to gather dust in a drawer. When the Air Force request arrived in 1977, they dusted off the finished prototypes and provided them for testing. The SSP bears much resemblance in certain features to the Petter pistol and the SIG-210. The slide moves in guides inside the grip, similarly to the SIG-210 or the Star Models 28 and 30. The entire firing pin mechanism is removable as a complete unit, also as in the two pistols mentioned. This proves to be good in practice, for no laborious dismantling of the weapon for cleaning or repairing is necessary.

The SSP pistols tested by the Air Force were reworked externally again: the trigger guard was enlarged to the front and the slide was given a matte rail on top. This model's fate was sad, for Colt finally could have offered something new with it.

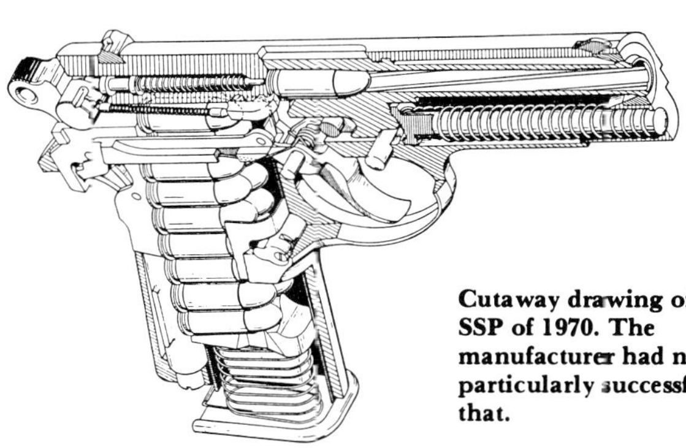

Cutaway drawing of the Colt SSP of 1970. The manufacturer had not been particularly successful before that.

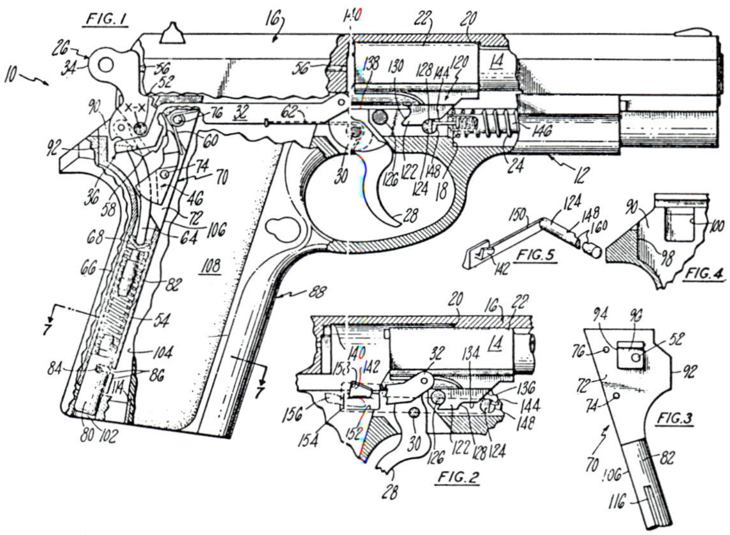

Excerpt from the patent documents for the Colt SSP, based on the work of Robert E. Roy.

The Air Force tests did not lead to a basic rearming, but definite data could be stored and used advantageously to help reach a decision in later tests. All in all, it was seen that a goodly number of practical alternatives to the venerable M 1911 A 1 were available.

The XM-9 Program

A particularly tedious and disappointing process for the participants was the U.S. Army's search for a new service pistol that was to be of 9 mm Parabellum caliber. It was disappointing for the participants because definite information about the results of the tests was withheld from them for a long time, and also because demands were made that were illusory rather than realistic.

The competition was made public in September of 1981. The "U.S. Army Armament Material Readiness Command" had announced on June 15, 1981 its decision to obtain a supply of 217,439 XM-9 pistols in 9 mm NATO caliber (identical to 9 mm Parabellum or Luger). These pistols were to be the new regular side arm for various units subordinate to the Department of Defense as well as for the Coast Guard.

For the first phase of testing, the interested manufacturers were required to make thirty examples of their pistol models available by September 15, 1981. The weapons had to follow the PDW (Personal Defense Weapon) guidelines. In addition, 360 magazines and any necessary spare parts had to be delivered with the pistols in sufficient quantities for 70,000 shots to be fired with twenty of each of the supplied weapons. Three to five of the test weapons were to be subjected to endurance shooting, to the extent of 7000 to 11,000 shots each.

The prize-giving or contract-issuing was to take place on December 18, 1981, and the first deliveries to the Coast Guard were planned for the middle of 1982.

The following characteristics or features were part of the established requirements:

— 9 mm NATO caliber.
— Maximum weight with filled magazine 1255 grams.
— Maximum length 221 mm.
— Maximum height 147 mm with magazine in place.
— The safety was to be operated simply in the same manner by left-and right-handed shooters, without changing the position of the weapon or the way it was held. The safety was to bolt, lock or otherwise block the firing pin, and to release so quietly that it could not be heard at a distance of five meters in open country.
— The trigger was to function without scratching and with a resistance of no more than 2265 kg, and no less than 1800 kg, in single-action operation. For double-action operation, the values were no more than 6340 kg and no less than 3625 kg.
— The magazine was to have a capacity of no fewer than ten rounds and was, after the magazine catch was released, to fall out of the grip by itself without having to be pulled out. A removable magazine base was required to make cleaning easier.
— The magazine catch was to be operable by either a left- or right-handed shooter with the holding hand without changing the weapon's position. It could be extended on either side or made so that the user could insert a magazine "in the field."
— Removing the magazine was not to prevent shooting.
— The foresight was to be rectangular in shape with a width of approximately 3.2 mm and a height of 3.2 to 6.3 mm.
— The sight was to be adjustable with a screwdriver, rectangular in form and with a sufficiently large light notch on each side of the foresight.
— The slide was to stay at the rear after the last shot, likewise after the removal of the magazine. The catch lever was to be capable of being set automatically or manually. A two-sided version, or an adjustable type that could be operated easily "in the field", was wanted.

Operation was not to require any change in holding the weapon.
— A ring eye was to be attached to the grip, and the grip panels could not have a smooth surface.
— The trigger guard was to be big enough to allow shooting while wearing heavy winter gloves.
— All parts were to be interchangeable without needing any reworking by hand or machine. After exchanging parts, no decrease in functioning or safety was to result.
— The screws were not to loosen by themselves before 5000 shots were fired, and no adhesive was to be put in the screw holes.
— The weapon could have no sharp angles or projections that could catch on clothing or cause injury to the user.
— Dismantling for cleaning was to be as simple to carry out as in the Colt 1911 A 1.
— The distance from the front edge of the trigger tongue to the rear angle of the grip back was not to exceed 70 mm with the single-action and 76 mm with the double-action trigger.
— All external surfaces of the weapon were to be dark, non-reflecting and corrosion-resistant.
— All internal parts were to be corrosion-resistant.
— The non-metallic parts could not be affected by insecticides or officially permitted lubricants.
— Functioning criteria: the pistol was to be capable of being loaded or unloaded without intermediate pulling of the trigger; the hammer should be releasable without pulling the trigger and without the danger of an unwanted shot being fired, the safety was to be checkable by feel as well as by sight, and with the holding hand without reaching, it was not to be possible to fire more than one shot intentionally or unintentionally with one pulling of the trigger, the weapon must be capable of being carried fully safely when loaded, it must be capable of being fired without using more than one hand. The functioning should normally be single action, with double action only for the first shot in the event of a failed ignition of a cartridge. Precision: the median dispersion circle diameter for ten series of ten shots each should not exceed a value of 35.6 mm at a distance of 50 meters; the groups should be fired with normal cartridges from a test barrel. The point of impact should not be more than 10 cm in height from the aiming point at a distance of 50 meters.

(At this point it should be noted that, outside the involved American testing facilities, some of the requirements had no relation to practice worth mentioning and were, in part, quite exaggerated. Groups of ten within 35.6 mm at a distance of 50 meters were scarcely attainable even with a technically optimal weapon such as the SIG-210 with the most careful selection of charges. A pistol for ordinary military use at short ranges has absolutely no need for such shooting precision.)

Additional Desirable Characteristics

— Magazine capacity 15 cartridges.
— Corrosion resistance under naval conditions, including full immersion in salt water.
— Functioning capability without manual assistance under unfavorable environmental conditions such as in sand or mud.
— Loading indicator for the completely filled magazine or for when the magazine held no more than five cartridges.
— Loading indicator visible and tangible.
— Trigger guard curved forward for two-handed shooting.
— Targeting apparatus with light markings for poor light.
— Effective range over 100 meters.
— Functioning safety with American and foreign 9 x 19 cartridges loaded with usual jacketed bullets.
— Capability of being marked on the magazine with a scratching tool.
— Removable foresight which can be replaced by the troops in case of damage.
— Finally, the possible availability of a compact version of the XM-9 in the same caliber and with the same technology. Military Police units which presently carry a short-barreled revolver should eventually be equipped with it.

A compact version was wanted as a service weapon in the USA. The Beretta 92 F-Compact was able to fulfill the requirements.

The XM-9 Program

This was an elaborate statement of all the requirements, some of them contradicting each other, for a weapon whose creation would require all the available artistry, for such a weapon had never yet existed. The requirements did a thorough job of scaring off all of those who may have been convinced of the quality of their previous weapons. For this reason, after the first tests only the Beretta Model 92 SB, made in Italy, and the American-made Smith & Wesson Model 459 A, which had been modified slightly, were left.

The extent of the contract, and the very prestige of coming through this competition successfully, did not leave the world's well-known manufacturers unmoved. After all, the prize was an original contract for $43,500,000 for the manufacturer and a sales value of $87,000,000. Whoever emerged victorious would find the private market far more open to him in many ways than to someone whose weapons had not passed the test. This at least must have been more or less the outlook of the other competitors.

Heckler & Koch had, shortly before, been successful when their P 7 pistol had been chosen as a German police weapon, and now they entered the competition with a modified version that had a 13-shot magazine; this was the P 7 M 13 version, a pistol with a gas-delayed breech without further locking, and a new hand-cocking system in the front of the grip. SIG-Sauer entered the Model P 226 with a 15-shot magazine. This pistol was technically almost identical to the P 220, which was introduced in Switzerland as an army pistol, and the P 225 pistol introduced very successfully by the German police.

A further requirement by the competent authorities was the possibility of production in their own country, perhaps meaning production in branch facilities. At this time Beretta and Heckler & Koch already owned production plants in the USA. SIG-Sauer intended to license the firm of Maremont in the event that their pistol was accepted.

At this time Colt was not in a position to provide 30 examples of its SSP (Stainless Steel Pistol), for this design had done poorly in previous tests in terms of precision, functioning safety and maintenance as well as servicing. For that reason Colt, in Hartford, resurrected an idea that had been developed along with the Kart Sporting Arms Corporation in a previous year: re-equipping the existing Colt 1911 A 1 for the 9 mm Parabellum caliber, installing a two-sided safety, and improving the sights. This was to cost only $70 per pistol, in comparison to which the expected price for an XM-9 pistol was $200, and adding all the resulting costs and supplies of spare parts raised it to $400.

The result of this thinking was the Government Model Mark IV, Series 80, which is now on the private market. Along with the already noted improvements, this pistol has an additional inner safety, which releases the firing pin only by activating the trigger.

The Colt firm's suggestion found no favor, and so Colt began, in the winter of 1981-82 and under the strictest secrecy, with the practical testing of the XM-9.

Things must not have gone quite right from then on, for it came as an unpleasant surprise to all participants when, on February 19, 1982, the U.S. Army stated, "The Army as executive organ of the Defense Department responsible for supplying a 9 mm pistol has given up this endeavor. It was in fact not possible to award a contract, for all of the offered weapons failed to meet the requirements of the description. The Defense Department has the intention of rethinking its requirements and focusing on a new type of pistol."

This decision naturally inspired righteous indignation, as the military had given absolutely no detailed reasons for its decision. It had simply eliminated the weapons of the world's four best manufacturers, including an American competitor, and no one knew why.

For the firm of Colt this was really a bitter pill, and in Hartford the old suggestion of either modifying 350,000 of the 1911 A 1 pistols as mentioned above, or providing acceptable prototypes of the SSP, as soon as the authorities wanted to begin testing again. The representatives of Beretta and Heckler & Koch restrained themselves discreetly, but the spokesman of Maremont, as the US representative of the SIG-Sauer firm, expressed himself very dejectedly, "We are disappointed, and we still do not understand the reasons for this decision."

A different comment came from the firm of Smith & Wesson, and its reaction was considerably colder. Robert Hass, the President of the Marketing Department, explained to the press, "We have examined our pistols carefully as to their agreement with the established requirements and compared them with the other weapons. It is impossible that they do not live up to the requirements in terms of their quality."

He disposed of the subject once and for all when he demanded that the technical testing results be made public under the "Freedom of Information Act." The Army authorities were so distracted that they claimed that all candidates had failed to pass the three essential parts of the test: functioning safety at low temperatures, in sand and in mud. No further concrete information followed.

As a logical result of all this, the military was accused of improper procedure with the intention of keeping the old .45 ACP caliber Colt 1911 A 1. Rumors surfaced that claimed the Colt 1911 A 1 had been the best weapon in the evaluation, but it is easy to suspect that this pistol must rather have finished a dead last in the evaluation. In terms of precision alone, its normal version is certainly not a good pistol.

Further rumors claimed that none of the pistols had stood more than 600 shots in the coldness, sand and mud tests without malfunctioning, while the criterion of 1000 shots, or at least a minimum of 800 shots, had been called for under these conditions.

In the end, the U.S. Army made a precise statement: None of the candidates had been able to score more than 11 of the required 71 points. That was the best they could do.

This led to another round of very different reactions, for now Congress felt that it had been deceived. It had, after all, made the sum of $1,900,000 available to the Army for the search for a new pistol in 9 mm Parabellum caliber. The House Committee on Appropriations published, under number 97-943, a report that was meant to bring the contrary military into line again. Its contents will be summed up here: . . . for five years the Defense Department committee had ordered a standardization of its handguns as well as their ammunition, in order to simplify supplying and lowering the cost of training. The assortment of weapons and ammunition then in use was unnecessary, impractical and indefensible.

Two years have passed since the committee was informed by the Defense Department that a pistol in 9 mm caliber was to be introduced uniformly and an appropriate description was circulated. The weapons were offered and tested, and the decision was promised by last February. But on February 19 the land forces (Army) had said that the search had been invalidated because none of the offered weapons had corresponded to the established criteria. After all, though, the committee had learned that all the offered pistols in 9 mm caliber had been better than the introduced pistol in .45 caliber which had served as a basis of comparison. In addition, the description had applied to a weapon whose manufacture was impossible anywhere in the world by the present-day standards of technology. Finally, the entire testing program and the way in which it was carried out had been called in question.

In May the committee was informed that the Defense Department had again empowered the Army to set up a program for testing and subsequent supplying. The evaluations were to take place in June and the decision in July of 1983. The description appeared only in August, and the establishment of a testing program has not yet taken place.

While these delays continue, the urgent need of the Coast Guard and the Air Force for a new pistol has not yet been satisfied. As a further indication of the illegal behavior of the Army, Congress has made known that it canceled all expenditures for purchasing and transferred them to the 1984 fiscal year. The House Committee expressed itself as being disappointed and annoyed at this inactivity. Perhaps the time has come to take this program out of the Army's jurisdiction and turn it over to the Defense Department or some other arm of the service.

To bring the Army's delaying action to an end, the Committee sees no other possible means than using financial pressure to force the necessary obedience to the will of Congress. For this reason the Committee suggests abolishing the budget of $7,100,000 for the acquisition of weapons and ammunition (handguns), as well as the amount of one million dollars for the acquisition of spare parts. As soon as the Defense Department is in a position to envisage a new program, the Committee will make the funding for the urgently needed weapons available in the proper manner . . .

In order to show that they were not joking, Mr. Stevens, as Speaker of the Committee, declared on September 8, 1982 that, in accordance with the law, the means to procurement of the 9 mm pistols would be made available only in 1983.

After being properly put in its place, the Army set out to do its job — the weapons for the new test had to be made available by January 31, 1983.

As was to be expected, the firms of Beretta, Heckler & Koch and SIG-Sauer (through Maremont) took part in the new competition with the pistols they had offered before. The Belgian firm of Fabrique Nationale of Herstal, successful with its MINIMI light machine gun model, offered a modified version of the Hi-Power with double-action trigger. This was the pistol that was always displayed at exhibitions and trade fairs, or shown as a picture in the press but never went into series production for lack of large-scale contracts, not even in its shortened version.

The Austrian manufacturer Steyr-Daimler-Puch entered the Model GB, an 18-shot pistol with a gas-delayed slide similar to the type used by Heckler & Koch, who offered their P 7 M 13, a new development based on the P 7 A 13. The Walther firm, located in Ulm on the Danube, developed the Model P 88 and offered pre-series weapons for testing. The Colt firm again offered the SSP, Sturm & Ruger presented a new development, and there was also a Bren-Ten in 9 mm Parabellum caliber; and then suddenly all was quiet again about all these pistols.

The requirements were now somewhat simplified and were to be tested in twelve stages:

1. Checking the weapons and testing their resistance to chemical substances.

A proud moment for Beretta, but displeasure at this contract came later has not ended yet.

2. Checking interchange capability of parts, whereby the weapons were to be dismantled as if for repair. Then shooting three groups of ten shots each from the shooting machine to determine average dispersion.
3. Testing durability; shooting 35,000 rounds per model, limited to weapons that had passed points 1 and 2.
4. Ammunition suitability. Each weapon would fire 300 cartridges with various charges, the choice being representative of cartridges meeting the NATO standards.
5. Temperature testing. Shooting 1000 cartridges at +60 degrees C and -40 degrees C with three pistols of each type. Shooting from two filled magazines with weapons that were formerly immersed in salt water. Then testing in dampness over a period of ten days.
6. Testing under disadvantageous conditions:
— Shooting with two clean and dry pistols in sandy environment.
— Placing the weapon in thinned mud, cleaning by hand, and then functioning test firing.
— Shooting 500 cartridges from a dry, unoiled weapon. Cooling the weapon after every fifty shots.
— Steady movement of the slide for a period of nine minutes, with spraying of imitation rain, then shooting until the full magazine is empty.
7. Precision: Shooting with five weapons of each type in ten series of ten shots each from the shooting machine. Distance 50 meters, average allowable dispersion 102 mm in diameter.
8. Falling safety. Weapon is dropped with cocked hammer and with safety set, with magazine filled and a cartridge in the chamber, from a height of 1.2 meters, onto a steel plate, repeated six times from six different positions.
9. Accuracy: shooting with six pistols of each type at a distance of 50 meters at a half-figure target, by representative shooters with varying training.
10. Safety: listing and evaluating all incidents during testing that concern the safety of the weapon and the danger to the shooter.
11. Human factors; personal impressions of the shooters.
12. Conference; evaluation of all resulting costs.This was certainly a stringent test, but it can be said here that the type of testing was based more on practice and no longer (see precision) based on imposed conceptions. It was advantageous that standardized cartridges of various origin were used. It was also good that there were always several weapons used in a test, thus avoiding the danger of ruining the average results with a "champion" or a

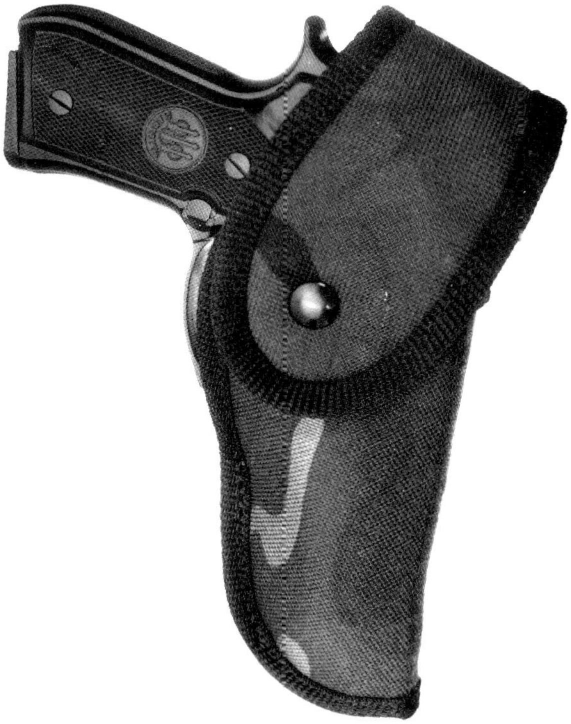

The Beretta 92 F in a modern nylon holster, which does not go with the military model.

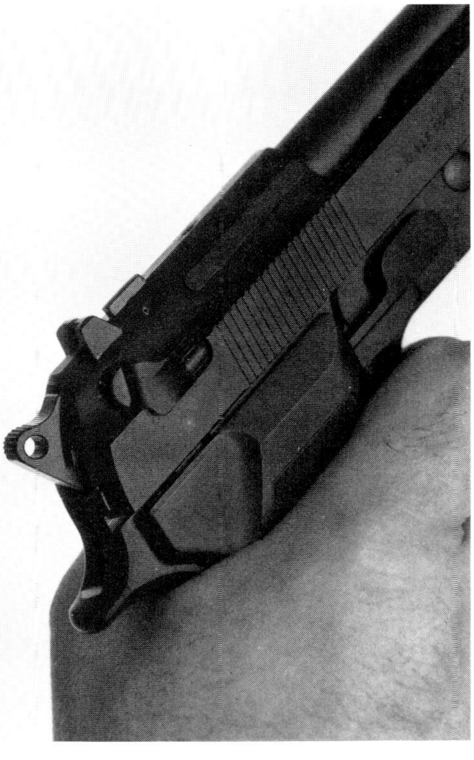

Safeties on both sides were required. As soon as the trigger is pulled all the way, the automatic firing pin block rises and emerges visibly from the top of the slide.

"clunker."

The decision to accept the Beretta 92 F was announced on January 15, 1985. It is understandable that not everyone was happy about the results, and soon enough dissatisfied voices were heard, including in the USA. The first part of the delivery was to consist of 50,000 pistols made in Italy, after which a change should be made to manufacturing in the American Beretta factory.

How did the pistols actually rank, when tested? The BERETTA 92 F had the Model 92 SB as its immediate ancestor. At this time, the Italian and Brazilian armies have more than 100,000 of them in service, showing that the manufacturer has ample practical experience. In addition, Beretta has been able to draw on much experience from previous tests, and had already put this pistol on the private market successfully. In all, the Beretta pistol had a very good reputation in the USA at that time. A compact version available at the same time with a smaller magazine capacity was a sensible means of filling out the firm's program.

Precise, safe, elegant in appearance, pleasantly balanced in the hand, practical for service and maintenance and made to withstand 20,000 shots; the 92 was a pistol that corresponded to the details of the specifications to a high degree.

The SMITH & WESSON Model 459 was practically the oldest participant in the test but had been improved steadily in terms of sturdiness and safety since it appeared in 1971. The alternative frames made of aluminum, steel or stainless steel made sense. The sights were also improved. Here too, a compact version was available, and was shortly thereafter put on the private market in various versions as the Mini Gun Model 469, with a magazine for twelve cartridges.

The HECKLER & KOCH P 7 M 13 was a completely new design made completely of steel and had already proved itself as a service pistol for part of the German police, used there with a magazine for eight cartridges. It is small, handy and pleasant to use once one gets used to it. At this time, Heckler & Koch was already filling other orders for the American armed forces and had an excellent reputation as a manufacturer.

The SIG-SAUER P 226 could also look back on success, and was the successor to such renowned pistols as the P 220 and P 225, which had been in production for more than ten years. Its safety features are remarkably good and simple to operate. Its position in the hand is simply excellent, as are the trigger and the sights. It sits high in the hand; its grip is a new development.

The Browning GP-DA has retained many good features of the earlier GP, plus its solid construction and good workmanship. The magazine capacity was expanded to 14 cartridges without having to increase the length of the magazine. The decocking levers are on both sides, but function a bit unusually, for they are pushed upward and not downward.

Or back to the Colt 1911 A 1 again . . .

In mid-1986 the rumor mill went into action again on the subject of the future army pistol. On the basis of a secret project, it was said that U.S. Army suggestions were being worked on that would make it possible to retain the beloved (and perhaps time-tested) M 1911 A 1. The change to the new Beretta 92 F displeased many Americans, and the lobby may have played an influential role. There was little confidence in the 9 mm cartridge and much fear of retraining and possible accidents as a result. Another reason, so it was said, was the high final cost, which was said to amount to $1500 per pistol in view of manufacture, stocks of spare parts, tools, ammunition, training and retraining of personnel. On this basis, the firm of Colt was supposed (in mid-1986) to have proposed a new alternative. The result was to be a Model 1911 A 2 version with the following improvements.

— Retention of the .45 ACP caliber
— Improved combat sights
— A match barrel for the use of all .45 charges
— An enlarged ejection window
— A safety lever on each side
— A lengthened grip safety
— Neoprene grip panels by Pachmayr (without a central piece)
— Ribbing on the front of the grip
— A new-shape spring housing at the back of the grip
— A new type of entry to the magazine shaft
— A trigger lengthened to the front

Several examples of this version were said to have been turned over to the army for testing; performance and handling were highly rated. At this time only 35,000 of the 92 F had been finished, and their production was said to have been halted, which was confirmed a short time later.

It must have been a truly difficult decision to take such a venerable pistol out of service . . . and replace it with a device not developed in the USA. But it also seems to have been difficult for a world-renowned firm to finally offer a really modern pistol.

In October 1986, the procurement merry-go-round began to turn again, and a new test was ordered. Thus after some 320,000 Beretta pistols had been ordered, another fifteen million or so dollars had to be spent on further tests, and a result could hardly be expected before 1990.

If all goes according to the will of the lawmakers, a second pistol will be introduced as well: a Smith & Wesson Model 459 X-9. Smith & Wesson had made successful use of the slogan "buy American." And the S & W pistol was one of those that had actually failed the test for decisive reasons. There was dissatisfaction with its durability and life expectancy, and there were also problems with ignition. It can scarcely be imagined that such decisions will be based solely on the results of an expensive test, for then the P 226 would more likely have gone on to the level of "technically acceptable finalist", but the Beretta 92 had then reached the level of "acceptable finalist and winner."

The manufacturer, the Fabrique Nationale of Herstal, is well established in the USA and manufactures various systems for the American armed forces, particularly automatic weapons.

The STEYR GB was produced in the USA for some years under the name of Rogack. The GB is a very modern weapon, though it has grown rather large and almost unhandy. The magazine holds 18 cartridges, the slide is delayed by gas conducted out of the barrel. The production of the weapon is quite unusual as compared to Colt or Smith & Wesson practices.

The WALTHER Model P 88 can be regarded as the most perfect weapon of the time, for it has a remarkably clear and simple operation and an equally simple safety system. As is always true of weapons from Ulm, the workmanship is superb. The characteristics of the trigger are regarded as less favorable, a criticism that the author cannot personally agree to. In the P 88, Walther departed from the swinging bolt for the first time and modified a Browning-type lock, while other features are similar to those of the dependable P 5. The P 88 was put on the private market in 1986, and at the same time this manufacturer offered the P 38 alternatively with a steel frame for those who prefer heavy pistols.

The decision was not easy, and the results will carry much weight, for when all is said and done there will be at least 600,000 pistols made, plus spare parts and accessories such as holsters. In addition, a successful pistol in this test will do well on the private market, and the manufacturer will be able to do well in very different markets too. Whether the Beretta 92 F is really the best pistol in the world on the basis of this decision may be debatable. Economic and political reasons always play a major role in decisions of this magnitude. For the private user and the collector, this is completely advantageous, for one can relate to an expanded program in this practical caliber.

Choosing Your Own Weapon

The views on no other question diverge as much as those on the question choosing a weapon. The basic decision between a revolver and a (self-loading) pistol is perhaps not very consequential, as the selection of suitable revolvers in 9 mm Parabellum caliber is not very great. On the other hand, the legal basis of the potential buyer plays a not inconsiderable role. Whoever has only a single weapon allowed by law has a very different decision to make than someone who can or may buy several weapons within one caliber, but more of this later. The revolver-or-pistol question was debated hotly for years, not without numerous arguments from the USA, the land of the revolver. Much was said and constantly repeated without gaining any justification. A few basic differences will be noted briefly here.

The majority of authors, testers, trainers and advisors of police units clearly incline toward the pistol, and not only in Germany, a country in which the revolver has always played a very subordinate role. The typical American handgun was and is the revolver, specifically the single-action revolver as the weapon of popular western heroes. Films and novels have done their best to see that no other kind of weapon could gain as much popularity. The six-shooter is a concept that has been dominant for years. Large-caliber pistols were used by the military in the USA, and small-caliber .22 pistols were reserved for sport shooting and the like. For a time there was no practical connection between them. On the other hand, numerous Americans bought reasonably-priced or downright cheap small pistols for their personal safety. There was a lot of junk involved, from a technical point of view, and this seems to have added to the viewpoint that self-loading pistols were not sufficiently reliable. Unfortunately, this was repeated frequently, and became the dominant opinion, of those lacking personal experience with well-built pistols. Another reason for the unfavorable opinion of self-loading pistols (in the USA) was the inadequate quality of domestic ammunition, especially in 9 mm Parabellum caliber. Also involved was the problem with the tests for a future army pistol. The 9 mm ammunition that was on the market was absolutely not capable of fulfilling the requirements in precision, and the manufacturers had to have a specific contract before taking action. Today the situation looks much better, and the norms that are valid in Europe, such as the NATO standards, have also been accepted in the USA. There have often been problems with the legendary Luger pistol, which enjoys a very good reputation there but would not shoot without malfunctions on account of the domestic ammunition. It was also problematic with normal German or other European ammunition, for the Luger pistol needs a slightly weaker charge, which is no great problem for capable reloaders. It should be noted at this point that the Luger and other Parabellum pistols functioned excellently and shot precisely with the earlier German police cartridge (with blue ring groove, often called "Polizei-Schlapp").

After World War II, there was a new wave of opposition to pistols, which were regarded as unreliable. Many soldiers had brought back captured pistols, and most of them were no longer in the best of condition — they were often weapons made in the last years of the war. When they were used with cartridges from armed forces overstocks, the results had to include many malfunctions.

Meanwhile, while the question of pistol reliability began to fade into the past, the idea of firing over 5000 shots with normal ammunition without problems was to be regarded as normal.

The size and stability of the individual parts of a modern revolver and pistol should be compared. Here too, many revolvers will look the worse for their many small pins and springs, all the more so when dirt gets into them.

A revolver, especially in .357 Magnum or .38 SPL caliber, can be basically smaller and more delicate than a 9 mm caliber pistol. However, the situation becomes very different when the same barrel lengths are used in these calibers. A revolver with the same barrel length is thicker and longer. The Smith & Wesson M 39 has a barrel 102 mm long and an overall length of 189 mm. The M 19 Combat Magnum is 191 mm long, but its barrel length is only 64 mm. With a 102 mm barrel, the same revolver would be 241 mm long.

The difference becomes quite glaring when one considers the cylinder or magazine capacity. A cylinder, even in the best of cases, can hold only five or six large-caliber cartridges, while a pistol of the same length can hold at least eight cartridges without having an overly thick grip, and the newer weapons can safely hold up to 15 cartridges plus an additional one in the barrel. Reloading is also very different, even when a quick loader is used for a revolver — changing a magazine is certainly faster and easier to do. If the user of a modern pistol carries two filled replacement magazines with him in a small pouch, he has the capacity of 15 + 15 + 15 + 1 = 46 cartridges — to equal this, a revolver would have to be reloaded more than seven times.

Present-day pistols have attained a high degree of operating comfort, when one thinks of such modern weapons as the Astra A 80, Walther P 5, Heckler & Koch PSP or P 7 pistol, and the pistols of SIG-Sauer. Simple dismantling, high magazine capacity and absolute safety, plus a good arrangement of the moving parts, make them superior to any revolver.

On the other hand, the revolver has two advantages of its own: it can be seen at a glance whether there are cartridges in the cylinder, and the most varying charges can be fired without concern for functioning disturbances. It cannot be denied that at short ranges, the small, handy revolver can provide sufficient accuracy and effect on the target. But one should avoid prejudice, for the charge that self-loading pistols are lacking in reliability can no longer be valid.

When choosing one's own weapon, the question of how it is to be used is worthy of special consideration. Most weapons are bought today for spare-time use in sport or pleasure shooting, a perfectly good purpose. Whoever buys a weapon for this purpose has little reason for concern about absolute safety of the old type (for example, the Star 30), for in his activities he always has sufficient time. Nor does it play any role if there is no good holster available for a pistol, or if the weapon is rather large. In this case one might well be inclined toward a steel frame, for one does not have to carry the weapon all the time. Many of the criteria stated briefly in the text below apply to someone who has to choose a weapon to carry for long periods and always be ready to defend himself.

Weapon Weight

A not overly heavy weapon is an important prerequisite for comfortable carrying, but weight savings are not to be overvalued. An overly light weapon's muzzle tends to jump up when fired and has to be brought back into line, and a light weapon also recoils harder into one's hand when fired. In 9 mm Parabellum caliber, weapon weights between 650 and 720 grams are normal, the recoil is bearable, and carrying is not too tiring. Pistols like the Walther P 5, SIG-Sauer P 6 or Heckler & Koch P 7 weigh about 800 grams unloaded and rank among the pistols that can be carried comfortably and even concealed.

In this respect, the choice between an aluminum or steel frame has to be considered. The lighter grip results in a saving of 200 grams or more, which is significant for someone who has to carry a weapon constantly. There is no longer any concern today about the durability of aluminum frames.

Compactness

This too is a very personal concept, influenced by one's own sensitivity. What is small and compact for .45 ACP caliber is too weighty for 9 mm caliber. Compactness thus has its limits, beyond which the weapon can no longer be carried safely. The small grip of a 6.35 pistol is impossible in 9 mm Parabellum caliber, for the weapon could not be held onto when firing. The grip must be long enough to hold sufficient cartridges, but not too wide. The barrel has a necessary minimum length to even come near utilizing the ballistic performance of the cartridge and to give a sufficient impulse for the self-loading function. Compactness is also a question of stability, for the more one slims down a weapon, the smaller, more delicate and more sensitive some of the moving parts become.

Pistols like the P 7 are very compact already as production weapons, and a good job was done by Smith & Wesson with their Mini-Gun, which despite holding 12 cartridges is neither too big nor too wide. On the other hand, the compactness of a pistol like the Detonics Pocket 9 seems somewhat exaggerated. The weapon recoils into the hand so hard when fired that one is happy to stop shooting.

Magazine Capacity

A sufficiently large magazine capacity is important but should not be exaggerated as a requirement, especially for a light and easily carried weapon. Naturally a similarly built pistol in a larger caliber will hold fewer cartridges than in a smaller caliber. Experience shows that the targeting accuracy of the first two or three shots is decisive, not that of the subsequent series of up to fifteen shots.

Thickness of the grip sets a clearly tangible limit, for when two rows of cartridges are held in the magazine, a grip can be overly thick and unhandy. Pistols like the Mini-Gun or the Smith & Wesson M 59 or the P 226 have

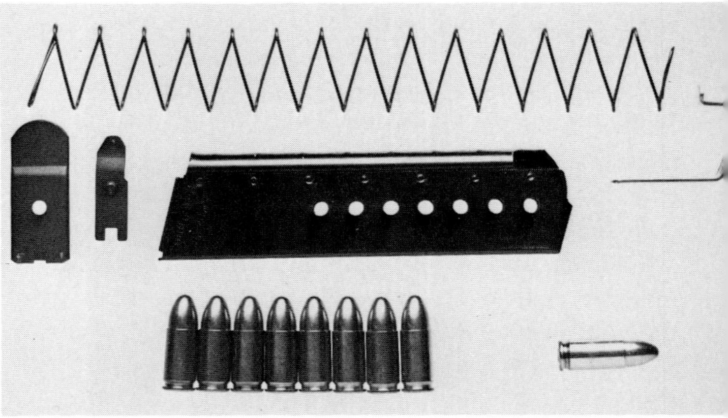

A magazine capacity of eight cartridges plus one more in the barrel are enough; "firepower" need not be overdone.

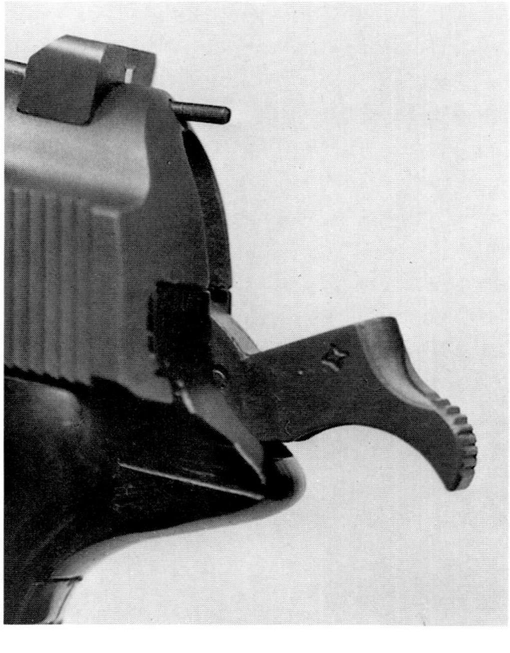

A signal rod comes out the back of the P 38 when there is a cartridge in the chamber. This clear indication makes the pistol considerably safer.

very thin grips, no thinner than the usual grips of weapons that hold one row of cartridges. How a grip can become too wide is shown by the handsome wooden grip panels of the P 226, which make the grip rather unhandy for even big hands. A magazine capacity of eight cartridges is sufficient and normal.

Safety Mechanisms

Malfunctions in critical situations can never be completely ruled out, but practical safety systems can prevent them to a great degree. A manual safety system that is not present cannot be used wrongly. This was precisely the trend in the last few decades. The modern pistols were made deliberately without a manually activated safety system, but they did not become at all dangerous — on the contrary.

The present-day ideal is the system that releases the firing pin only when the trigger is pulled and is almost in its rearmost position. A fine example of this is the P 5 pistol, where the firing pin is swung into the area where it can be struck by the hammer only when the trigger is pulled. Other modern pistols also show very well-designed, independently acting safeties and do without the earlier lateral wing safety.

A part of the good mechanical safety system is the possibility of being able to decock a cocked hammer without any risk of causing a shot to be fired. Here too, the modern pistols offer good alternatives. The old-type safeties were less practical, for there one had to consider what position they were supposed to be in. One not only had to pay attention to their markings but also see that the wing of the safety indicated the released position when preparing to shoot.

Devices such as the short firing pin, broad and strong safety and striking rests, a wide hammer spur with an easily gripped surface, a stable safety pivot, and especially a sufficiently sturdy arrangement of all these parts, are also important.

Devices that show whether a cartridge is in the chamber are also important, even though one should not carelessly rely on them. Depending on the type of weapon, there may be no such devices, or there may be very practical ones, such as the signal rod of the P 38 and similar models.

The clear safety system of the Walther P 5 can stand any comparison.

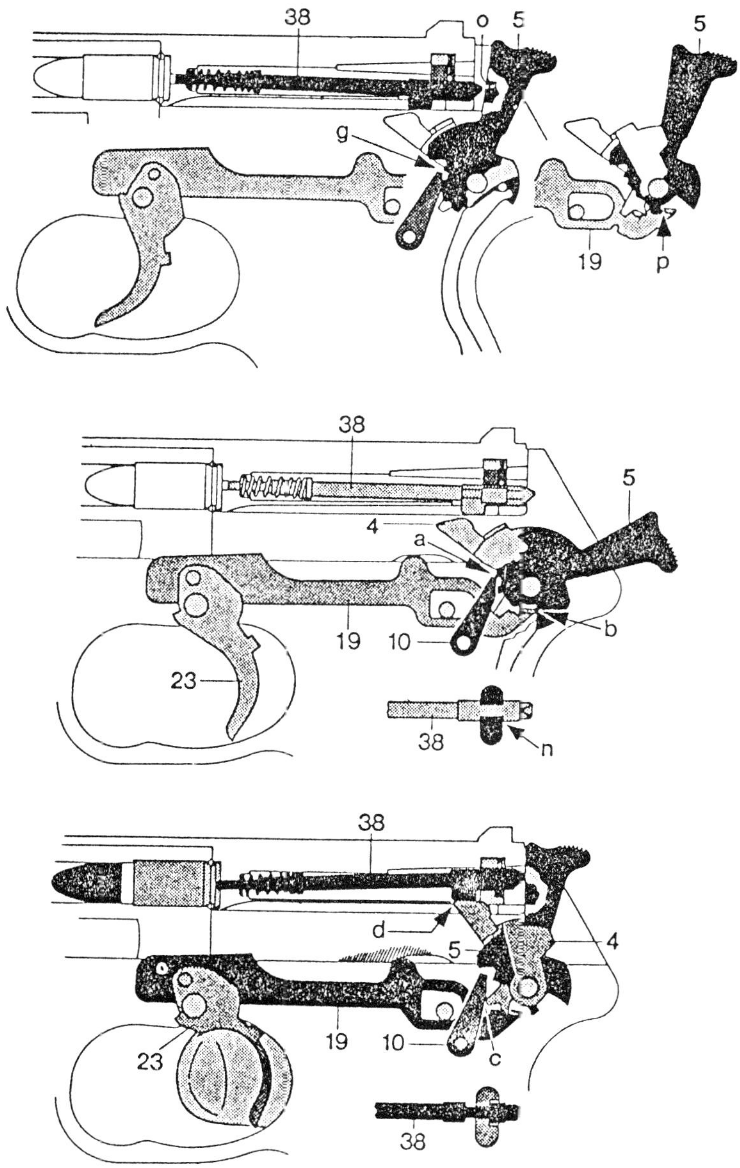

Types of Triggers

Whether one should prefer the somewhat archaic single-action trigger or the more versatile double action trigger appears to be a problem of the past. Today no manufacturer would think of putting a pistol in a popular caliber on the market without a double action trigger. The opponents of the cocking trigger like to make to claim that there is a very great difference between the firing of the first shot (via the double action trigger) and that of the second shot (via the pre-cocked hammer). This cannot be regarded as that simple, for it is a matter of practice, and many shooters do not shoot much worse with a double action trigger than with a pre-cocked hammer.

Of course it cannot be denied that many pistols have an extremely bad double action trigger with a poor transmission of power that hardly makes a well-placed first shot possible. If one compares the double action trigger of the P 5 with that of the Astra A-80, one sees a difference like that between day and night. Often the distance is too long, the weight to be overcome too great and the falling of the trigger after firing the shot too far. Here it is a matter of trying a weapon critically oneself and considering the possibility of having it reworked by an expert.

Simple Dismantling

Dismantling without special tools is the norm today, and few manufacturere deviate from it. For checking and cleaning, no tool should be necessary, and in this respect most pistols are more than excellent. Despite its slightly antiquated safety, the Star 30 is optimal in terms of dismantling. To remove the entire firing pin housing one needs only the rounded tip of the catch lever — the individual pins can also be pushed out with it. Reassembly, though, is not so simple in the event that one has removed the mainspring, hammer and/or sear, for which a flat pair of pliers is helpful. The catch lever is also needed to remove the firing pin. With the firing pin one can push in the block of the right safety wing and, after removing this part, take all the remaining parts out of the slide without a tool. The criterion for a tool-free, simple dismantling should not be the dismantling of all the small parts, but rather the state of dismantling necessary for inspection and cleaning.

Light Recoil

The less a weapon recoils in the hand when fired and the less the muzzle jumps, the more easily quick series and good groups can be fired. When practicing with a revolver set up for the 9 mm cartridge, lighter charges can be used, but this leads over a period of time to a false impression and to no better results. The recoil must be opposed by a certain firmness in holding the weapon and a certain stability of the wrist, and that can be practiced best with the right charge. In the case of the 9 mm cartridge, the recoil is heavy only with small weapons — it would be felt as somewhat stronger with a gas-delayed pistol such as the P 7.

On the other hand, expecting a hard recoil leads to holding the weapon more firmly, which is more likely to help than hinder firing good groups if it is not overdone.

Fixed Sights

Much money has been spent on sights that are adjustable to all sides, but their purpose in defensive weapons is more than disputed by experts — the situation is different for sporting use. The foresight may not be cut back or stick out so far that the weapon gets caught in the holster or the clothing. A not overly high foresight with a light incline in the shooting direction is very beneficial.

The backsight is, at best, either fixed or only laterally adjustable, as is the case on many of our modern pistols. With backsight leaves or foresights of differing heights, an optimal adjustment to any cartridge and personal sighting habits can be attained. On the other hand, fully adjustable sights can easily get out of adjustment, for one never knows whether anyone might have adjusted them.

Light markings on the foresight and/or on both sides of the backsight notch are advantageous — the light markings allow quick targeting even in poor light, and such markings have prevailed in recent years. Defensive situations, as experience has shown, generally take place at ranges of less than ten meters, and usually even within a limit of five meters. Sporting sights are quite unimportant in such situations. It is more important to have clearly and quickly visible sights whose outlines remain recognizable against any background.

Functioning Safety

This should go without saying in a weapon, but often it does not. Authors like G. Nonte were right to call for a proper "running-in time" of several hundred shots for a weapon on whose functioning a life can depend.

Many weapon carriers will, fortunately, never use their weapons against an attacker, but if this situation should occur, then there should be no doubt about its safe functioning. Testing the functioning safety is necessary after every disassembly, and especially after any modification to the trigger or hammer, or their rests.

It is not overdoing it to break in one's own weapon properly.

On this score, two of the pistols shown here can be evaluated more than critically: a modification by the Joniskeit firm and the Pocket 9 by Detonics. The modification was only to be used as a single-loader, and that with weak, medium and strong cartridges. At one of these levels there would have had to be a malfunction. Factory-made cartridges would not have made the situation any better.

We found the depicted early Pocket 9 to be a real failure. Its breech delaying is located in an extension of the housings inside a cartridge-chamber bulge. Cartridges with thin-walled cases made the pistol produce a mighty noise, cartridges with thick cases did not function — every case had to be driven out of the barrel with a tool.

Ammunition Suitability

The trouble-free reaction of a self-loading pistol to differing types and charges can never be as great as that of a revolver. In other words, everything that is of the right caliber to fit into the cylinder can be fired from a revolver with no trouble. As for the strength of the charges, the upper loading limit is assuredly better than experiments at the lower limit. The situation is different when it is only a question of measurable sporting precision. As shown elsewhere with the SIG 210 and MP 3 S as examples, the precision is clearly better in the lower range of charges. But this cannot be tested in any way for a weapon used for defense, for the uncertainty is simply too great. It would not be any different with a shortening or weakening of the mainspring to enable a minimal charge to be fired without problems.

Short-range precision does not need to be overstressed. Good pistols maintain a diameter of 10 cm at 25 meters with most cartridges, and thus fire at practically the same spot from one shot to another at five to eight meters.

It is important to decide on a certain cartridge and break in the weapon with the sights on it. Doubts as to a possibly changing targeting point should never occur. The differences, depending on the cartridges, are very considerable at 25 meters.

Difficulties may be caused by different bullet shapes, but the 9 mm Parabellum ogival bullet is problem-free. The situation is different with semi-jacketed and flat-headed bullets that can go awry on the way into the chamber. Here an expert evaluation makes sense, and a slight reworking of the ramp usually helps. As always, with the finally selected cartridge and with normal cartridges available everywhere, the weapon should not have any problems.

Ease of Handling

Functioning reliability, precision and effect on the target cannot be utilized fully if the weapon cannot be handled and operated smoothly. In short, a weapon for self-defense must be operable with one hand — the other hand should be required only to insert a new magazine.

This is nowhere near as self-evident as it sounds. It is scarcely possible to operate the safety, and thus decock the hammer, of a pistol like the Llama 82 with the thumb of the right hand (when held with the right hand). This may not be of any great importance, however one must at least be able to cock the hammer with the right thumb.

The size of the grip, the releasing of the grip horn and the gap with the trigger in its foremost position must fit the hand — someone with small hands and short fingers simply cannot use many of the modern fifteen-shot pistols. The length of the magazine catch is important. A magazine catch at the top of the grip surely gives a small time advantage for fast changing, but many catches have such weak springs that the magazine can also be released accidentally. If the pistol also has a magazine safety, then this can cause a big surprise in the middle of a series.

We do not mean to carry coals to Newcastle, but as far as handling goes, the police pistols introduced in Germany may well be the best weapons of their kind in the world.

Availability of Spare Parts

Official procurers pay great attention to the interchange capability of parts for the same weapon. In this way, the replacement of a defective part can be done quickly and economically. There is always the possibility of "cannibalizing", of sacrificing another weapon to obtain spare parts.

The first step is the decision of what to buy. Whoever buys a weapon with good service available can rely on the service of its manufacturer or importer. But if, on the other hand, one has bought an "exotic" weapon, one often finds out very soon that the manufacturer no longer exists. Spare parts then either do not exist at all or have to be made especially at a high price.

Precision

This is a subject on which opinions differ sharply. In many ways, expectations of precision are simply too high. Precision is a blend of many individual factors: the inherent precision of the cartridge, the precision of the cartridge in a given weapon, the precision of the barrel, the precision derived from the mounting of the barrel, and finally what the position in the hand and the trigger contribute to measurable precision. Many weapons can be said to have excellent precision when tested in a shooting machine, but when fired by hand, their pre-

Defense pistols are not sport pistols. This target with ten shots was made sitting at 20 meters. It is easy to see and is well above average performance.

cision is often less than satisfactory. A stiff-moving, scratching and then long-falling trigger can nullify everything else. To determine precision for the cartridge-barrel-barrel mounting combination, supported shooting from a sitting position or the use of a shooting machine is inviting. Only shooting from the hand, one hand or both, with and without time pressure, gives an impression of the actual precision.

Sporting standards have no validity for a defensive weapon. A group of five in a circle with a diameter of about 60 mm at 20 meters, or in a circle with a 120 mm diameter at 40 meters, would be an acceptable performance for the cartridge, weapon and shooter. It does not make much sense to improve the precision of the weapon slightly through expensive modifications if, for one thing, no choice (or self-loaded charge) of cartridges brings success, or if one does not get enough practice, and under realistic conditions, with the weapon.

A Sure Grip

The grip must fit into the hand without sliding, even when the hand is dirty, oily or sweaty. Grip panels made of wood, plastic, hard rubber, nylon, ivory, horn or metal may make a good appearance, but they often do not provide a sure handhold for the weapon, even if a herringbone pattern is cut or pressed into them. Grip panels made of wood are often better than the same panels made of plastic, and they are usually available as accessories. Painted surfaces are troublesome. The paint can be removed with fine sandpaper plus an application of good shaft oil such as Roolin-II — the matted surface not only looks better, but also, and above all, fits into the hand better. Caution must be exercised when wooden grip panels are substituted. Here is a personal experience: to a P 5 the author added wooden grip panels marketed by the Walther firm, and screwed them on firmly. As a result of this, the trigger bar, guided from outside, got stuck and the trigger no longer moved forward after being pulled — in this area wood had to be cut away cautiously. On both sides, the grip panels were so binding that even the slide could no longer move freely. This became noticeable only after several days, for the wood had apparently bent just a little bit. There too some material had to be removed. The Pachmayr grips made of neoprene rubber offer a good alternative — they have an inlaid steel reinforcement and are currently available for many of the pistols and revolvers on the market. They offer even a sweaty hand a secure, non-skid grip.

Smooth Contours

A weapon in a holster must have smooth external contours so that it does not snag when being drawn. An adjustable sight often projects too far out, and operating levers should not stick too far out at the side. This is often the case when weapons are modified, for example with all the lengthened levers added to the Colt Government or Commander, or when they are switched from left-to right-hand operation.

Sights with their angles rounded, and rounded magazine bases, can be added by the owner in some cases. After talking it over with an experienced gunsmith, it may be found that rounding the sharp corners at the rear of the slide may be an improvement in some cases.

Handy, high-performance caliber, smooth contours, clear safeties: the Walther P 5-Compact fulfills all these requirements.

Calibers

The 9 mm Parabellum caliber has stabilized its position as the universal cartridge in recent years — only in the USA did it take a very long time before it was finally accepted for service use. This cartridge is available everywhere and is a good compromise between penetrating power and retarding power, depending on the charge and the bullet.

Aiming Quality

Under stressful conditions there is often scarcely any time to aim — the weapon has to be fired instinctively, and one depends on the muzzle pointing in the direction that the hand holding the weapon points. Just as one points at something with an outstretched index finger, the muzzle of the weapon points at the target.

A prerequisite for this is the correct grip angle. Take any pistol you choose in your hand and stretch out your index finger alongside the grip. Does the muzzle of the weapon point where the finger is pointing?

Many pistols have an excellent aiming quality, meaning that they point at the target as if by themselves. It is a question of the grip angle, and naturally a question of getting accustomed. Whoever may find himself in a critical situation of this kind one day should practice sufficiently, both with and without live bullets. Sigfried F. Hübner has written a series of highly regarded and very appreciated (even outside Germany) works on this subject — in his books one will find countless bits of advice and concrete practice suggestions for defensive and combat shooting.

A new possibility for use is represented by the very natural pistols based on the SOFTAIR principle. The nylon bullets are fired at short ranges with little energy.

CLEANING AND MAINTENANCE

The cleaning and care of a handgun has two purposes: maintenance of safe functioning and maintenance of condition — the latter will be of major interest to the collector. A poorly or wrongly treated weapon becomes a risk for the user, and this, of course, does not decrease the import of the expression, coming from practice, that meany more weapons are ruined by cleaning than by shooting. Even the frequent pressing and releasing of the hammer without buffer cartridges does the weapon much more harm than normal use. Buffer cartridges are now available for every caliber (with the exception of some rather exotic calibers or the 7.65 mm Parabellum), and should really be used. Their clear identification and markings are important in that they cannot be confused, either by sight or by feel.

Many weapon users are of the opinion that a lot of oil or lubricant in a weapon will assure its functioning —this must be disagreed with, for a lot of oil alone is no guarantee of proper functioning.

Here are several basic rules to keep in mind for the maintenance of safe functioning of every weapon:

— Do not leave the weapon in a damp or clammy holster or other container for a long period of time. Residues of tannic acid in the leather or emanations from plastics attack the burnishing and work their way inside the weapon.

— Never lay down a weapon just out of a holster or a case without unloading it and making a safety check.

— Never tighten the screws of the grip or grip panels too tightly as it is better to maintain their normal tightness and check them regularly. Check immediately after use in a damp atmosphere to see whether a wooden grip panel may be blocking an external trigger bar, it is always possible to trim the wood slightly.

— Never play with the adjustment screws of the sights, otherwise it cannot be told whether the sights are set correctly.

— Do not flood the interior of the weapon with oil — it is enough to lubricate the moving surfaces and rests. Be sure to choose a really good and, above all, non-adhering or hardening oil. Not every oil does what its advertising claims. Oil hardening around the firing pin can have bad results.

— Do not douse the grip panels with oil, and see whether plastic grip panels are really resistant to the kind of oil you use.

— Completely dismantle the weapon only when you have good tools and good knowledge. Complete dismantling is usually done by a gunsmith whom you should supply with the technical data on your gun.

— Keep the gun away from dust and sand as much as its use allows.

— Avoid direct contact of oil and lubricants with cartridges and particularly with percussion caps. Powder can become partially powerless when oil gets into it.

— Always dismantle the weapon only as much as is necessary for a thorough cleaning. Usually the typical dismantling into grip, slide, barrel and recoil spring is sufficient.

— Do not use any parts that do not fit the weapon and that you have not tried personally.

— Avoid technical work which you have neither the ability nor the legal right to do. The reworking of triggers is still easy to do in a revolver, but usually not in a self-loading pistol, the trigger weight of which is often determined partly by its angle on the rest. The hard surface of the rest is usually very thin, and removing material will destroy the thin hardened area.

— Keep the weapon dry inside and out, and use as little oil as possible.

— Check the safe functioning of the weapon in all areas calmly before and after long periods of shooting.

— Clean the inside of the holster now and then, otherwise dirt will get into the muzzle.

— Oil the inside of the magazine and cylinder holes only minimally — too much oil may get on and into the cartridges.

— Get a good cleaning tool and keep it clean.

— Fire a whole magazine from time to time and check the pressure of the magazine spring with the help of a wooden stick.

— Check the safe seating of screws and pins from time to time.

Whenever a weapon is cleaned, it should also be inspected in all the places that may show increased wear. Taking a large-caliber pistol like the Colt Government or the M 39 as an example, let us discuss a few steps in detail.

It always begins with a conscientious safety check with a look into the chamber, then it proceeds to the removal of the magazine, from which any cartridges which are still present should be pushed out by hand. One looks at every single cartridge to see if it shows any damage, of if there is any oil in the area of the percussion cap. Such cartridges should be set aside and used in one's next training session. The magazine is dismantled, its individual parts are cleaned and lightly rubbed with oil. The inside of the magazine is wiped out with a sufficiently thick woolen wiper and likewise treated lightly with oil. After reassembling the magazine, always make a test with the help of a stick or reversed screwdriver.

Next take the grip panels off and look to see whether dirt has gotten into the inner area of the grip. The magazine shaft is likewise cleaned with a woolen wiper — the magazine must be able to be inserted without scratching and must slide out easily.

Then remove the barrel according to the usual way of dismantling this weapon. The recoil spring is pulled out and cleaned, along with its guiding rod, and then lightly oiled again (If the weapon has a too poorly polished recoil spring rod, then some work is called for).

One checks the condition of the barrel optically, looking for not very bright surfaces or dispersed light. If the weapon has not been fired, then wiping the barrel several times with a lightly oiled woolen wiper and then pulling an unoiled wiper or felt wadding through it will suffice.

If the barrel is badly dirtied by lead or residue from bullet jackets, it must be cleaned thoroughly. Solvents for residues of powder and tombac are available on the market, though it is important that they be applied evenly and thoroughly with a soft brush and allowed to act long enough. Sometimes it is appropriate to plug the barrel with small corks and let it stand for a few days with the solvent in it. Metallic deposits on the rifling angles can often be removed only mechanically, by being rubbed with a bronze brush that fits the caliber. Deposits of lead decrease the precision very much and must be removed completely, and the typical lead solvents on the market generally are not much help. Lead-Remover has a very good effect — it pulls the lead out of the barrel in long strips with an inserted disc of bronze gauze. The barrel must not be treated with oil — that is done only after working on it with Lead-Remover. At least once a year the firing pin should be removed and thoroughly degreased with all its moving parts, checked for wear and put back in carefully. For most weapons this job can be done quickly.

The inside of the slide is wiped out thoroughly — small sticks with wadding or bent pipe cleaners do a good and economical job.

The course of the slide, the contact area between the slide and the frame, must be kept clean and oiled regularly. Several oils that do not run off too quickly are suitable. A particularly effective lubricant is the Tri-Flow shown in the picture — it contains very small balls of teflon, which settle into the raw depths of the surfaces to be lubricated and provide a proper ball-bearing effect. These balls can be seen only microscopically in a water suspension. The application of Tri-Flow is even more practical when one lets it thicken somewhat and then uses it as a grease. First, though, all the parts must be degreased carefully.

Stainless weapons are thought to be easy to maintain, at least in the sense that they rarely show rust. One does, of course, have to lubricate such weapons well, for which the manufacturers often sell lubricants made especially for stainless steel. Here too, Tri-Flow shows good results.

Special attention should be given to the strike plate, where residues of powder and percussion-cap paint stick fast. These should be worked on with a stiff brush with solvent added. After every cleaning, the weapon should be reassembled properly and its functioning should be checked to make sure all parts move smoothly. The cleaning of a revolver is no different in principle. Here special attention should be given to the cylinder bore-holes, the attachment of the barrel (this is exactly where lead begins to be deposited) and the cylinder gear. This is best cleaned with a stiff brush or other small brush, so that it can always sink completely into its orifice in the cylinder. The crane of the cylinder should be cleaned of oil and oiled anew regularly. After the side plate is removed, the few moving parts are easy to reach — they do not always need to be removed.

The value of a collector's weapon depends on its state of preservation, and this condition should be maintained for as long as possible. When used weapons are obtained from arsenals, they are usually received covered with grease and dirt. This always requires a complete dismantling, down to the last and smallest parts if possible. Every part is rid of adhering dirt, which cannot be done without mechanical means. But it must always be kept

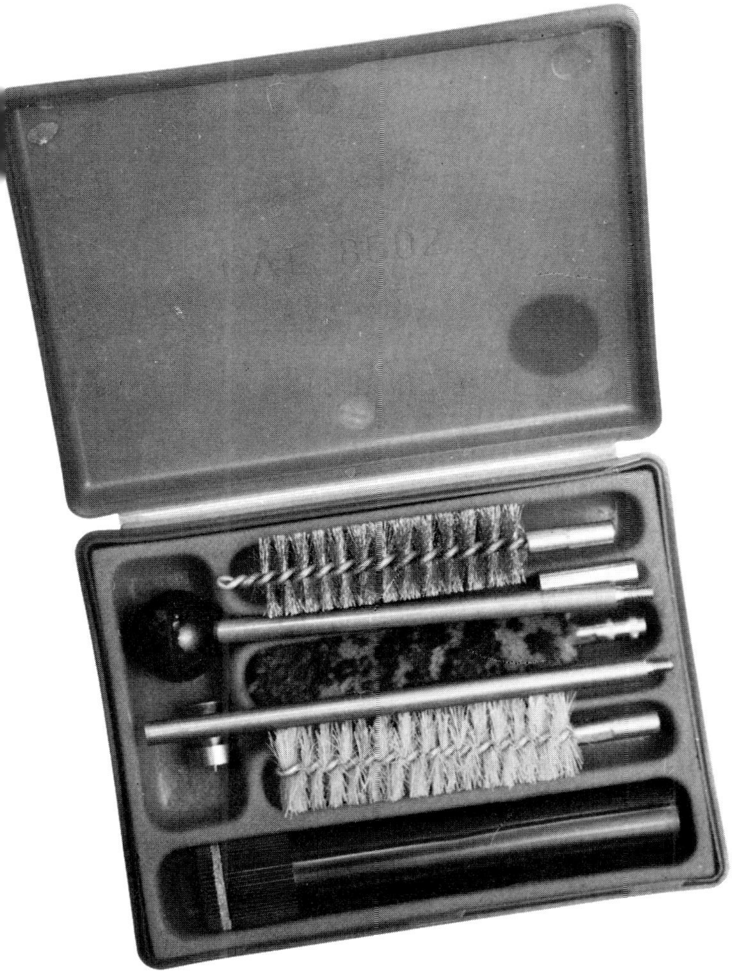

For simple cleaning, simple equipment such as the usual brushes will suffice. Such brushes scarcely help to remove lead from the barrel.

Tri Flow contains many little balls of teflon. Parts coated with it slide as if on ball bearings.

in mind that the original condition of a part must not be falsified by personal reworking. Smooth parts remain smooth, burnished parts remain burnished and may not be treated with polishes or wire brushes.

Dirt in a complicated frame can sometimes be removed only by boiling in hot water (with some detergent) or by washing with cleaning gasoline. In every case, though, one should first test the dirty spot to see whether the burnishing may have been attacked. Smooth parts can be cleaned well with the finest steel wool, and depending on the gloss of the surface, polishing can be done practically with felt and paste. Here it is important to use "soft" substances such as car wax or chrome-cleaning paste. If very fine rust needs to be removed, it is quite possible that burnished surfaces can be rubbed with the finest steel wool, number 000, thoroughly soaked in oil. The burnishing will not be visibly damaged then.

The dismantled weapon should be oiled sufficiently and then reassembled and checked for functioning. Dirt from cut grip patterns can often be removed only partly with a stiff toothbrush, which must always be used in the direction of the herringbone cuts.

Good collectors' pieces should not be packed away without protection. Many people have an excess of acid in the sweat on their hands, and if this is not counteracted, it can lead in a few days to rusty marks on the unprotected surfaces. It is best to keep cloth gloves in one's weapon cabinet and put them on in advance.

Stainless steel weapons are easy to maintain, but in the areas of their moving parts they absolutely need good and lasting lubrication.

Various brushes, emery and felt discs can be used to treat slightly rusty spots on weapons effectively.

Special Characteristics of Stainless Steel

Weapons made of stainless steel are not as sensitive as weapons made of burnished steel, yet they can develop problems according to how they are used and stored. Sometimes one notices discoloration on the surface, especially on the grip. These are reactions to sweaty hands or substances contained in the leather as residues of tannic acid. Salty air, high humidity and chemicals have a negative effect. Smaller discolorations, which are oxide layers, can be rubbed away with the finest steel wool. Various auto polishes and cleaners such as are used on chrome or precious metals can be of help. The outer surfaces are rubbed away by them, the cream is allowed to dry, and then everything else is rubbed away cleanly with a dry cloth. Even when it is stainless steel, some oil on the surface is helpful. Stainless steel is in principle not completely rust-free, but only rust-resistant. Weapons that are used often can, according to instructions from the firm of Sturm & Ruger, be treated with protective wax, but it must not get into the parts of the breech. There are special lubricants for treating moving parts — an example is MINUTEMAN. It has a thicker consistency and stays on moving parts better than ordinary oils can.

MODEL WEAPONS

It may not exactly fit into the framework of this portrayal, but they are basically worth a brief look too: model weapons. One need not necessarily take them seriously as a typical product of the times, and a serious collector will scarcely want to include them in his collection either. On the other hand, model weapons have a certain function as substitutes, for many interested parties will never receive official permission to obtain handguns, in which case a model weapon may well offer a small substitute, though only a meager one.

Many weapons or devices that resemble them come and go because of a very definite legal situation, and the same is true of model weapons, almost all of which are made in Japan. Scarcely any other land was as strictly

A readymade P 38 pistol. The lettering has no relation to that of the original.

A readymade 08 pistol, made as a model in Japan. It dismantles almost like the original, but the workmanship is much worse.

deprived of weapons after losing a war as was Japan — only the Eastern Bloc countries may have even stricter gun regulations. In Japan this situation resulted in clearly recognizable substitutes, of which the model weapon is only one. Not only are weapons made of plastic and metal as representations of well-known real ones, but so are "weapons", up to the level of the machine pistol, that are capable of firing lightly-charged bullets with little energy. People get together for realistic war games, put on camouflage suits, protect their faces with special masks, and fire at each other just as children play cowboys and Indians.

The model weapon definitely can have a certain charm for the collector, for who will still know after many long years why there was a P 38 or a Smith & Wesson M 439 made of plastic. Then too, the well-made model weapons show still another purpose. They are put together according to a detailed plan from parts of a carefully planned kit. Many parts differ from the real thing only in the type of material used, and sometimes the similarity is so great that parts can be exchanged. The magazine of a model M 439 will fit into the real pistol without any functioning loss. It is not an education for hostility or for war when children or young people first learn the technical basis of a weapon from such models. Assembling the kit calls for precise understanding of plans, and often for very nimble fingers too, no differently from totally disassembled real weapons. Whoever intends to pass his own collection on to his children one day is making no mistake when he introduces the future weapon owners carefully to their technology and the responsibility that goes with owning them.

A plastic M 439. One can scarcely tell if it is the real thing or not . . .

. . . that can be seen in the picture only when one looks at the right side. Many parts can be exchanged with those of the real thing.

In the world of model weapons there are two large groups that differ considerably in quality. The one group consists of ready-made, fully assembled weapons made of darkened die-cast metal. They need no extra work and can be dismantled more or less like the real weapons. The workmanship of this group is not quite as good as that of the kit models, but they may do very well as decorations.

The other group requires personal assembly. The parts are made of a moderately hard black plastic, though some die-cast metal parts may also be included. These weapons even "shoot", and the Japanese manufacturers make special bullets for them, with a small percussion cap included. The gas pressure is sufficient for a medium-loud bang, the slide moves back and injects the next cartridge.

A nice feature of these kits, whose quality depends somewhat on their price, is the precision of the manu-

The model weapon's magazine. It fits into the real pistol and functions properly there too.

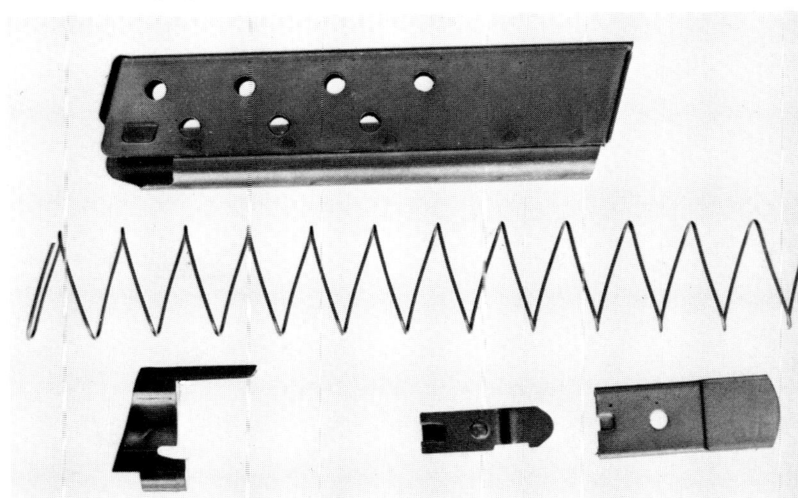

factured parts and the precision of the instructions that come with the plans. Down to the last and slightest detail, everything is there. This is precisely what gives such kits their value: every part requires a thorough study of the plans. The functioning of the model weapons from the second group is problem-free but not built to stand heavy use. They too are meant to be more of a decoration.

The market for model weapons seems to be worldwide, for the Japanese manufacturers are expanding their programs constantly, as well as improving their quality noticeably. The best kits at this time are the machine-pistol and assault-carbine kits that make it possible to hang an UZI or an MP 40 on the wall — only when one holds it in one's hands and goes through the process of loading it does one notice that it is a copy. There are as yet no limitations on obtaining such kits, though assembling them is illegal in Germany and Austria, because the assembled models give the impression of being fully automatic weapons of war. How true to life they are is shown by the plans for the UZI machine pistol, the kit for which is composed for the most part of precisely made cast metal parts.

A model of an UZI machine pistol made from a kit. In Germany and Austria the kit may be bought legally but not assembled.

The original and the model become more and more alike. This can be dangerous, for criminals often use model weapons. The victim does not know what is pointed at him.

Diagram of the UZI machine pistol from a Japanese kit. Most of the parts are made of metal.

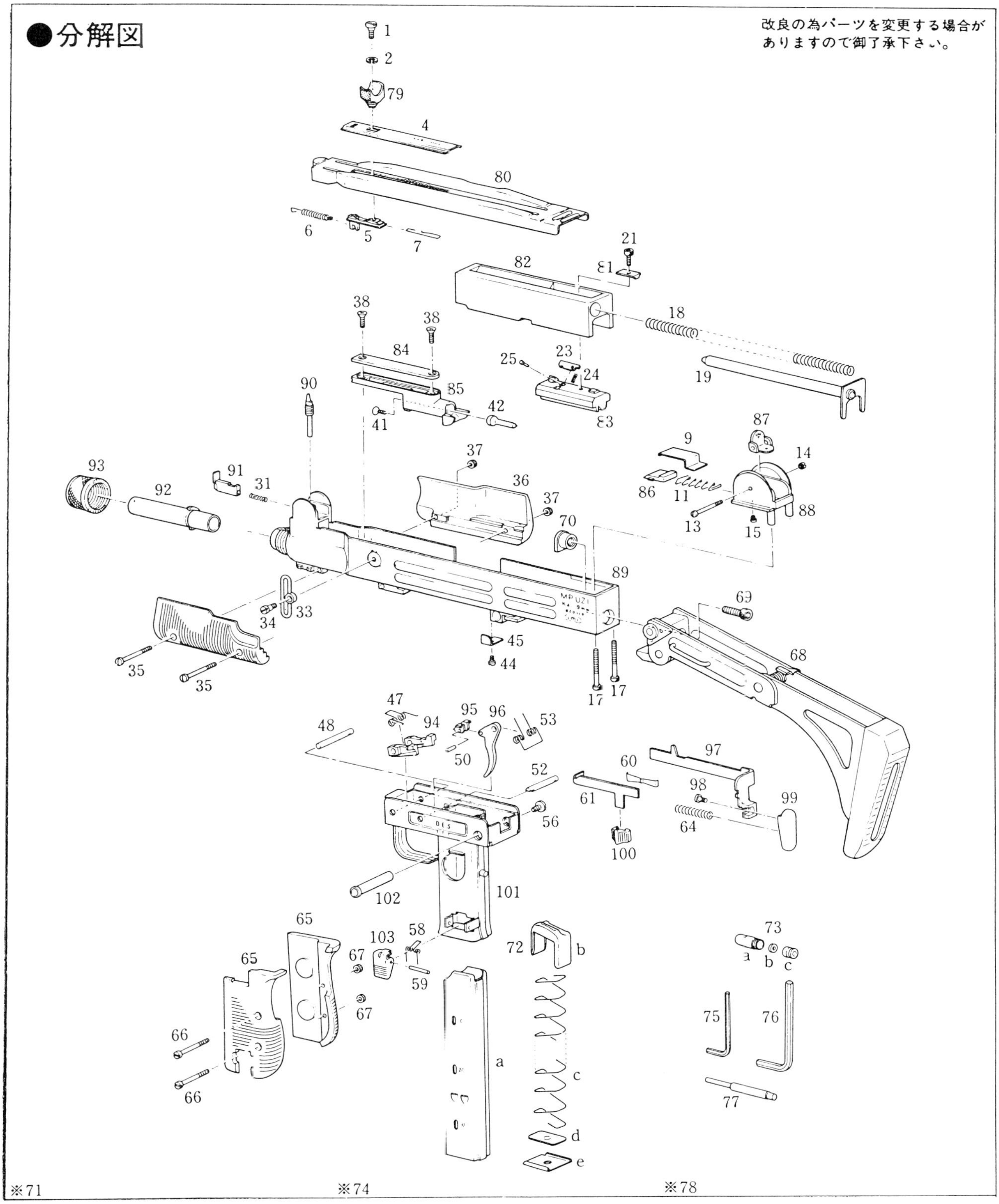